The Rules of
Globalization

Case Book

4 World Scientific
Studies in
International
Economics

THE RULES OF
Globalization
CASE BOOK

EDITOR

RAWI ABDELAL
Harvard University, USA

World Scientific

NEW JERSEY · LONDON · SINGAPORE · BEIJING · SHANGHAI · HONG KONG · TAIPEI · CHENNAI

Published by

World Scientific Publishing Co. Pte. Ltd.

5 Toh Tuck Link, Singapore 596224

USA office: 27 Warren Street, Suite 401-402, Hackensack, NJ 07601

UK office: 57 Shelton Street, Covent Garden, London WC2H 9HE

British Library Cataloguing-in-Publication Data
A catalogue record for this book is available from the British Library.

THE RULES OF GLOBALIZATION (Casebook)

by Rawi Abdelal

ISBN-13 978-981-270-927-1 (pbk)
ISBN-10 981-270-927-4 (pbk)

Printed in Singapore.

LIST OF CASES

INTRODUCTION: SEEING THE POLITICS OF GLOBALIZATION THROUGH THE EYES OF MANAGERS

Rawi Abdelal

Globalization is neither inexorable nor inevitable. Although this era of globalization has fundamentally reshaped the environment in which many of the world's firms operate, managers must recognize that this highly internationalized economy — in which goods, services, and capital flow across country borders — rest on institutional and inescapably political foundations. Politics are, therefore, ever present. In the early years of the new century, those politics are, perhaps paradoxically, making this globalized world economy more complicated for managers. Markets and industries still vary dramatically across national borders. Politics and rules have become increasingly important to the success of firms' selling, buying, and investing abroad.

The central theme of this case book is that the institutional foundations of globalization are undergoing a fundamental transformation within individual countries and at the level of the entire system. Rules should therefore be an integral part of strategy for internationalizing firms. The cases in this book are organized into four parts.

Part I: The Emerging Challenge of Globalization

The first part explores the emerging challenge of globalization. *American Outsourcing* describes the phenomenon of outsourcing and offshoring and explores the broader implications for an American economy that has heretofore remained open to the process by which trade in services essentially locates certain functions outside of the United States. A national debate has raged over whether on balance, and in the long run, the U.S. economy and its workers will benefit, and if the benefits outweigh the costs whether the distributional implications might undermine American public support for globalization.

A series of cases on Porsche — *True to Brand?* And *Made in Germany* — then explores similar themes in Germany and its automotive sector. Highlighting Porsche's decision to enter the SUV market with the Cayenne and share much of the production platform with the Volkswagen Touareg, the cases demonstrate that Germans, too, are increasingly concerned about how their country relates to patterns of production. With much of the assembly ultimately taking place in central Europe, Porsche seems to be straining a core element of its brand — "Made in Germany." A broader question is at stake: As production internationalizes, are there products for which country of origin, however defined, will remain central to their brands?

Part II: The Domestic Politics of Globalization

The next five chapters comprise the second part of the book, which explores the challenges for firms from various kinds of domestic politics. The *Journey to Sakhalin* series offers a narrative that connects developments in Russia to the experience of the country's largest foreign investor, Royal Dutch/Shell. As the Russian government centralizes power and reasserts control over the energy sector, foreign firms such as Royal Dutch/Shell must struggle to find their place in an evolving Russian national interest.

The unhappy experience of Wal-Mart's foray into Germany shows how a collection of formal European rules and informal, societal norms can affect the performance of a company that is generally considered to have been a juggernaut. Again, managers find their strategies to be inconsistent with prevailing rules, and the price they pay is a heavy one: failure. The experience of managers in *deCODE Genetics* offers a fascinating contrast: whereas the firm had successfully influenced the codification of rules favorable to their enterprise, a societal backlash threatens to undermine that success.

In *Infosys in India: Building a Software Giant in a Corrupt Environment*, students are encouraged to consider the challenges faced by managers of an aggressively internationalizing firm that is based in a local institutional environment rife with petty corruption. Although Infosys has managed to cultivate an impeccable reputation for cleanliness and honesty, the challenges for other Indian firms to replicate that successful strategy may turn out to be even more daunting. Here, the informal rules in India threaten to constrain the success of many promising firms.

Finally, *The Dubai Ports World Debacle* and its Aftermath narrates the ill-fated attempt by a Dubai-based firm, DP World, to manage a handful of American ports whose operations were inherited from a firm it acquired. Although the formal processes governing this cross-border investment had gone very smoothly, the informal political and societal reaction to the deal ultimately undermined it.

Part III: The International Financial Architecture

The next two parts of the book explore politics and rules at the level of the international system. First is the collection of norms and rules that underpins the movement of capital across country borders — that is, the international financial architecture.

International capitalism has always, paradoxically, had an uneasy relationship to capital itself. The international financial architecture — the collection of norms and rules that structure the interactions between governments and international financial markets — has changed dramatically more than once. Capital has alternately been extraordinarily free and fundamentally constrained as international capitalism has evolved over time. No arrangement or orthodoxy has been permanent, although illusions of permanence, inevitability, and inexorability have defined each historical moment.

The first era of globalization, circa 1870–1914, was built upon fundamentally liberal institutional foundations embodied in the practices of the classical gold standard. Policy makers understood that to restrict freedom of capital violated the rules, *albeit* unwritten, of the gold standard. Restrictions being neither normal nor legitimate, capital was as free to flow from one country to another as it has ever been. Bankers, managers, and investors thus enjoyed an age of extraordinary freedom and opportunity.

The first world war, the decade of recurrent international financial crises that followed, and the Great Depression destroyed that liberal order. Then, during the 1940s and 1950s, the rules of the international financial architecture were rewritten to be restrictive by design and doctrine. At that time members of the international financial community collectively shared a set of beliefs about the destabilizing consequences of short-term, speculative capital flows, or "hot money," and the need for government autonomy from international financial markets. To regulate and control capital became the prevailing orthodoxy. Policy makers then wrote their new consensus into the international financial architecture. The right of International Monetary Fund (IMF), European Community (EC), and Organization for Economic Cooperation and Development (OECD) members to regulate movements of capital was protected by the IMF's Articles of Agreement (1945), the EC's Treaty of Rome (1957), and the OECD's Code of Liberalization of Capital Movements (1961).

As the rules were liberalized in the decades that followed, managers and investors enjoyed another era of freedom, one that spurred massive growth in global financial markets. Freedom for capital movements became the new orthodoxy once again. Unlike the first era of globalization, formal, codified rules explicitly defined these liberal principles and policy practices. The rules of the European Union (EU) and the OECD were rewritten to oblige members, the world's thirty or so richest countries, to allow virtually all cross-border flows of capital. The IMF began informally to promote capital liberalization among its membership, which was nearly universal, and some policy makers sought to amend the Articles of Agreement to oblige members to liberalize capital movements. Central bankers meeting in Basel at the Bank for International Settlements (BIS) endorsed this liberal evolution of government practices. And private credit rating agencies, such as Moody's and Standard & Poor's (S&P) propagated these liberal ideas in their evaluations of sovereign borrowers.

Subsequently, the new orthodoxy of capital mobility was again undermined, this time by a wave of financial crises that struck emerging markets in the 1990s. The EU, OECD, and IMF have since begun a general rethinking within the international financial community of the risks and benefits of capital liberalization. The policy debate on the causes of the financial crises has been heated, and a new consensus appears unlikely. With the very idea of unrestricted capital now suffering a crisis of legitimacy, the managerial implications are dramatic and perplexing, and sure to grow all the more so.

The first set of readings in the module explores the important, but widely misunderstood, place of the credit rating agencies in the international financial architecture. Although few observers deny that Moody's and S&P exercise significant influence over the borrowing practices of sovereign governments and firms around the world, that influence has, until recently, not been the subject of sustained scholarly inquiry. These agencies derive their influence from two sources. The first is the information content of their ratings, and this is reasonably straightforward for students to understand. The second is both more profound and vastly more problematic: ratings are incorporated into financial regulations in the United States and around the world. As a result, these ratings, particularly on the margin between investment-grade and non-investment-grade, literally carry the force of law. A case on S&P's sovereign credit ratings business and an accompanying note on scales and process within the firm allow for a discussion of how S&P managers understand their own ideological assumptions and influence on international capital markets. Because the credit rating agencies are empowered by domestic financial regulations, primarily in the United States, they are the epitome of *ad hoc* globalization. The case suggests that the current regulatory environment is not likely to be a stable political equilibrium, and students are thus encouraged to make informed predictions about how financial regulations in the United States and Europe, especially, will affect the role of the agencies in the coming years.

The second and third sets of readings are designed to introduce students to the causes and effects of European policy makers' embrace of the doctrine of organized, or "managed," globalization. *Bohemian Crowns* is about the experience of one of the Czech Republic's four largest banks during the country's accession to the OECD and the capital liberalization obliged by the organization's Code of Liberalization of Capital Movements. The combination of a fixed exchange rate, rapid liberalization, and a poorly governed banking system turned out to be disastrous for the Czech Republic, leading to a financial crisis that cost the government more than 10% of GDP to resolve. What is most fascinating, however, is that this bank, ČSOB, stood apart from the credit bubble that precipitated the crisis. Students are encouraged to consider the banks' incentives to borrow and lend while under pressure from the government to avoid domestic adjustment, as well as to understand why ČSOB's executives chose to manage their bank more prudently and the institutional mechanisms that allowed them to do so.

Politics and Prudential Supervision and *European Financial Integration* evaluate students to one of the most important bargains in the history of the decades-old European integration project: a new obligation in 1988 to allow nearly complete freedom for capital movements, *erga omnes* (that is, toward all — non-EU members as well). Europe's rules for capital freedom at one stroke became the most liberal the world has ever known. Moreover, this European rule made an entire world of integrated capital markets possible. During the late 1980s, Europe faced a turning point: it could create a single financial space that was European, or it could create a financial space that was integrated with the rest of the world economy. Because they chose the latter, the EU provided one of the most important institutional foundations for global capital markets. Major developments followed this move, including a common money and wholesale banking integration. Yet European rules were written with one important carve-out: national banking supervisors could prioritize "sound and prudent management," even if doing so meant blocking cross-border banking mergers.

The case explores the most famous, even notorious, effort by the Italian central bank governor to prevent the purchase of an Italian bank, Antonveneta, by a Dutch bank, ABN Amro. Written from the perspective of ABN Amro's executives, the case explores the logic of the Italian central bank governor's concerns about foreign ownership of Italy's banks, describes how the Dutch bank navigated between European and Italian norms and rules, and reflects on the implications for national models of capitalism of European financial integration. In particular, the Italian model has been built upon small to medium-size, family-controlled firms traditionally reliant on bank financing and close relationships with their local bankers in one of the most highly fragmented banking systems in the world. Changing the ways in which Italian banks operate is very likely to transform the practices of Italian firms, and thus Italian capitalism, as well. With Italian resentment against the euro also on the rise, the case can be interpreted as a struggle for the soul of the European project.

The final case in the module focuses on another case, *Chrysanthemum and Dragon*, that explores the influence of the Chinese capital controls regime on the opportunities for and practices of foreign venture capital and private equity firms. Because the case takes the perspective of JAFCO Asia, one of the only Japanese venture capital firms active in China, the political stakes are increased significantly. Ongoing political tensions between the Chinese and Japanese governments set the context for growing economic ties; in the region the phenomenon was described as "hot economics, cool politics." The case is an excellent coda to the module because China, unlike the other national and regional settings explored in the module, continues to maintain a strict capital controls regime. Not having been obliged by membership in any international organization to liberalize capital flows, China remains a challenging country in which to invest. The case explores the advantages and disadvantages of what has become the most common practice for foreign venture capital and private equity firms investing in China: to invest in China indirectly, through complex offshore holding company structures permitting the investment and exit (via offshore exchanges) to occur entirely outside mainland China. Here again is *ad hoc* globalization the defining process, based on largely unilateral decisions by Chinese policy makers to begin to engage international capital markets on terms they define differently over time.

Part IV: The Politics and Rules of International Trade

The final part of the book explores the politics and rules that both enable and constrain trade in goods and service. Unlike the international financial architecture, the organizations that govern trade are relatively weak, and protectionism remains a recurrent feature of world markets.

The first two cases explore the logic of developed-country protectionism and how it influences the prospects for industrial development in Asia and Africa. *The Delta Blues* explores the paradox of American protectionism against imports of aquaculture from Vietnam just as the United States and Vietnam embrace a greater political rapprochement after decades of enmity. The political logic of this protectionism runs, however, in contrast to the logic that often informs explanations for such protection — namely, that powerful import-competing producers organize to redistribute the diffuse costs of protection to consumers to themselves. In the United States, other logics are often at work. In addition to the high politics of national security, are more traditional "low politics," putatively prosaic in comparison. In this and many other cases, protectionism seems to serve as a kind of politically acceptable social welfare, in which Americans seem much more willing to protect the unlucky. Naturally, this kind of in-group altruism of Americans comes at the unhappy expense of the Vietnamese, who find their development trajectory undermined by American promises of greater openness that fall apart.

In the next case, *The Market and the Mountain Kingdom*, the effects of developed-country protectionism in the textile and garment industry manifest themselves in the fits and starts of a momentarily booming industry in sub-Saharan Africa, and in the tiny mountain kingdom of Lesotho most speficially. With the end of the decades-old Multi-Fiber Arrangement in 2005, many developing countries were poised to take advantage of what they hoped would be greater market access. Yet protectionism in the United States continues to disappoint developing-country managers in the industry, who must navigate an increasingly complex patchwork of rules that determine which societies and firms get privileged access and on which terms. The American African Growth and Opportunity simultaneously carves out greater market space for the poorest of African countries, and yet its temporariness makes long-term planning difficult.

The next two cases deal with the needs of multinational corporations to protect their intellectual property rights in both the developing world and in Europe. In *Life, Death, and Property Rights*, Western pharmaceutical firms face a growing backlash against their pricing policies for AIDS drugs as a pandemic threatens Africa in particular. Those firms must decide just how much of their intellectual property they are prepared to give away before developing-country governments ultimately take away more. The stakes are huge for all involved.

In *Competition Policy in the European Union and the Power of Microsoft*, one of the world's most powerful firms — Microsoft — must deal with the increasing role of antitrust authorities in Europe in defining the institutional landscape of their markets. Having overcome such a regulatory challenge in the United States, Microsoft executives seem to have been taken unawares by European competition authorities who are much more aggressive and intrusive into the Microsoft business model. Competition law is necessarily vague, and so it is clear that the interpreters of that imposing legal authority matters a great deal. EU-style competition policy emerges in the case as quite distinct in both logic and implication from American policy. The broadest implication is that, with the integration of Europe, large multinational firms must have not one, but two strategies for dealing with competition law, competition policy, and regulators.

Thus all of the cases highlight how important the institutions of globalization — informal and formal rules at the level of both countries and the system as a whole — constrain and enable the very firms that reproduce globalization daily. Understanding those rules is one of the central managerial challenges of our time.

Part I

THE EMERGING CHALLENGE OF GLOBALIZATION

RICHARD H.K. VIETOR

ALEXANDER VEYTSMAN

American Outsourcing

There are people looking for work because jobs have gone overseas, and we need to act in this country.[1]
— George W. Bush

Half of our sales are outside the United States. If you want to sell in places like China, India and Europe you've got to employ people there. GE is a global company.[2]
— Jeff Immelt

As the 2004 presidential campaign undertook its tumultuous path, the recent losses of American jobs were a major issue for both President George W. Bush and Senator John Kerry. Neither candidate disagreed that outsourcing of U.S. jobs had aggravated the loss of more than 2.5 million jobs since 2001. In addition to NAFTA-driven outsourcing to Mexico, U.S. corporations shipped jobs to Asia and India, both reducing costs and serving Asian markets. Critics viewed outsourcing as the chief reason behind domestic employment woes. CNN's Lou Dobbs, among the most vocal of critics, asserted that the debate over outsourcing revealed a "too comfortable alliance between multinational corporations and government, which has resulted in Corporate America's dominance over Washington."[3]

Mexico's *maquiladoras*, China's Special Economic Areas (SEAs), and software outsourcing to India had attracted billions of dollars in foreign direct investment (FDI). The Mexican maquiladoras had existed since the 1960s, but became especially popular in the 10 years after the passage of NAFTA in 1993. The Chinese SEAs were formed in conjunction with reforms of the post-Maoist era to usher in gradual economic openness and trade with the West. India's intellectual capital created a potential for cheap white-collar labor in the aftermath of the "Washington Consensus" program. The governments in all three countries created favorable business environments, in which companies like GE could prosper by seizing sales-growth or cost-reduction opportunities not available in their home countries. In turn, Mexico, China, and India sought to increase inflows of FDI, which contributed to growth, employment, and the acquisition of management skills and technology.

Global Outsourcing

Outsourcing in America involved the transfer of manufacturing or service jobs abroad, generally to attain lower labor costs, for sales back to the United States. Sectors affected include assembly and related manufacturing, business functions (e.g., human resources, marketing, payroll, billing), and the provision of business infrastructure (e.g., information systems, security systems, telecommunications networks) and operating processes (e.g., procurement of raw materials, industrial production, operation of a telecommunications network). Some people used the term "offshoring" to describe manufacturing abroad (replacing U.S. exports) for sales abroad. Others, especially in the corporate world, preferred the term "right-sourcing" to describe the optimal combination of locational manufacturing for the firm.

Outsourcing did not necessarily guarantee higher profits for a particular business. The success of the outsourcing activity would in many respects be driven by the firm's ability to manage in remote locations and by the caliber and skill sets of the local labor force. In addition, there were such exogenous factors as political stability, language skills, infrastructure, and enforceability of intellectual property rights and business contracts that all affected the success of an outsourced operation.

Saving in labor costs was the major incentive for companies that chose to outsource. In services, for example, a financial analyst who earned $35 per hour in the U.S. might receive $10 in India. In the manufacturing sector, the disparity was greater. Workers who earned between $11–$20 per hour in the U.S. were replaced by similar employees who were willing to work for $1–$2.50 per hour in China and Mexico.

The opponents of outsourcing viewed it as a grave threat to American jobs. Between 2000 and 2004, the practice of sending U.S. jobs abroad had begun hurting employment in such sectors as professional and business services, information industries, textiles and apparel, computers and electronics, furniture, vehicles, and fabricated metals. A 2003 study at the University of California Berkeley found that "employment in these sectors has plummeted by 15.5% nationally, with California experiencing a particularly acute 21% reduction in employment. In these sectors alone, between the first quarter of 2001 and the second quarter of 2003, more than 1 million jobs in the U.S. as a whole and 200,000 jobs in California have been lost."[4] In the auto industry the results were just as alarming. Employment dropped by 200,000 jobs over the past four years. During the same time, "imports of Chinese auto parts have doubled."[5]

The phenomenon of outsourcing had scarcely slowed, even with the improvements in the U.S. economy. In 2004 Patrick Buchanan wrote: "In 2004 Siemens announced it was moving 15,000 software programming jobs out of the United States and Europe to China, India and Eastern Europe. . . . According to an AP story in February 2004, professional accountants in India prepared 1,000 U.S. tax returns in 2002, 20,000 in 2003, and 150,000 to 200,000 in 2004."[6] Lou Dobbs claimed that over 840 U.S. companies were "exporting America" at present. These companies were "either sending American jobs overseas or choosing to employ cheap overseas labor instead of American workers."[7]

Critics of outsourcing feared not only job losses but also downward pressures on effective wages. As low-skilled workers lost their jobs to foreign markets, they were usually able to find replacement jobs that paid 20%–40% less than their previous earnings. And newly expanding firms, according to the American Policy Institute, were less likely to provide workers with health insurance than firms that were cutting jobs. Such employment situations contributed to rising income inequality in the U.S. The Gini coefficient kept creeping upward, as low- and middle-income households experienced declining household incomes, while wealthier families prospered.[8] There were estimates that by 2015, $151 billion in wages would shift from the U.S. to countries with cheaper labor costs.[9] Heightened mobility of employers also appeared to hurt workers by decreasing their bargaining power.

But the outsourcing of U.S. jobs also had its supporters. "Just as consumers inthe United States have enjoyed lower prices from foreign manufacturers, so too should they benefit from services being offered by overseas companies that have lower labor costs,"[10] claimed Gregory Mankiw, chairman of the White House Council of Economic Advisers (CEA). Mankiw cited outsourcing of health-care jobs as an example of beneficial outsourcing, concluding that such a practice would help control rising medical costs. Some pharmaceutical companies could save up to 50% in operational expenses, he argued. According to the Council of Economic Advisors:

> Outsourcing of professional services is a prominent example of a new type of trade. The gains from trade that take place over the Internet or telephone lines are no different than the gains from trade in physical goods transported by ship or plane. When a good or service is produced at lower cost in another country, it makes sense to import it rather than to produce it domestically. This allows the United States to devote its resources to more productive purposes.[11]

The supporters of outsourcing service jobs also claimed that outsourcing ultimately created jobs in the U.S. export sector, lowered domestic firms' costs, and provided services to consumers at lower prices. According to one economist, "instead of altering the number of jobs, free trade changes the mix of jobs in the country to reflect those areas in which we have the greatest competitive advantage over other countries. International trade in services expands the process of job specialization and raises living standards."[12]

Mexico: Maquiladoras

A maquiladora is a labor-intensive assembly operation that imports inputs from a foreign country, processes these inputs, and then ships them back to the country of origin. The term has its roots in colonial Mexico, when millers charged a "maquila" for processing other people's grain. Maquiladoras were generally owned by non-Mexican corporations that took advantage of low-cost Mexican labor, advantageous tariff regulations, and close proximity to U.S markets. Maquiladoras were one of Mexico's primary sources of foreign exchange. The Mexican government allowed duty-free, temporary importation of raw materials, supplies, machinery, and equipment, as long as the product assembled or manufactured in Mexico was exported.

In 2003, American firms accounted for 90% of maquila ownership. Among the high-profile U.S. companies that claimed ownership in Mexico were General Electric, Delphi, Ford Motor Company, Tyco, General Instruments, Johnson & Johnson, and ITT. Seventy-nine percent of the top 100 maquiladora employers were from the United States.[13] Nearly 26,000 U.S. companies supplied maquiladoras with machinery, equipment, and materials.

Historical Background

The genesis of the Maquiladora program in Mexico went back to the demise of the 23-year-old Bracero program in 1964. The Bracero program had allowed Mexican agricultural workers to work legally in the U.S. on a seasonal basis. But the Johnson administration's Great Society policies abolished such practices in order to benefit low-wage American workers, and the Bracero program was terminated. The Mexican government then moved to implement the Maquiladora program, also known as the Border Industrialization Program (BIP), to alleviate the rising unemployment burden along the border.

The substantial devaluations of the peso, coupled with changes in the U.S. customs laws, eventually made Mexico an attractive location for foreign investment by American firms. As many firms were increasingly squeezed by Asian competitors, they turned to Mexico for lower labor costs. The maquiladoras began to experience steady growth after 1985, when Mexico's government issued a decree to recognize formally and to regulate the maquila industry. As part of its structural adjustment, Mexico gradually opened its economy to foreign direct investment. In 1986, Mexico entered the GATT (General Agreement on Trade and Tariffs), and in 1989 it eliminated most barriers to FDI. A momentous milestone for the Maquila industry came during the Salinas administration, with the enactment of the North American Free Trade Agreement, effective January 1, 1994.

Impact of NAFTA

NAFTA, implemented over 15 years, created a free-trade zone in North America. During the five years before NAFTA, maquila employment grew 47%. But in the first five years after NAFTA, employment growth soared 86%.[14] The number of maquila plants grew in tandem, from about 2,700 in 1997 to a peak of about 3,700 in 2001. (See **Exhibit 1**.) Ten years after NAFTA's initiation, analysts cited the textile and apparel sectors as key determinants of growth of maquiladoras.[15]

Critics of NAFTA charged that it was a chief contributor to outsourcing. According to Lou Dobbs, "At least 750,000 American jobs were lost as a direct result of NAFTA."[16] Pat Buchanan echoed: "By 2000, more than a million Mexicans were at work in maquiladora plants at jobs once held by Americans." He claimed that NAFTA had first taken away jobs from the apparel and textile sectors, then from the auto industry, then from aerospace. The latter industry, especially high-tech, involved giants such as Boeing Corporation, General Dynamics, Honeywell International, and GE Aircraft Engines moving to Mexico. As an executive of Smith West, a GE supplier, observed: "you can only cut costs so much with new machinery. Pretty soon you need to lower labor costs, too."[17]

Supporters of NAFTA attributed a number of successes to freer trade. First, they highlighted NAFTA as the largest free trade area, linking 426 million people and a $12 trillion GDP in a single market. (Despite the European Union's expansion in 2002, its cumulative GDP is still lower than that of the NAFTA members.) Second, NAFTA expanded Mexico's global export market, with the United States constituting its greatest export share. (See **Exhibit 4**.) The total volume of trade among the three NAFTA partners had grown from $289.3 billion in 1993 to $623.1 billion in 2003. Third, NAFTA proponents claimed that NAFTA benefited U.S. households. According to the USTR (United States Trade Representative), rising U.S. manufacturing output, income gains, and tax cuts from NAFTA were worth up to $930 each year for the average family of four. Fourth, NAFTA was viewed as a catalyst for enforcement of environmental laws; the Commission for Environmental Protection (CEP) was NAFTA's direct offshoot.[18]

Finally, NAFTA had benefited Mexico's infrastructure with the inflow of foreign direct investment. From 1993 to 2003, Mexico increased its number of highways and toll freeways. The country's power generation almost doubled. Cell phone lines grew from 300,000 to over 28 million. As a percent of GDP, commercial exchange (exports and imports as a share of GDP) increased from 29.1% to 45.5%. The foreign direct investment into Mexico also rose sharply. In 1993, it stood at around $4.4 billion, while by 2003 FDI into Mexico was almost $11.4 billion. (See **Exhibit 3**.)

Structure of Maquiladoras

In the 1970s most maquiladoras clustered around Mexico's Northern border with the U.S.; however, by 1994 over 50% of new plants were opening within Mexico's interior regions. One academic study concluded, "This movement to the interior is important in that it helps spread the employment benefits of foreign investment throughout the country and fosters backward linkages to domestic industry."[19] Although border plants still outnumbered interior plants by a factor of approximately 3 to 1 (**Exhibit 1**), maquila plants nonetheless spread throughout the country. (See **Exhibit 4**.) The average size of maquiladoras varied by region. For instance, Chihuahua hosted many plants with over 1,000 workers, while in Baja California Norte the majority of plants had 100 employees or less.

Size and locational differences also varied by sector. In Juarez, for example, the biggest plants were in electronics, apparel, and business services. In Tijuana, the concentration of electronics was also significant, focusing mostly on television production. Apparel operations were also among the largest in Juarez, yet they were inconsequential in Tijuana.

Maquiladora employment had grown 300-fold since 1967, and in 2005 maquiladora exports accounted for half of Mexico's total exports. Some maquiladoras evolved from first-generation plants—labor-intensive with limited technology—to third-generation businesses that performed research, product design, and development. In a typical maquiladora, administrative employees constituted 7% of the workforce, technicians 12%, and production workers 81%. Fifty-six percent of production workers were female.

The electrical and electronics industry was the largest among maquilas. The automotive and metal mechanics sectors came next. Textile, medical, and chemical plants were smaller. This pattern translated into Mexico's foreign trade by industry. Electrical and electronics industry led Mexico's imports and exports, with over $55 billion in exports and almost $40 billion in imports in 2003. The automotive sector was next, with about $32 billion in exports and $21 billion in imports. The textile sector was far behind, with $9 billion in exports and $5 billion in imports. But even without this distribution, all three sectors experienced significant growth since NAFTA's initiation.

Tax Advantages

Maquiladoras enjoyed a number of advantages that helped attract foreign capital to Mexico. The Maquiladora Decree established four categories of duty-free imports. The following items were excluded from the duties:

1. Raw materials, containers, packing material, labels, and brochures necessary to complement production;

2. Tools, equipment, and accessories for industrial production and security, products necessary for hygiene and sanitation, pollution control equipment, work manuals, telecommunication and computation equipment;

3. Machinery, apparatus, instruments, and spare parts for the production process, laboratory and testing equipment, and information and products necessary to ensure quality control, train personnel, and manage the business; and

4. Trailer bodies and containers.[20]

Maquiladoras also benefited from a reduced impact of Mexican laws on Income Tax and Assets Tax. Since those plants represented cost centers that drew much of necessary materials, components, and equipment from the parent company, the profits were marginal and hence, hardly affected by the Income Tax law. However, the rate on products that maquiladoras bought in Mexico was zero. While services were taxable, maquiladoras were able to obtain refunds for those used in exports.[21]

Economic Impact of the Maquiladoras

Mexico seemed like a winner from the maquila policies. Maquiladoras grew from being 44% of total U.S.-Mexico trade in 1994 to 54% in 2004. While Mexico's FDI was unstable before NAFTA, since then it grew steadily at $12–$16 billion per year. Even during the recessionary 2001–2002 period, FDI grew from $12.8 to $14.4 billion. Maquiladoras accounted for about 10% of FDI. Investment specific to the maquiladora industry more than doubled from about $900 million in 1995 to over $2 billion in 2002. About half of FDI was concentrated in the manufacturing industry, a fourth in financial services, and the remaining quarter in communication and transportation, retail trade, construction, electricity, and water. Much of the newer investment went to central Mexico. The United States remained the major contributor, accounting for about 65% of total FDI. (See **Exhibit 5**.)

The maquila industry had become an important source of foreign exchange. It consistently accounted for at least 40% of the country's total export earnings. Maquilas obviously ran a consistent trade surplus.[22] According to a U.S. government report, "In 2001, 79% of maquiladora imports of components and parts for production were from the U.S. and 98% of their exported products were destined for the U.S. market."[23] The export figures did not differ much from Mexico's global exports. In 2003, Mexico exported nearly 89% to the U.S. (See **Exhibit 2**.)

As the maquila sector grew, so did jobs. In 1997, 904,000 people were employed at maquilas. By 2001, employment rose to almost 1.3 million. (See **Exhibit 6**.) Although employment declined with the downturn in 2001–2002, at least a quarter of total manufacturing jobs in Mexico were still maquila-related. Most major Mexican border regions experienced growth in jobs, with some regions and sectors growing faster than others. The U.S. government report continued, "Tijuana and Mexicali tripled their maquiladora employment, and the electronics industry more than doubled its maquiladora employment in the border region."[24]

With regard to social welfare, the work week in Mexico was limited to 48 hours, with Sunday a fully paid holiday. Maquiladoras usually had five nine-hour workdays; workers ended up spending 45 hours at the plant and getting paid for 56 hours. Some employers also offered generous overtime opportunities, which resulted in doubling or tripling the regular wage. Mexico did not have unemployment insurance, but upon a worker's termination at a plant, he or she usually received 90 days' pay, in addition to accrued vacation and seniority premiums. The maquiladoras were also required to provide for retirement and social security benefits, accident coverage, and 12 weeks of maternity leave.

Maquiladora Downturn?

Between October 2000 and March 2002, the maquila industry experienced a 21% decline in employment, which translated to about 278,000 Mexican jobs. In 2001, there were a total of 3,684 plants nationwide. By 2003 the total was down to 2,829 plants. The decrease was sharpest along the border. (See **Exhibit 1**.) The electronics industry was particularly affected.[25] In most regions of Mexico (Baja California, Nuevo Leon, Chihuahua), increases in the fully-loaded wage also moderated or simply leveled out. In the region of Jalisco, wages underwent a substantial decline. (See **Exhibit 7**.)

The leading reason for this downturn was the U.S. recession. Since most maquila production was destined for the U.S. market, its sensitivity to the U.S. economy was overwhelming. Historically, maquiladora growth was tied to the growth of the U.S. GDP. As the U.S. economy slipped into recession in 1981, 1991, and 2000, the maquiladora industry suffered in turn. (See **Exhibit 13**.)

But a second, more ominous reason for the downturn was the loss of competitiveness of the maquiladoras. After the Tequila Crisis in 1994–95, Mexican real wages rose during the later-NAFTA period, while the peso remained relatively strong. Relative productivity, meanwhile, fell. Some attributed these developments to the rising costs of maintaining an average worker in Mexico, because of the generous employment benefits that were mandated by law. In many instances employers were required to guarantee workers transportation and food subsidies, in addition to affordable housing.

Finally, the rise of new geographic markets, with especially low wages and more fiscal certainty (e.g., relatively stable deficits) had opened alternative opportunities for multinational corporations (MNCs). While the competition from Singapore, Malaysia, India, and Pakistan was severe, it was China, with its Special Economic Areas, that posed the largest threat.

China: Special Economic Areas

A Special Economic Area is a geographical region that has economic laws which are different from the country's typical economic laws. In the People's Republic of China, the word "special" denoted economic and political independence for the foreign firm.

Historical Background

After the death of Chairman Mao Zedong in 1976, the People's Republic of China started on its path toward gradual capitalist-oriented reforms. In 1978 the Third Plenary Session of the 11th CPC Central Committee concluded that China needed greater openness towards the global economy. One of the key reforms implemented during the next several years, under Deng Xioaping, was the establishment of Special Economic Areas. SEAs were treated separately in national planning and had province-level authority in their economic administration.

The main purpose behind the newly created SEAs was to attract foreign investors, which would create jobs and generate exports. After Mao's demise, China's official policy of "self-reliance" eroded quickly. By 1988 China's opening to foreign companies was extended to coastal areas along the Yangtze River Delta, Pearl River Delta, Xiamen-Zhangzhou-Quanzhou Triangle in south Fujian, Shangdong Peninsula, and Liaodong Peninsula (Liaoning Province, Hebei and Guangxi). Together, these SEAs functioned as catalysts for developing the foreign-oriented economy, generating commerce through exporting products, and importing technologies and management skills to accelerate China's economic development.

Tax Advantages for Foreigners

Just like Mexican maquiladoras, Special Economic Areas offered substantial tax advantages to foreign investors. A typical manufacturing plant could expect corporate income taxation privileges in accordance with the following schedule:

- No tax during start-up years before making a profit.

- The first year that an operation makes a profit starts the "tax clock."

- The first and second year after the tax clock starts, there is no tax.

- For years three and four, half the normal tax rate applies.

- From the fifth year, the company pays the full tax rate.[26]

Even more than Mexico, China lacked solid and permanent rules for foreign investors. According to Sergio Ornelas from *MexicoNow*, "As the provinces and cities competed for FDI, investors discovered significant variances in local tax incentives, labor benefits, and other business conditions."[27] Chinese government officials strove to create comfortable conditions for foreign direct investors. The changes had so far been beneficial to foreign capital, without the economic uncertainty that prevailed in Mexico.

Even beyond tax advantages, foreign investors enjoyed preferential treatment when it came to operating their businesses in China. Administrative procedures were greatly simplified in the SEA domains. Special administrative committees held approval power for foreign investment that would ordinarily be relegated to provincial governments. Companies operating in SEAs could expeditiously win approval in the "customs office, bureau of commerce and industry, administration of foreign exchange [and] administration of taxation."[28]

Wage Advantages

China offered very low wages to foreign investors. The fully-loaded salaries for Chinese were considerably less than $1 per hour. The average employee required fewer benefits and holidays than in other outsourcing countries. For instance, a Chinese worker had lower bonuses and lacked the program for food coupons that prevailed in Mexico. Social security and insurance policies were not available for most Chinese plants, in part due to the lack of unionization. At the same time, an average Chinese worker spent 2,930 hours per year at the SEA, or 25% more time than what the average Mexican committed to maquilas. (See **Exhibit 8**.)

FDI and Trade

The economic impact of the Special Economic Areas had thus far encouraged FDI inflows that reached $60 billion in 2004. China surpassed the U.S. as the world's largest recipient of FDI.[29] (See **Exhibit 9**.) The growth in FDI had a strong direct proportional link to the rise in plants and other facilities in China's 40 existing Special Economic Areas. The province of Guangzhou alone boasted 900 facilities.[30]

In 1994 China unified its cumbersome, dual exchange-rate system. At the same time, it devalued the currency (Renminbi, or Yuan) from 5.75 to 8.7 yuan per dollar. In November 1994 the exchange rate was stabilized at 8.3, where it has remained ever since.

China's successful, albeit gradual, opening had generated more than $400 billion in cumulative trade surpluses. Its trade relationship with the United States, however, was anything but symmetric. While the U.S. bought about 40% of China's exports, China bought but 3% of U.S. exports. In 2002, Americans purchased 10% of China's entire GDP, while China purchased about one-fifth of 1% of the U.S. GDP. This resulted in a bilateral trade imbalance of $124 billion, reaching $153 billion in 2004.

China's total trade volume had witnessed a remarkable growth and was currently projected to reach almost $2 trillion by 2008. (See **Exhibit 10**.) Outward-bound exports from foreign enterprises had exceeded 50% of total exports by 2001. This growth in exports obviously contributed to China's incredible GDP growth, which was 9.1% in 2003.

Critics of Special Economic Areas

Despite the positive developments for the Chinese economy and the improvement of Sino-U.S. relations, there were vocal critics on the U.S. side of Special Economic Areas. Primarily, the critics highlighted the myriad American jobs that had been shipped overseas through SEA-driven outsourcing. Factories and plants were closing in the U.S. in large numbers, contributing to the de-industrialization of its economy. Opponents of SEAs and the WTO claimed that globalization hurt workers in the manufacturing sector, as employers were lured by lower labor costs and lucrative tax advantages in China.

Again from Pat Buchanan: "In 2002, the U.S. trade deficit with China was $103 billion. In 2003, it hit $124 billion, the largest trade deficit between the two nations in history."[31] Other critics cited additional malaises. They attributed the falling dollar and the diminution of American income to the expansion of the Chinese market. Free trade was associated with eroding national self-sufficiency and dependence on foreign sources for vital goods.

Political risk was another area frequently cited by critics. One was the risk associated with Taiwan, given the U.S.'s tacit support of Taiwan. Another challenge was China's severe shortage of energy and power, which had to be resolved if growth was to continue at its present pace. Furthermore, China had a rather dismal reputation for corruption—even worse than Mexico. The prospect of SARS, or other similar shocks, added to operational risks.

India's Software and Services

Recent Economic Reforms

The present outsourcing trend was expedited by the so-called "Washington Consensus" in India. The Washington Consensus was a set of economic policies that sought to heal the ailing Indian economy, ultimately orienting the country toward globalization. In 1991, India faced a substantial balance-of-payments crisis, which compelled the government to seek help from the International Monetary Fund in 1991. The IMF granted the loans and prescribed various policies for market reform in India. Among them were "fiscal discipline, increased public expenditure on health and education, tax reform, interest rate liberalization, a competitive exchange rate, the removal of barriers to trade and barriers to foreign investment, deregulation, and secure property rights."[32]

While the results of the Washington Consensus were mixed, these policies certainly contributed to the rise of Indian entrepreneurs, such as Wipro, Tata Consultancy Services, and Infosys Technologies. Meanwhile, FDI trickled into India, eventually rising to $4.4 billion in 2004. According to an A.T. Kearney report, "India displaced Mexico to become the third most attractive destination worldwide and is increasingly perceived as a R&D hub for a wide range of industries."[33] The conditions were ripe for foreign firms to focus on India's manufacturing and intellectual markets.

The privatization campaign was another vital feature of the Washington Consensus that facilitated outsourcing. Few foreign firms were willing to open plants in a country that did not have solid private property rules. As India's Secretary of Disinvestment, Pradip Baijal, noted at the time, "Our privatization policy is clear. Other than defense, railway, and atomic energy, all sectors are being privatized."[34] While major state enterprises were kept away from private hands, at least the process of privatization was unfolding. The multinational companies were also encouraged to participate. For instance, foreign investors were given an opportunity to own up to 40% in Indian banks. In 2003, the government offered a third of the stake in national oil companies.

Toward Outsourcing

The news about George W. Bush's reelection in 2004 was taken very positively in India. "This is great news for the offshoring industry. . . . The trend toward outsourcing will now become even more inexorable," said Nandan Nilekani, chief executive of Infosys Technologies. "The President's track record has been of recognizing the advantages of the free trade," said Kiran Karnik, president of the industry group Nasscom, or National Association of Software and Service Companies. Major Indian executives expected more and more firms to outsource to India, since the Bush administration did not plan to punish the "Benedict Arnold" American companies, to use John Kerry's campaign parlance.[35]

For over a decade, Indian software vendors performed work for top American and European companies, such as General Electric and Citigroup. Inexpensive skilled labor in India was readily available. The high-tech boom of the 1990s heightened the demand for software engineers in the United States. As the boom turned into bust, major U.S. companies became more sensitive about the costs of labor. Moreover, leading outsourcing companies earned close to two-thirds of their revenue from non-U.S. customers.

India's outsourcing industry employed over 800,000 people. The software and back-office services industries posted $12.5 billion in export revenues for fiscal year 2003. That figure represented a 30% increase over the previous year, as the global demand for India's services grew. Credit card and billing services rose rapidly in India, with companies like Ernst Young taking advantage of low costs. Readily available intellectual capital made India a viable market for outsourcing of services.[36]

General Electric, Inc.

A firm known to have spread its work in manufacturing and services throughout the world is the General Electric Company (GE). GE was prominent in such sectors as jet engines, plastics, power generation, medical equipment, and financial services, to name a few.[37] In 2004, GE was the largest company by market capitalization in the world; it employed about 315,000 people.

GE had established a powerful international presence over the past 15 years. Tens of thousands of jobs had been created in Asia, India, Latin America, and Europe. In Mexico, GE operated 30 plants including joint ventures, many of which were maquiladoras. In China, GE had invested in a dozen operations, mostly in Special Economic Areas. GE sold products in China and purchased products to supply its U.S. operations. In India, GE established its position in the software sector, taking advantage of the availability of human capital.

Over the last century and a quarter, GE established itself in more than 100 countries. It was one of the largest foreign investors in Japan, it had an enormous presence in Europe, employed more than 20,000 in India, and was widely present in Latin America. Headquartered in Fairfield, Connecticut, General Electric comprised 11 business units: (1) Advanced Materials, (2) Commercial Finance, (3) Consumer Finance, (4) Consumer & Industrial, (5) Energy, (6) Equipment Services, (7) Healthcare, (8) Infrastructure, (9) Insurance, (10) NBC Universal, and (11) Transportation Systems. Almost half of GE's net income came from financial services.

For the calendar year 2003, GE Insurance, GE Commercial Finance, and GE Energy were the businesses with the greatest revenue: $26.2 billion, $20.8 billion, and $19.0 billion, respectively. (See **Exhibit 11.**) Jeff Immelt served as the current chairman of GE. Under his leadership, GE revenues reached $134.2 billion in 2003. International revenues contributed 45% of the total. Immelt placed a strong emphasis on growing international markets: "The bet has to be that China is going to figure out micro-economic practices and India is going to fix its infrastructure, and therefore both of them will be tremendously competitive over time."[38]

GE Mexico

GE had established itself in Mexico over the previous 108 years. While its presence in 1985 consisted merely of several plants, by 2003 GE Mexico had expanded its production to over 30 plants and the employment of over 30,000 people. In 1985, all of GE's Mexican plants were located in the north. The plants in Juarez were responsible for production of capacitors, electric motors, and control devices, while the plant in Monterrey was responsible for lighting products. By 2004, GE's geography had mushroomed throughout Mexico. In Monterrey alone there were 10 plants, six of which were joint ventures. There were GE maquilas in Chihuahua, Tampico, and Queretaro.

GE Mexico was GE's largest operation outside of the United States. Under the leadership of country manager Edmundo Vallejo, GE worked closely with the Mexican government to make sure that GE's target of 6% productivity growth was met. Some of GE's businesses in Mexico were clear winners. For instance, GE's Real Estate sector was a clear winner, with over $1 billion in financing in Mexico. GE had thus become Mexico's top real estate lender.

Mexico's languages—Spanish and English—facilitated business relationships with GE USA. Technicians from America could visit Mexico, and vice versa, to work on system and technological improvements. Doing so in China, of course, entailed greater expense and significant language difficulties. Even for a phone call, China was 12 hours away. And finally, Mexico's domestic market, with incomes of more than $6,000 per capita and a population over 100 million, was another attraction for GE. "That's why financial services are growing," explained Vallejo, "and we are definitely trying to grow more in the businesses that depend on infrastructure investment."[39] GE Financial Services, for example, was eager to challenge the large foreign-owned banks in consumer lending, mortgages, credit cards, and a host of commercial-loan sectors.

Some factors, however, were less conducive to GE operations in Mexico. The wages and turnover costs, in addition to the costs of land, construction, water, gas, and electricity were high when compared with similar costs in China. And there were also macroeconomic factors that needed improvement. While Mexico's inflation rate had dropped from 35% (1996) to 5% (2003), the country was still not ideal for FDI due to the currency's vulnerability to fluctuations. Mexico's GNP growth was on the rebound after its steep decline in 2000–2001, but at 4.2% for 2004 it was still low compared with Asian markets.

Mexico had recently instituted scholarships and support programs for "On the Job Training." It had put in place a South-East Development Program, colloquially known as "March to the South." There were also "Smart Borders" and "Reliable Trader" programs, which were implemented by a Presidential Council for Competitiveness. These initiatives were designed to improve Mexico's reputation as a worthy investment and trading partner. In addition, the Mexican government was trying to improve schools, labor-force training, and the workings of its courts.

Edmundo Vallejo remained cautiously optimistic about Mexico's GE potential, at the same time recognizing that GE China was a worthy investment target. "We certainly have been impacted negatively by the economic downturn," said Vallejo:

> I would attribute the majority of what we suffered the last two or three years to the global slowdown. But my concern is the projects looking ahead in terms of them going somewhere else and certainly as a somewhere else, China is a huge possibility. That worries me and that is why we are trying to understand better what are the advantages of Mexico. We work with the government to explain to them that when the economy picks up and when the global demand picks up, we have to be ready so that companies will again look at Mexico as a source of opportunity.[40]

GE China

General Electric's relationship with China dated back to 1910, when the first GE light bulb was produced there. Almost a century later, GE presence in China entailed $1.5 billion in investments, employment of more than 12,000, and formation of more than a dozen joint ventures. These ventures thrived in high-technology industries (which included medical systems, plastics, and lighting products), and in aircraft engine maintenance facilities, training, and component manufacturing. GE had recently opened a huge research facility in Shanghai, to perform specialized research for Asian product development.[41]

GE plants were located throughout coastal China. The Eastern and Southern corridors were especially heavily populated with GE plants. The Power Services joint ventures were located in Harbin, while Fine Silicones were in Shenzhen, Shenjang, and Shanghai. Wuhi housed GEMS Ultrasound, while Shenyang had SBW Turbo-machinery. (See **Exhibit 12**.) GE was trying to build more plants inland, where land was cheaper.

China exhibited a synergy between customers and markets in the areas of electronics, telecommunications, transportation, and healthcare, among others. Metalwork, small appliances, and tooling were other examples of successful sectors in GE China. The manufacturing sector alone claimed only 4,000 employees. The research and development, sourcing, and distribution presence in China was substantial.[42]

GE China successfully led in innovation. In March 2004, for example, GE became the first foreign company to announce a subsidiary in China to engage in leasing. As Geoff Li, a spokesman at GE China, noted, "We used to have some reservations about the Chinese market because of the potential high risks. However, we are now convinced that in the long run the advantages of entering the China market will outweigh the risks."[43] Numerous other foreign companies had followed GE China's lead, positioning themselves to become viable global competitors.

In 2002, Jeff Immelt identified China as GE's major target for international growth. His objective would be $5 billion in sales and $5 billion in sourcing by 2005. "Our China strategy has always been about growth in sales, sourcing and expanding the manufacturing capability to serve our customers in China and around the world," said Steve Schneider, chairman and CEO of GE China.[44] The company had formed a "One GE" strategic and practical approach to China. It involved four components. There was a sourcing component, in which GE would source parts and goods from domestic producers where cost savings exceeded 10%. Most of GE China's sourcing to date was in consumer products, but not those that competed with GE Mexico. (See **Exhibit 13**.)

GE's other three components were focused on China's own swelling markets. GE planned to manufacture products for China, develop distributional channels for selling, and build up its services—both product-related services such as locomotive repairs and jet engine services, and eventually GE Capital's more sophisticated financial services. (See **Exhibit 14**.)

GE India

General Electric had a presence in India since 1902, when India's first hydro power plant was installed by the company. In 1930, the International General Electric established sales of GE products and services by GE businesses that were not represented in India. Seventy years later, GE enjoyed a major presence in India, which extended to aircraft engines, capital services, medical systems, industrial, systems, plastics, power systems, broadcasting, and others. In 2002, revenues and orders exceeded US $1 billion for GE India. As of 2006 Scott R. Bayman was president and CEO of GE India.

The company employed over 22,000 people in the country. Major locations were in Gurgaon, Hyderabad, Bangalore, and Jaipur.[45] The *Wall Street Journal* explained that "GE's technology partnership with India came amid the country's economic opening, which began in 1991 when New Delhi began systematically dismantling tariff and export controls."[46]

When in 1989 Jack Welch traveled to India to seek a business partnership, he was surprised to learn that India needed business for its embryonic high-tech sector. "We want to sell you software," he was told by Sam Pitroda, chief technology adviser to the late Indian Premier Rajiv Gandhi.[47] This meeting was the foundation for the strategic outsourcing relationship between the company conglomerate and the nation populated with talent.

Since then General Electric successfully placed an emphasis on human capital in India. (See **Exhibit 15**.) Nigel Andrews, a former top GE Capital executive who oversaw India, claimed that India's 100 million English speakers offered a vast pool of inexpensive, educated labor. Nevertheless, training had to be done. The GE Indian program for training managers was instrumental in bringing up local talent. This strategy also allowed greater remote monitoring and maintenance in India. The vast majority of employees who filled the white-collar jobs had a university-level education. The Offshore Development Centers, which pioneered the idea of software sourcing in India, was largely responsible for promoting the educational zeal. The John F. Welch Technology Center was the most famous example, being the first and the largest multidisciplinary research facility in India. In addition to avoiding educational orientation, the Center provided critical technology, research, and development, and financing techniques. In 2005 the *Wall Street Journal* stated that "This year the conglomerate plans to spend about $600 million on computer-software development from Indian companies, according to a recent company report. The company estimates that similar products would cost it as much as $1.2 billion in the U.S."[48]

GE Capital Services served diverse needs of a global business via its outsourcing services which included transaction processing, finance and accounting services, call center services, customer fulfillment activities and processes, data modeling and analytics support, managed IT services, software solutions, and e-learning. GE Capital Services India's financing businesses was composed of commercial finance (GE Commercial Finance) and consumer finance (GE Countrywide and GE-SBI). GE Commercial Finance had $1.2 billion in assets, offering financial solutions to corporate and retail customers. GE Countrywide represented India's leading consumer finance company, "with one of the widest retail distribution networks covering over 5,000 outlets across India, and operating out of 44 locations in the country." GE-SBI, a joint venture with the State Bank of India, was in 2005 the largest provider of VISA cards in India. Crisil and Fitch assigned Capital India a favorable credit rating of AAA. "Capital India's Business Process Outsourcing (BPO) arm, Capital International Services (CIS), provides outsourcing services, including finance and accounting services, collection services, insurance services, customer fulfillment activities and processes, data modeling and analytics support, managed IT services, software solutions, e-learning and remote-marketing. GECIS is a global company headquartered in India with operations in China, Hungary, and Mexico."[49]

General Electric was successful in sourcing products, services, and intellectual talent from India for its global businesses. In the sphere of intellectual sourcing, GE India presented very low costs, offering substantial savings in comparison with English-speaking countries, while retaining high quality. GE India sales and sourcing had blossomed to $0.7 billion and $2.0 billion, respectively, in 2003. The current estimates predicted at least a 20% growth for both sales and sourcing by 2005. (See **Exhibit 16**.) The savings in services was especially significant.[50] As white-collar jobs migrated to India, the rationale for the cost-cutting benefits of outsourcing was serious. For instance, Hewitt Associates estimated that a computer programmer with two to four years of experience earned annually about $10,000 in India, while earning $62,000 in the U.S.

As an outsourcing market, India took away the highest-paying U.S. jobs. Management at GE, however, had a different perspective on this process. According to CEO Jeff Immelt, "India is playing a key role in GE's globalization initiative. Our research and development, engineering design and software development centers in India are fully integrated into GE's global centers. The back room centers of excellence spread across India are raising quality levels, improving cycle times and lowering GE's cost of operations."[51] The popular executive attitude toward outsourcing to India was best summarized by Raman Roy, the founder of Wipro's call-center operation: "[t]echnology companies and outsourcing firms in India need to recognize that if it wasn't for GE, they wouldn't be here today."[52]

In Conclusion

In the domain of outsourcing, an inherent competition existed between Mexico, China, and India as of 2006. The business interests of these countries competed for the attention of key American companies, such as General Electric. Their governments strove to make the financial climate more accommodating in order to enhance the investor relations of outsourcing, and to create jobs.

For instance, one could see how Mexico's maquiladoras and China's Special Economic Areas competed for the manufacturing market. As David Luhnow of the *Wall Street Journal* observed:

> What's happening in Mexico illustrates how globalization is a double threat to blue-collar workers in wealthy countries such as the U.S. . . . low-skill factory jobs migrate directly to China and countries such as Mexico accelerate their competitiveness for their own survival. By playing the role of upstart global entrepreneur, China isn't just drawing in jobs but forcing factories throughout the world to become more efficient.[53]

China had a number of advantages that had made it attractive for sourcing, among them, low labor and electricity costs. A market research firm reported that "the average wage of a semi-skilled employee in China is \$0.50 per hour whereas it ranges from \$2.00 to \$2.50 in Mexico[54] [and] electricity costs \$0.03 per kWh in China whereas it costs \$0.08 in Mexico."[55] However, because of productivity differences, unit labor costs in China appeared to be somewhat higher than those in Mexico. (See **Exhibit 17.**)

Mexico, on its end, still possessed several advantages that contributed to attracting foreign capital. It had a geographic proximity to the U.S., which gave it a reliable and inexpensive shipping advantage, in addition to swift transit time. Mexico also provided greater protection of intellectual property than China and had a greater transparency in regulation and administration of the maquila industry. Mexico had reformed and refinanced its banking system, while China's banks were broke. Finally, Mexico's legal system recognized the rule of law, while China was just beginning to move beyond its system of guanxi ("relationships"). The peso floated, while the yuan had been fixed since 1994, and was probably undervalued. (See **Exhibit 18.**)

What are the longer-term prospects for the U.S.-Mexican NAFTA relationship? Will the low costs in China further contribute to channeling away manufacturing processes to the communist country? In this context, did the advantage of market proximity become less important?

As of 2006, another powerful competition for outsourcing currently existed between China and India. Although India was the undisputed leader in IT outsourcing, some studies, like that of Horasis' Global Outsourcing Report, predicted that China would converge onto India within the next 10 years, and ultimately overtake its leadership in software and services.[56] India and China already substantially competed for FDI. According to the A.T. Kearney study, "China and India dominate the top two positions for most positive investor outlook, likely first-time investments, and most preferred offshore investment locations for business processing functions and IT services."[57] (**See Exhibits 19 a & b.**)

At the same time, General Electric maintained strong positions in both India and China, although its Chinese market had global revenues four times higher than those of India. (See **Exhibit 20.**) There were sourcing opportunities for GE in both countries. In 2006 India was at the beginning of its major growth cycle. Little financial investment was needed in India, since the intellectual talent was quite abundant. China also provided substantial growth opportunities. As China prepared for the 2008 Beijing Olympics, the opportunities for sourcing would continue to expand.

Will the dominance in software and services outsourcing shift toward China? How will such a pattern affect China's manufacturing capabilities? Would a GE-like company find it ideal to limit the outsourcing of manufacturing and services to one country?

In the United States, the overwhelming domestic question of American Outsourcing was that of jobs. Despite moderately rising jobs numbers, in 2005 this topic remained as acute as ever before. Forrester Research estimated that 40% of Fortune 1000 firms had already outsourced some work abroad, and that another 3 million jobs would leave the United States by 2015. A 2005 Berkeley study indicated that 14 million U.S. jobs, or 11% of total labor force, were currently vulnerable to outsourcing.[58]

With the downward pressures on wages and the quality of jobs deteriorating, both blue- and white-collar workers were in jeopardy. Low-skilled workers were more willing to accept jobs without health insurance. Skilled professionals with university education were receiving fewer financial returns for their educational investment. As outsourcing markets to Mexico, China, and India continued to expand, the loss of jobs was likely to affect different income cohorts. On another hand, the practice of outsourcing helped free trade and thus boosted domestic GDP.

Will the American employment losses continue in the short-run? Will the outsourcing trend ultimately bring in more jobs in the longer run? Is it time for the U.S. government to step in with the outsourcing regulation? Or should the outsourcing market be allowed to prosper without Uncle Sam's intervention?

Exhibit 1   Total Maquila Plants in Mexico

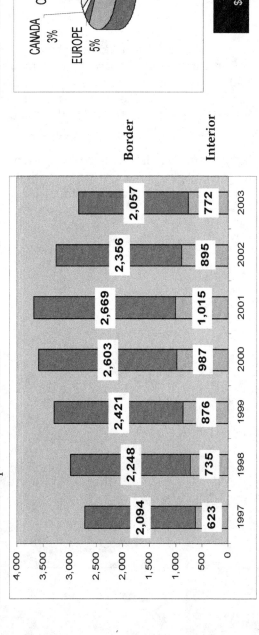

Source: INEGI, SE (from *Mexico Now*, 2004, Number 9).

Exhibit 2   Mexico's Global Exports Markets (US$ billions)

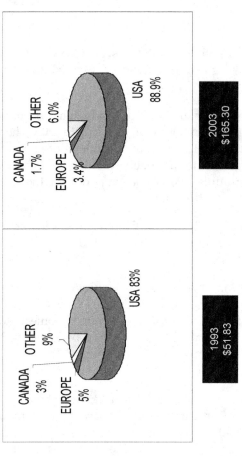

Source: SE, Banco de Mexico, INEGI (from *Mexico Now*, 2004, Number 9).

Exhibit 3   The Impact of NAFTA on Mexico

Trade

	'93	'03
Total Imports (US$Billion)	65	171
Total Exports (US$Billion)	52	165
Exports to US (% from total)	83	90
Agriculture Exp. (US$Billion)	3.3	5.6

Infrastructure

	'93	'03
Highways ('000 of Mi)	191	217
Toll Freeways ('000 of Mi)	0.9	3.1
Power Generation ('000 of Mi)	135	263
Cellphone Lines (Million)	0.3	28.1

Commercial Exchange
(as % of GDP)

1993 29.1%
2003 49.5%

FDI
(US$Million)

1993 4,389
2003 11,372

Source: INEGI, Banxico.

Exhibit 4   Map of Mexico Showing Share of Maquiladora Establishments, by State

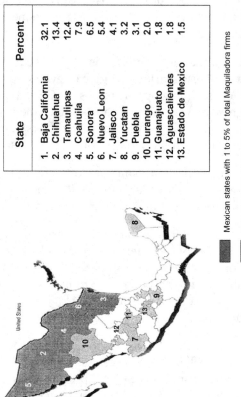

State	Percent
1. Baja California	32.1
2. Chihuahua	13.4
3. Tamaulipas	12.4
4. Coahuila	7.9
5. Sonora	6.5
6. Nuevo Leon	5.4
7. Jalisco	4.1
8. Yucatan	3.2
9. Puebla	3.1
10. Durango	2.0
11. Guanajuato	1.8
12. Aguascalientes	1.8
13. Estado de Mexico	1.5

▮ Mexican states with 1 to 5% of total Maquiladora firms

▯ Mexican states with more than 5% of total Maquiladora firms

Source: Center for Analysis and Economic Projections of Mexico.

Exhibit 5   Mexico's Top 10 Foreign Investors (FDI %)

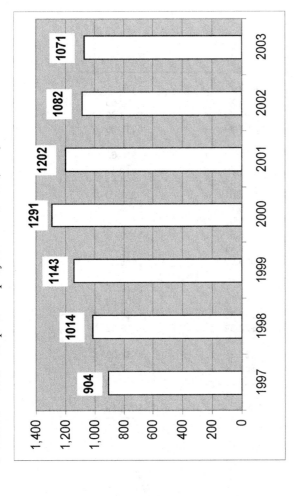

Source: INEGI, SE (from *Mexico Now*, 2004, Number 9.)

Exhibit 6   Total Maquila Employees in Mexico (000s)

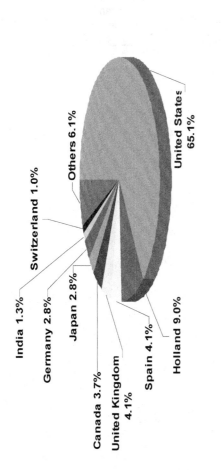

Source: INEGI, SE (from *Mexico Now*, 2004, Number 9.)

Exhibit 7   Direct Labor Wage Fully Loaded (Dollar/Hour)

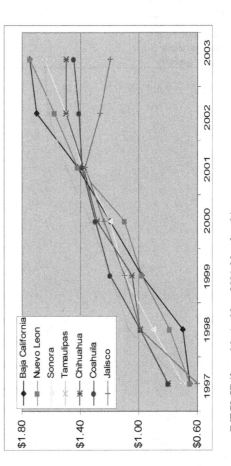

Source: INEGI, SE (from *Mexico Now*, 2004, Number 9.)

Exhibit 8   Salary Breakdown

	Mexico	China
Base Salary per Day	$6.24	$2.53
Base Salary per year	$2,197.49	$513.66
SUBTOTAL	**$2,197.49**	**$513.66**
BASIC BENEFITS		
Vacation Days	$31.21	$14.63
Vacation Premium	$7.80	$6.10
Holidays	$36.41	$26.83
New Year/Christmas Bonus	$78.01	$37.80
Savings Fund	$246.79	$189.02
Food Coupons (Year)	$325.00	
Attendance Bonus (Year)	$278.57	$280.49
Profit Sharing (Year)	$62.41	$31.34
SUBTOTAL	**$1,066.19**	**$586.21**
ADDITIONAL BENEFITS		
Housing		$170.75
Cafeteria (Year)	$557.14	$804.88
Life Insurance (Year)	$26.79	$8.29
Uniforms (Year)	$22.32	$6.22
Transportation	$232.14	
Medicines (Year)	$31.25	$7.93
Social /Sport Activities (Year)	$58.04	$7.56
SUBTOTAL	**$927.68**	**$1,005.63**
FISCAL COST		
Social Security	$496.63	$326.59
Wage Tax		$30.57
Housing Program	$113.93	
State Tax	$115.00	
Half-Yearly Tax	$3.76	
SUBTOTAL	**$729.32**	**$357.16**
TOTAL ANNUAL	**$4,920.68**	**$2,462.66**
Hours per Year	**2,223**	**2,930**
Cost per Hour	**$2.21**	**$0.84**
Exchange Rate	**11.2 P/$**	**8.2 Y/$**

Source: *Mexico Now*, 2004, Number 11.

Exhibit 9   China's FDI Inflows (US$ billions)

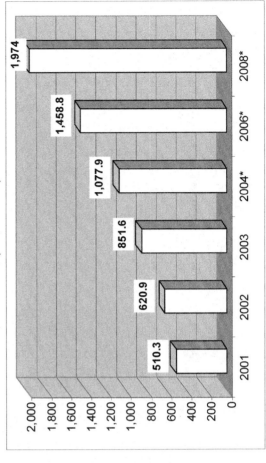

Source: *The Economist:* EIU for China, January 2005, based on data from China's Ministry of Foreign Trade and Economic Cooperation.

Exhibit 10   China's Total Trade (US$ billions)

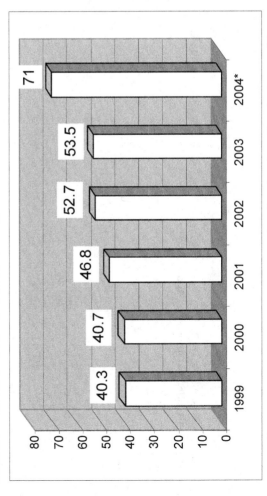

Source: *Global Insight,* U.S. Department of Commerce, U.S. International Trade Commission.
*estimated

Exhibit 11   GE Revenues by Business Unit, 2004

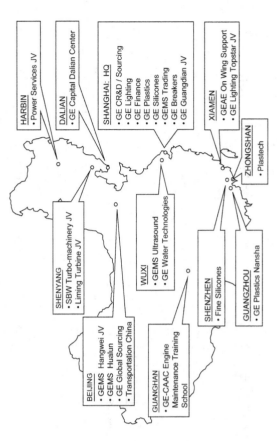

Source: General Electric 2004 Annual Report.

Exhibit 12   GE Investments in China

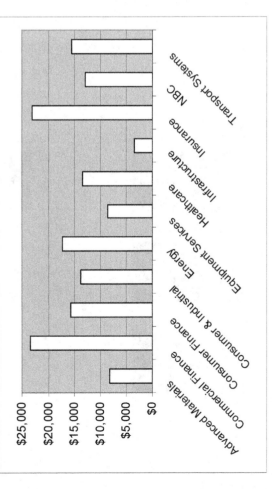

Source: Gary Reiner, *Global Update India & China,* October 18, 2004.

Exhibit 14 "One GE" in China: "Strategic and Practical" Approach

"One GE" in China: "Strategic and Practical" Approach

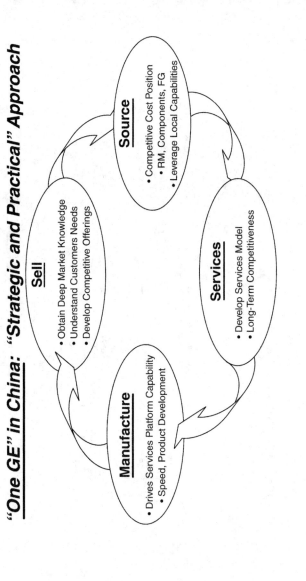

Sell
- Obtain Deep Market Knowledge
- Understand Customers Needs
- Develop Competitive Offerings

Source
- Competitive Cost Position
- RM, Components, FG
- Leverage Local Capabilities

Manufacture
- Drives Services Platform Capability
- Speed, Product Development

Services
- Develop Services Model
- Long-Term Competitiveness

Exhibit 13 China's Sales and Sourcing Trend

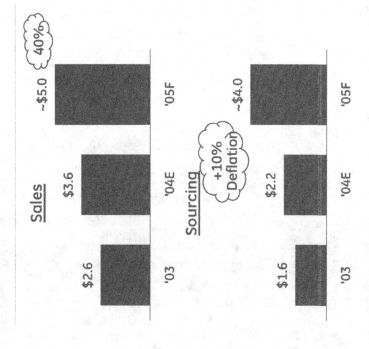

Sales

~$5.0 40%

$3.6

$2.6

'03   '04E   '05F

Sourcing +10% Deflation

~$4.0

$2.2

$1.6

'03   '04E   '05F

Source for both exhibits: Gary Reiner (GE's SVP CIO), *Global Update India & China*, October 18, 2004, http://www.ge.com/files/usa/company/investor/downloads/gary_reiner_update_on_china_india_10182004.pdf, accessed April 9, 2005.

Exhibit 15   India's Intellectual Capital

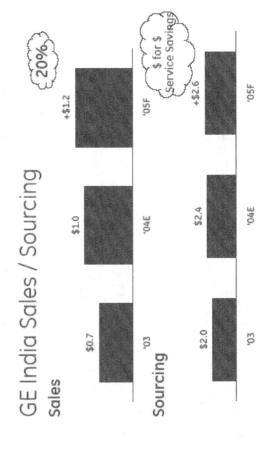

- Entry level leadership programs ... 400+
- Audit staff assignments 50+ in 2003
- Cross business moves in India ... 400+ last 2 yrs
- Global assignments .... 200+
- 1005+ with options

Source: Gary Reiner, *Global Update India & China*, October 2004.

Exhibit 16   India's Sales and Sourcing Trend

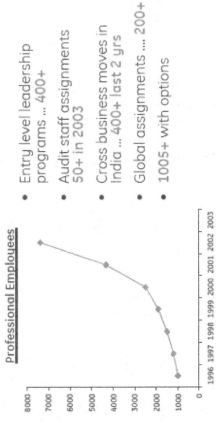

Source: Gary Reiner, *Global Update India & China*, October 2004.

Exhibit 17   Unit Labor Cost by Country: Comparison with U.S.

	Wages (A)	Labor Productivity (B)	Unit Labor Cost (A/B*100)
U.S.	100.0	100.0	100.0
Sweden	74.5	53.8	138.5
Japan	62.6	67.8	92.3
Singapore	49.0	49.0	100.0
Taiwan	43.1	24.4	176.9
Korea	27.0	43.9	61.5
Chile	26.2	42.5	61.5
Mexico	16.3	30.3	53.8
Turkey	15.7	22.7	69.2
Malaysia	10.9	12.9	84.6
Philippines	8.6	15.9	53.8
Bolivia	7.7	16.8	46.2
Egypt	5.9	5.1	115.4
Kenya	5.4	3.5	153.8
Indonesia	4.6	6.6	69.2
Zimbabwe	4.6	5.0	92.3
India	3.1	2.9	107.7
China	2.1	2.7	76.9

Source: United Nations Conference on Trade and Development (UNCTAD), Trade and Development Report, 2002.

Exhibit 18   Mexico, China, India: Macro Variables

Mexico

	1999	2000	2001	2002	2003	2004
GDP Growth	3.70%	6.90%	-0.30%	0.70%	1.30%	4.40%
Inflation Rate	16.50%	9.50%	6.00%	5.00%	4.50%	4.70%
Exchange Rate (Peso/$US)	9.6	9.5	9.3	9.8	10.8	11.3
Total Trade ($US BN)	278.4	340.9	370.5	330.2	336.2	385.8

China

	1999	2000	2001	2002	2003	2004
GDP Growth	7.10%	8.00%	7.30%	8.00%	9.10%	9.50%
Inflation Rate	-1.30%	-1.00%	0.40%	-0.80%	3.00%	3.90%
Exchange Rate (Yuan/$US)	8.3	8.3	8.3	8.3	8.3	8.3
Total Trade ($US BN)	362.5	445	510.3	620.9	851.6	1,135.5

India

	1999	2000	2001	2002	2003	2004
GDP Growth	7.10%	3.90%	5.20%	4.10%	8.60%	6.80%
Inflation Rate	4.70%	4.00%	3.80%	4.30%	3.80%	3.80%
Exchange Rate (Yuan/$US)	43	44.9	47.2	48.6	46.6	45.3
Total Trade ($US BN)	82.4	98.4	96.6	107.8	127.1	160.9

Source: Compiled by casewriter from National Bureau of Statistics of China, Global Insight, U.S. Department of Commerce (*Mexico Now*, 2004, Numbers 9 and 11); *Latin Business Chronicle*; *CIA World Fact Book*; OECD *Economic Outlook*, 2004.

Exhibit 19a Ranking of FDI Confidence Index

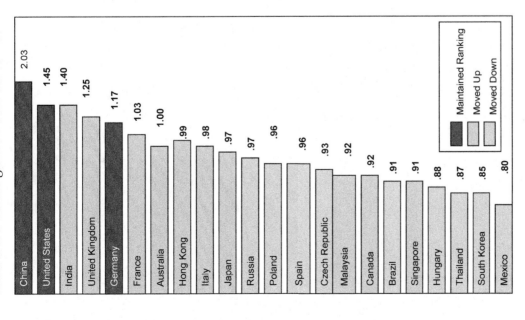

Exhibit 19b Which is more attractive for the following FDI attributes—China or India

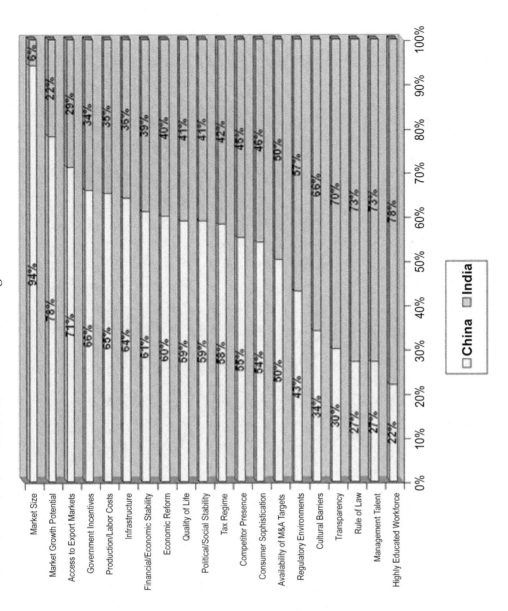

Source: Compiled from A.T. Kearney data.

Exhibit 20   General Electric's Worldwide Presence

Source: Gary Reiner, *Global Update India & China*, October 2004.   Accessed 4/9/05.   Available at http://www.ge.com/files/usa/company/investor/downloads/gary_reiner_update_on
_china_india_10182004.pdf.

Endnotes

[1] CNN website, "Bush promotes job creation on PA trip," Associated Press, http://www.cnn.com/2004/ALLPOLITICS/02/12/elec04.prez.bush.ap/, February 12, 2004.

[2] GE website, "General Electric Executive Defends Outsourcing Policies," April 29, 2004, http://www.gecapitalindia.com/gecapital/news.htm.

[3] Lou Dobbs, *Exporting America* (New York: Warner Books, 2004), p. 1.

[4] Craig Richards and Lori Margolis, "U.S.: Outsourcing threatens one in six jobs in Silicon Valley," May 5, 2004, World Socialist website, http://www.wsws.org.

[5] Lou Dobbs, *Exporting America*, p. 10.

[6] Patrick J. Buchanan, *Where the Right Went Wrong* (New York: St. Martin's Press), 2004.

[7] Lou Dobbs, *Exporting America*, pp. 167–196.

[8] Economic Policy Institute, Open Letter to the President, October 4, 2004.

[9] Lou Dobbs, *Exporting America*.

[10] Warren Vieth, "Fed Chief Warns of Barriers to Growth," *Los Angeles Times*, February 12, 2004, p. C-1.

[11] Council of Economic Advisers, 2004 Economic Report of the President, U.S. Govt. Printing Office, p. 30.

[12] Benjamin Powell, "Outsourcing Benefits Silicon Valley," April 9, 2004, Pacific Research Institute, www.pacificresearch.org.

[13] William C. Gruben et al., "NAFTA and Maquiladoras: Is the Growth Connected?" Federal Reserve Bank of Dallas, www.dallasfed.org, June 2001.

[14] Ibid.

[15] Ibid.

[16] Lou Dobbs, *Exporting America*.

[17] Patrick J. Buchanan, *Where the Right Went Wrong*.

[18] United States Trade Representative, "NAFTA: A Decade of Success," July 1, 2004, www.ustr.gov.

[19] Staci Warden, "Assessing Export Platforms: The Case of the Maquiladora Sector in Mexico," CAER Discussion Paper No. 78, 2002.

[20] Trade Commission of Mexico in Los Angeles website, "Mexican Business Opportunities and Legal Framework/Maquiladora Program (In-bound Program)," http://www.mexico-trade.com/exports.html.

[21] Aureliano Gonzalez Baz, "What Is a Maquiladora?" http://www.udel.edu/leipzig/texts2/vox128.htm.

[22] Staci Warden, "Assessing Export Platforms: The Case of the Maquiladora Sector in Mexico."

[23] U.S. General Accounting Office, Report to Congressional Requesters, "Mexico's Maquiladora Decline Affects U.S.-Mexico Border Communities and Trade; Recovery Depends in Part on Mexico's Actions," July 2003, GAO-03-891, p. 8.

[24] Ibid.

[25] Ibid.

[26] "Special Economic Zones in China," http://chinaunique.com/business/sez.htm.

[27] Ibid.

[28] Memorandum from CHEN Quiang to Mr. Paul Thaler on "Special Zones," July 2003.

[29] Patrick J. Buchanan, *Where the Right Went Wrong*, p. 167.

[30] Sergio L. Ornelas, "Important Tax Procedures for Maquiladoras in 2004," Mexico*Now*, Number 11, July–August 2004, p. 15.

[31] Patrick J. Buchanan, *Where the Right Went Wrong* (New York: St. Martin's Press, 2004), p. 167.

[32] Richard H.K. Vietor and Emily J. Thompson, "India on the Move," HBS No. 703-050.

[33] A.T. Kearney study, 2004.

[34] Richard H.K. Vietor and Emily J. Thompson, "India on the Move," HBS No. 703-050.

[35] Saritha Rai, "In India, outsourcing firms rejoice," *The New York Times*, November 5,2004.

[36] Patrick Thibodeau, "India's Outsourcing Firms Report a Surge in Hiring," Computer World, October 15, 2004, www.computerworld.com.

[37] GE website, http://www.ge.com/en/company/index.htm.

[38] Carmel Crimmins, "G7 company CEOs see rise of China, India predators," February 4, 2005, http://in.news.yahoo.com/050204/137/2jf5o.html.

[39] Edmundo Vallejo quoted in Matthew Brayman, "15 Minutes with Edmundo Vallejo," *Business Mexico*. October 2003.

[40] Ibid.

[41] GE website, http://www.ge.com/stories/en/10794.html.

[42] Consumer and Industrial Asia Pacific Presentation, 2003.

[43] Liang Yu, "GE blazes trail in leasing bix," March 16, 2004, www.chinadaily.com.cn/chinagate/doc/2004-03/16/content_315350.htm.

[44] GE press release, "GE Opens Technology Center in China," PR Newswire, October 23, 2003.

[45] GE website, www.ge.com.

[46] "In India's Outsourcing Boom, GE Played a Starring Role," *Wall Street Journal*, March 23, 2005.

[47] Ibid.

[48] Ibid.

[49] General Electric website, www.ge.com.

[50] Gary Reiner (GE's SVP CIO), "Global Update India & China," October 18, 2004, http://www.ge.com/files/usa/company/investor/downloads/gary_reiner_update_on_china_india_10182004.pdf.

[51] Ibid.

[52] "In India's Outsourcing Boom, GE Played a Starring Role," *Wall Street Journal*, March 23, 2005.

[53] David Luhnow, "Up the Food Chain: As Jobs Move East, Plants in Mexico Retool to Compete," *Wall Street Journal*, March 5, 2004.

[54] Strategic "Strategic Evaluation Electronic Manufacturing Services Provider Market China Versus Mexico," http://www.marketresearch.com/product/display.asp?ProductID=965193.

[55] Ibid.

[56] Ibid.

[57] A.T. Kearney study, 2004.

[58] Sarah Anderson and John Cavanagh, "*Outsourcing: A Policy Agenda*," Foreign Policy in Focus, Vol. 9, No. 2, April 2004.

JEFFREY FEAR

CARIN-ISABEL KNOOP

Dr. Ing. h.c. F. Porsche AG (A): True to Brand?

I do not copy any Harvard blueprint; instead I try every day to lead my team through fact-based discussions. In this process it helps that people feel how enthusiastic I am. I stand behind every decision. My colleagues learn that immediately.

—Wendelin Wiedeking[1]

Porsche . . . there is no substitute.

—Porsche advertising slogan[2]

[Location] is not an uncritical issue. People think that as a car comes off the line at Zuffenhausen, [company founder] Ferdinand Porsche comes by and caresses the car with his hand, and that makes it an official Porsche. Of course, Ferdinand Porsche hasn't been doing that for some time.

—Porsche spokesman[3]

In August 1996, legendary sports car maker Dr. Ing. h.c. F. Porsche A.G. (Porsche)[4] launched the Boxster, a zippy new two-seater with an "entry-level" price of $40,000. At the same time, Porsche chairman and CEO Wendelin Wiedeking stunned the automotive world by announcing that as of September 1997 the Boxster would be assembled in Finland, rather than at Porsche's main Zuffenhausen plant, which was already operating beyond capacity. In spring of 1998, just months after the controversial move to Finland, Wiedeking shocked observers yet again by confirming rumors that Porsche would enter the fast growing sport-utility vehicle (SUV) market by 2002. The company would also be looking for a production site for this new model.

This one-two punch immediately sparked a debate about whether Porsche would or could remain true to its brand and its "made in Germany" imprimatur. Could the Porsche brand ever align with an SUV concept? Could the small German company become a major player in the already very competitive—and chiefly U.S.-oriented—SUV market? Would luxury SUV sales expand beyond North America to markets that had neither the roads and parking nor the cheap energy for oversized vehicles? And would SUV production be located in Germany or elsewhere? Launching a new model series was risky for any manufacturer, but especially risky for a small player such as Porsche.

If Porsche went ahead with an SUV, there were several options for development and production. It could partner with a major manufacturer to gain development and manufacturing efficiencies as well as production slots. Porsche could also follow the course of its German compatriots BMW and Mercedes-Benz, who had established manufacturing bases in the United States, the largest SUV market in the world. But Porsche would need to decide if "made in Germany" was integral to its global appeal. However, making SUVs in Germany—with its strong unions, high and rising labor costs, and appreciating currency—could push the luxury product prices even higher, and posed other challenges as well. But how important was it for the new model to actually be "made in Germany?"

The responsibility for these decisions lay with Wiedeking, a relentless efficiency expert who, in the mid-1990s, had steered Porsche through one of the most noteworthy turnarounds in industry history. He staved off bankruptcy by cutting costs, paring the product line to two models, and expanding into 70 global markets—30 more than in 1993.[5] By the time of the 1998 SUV announcement, the 50-year old firm was back on solid financial footing and its stock price beat the national DAX index by 180% in the previous two years (see **Exhibits 1** and **2** for stock and financial information).

But the company still needed to manage risk sensibly. Analysts fretted about the dilutive impact an SUV might have on the Porsche name, and worried that the DM 1 billion investment (ca. $550 million in 1998) was a huge bet for a small player like Porsche. Meanwhile, competition within Porsche's core business was expected to increase with the coming launch of a sporty two-seater from Audi, positioned at an equal performance level but priced 15% below the Boxster.[6]

The Legacy

Ferdinand Porsche was born on September 3, 1875, in Maffersdorf, Bohemia, in the former Austro-Hungarian Empire (now Vratislavice in the Czech Republic). After a brief stint as Daimler-Benz's technical director, he left the company, which did not want to build small, fast cars for the public. Unemployed at 55, Porsche started his own design firm for all sorts of vehicles. His son, Ferdinand Anton Ernst "Ferry" Porsche, and his son-in-law, Anton Piëch,[7] joined him, along with key engineers. Ferry became head of R&D. The senior Porsche, renowned for his temper and single-mindedness, imbued the firm with a spirit of fierce independence.

In 1934, Adolf Hitler tasked Porsche to develop a family car that was both cheap and reliable—yielding the "people's car" or Volkswagen, whose design was intended to evoke the German infantry helmet and honor National Socialist ideals. During wartime, the company focused on tank design, including the formidable "Tiger." In June 1948, Porsche launched the *356*, the first automobile to carry the Porsche name. Volkswagen manufactured the 356, with its tubular space-frame chassis, aluminum body, and rear-mounted four-cylinder engine, until Porsche opened its own production facility in Stuttgart-Zuffenhausen in 1950.[8] See **Exhibit 3** for company milestones.

In 1953, Porsche produced its first car specifically for racing, the *550*. In 1964 came the *911*, also a racing car. Designed by Ferry's eldest son, Ferdinand Alexander "Butzi" Porsche, the vehicle became a twentieth-century design milestone. In the 1970s Porsche and Volkswagen collaborated on launching the *914*. In 1972, Porsche became a joint stock company (Porsche AG) with the Porsche and Piëch families on the supervisory board. Butzi left the company at the same time to found his own design studio for other products, called "Porsche Design."

Porsche AG was nearly derailed by the U.S. economy's tailspin and stock market crash in 1987. Sales volume collapsed from a peak of 50,000 cars in 1986 to 14,000 in 1993.[9] The culprits were global recession—particularly in the United States, Porsche's most important market—and a stagnant product line. Leadership problems also affected company performance during this period. In 1990 Butzi succeeded Ferry as chairman of the supervisory board, but lasted only until early 1993. He was replaced by Helmut Sihler, one of the most respected men in German business. Moreover, between 1987 and 1992, four chairmen of the managing board left in disputes with the controlling Porsche and

Piëch families about how to run the company.[10] Sihler named Wendelin Wiedeking, a 38-year-old engineer from central-western Germany, executive director (CEO) of the group in 1993.

New Leadership

An avid car enthusiast since childhood, Wiedeking first drove at age 11, and built over 1,500 model cars as a boy. After completing his doctorate in engineering, he joined Porsche in 1983 as an assistant to the production director. He left in 1988 to head a maker of automotive ball bearings, where he was exposed to Japanese and American production methods and management strategies. In 1991 he returned to Porsche as production and materials management director, and was soon promoted to spokesman of the executive board, and then President and CEO.

Wiedeking claimed that the most important quality in leading a manufacturing operation was "clear direction." Since the age of 15, after his father's death, his goals had been clear: "I have always known what I wanted and have also realized it—without regard for the hesitant and the doubtful."[11] He believed that an effective manager had to "make everybody know about the strategy. In bad times, you must talk very openly about the problems you're facing. Say what you really mean. Put everything on the table. Good things as well as bad things. And then do it. Just do it." He was also said to like and live by two German proverbs: "You sweep the steps from the top down" and "He who barks must also bite." Finally, while rival brands such as Jaguar, Ferrari, Lamborghini, Lotus, Alfa Romeo and Aston Martin had allowed themselves to be sold to mass marketers such as Ford, Fiat, Chrysler and General Motors, Wiedeking remained as independent as the company he led, explaining "Size alone is not a prerequisite for survival."

Wiedeking quickly made his mark inside and outside the company. He emerged as one of the most admired, but outspoken and unconventional CEOs in Germany, challenging the very tenets of shareholder value, and questioning the necessity of issuing quarterly reports and forecasts. "Yes certainly, we [Porsche] too have already heard about shareholder value," he explained. "That changes nothing for us because our customer comes first, then our employees, then our business partners, suppliers, dealers and afterward our shareholders. It is completely inappropriate to place the shareholder first. It will limit the strength of the enterprise. You will achieve the opposite goal and spiral downwards."[12] Such tough talk and bold decision making was quickly turning Wiedeking into a "brand"[13] himself, like Chrysler's Lee Iacocca in the 1980s.

Lean Production

Together with a global brand name and a highly skilled workforce, Wiedeking inherited a bloated management roster, an inefficient production process, and a record $150 million loss widely blamed on management complacency.[14] Early into his tenure as CEO he promised to cut production costs by 30%. Porsche's chairman at the time (Butzi Porsche) declared such a feat impossible. "But I said, 'No, I offered it, I'll bring it,'" Wiedeking reminisced, "and I brought it."[15]

Wiedeking benchmarked every aspect of production to find out how much time, effort, and money went into making every Porsche. His goal was to emulate modern "lean production" or "just in time"[16] manufacturing methods to cut costs and increase productivity. Lean production moved away from the principles of specialization, where individual production line workers had a deep knowledge of one specific task. Instead, lean production environments called for highly skilled and flexible workers who could operate multi-purpose machinery with minimal supervision.[17] Workers' ability to be productive in a team environment became imperative, along with a focus on continuous improvement throughout the entire operation.

In 1992 Wiedeking took key managers on a tour of Toyota, Honda, and Nissan production facilities to show how fat and wasteful Porsche's production process was in comparison. He hired a leading Japanese automotive consultant who, during a plant visit, described the Zuffenhausen plant as more of a warehouse than a factory. He then handed Wiedeking a circular saw and told him to cut the storage shelves in half.[18]

Once trained in the principles of lean production, Porsche employees passed them on to major suppliers to help them lower waste and production cycle time, thus reducing component prices for Porsche.[19] The new strategy reduced manufacturing defects and inventory (from 7 days' worth to 1 day). Revenue per employee rose 53% from FY92 to FY97. The number of cars per production employee per year almost doubled over the same period from 4.9 to 9.1 cars. In FY92 the old 911 (then type 993) took 128 hours to produce; five years later, only 70 hours. The new 911 took 56 to 58 hours to produce.[20]

Wiedeking dismissed a third of the company's middle managers and established the Porsche Improvement Program, designed to measure quality and efficiency and eliminate waste: "I had to cut 2,000 jobs to save 6,000," he explained.[21] Employee participation picked up and improvement suggestions increased from 0.09 to 4 per person. Wiedeking rewarded employee suggestions with cash (DM 100 for a good idea that was implemented) or with gifts, like trips or motorcycles.[22]

New Models

In 1991, a year before Wiedeking became CEO, Porsche launched the first of several cars at lower price points than traditionally associated with the Porsche brand. The 911 RS America was a no-frills version of the long-running rear-engine 911 model; priced at $54,000, it ran about $10,000 under traditional Porsche prices. This was followed by the entry-level 968 at about $40,000, close to the $37,000 Nissan 300ZX Turbo or the $33,000 Mazda RX-7.[23]

By early 1992, Porsche postponed the launch of a larger, luxury Porsche 989 for aging baby boomers when it became clear that its total cost would be 30% higher than the price it could command in the market.[24] The company wrote off significant development costs for the 989 and geared up for its $40,000 two-seat Boxster, to launch by 1996. In an important departure from Porsche practice, the Boxster would share 40% of its parts with the 996.[25] Changes continued in 1992 with a revamped, water-cooled 911. Moving away from the traditional air-cooled engine was another break with the past—and sacrilege to many Porsche purists.

The redesigned 911 and the Boxster were developed simultaneously in a record 37 months, and at a greatly reduced cost. Design engineers made extensive use of computer simulation, which cut the prototype development time and kept costs down. The new 911 used components developed for the 986, reducing costs by 15%.[26] In addition, the Boxster and the new 911 shared the same basic engine, the same basic body structure, and a similar design for chassis and suspension. The result was a higher production volume for individual parts, and an assembly line common to both cars.

The SUV Bet

The Porsche SUV would be the company's third series, and the first developed and launched entirely under Wiedeking's watch. He wanted the vehicle to combine traditional Porsche styling and performance with off-road driving capability and a spacious interior, placing more emphasis on "sports" than "utility." The new car had to retain the brand's style and panache while accommodating family, outdoor, and transport activities. Wiedeking felt that SUVs were "nearer to the sports car business than sedans. We also looked at minivans, but we do not want an eighth 'me-too' product. It has to be a real Porsche in terms of chassis, performance, and design"—Porsche's key strengths.[27] Wiedeking continued: "We know from our surveys that a lot of our customers are waiting for a Porsche SUV. Then there will be no doubt that customers can proudly park their SUV next to a Mercedes S-Class and other cars like that."[28] The average Porsche customer already owned three cars: an SUV, a limousine or sedan, and a sports car.[29]

Much of the SUV sales boom after 1996 occurred in the so-called Premium SUV market. For example, the immediate success of the 1996 Mercedes off-roader M-Class demonstrated a demand for luxury SUVs (see **Exhibit** 4 for SUV market information). Porsche wanted to leverage its "premium" brand to enter that market, emulating Ford Motor Company's achievement with its GT sports car and BMW with its 7- and 5-series luxury vehicles. SUV optimists argued that Porsche had found a solution to diversify its "aging model range" in an oversaturated market. They estimated a breakeven number of 10,000 units priced between DM 100,000 and DM 120,000. By building 20,000 SUVs a year, Porsche could boost its total sales by 50%.[30]

But many Porsche enthusiasts feared that instead of rejuvenating the company, the SUV would cheapen the Porsche image. Some saw the move as near sacrilege.[31] Porsche family shareholders cringed, fearing the company's pure breed sports car tradition and exclusivity were not befitting bulky off-roaders. Wiedeking countered: "Our new sport utility vehicle will not only correspond in full with Porsche's high technical and visual standards, but will also pave the way for future growth potential in the sales, turnover and earnings areas" he promised.[32] An SUV would give Porsche "a new dimension in both profit and revenues."[33]

The automotive press reported that Porsche saw the SUV as its chance to balance the risks of its exchange rate position. Porsche was particularly sensitive to the value of the dollar because 44% of its cars in 1997 were sold in the United States (see **Exhibit 5**).[34] While Porsche had improved its hedging operations since its liquidity crisis of the late 1990s, the company remained highly exposed to the U.S. market and dollar fluctuations. In 1998, 23% of its sales came from the United States (and 37% from Germany).[35] About 80% of its sales came from its vehicles and 9% from spare parts.[36]

The SUVs' popularity with U.S. drivers was attributed to the nation's historic affinity for larger cars and trucks that could serve for both work and personal use. This new breed of vehicle was viewed as innately "American": the rugged and powerful appearance, and the promise to combine the carrying capacity of station wagons with the off-road capability of pick-ups, offered an alternative to old fashioned family suburban and rural utility vehicles. The sporty and aggressive design appealed even to those who would never dream of taking a car into rough terrain, namely preppy, youthful professionals, including working women who preferred not to be associated with station-wagon moms. Luxury/crossover SUVs targeted the high-end market with top quality interior amenities such as navigation systems and DVD players, stylish materials (wood and leather), and lowered suspensions. After Ford's successful launch of the Explorer, other leading manufacturers both in the United States and abroad (Japan, Germany) followed with their own models.

To cut down development and manufacturing costs, SUV bodies tended to be less sophisticated than the newer smaller cars. Most cars employed unibody construction, with a steel body shell designed to absorb the impact of collisions and crumple without injuring the passengers. Many (not all) SUVs were built in the tradition of light trucks, using a "body-on-frame" method which provided a lower level of safety but better maneuverability.

Porsche's SUV would join an already crowded market, estimated at about two million units in early 1998. Still, the category ranged from pick-ups, light trucks, and small jeeps to high-end entries such as the Suzuki LJ. Range Rover—the only SUV with a base price over DM 100,000.[37] A successful high-end, high-performance Porsche SUV could trigger me-too follow-ons within two to three years, thanks to the compression of development intervals within the automobile industry. Already, Mercedes Benz was rumored to be considering an M-Class vehicle with a 300-plus horsepower engine. BMW was also rumored to be interested in developing what would later become the X5. The potential for such new entrants threatened the sustainability of Porsche's sales forecasts of 20,000 SUVs each year.[38] Finally, some observers questioned the long-term attractiveness of the SUV segment, predicting a move towards smaller, more fuel-efficient cars.[39]

In the context of the broad demographic that could afford only lower priced vehicles, Porsche's decision to go forward with a luxury SUV seemed particularly puzzling. And though SUVs had emerged as the most profitable segment of the industry in the 1990s, they lacked the agility and performance synonymous with Porsche. The challenge was now to close the perceptual gap between Porsche attributes and those associated with SUVs.

Location Decisions

One thing was certain—Porsche lacked production capacity for a new SUV. In 1998, the Zuffenhausen factory, originally designed to produce 20,000 cars annually, worked three shifts six days a week and had reached a capacity of about 40,000 cars per year.[40] The location of a new factory had to satisfy multiple criteria and posed a serious challenge to Wiedeking. Since outsourced parts would make up approximately 80% of the finished product, easy access to suppliers was imperative;[41] other factors included labor costs (hourly wages as well as additional expenses such as healthcare, retirement benefits, etc.); the quality, skills, and flexibility of the local labor pool; proximity to major or high quality ports and airports; favorable tariff structures for imported components and exports of finished product; and access to a large local market.[42] The site decision would also consider nonfinancial support of local authorities, the location's fertility as a learning ground, and its potential impact on the Porsche brand.

Until the 1990s, the labor-intensive automobile industry had been largely a national affair regarding technology, parts supply, and skill base. Several factors propelled automotive manufacturers beyond their borders, including the expansion of the Central and Eastern European markets after the end of the Cold War, and the emergence of potentially large new markets such as China, India, and other countries in Asia, Central and South America.[43]

Manufacturers adopted one of four strategies for internationalization, encompassing various levels of local content. The first option was to export complete cars. The second was to export slightly disassembled cars, known in the sector as semi-knocked-down or SKD kits. The third option was substantial local assembly of cars (or completely-knocked-down kits or CKD) and fourth, the use of integrated local manufacturing.[44]

Typically, manufacturers chose one of three approaches to locate facilities abroad. First they could choose to locate in emerging large market areas (e.g., China, Russia and India) or established ones (e.g., the United States, northern Europe and Japan). They could also locate close to such large markets, exporting to them from peripheral countries such as Mexico, Spain, Portugal, Canada and Central and Eastern Europe. Finally, domestic facilities could also be expanded to serve the global markets from the home base.[45] According to a study, emerging larger markets or peripheral markets accounted for 51% of the world's plants, but only 23% of its capacity. Players aimed to either maximize economies of scale or adopt a more flexible production system when defining their international strategy. The latter had been Porsche's approach.

In 1992 and 1993 BMW and Mercedes Benz moved about 10% of their production to the United States.[46] In turn, they pressured suppliers to locate component factories closer to U.S. plants, much as Toyota and Nissan had before them. Thus, the 1990s marked the rise of the global supplier, created through an intense wave of M&A and joint venture activities and international expansion. European automobile manufacturers developed an ever-increasing length and globalization of supply networks, especially into Central and Eastern Europe.[47] Several major mergers and alliances, such as Daimler-Chrysler and Nissan-Renault, reinforced the prevailing argument that any manufacturer unable to produce four million cars a year could not survive on its own.[48]

Porsche's options spanned the compass: SUV production could follow the Boxster's path to Finland or go across the southeastern border to the emerging Czech and Slovak automotive markets; or it could follow competitors to North America. "There is plenty of spare capacity around the world," Wiedeking said in May 1997. "The main investment [for the Porsche SUV] is in the design and manufacturing equipment."[49] Porsche was expected to spend about $830 million in design and development of the new model.[50] **Exhibit 6** provides more information on labor costs, additional labor expenses, and working hours in the manufacturing sector in selected countries.

Replicate the Boxster Solution?

One option for assembling the new SUV was to outsource it to a third party, as Porsche had done in 1997 for its Boxster model. At the time of the SUV decision, it was not widely known that Porsche already produced only about 70% of its cars in German factories; the Finnish company, Valmet Automotive, manufactured the rest.[51] The controversial decision arose when Boxster sales forecasts reached 20,000 for 1998, following actual sales of nearly 16,000 in 1996/97 (about 6,450 in the United States).[52] Porsche's Zuffenhausen plant was running at full capacity to meet the surging demand for the revamped 911 Turbo.[53] In a surprising move, Porsche outsourced some of the production to Valmet, an independent European contract manufacturer of premium specialty cars. "We had no choice," said Wiedeking, stressing that on-site German assemblers and engineers ensured that the Boxsters assembled in Finland were "100% Porsche" and just as good as those made in Germany. Porsche leaders also cited high German labor costs to justify the move,[54] along with fixed costs, which Wiedeking professed to abhor.[55]

With that stroke, Porsche joined automakers such as Chrysler, Fiat, Peugeot Citroen, and Saab, which had outsourced the entire assembly of models either too specialized or time-consuming to be produced in their own plants. For Saab, it was cheaper to ship body panels and engines for its convertibles to Valmet than to disrupt its own production lines with the tooling and engineering required for soft-top models.[56] Although the Finland decision was widely reported as Porsche's first overseas production move, between 60 and 80 individual 911s had already been assembled annually in Mexico since 1995, with still others manufactured in Indonesia.[57]

Despite living in the shadow of the Soviet Union for decades, Finland had become the world's 15th-largest economy, growing at a robust 5% per year in the 1990s. Home to five million inhabitants and a number of international companies such as telecom giant Nokia, Finland was the last country to join the EU in 1995 but one of the first to qualify for the common currency scheduled to take effect in 1999. In July 1997 the European Commission approved a regional aid package to Valmet (Finland's only car assembly company) located in Western Finland, where unemployment was high. The ratio of aid to investment reached 18%, with $12 million allocated for Porsche.[58] The aid package would enable Valmet to produce 5,000 Boxsters per year.

Most Valmet assembly workers were female.[59] They assembled 35,000 cars in 1997, up from 30,000 in 1996, and aimed for 40,000 in 1998. Vehicles produced included Saab 900 cabriolets, as well as Russian-designed Lada Samara hatchbacks. Production at Valmet was highly flexible, a manager explained, designed in the image of Toyota.[60] "Nowhere else will you see assembly workers moving from a mid-engine Porsche to a front-wheel drive Saab. Flexibility in this business is the key to success."[61] Valmet was also quick—with Porsche it had moved from proposal to commercial production in just eight months.[62] Over 15,000 Boxsters were produced that first year.

The solution was not without risk for both parties. Carmakers that outsourced production lost some control over the final assembly and had to anticipate and manage the risks of customer dissatisfaction and brand dilution. Assemblers risked losing contracts if outsourced models were discontinued or if capacity in the parent plants became available. In this risky environment Valmet boasted a 19% profit margin, consistently above industry averages.[63] In September 1998, a Porsche manager noted that while the firm was planning to increase production, "this increase [could] only come in Finland."[64] Fortunately, in the case of the Boxster, it seemed that the origin of the actual car mattered little to impatient customers. "Dealers just want the [Boxster]. They could build it on the moon for all we care," said the president and CEO of Porsche Cars North America in early 1998.[65] Most initially skeptical observers eventually deemed the outsourcing strategy a success.

It was unclear, however, how extensively Porsche could outsource without backlash. And if Porsche managers chose Valmet to assemble the SUV, the firm would become very dependent on one assembler and expose itself to risks associated with Valmet's success and performance. Moreover, the SUV was different from the typical cars Porsche had brought to market over the years. As such, there would be learning associated with the launch that Porsche would want to capture and that would be difficult with a third party assembler. Nevertheless, Valmet would likely provide the fastest ramp-up and lowest production risk, two highly desirable qualities to launch its most controversial model to date. Valmet had also indicated a willingness to accommodate the new Porsche SUV.

Stay Home?

Many consumers associated high quality cars with Germany, and its auto sector was of major importance to both the country's industrial fabric and its global reputation for highly-engineered, high-performance, high-quality products. Despite very high production costs, Germany competed successfully in exporting advanced engineered, quality products backed by excellent service. In 1997 German manufacturers increased their worldwide exports of automobiles by 6.3%, with 27.7% of cars going to the United States and 25% to Eastern Europe.[66] Daimler-Benz and Porsche alone exported 20% and 36% of their production, respectively, to the United States.

Nearly one-third of all German tax revenue came from the automobile sector. German manufacturers were also responsible for one of three auto-related patents issued worldwide, nearly one-third of automotive production within the EU, and one-seventh of world production. German-branded vehicles satisfied 17% of worldwide demand.[67] The German automobile industry benefited greatly from the fall of the German mark from DM 0.55 to the dollar in 1991 to DM 0.72 to the dollar in 1995. But on the eve of the Euro's introduction, there was considerable uncertainty around how the common European currency would move in relationship to the dollar. Many disparaged the attempt to create one currency for such a diverse set of European countries and expected a weak Euro.

By the late 1990s, however, globalization and rising Asian competition in the higher-end automotive market segments were straining the traditional German model of exporting from domestic factories. Porsche and its peers grew concerned with the limitations of Germany's "social market economy"—a model of cooperative industrial relations between management, strong unions, and skilled workers—which encouraged overall social cohesion but created high domestic production costs. Legislators, trade unions, and employer associations set minimum wage rates and other conditions of employment at the regional level. Most observers associated high German labor costs with the concessions the unions had extracted over the years, such as the lowest number of yearly working hours of any industrialized country (1,648) with six weeks of annual vacation, holidays and paid sick leave.[68] For instance, in the highly unionized coal mining industry, German taxpayers effectively spent nearly $60,000 a year in subsidies for each of 85,000 jobs while paying three times more for their coal than they would on the world market.[69] In 1995, the standard workweek was further reduced from 40 to 35 hours.[70]

Rising unemployment was becoming a major economic and political challenge. In January 1996, government, industry, and labor leaders developed a "Fifty-Point Action Plan" to halve unemployment by 2000. In spring 1997, with unemployment figures at their highest level since 1933, nearly one in eight of Germany's working population received some form of support. Massive layoffs by some of the country's biggest firms spawned a feeling of insecurity. The ThyssenKrupp combination in March 1997, for example, called for the elimination of 25% of the 40,000-person workforce. As a result, German unions began reviewing wage restraints in an attempt to secure jobs. Germans were even tolerating changes such as longer shopping hours, discussing aviation and telecommunications deregulation, and considering retirement reform.

Go East?

One way to preserve the "made in Germany" cachet for high quality engineering, but partially avoid the country's high labor costs, was to build a factory in the former Eastern Germany. However, that might leave Porsche with the worst of two worlds: the high cost/high rigidity of German labor and industrial relations framework, without its advantages of a trained and highly skilled workforce with years of experience in an export-oriented market economy.

In 1991, average wages in East Germany amounted to 46.7% of the West German wage level, while relative labor productivity was 31%. Seven years later these trends held true.[71] In fact, a 1996 JP Morgan study found that although manufacturing sector wages in the East were lower than those of the West, they still approached the national average when it came to calculating the actual cost per item, because efficiency was so much poorer in the East.[72]

Furthermore, East German workers were widely seen as less skilled and employed older machinery than their counterparts in the West.[73] The poor condition of the basic infrastructure, widespread environmental damage, and lower-than-expected levels of private investment in the East had complicated the process of economic integration. Private investment in eastern Germany was slower than expected mostly because of restitution and property rights issues. Indeed, nearly a decade after German reunification in 1989, economic and social integration remained incomplete. The one-to-one post reunification currency exchange level had made eastern German goods too expensive to be competitive as exports. Their former eastern European markets vanished. Reunification meant deindustrialization for many regions, and it strained German public finances.[74] Annual transfer payments to Eastern states reached around €90 billion per year. To contain inflation, the Bundesbank kept interest rates high, further dampening investment and economic activity.

Total employment in eastern Germany fell dramatically from almost nine million employed people to fewer than six million at the end of the nineties.[75] In 1997 eastern German unemployment was estimated at 20%, about twice the Western level, and even higher in some areas. Overall, in April 1998 4.4 million Germans were out of work, fully 11.4% of the country's work force. Many viewed as futile the income support programs meant to stimulate the East German economy. To attract investment, many firms establishing factories in former East Germany benefited greatly from subsidies. Wiedeking decried this practice, especially denouncing companies with "golden balance sheets" that accepted such handouts. Porsche ensured that it would accept no subsidies.[76]

Political shifts were also afoot: former Communists, now reincarnated as the Party of Democratic Socialism (PDS), were expected to confirm a comeback in the region in the September 1998 elections.[77] Xenophobic parties of the far right were also expected to draw support from citizens disgruntled by the evolution in the former East Germany. Federal elections set for October 1998 were expected to mark the end of conservative Chancellor Helmut Kohl's 16-year reign.

Despite all the problems, the town of Leipzig (population nearly 500,000) was a strong candidate for a new Porsche plant. Located in the German federal state of Saxony, the country's sixth largest and one of its former eastern states, Leipzig had some attractive features. It would provide easy access to two major seaports (Emden and Bremerhaven). It had a brand new international airport and convention hall. Saxony's 1997 per capita income was about three-quarters of the national average, with an average gross monthly wage per employee of €1,600, compared to the western state average of €2,100.[78] Furthermore, Saxony had a long industrial history, dating back to the 1830s. It boasted four state universities, five specialized colleges in business and technology, and numerous other educational and training institutions. Highly productive before World War II, the region had accounted for 40% of the former East Germany's industrial output.[79] A Leipzig plant could source motors from Stuttgart-Zuffenhausen and axles from Braunschweig (located between Bremen and Berlin), and possibly other parts from the Volkswagen plant in Bratislava, Slovakia. See **Exhibit 7** for a map of Europe.

Partner with Volkswagen and Go Southeast?

Yet another option was to follow Volkswagen's lead and build a new plant in Eastern Europe. In early 1998 Volkswagen moved its entire four-wheel-drive Golf production facility from Wolfsburg, Germany to Bratislava, Slovakia, where it announced an output of 120,000 units, nearly three times as many as the peak of 40,822 in 1997.[80] Bratislava, Slovakia's capital and largest city with 450,000 of the country's 5.3 million inhabitants, was located less than an hour from Vienna. French automotive group PSA Peugeot Citroen had recently chosen Slovakia as the location for its manufacturing plant in Central and Eastern Europe, rejecting bids from Poland and Hungary. PSA's decision had helped Slovakia become one of the leaders in automotive manufacturing in Central and Eastern Europe.[81] Labor cost per hour in the automotive sector were close to the Czech Republics, $3.11 in 1996, falling to $2.55 in 1997, before recovering to $3.32 in 1998.[82]

By spring 1998 Porsche was rumored to be negotiating with Volkswagen. The Piëch family already had strong ownership stakes in Porsche and VW, with Piëch officiating on Porsche's supervisory board. Under the proposed arrangement Porsche would undertake the research and development of the SUV and Volkswagen would invest about $657 million in the project.[83] The first SUVs would be available in 2002. Porsche intended to manufacture 20,000 SUVs a year and Volkswagen planned to make 80,000, probably in the Slovakian facility where it already made Golfs.[84] Of course, the Porsche SUV would target the luxury market at price points 40% to 100% above Volkswagen's SUV, which would fall somewhere between DM 60,000 to DM 80,000.[85] Although VW and Porsche had longstanding historical ties, Wiedeking had to weigh the issue of being so closely associated with a mass production car maker as well as a cheaper SUV.

Alternatively, Porsche could explore another emerging automotive power, Slovakia's neighbor, the Czech Republic. It had been among the leading recipients of foreign direct investment (FDI) in East-Central Europe in the 1990s, attracted by the country's long manufacturing tradition and relatively skilled, well-educated, and low-cost labor force.[86] Average labor costs in manufacturing were only about 10% of levels in the former West Germany, and its proximity to Germany and Austria encouraged cross border, export-oriented investments capitalizing on low-cost production. The Czech Republic also served as a bridgehead to East-Central European markets.

Although the Czech Republic was one of the larger Central and Eastern European countries, its relatively small domestic market made an ideal base for exports. Its central location provided easy access to all European markets including Russia. Compared to its immediate neighbors it had a well-developed infrastructure, as well as a dense network of automotive suppliers catering to Skoda, its national car company founded in 1895 and acquired by Volkswagen in 1991. With a 40-hour work week, and average hourly wages in the automotive sector around $4 in 1998, a Czech plant near VW might prove a viable solution for SUV production. But while Skoda's reputation and reliability improved steadily under Volkswagen's ownership, moving Porsche's factory to the home of a lower quality car might mar Porsche's reputation for excellence and best-in-class craftsmanship.

Moreover, by 1997 the country's political and economic stability had deteriorated and investment conditions became increasingly uncertain. Annual GDP growth declined to 1.2%, the Czech *koruna* lost 21% of its value against the U.S. dollar, the inflation rate increased and privatization slowed. This situation contributed to a drop in FDI, from more than $2.5 billion in 1995 to only $1.3 billion by 1997. The British rating agency IBCA lowered the credit-risk rating for the Czech Republic in November 1997, and several multinational companies, including General Motors, Toyota and Coca-Cola, relocated their investments elsewhere.[87]

Follow the Market?

In the late 1980s, the Ford Explorer legitimized the SUV as the quintessential American family vehicle. By the late 1990s the SUV market was deemed intensely competitive,[88] as many manufacturers strove to offer SUVs with car-like agility, the space of a mini-van and the utility options of a sport vehicle. Fortunately for owners of such large cars (SUVs weighed 4,000 to 6,000 pounds; cars 2,000 to 4,000 pounds), gasoline prices in the United States remained very low by global standards. In 1998 light trucks, including SUVs, captured 51% of the new U.S. vehicle market, double the share they had 20 years before, propelled by a strong economy, demand for roominess (some even had 10 cup-holders) and the perception of enhanced driver visibility and safety. Sales of high-end SUVs—those costing between $43,000 and $49,000—were expected to reach 300,000 in 1998 (up from 75,000 in 1995)[89] as baby boomers opted for Lincoln Navigators and Mercedes-Benz M-class SUVs. **Exhibit 8** shows SUV sale forecasts by region.

Fierce competition in luxury SUVs was dominated by major Asian players. Lexus, Toyota's luxury auto division, saw its small LX 450 SUV grow to nearly 30% of all U.S. Lexus sales in just a few years. The company was said to be considering a plant for manufacturing SUVs in North America. Acura (Honda), Infiniti (Nissan), and Mitsubishi already had luxury offerings in the U.S. market. Nissan's Xterra SUV, to be built in Tennessee, was planned for 2000.[90] Finally, Cadillac was expected to launch an SUV in late 1999, and Ford was testing a 19-foot "crew wagon" with a V10 engine.

Overall, U.S. car buyers were increasingly favoring European makes. Total vehicle sales were up 2% during the mid-1990s but European automakers, which accounted for only 5% of the total U.S. market, posted 24% gains.[91] But Germany's luxury carmakers had suffered a few setbacks in the American market. First, the strong German mark significantly raised the entry-level price for German luxury cars, negatively impacting sales overseas. Next, higher-end Japanese models such as Toyota's Lexus and Nissan's Infiniti made design and marketing inroads that were attractive to consumers. Finally, the U.S. Department of State made the environment for German auto sales more inhospitable by imposing a new luxury tax on all cars,[92] and requiring more U.S.-made parts in German vehicles sold in the United States. This forced German manufacturers such as Mercedes, BMW and Porsche to increase their parts purchases from U.S. companies. In response, Audi was considering opening a new plant in North America, probably in the United States. [93]

Prior German efforts to produce vehicles in the United States had met with mixed results. Volkswagen took over a plant at Westmoreland, Pa., in the late 1970s but the Rabbits produced there were plagued by quality problems. VW closed the plant a decade later after piling up $1.5 billion in losses, a raft of customer complaints, and bad press.[94] The company's purchase of a former General Motors plant in Ohio, with a unionized local workforce, had also run into problems. VW had compounded its problems by hiring a largely American management, reasoning that a U.S. workforce would not respond to Teutonic discipline. The result was a failure to instill a respect for quality, further negatively impacting VW's reputation.

VW's challenges did not deter Mercedes-Benz and BMW. In 1995, BMW set up a plant in Spartanburg, South Carolina, that experienced strong success (see **Appendix**). In 1994, Mercedes-Benz selected Vance, Alabama, for the site of a $300 million M-Class SUV plant. Initial production capacity of about 50,000 units a year would increase to 65,000 units after completion of a 1999 expansion.[95] With building a factory considered a "second step,"[96] Porsche had explored the possibility of producing its cars with Mercedes at the Vance facility. However, a potential deal collapsed in January 1997 when Mercedes demanded a stake in Porsche and Daimler head Helmut Werner stepped down. "The Mercedes decision put us back in charge of our own destiny," a Porsche manager noted.[97] Discussions with GM and Chrysler followed, though the latter had indicated that it would only make a deal with BMW.

While Porsche was weighing its options, German companies were pushing ahead to exploit opportunities in the North American market. NAFTA also created a new investment landscape. Direct investment by German companies in the United States reached $7 billion in 1997—eight times 1992 levels—fueled by a strong American economy, a robust dollar, and the notion that a U.S. foothold was imperative to global competition.[98] Siemens, the German electronics giant, agreed to buy Westinghouse's non-nuclear power generation business in 1997 for $1.53 billion; chemical manufacturer Hoechst AG took over American icon Marion Merrell Dow Inc. in 1997 for $7.26 billion. In March 1998 Bertelsmann AG spent over $1 billion for Random House, the biggest U.S. book publisher; by April 1998, more Americans (about 230,000) were working for companies at least partially owned by German corporations than by any other foreign nation. Daimler's purchase of Chrysler in May 1998 added another 94,300 to this total.[99]

Doing the Seemingly Impossible

In spring 1998, Wiedeking indicated that, while his team did not know where and when to build the controversial SUV, "we know precisely all the labor, land, and building costs around the world. More or less every U.S. state governor has been here to put an offer on the table."[100] "We have to think much harder if we're going to do it ourselves," he continued. "The investment would be much higher."[101] While Porsche could self-finance the investment, he explained, "What do we want to spend our money on? You can only spend it once and I don't like too much risk."[102] However, Porsche's website described the company's mission as "combining the doable with the seemingly impossible."[103]

The careful but decisive Wiedeking had surprised observers and investors before, and they expected more of the same in the future. Above all, Porsche had to remain true to the brand:

> Porsche is fascination. Porsche not only promises a world of experience, Porsche's products and services guarantee it. This has produced a company culture which is transferred from the employees via the vehicles to the customers. The myth becomes reality. Only then can you feel the power that is unique to Porsche—both active and attractive. The brand thus embodies the epitome of sporty driving and thinking. [104]

Exhibit 1   Porsche Relative Stock-Price Performance, January 1990–April 1998

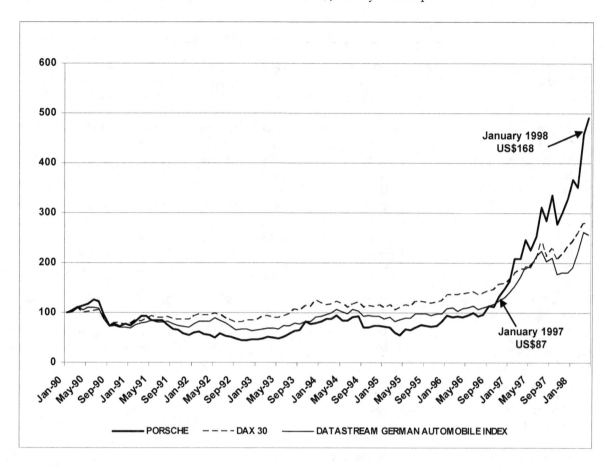

Source: Thomson Financial Datastream.

Exhibit 2   Porsche Group Highlights 1993–1997

		1993–1994	1994–1995	1995–1996	1996–1997	1997–1998
Sales	**million**	**1,194.2**	**1,332.9**	**1,437.7**	**2,093.3**	**2,519.4**
Domestic	million	554.1	569.7	527.7	671.9	735.5
Export	million	640.1	763.2	910.0	1,421.4	1,783.9
Vehicle Sales	**Units**	**18,402**	**21,124**	**19,262**	**32,383**	**36,686**
Domestic Porsche	Units	5,574	6,420	5,873	9,670	9,174
Export Porsche	Units	10,269	11,992	13,346	22,713	27,512
Other Models	Units	2,559	2,712	43	—	—
Vehicle Sales Porsche	Units	15,843	18,412	19,219	32,383	36,686
911	Units	13,010	17,407	19,096	16,507	17,869
928	Units	509	510	104	—	—
944/968	Units	2,324	495	—	—	—
Boxster	Units	—	—	19	15,876	18,817
Cayenne	Units	—	—	—	—	—
Production	**Units**	**19,348**	**20,791**	**20,242**	**32,390**	**38,007**
Porsche total	Units	16,789	18,079	20,242	32,390	38,007
911	Units	13,771	17,293	20,132	16,488	19,120
Carrera GT	Units	—	—	—	—	—
928	Units	633	470	28	—	—
944/968	Units	2,385	316	—	—	—
Boxster	Units	—	—	82	15,902	18,887
Cayenne	Units	—	—	—	—	—
Other Models	Units	2,559	2,712	—	—	—
Employees	**At year-end**	**6,970**	**6,847**	**7,107**	**7,959**	**8,151**
Personnel expenses	million	343.6	363.7	392.1	464.4	528.2
Balance Sheet						
Total Assets	million	795.6	836.7	951.4	1,249.7	1,490.9
Shareholders' Equity	**million**	**218.2**	**210.5**	**239.1**	**298.1**	**415.8**
Fixed Assets	million	351.4	353.2	482.5	565.3	579.6
Capital Expenditures	million	63.0	83.9	213.6	234.8	175.8
Depreciation	million	76.6	55.2	67.7	107.6	157.1
Extended Cash Flow	million					413.1
Net income/loss before taxes	**million**	**-73.9**	**5.8**	**27.9**	**84.5**	**165.9**
Net income/loss after taxes	million	-76.8	1.1	24.6	71.3	141.6
Dividends	**million**	**1.0**	**1.1**	**1.8**	**13.0**	**21.9**

Source: Porsche website, accessed April 29, 2004.

Exhibit 3   Porsche Milestones

1875	Ferdinand Porsche born Sept. 3 in Maffersdorf, Austria-Hungary.
1909	Ferdinand Anton Ernst ("Ferry") Porsche born Sept. 19, in Wiener Neustadt, Austria.
1950	Porsche begins *356* production in Stuttgart-Zuffenhausen.
1951	The senior Ferdinand Porsche dies at age 75.
1953	Porsche introduces the *550*, its first racing-specific car, which meets immediate success.
1964	Porsche introduces the *911*. The company had produced 78,000 Type *356*s in 14 years.
1972	Porsche KG becomes a joint stock company (AG). Ferry Porsche, chairman of the supervisory board, precludes all family members, including himself, from direct management roles.
1984	A third of Porsche AG's capital is offered to the public in the form of nonvoting preference shares on April 25. On Sept. 19, his 75th birthday, Porsche receives the honorary title of "Professor."
1989	Porsche AG presents Ferry Porsche with the birthday present of a two-seat Panamericana roadster, "a boy's car for an 80-year-old man."
1990	Butzi Porsche (Ferdinand A.) succeeds Ferry Porsche as chairman of Porsche AG's supervisory board. Butzi began his own firm, Porsche Design, in 1972.
1992	Wendelin Wiedeking becomes CEO of Porsche.
1996	Launch of the Boxster.
1997	Porsche introduces its all-new, liquid-cooled *911* at the Frankfurt Motor Show.
1998	The company prepares to celebrate 50 years of building sports cars with the Porsche name. Ferry Porsche, honorary president of the Porsche AG supervisory board since 1990, dies March 27 at the age of 88.

Source: "Porsche Timeline," *AutoWeek*, April 6, 1998.

Exhibit 4   Premium SUV Market Information (1996–1998 forecast) (in units)

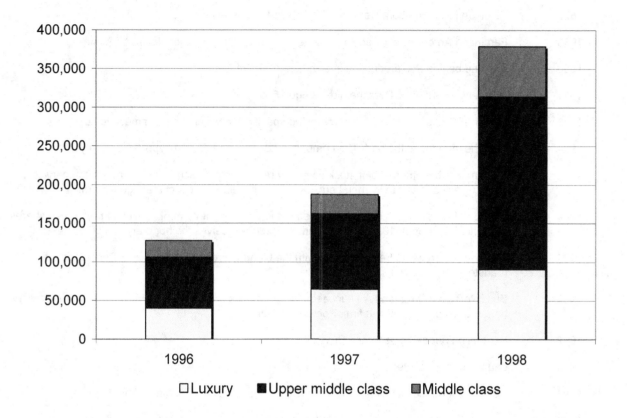

Source: Global Insights.

Exhibit 5   Exchange Rate Fluctuations—DM to Major Currencies, 1990–1998

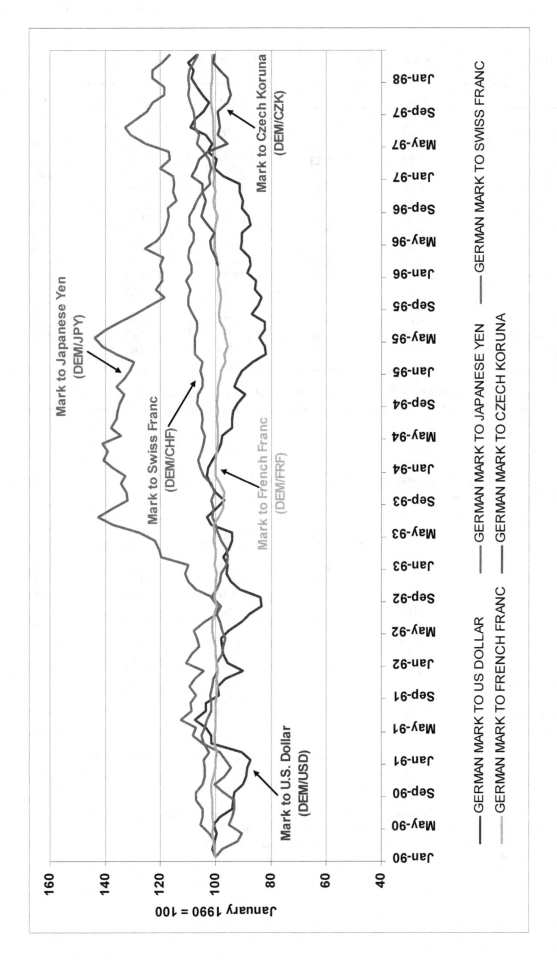

Source: Thomson Financial Datastream.

Exhibit 6a   Hourly Compensation Costs in U.S. Dollars for Production Workers All Manufacturing

	1980	1985	1990	1995	2000
United States	9.87	13.01	14.91	17.19	19.76
Japan	5.52	6.34	12.70	23.73	22.27
Korea	0.96	1.23	3.71	7.29	8.19
Finland	8.33	8.25	21.25	24.32	19.45
France	8.94	7.52	15.49	19.38	15.70
Germany	12.21	9.50	21.81	30.26	23.38
Sweden	12.51	9.66	20.93	21.44	20.14
Italy	8.15	7.63	17.45	16.22	14.01
United Kingdom	7.56	6.27	12.70	13.78	16.45
Belgium	13.11	8.97	19.17	27.62	21.59
Netherlands	12.06	8.75	18.06	24.12	19.44
Austria	8.88	7.58	17.75	25.32	19.46
Portugal	2.06	1.53	3.77	5.37	4.75
Spain	5.89	4.66	11.38	12.80	10.78
Czech Republic	NA	NA	NA	2.53	2.83
Hungary	NA	NA	NA	2.69	2.79

Source: U.S. Bureau of Labor Statistics, ftp://ftp.bls.gov/pub/special.requests/ForeignLabor/industry.txt.

Note: Data for Germany Prior to 1995 for Former West Germany only. Nineteen ninety-five onward is for Germany (unified).

Exhibit 6b   Hourly Compensation Costs in U.S. Dollars for Production Workers Motor Vehicles and Equipment Manufacturing

	1980	1985	1990	1995	2000
United States	15.96	19.71	22.48	26.55	27.99
Japan	6.97	8.09	15.68	29.12	27.77
Korea	1.15	1.62	5.48	10.85	11.75
Finland	NA	NA	NA	25.84	18.78
France	9.98	8.31	16.37	20.04	16.65
Germany	15.03	11.70	26.98	40.83	31.63
Sweden	12.70	10.14	21.13	22.30	21.27
Italy	8.45	8.19	18.29	17.22	15.12
United Kingdom	8.50	7.18	14.93	16.78	19.45
Belgium	14.27	9.87	21.30	30.36	23.46
Netherlands	11.64	8.21	16.29	NA	NA
Austria	NA	NA	NA	26.89	20.82
Portugal	NA	NA	NA	NA	NA
Spain	NA	NA	15.02	16.89	13.72
Czech Republic	NA	NA	NA	NA	3.20

Source: U.S.   Bureau   of   Labor   Statistics,   ftp://ftp.bls.gov/pub/special.requests/ForeignLabor/industry.txt; ftp://ftp.bls.gov/pub/special.requests/ForeignLabor/ind336naics.txt.

Note: Data for Germany Prior to 1995 for Former West Germany only. Nineteen ninety-five onward is for Germany (unified).

Exhibit 6c GDP per head ($ at PPP)

	1980	1985	1990	1995	2000
Austria	10,233.40	14,253.10	19,101.90	23,032.10	28,371.40
Finland	9,274.20	13,526.70	18,102.90	19,258.70	25,868.40
France	10,084.40	14,136.70	18,769.00	21,546.60	26,531.40
Germany	10,914.10	14,994.00	15,870.30	22,062.80	25,558.70
Italy	9,288.30	12,973.20	17,452.10	20,806.90	25,031.10
Japan	8,928.30	12,986.20	18,828.10	22,420.00	25,557.30
Netherlands	10,096.00	13,430.50	18,011.60	21,759.90	27,429.80
South Korea	NA	4,621.60	8,215.30	12,802.40	16,347.00
Sweden	10,307.00	14,526.70	18,740.70	21,324.40	26,887.50
United Kingdom	8,517.90	12,116.50	16,474.80	19,904.50	25,622.80
United States	12,249.50	17,697.50	23,200.10	27,752.60	34,770.20
Portugal	5,303.30	6,967.70	10,798.30	13,842.10	18,270.50
Spain	NA	9,085.40	13,105.30	16,054.80	21,208.90
Czech Republic	NA	NA	NA	11,772.70	13,807.90
Hungary	NA	NA	8,922.30	9,002.00	12,083.50

Source: Economist Intelligence Unit Country Data Database.

Exhibit 6d Hours Actually Worked per Week by Wage Earners in Motor Vehicle Manufacturing Industry

	1975	1980	1985	1990	1995	2000
Austria	33.3	30.5	34.7	33.9	33.8	33.6
Belgium	35.7	34.8	32.1	35.7	39.4	NA
Finland	34.0	32.8	31.0	31.6	39.5	40.3
France	41.6	40.5	39.5	40.3	36.6	36.4
Germany[a]	39.3	40.7	40.2	38.7	35.8	35.1
Italy	NA	NA	NA	NA	40.1	40.4
Japan	39.1	42.7	42.9	43.0	38.6	39.2
Korea	49.1	50.8	52.5	48.4	49.7	46.5
Netherlands[a]	41.1	40.9	40.5	40.1	38.2	37.6
Sweden	NA	NA	NA	NA	32.5	31.4
United Kingdom[a]	NA	NA	41.0	43.7	42.9	42.1
United States[a]	40.4	40.6	42.6	42.0	43.8	43.4
Portugal	41.6	37.8	35.4	NA	38.8	37.0
Spain	NA	NA	35.1	36.0	35.9	34.8
Czech Republic	NA	NA	NA	NA	39.5	41.8
Hungary	40.3	40.5	36.5	35.5	36.4	37.7

Source: International Labor Organization LABORSTA Database, http://laborsta.ilo.org/.

[a]Series is Hours per Week Paid to Wage Earners in Motor Vehicle Manufacturing.

Exhibit 7   Map of Europe

Source: University of Texas website.

Exhibit 8   SUV Sales by Region (actual and forecast)

REGION	1990	1991	1992	1993	1994	1995	1996	1997	1998	1999	2000	2001	2002	2003
AFRICA	-	-	-	-	-	-	108,960	122,526	131,645	39,862	32,629	33,214	35,418	40,329
ASIA	222,968	222,692	209,285	201,318	224,047	468,038	1,044,178	930,311	802,585	853,460	870,771	927,113	1,075,526	1,211,453
CENTRAL AMERICA AND CARIBBEAN							1,905	1,672	1,937	1,811	1,354	954	1,280	1,452
EAST EUROPE							117,543	146,086	127,012	129,675	138,157	150,850	142,375	164,572
MIDDLE EAST							53,786	65,862	83,183	74,246	79,328	97,167	116,676	132,105
NORTH AMERICA	929,066	909,577	1,133,137	1,379,806	1,556,075	1,753,404	2,255,726	2,615,633	2,988,725	3,434,365	3,616,924	4,019,735	4,329,701	4,660,994
OTHER							22,209	20,714	16,640	16,472	16,365	14,393	17,373	19,790
SOUTH AMERICA							85,436	121,205	121,741	101,523	104,024	125,456	100,498	117,531
WESTERN EUROPE	272,268	282,712	292,973	302,809	309,044	336,113	341,839	367,080	466,413	591,989	603,289	624,917	702,301	806,093
TOTAL	1,424,302	1,414,981	1,635,395	1,883,933	2,089,166	2,557,555	4,031,582	4,391,089	4,739,881	5,243,403	5,462,841	5,993,799	6,521,148	7,154,319

REGION	2004	2005	2006	2007	2008	2009	2010	2011	2012	2013	2014	2015	2016	2017	2018
AFRICA	50,139	50,817	53,009	55,981	55,186	54,547	54,506	58,206	58,604	57,854	59,046	61,543	61,784	63,106	64,174
ASIA	1,235,298	1,415,096	1,568,204	1,797,321	1,976,001	2,047,728	2,128,306	2,254,793	2,352,158	2,465,585	2,582,540	2,700,761	2,808,717	2,960,189	3,081,801
CENTRAL AMERICA AND CARIBBEAN	1,714	1,911	2,336	2,493	2,685	2,263	2,572	2,463	2,267	2,455	2,997	3,259	3,241	3,460	3,687
EAST EUROPE	220,522	262,094	262,047	284,475	296,241	304,658	317,405	325,166	336,930	353,962	373,505	397,577	422,095	445,923	465,426
MIDDLE EAST	135,259	146,121	146,324	157,758	164,281	173,540	192,578	189,283	183,859	180,047	172,971	184,509	193,631	202,134	209,677
NORTH AMERICA	4,862,792	5,035,576	5,189,639	5,519,368	5,616,647	5,780,657	5,820,586	5,818,371	5,740,861	5,645,049	5,749,167	5,977,377	5,952,067	5,877,672	5,844,286
OTHER	20,741	21,183	21,253	19,633	20,615	20,946	21,935	21,742	21,679	21,573	26,870	26,210	26,308	26,652	26,393
SOUTH AMERICA	167,761	177,363	182,982	211,833	229,733	259,277	247,787	267,100	285,939	296,723	299,531	321,795	342,878	329,765	345,196
WESTERN EUROPE	925,777	957,200	1,034,870	1,153,726	1,287,680	1,294,649	1,308,540	1,329,588	1,315,833	1,320,816	1,348,453	1,390,120	1,419,399	1,418,548	1,399,331
TOTAL	7,620,003	8,067,361	8,460,664	9,202,588	9,649,069	9,938,265	10,094,215	10,266,712	10,298,130	10,344,064	10,615,080	11,063,151	11,230,120	11,327,449	11,439,971

Source: Global Insights.

Appendix

The BMW Precedent

In 1995 BMW became the 82nd internationally headquartered company to set up shop in Spartanburg, South Carolina (a town of 250,000 in a state of 3.5 million people). From 1995 onward, the $400 million factory would make 30,000 BMWs a year, rising to 70,000 by the year 2000—more than BMW had sold in the United States in any year since 1988. BMW's CEO explained that the move aimed to maintain, secure, and build BMW's position in the American luxury-car market, the world's largest.[105] The decision to set up its first plant outside of Germany had been based on a combination of factors: the German plants were clearly going to burst at the seams and BMW was anxious to hedge an appreciating German Mark.

Spartanburg was conveniently located only a couple of hundred miles from a deep-water port and at the crossroads of many key U.S. rail lines and interstate highways. And crucially, Spartanburg was prepared to create an 800-acre contiguous site near the local airport by paying $40 million to acquire land from more than 100 owners. Indeed, just three months before the decision was due, BMW requested that any prospective site have direct access to an airport big enough to accommodate everything from business jets ferrying company executives to and from Bavaria to jumbo transports loaded with car engines, drive trains, gearboxes and axles airlifted from the factory there. These could then be driven by semi-truck into the factory. The press reported that BMW refused to contemplate a comparable site less than a mile away, for $20 million less. Shipping costs would drop by up to $2,500 for each car made and sold in the United States.[106]

As part of the deal South Carolina would extend the Greenville-Spartanburg airport's free-trade-zone status to the 900-acre plant site, meaning BMW would not have to pay duties on parts imported from Germany or elsewhere. BMW planned to export half of the plant's output to Japan and Europe. The cars would first be assembled mainly from German parts. As BMW transitioned to parts manufactured locally, it planned to rely heavily on the American units of trusted German suppliers such as Robert Bosch, producer of brakes and other parts. Even after U.S.-made parts reached 50% to 70% by the late 1990s, key components such as engines and axles would still come from Germany.[107]

Assuming the UAW failed to organize Spartanburg, BMW figured that initial labor costs would be at least one-third lower than the $28 an hour, including fringe benefits, that BMW paid at home. Lower wages plus production efficiencies could save BMW $2,000 to $3,000 per car, a significant number for cars starting at $22,000.[108] However, as one BMW insider pointed out: "If the cost structure had been the only consideration, then Spain would have been the obvious choice," or Mexico, countries that could offer lower wages than the $13–$18 an hour BMW would pay in the United States.

Key to the decision seemed to have been "the uniformly friendly atmosphere" BMW encountered in the town. A number of suppliers, among them Hewlett-Packard, had already announced intentions to set up nearby factories to supply BMW with a variety of parts, in line with BMW's pledge "to do its best to attract suppliers to South Carolina." German auto manufacturers had always been keen on preserving the reputation of high-quality German engineering. BMW therefore paired German technicians and production experts with a handful of American executives, recruited from a plant Honda had successfully set up in Kentucky in the late 1970s.

Endnotes

[1] Stefanie Winter, *Die Porsche Methode* (Frankfurt: Carl Ueberreuter Wirtschaft, 2000), p. 13.

[2] "Now It's the Cars That Make the Characters Go," *The New York Times,* April 21, 1996, available on Factiva, accessed December 6, 2005.

[3] "Porsche doubles Finnish output of popular Boxster," *Automotive News*, January 12, 1998, available on Factiva, accessed April 19, 2004.

[4] Germans tended to pronounce "Porsche" as *porsh-uh*. In English, the German form was often heard from official Porsche sources and from some Porsche owners and enthusiasts. Americans tended to overcompensate the *e*, resulting in *Pors-scha*. Outside of these groups however, the pronunciation *porsh* was standard.

[5] Jeremy Cato, "Will the 911 Carrera 4 Boost Porsche's Bottom Line?" *The Globe and Mail*, November 6, 1998, available on Factiva, accessed April 21, 2004.

[6] "Porsche," B. Metzler Seel Sohn & Co research report, July 10, 1998, available on Investext, accessed November 29, 2005, p. 3.

[7] Anton was the father of Ferdinand Piëch, the supervisory board chairman of Volkswagen in 1998.

[8] Stefan Nicola, "David saves Goliath," Washington Times, available on http://washingtontimes.com/upi/20050927-085542-8230r.htm, accessed November 11, 2005.

[9] Tom Mudd, "Back In High Gear," *Industry Week*, February 21, 2000.

[10] See http://www.fischetti.com/porsche_history.html, accessed February 8, 2006.

[11] Tom Mudd.

[12] All quotes from Tom Mudd, "Back In High Gear," *Industry Week*, February 21, 2000. "Geiz ist eine Todsünde," Wendelin Wiedeking, *Die Zeit*, 18/2005, zeus.zeit.de/text/2005/18/W_Wiedeking, accessed 8 Aug. 2005. Paul Gallagher, "Porsche Expects Growth if No Global Downturn," *Reuters News*, December 3, 1998.

[13] Michael Freitag and Dietmar Student, "Die Stille Macht," *Manager Magazin*, Vol. 6, May 27, 2005.

[14] Tom Mudd, "Back In High Gear," *Industry Week*, February 21, 2000.

[15] Tom Mudd, "Back In High Gear," *Industry Week*, February 21, 2000.

[16] In a just in time system, items only moved through the production system as and when they were needed. The main focus was the elimination of waste and inventory reduction. For more details see http://mscmga.ms.ic.ac.uk/jeb/or/jit.html, accessed May 26, 2004.

[17] *The German Skills Machine*, Pepper D. Culpepper and David Finegold (eds.) (New York: Berghahn Books, 1999), p. 10.

[18] Tom Mudd, "Back In High Gear," *Industry Week*, February 21, 2000.

[19] Tom Mudd, "Back In High Gear," *Industry Week*, February 21, 2000.

[20] Gavin Launder and Xavier Gunner, "Porsche," Warburg Dillon Read, August 11, 1998, p. 4, available on Investext, accessed December 19, 2005.

[21] Tom Mudd, "Back In High Gear," *Industry Week*, February 21, 2000.

[22] Winter, p. 77.

[23] James R. Healey, "Porsche chairman quits over dispute," *USA Today*, September 24, 1992, available on Factiva, accessed December 2, 2005.

[24] "Bohn must now get Porsche back on its feet," *Frankfurter Allgemeine Zeitung*, February 27, 1992, available on Factiva, accessed December 3, 2005.

[25] Jeremy Cato, "Will the 911 Carrera 4 Boost Porsche's Bottom Line?" *The Globe and Mail*, November 6, 1998 available on Factiva, accessed April 21, 2004.

[26] "Bohn must now get Porsche back on its feet," *Frankfurter Allgemeine Zeitung*, February 27, 1992, available on Factiva, accessed December 3, 2005.

[27] "Soaring Porsche considers SUV," *Automotive News Europe*, July 7, 1997, available on Factiva, accessed April 18, 2004.

[28] Mudd (2000)

[29] "A Chat with Porsche's Wendelin Weideking," *BusinessWeek*, January 12, 2001.

[30] "Porsche looking to outsource SUV assembly," *Automotive Industries*, May 1, 1997, available on Factiva, accessed April 16, 2004.

[31] Peter Bohr, "Cayenne is Indeed a Real Porsche: SUV has much of the automaker's trademark styling and handling," *The Press Enterprise*, October 22, 2005, available on Factiva, accessed November 30, 2005.

[32] "Special Feature: Executive Cars (Arrive in Style): Porsche to build sport utility vehicle," *BusinessWorld*, August 31, 1998.

[33] Paul Gallagher, "Porsche Expects Growth if No Global Downturn," *Reuters News*, December 3, 1998.

[34] Paul Gallagher, "Porsche Expects Growth if No Global Downturn," *Reuters News*, December 3, 1998.

[35] "Porsche," B. Metzler Seel Sohn & Co research report, July 10, 1998, available on Investext, accessed November 29, 2005, p. 6.

[36] "Porsche," B. Metzler Seel Sohn & Co research report, July 10, 1998, available on Investext, accessed November 29, 2005, p. 6.

[37] "Porsche," B. Metzler Seel Sohn & Co research report, July 10, 1998, available on Investext, accessed November 29, 2005, p. 6.

[38] "Porsche," B. Metzler Seel Sohn & Co research report, July 10, 1998, available on Investext, accessed November 29, 2005, p. 8.

[39] "Extinction of the predator," *The Economist*, September 8, 2005.

[40] "Porsche doubles Finnish output of popular Boxster," *Automotive News*, January 12, 1998, available on Factiva, accessed April 19, 2004.

[41] "Porsche unable to meet runaway demand," *The Financial Post*, December 5, 1997, available on Factiva, accessed April 19, 2004.

[42] "Nothing Finer Than A Plant In Carolina—BMW," *Independent On Sunday*, May 9, 1993, available on Factiva, accessed July 15, 2004.

[43] Shimokawa, p. 5.

[44] Rob van Tulder and Winfried Ruigrok, "International Production Networks in the Auto Industry: Central and Eastern Europe as the Low End of the West European Car Complexes," repositories.cdlib.org/cgi/viewcontent.cgi?article=1082&context=uciaspubs/research, accessed December 16, 2005.

[45] Timothy J. Sturgeon, "Globalization and Jobs in the Automotive Industry: A Locational Typology," Research Note #5, Paper for the GERPISA Colloquium in Paris France (June 18-20, 1999), ipc-lis.mit.edu/globalization/typology.pdf, accessed on December 16, 2005.

[46] Rob van Tulder and Winfried Ruigrok, "International Production Networks in the Auto Industry: Central and Eastern Europe as the Low End of the West European Car Complexes," repositories.cdlib.org/cgi/viewcontent.cgi?article=1082&context=uciaspubs/research, accessed December 16, 2005.

[47] Timothy J. Sturgeon, "Globalization and Jobs in the Automotive Industry: A Locational Typology," Research Note #5, Paper for the GERPISA Colloquium in Paris France (June 18–20, 1999), ipc-lis.mit.edu/globalization/typology.pdf, accessed on December 16, 2005. Rob van Tulder and Winfried Ruigrok, "International Production Networks in the Auto Industry: Central and Eastern Europe as the Low End of the West European Car Complexes," repositories.cdlib.org/cgi/viewcontent.cgi?article=1082&context=uciaspubs/research, accessed December 16, 2005.

[48] Koichi Shimokawa, "Reorganization of the Global Automobile Industry and Structural Change of the Automobile Component Industry," repositories.cdlib.org/cgi/viewcontent.cgi?article=1082&context=uciaspubs/research, accessed December 16, 2005.

[49] "Porsche looking to outsource SUV assembly," *Automotive Industries*, May 1, 1997, available on Factiva, accessed April 16, 2004.

[50] Mike Duffy, "Off the autobahn," *Sunday Telegraph*, October 17, 1999, available on Factiva, accessed April 18, 2004. Stuart Birch, "Global Development: Part II Europe," *Automotive Engineering International*, June 1, 1999, available from Factiva, accessed November 10, 2005.

[51] "Porsche," B. Metzler Seel Sohn & Co research report, July 10, 1998, available on Investext, accessed November 29, 2005, p. 3.

[52] "Porsche doubles Finnish output of popular Boxster," *Automotive News*, January 12, 1998, available on Factiva, accessed April 19, 2004.

[53] Christine Tierney, "A Niche Carved Out of Dreams," *Birmingham Post*, December 29, 1999.

[54] "Porsche Backs away from costly Germans," *The Christ Church Press*, July 2, 1997.

[55] "Porsche doubles Finnish output of popular Boxster," *Automotive News*, January 12, 1998, available on Factiva, accessed April 19, 2004.

[56] "In Finland, Boxsters, Ladas share quarters," *The Financial Post*, April 17, 1998.

[57] Winter, p. 105.

[58] "EU clears regional aid to Valmet unit, *Reuters News*, July 15, 1997, available on Factiva, accessed April 19, 2004. "EU/State Aid—Approval of Finnish Aid to Valmet Automotive," *Agence Europe*, July 19, 1997. "Porsche doubles Finnish output of popular Boxster," *Automotive News*, January 12, 1998, available on Factiva, accessed April 19, 2004.

[59] "EU clears regional aid to Valmet unit," Reuters News, July 15, 1997, available on Factiva, accessed April 19, 2004. "In Finland, Boxsters, Ladas share quarters," *The Financial Post*, April 17, 1998.

[60] "Porsche doubles Finnish output of popular Boxster," *Automotive News*, January 12, 1998, available on Factiva, accessed April 19, 2004.

[61] "In Finland, Boxsters, Ladas share quarters," *The Financial Post*, April 17, 1998.

[62] "Porsche doubles Finnish output of popular Boxster," *Automotive News*, January 12, 1998, available on Factiva, accessed April 19, 2004.

[63] "In Finland, Boxsters, Ladas share quarters," *The Financial Post*, April 17, 1998.

[64] "Porsche Plans to Raise Finnish Boxster Production," *Reuters News*, September 9, 1998, available on Factiva, accessed April 19, 2004.

[65] "Porsche doubles Finnish output of popular Boxster," *Automotive News*, January 12, 1998, available on Factiva, accessed April 19, 2004.

[66] "Germany—Automotive Parts and Service Market," *Industry Sector Analysis*, Chamber World Network, June 2, 1998.

[67] "Germany—Car Industry Having A Banner Year," *International Market Insight Reports*, February 11, 2000.

[68] As per 1990 agreements, Smith, p. 282. The comparable U.K. number was 1,769.

[69] William Drozdiak, "Germany's Lost Luster; Economy Beset by Welfare Burden, World Trade," *The Washington Post*, October 11, 1997.

[70] Culpepper, p. 49.

[71] "Germany—Industry" (1998), available from Cambridge International Forecasts, available on Factiva, accessed March 2, 2004.

[72] "Germany—Industry" (1998), available from Cambridge International Forecasts, available on Factiva, accessed March 2, 2004.

[73] Culpepper, 39.

[74] Culpepper, p 40.

[75] Viktor Steiner, "How is Germany's Labor Market Coping with Unification?" Paper prepared for the conference "Labor, Employment and Social Policies in the EU Enlargement Process: Changing Perspectives and Policy Options," Baden/Vienna, June 28-30, 2001.

[76] Winter, p. 93.

[77] Cacilie Rohwedder, "Polls Apart," *The Wall Street Journal,* September 9, 1998.

[78] "Basic Economic Data for the Free State of Saxony," Saxony State Ministry of Economic Affairs and Labor, February 25, 2004.

[79] From a speech presented by Professor Kurt Biedenkopf, "Leading the Transition to a Market Economy on a State Level," delivered at Harvard Business School, April 17, 2004.

[80] "Germany—Industry" (1998), available from Cambridge International Forecasts, available on Factiva, accessed March 2, 2004.

[81] "Polish Car Industry Suffers Blow," *Polish News Bulletin*, January 21, 2003, available on Factiva, accessed November 10, 2005.

[82] United Nations International Labour Organization; http://laborsta.ilo.org/, accessed December 12, 2005.

[83] "FOCUS-Porsche says no decision on VW tie-in," *Reuters News*, March 19, 1998, available on Factiva, accessed April 19, 2004.

[84] Wayne Webster, "Off-Road Gamble," *The Daily Telegraph* (December 4, 1998): 58, available on Factiva, accessed March 31, 2004).

[85] "FOCUS-Porsche says no decision on VW tie-in," *Reuters News*, March 19, 1998, available on Factiva, accessed April 19, 2004.

[86] Petr Pavlinek, "Contrasting geographies of inward investment in the Czech and Slovak Republics," *SN Regional Studies,* October 1, 1998, available on Factiva, accessed November 10, 2005.

[87] Petr Pavlinek, "Contrasting geographies of inward investment in the Czech and Slovak Republics," *SN Regional Studies,* October 1, 1998, available on Factiva, accessed November 10, 2005.

[88] Suzanne Christiansen, "Living large—the sports utility," *Metal Bulletin Monthly,* December 8, 1998, available on Factiva, accessed May 2, 2004.

[89] Cindy Starr, "Kings of the road Big cars win buyers' hearts," *The Cincinnati Post,* January 28, 1998, available on Factiva, accessed May 2, 2004.

[90] Suzanne Christiansen, "Living large—the sports utility," *Metal Bulletin Monthly,* December 8, 1998, available on Factiva, accessed May 2, 2004.

[91] Brian Akre, "Truck sales outpace cars for first time," *Chicago Sun-Times,* December 7, 1998, available on Factiva, accessed May 1, 2004.

[92] John Templeman and David Woodruff, "The Beemer Spotlight Falls On Spartanburg, USA—BMW Decides The Math Of Building Its First U.S. Plant Finally Adds Up," *Business Week,* July 6, 1992, available on Factiva, accessed July 15, 2004.

[93] "Germany—Automotive Parts and Service Market" (1998). Available from Chamber World Network, available on Factiva, accessed March 2, 2004. "Porsche looking to outsource SUV assembly," *Automotive Industries,* May 1, 1997, available on Factiva, accessed April 16, 2004.

[94] John Templeman and David Woodruff, "The Beemer Spotlight Falls On Spartanburg, USA—BMW Decides The Math Of Building Its First U.S. Plant Finally Adds Up," *Business Week,* July 6, 1992, available on www.factiva.com, accessed July 15, 2004.

[95] Lindsay Chappell, "Mercedes Eyes More Alabama Growth," *Automotive News,* January 19, 1998.

[96] "Porsche looks at a plant in the US for its Sport-Ute," *Automotive News,* March 31, 1997, available from Factiva, April 16, 2004.

[97] "Porsche looking to outsource SUV assembly," *Automotive Industries,* May 1, 1997, available from Factiva, April 16, 2004.

[98] Paul Geitner, "German companies are buying American," *Associated Press Newswire,* May 10, 1998, accessed May 26, available on Factiva.

[99] "Soaring Porsche considers SUV," *Automotive News Europe,* July 7, 1997, available from Factiva, April 18, 2004.

[100] "Soaring Porsche considers SUV," *Automotive News Europe,* July 7, 1997, available on Factiva, accessed April 18, 2004.

[101] Ibid.

[102] Ibid.

[103] http://content3.us.porsche.com/prod/company/philosophy.nsf/usaenglish/whowearestandard, accessed April 14, 2004.

[104] http://www.porsche.com/usa/aboutporsche/porschephilosophy/whoweare/aps1245/, accessed February 24, 2006.

[105] "Nothing Finer Than A Plant In Carolina—BMW." *Independent On Sunday,* May 9, 1993, available on Factiva, accessed July 15, 2004.

[106] "Nothing Finer Than A Plant In Carolina—BMW," *Independent On Sunday,* May 9, 1993, available on www.factiva.com, accessed July 15, 2004. John Templeman and David Woodruff, "The Beemer Spotlight Falls On Spartanburg, USA—BMW Decides The Math Of Building Its First U.S. Plant Finally Adds Up," *Business Week,* July 6, 1992, available on Factiva, accessed July 15, 2004.

[107] John Templeman and David Woodruff, "The Beemer Spotlight Falls On Spartanburg, USA—BMW Decides The Math Of Building Its First U.S. Plant Finally Adds Up," *Business Week*, July 6, 1992, available on Factiva, accessed July 15, 2004.

[108] John Templeman and David Woodruff, "The Beemer Spotlight Falls On Spartanburg, USA—BMW Decides The Math Of Building Its First U.S. Plant Finally Adds Up," *Business Week*, July 6, 1992, available on Factiva, accessed July 15, 2004.

JEFFREY FEAR

CARIN-ISABEL KNOOP

Dr. Ing. h.c. F. Porsche AG (B): Made in Germany

Our customers really want a product made in Germany. They're ready to pay more for that. . . It's an exclusive kind of product and lot of emotion is attached to it.[1]

—Wendelin Wiedeking, CEO and Chairman

In 2002 Porsche AG opened a state-of-the-art assembly facility for its new Cayenne SUV in Leipzig, Germany, following a prolonged search for the best location. At the August dedication ceremony attended by German Chancellor Gerhard Schröder, Porsche CEO Wendelin Wiedeking proclaimed: "Here in Leipzig, the smallest independent automobile manufacturer in the world is about to move forward in an entirely new direction."[2] In January 2004 Porsche held its annual shareholders' meeting in Leipzig, the first time ever away from its headquarters close to Stuttgart. In June 2005 the 100,000th Cayenne rolled off the Leipzig assembly lines. The Cayenne was the firm's best-selling automobile ever, towing the entire company along with it. Porsche's profit levels had more than doubled since 2001 and the firm enjoyed exceptionally strong free cash flow (see **Exhibit 1**). In September 2005, Porsche's stock topped €650 per share, an all-time record (see **Exhibit 2**).

Investors and consumers had initially balked when Porsche announced its intention to enter the family-friendly SUV segment, fearing the company's sportscar tradition and exclusive brand name did not befit bulky off-roaders.[3] Loyal Porsche enthusiasts in particular, reacted with extreme skepticism. Over its 50-year history, the automaker had carefully built a simple, emblematic brand, producing limited numbers of sports cars like the "legendary" *911* and the "sexy" Boxster. Despite withering criticism from Porsche fans and business analysts, Wiedeking claimed he was not concerned: "A lot of top management [spends too much] time on whether a decision will have a negative impact on their careers. As a top manager, I think, you have to build a balance between the interests of your employees—because their families, their children are part of your responsibility— and shareholders. To focus only on shareholder value and dividends is not enough."[4]

Entering the fast-growing but highly competitive SUV market was an expensive bet for one of the world's smaller car companies. R&D alone amounted to €300 million and capital expenditures for new plant and equipment tripled between 2000 and 2002. In 2004 Wiedeking initiated a companywide efficiency drive and tackled to address the company's ongoing challenges with characteristic zeal.[5]

Wiedeking's achievements, combined with his irreverent and unusually colorful rhetoric, made him a star among corporate CEOs. He regularly ranked as Germany's top chief executive, and attracted both admiration and controversy. For one, he refused to disclose his compensation as

---

recommended by the German corporate governance commission on which he sat. Porsche also issued semiannual reports, not quarterly ones, causing the Deutsche Börse to delist it from its mid-size stock index. In mid-2005, Wiedeking publicly criticized Josef Ackermann, the CEO of Deutsche Bank, for his lack of "social responsibility." Ackermann was Germany's major advocate of shareholder value. Under his leadership, Deutsche Bank turned around to earn over €4 billion of pretax profit in 2004, achieving a pretax return of 17% on equity and a 30% increase in share price in 2005. At the same time, Ackermann announced a restructuring that would eliminate 6,400 jobs. Amidst the ensuing widespread dismay, Wiedeking opined that "even if firms are obligated to their shareholders, we have taken on a high amount of social responsibility. In a social market economy, we have to find a balance between capital and labor, and that attempt is missing at many corporations today."[6]

Just as Porsche reached the height of acclaim, Wiedeking once again stunned everyone by announcing that Porsche, the smallest independent carmaker in the world, had suddenly become the largest shareholder of Volkswagen (VW), the fourth-largest automaker. VW, however, was troubled by corporate governance scandals. Investors decried the interlocking directories of Porsche and VW controlled by the Piëch family, creating a conflict of interest. Then, a controversy ensued over the question whether the Cayenne was really "made in Germany."

Product and Partner

In June 1998 Porsche announced that it would design its SUV together with VW, a company that had been closely allied to Porsche since 1934 when Porsche's chief designer developed the body for the original VW Beetle. The core project team of designers, managers, logisticians, and partners shared workspace on three floors of a striking, cylindrical office building in Leipzig. The team locked down the exterior design of the vehicle in 1999, and finalized the initial interior design soon after that.

The new SUVs would share the same chassis and some technologies, but showcase very different exterior stylings, engines, and chassis tuning. Porsche would develop the two models as well as the common platform. VW would be responsible for major aspects of production in Bratislava, with final Cayenne assembly to take place in Leipzig. Beginning in 2002, Porsche planned to produce 20,000 Cayennes annually while VW would produce 80,000 to 100,000 Touaregs, with very different market positions and price points.

The Cayenne and Touareg shared close to 65% of their parts and modules. The price differential between the two models covered Porsche's incremental cost for the motor, rear end synchronization, and body.[7] A great safety proponent, and one of the first companies to install antilock brakes and dual front airbags, Porsche chose to encase Cayennes (classified as a cross/utility vehicle) in a very rigid unibody construction with a lower center of gravity to reduce sway and limit the SUV's tendency to roll as a result of tight turns. This raised development and manufacturing costs. As a further safety feature, the Cayenne would be outfitted with high-performance tires used by aircraft.[8]

Partnering with VW was "an ingenious coup," an observer noted in 2005: "Half of Porsche's profits come from the Cayenne. That model was developed in collaboration with VW and was built in VW plants. The car is 90 percent VW and 10 percent Porsche."[9] Skeptics worried about paying Porsche prices for a VW, but were assured that the R&D of the new model was purely Porsche's domain, while its partner would oversee only the production of some major components, excluding the engine.[10] But as one financial analyst opined, the Cayenne would "push Porsche's brand credibility to the absolute limit."[11] Other exclusive carmakers, such as Aston Martin, declared that Porsche was "no longer a sports car brand because the company [was] now making light trucks [...] and with sales of 100,000 a year, they are no longer exclusive."[12]

The Plant

The largest city in Saxony, in the former eastern territories midway between Stuttgart and Bratislava, Leipzig had lower minimum wages as well as a skilled workforce and a regional reputation closely tied to the automotive industry. Saxony and Thuringia had been the heart of car and motorcycle manufacturing since the early 20th century. BMW's automobile production began there. Audi's "four-ring" logo stood for the defunct Auto-Union, a merger of four prewar companies formerly based in the area. Even in the time of the communist German Democratic Republic, Saxony remained a center for automobile construction and microelectronics.

With about 400 direct employees, the Leipzig plant was responsible for mounting the engine, steering, and other final components, along with testing the finished cars. Porsche adopted the same Japanese production model, tried and tested at the home plant: lean production principles and the just-in-time method in which the loading sequences of car bodies delivered to Leipzig by train were synchronized with the production schedule. All system suppliers simultaneously delivered the components for production of the Cayenne straight to the assembly line; the bodies and components were processed immediately without interim storage, allowing for production without forklifts. Close collaboration with well-established service providers assisted the adaptable production process. According to Porsche, the Leipzig plant contributed 12% of the production value of a Cayenne.[13]

Located 289 miles north of the Zuffenhausen plant, the new compound measured 195,903 sq. ft. Its L-shaped, one-floor production facility was surrounded by loading docks for delivery of parts from more than 300 contractors. The compound also included a modern five-story Customer Center for special functions and delivery of vehicles to customers, as well as a custom-designed, Formula One accredited racing track upon which Wiedeking himself could often be found.[14] Enhancing access for customers, the facility was located just minutes by car from the new Leipzig-Halle international airport. The facility produced just under 25,000 Cayennes (with price tags between $56,000 and $110,000) in its first full year of operations, and later added a new limited edition sport car, the Carrera GT.[15] Break-even for the new plant was 5,000 units a year.

The Leipzig plant contributed to the revitalization of the region. By the mid-2000s, Saxony had one of the most vibrant economies among the former GDR states. Its 2.1% growth in 2004 made it the only eastern state to exceed the national average.[16] A 2005 study of "economic dynamism" in German states ranked Saxony as a national leader, applauding state government and lobby efforts in attracting western companies to the region with a skilled workforce and sound infrastructure. "The foundation for this [success] is excellent education and know-how," Wiedeking said. "Our politicians have to guarantee through clear, fast reforms that we'll keep our world-class manufacturing status."[17]

Going East

The automotive production business was booming throughout Central and Eastern Europe. Countries like Slovakia, the Czech Republic, Romania, and Russia offered low labor costs, attractive locations, and highly qualified employees. More than 20 of the largest international suppliers of various car parts from air-conditioning systems to seatbelt webbing and car body parts opened over 150 production locations there. From zero cars produced in Central Europe in 1990, output rose to over 730,000 in 2003. In 2004 the region accounted for 6.1% of global car production.

German manufacturers were also investing in the area, with German FDI stock in Central and Eastern Europe rising almost fivefold from 1995 to €5.4 billion in 2002 (with 80% directed to Poland, Hungary, and the Czech Republic). In 2003, labor costs in the four major host countries were about one-sixth of the labor costs in Germany, and by 2004, the exodus of capital and jobs pressured German unions to accept wage restraints and longer working hours.[18]

Host countries pursued various strategies to attract automobile manufacturers. For example, Slovakia hoped to focus on the higher end. According to the country's minister of the economy, Slovakia was not looking for big investors, rather higher quality projects related to R&D; incentives were tailored accordingly.[19] While Belgium produced the largest number of cars per capita within the EU in 2004, Slovakia was poised to become a major car producer with the opening of new Peugeot-Citroen and KIA production plants.[20] And of course VW had been operating its plant in Bratislava long before other foreign automakers broke ground on their Slovak plants.

New plants producing cars and automobile components also sprang up all over Bohemia. Bosch Diesel, a producer of high-pressure pumps for diesel engines, settled in Koprivnice and supplied carmakers all over Europe, including BMW, Faurecia, Volvo, and others.[21] The VW group's Czech automotive company, Skoda Auto, became a star performer. Offering high-quality compact cars at low price, it increased car sales by nearly 7% between 2004 and 2005 due to export growth to West Europe, primarily to Germany. Audi chose Györ in Hungary to produce its TT/TTS sports coupe.

Meanwhile, Asian automakers (Japanese, Korean, and finally Chinese) offered stiff competition to Europeans, using central Europe as a launching pad to produce cheaper but high quality models destined for Western Europe. Hyundai Motor Co., the largest South Korean carmaker, considered opening a plant in the Czech Republic and its subsidiary, KIA Motors Corp., was building a new plant in Slovakia due to become operational in 2006 with annual capacity of 200,000 units.[22]

Porsche's Driving Future

The Cayenne was a success from its launch, with more than 20,000 units sold in the first year of production. Porsche revenue for 2002–2003 amounted to €5,582 million—a 4.86% increase over the previous year—primarily due to SUV sales. Net profits grew by 22% over the same period (refer to **Exhibit 1**). By 2003/04, "every second Porsche sold in the world"[23] was a Cayenne, according to a company spokesperson, "a bonus at a time when the United States, our biggest market, and Germany, our second biggest, have economic problems."[24] Indeed, Cayenne sales in North America rose from 13,607 units in 2004 to 18,117 in 2005.[25]

However, in the mid-2000s the popularity of the large-engine, inefficient, polluting SUVs was called into question for several reasons. Some safety issues persisted, with reports that SUVs' raised center of gravity precipitated vehicle rollovers upon impact. Rocketing gas prices (reaching $3.17 per gallon in the United States in September 2005),[26] undermined new sales and lowered resale value. American automakers had been particularly reliant on SUV sales, and their earnings suffered accordingly. Rising demand for crossover SUVs (spacious yet more fuel efficient vehicles) translated into a significant decline in demand for full-size SUVs. With billions of dollars invested in product development, American auto manufacturers like GM, Ford and DaimlerChrysler began exploring seven-person SUVs with hybrid engines.[27] In the fall of 2005, Porsche announced a future hybrid SUV.

In the summer of 2005 Porsche revealed plans for its first ever four-door auto, the Panamera, expected to go on sale in 2009. Estimated development costs for the brand new model featuring a V8 engine were $1.2 billion.[28] Envisioned as a rival to Maserati, BMW, Audi and Jaguar sedans, Panamera would "uphold the philosophy of Porsche in terms of a premium on performance." "The Panamera is a perfect fit for Porsche," Wiedeking professed. "It has all the typical DNA characteristics of a genuine sports car. In terms of performance, design, and driving dynamics, it meets Porsche's high standards in every respect."[29] Porsche was considering using its Leipzig plant to produce this fourth series that would share a number of modules and components with the Cayenne, thereby leveraging certain efficiencies and creating 600 potential new jobs in Germany. The yet unpriced four-seater was expected to sell up to 20,000 units annually worldwide.

The announcement was not surprising given that sales of Porsche core models—the 911 and the Boxster—were waning, leaving the company overly dependent on the Cayenne line. Perhaps even more troubling was a May 2005 report by JD Power, an organization known for its quality audits in the automotive industry, placing Porsche as below average in its rankings.[30]

In November 2005, Porsche started selling a new two-door sports car, the Cayman S, priced in the U.S. market at $59,800, between the Boxster at $45,000 and the 911, starting at $81,400. The next month, Wiedeking explained to the press that it "was not enough to cook in your own customer base." He acknowledged that Porsche would endure "enormous development costs" for the new four-door coupe and a new hybrid motor for the Cayenne.[31]

Family Matters

Porsche had jolted the investment world yet again on a Sunday, September 25, 2005, when Wiedeking announced that Porsche would invest around €3 billion in VW and assume an 18% stake in the company, with the option of purchasing additional stock. When its holdings rose to 20%, Porsche suddenly became VW's largest shareholder—a major move for a company with $8 billion in sales. VW, by contrast, was the largest European carmaker and the fourth largest in the world with annual sales exceeding $107 billion and an output of about 5 million cars a year, compared to Porsche's 90,000 units.

Porsche and VW pointed out numerous synergies between the two companies, including the Cayenne and Touareg, the opportunity to pool purchasing volumes, cooperation in hybrid and electric engines, and the new Panamera, as well as other parts and components. Porsche's move also preempted a negative EU ruling on a special VW law requiring an 80% majority to approve major corporate decisions. Taken together, Porsche's investment and VW-owned shares (13%) were enough to shield VW from a potential "hostile takeover." Wiedeking said: "We want to secure our business relations with VW and safeguard an essential part of our future planning over the long term."[32] A stable shareholder structure would support a long-term vision.

But critics were not convinced of the move's financial attractiveness. Some spoke of a return to protectionism and cozy interlocking directorates that blocked real change. In particular, Ferdinand Piëch sat on the supervisory boards of both companies (in VW as chairman), which raised the possibility of conflict of interest. Many criticized Porsche's maneuver as family- rather than profitability-driven. The Piëch and Porsche families could strongly influence the supervisory board of VW. Each family held 50% of common stock in Porsche; external investors owned the preferred, listed shares but had no voting rights. The Piëch family also owned Porsche Holding, the major distributor of VW and Audi in Austria and Eastern Europe. They could potentially exert substantial influence in VW decisions for future contracts between VW and Porsche Holding.[33]

VW was also a troubled company, suffering from falling profitability, quality problems, poor sales in new luxury vehicles (Phaeton), and high labor costs at its core Wolfsburg site. And since July 2005, the company had been rocked by allegations of bribery and fraud after labor representatives on the supervisory board allegedly received "pleasure trips" to Brazil that included prostitutes. As one VW employee put it: "For years employees have been trimmed down to zero pay increases in negotiations, while the works council goes to brothels."[34] The scandal raised questions about Germany's system of codetermination, which placed labor representatives on boards. The state of Lower Saxony, formerly VW's largest shareholder at 18%, had tried for a year to force Piëch off of VW's supervisory board, but Piëch fought the attempt by allying himself with trade union leaders and offering them positions as labor directors—against the wishes of shareholders and some members of the executive board.

Eventually analysts downgraded Porsche's stock, and the market followed: over a month, VW share prices fell about 14% (ca. €52–45) and Porsche's about 12% (ca. €690–600). A J.P. Morgan analyst described the new strategy as a move from "under-investing to over-investing,"[35] estimating that Porsche spent 40% more on its VW stake than it would have paid for the equivalent assets.

Wiedeking brushed off such criticisms as "nonsense," adding that there was no conflict of interest with Porsche as an investor: "Moving into VW was my idea, whatever others may think." Many U.S. practices, such as combining the positions of CEO and board chairman and including company CEOs and other executives on boards of directors, were frowned upon in Germany, but Wiedeking and his chief financial officer desired seats on VW's supervisory board. He argued that "the savings we expect from our investment in VW will certainly not help us in [improving profitability] in the short-term, but definitely will in the long run."[36]

Skeptics remained unconvinced. "I just always questioned what [Porsche] management wanted to really do with all of that money," a Fidelity fund manager spoke for many. "As an investor I would have hoped for a higher dividend or an acquisition that made more sense. […] From the outside it is difficult to understand why Porsche needs 20% of Volkswagen."[37] Tweedy Browne, a U.S. investment firm that owned about 2% of VW and 1.4% of Porsche, was so concerned about VW's poor performance, the role of Piëch, and Porsche's newfound role, that he considered scrapping all of his German investments. He found the situation "intolerable"; such arrangements would be only possible in Germany—or China.[38]

The boardroom controversy grew so great that on January 20, 2006, Piëch stepped down after reaching a compromise with VW's other major shareholder, the state of Lower Saxony, represented by Governor Christian Wulff. Wulff commissioned a J.P. Morgan report on corporate governance that argued that no Porsche shareholder or executive should be on the board. As a compromise, two Porsche executives, including Wiedeking, entered the supervisory board, but gave up their claims to the chair, as did the state of Lower Saxony. Browne remained unsatisfied with two Porsche executives ("one would have been adequate"), but was happy to see Piëch leave.[39] And just two days before the Piëch departure, Porsche announced it would sell $1 billion of hybrid bonds (treated as equity) to shore up its capital structure, raise its cash liquidity, and act as a dollar hedge. An analyst commented: "This is the biggest hybrid transaction by an unrated European company to date, helped by the strong brand recognition of Porsche and the company's financial track record."[40]

Made in Germany?

As this corporate governance controversy filled world newspapers, more mudslinging erupted when Germany's leading conservative public economist, Hans-Werner Sinn (roughly equivalent to Paul Krugman of the *New York Times*), made the Cayenne the showcase exhibit for what he called the "Bazaar-Economy." Sinn argued that, in effect, Germany was only a trading or export platform for goods actually made elsewhere, then touched up and pasted with a "Made in Germany" label: "Customers from all over the world, who buy a Porsche or VW, have the feeling that they are purchasing a German automobile, but in reality they are taken in by false advertising." By his rough calculations, a Cayenne's value was only 38% German.[41]

Porsche's press relations officer quickly shot back, calling Sinn's figures "economic poetry" based upon deliberately misleading calculations chosen to bolster the argument. In the press, Porsche asserted that 55% of a Cayenne's value was "made in Germany," and 60% if one added all of the one-time costs for development and equipment, plus the parts that Porsche and other German suppliers sent from Germany to Bratislava.[42] Most of the suppliers of the SUV's larger modules, such as ThyssenKrupp, Brose, and Behr GmBH, were based in Germany.

Yet another voice weighed into the debate as Ferdinand Dudenhöffer, an economics professor so expert in the automobile industry that he was known as the "Auto-Pope," felt it near impossible (even for Porsche) to estimate the German content because of the long subcontracting chain behind German automobile makers and their suppliers. Dudenhöffer's own calculations found that only about one-third of a Cayenne was "made in Germany," even lower than Audi, BMW, or Mercedes.[43]

Whatever the actual content was, the question remained whether it mattered at all.

Exhibit 1   Select Porsche Financials, 1999–2005

		1995/96 HGB	1996/97 HGB	1997/98 HGB	1998/99 HGB	1999/00 HGB	2000/01 HGB	2001/02 HGB	2002/03 HGB	2003/04 IFRS	2004/05 IFRS	
Sales	**€ million**	**1,437.70**	**2,093.30**	**2,519.40**	**3,161.30**	**3,647.70**	**4,441.50**	**4,857.30**	**5,582.00**	**6,147.70**	**6,574.00**	**Sales**
Domestic	€ million	527.7	671.9	735.5	955.6	893.2	1,001.30	1,121.00	1,482.50	1,213.60	1,267.00	Domestic
Export	€ million	910	1,421.40	1,783.90	2,205.70	2,754.50	3,440.20	3,736.30	4,099.50	4,934.10	5,307.00	Domestic
Vehicle sales (new cars)	**units**	**19,262**	**32,383**	**36,686**	**43,982**	**48,797**	**54,586**	**54,234**	**66,803**	**76,827**	**88,379**	**Vehicle sales (new cars)**
Domestic Porsche	units	5,873	9,670	9,174	10,607	11,754	12,401	12,825	13,896	12,176	13,902	Domestic Porsche
Export Porsche	units	13,346	22,713	27,512	33,375	37,043	42,185	41,409	52,907	64,651	74,477	Export Porsche
Other Models	units	43	-	-	-	-	-	-	-	-	-	Other Models
Vehicle Sales Porsche	units	19,219	32,383	36,686	43,982	48,797	54,586	54,234	66,803	76,827	88,379	Vehicle Sales Porsche
911	units	19,096	16,507	17,869	23,090	23,050	26,721	32,337	27,789	23,704	27,826	911
928	units	104	-	-	-	-	-	-	-	-	-	928
Boxster	units	19	15,876	18,817	20,892	25,747	27,865	21,897	18,411	12,988	18,009	Boxster
Carrera GT	units	-	-	-	-	-	-	-	-	222	660	Carrera GT
Cayenne	units	-	-	-	-	-	-	-	20,603	39,913	41,884	Cayenne
Production	**units**	**20,242**	**32,390**	**38,007**	**45,119**	**48,815**	**55,782**	**55,050**	**73,284**	**81,531**	**90,954**	**Production**
Porsche total	units	20,242	32,390	38,007	45,119	48,815	55,782	55,050	73,284	81,531	90,954	Porsche total
911	units	20,132	16,488	19,120	23,056	22,950	27,325	33,061	29,564	26,650	28,619	911
Carrera GT	units	-	-	-	-	-	-	-	7	270	715	Carrera GT
928	units	28	-	-	-	-	-	-	-	-	-	928
Boxster	units	82	15,902	18,887	22,063	25,865	28,457	21,989	18,788	13,462	20,321	Boxster
Cayenne	units	-	-	-	-	-	-	-	24,925	41,149	41,299	Cayenne
Employees	**at year-end**	**7,107**	**7,959**	**8,151**	**8,712**	**9,320**	**9,752**	**10,143**	**10,699**	**11,668**	**11,878**	**Employees**
Personnel expenses	€ million	392.1	464.4	528.2	574.9	631.3	709.9	799.4	849.5	949.7	964.8	Personnel expenses
Balance Sheet												
Total Assets	€ million	951.4	1,249.70	1,409.90	1,916.10	2,205.40	2,891.60	5,408.70	6,315	9,014.30	9,710.10	Total Assets
Shareholder's Equity	**€ million**	**239.1**	**298.1**	**415.8**	**587.4**	**782**	**1,053.30**	**1,466.80**	**1,754.50**	**2,920.80**	**3,420.20**	**Shareholder's Equity**
Fixed Assets	€ million	482.5	565.3	579.6	525.6	577.7	731.8	2,207.70	2,663.30	2,380.10	2,428.40	Fixed Assets
Capital Expenditures	€ million	213.6	234.8	175.8	155	243.7	293.8	1,119.50	1,295.20	1,111.10	919.00	Capital Expenditures
Depreciation	€ million	67.7	107.6	157.1	183.7	196.6	132.7	278.80	392.20	381.50	510.50	Depreciation
Cash Flow	€ million	123.6	205.5	305	407.8	424.7	418.4	781.50	1,007.90	1,120.40	1,335.30	Cash Flow
Extended Cash Flow	€ million			413.1	592.5	506.5	764.4	1,067.30	1,389.60	1,511.70	1,332.10	Extended Cash Flow
Income	**€ million**	**27.9**	**84.5**	**165.9**	**357**	**433.8**	**592.4**	**828.90**	**933.00**	**1,137**	**1,238**	**Income**
Net Income	€ million	24.6	71.3	141.6	190.9	210	270.5	462.00	565.00	690.00	779.00	Net Income
Dividends	**€ million**	**1.8**	**13**	**21.9**	**21.9**	**26.4**	**45**	**297.00**	**59.00**	**69.50**	**87.00**	**Dividends**

Source: Porsche website.

Note: HGB and IFRS denote accounting standards. In 2003 Porsche adopted IFRS, or International Financial Reporting Standards.

Exhibit 2   Porsche Relative Stock Price Performance, January 1990–November 2005

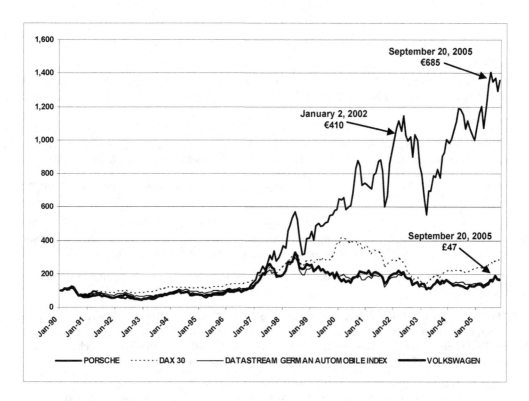

Source: Thomson Financial Datastream.

Endnotes

[1] Christine Tierney, "A niche carved out of dreams," *Birmingham Post*, December 20, 1999, available on Factiva April 20, 2004.

[2] Kevin Kelly, "Leipzig in Porsche's crown jewel," *Ward's Auto World*, October 2002, available from ProQuest, www.proquest.com, accessed November 8, 2005.

[3] Edmondson.

[4] Hanns-Bruno Kammertoens and Stephan Lebert interview with Wendelin Wiedeking, "Geiz ist eine Todsuende," reproduced in www.zeit.de/text/2005/18/W_Wiedeking, accessed May 24, 2005.

[5] Philippe Houchois, "Porsche AG," JP Morgan, November 23, 2005, available on Investext, accessed December 18, 2005.

[6] "Ackermann ist kein Vorbild," *manager-magazin.de*, March 21, 2004, www.manager-magazin.de/unternehmen/boersenbarometer, accessed December 16, 2005. "Geiz ist eine Todsünde," *Die Zeit* 18 (2005), zeus.zeit.de/text/2005/18/W_Wiedeking, accessed December 14, 2005.

[7] "Porsche," B. Metzler Seel Sohn & Co research report, July 10, 1998, available on Investext, accessed November 29, 2005, p. 8.

[8] "Porsche enters the SUV market with Cayenne Model," *Business World*, February 19, 2003, p. 1, available from ProQuest, http://proquest.umi.com.ezp1.harvard.edu/, accessed November 8, 2005. Andrew Luu, "Laying Down Fresh Rubber; Yokohama Expands Its Lineup and Horizons," *Autoweek*, 55:6, February 7, 2005, available from Factiva, http://www.factiva.com, accessed December 6, 2005.

[9] Stefan Nicola, "David saves Goliath," Washington Times, September 27, 2005, available on http://washingtontimes.com/upi/20050927-085542-8230r.htm, accessed November 10, 2005.

[10] Scott Miller, "Road more Traveled: Long Used to Going It Alone, Porsche Joins the SUV Crowd," *The Wall Street Journal*, August 21, 2002, p. A.1, available from ProQuest, http://proquest.umi.com.ezp1.harvard.edu/, accessed November 8, 2005.

[11] Jens Meiners, "Porsche moves further from its sports car roots," *Automotive News*, December 1, 2003, available on ABI/Inform, www.proquest.com, accessed November 5, 2005.

[12] Meiners.

[13] Dr. Ing. H.c.F. Porsche AG, "Logistics Concept," Porsche Leipzig GmbH website, http://www.porscheleipzig.com/en/produzieren/logistikkonzept.htm, accessed March 10, 2004. Ferdinand Dudenhöffer, "Wie viel Deutschland Steckt im Porsche?," *ifo Schnelldienst* 24/2005, pp. 3–5, www.cesifo-group.de, accessed January 17, 2006.

[14] Edmondson, Kelly.

[15] Edmondson.

[16] Wikipedia, "Saxony," http://en.wikipedia.org/wiki/Saxony, accessed November 13, 2005.

[17] Edmondson.

[18] Peter Nunnenkamp, "The German Automobile Industry and Central Europe's Integration into the International Division of Labour: Foreign Production, Intra-industry Trade, and Labour Market Repercussions," ipc-lis.mit.edu/globalization/typology.pdf, accessed on December 16, 2005.

[19] "Slovakia to prefer R&D projects to new plants," *Business News*, November 4, 2005, available from ProQuest, http://proquest.umi.com.ezp1.harvard.edu/, accessed November 11, 2005.

[20] Jurgen Reers, "Going East: Auto Industry Growth in Russia," *Automotive Design & Production,* August 2005, available from ProQuest, http://proquest.umi.com.ezp1.harvard.edu/, accessed November 11, 2005; "Czechrep, Slovakia likely to produce most cards per head in EU," *Business News,* September 27, 2005, available from Factiva, http://global.factiva.com, accessed November 11, 2005.

[21] "New Factory Opens in Eastern Europe," *Ward's Auto World,* July/August 2005, available from ProQuest, accessed November 11, 2005.

[22] Keith Crain, "Europe faces a deluge of imports," *Automotive News,* May 2, 2005, available from ProQuest, accessed November 11, 2005. Norman Thorpe, Lyle Frink, "Hyundai may build 2nd Europe plant," *Automotive news,* September 19, 2005, available from ProQuest, accessed November 11, 2005. "Hyundai Motor to Build $1.2 billion Czech car plant," *AK&M,* September 30, 2005, available from ProQuest, accessed November 11, 2005.

[23] Meiners.

[24] Meiners.

[25] Kammertoens and Lebert.

[26] "U.S. Retail Gasoline Prices Fall to Lowest Since June 13," *AFX Asia,* December 6, 2005, available from Factiva, accessed December 6, 2005.

[27] Eric Mayne, "Big 3 SUV blitz could backfire: Automakers forge ahead despite high gas prices, changing consumer tastes," *The Detroit News,* May 2, 2005, http://www.detnews.com/2005/autoinsider/0505/02/A01-168587.htm, accessed December 2, 2005

[28] Tom Incantalupo, "Porsche to unveil first Four-door car in 2009," *Knight Ridder Tribune Business News,* July 28, 2005, p.1, available from ProQuest, accessed November 8, 2005.

[29] "Porsche Will Build Fourth Model Line: Porsche Panamera; board Approves Four-Door Sports Coupe for 2009 Launch," *Business Wire,* July 27, 2005, available on Factiva, accessed November 8, 2005.

[30] Stephen Power, "Porsche's Road to Growth Has Real Hazards," *Wall Street Journal,* December 8, 2005.

[31] Power.

[32] "Porsche Buying into VW," *Sydney Morning Herald,* September 27, 2005, www.smh.com.au, accessed December 16, 2005.

[33] Michael Freitag and Dietmar Student, "Die Stille Macht," *Manager Magazin,* Vol. 6, May 27, 2005.

[34] "Wolfsburg fürchtet den Verlust von 1000 Arbeitsplätzen," Frankfurter Allgemeine Zeitung, 1 Sept. 2005, S. 14. "VW's Woes Mount Amid Claims of Sex Junkets for Union Chiefs," *The Wall Street Journal,* November 17, 2005, p. 1.

[35] Philippe Houchois, "Porsche AG," JP Morgan, November 23, 2005, available on Investext, accessed December 18, 2005.

[36] "Porsche chief rounds on critics," and "Wiedeking breaks silence on long-term strategy," *The Financial Times,* December 8, 2005. "VW Einstieg war meine Idee," *manager-magazin.de,* December 8, 2005, accessed December 17, 2005.

[37] "Ich verstehe nicht, warum Porsche VW-Aktien kauft," October 2, 2005, *FAZ.Net,* accessed December 17, 2005.

[38] "US' Tweedy Browne Wants Piech Removed as VW Supervisory Board Chairman," *The Financial Times,* December 13, 2005.

[39] "Volkswagen Chairman Will Step Down," *New York Times,* January 21, 2006, B3. Quote from "Porsche's $1bn Hybrids," *Financial Times,* January 19, 2006.

[40] Quote from "Porsche's $1bn Hybrids," *Financial Times*, January 19, 2006.

[41] Hans-Werner Sinn, *Die Basar-Ökonomie. Deutschland: Exportweltmeister oder Schlusslicht?* (Berlin: Econ-Verlag, 2005), p. 92 and p. 230, ftn. 44. The debate is available at www.cesifo-group.de, accessed January 17, 2006.

[42] Anton Hunger, "Wir Bleiben Deutsch," *Frankfurter Allgemeine Sonntagszeitung*, Nr. 41, October 16, 2005, p. 42, faz-archiv.faz.net, accessed January 18, 2006.

[43] Ferdinand Dudenhöffer, "Wie viel Deutschland Steckt im Porsche?," *ifo Schnelldienst* 24/2005, pp. 3–5, www.cesifo-group.de, accessed January 17, 2006.

Part II

THE DOMESTIC POLITICS OF GLOBALIZATION

RAWI ABDELAL

Journey to Sakhalin: Royal Dutch/Shell in Russia (A)

I have seen Ceylon, and it is heaven, and now I have seen Sakhalin, and it is hell.

— Anton Chekhov

Sir Philip Watts waited patiently for a letter from Russian Prime Minister Mikhail Kasyanov. As chairman of the Committee of Managing Directors of the Royal Dutch/Shell Group, as well as chairman of the Shell Transport and Trading Company, Watts bore great responsibility for the future of the Anglo-Dutch energy giant. Kasyanov, for his part, sought to protect the interests of Russia. At stake was an investment project—Sakhalin II—that would be profoundly consequential for the company, the country, and the entire Asian region. Worth approximately $10 billion, the second phase of Sakhalin II would be the single largest investment decision in the company's history and the single largest foreign direct investment in Russia's history. Sakhalin II was the very reason for the existence of the Sakhalin Energy Investment Company (SEIC), owned by Shell (55%) and its Japanese partners Mitsui (25%) and Mitsubishi (20%). Sakhalin II would be the largest single integrated oil and gas project in the world.

By May 15, 2003, the project had already come a long way since its inception more than a decade earlier. Yet on that day its future hung in the balance. Sakhalin II was governed by a production-sharing agreement (PSA), a commercial contract between a foreign investor and host government that replaces the country's tax and license regimes for the life of the project.[1] Although Sakhalin II's PSA enjoyed the status of Russian law, other Russian laws conflicted with the terms of the PSA. PSAs had also become controversial within Russia during the previous few years, as some Russian politicians and business leaders openly questioned the usefulness of these separate contracts with foreign investors. After several years of waiting for what they called "legal stabilization"—new PSA legislation that would clarify the place of such contracts in the Russian legal system and eliminate remaining contradictions with other laws—Shell, Mitsui, Mitsubishi, and SEIC executives realized in March 2003 that there would be no change in Russian institutions before they had to decide whether the project should go forward. Prime Minister Kasyanov offered them a letter instead to assure them that the government intended to honor the PSA. Shell, Mitsui, Mitsubishi, and SEIC settled for the promise of such a letter.

SEIC had set May 15 as the declaration-of-development date for the Lunskoe field, the decision that would mark the official launch of the second phase of Sakhalin II. Expecting the letter from Kasyanov, Watts and his colleagues prepared to announce publicly SEIC's massive investment. But by the morning of May 15 the letter still had not arrived. Shell, Mitsubishi, Mitsui, and SEIC executives, Russian politicians, and the media waited at the President Hotel in Moscow for the announcement. Hours passed, and still there was no word from Kasyanov. By 3:00 p.m. a few of those present were starting to become concerned.

Royal Dutch/Shell Company Background

Royal Dutch/Shell has had a colorful history.[2] In the late nineteenth century the Anglo and Dutch pieces of the firm evolved independently. Marcus Samuel inherited a stake in his father's trading company in 1870. The company had been successful, but only modestly ambitious, importing seashells from Asia. Samuel, foreseeing opportunities in the provision of energy, expanded the business, and eventually began buying Russian oil and selling kerosene in Asia. In 1897 Samuel officially created the "Shell" Transport and Trading Company. Meanwhile, the Dutch progenitor of the energy giant made its way in southeast Asia. After discovering oil in Sumatra, Aelijko Ziljker formed the Royal Dutch Petroleum Company in 1890.

A budding relationship between Shell and Royal Dutch was arranged with the help of the Rothschilds in 1903, when the two firms created a marketing alliance called Asiatic Petroleum. The marriage of the two firms was completed in 1907, when a merger created the Royal Dutch/Shell group of companies; Royal Dutch's share of the group was 60%, and Shell's 40%. By 2003 Royal Dutch/Shell had enjoyed a century of extraordinary financial success and employed more than 111,000 people around the world. (See **Exhibit 1** on the group's financial performance; see **Exhibit 2** on the group's structure.)

Russia in Transition

The 1990s had not been kind to the Russian economy. (See **Exhibit 3** on the Russian economy.) After emerging from the ruins of the Soviet economic system in December 1991, the Russian government and public hoped for a prosperous, capitalist economy, a democratic regime, and an effective state. The economy, certainly, was a disappointment. Between 1991 and 1998 Russian gross domestic product (GDP) fell by half, and the proportion of Russians living below the poverty line increased from 2% to 50%. The Soviet system, for all its faults, had created an equality of income, which was undone in only a few years as Russia's Gini coefficient, a measure of inequality, increased from 0.27 to 0.48. Many Russians and foreign observers hoped that President Vladimir Putin, who took office in May 2000, would reverse Russia's economic decline. For those who believed that the weakness of Russia's political and economic institutions was the root of the country's troubles, Putin's efforts to rebuild the autonomy, capacity, and legitimacy of the Russian state held great promise.[3]

Russian Oil and Gas

The Soviet Union was endowed with enormous oil and natural gas reserves, which Soviet planners used to promote industrialization, regional integration, and state-building. While the constituent republics of the Soviet Union and the east European satellite states were allocated oil and gas by planners at effective prices far below those of the world market, energy exports fetched much higher prices. As a result, oil and gas dominated Soviet export earnings, reaching as high as 75% of the total. Gas was particularly important for the industrial sectors of the Soviet republics and eventually became the single most important resource in the regional economy. Moreover, after the Soviet Union disintegrated in December 1991, it was precisely gas—and the thousands of miles of pipelines that transported it—that continued to tie the new states' economies together. (See **Exhibit 4** for a graphic depiction of these links.) It was also in gas that Russia was destined to be a dominant player in world markets: with 1,700 trillion cubic feet of proven natural gas reserves, Russia controlled the largest concentrated supply in any country, constituting 30% of the world's total reserves. Oil, in contrast, was not as important for industrial firms, nor was its supply in Russia, proven reserves of 60 billion barrels, nearly so enormous, constituting the eighth-largest concentration of oil. Energy was a critical component of the Russian economy, making up 20% of GDP, 55% of export revenues, and 40% of fiscal revenues.

Russia's efforts to privatize state-owned energy firms also produced contrasting patterns in oil and gas. The oil industry produced a number of firms, such as Sidanko and Sibneft, that came to be dominated by businesspeople close to the Russian political establishment. The dominant firms in the Russian oil industry—Lukoil, Yukos, Surgutneftegaz, the Tiumen Oil Company (TNK), Sibneft, Slavneft, and Rosneft—were vertically integrated.

The gas industry was in some respects more straightforward, though not, by the end of the 1990s, less notorious for problematic corporate governance. In gas there was only one significant firm, Gazprom, the largest gas company in the world, in which the Russian government retained a 38% stake. By any measure Gazprom was an enormous player in world energy. Employing approximately 300,000 people and involved in 258 subsidiaries within Russia and abroad, Gazprom was the largest gas-producing company in the world, constituting 20% of the world's and 90% of Russia's gas production, and was itself responsible for 8% of Russia's GDP. The Russian government's equity stake and close relationship to the Gazprom board of directors led some scholars to suggest that the firm often acted as another policy lever for the president.[4] According to the Russian Natural Gas Law of 1999, Gazprom had to supply the Russian market, regardless of profitability, at regulated prices that were, at times, one-tenth of the world price. However, at other times, particularly in Russian domestic politics, it seemed that the Russian government acted on behalf of Gazprom in its international dealings.

Energy, moreover, was certain to dominate the future of Russia's international relations. Already the main gas provider for almost all of the countries of the Commonwealth of Independent States and a supplier of one-quarter of the gas needs of the European Union, Russia sought to play a larger role in Asia. As SEIC's Andy Calitz described: "In contrast to the vast success of Russia's energy diplomacy in Europe and the Commonwealth of Independent States, Russia has so far been unable to get an oil or gas pipeline to China, unable to develop significant energy exports to Japan, and unable to create energy links to North or South Korea."[5] Putin emphasized these priorities regularly, and at the Asia Pacific Economic Forum meeting in Bangkok in October 2003 referred specifically to the promise of SEIC on Sakhalin: "Russia is also prepared to make its contribution to creating a new energy configuration in the Asian and Pacific region. For example, in 2007 it is planned to open a [plant] for liquefying natural gas on Sakhalin—one of the largest LNG [plants] in the world." Clearly, however, for Russia to embrace fully its role in world energy markets it would need massive amounts of capital to develop its resources. With the challenges of economic transition still weighing heavily on Russia, it seemed that foreign energy firms, which had fully developed many of their reserves or exhibited reluctance about investing in a volatile Middle East, and Russian energy were a perfect match.

Foreign Direct Investment (FDI)

The challenges faced by foreign investors in the Russian energy sector were serious, however. "In Russia," Calitz explained, "the issue is not the existence of energy resources. They are here. Investors are almost giddy about the resources. The issue is transportation, which is the biggest single stumbling block for FDI in the Russian energy sector."[6] Furthermore, foreign firms were obliged to create innovative strategies to manage the substantial political risk of investment in Russia.[7] Despite the promise, foreign investment in Russia's energy sector was modest during the 1990s. (See **Exhibit 5** on foreign investment in the Russian energy sector.) Foreign investment in Russian oil firms had been limited, while foreign investment in the development of Russian natural gas was practically nonexistent.

It was not difficult to understand why. The experience of one western firm, BP Amoco, made the new Russia notorious for corporate governance scandals: BP, a minority investor in the Russian oil company Sidanko, watched helplessly as several of Sidanko's prized assets were seized through rival TNK's manipulation of Russia's weak bankruptcy courts.[8] After years of wrangling in the Russian legal system and complaining to the western media, BP announced in 2003 that it would invest another $6.15 billion in Russia, in addition to its initial $500 million, for a 10% stake in Sidanko. Like its first investment in Sidanko, BP's new deal would be an acquisition, rather than greenfield. Many observers were surprised that the newly created firm—TNK-BP—was the result of a joint venture with TNK, the Russian firm with which BP had struggled so much during the late 1990s.[9]

In an effort to attract foreign investment, the Russian Parliament sought to allay foreign firms' concerns about political risk with legislation to allow PSAs. PSAs were seen as very useful for large, long-term, greenfield investment projects, particularly for areas with proven reserves that had gone undeveloped for technical or logistical reasons. Russia passed legislation regulating PSAs in December 1995 and "grandfathered" the few PSAs that had been signed in the early 1990s. More detailed PSA legislation emerged in 1999, but much legal work remained to be done to bring greater consistency among the laws regulating the energy sector.

A number of powerful domestic firms and businesspeople opposed PSAs, insisting that they unfairly favored foreign firms. Mikhail Khodorkovskii, then chairman and CEO of Yukos, argued that the TNK-BP deal "shows that large international oil companies are willing to work in Russia under the present tax system."[10] Khodorkovskii, an opponent of new PSA legislation, was widely known to have lobbied the Duma against PSAs very intensely.[11] In May 2003, the Duma tightened requirements for new PSAs, making them all but impossible to acquire.[12] Some observers felt that this move signaled the end of large, foreign-operated greenfield investments and the beginning of a new wave of corporate foreign investment deals.[13] As of 2004, although the Russian government had received 26 applications, only three oil and gas fields were being developed under a PSA: an Arctic oil field, Kharyaga, controlled by the French firm Total and Norwegian Norsk Hydro; the Exxon-Mobil-led Sakhalin I project; and Shell-led Sakhalin II.

Sakhalin

By the time Russian author Anton Chekhov visited Sakhalin in the Russian far east in 1890, the island was already legendary. Just north of Hokkaido, Japan's northernmost island, Sakhalin was a place of extremes. Sakhalin's natural physical beauty was balanced by its extremely harsh weather. The island was covered with mountains, more than 60,000 rivers and streams, and 16,000 lakes. Sakhalin also rested upon a number of seismic fault lines, and the city of Neftegorsk was devastated by an earthquake in 1995. The island was home to the native Nivkhi, also known as Gilyak.[14]

Russian leaders who had always considered their country to be a European power saw Sakhalin, with pride, as an extension of the West into the East. Many Japanese leaders shared this interpretation, though for them it was a source of frustration. The Russians officially arrived on Sakhalin in October 1806, when Captain Nikolai Khvostov destroyed Japanese settlements in the southern half of the island and proclaimed Sakhalin a Russian possession. Two centuries of Russo-

Japanese disagreement and armed conflict over the border between the countries followed. In 1875 Russia ceded the Kuril Islands to Japan in exchange for Sakhalin. Thirty years later, Russia's defeat in the Russo-Japanese War saw Japan seize the southern half of the island and even briefly occupy the northern half between 1920 and 1925. Near the end of the Second World War, the Soviet Union took the southern half of Sakhalin, as well as four islands in the Kuril chain. In 1946 many Japanese residents of Sakhalin were repatriated, and by 2004 Russia and Japan still had not signed a peace treaty.

The tsarist government had meanwhile populated the island with criminals and exiles. Although the first Russian exile had already arrived on Sakhalin in 1858, in 1869 the tsarist government declared the island to be a zone of penal servitude and exile. Chekhov's 1890 visit to Sakhalin produced a startling exposé of the misery of the island's inhabitants. Chekhov related a legend, told to him by the doctor with whom he was staying: "When the Russians occupied the island and began to offend the Gilyaks, the Gilyak Shaman cursed Sakhalin and predicted that no good would ever come of it. 'So it has come to pass,' sighed the doctor."[15] In subsequent years Chekhov's *Island of Sakhalin* was often published alongside an account of his travels there, *Across Siberia*, in a single volume: *A Journey to Sakhalin*.

The Russian government ended penal servitude and exile on Sakhalin in 1906 and in 1908 declared the island open to free settlement. But by the end of the first post-Soviet decade, life on Sakhalin remained difficult. It was sometimes said that although the Soviet Union no longer existed, one could get a sense of what it was like by traveling outside Moscow—the further away from Moscow one traveled, the further back in time the traveler was transported. Sakhalin was about as far from Moscow as one could travel and still be in Russia. The contrast between beautiful and elegant Moscow and Yuzhno-Sakhalinsk, the capital of Sakhalin, could not have been starker. As described by a *Time* reporter, "Forgotten by successive Russian governments and weather-beaten by violent winter storms, Yuzhno is a mix of degraded Soviet architecture, dusty, potholed streets, and makeshift stalls."[16] Between 1990 and 2000 Sakhalin's population declined by almost one-quarter and in 2003 stood at 546,000.

There was little to keep Russians on Sakhalin. The local fishing industry was vibrant. The island enjoyed abundant coal and timber. But Soviet developers had largely forgotten Sakhalin, as had the presidential administration of Boris Yeltsin. Only in the late 1990s did Russians' own interest in Sakhalin revive significantly, and then it followed the rising interest of the rest of the world. Just off the coast of Sakhalin were some of the largest oil and gas reserves in the world—untapped, and on the doorstep of Asia. Someone would, however, have to spend the tens of billions of dollars necessary to develop the offshore reserves, which presented a technical challenge no one in Russia had ever surmounted.

The Sakhalin Energy Investment Company

In May 1991, months before the entire Soviet Union collapsed, the Soviet government invited international energy companies to tender for the right to conduct a feasibility study for the development of two fields off the coast of Sakhalin: the Piltun-Astokhskoe and the Lunskoe. Piltun-Astokhskoe was primarily an oil field with associated gas, while Lunskoe was primarily a gas field with associated condensate. Three firms—Marathon, McDermott, and Mitsui—conducted the study in 1992, at which point Royal Dutch/Shell and Mitsubishi joined the development consortium. After the Russian government approved the study in 1993, the five foreign firms formed SEIC in April 1994. SEIC signed the first ever PSA in Russia, on June 22, 1994, to develop the estimated 4.6 billion barrels of crude oil and 24 trillion cubic feet of natural gas that lay within the two fields under the Sea of Okhotsk. The development became known as Sakhalin II.

Shortly thereafter, McDermott sold its 20% stake in SEIC to the remaining shareholders on a *pro rata* basis, leaving only Mitsui, Mitsubishi, Royal Dutch/Shell, and Marathon, which controlled 37.5% of SEIC and remained the operator of the project. By 2000, however, the operatorship of SEIC had changed, and another of the original partners had left the consortium. (See **Exhibit 6** for the changing equity shares of SEIC.) By 2003 SEIC employed 760 people on Sakhalin, 226 in Rijswijk, 82 in Moscow, and 94 elsewhere.

Project Roberta

The story of Shell's ascendance within and Marathon's departure from SEIC was remarkable. It even had a code name for Shell managers: Project Roberta. Shell's plan to buy enough of Marathon's share of SEIC to become the lead partner and operator of the Sakhalin II development was launched in 1997.

Shell's Rein Tamboezer and Philip Watts initiated Project Roberta. "We were after operatorship of the project," Tamboezer explained, "not Marathon's share per se." Shell originally offered to buy out 17.5% of Marathon's share, leaving the American firm 20%. According to Tamboezer, "We wouldn't have minded, and it would have been nice to keep an American presence in the project, in part to have access to U.S. influence should this be beneficial to the project."[17]

Watts approached Marathon CEO Vic Beghini with Shell's offer. Watts had "two or three dinners with Beghini to attempt to persuade him to sell us their share of Sakhalin II. But he just wouldn't. It was his baby."[18] Having been involved in the development of Sakhalin II since the early stages, Beghini apparently felt personally committed to Marathon's involvement.

In autumn 1999, however, Beghini retired, and Marathon struggled to find his successor. Eventually Tom Usher, the CEO of USX, Marathon's parent company, decided to become acting CEO of Marathon. Marathon's interregnum presented another opportunity. As Tamboezer recalled, "I said to Phil, 'We have a great opportunity now.'"[19] So in December 1999 Watts flew to Washington to meet Usher for dinner at one of the city's steak houses. Usher agreed in principle to the deal, which the incoming Marathon CEO, Clarence Cazalot, finalized in 2000 and which went into effect in December 2000.

In exchange for Marathon's stake in SEIC, Shell gave up its 28% interest in the BP-operated Foinaven field west of the Shetland Islands, all of its interests in discoveries adjacent to Foinaven, and a 3.5% royalty for an eight-block area in the Gulf of Mexico. Additionally, Shell reimbursed Marathon for its 2000 expenses on the Sakhalin II project. Then, in December 2000, Shell sold 7.5% of SEIC to Mitsubishi, resulting in one more reshuffling but still leaving Shell, at 55%, the majority shareholder in SEIC.

Project Roberta, according to Watts, "was a crucial step. It injected Shell into SEIC in a significant way. It took us about two months to second the necessary Shell staff to SEIC and make available Shell resources to the company."[20] SEIC was now, according to David Greer, the Sakhalin II project director, "a Shell-affiliated company. Period. Shell standards apply."[21] From then on SEIC would be run according to Shell's business principles, with a staff heavily trained in Shell leadership.

The First and Second Phases of Sakhalin II

The first phase of Sakhalin II involved the development of the Piltun-Astokhskoe field. This was the more modest of the two projects. But it was still beset by serious challenges. Phase 1 was the first offshore oil development in Russia, as well as the first project to begin operation under a Russian PSA. SEIC began producing oil in the Piltun-Astokhskoe field in 1999, but only during the summer. During the rest of the year the Vityaz production complex was embedded in ice.

The planning of the second phase was a daunting prospect, and from the beginning it was clear that the development would cost many billions of dollars more than the $1.6 billion necessary to complete Phase 1. The focus of Phase 2 was the development of the Lunskoe gas field. (See **Exhibit 7** for a map of the Sakhalin II project.) Early on SEIC had to decide whether to build a natural gas pipeline from Sakhalin to target markets, or whether to build an LNG plant on the island.

The technical and logistical consequences of SEIC's decision to export LNG were enormous. Natural gas and crude oil produced offshore in the north of the island would have to be brought by pipelines, which did not yet exist, to the southern tip of Sakhalin. The pipelines would run through the island, crossing 1,100 rivers and streams and seven active seismic faults. SEIC engineers and construction workers could expect to encounter unexploded ordnance and war dead from 50 years earlier.

SEIC would then build an LNG plant, as well as an export terminal, on Aniva Bay, where the weather was not as harsh as in the north. Jon Edmondson, SEIC's head of project services for the onshore processing facility, highlighted just a few of the challenges: "What we are talking about is an enormous, world-class gas plant in the middle of a peat bog in the wilderness. The challenges are about as daunting as you can imagine. Uncharted land, escalating costs, abysmal weather, and then, of course, there were the approvals."[22] As described by SEIC's Calitz, "The technical complexity is extraordinary. This will be one of the industrial feats of the century."[23]

The Production-Sharing Agreement

The Sakhalin II project was governed by a PSA, which created a legal framework separate from Russian law. Although many of the details were covered by a confidentiality agreement, some key features were widely known. The PSA, which commenced in June 1994, would last for the life of the Sakhalin II project, which was expected to be well over 30 years. A supervisory board for the PSA met regularly, with half of its 12 members appointed by the Russian government and the other half by SEIC. Other important aspects of the PSA included:

- Preference to duly qualified Russian firms for contracts. Best effort to achieve 70% Russian labor and goods and services over the life of the project. Russian content to be measured by volume of materials and equipment and man-hours of services.
- Exemption from value-added tax (VAT) and customs, road users', and property taxes for PSA investors, contractors, and many subcontractors.
- 100% cost recovery for PSA investors. Remaining production to be allocated to SEIC, the Russian federal government, and the Sakhalin oblast government based on a formula determined by the profitability of the project.
- The Russian federal government and Sakhalin oblast government receive a royalty (in the form of gas) of 6% of the oil and gas produced for the life of the project.
- Title on project assets held by SEIC until full cost recovery has been achieved, at which point title is transferred to the Russian federal government. SEIC retains the right of exclusive use for as long as the company deems operations to be economic.

- Fixed profit tax rate.
- PSA to be governed by the law of New York, with arbitration in Stockholm per United Nations Commission on International Trade Law (UNCITRAL) rules.

According to many within Shell and SEIC, the PSA was the very foundation of the Sakhalin II project. Shell's Tamboezer insisted, "Sakhalin II simply would not have happened without the PSA."[24] Similarly, Engel van Spronsen, the Sakhalin II technical director, argued that the PSA was "absolutely the basis for investing approximately $10 billion in Russia. We wouldn't do this project without the PSA—not a $10 billion greenfield project like this."[25]

The advantage of the PSA was twofold. First, in an institutional environment as fluid and uncertain as Russia's, the agreement protected SEIC from changes in Russia's tax and regulatory regimes. Second, the specific details of the Sakhalin II PSA were widely considered to be favorable for SEIC. As Russia's first PSA, designed to attract foreign firms to invest in risky, technically challenging, and long-term projects, the Sakhalin II agreement was designed to be attractive to the investors. "The first PSA," argued van Spronsen, "always has the best conditions for the foreign investor."[26] McVeigh, SEIC CEO, concurred: Sakhalin II had the "best PSA terms that you'll ever get in Russia, certainly in the future." The PSA, McVeigh continued, "helps to ensure that SEIC receives reasonable, but not excessive, returns."[27] The benefits to Russia were also expected to be significant. According to Watts, Sakhalin II was "a real win-win. This is real FDI, not just the purchase of shares. We are building billions of dollars worth of assets that, under the terms of the PSA, are to belong to the Russian state."[28]

Unfortunately for SEIC, the PSA required management. One problem was the lack of civil service infrastructure to implement the terms of the PSA. Customs officers on the island often challenged SEIC's customs-free importation of project materials.[29] Similar problems were common elsewhere within the Russian bureaucracy, including the absence of a mechanism for the tax ministry to refund VAT payments.

More worrisome, however, was the politicization of the terms of the PSA and, occasionally, the agreement itself. The more modest form of this politicization was the contesting of the meaning of "Russian content." The PSA defined Russian content specifically as man-hours and the volume of materials, not ruble or dollar amounts. What was left undefined, however, was how to total man-hours and material volumes.[30] SEIC had a Russian content manager to deal with the intricacies of the terms of the PSA.[31] Concerns about local content were not unique to Russia, reminded SEIC's contracting and procurement manager Nick Binks. Indeed, the politics of local content were sometimes even more extreme, such as in Malaysia, where affirmative action for local firms was the rule in such projects. The central complication with regard to Russia's interest in local content was that in energy projects there were Russian firms that produced many of the goods and services necessary. However, Russian industry had little or no experience with offshore production facilities and operations and no experience with building LNG plants. Therefore, their ability to supply certain equipment and services was constrained. This coupled with the obligation to meet SEIC's requirements on quality, price, timeliness, health, safety, and the environment made it difficult for Russian industry to maximize its participation.[32]

The very constitutionality of the PSA was challenged by some members of the Russian Parliament. This was not a matter of interpretation but whether the terms of the PSA should be upheld by Russia at all. While these sorts of concerns never seemed very likely actually to overturn the PSA, they obliged Shell and SEIC managers to maintain a close watch on political developments in Russia and particularly within the Duma. "Threats to the PSA," Shell's John Barry explained, "will be vigorously resisted. We will defend the PSA with all our strength."[33]

Community Outreach

SEIC's efforts to construct a harmonious relationship with Sakhalin's residents were substantial. "Stakeholder engagement is the key issue in a massive project like this," explained David Greer, the Sakhalin II project director. "The technical challenges can always be surmounted." The crucial issues, therefore, in managing this project "are health, safety, and the environment, sustainable development in general, as well as the management of our relationships with all stakeholders."[34] Toward this end SEIC created a number of programs managed by a number of community liaison officers throughout the island, all of whom were Russian nationals. The programs included:

- Support for the monthly *Nivkh Dif* newspaper in the language of the indigenous Nivkh people, as well as new costumes for native folk groups
- Annual support for an environmental education program at the Yuzhno-Sakhalinsk school
- The Young Talents of Sakhalin, a collection of scholarships and funds for projects
- Scholarships for native students
- A Small Grants, Big Deeds program to supply grants for a wide range of community and environmental activities to organizations throughout the island

Although these programs enjoyed great popularity on the island, SEIC's approach to sustainable development would be the longest-lasting impact of Sakhalin II. "You must always," observed Greer, "be conscious of the fact that we as project managers are only temporary guests in this great country. When we leave and project execution is complete, some sources of employment will disappear also. So what we must do is ensure that nobody is left worse off than before we started the project and that new skills and opportunities for further development are left behind."[35]

Relations with the Island Government

SEIC's relationship with the Sakhalin government was the single most important external determinant of the project's success, particularly because the late governor, Igor Farkhutdinov, supported the project both on the island and in Moscow, where he was politically influential as well. As Shell chairman Watts explained, "Governor Farkhutdinov was absolutely critical to our success so far with Sakhalin II."[36] More broadly, SEIC CEO McVeigh described the firm's "remarkable synergy with the local administration."[37] For Sakhalin II to succeed it would be vital that the interests of the Sakhalin government and the needs of SEIC remain complementary.

In addition to the development and employment that the Sakhalin II project would bring to the island, SEIC improved its relationship with the local government in more direct ways as well. SEIC contributed $100 million to the Sakhalin Development Fund—$20 million per year between 1997 and 2001. SEIC also moved its headquarters from Moscow to Yuzhno in 2000, in part to clarify the commitment of the firm to the island's economy.[38]

Another visible example was SEIC's upgrading of the island's infrastructure, which was woefully inadequate for the needs of a project the size of Sakhalin II. Significantly, SEIC decided that the infrastructure upgrade project could be used to improve the lives of many of Sakhalin's residents in addition to laying the groundwork for meeting the logistical challenges of Sakhalin II. SEIC, in order to be inclusive, sent its social performance monitors to listen to the requests of the island's residents. This approach, sound from a public relations perspective, created some other managerial challenges, however. When public consultation teams visited every community during the planning of the island infrastructure upgrade project, the teams collected concerns but perhaps did not clarify sufficiently what could realistically be expected. As a result, "SEIC's endeavor to be inclusive may have contributed to rising expectations."[39] Many of the island's communities hoped, and even expected, that the upgrade project would involve new roads throughout the island and possibly new buildings and local-use facilities such as swimming pools. Governor Farkhutdinov, for his part, presented SEIC with a wish-list of infrastructure upgrades worth $1 billion.[40] When SEIC announced what the infrastructure upgrade would actually entail, its managers also had to manage community expectations downward again. Still, the upgrade was extraordinarily ambitious, including:

- $180 million to upgrade existing roads; $80 million for new roads
- $10 million to upgrade the Nogliki airport
- $20 million to upgrade ports, including the Kholmsk fishing port, to handle the influx of equipment and supplies
- $20 million for project-specific upgrades to rail facilities
- $7 million to improve hospitals
- $4 million to improve the island's waste-disposal facilities

Even in its more modest form, the infrastructure upgrade proved to be popular on the island. "One of the most important things," Shell executive Barry explained, "is to recognize in managing relations with friends of the project you must use the appropriate horses for the appropriate courses. Convincing President Putin of the worth of Sakhalin II revolves around the geopolitics of Asia. The governor of the island, in contrast, is worried about jobs and the infrastructure required to develop the island."[41]

On August 20, 2003, Farkhutdinov was killed in a helicopter crash. Farkhutdinov's first vice governor, Ivan Malakhov, a supporter of Sakhalin II, won the island's election for a new governor by a comfortable margin.[42] SEIC managers expected to be able to work as well with Malakhov, who promised to continue Farkhutdinov's support of Sakhalin II.

Approvals

For SEIC, the management of "approvals" was of vital importance, a demanding job that caught the attention of other senior executives only when things went awry. Approvals were what SEIC called regulatory compliance, and in Russia regulatory compliance was, in addition to "a full understanding of codes and standards," a matter of "relationships." This was according to Bernt Granas, SEIC's general approvals manager, who oversaw a staff of 24 (half in Moscow and half in Yuzhno-Sakhalinsk) to ensure that Sakhalin II stayed on track. Granas, a former Shell engineer, had already learned a great deal about foreign firms operating in Russia—what worked and what did not: "The biggest mistake western firms make in doing business in an environment like Russia's is to think that if you go high enough in the government you will be fine. Many managers in these firms think that if you have the ear of the president or prime minister that they can always solve problems further down in the bureaucracy, or that if you can just get the right presidential decree all will be well. This is absolutely not the case." The regulatory environment in Russia was enormously complex, and any project could be delayed, even derailed, by just one of the hundreds of civil servants who oversaw commercial activity. Although power in Russia had been recentralized since the chaotic years of the 1990s, "President Putin," Granas observed, "does not sit in his office with a silver bullet."[43]

By the time Putin took office Russia's governance had become extremely decentralized, and great effort was taken to reestablish central political authority in Moscow. Shell and SEIC executives witnessed the transformation firsthand. As Tamboezer recalled, there was "a total reversal of who called the shots on Sakhalin; it had been the local authorities, but it became the federal authorities.

Under Yeltsin, the governor called the shots. But under Putin, the local government was pushed more to the side. What continued to help was that Governor Farkhutdinov still had high personal standing and was very influential in Moscow as well."[44] SEIC's Granas agreed: "The political influencing of SEIC's progress is primarily driven through the Moscow institutions."[45]

The central challenge of approvals for SEIC was the acquisition of a technical and economic substantiation for construction (TEOC). The TEOC constituted official approval of SEIC's plans for the Sakhalin II project, and it consisted of over 50 different approvals by local and federal Russian regulatory agencies. SEIC formally began the process of acquiring a TEOC in February 2002 after receiving preapprovals for construction at the local and federal level. SEIC could not proceed with the more ambitious and technically challenging pieces of the project without the TEOC. And SEIC's shareholders insisted that the TEOC be in place before committing approximately $10 billion to Sakhalin II. The TEOC was undoubtedly one of SEIC's highest priorities. The first step was to complete the TEOC application, which turned out to be more than 100,000 pages. "The challenge," according to Shell's Barry, "is to acquire the TEOC according to our business principles."[46] In a country where corruption and bribery were not uncommon, this was a challenge indeed. In addition to Shell's own business principles, U.S. law further restrained Shell and SEIC managers, as the Americans among them were subject to the Foreign Corrupt Practices Act. As SEIC's Elena Zolotareva insisted, "We never paid a ruble to get anything done—everything was done in compliance with the rules."[47]

Yet the TEOC approvals came very slowly, and it appeared that those within Russia who opposed the Sakhalin II project could potentially undermine its progress within individual federal agencies. It was clear that Sakhalin II had powerful enemies within Russia. "You must realize," Granas explained, "that in Russia Sakhalin Energy is not just a company; it is also a political statement" about the future and possible success of foreign investment in the country's fast-growing energy sector.[48] SEIC would have to consider how to manage Sakhalin II's opposition. A first step, according to SEIC's van Spronsen, was to categorize the opposition into "first, groups that can be turned; second, groups that can be neutralized; and third, groups that will never support the project."[49]

A second, more important step was to understand the political dynamics within each of the regulatory bodies from which SEIC needed approval for the TEOC. This involved much more than simply making sure that SEIC followed the letter of Russian law, which was often ambiguous and contradictory. "You therefore," Granas explained, "need a very close dialogue with the relevant civil servant, to understand his concerns and to allow immediate interaction if other pressure groups are trying to influence him on your case. You need to consider the individual official within each of the ministries. What is he worrying about? How can I make him feel confident that the approval he is signing is correct and justified? To what pressures has he been subjected? To whom is he talking? What is his social network?"[50] Other SEIC managers elaborated on this theme. Zolotareva, SEIC's eyes and ears in Moscow, explained the importance of interacting with individual officials in the Russian government: "It is necessary to work with middle-level staff who draft papers for their superiors. The superiors usually put their signature on what the middle-level staff give to them."[51] Thus, Zolotareva argued, "You have to work from the bottom up."[52] From London, Watts could see how crucial this was: "It is absolutely essential that you have the proper—and I mean that in the truest sense of the word—relationships with every level of the government. You must be meticulous."[53]

Knowing individual Russian officials was necessary but not sufficient, however. Just as important was figuring out how to win support for the project. As SEIC's van Spronsen explained, "It is absolutely critical to use your supporters to combat the opposition."[54] Granas described the subtlety of this process: "You must figure out who your supporters will be. You must ask yourself, 'Who has an interest in our success?' And, 'Who will fight for us?' The foreign investor in Russia cannot possibly win by fighting for himself."[55] Therefore, a successful foreign investor in Russia also needed "serious Russian knowledge" and to "understand processes." Most important, according to Granas, "is that you have to have a fine touch, a *fingerspitzengefühl*. You do not solve your problems with the Russian government by pounding your fist on the table with indignation."[56]

On the wall of Granas's office in Yuzhno were 20 or so organization charts for the local and federal ministries and Duma committees with which SEIC was dealing. Granas stood and pointed out, box by box, the various alliances within the ministries and committees, outlining the social networks motivations of the key figures. This appeared to be *fingerspitzengefühl* at work.

NGOs and the Environment

Another challenge for SEIC was to operate efficiently and profitably in one of the most pristine natural environments in the world. Sakhalin's rivers and streams were home to salmon and their yearly spawning. The Western Gray Whale, an endangered species, migrated to summer feeding grounds off the northeast coast of the island. In addition to developing the Western Gray Whale Protection Program in 2001, SEIC would have to find sound, technically viable ways to ensure that Sakhalin II did not upset many of the island's natural balances. This meant keeping a careful eye on SEIC's contractors, who were obliged to meet high standards on health, safety, and the environment (HSE). "We need to ensure that contractors are up to Shell standards," according to SEIC's Binks. Indeed, Binks continued, "On HSE performance SEIC is vulnerable to contractors, as well as to contractors' choice of subcontractors."[57]

Several environmental nongovernmental organizations (NGOs) looked over SEIC's shoulder and were not always pleased with what they found. Indeed, several NGOs, including Sakhalin Environment Watch, opposed SEIC's development plans altogether. They first targeted the government-sponsored environmental expertise board. When the board approved the plans, the NGOs urged the buyers of SEIC's LNG in Japan not to purchase from SEIC. Finally, as SEIC signed several long-term contracts with Japanese utilities, the NGOs turned their attention to the international lenders from whom SEIC sought project finance for Sakhalin II.[58] Citing the island's seismic activity, concerns over the health of the Western Gray Whale, and the possible impact on Sakhalin's vibrant fishing industry, Sakhalin Environmental Watch warned lenders to "Stop Shell Ruining Sakhalin Island."[59]

Project Finance

SEIC approached Export-Import Bank of the United States, the European Bank for Reconstruction and Development (EBRD), the Japan Bank for International Cooperation (JBIC), and the Export Credits Guarantee Department (ECGD) of the U.K. to finance perhaps 50% of the nearly $10 billion required to complete Sakhalin II. SEIC managers hoped that the lenders would not be swayed by the arguments of the NGOs that opposed the project. Although the project financing was considered by SEIC managers to be useful for political risk mitigation, it was not necessary for Sakhalin II to move forward.[60] Tamboezer explained, "Project finance was never a *sine qua non* for this deal from a Shell point of view. We always make investment decisions as if we are equity financing them."[61]

Gazprom, Salym, and St. Petersburg

Sakhalin II was by far the most important piece of Shell's strategy in Russia, but it was not the only one. Investing on Sakhalin fit what Tamboezer described as Shell's "peripheral strategy" for Russia—to be literally on the periphery of the country, rather than in the heartland, and to be producing for the export market, rather than the Russian domestic market.[62]

Shell managers also hoped that a strategic alliance with Gazprom, Russia's natural gas monopoly, would bear fruit. In November 1997, Gazprom and Shell announced their alliance, which at the time included an agreement to develop jointly the Zapoliarnoe gas field in the Northern Siberian Yamal-Nemets region. The alliance also involved Shell's cooperation in a large issuance of convertible Gazprom bonds.[63] Gazprom officials saw early on that Shell's play in Russia would be massive. According to then deputy chairman Piotr Rodionov, for Gazprom "Shell is bigger than BP."[64] The Zapoliarnoe gas field was "Gazprom's present biggest hope."[65] Shell's alliance with Gazprom, according to SEIC's Calitz, was "an arranged marriage by Dresdner Kleinwort Benson [now Wasserstein], driven by our desire to be the first international company to export Russian gas and by Gazprom's desire to diversify and for capital."[66]

After six years, however, the alliance had yet to bear fruit for either party. The daunting challenges of undertaking corporate deals in Russia undermined early plans for cooperation. On November 28, 1997, Shell, Gazprom, and the Russian energy firm Lukoil announced their intention to bid jointly on Rosneft, a state-owned energy company that was about to be privatized. But Shell ultimately balked at the deal in the summer of 1998. "We decided it was too risky a deal," recalled Tamboezer. The central concern with such a corporate deal as the basis for foreign direct investment was that "at the end of the day, you often don't really know what you're buying. You have to be aware of what you're buying liability wise. The foreigner's interest in Russia is mostly upstream, but corporate deals in Russia come with all sorts of unrelated downstream assets—restaurants, hunting lodges. Then you have to sort out what you will divest and what you will try to manage."[67] Russia's August 1998 financial crisis also put the Gazprom bond issue on hold indefinitely, so that Zapoliarnoe remained the only ongoing project of the alliance.

Still, Shell managers remained optimistic about the relationship with Gazprom, despite the complexity of relations with such a huge and opaque partner. "There is not only one Gazprom," reminded Tamboezer. "There are many Gazproms within Gazprom."[68] Although Shell offered Gazprom a share of Sakhalin II, they were unable to come to an agreement on a deal. In 2004, after the final investment decision was taken, Gazprom made overtures to become part of the project again. Recasting the shares of SEIC in 2004, however, promised to be awkward for the marketing of LNG in Asia and would certainly raise problems with the project finance.[69] In early 2004 Shell and Gazprom continued to work to find common ground. Reflecting on Gazprom's enviable record of delivery without a single day missed in its European gas business in more than 30 years, Shell's Clive Mather noted that "the Russians haven't let us down yet."[70] Moreover, regardless of the state of any particular joint project, it seemed clear that having such a powerful ally in Moscow, and within the Russian government, was extremely useful for Shell's operations in Russia.

Shell proceeded with two other projects in Russia. Together with Russian partner Evikhon, its (50%-50%) subsidiary Salym Petroleum Development B.V. held licenses for the Salym group of oil fields in western Siberia. In September 2003, Salym Petroleum Development announced a $1 billion development plan for the Salym fields, which held 600 million barrels of crude oil. Although Shell had hoped that the Salym development would also acquire a PSA, by 2003 it was clear that the project would be governed by the general Russian tax and royalty regime instead.[71] Shell also constructed and operated a small retail refilling station network in St. Petersburg, primarily as a way to learn more about the retail business in Russia.

The Final Investment Decision (FID)

"We were prepared in May 2003 not to go forward without a letter from the Prime Minister of the Russian government," recalled Watts.[72] The "letter of assurance" from Kasyanov was delivered by Khristenko to Watts at 3:45 p.m. Shell and SEIC executives took some time to review the letter. "It is a good letter," explained Tamboezer. "While of course not as conclusive as clear legislation, the letter shows the government's clear understanding that the Sakhalin II PSA is grandfathered and sets out the legal justification for this view."[73] At long last the second phase of Sakhalin II was ready to go. SEIC declared the development date for the Lunksoe field, announced sales of Russian gas into Asia-Pacific markets, launched the project financing, and awarded several major Phase 2 contracts.

All of this was done, however, without many of the requirements set forth by SEIC shareholders. Three had loomed particularly large: SEIC's TEOC still had not been approved, a number of Russian laws still conflicted with the PSA, and only a few long-term contracts for SEIC's LNG production had been signed. Barry explained, "We went forward with FID without all of the requirements having been met on the basis of our confidence that we would be able to fix any problems, and our recognition of the fact that Russia is not the only sometimes difficult place in the world we do business."[74] By the time FID was taken, SEIC had already put $200 million into the ground for the second phase of Sakhalin II. "Our commitment to the project," according to shareholder advisor Paul Pickering, "was clear, and all efforts would be expended to avoid any situation in which we would be forced to walk away."[75]

Legal Stabilization

When, in June 2001, SEIC announced its plans for the second phase of Sakhalin II, its shareholders had made clear that the project could not go forward without revisions to Russia's legal code. The shareholders authorized enough money to take SEIC through March 2003. If legal stabilization had not taken place by then, the shareholders insisted, Phase 2 development would be in doubt.

By November 2002, the frustration of SEIC's managers at the lack of progress in legal stabilization was mounting. At the Sakhalin Oil and Gas Conference in London, McVeigh raised the stakes:

> We expect the Russian government to come through on approvals of the TEOC and PSA legal stabilization measures . . . by the first quarter of next year. Both of these actions are on the project schedule critical path so every day delayed by lack of government action causes a one-day delay in the start of new production. . . . But these benefits will not accrue to the Russian government until and unless we secure legal stabilization of our "grandfathered" PSA. There are a number of current and proposed laws that directly conflict with investor rights guaranteed in our PSA. First, the Anti-Monopoly Law gives the government the right to force third-party allocation into oil and gas facilities such as pipelines at government-determined tariffs vs. arm-length commercial arrangements such as provided in our PSA. The Gas Supply Law allows the government to force a private gas pipeline company to sell gas to third parties at government-determined prices. The current Draft Trunk Pipeline Law under consideration by the Duma would bar foreign ownership of oil and gas export pipelines. And finally, passage of the PSA chapter of the tax code is necessary to clarify and anchor the means for reimbursement of VAT to the investor as provided in the PSA. These laws must be amended or

passed to guarantee our PSA rights. . . . There is a plan, currently being worked on in the Duma, that could resolve these matters in the coming months, but the bottom line is that if the laws are not amended, the Phase 2 project will not proceed on schedule.[76]

Amid speculation in the Russian press that McVeigh's speech marked the end of Phase 2, SEIC issued a press release to clarify: "The speech given at the Sakhalin Oil and Gas Conference in London dealt with some of the issues we are facing in developing Phase 2 of the project. One of the most important is that the terms of the Sakhalin II PSA conflict with some Russian laws. This issue is not new and needs resolving quickly if the project is to proceed on schedule, as both SEIC and the Russian Party are aware. The CEO's speech emphasized the need for urgency in resolving this."[77]

By the winter of 2002 passage of the proposed PSA legislation by the Duma appeared increasingly unlikely. Among others, Yukos and its outspoken chairman Mikhail Khodorkovskii had lobbied against the legislation. Khodorkovskii and his allies insisted that PSAs created deals that privileged foreign over domestic energy firms. As Shell and SEIC managers witnessed the end of their hopes for legal stabilization, time was clearly running out on Phase 2.

Shell's senior managers decided to approach the head of the Russian government. As Watts recalled, "PSAs had become increasingly controversial in Russian politics, and especially the Duma. We decided that this was an important enough problem to engage the president and prime minister. We wanted to be reassured. We asked for a meeting with Prime Minister Kasyanov, and then for a meeting with Kasyanov and Viktor Khristenko, head of the PSA commission."[78] In February 2003 Kasyanov and Khristenko met with Watts, Tamboezer, and Walter van de Vijver of Shell. Shell's leadership made it clear that the summer 2003 construction season would have to be used if the 2007 production schedule were to be met, and that they were eager for reassurance on legal matters. Such reassurance would be useful not only for SEIC shareholders but also for potential lenders, such as JBIC. Kasyanov and Khristenko worried about the precedent of undertaking legal changes for specific foreign firms. Instead, Kasyanov suggested that the Shell representatives submit the language that they and their lenders would need in the form of a "comfort letter." "By March 2003," according to Watts, "we had decided that a letter from the prime minister would be enough to reassure us. But time was of the essence."[79]

Three days before the May holidays, Watts wrote to Kasyanov agreeing to such a letter and offering suggestions for the kind of letter that would reassure his investors and lenders. Watts continued:

> We had hoped for legal stabilization, by which we meant the reconciling and solidifying of Russia's legislation surrounding the PSA. In the absence of legal stabilization, we at least wanted some formal reassurance from the prime minister's office that the government intended to honor our PSA. It is pretty reasonable, of course, that you want to have some comfort for the avoidance of doubt. We were not asking for anything more. But this all had to happen before May 2003, when SEIC needed to announce a declaration date for Lunskoe to enable us to launch the start of construction on Phase 2.[80]

Sales

Lining up long-term sales contracts was another pressing concern in the months before FID. Unlike oil markets, which were well integrated and increasingly global, gas markets were much more disparate and local. In the extreme the image of a market for gas was simply misleading because delivery completely depended on the pipeline infrastructure. Gas was sold, therefore, only where the pipelines ended. The emergence of the technology to liquefy natural gas, thereby making it transportable by ship, transformed gas markets. Still, to liquefy and gasify natural gas was expensive, and LNG remained a rich country's fuel, clean, safe, and pricey. Long-term supply contracts remained crucial for LNG projects. As Watts described the difference, "You push oil; gas is pulled."[81] SEIC executives were hoping that Japan, just to the south, would pull the LNG from Sakhalin II.[82] In the longer term SEIC intended to sell LNG to China, Korea, and the U.S.

By May 2003, however, sales had not progressed as far as SEIC executives had hoped. Still, they were confident that more would come. Tamboezer explained, "We took a leap of faith on the sales."[83] Just before FID, on May 12, SEIC and Tokyo Gas signed a Heads of Agreement (HOA), the precursor to a full purchase and supply agreement, for 1.1 million tons of LNG from 2007 for 24 years. With other deals in the works, SEIC could approach the May 15 FID with some confidence. A few days later, on May 19, SEIC and Tokyo Electric signed an HOA for 1.2 million tons of LNG per year from 2007 for 22 years. And July brought an HOA with Kyushu Electric for 0.5 million tons of LNG per year from 2010 for 21 years. Together these deals would make up 30% of the output of the LNG plant. The marketing success of SEIC not only ensured future success in the region and reassured shareholders and lenders, it also served to dissuade competitors on the island from building gas pipelines to Japanese markets.

The dominant factor in SEIC's success in marketing LNG in 2003 was, according to Calitz, "proximity, proximity, proximity." A number of other factors were at work as well: increasing uncertainty about other sources, especially the Middle East and Indonesia; the "marketing power and credibility of a combination of Mitsubishi, Mitsui, and Shell," particularly in Japan; and the Russian government's increasing willingness to promote Sakhalin LNG jointly with Sakhalin Energy, "such as President Putin's mentioning Sakhalin II at APEC."[84]

The Future of Sakhalin II and the Art of Project Management

FID had been a giant step toward the realization of Phase 2, but it had still been only one of the first steps. Having moved forward without legal stabilization, SEIC executives remained concerned that the politics of the Duma and the approvals process would continue to threaten the success of Sakhalin II. It was clear, for example, that there were still powerful enemies of Sakhalin II within the Duma, some of whom continued to attempt to undo SEIC's PSA.[85] Even the day-to-day operations of the development could be affected. In November 2003 SEIC was issued a stop order on some early construction activities on the onshore processing facility when its temporary construction permit was rescinded ostensibly over concerns about how the drawings were approved. Approval of the TEOC for Phase 2, several years in the making and one of the original requirements for FID, eluded SEIC until December 24, 2003, which was about as close to being the last possible moment as one could imagine. As Tamboezer explained, doing business in Russia was an exhilarating process, and he advised: "Always expect a surprise at the end."[86]

SEIC needed someone of extraordinary ability to see Phase 2 development to its completion in 2007, and Watts turned to David Greer, one of Shell's most successful project managers. Greer relocated to Sakhalin and immediately impressed his new SEIC colleagues with his knowledge, enthusiasm, and charisma. "Project management," explained Greer, "is both an art and a science; mastering the science of project management provides a foundation for the art of leadership. The necessary skills are common to both. There is no question that the best project managers are also outstanding leaders. They have vision, they motivate, they bring people together, and most of all, they accomplish great things."[87]

SEIC's bold decision to move ahead with Phase 2 had been hailed by observers of world energy markets as the beginning of a new era for the Asia-Pacific region, and perhaps for gas markets as far away as the U.S. In 2007 LNG would, for the first time, leave Russia for Japan. "Yes," admitted Greer, "the declaration of development was very exciting. Everyone anticipates great things from Sakhalin II. Whilst many people were rightly celebrating the declaration of development with glasses of champagne, I chose to drink a cup of cold, black coffee. There is so much still to do. We are after all but in the foothills of this huge undertaking."[88]

Exhibit 1   Royal Dutch/Shell Financial Summary, 1998–2002 (US$ million)

	2002	2001	2000	1999	1998
INCOME DATA					
Sales proceeds					
Exploration and Production	18,525	21,094	22,123	10,098	8,956
Gas and Power	17,302	16,092	16,281	9,940	7,990
Oil Products	184,345	125,739	136,968	115,434	107,766
Chemicals	14,659	13,767	15,658	13,408	12,795
Other	767	589	481	826	767
Gross proceeds	235,598	177,281	191,511	149,706	138,274
Sales tax, excise duties and similar levies	56,167	42,070	42,365	44,340	44,582
Net proceeds	179,431	135,211	149,146	105,366	93,692
Cost of Sales	151,214	107,839	118,328	81,839	76,674
Gross Profit	28,217	27,372	30,818	23,527	17,018
SGA, exploration, R&D, other	10,394	7,370	6,318	8,295	13,914
Operating Profit	17,823	20,002	24,500	15,232	3,104
Interest income/expense, forex gain/loss	629	104	464	711	699
Income before taxation	17,194	19,898	24,036	14,521	2,405
Taxation	7,775	9,046	11,317	5,937	55
Net Income	9,419	10,852	12,719	8,584	350
BALANCE SHEET DATA					
Total fixed and current assets	145,392	103,827	115,660	108,921	105,357
Net current assets (liabilities)	(14,569)	(2,989)	3,232	(3,071)	(8,541)
Total debt	68,050	39,814	50,771	42,715	39,819
Parent companies' interests in group net assets	60,064	56,160	57,086	56,171	54,962
Royal Dutch (60% interest)	36,038	33,696	34,252	33,703	32,977
Shell Transport (40% interest)	24,026	22,464	22,834	22,468	21,985
Capital employed	83,317	65,457	67,394	71,944	71,473
CAPITAL FLOW DATA					
Cash flow from operations	16,365	16,933	18,359	11,059	14,729
Capital expenditure (including capitalized leases)	(12,184)	(9,626)	(6,209)	(7,409)	(12,859)
Cash flow used in investing activities	(20,715)	(9,108)	(1,571)	(3,023)	(12,500)
Cash flow used in financing activities	(53)	(11,562)	(9,125)	(6,256)	(3,582)
Dividends paid to parents and minority interests	7,189	9,627	5,501	5,611	5,993
Increase (decrease) in cash and equivalents	(5,114)	(4,761)	7,388	1,326	(1,589)

Source: Casewriter compilation from Royal Dutch/Shell Annual Report 2002, pp. 4–6, available at www.shell.com, accessed March 4, 2004.

Exhibit 2   Royal Dutch/Shell Group Structure, 2003

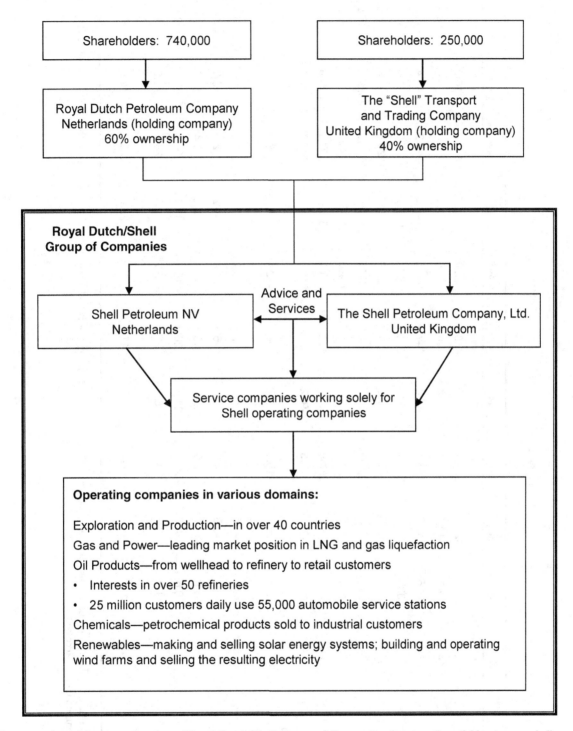

Source: Adapted by casewriter from "Royal Dutch/Shell Group of Companies: Structure," available at www.shell.com/
home/Framework?siteId=royal-en&FC2=/royaln/html/iwgen/who_we_are/structure_of_shell/zzz_lhn.html&FC3
=/royal-en/html/iwgen/who_we_are/structure_of_shell/structure_of_shell.html, accessed March 4, 2004.

Exhibit 3   Russian Federation, Summary Economic Indicators, 1992–2003

	1992	1993	1994	1995	1996	1997	1998	1999	2000	2001	2002	2003
GDP (current $ billion)	442.0	393.5	325.9	337.7	418.6	428.5	282.4	193.6	259.6	310.0	346.5	427.0
Annual GDP growth	-14.5	-8.7	-12.6	-4.1	-3.4	0.9	-4.9	5.4	9.0	5.0	4.3	6.7
Population (mn)	148.6	148.5	148.3	148.1	147.8	147.4	146.5	145.6	145.2	144.4	145.3	144.9
GDP per capita, PPP (current $)	7,742	7,038	6,212	6,171	6,045	6,127	5,918	6,533	7,260	7,653	7,926	8,130
Annual CPI (%)	1,583.9	875.2	307.5	197.5	47.9	14.7	27.8	85.7	20.8	21.6	16.0	13.6
Current-account balance	4,179	7,500	7,844	6,965	10,847	-80	216	24,611	46,840	33,572	29,905	39,093
Net FDI (BoP, current $)	n.a.	n.a.	409	1,460	1,657	1,678	1,496	1,103	-464	-65	-863	n.a.
Inward direct investment	n.a.	n.a.	690	2,065	2,579	4,864	2,764	3,309	2,713	2,469	3,008	5,000
Outward direct investment	n.a.	n.a.	-281	-605	-922	-3,186	-1,268	-2,206	-3,177	-2,532	-3,491	-4,500
Annual change in gross fixed investment (%)	-41.5	-25.8	-26.0	-15.3	-21.2	-8.0	-12.4	6.3	18.1	10.5	3.0	12.0
Annual change in industrial production (%)	n.a.	n.a.	-8.5	-3.6	-5.3	2.1	-5.2	11.1	11.8	5.0	3.8	6.9
Budget balance/GDP	-10.3	-5.7	-9.8	-4.9	-7.4	-6.4	-4.8	-1.2	2.4	3.0	1.7	1.6
Budget revenue/GDP	15.8	14.9	14.1	15.8	14.0	13.8	11.4	12.6	15.4	17.7	20.4	19.8
Budget expenditure/GDP	26.1	20.6	24.0	20.7	21.4	20.2	16.2	13.8	13.1	14.6	18.8	18.2
Exchange rate (ruble/$)	0.2	1.0	2.2	4.6	5.1	5.8	9.7	24.6	28.1	29.2	31.3	30.7
Russian 12.75% government bond of 06-24-2028	n.a.	n.a.	n.a.	n.a.	12.3	11.3	41.1	20.8	16.7	11.5	9.3	7.4

Source: Casewriter compilation of data available from Economist Intelligence Unit, www.eiu.com; *World Development Indicators*, World Bank, www.worldbank.org/data/wdi2003/index.htm; *Global Financial Data*, www.globalfindata.com, accessed March 3, 2004.

Note: Figures are in US$ million unless otherwise stated.

Exhibit 4   Map of Natural Gas Assets, Russia and Vicinity, 2002

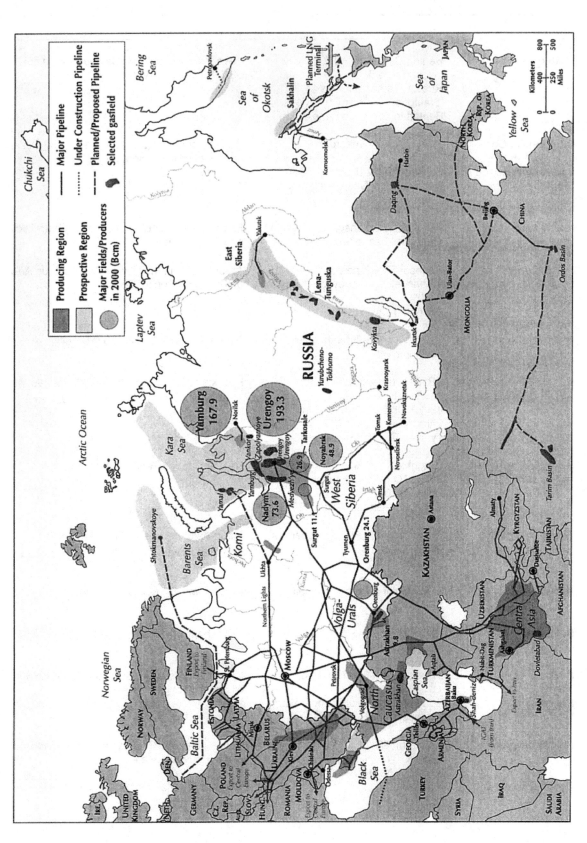

Source: *Russia Energy Survey 2002*, OECD, International Energy Agency, available at www.iea.org/public/studies/russia02.htm.

Exhibit 5   International Oil and Gas Production Projects in Russia, 2002

Name	Ownership	Fields and Estimated Reserves
Arktikgaz	Benton Oil & Gas: 60% Gazprom: 12% Russia (Yamalo-Nenets autonomous district): 28% Benton to sell its share to Yukos.	Yevo-Yakhinskoye and Samburgskoye fields; 35.3 Tcf gas reserves
Caspian Oil Co.	Yukos, Lukoil, Gazprom	Russian sector of Caspian Sea; 15–30 billion barrels of oil equivalent
Chayandinovskoe Field	Sakhaneftegaz (Russia), China National Oil & Gas Development Corp.	43 Tcf gas
North Astrakhan PSA	ENI-Agip, Stoitransgaz (Russia), and Astrakhannefteprom (Russia)	Recoverable reserves of 3.4 billion barrels oil and 5.1 Tcf gas
Polar Lights	Conoco: 50% (operator) Arkhangelskgeoldobycha (Russia): 30% Rosneft (Russia): 20%	Ardalin fields in the Nenets Autonomous Area of the Timan Pechora Basin
Prirazlomnoe Field	Gazprom and Wintershall, joint development	Pechora Sea; 608 million barrels oil
Russia Petroleum	BP: 31% (operator) Interros (Russia): 24% Irkutsk Oblast Property Fund: 14% Vitra Holdings Co.: 13% Tyumen Oil: 18%	Kovykta field, eastern Siberia; 49 Tcf gas
Sakhalin I	ExxonMobil: 30% SODECO (Japan consortium) 30% Rosneft: 20% ONGC Videsh Ltd. (India): 20%	Chayvo, Odoptu, and Arkutun-Dagi fields; 17.1 Tcf gas
Sakhalin II (SEIC)	Royal Dutch/Shell: 55% (operator) Mitsui: 25% Mitsubishi: 20%	Piltun-Astokhskoye and Lunskoye fields; 4 billion barrels oil and over 20 Tcf gas
Sakhalin III	ExxonMobil, Texaco, Rosneft- SMNG	Ayyash and Eastern Odoptu fields
Sakhalin IV	Rosneft: 50% Rosneft-SMNG: 50%	Astrakhanovsky block; 3.53 Tcf gas
Sakhalin V	BP and Rosneft to tender jointly	East Schmidtovsky blocks; 4.4 billion barrels oil and 21 Tcf gas
Sakhalin VI	Rosneft, ExxonMobil, and Texaco to tender jointly	--
Shtokmanskoe Field	Gazprom: 50%, Fortum (Finland), Conoco, TotalFinaElf (France), Norsk Hydro (Norway)	Barents Sea; 113 Tcf gas and 440 million barrels of condensate
Zapoliarnoe Field	Gazprom	Western Siberia

Name	Ownership	Fields and Estimated Reserves
Caspian Pipeline Consortium (Oil)	Russia: 24% Kazakhstan: 19% Chevron: 15% LukArco: 12.5% Rosneft-Shell: 7.5% ExxonMobil: 7.5% Oman: 7% Agip: 2% BG: 2% Kazakh Pipelines: 1.75% Oryx: 1.75%	900-mile oil pipeline from Tengiz oil field in Kazakhstan to Novorossiisk; Phase I 565,000 bbl/d capacity, rising in 2015 to Phase II capacity of 1.34 million bbl/d
China Natural Gas Pipeline	China National Petroleum Corp., Sakha (Russian Republic); Gazprom as operator?	1,700-mile pipeline, Chayandinovskoye gas field to Xinjiang, (about 550 miles southwest of Beijing in northern China)
China-South Korea Natural Gas Pipeline	BP, Tyumen Oil	2,000–2,700-mile pipeline from Kovykta gas field in Irkutsk to northeastern China (possibly via Mongolia), terminating in South Korea via a sub-sea pipeline across the East China Sea
China Oil Pipeline	Yukos, Transneft, China National Oil Corp.	1,400–1,500-mile pipeline from Angarsk, East Siberia to Beijing (possibly via Mongolia); initial 400,000 bbl/d capacity rising to 600,000 bbl/d in 2010
Japan Natural Gas Pipeline	ExxonMobil, SODECO (Japan consortium)	Proposed 120-mile pipeline from the Sakhalin I field to Sapporo, on Japan's northernmost island of Hokkaido; possible extension to Tokyo
North Trans Gas Pipeline	Gazprom: 50% Fortum (Finland): 50% Wintershall and Ruhrgas (Germany) may join	1,800-mile gas export pipeline from Vyborg on Russia's Gulf of Finland coast under the Baltic Sea to northern Germany; planned annual capacity of 706 Bcf
Yamal-Europe Pipeline	Gazprom (Russian and Belarussian sections), EuroPolGaz consortium (Polish section), Germany	Natural gas export pipeline from Russia across Belarus through Poland and on to Germany; proposed 373-mile "Yamal-Europe II" pipeline from Russia through Belarus, then connecting Brzesc, Poland to Velke Kapusany, Slovakia

Source: U.S. Department of Energy, Energy Information Administration, Office of Energy Markets and End Use, Country Analysis Briefs, *Russia: International Oil and Gas Projects*, Table 1: International Oil and Natural Gas Production Projects, November 2002, available at www.eia.doe.gov/emeu/cabs/russproj.html#PIPE, accessed March 3, 2004.

Exhibit 6   Changing Equity Shares in SEIC, 1994–2003

Date	Investor	Percentage Ownership
June 1994	Marathon	30%
	McDermott	20%
	Mitsui	20%
	Shell	20%
	Mitsubishi	10%
April 1997	Marathon	37.5%
	Shell	25%
	Mitsui	25%
	Mitsubishi	12.5%
December 6, 2000	Shell	62.5%
	Mitsui	25%
	Mitsubishi	12.5%
December 15, 2000	Shell	55%
	Mitsui	25%
	Mitsubishi	20%

Source: Company document.

Exhibit 7   Map of Sakhalin II Project

Phase 2 development

- Piltun -B platform
- Astokh year round production
- Lunskoye A platform
- Onshore processing facility
- Oil and gas pipelines
- LNG plant and oil export terminal

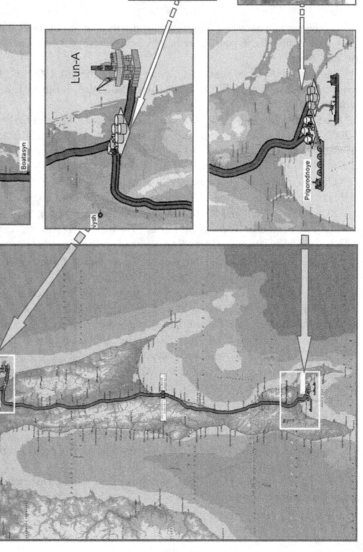

Source: Company document.

Endnotes

[1] The phrase production-sharing agreement has undergone a significant evolution. Originally reserved for arrangements in which a foreign firm and host government share the output of a project in specific proportions, the phrase has come to refer to almost any agreement between foreign firms and host governments that creates exceptions from the country's standard legal regime and opens the possibility of the host government receiving benefits from the project in kind. Many foreign investors based in the U.S. prefer not to replace the local tax regime for purposes of U.S. income tax. Also, many PSAs are contractual relationships between foreign investors and host country state-owned enterprises, relationships in which the title of assets is vested in the SOE from the beginning of the project. I am grateful to Louis Wells for conversations to clarify these points.

[2] For several insightful discussions of Royal Dutch/Shell's operations in general and in a specific country context, see Lynn Sharp Paine, "Royal Dutch/Shell in Transition (A)," HBS Case No. 300-039, October 4, 1999; Paine, "Royal Dutch/Shell in Transition (B)," HBS Case No. 300-040, October 25, 1999; Paine, "Royal Dutch/Shell in Nigeria (A)," HBS Case No. 399-126, Rev. April 20, 2000; and Paine, "Royal Dutch/Shell in Nigeria (B)," HBS Case No. 399-127, Rev. June 14, 2000.

[3] For an overview and citations to the relevant scholarly literature, see Rawi Abdelal, "Russia: The End of a Time of Troubles?" HBS Case No. 701-076, Rev. May 24, 2001.

[4] See, for example, Jan S. Adams, "Russia's Gas Diplomacy," *Problems of Post-Communism*, vol. 49, no. 3 (2002): 14–22.

[5] Author's interview with Andy Calitz, commercial director, Sakhalin Energy Investment Company, Yuzhno-Sakhalinsk, November 3, 2003.

[6] Ibid.

[7] On the management of political risk in the Russian oil industry, see Debora L. Spar, William W. Jarosz, and Julia Kou, "White Nights and Polar Lights: Investing in the Russian Oil Industry," HBS Case No. 795-022, Rev. June 26, 1996.

[8] See "Russia: Rules of War," *The Economist*, December 4, 1999; and Bhushan Bahree, "How Siberian Oil Field Turned into a Minefield—BP Amoco Learns Bruising Lesson on Investing in Russia," *The Wall Street Journal*, February 9, 2000.

[9] See Sabrina Tavernise, "BP Adds to Stake in Russia, Despite Earlier Legal Battle," *The New York Times*, April 17, 2002; "Gluttons for Punishment?" *The Economist*, April 20, 2002; Andrew Jack, "A Rare Hybrid Takes on a Very Russian Battle," *The Financial Times*, June 12, 2002; and Heather Timmons, "BP Signs Deal with Russians for Venture in Oil and Gas," *The New York Times*, June 27, 2003.

[10] Quoted in Maureen Lorenzetti, "Russian Resurgence," *Oil & Gas Journal*, March 3, 2003.

[11] See, for example, "Russia," *Petroleum Economist*, June 1, 2003.

[12] "Lawmakers Tighten PSA Rules," *RFE/RL Business Watch*, May 20, 2003. See also Jeanne Whalen, "Russia to Scrap Pacts Protecting Foreign Oil Firms," *The Wall Street Journal*, April 2, 2003.

[13] Sam Fletcher, "Mergers, not PSAs, Key to Foreign Russian Investment," *Oil & Gas Journal*, June 2, 2003.

[14] On the native Nivkhi of Sakhalin, see Bruce Grant, *In the Soviet House of Culture: A Century of Perestroikas* (Princeton, N.J.: Princeton University Press, 1995).

[15] Anton Chekhov, *The Island of Sakhalin*, trans. Luba and Michael Terpak (London: Folio, 1989), p. 15.

[16] Shawn M. Clankie, "Once a Penal Colony, Sakhalin Still Captivates Its Visitors," *Time Asia*, June 3, 2002. Also see James Brooke, "On Sakhalin, the Cold War is Ending," *The New York Times*, October 5, 2003.

[17] Author's interview with Rein Tamboezer, EP global divestment manager, Royal Dutch/Shell Group of Companies, The Hague, November 7, 2003.

[18] Author's interview with Sir Philip Watts, chairman of the Committee of Managing Directors of the Royal Dutch/Shell Group of Companies and chairman of the Shell Transport and Trading Company, London, November 6, 2003.

[19] Author's interview with Tamboezer, The Hague, November 7, 2003.

[20] Author's interview with Watts, London, November 6, 2003.

[21] Author's interview with David J. Greer, Sakhalin II project director and deputy CEO, Sakhalin Energy Investment Company, Moscow, November 5, 2003.

[22] Author's interview with Jon Edmondson, SEIC head of project services—onshore processing facility, Yuzhno-Sakhalinsk, November 3, 2003.

[23] Author's interview Calitz, Yuzhno-Sakhalinsk, November 3, 2003.

[24] Author's interview with Tamboezer, The Hague, November 7, 2003.

[25] Author's interview with Engel van Spronsen, technical director, Sakhalin Energy Investment Company, Yuzhno-Sakhalinsk, November 3, 2003.

[26] Ibid.

[27] Author's interview with Steve McVeigh, CEO, Sakhalin Energy Investment Company, Yuzhno-Sakhalinsk, November 3, 2003.

[28] Author's interview with Watts, London, November 6, 2003.

[29] Author's interview with Nick Binks, head of contracting and procurement, Sakhalin Energy Investment Company, Yuzhno-Sakhalinsk, November 4, 2003.

[30] Ibid.

[31] Ibid.

[32] Ibid.

[33] Author's interview with John Barry, president and country chairman, Shell Exploration and Production Services (RF), Moscow, November 5, 2003.

[34] Author's interview with Greer, Moscow, November 5, 2003.

[35] Ibid.

[36] Author's interview with Watts, London, November 6, 2003.

[37] Author's interview with McVeigh, Yuzhno-Sakhalinsk, November 3, 2003.

[38] Ibid.

[39] Author's interview with David Meehan, project manager, infrastructure upgrade project, Sakhalin Energy Investment Company, Yuzhno-Sakhalinsk, November 4, 2003.

[40] Ibid.

[41] Author's interview with Barry, Moscow, November 5, 2003.

[42] "Malakhov elected Sakhalin Governor," *The Sakhalin Independent*, December 22–January 15, 2003–2004.

[43] Author's interview with Bernt Granas, general approvals manager, Sakhalin Energy Investment Company, Yuzhno-Sakhalinsk, November 3, 2003.

[44] Author's interview with Tamboezer, The Hague, November 7, 2003.

[45] Author's interview with Granas, Yuzhno-Sakhalinsk, November 3, 2003.

[46] Author's interview with Barry, Moscow, November 5, 2003.

[47] Author's interview with Elena Zolotareva, head of Moscow representation, Sakhalin Energy Investment Company, Moscow, November 5, 2003.

[48] Author's interview with Granas, Yuzhno-Sakhalinsk, November 3, 2003.

[49] Author's interview with van Spronsen, Yuzhno-Sakhalinsk, November 3, 2003.

[50] Author's interview with Granas, Yuzhno-Sakhalinsk, November 3, 2003.

[51] Author's interview with Zolotareva, Moscow, November 5, 2003.

[52] Author's interview with van Spronsen, Yuzhno-Sakhalinsk, November 3, 2003.

[53] Author's interview with Watts, London, November 6, 2003.

[54] Author's interview with van Spronsen, Yuzhno-Sakhalinsk, November 3, 2003.

[55] Author's interview with Granas, Yuzhno-Sakhalinsk, November 3, 2003.

[56] Ibid..

[57] Author's interview with Binks, Yuzhno-Sakhalinsk, November 4, 2003.

[58] Author's interview with McVeigh, Yuzhno-Sakhalinsk, November 3, 2003.

[59] "Stop Shell Ruining Sakhalin Island," Sakhalin Environmental Watch leaflet. See www.sakhalin.environment.ru.

[60] Author's interview with Barry, Moscow, November 5, 2003.

[61] Author's interview with Tamboezer, The Hague, November 7, 2003.

[62] Ibid.

[63] "Royal Dutch/Shell Forms Development Alliance with Gazprom," *Oil & Gas Journal*, November 24, 1997.

[64] Quoted in Robert Corzine, "Gazprom Pins Long-Term Hopes on Shell," *The Financial Times*, November 28, 1997.

[65] Ali Morteza Samsam Bakhtiari, "Russia's Gas Production, Exports Future Hinges on Dramatic Changes Needed at Gazprom," *Oil & Gas Journal*, March 10, 2003.

[66] Author's interview with Calitz, Yuzhno-Sakhalinsk, November 3, 2003.

[67] Author's interview with Tamboezer, The Hague, November 7, 2003.

[68] Ibid.

[69] Author's interview with Barry, Moscow, November 5, 2003.

[70] Author's interview with Clive Mather, head of global learning, Shell International Ltd., London, November 6, 2003.

[71] See Jeanne Whalen and Chip Cummins, "Shell Resurrects Development Plan for Siberian Field," *The Wall Street Journal*, September 17, 2003.

[72] Author's interview with Watts, London, November 6, 2003.

[73] Author's interview with Tamboezer, The Hague, November 7, 2003.

[74] Author's interview with Barry, Moscow, November 5, 2003.

[75] Author's interview with Paul Pickering, shareholder advisor, Shell Exploration and Production Services (RF), Moscow, November 5, 2003.

[76] Stephen McVeigh, "Sakhalin II—On Track to Phase 2," Sakhalin Oil and Gas Conference, London, November 18–19, 2002.

[77] Sakhalin Energy Investment Company, Press Statement, November 21, 2002.

[78] Author's interview with Watts, London, November 6, 2003.

[79] Ibid.

[80] Ibid.

[81] Ibid.

[82] Also see Alan Troner, "Russian Far East Natural Gas Searches for a Home," *Oil & Gas Journal*, March 5, 2001.

[83] Author's interview with Tamboezer, The Hague, November 7, 2003.

[84] Author's interview with Calitz, Yuzhno-Sakhalinsk, November 3, 2003.

[85] Author's interview with McVeigh, Yuzhno-Sakhalinsk, November 3, 2003.

[86] Author's interview with Tamboezer, The Hague, November 7, 2003.

[87] Author's interview with Greer, Moscow, November 5, 2003.

[88] Ibid.

RAWI ABDELAL

IRINA TARSIS

Journey to Sakhalin: Royal Dutch/Shell in Russia (B)

On April 7, 2005, after protracted negotiations, Gazprom and Royal Dutch/Shell reached an agreement to swap shares in two Russian oil and gas projects—Sakhalin II and Zapolyarnoe-Neokom. The deal was approved by the other shareholders of the Sakhalin Energy Investment Company (SEIC), Mitsubishi and Mitsui, and it represented one of the largest asset exchanges in the history of the energy industry. Two months later, Gazprom and Shell signed a memorandum of understanding (MOU), according to which Gazprom would receive a 25% stake plus one additional share in the Shell-led Sakhalin II natural gas project in return for 50% of its shares in the Zapolyarnoe-Neokom fields, the world's fifth-largest gas deposit, and Shell would remain the Sakhalin II project operator. Since the assets were not of equal value, one of the sides would have to settle the difference, and it was not yet clear which one it would be.

Sakhalin and Gazprom Monopoly

At the time of the case, six separate oil and gas projects were under way off the shores of Sakhalin, a cold, 589-mile-long island in the north Pacific that once served as a tsarist prison. In operation since 2001, Sakhalin I included three fields on the northeast shelf of the island. Operated by Exxon Neftegas Limited, an affiliate of ExxonMobil, it was run by a consortium of five international companies, two of them Russian. Sakhalin II, operated by Royal Dutch/Shell and the SEIC, was jointly owned by three non-Russian firms. Other Sakhalin projects (III, IV, V, and VI) were at earlier stages of development. However, tenders (written offers to contract services at a specified cost or rate) awarded to ExxonMobil and ChevronTexaco for developing Sakhalin III were annulled in 2004 because the Russian government found "irregularities in the auction documentation."[1]

On several occasions, the CEO/chairman of the management committee of state-run Gazprom, Alexei Miller, stated that his company had to establish strategic control on the island of Sakhalin.[2] According to Miller, Gazprom "wished to participate in all phases of exploration and drilling on the island."[3] In 2003, Rosneft transferred 20% of its shares in Sakhalin I to Gazpromneft, a fully owned subsidiary of Gazprom.[4] Although Gazprom reportedly sought operatorship of Sakhalin II, Shell negotiated to retain control of the project. Gazprom also planned to participate in a re-auction of the rights to develop Sakhalin III. U.S. companies ChevronTexaco and ExxonMobil were promised priority in buying up to a 49% stake if they would decide to take part in the new auction. Foreign investors in Russia's energy sector worried that Gazprom's encroachment on the Sakhalin contracts was part of a broader pattern of Russian policy, in which the government increasingly sought direct control over firms that dominated its oil and gas resources.

Professor Rawi Abdelal and Research Associate Irina Tarsis, Global Research Group, prepared this case. This case was developed from published sources. HBS cases are developed solely as the basis for class discussion. Cases are not intended to serve as endorsements, sources of primary data, or illustrations of effective or ineffective management.

In the most recent move toward consolidating the Russian energy industry, on September 28, 2005, Gazprom's board of directors approved a $13.1 billion acquisition of nearly all of Sibneft Oil stock owned by Russia's richest man, Roman Abramovich. At the time of the acquisition, Sibneft Oil was Russian's fifth-largest oil producer; its major assets included 731 million cubic meters of proved oil reserves and 137.4 billion cubic meters of proved liquefied natural gas (LNG) reserves.[5]

The Meaning of Yukos

In October 2003, Mikhail Khodorkovskii was arrested on charges of tax fraud and later sentenced to nine years in prison. This incident alarmed foreign investors. Prior to his arrest, Khodorkovskii was widely known as one of Russia's richest men and owner of Yukos, Russia's second-largest oil company. He was also one of the most vocal opponents of the administration of Russian President Vladimir Putin and government plans to allow foreign investors to develop Russian natural resources. In December 2004 his oil company was dismantled and bought by Gazprom. Less than two years later, another oil company, TNK-BP, a joint Russian-British venture, was presented with an "arbitrary $1 billion tax bill," which the company appeared inclined to pay.[6]

In February 2005, Russia's Minister of Natural Resources Yury Trutnev announced that neither foreign companies nor Russian companies managed from abroad would be allowed to participate in new auctions for rights to develop Russian natural resources. At the same time, the State Duma (Russia's supreme legislative body) was reviewing a tax code amendment that would levy additional taxes on firms transacting with offshore companies.[7] The regulations limiting foreign investors, as well as the Natural Resources Ministry's decision to stall ChevronTexaco and ExxonMobil's attempts to develop Sakhalin III, demonstrated the Russian government's interest in favoring domestic companies involved in national resource excavations. "We don't understand this situation at all," admitted Shell's press secretary following Trutnev's announcement.[8] In light of a reassertion of Russian government influence in the oil industry, some thought that the Sakhalin II MOU could be seen as a natural extension of Russian government influence in an industry that had until recently been dominated by large foreign energy firms.[9]

The View from Amsterdam and London

As old oil and gas fields around the world ran dry and national policies and technical challenges made the prospect of bringing new fields online less tenable, major oil-producing companies vied for new opportunities in which to invest and expand. Doing nothing to expand reserves literally meant losing assets.[10] Russian oil and gas fields looked promising, but foreign investors could never fully predict what new regulations the Russian government might impose and what additional overhead costs might be incurred as a result. In 2004 the Russian State Audit Department investigated Sakhalin Energy on charges of financial damages ($2.5 billion) that the company brought upon the Russian budget by not employing domestic workers. By inviting Gazprom to join Sakhalin Energy and via the equity swap, Shell hoped to lock in future opportunity and to gain access to other large Russian gas fields. Not only would the agreement boost Shell's natural gas reserves, but by joining forces with a state-run company, Shell would receive indirect Russian backing, which presumably would make its presence in the country more secure.

The Zapolyarnoe-Neokomian gas field, discovered in 1965, had an estimated reserve of 2.8 trillion cubic meters of gas; the commercial development of the site did not begin until the 1990s.[11] By 2004, the field was producing 100 billion cubic meters of gas per year. According to gas market experts, Neokom offered three times more fossil fuels than Sakhalin II. However, the upcoming share exchange held promise for both sides, as Gazprom was joining a project well under way, Sakhalin II investments had already exceeded $8.5 billion of an estimated $10 billion in total project costs, and Shell looked forward to exploring a new field.[12]

With Gazprom as its partner in the Sakhalin II project, Shell also hoped to gain a major stake in developing the Shtokman field in the Barents Sea. Discovered in 1988, the Shtokman gas field was estimated to contain up to 3.2 trillion cubic meters of LNG, with a development cost projected to reach $10 billion.[13] In exploring Barents Sea fields, Gazprom planned, however, to partner with smaller Norwegian companies such as Statoil ASA or Norsk Hydro. Other potential collaborators included French oil company Total SA and ChevronTexaco.[14]

Making Sense of the Agreement: "Strategically Important for Both Sides"

Both parties announced to the media that the deal was mutually beneficial. Miller argued that the swap would help his company become "a large shareholder of a fast-growing project for hydrocarbons development, LNG production, and sale to strategic markets."[15] His counterpart from the Royal Dutch/Shell side, Jeroen van der Veer, welcomed Gazprom as "a great Russian partner [that] will make significant contributions toward maximizing the long term value of the project." Furthermore, the agreement promised to build up Shell's position in western Siberia.[16]

External analysts viewed the exchange as beneficial for both sides. "[I]f the assets swap passes successfully it will increase probability of production growth in Russia for both parties. Gazprom has only one other joint production project with Wintershall AG and diversified production capabilities of Shell allow significant increase of production in Russia."[17] In exchange for the Zapolyarnoe-Neokomian field stake, Gazprom gained access to developed oil and gas sources on Sakhalin and the LNG market in Asia as early as 2007. Sakhalin Energy had signed contracts with Japanese and Korean customers, such as Tokyo Electric, Tokyo Gas, and Kogas. Gazprom's experience in laying pipelines could be an asset to SEIC, which was in the process of running two parallel pipelines north to south of the island underwater and over land to transport oil and gas to LNG plants and oil terminals.[18] Shell in turn received a powerful Russian partner, viewed as critical to continuing oil exploration within the country. An analyst saw "the exchange of shares with Gazprom was to a great degree a political deal [from Shell's perspective]. Since the government decided to keep foreigners from strategically important fields, collaboration with Gazprom in the Zapolyarnoe-Neokom field provides Shell with hopes of participation in other major projects in Russia."[19]

The Rising Cost of Sakhalin

A week after the memorandum of understanding was signed in June 2005, Royal Dutch/Shell announced that the anticipated costs of Sakhalin II were expected to double from the $10 billion estimate of 2003 and perhaps even exceed $20 billion. The revised projections were ascribed to flawed geological modeling, weather-related delays, and concerns brought by environmentalists who claimed the drilling operations on the seabed would disrupt salmon breeding areas and threaten endangered Western Gray whales. In response, Sakhalin Energy decided to reroute the undersea pipeline and bury it deeper in the ocean floor. "The need to increase capital spending and the delay in the first LNG shipment from the Sakhalin II project will certainly lead to a downward revision of Shell's assets value [in the swap]," professed the head of the Gazprom export entity.[20] Since the negotiations between Gazprom and Royal Dutch/Shell regarding other joint Russian projects were frozen, the increased Sakhalin expenses made Shell's position in Russia a central concern to company management.

Endnotes

[1] "People, Company, Miscellaneous," *Oil and Gas, Euroasia*, http://www.oge.ru/?action=Article&id=152, accessed September 14, 2005.

[2] "A Quarter of Sakhalin-2 Was Given for Half of the Zapolyarnoe: Gazprom and Shell Exchange Assets," *Kommersant*, July 8, 2005, http://www.komersant.com/doc.asp?id+589469, accessed August 30, 2005.

[3] Varvara Aglamishian, "Gazprom vukhodit na Sakhalin: Contsern chochet preobresti doli Rosnefit i Shell," *Izvestia*, June 15, 2005.

[4] Dmitry Butrin, "China Joins the Battle for Sakhalin with ExxonMobil's Help," *Kommersant*, November 3, 2004, http://www.kommersant.com/page.asp?id=521873, accessed September 14, 2005.

[5] "Gazprom Buys Abramovich's Sibneft for $13.1," *MosNews*, September 28, 2005, http://www.mosnews.com/money/2005/09/28/gazprombuyssibneft.shtml, accessed October 17, 2005; "Sibneft Oil Company," Mosnews.com, September 23, 2005, http://www.mosnews.com/mn-files/sibneft.shtml, accessed October 19, 2005.

[6] "Global or National?" *The Economist*, April 28, 2005, www.economist.com, accessed August 29, 2005.

[7] Andrey Bagrov and Irina Rybalchanko, "Dig In: Russian Companies Alone Admitted to the Earth's Entrails," *Kommersant*, February 11, 2005, http://kommersant.com/page.asp?id=546458, accessed September 13, 2005.

[8] Ibid.

[9] Ronald Smith and Veronika Lyssogorskaya, "Gazprom: Buy the Local/Sell the ADR," *Ing Wholesale Banking, Equity…, Russia,* September 21, 2005, www.investext.com, accessed October 19, 2005.

[10] "Global or National?" *The Economist.*

[11] Malcolm Brinded, *International Conference on Energy Security, 13-14 March 2006*, Centre for Energy Policy, Ministry of the Industry and Energy of the Russian Federation, p. 36, http://www.minprom.gov.ru /G8/eng/kit/G8_IntrConf_ENG_FIN_View.pdf, accessed January 8, 2007.

[12] "The Case of Yamal: What Can Shell Get from Gazprom in Exchange for Sakhalin?" *Kommersant*, October 13, 2004, http://kommersant.com/page.asp?id=514117, accessed October 19, 2005.

[13] Bente Bjorndal, "Russia's Klebanov Says Norsk Hydro, Statoil likely Partners in Shtokman Field," *AFX News*, August 22, 2005, http://uk.biz.yahoo.com/050822/323/fq61h.html, accessed September 14, 2005.

[14] "Gazprom says Total still in the running for Shtokman; sees Sakhalin-2 participation," *Forbes*, October 17, 2005, http://www.forbes.com/business/feeds/afx/2005/10/17/afx2279383.html, accessed October 17, 2005.

[15] Virginia Citrano, "Gazprom CEO Miller Hails LNG Deal with Shell," *Forbes*, July 7, 2005, http://www.forbes.com/facesinthenews/2005/07/07/0707autofacescan05.html, accessed August 29, 2005.

[16] "Gazprom and Shell Sign Memorandum of Understanding to Swap Shares in Zapolyarnoye-Neokomian and Sakhalin-2 projects," *Media Center*, July 7, 2005, http://www.shell.com, accessed September 13, 2005.

[17] Ibid.

[18] Benoit Faucon, "Shell Ties Woes of Russia to Lack of Data—Sakhalin II Exemplifies Challenges and the Costs Facing Major Oil Firms," *The Wall Street Journal*, September 12, 2005.

[19] "Shell priglashaet Gazprom na Sakhalin," www.lenta.ru, October 11, 2004, accessed August 23, 2005; "Gazprom i Shell obmenialis aktivami: Gazprom poluchil blokpaket v proekte Sakhalin 2," *Novosti*, July 8, 2005, http://www.e-xecutive.ru/print/news/piece_13709, accessed August 23, 2005.

[20] "Shifting Weight: Sakhalin-2 Cost Overruns Could Alter Gazprom-Shell Deal," *NEFTE Compass*, July 18, 2005, p. 1.

RAWI ABDELAL

MARINA N. VANDAMME

Journey to Sakhalin: Royal Dutch/Shell in Russia (C)

Obviously, political discussions are cheaper to conduct than engineering work.
— Oleg Mitvol, Deputy Head of the Federal Service for the Oversight of Natural Resources[1]

The cost overruns of Sakhalin II promised to make the lives of Sakhalin Energy executives significantly more difficult, as if the technical and political challenges of the project were not already extraordinary enough. The stakes were large for all parties involved. Sakhalin II was still Shell's most important investment. Alexei Miller, Gazprom's chief executive, continued to insist that his firm and the Russian government considered Sakhalin II "as one of its most serious projects."[2] And by 2006 Sakhalin Energy employed 17,000 people on the island. As the project developed, so, too, would Sakhalin.

Russian policymakers were disappointed that the project was going to cost so much more than the original estimate. Rather than a $10 billion project, Sakhalin II was to cost more than $20 billion. Because the Sakhalin II production sharing agreement (PSA) provided for 100% cost recovery for the Sakhalin Energy Investment Company (SEIC), the cost overruns meant that the time when the Russian government would reap large financial rewards from the project would be delayed. Rather then the roughly $2 billion per year the government was soon expecting, approximately $300 million would arrive until costs were recovered.[3] German Gref, Russia's economic development minister, suggested that the government would not support all proposals made by foreign companies for increased spending on Sakhalin's oil and gas projects.[4]

Gazprom executives also expressed displeasure that they had not been informed of the higher cost estimate before signing the spring 2005 deal to swap assets with Shell. The cost overruns seemed to have stalled negotiations. Gazprom offered a significantly smaller stake in the Zapolyarnoe-Neokomian field to Shell because, by Gazprom's estimation, the value of the Sakhalin asset had fallen.

Thus, by the summer of 2006, the development of Sakhalin II was proceeding apace, but in the background tensions with the Russian government and Gazprom continued to increase. The project, once privileged, was situated on ground that felt less and less firm.

Professor Rawi Abdelal and Research Associate Marina N. Vandamme prepared this case. This case was developed from published sources. HBS cases are developed solely as the basis for class discussion. Cases are not intended to serve as endorsements, sources of primary data, or illustrations of effective or ineffective management.

The Federal Service for the Oversight of Natural Resources

Meanwhile, concerns about the effects of Sakhalin II on the island's fragile ecosystem had spread to Russia's environmental watchdog, Rosprirodnadzor. Rosprirodnadzor claimed that Sakhalin Energy had consistently violated the terms of its permits for construction. Russia's environmental protection agency was taking legal action to revoke its July 15, 2003 order, No. 600, endorsing the conclusion of an expert commission that had compiled a technical and economic feasibility report on the integrated development of the Piltun-Astokhskoe and Lunskoe license area.[5]

Yuri Trutnev, Russia's natural resources minister, ordered an inspection of Sakhalin Energy's alleged violations of ecological legislation and project specifications by the Federal Service for the Oversight of Natural Resources. The Federal Service found what it considered to be numerous violations. Although the pipeline route was supposed to be no wider than 43 meters, other than for difficult terrain, the actual width was greater along portions of the 800-kilometer pipeline. Sakhalin Energy was also criticized for not having built anti-erosion facilities, disposing of excessive industrial wastewater from the Molikpaq offshore platform, illegal tree felling, damaging onshore water resources, illegal deepening of the sea bottom, dumping chemicals in the bay, and illegally routing a stretch of pipeline through a natural reserve. Ninety percent of the violations were related to the onshore pipeline.[6]

As a result of the inspection, Trutnev's ministry suspended 12 licenses for water use granted to Starstroi (a Russian-Italian joint venture building natural gas and oil export pipelines as a subcontractor of the Sakhalin Energy consortium) and annulled the examination results of the second stage of the project, which were a key permit for the positive project evaluation.[7] This meant that work in the licensed offshore areas had to be postponed at least until new examination results were announced. It gave the company two months to resolve the designated violations; otherwise, it would annul the licenses, which were mandatory for any construction affecting rivers and other water resources.[8]

Shell denied it had violated any Russian environmental laws. "Although there have been various environmental challenges on this project, these have been tackled and largely overcome," Shell insisted in a statement released in Moscow. "All concerns are being addressed expeditiously in cooperation with the relevant authorities and do not constitute any legal grounds for nullification."[9] Sakhalin Energy weighed in on the issue as well: "This would lead to significant delay of the project, extra costs and irreparable damage to the reputation of this venture and the Russian Federation as a whole."[10]

Russian authorities were not impressed, and the natural resources ministry estimated the ecological damage to be $50 billion. Oleg Mitvol claimed that Sakhalin Energy had done little to resolve the problems other than "resorting to political pressure from the company's friends inside the country, and no engineering solutions have been found."[11] Court proceedings on compensation for environmental damage inflicted by Sakhalin II were likely to start in March 2007. The proceedings were likely to be launched in various courts, in Russia, Sweden, Belgium, Britain, Italy, Japan, and possibly the United States. Russia would use international laws that envisaged triple compensation of damages plus payment of legal costs, the official added.[12]

Soon thereafter, the natural resources ministry also discovered numerous technical violations in the other two projects governed by PSAs, Sakhalin I (operated by ExxonMobil) and Kharyaga (operated by Total).[13] Although many Russians were critical of the PSAs, which were signed when energy prices were low and the country was desperate for foreign investment, economic development minister Gref insisted: "We should certainly honor the current agreement. I believe that the current investment climate in the country and the situation on the foreign market allow us to do without this regime and work on standard terms."[14]

Negotiations with Gazprom

Gazprom executives insisted that the firm would await the resolution of "all ecological accusations" before negotiating the final terms of its involvement in Sakhalin II.[15] Some observers saw the ecological concerns as a negotiating tactic, however, and not a very subtle one for the only wholly foreign-owned venture in the Russian energy industry.[16]

A spokesperson for the Russian energy giant said that Gazprom CEO Miller had a working meeting with Shell CEO Jeroen van der Veer on December 8, 2006, at which the Shell chief put forward proposals on Gazprom's participation in the project. The Anglo-Dutch Shell concern would turn over the controlling share in Sakhalin II to Gazprom. Under the proposed deal, Shell would cede up to 30% of its 55% holding. Mitsui and Mitsubishi could each sell 10% of their respective stakes of 25% and 20%, enabling Gazprom to secure a bare majority.[17] Mitsui and Mitsubishi began talks with Gazprom on the sale of smaller shares in the project.

Japan wanted guarantees that it would receive oil and gas from the Sakhalin II project on schedule, in view of Gazprom's slated involvement. Akira Amari told journalists, "In view of Gazprom's intention to gain a stake in the project, fears have arisen among Japanese business circles on the stability of supplies. It is therefore of the utmost importance that Japanese producers of electricity, and oil and gas companies, are given guarantees that the schedule would remain unchanged."[18]

On December 21, 2006, Gazprom, Royal Dutch Shell plc, Mitsui & Co., Ltd., and Mitsubishi Corporation signed a protocol to bring Gazprom into the Sakhalin Energy Investment Company Ltd. (SEIC) as a leading shareholder. Under the terms of the protocol, Gazprom would acquire a 50% stake plus one share in SEIC for a total cash purchase price of $7.45 billion. The current SEIC partners would each dilute their stakes by 50% to accommodate this transaction, with a proportionate share of the purchase price. Shell would retain a 27.5% stake, with Mitsui and Mitsubishi holding 12.5% and 10% stakes, respectively.[19]

Naturally, Gazprom was not joining the project for free. Yet the issue of Sakhalin Energy's appraisal by the Russian authorities worried analysts. Gazprom was expected to offer no more than $6 billion for its stake. SEIC's shareholders were reportedly surprised that the offer was so large.[20] The deal was expected to be finalized in February 2007.

Functions of the project's participants would remain unchanged. Sakhalin Energy would remain the operator; Royal Dutch/Shell would provide technical consultations and would continue taking part in the project management. Gazprom would be playing the leading role, of course. The Russian company would guarantee that the already signed contracts would be honored.

Exhibit 1   Royal Dutch/Shell Financial Summary, 2001–2005 (US$ million)

	2005	2004	2003	2002	2001
CONSOLIDATED STATEMENT OF INCOME					
Revenue[a]					
Exploration and Production	**23,970**	18,400	12,224	11,640	11,808
Gas and Power	**13,766**	9,625	7,377	4,254	5,947
Oil Products	**237,210**	210,424	159,075	132,681	90,862
Chemicals	**31,018**	26,877	18,843	14,125	13,260
Other	**767**	1,060	843	753	576
Gross Revenue[b]	**379,008**	338,756	263,889	218,287	163,361
Sales tax, excise duties and similar levies	**72,277**	72,370	65,527	54,834	40,908
Net Revenue	**306,731**	266,386	198,362	163,453	122,453
Cost of Sales	**252,622**	223,259	165,147	135,658	96,091
Gross Profit	**54,109**	43,127	33,215	27,795	26,362
SGA, exploration, R&D, other	**9,439**	11,044	11,909	9,947	7,461
Operating Profit	**44,670**	32,083	21,306	17,848	18,901
Interest income/expense, forex gain/loss	**103**	424	-441	534	-42
Income before taxation	**44,567**	31,659	21,747	17,314	18,943
Taxation	**19,256**	13,119	9,425	-441	8,622
Net income	**25,311**	18,540	12,322	9,671	10,321
CONSOLIDATED BALANCE SHEET					
Total assets	**219,516**	187,446	169,766	153,320	112,050
Net current assets/(liabilities)	**12,928**	7,197	-5,059	-7,627	3,930
Total debt	**121,592**	96,063	64,033	62,462	33,738
Parent companies' interests in group net assets	**97,924**	91,383	78,251	66,195	62,822
Royal Dutch (60% interest)	**58,754**	54,830	46,951	39,717	37,693
Shell Transport (40% interest)	**39,170**	36,553	31,300	26,478	25,129
Capital employed	**110,840**	105,975	101,335	88,845	72,108
CONSOLIDATED STATEMENT OF CASH FLOWS					
Cash flow from operation	**30,113**	26,537	21,983	15,768	16,936
Capital expenditure (including capitalized leases)	**-15,904**	-13,566	-12,252	-12,102	-9,598
Cash flow used in investing activities	**-8,761**	-5,964	-8,253	-20,632	-9,080
Cash flow used in financing activities	**18,573**	13,592	-12,864	10	-11,345
Dividends paid to parents and minority interests	**-10,849**	-7,655	-6,832	-5,750	-5,409
Increase (decrease) in cash and equivalents	**2,529**	7,094	408	-5,545	-4,552

Source: Casewriter compilation from Royal Dutch/Shell Financial and Operational Information 2001–2005, available at www.shell.com, accessed October 28, 2006.

Note: The 2005 and 2004 financial statements (FS) have been prepared in accordance with applicable laws in England and Wales and with International Financial Reporting Standards (IFRS) as adopted by the EU. There are no material differences with IFRS as issued by the International Accounting Standards Board. The 2003, 2002, and 2001 FS have been prepared in accordance with U.S. generally accepted accounting principles (U.S. GAAP), applied by the group prior to its transition date to IFRS.

[a] Revenue is stated after deducting sales tax, excise duties, and similar levies.

[b] Gross revenue is stated before deducting sales tax, excise duties, and similar levies.

Exhibit 2   Russian Federation, Summary Economic Indicators, 2000–2006

	2000	2001	2002	2003	2004	2005	2006[a]
GDP (current $ billion)	259.72	306.62	345.07	431.49	588.83	763.60	974.64
Annual GDP growth	10.00	5.10	4.70	7.25	7.16	6.41	6.50
Population (mn)	146.30	145.65	144.96	144.17	143.47	142.80	142.35
GDP per capita, PPP (current $)	7,144.10	7,722.60	8,256.00	9,075.00	9,890.80	10,894.50	11,980.00
Annual CPI (%)	20.80	21.47	15.79	13.65	10.91	12.70	9.80
Current-account balance	46,840.00	33,795.00	29,116.00	35,410.00	59,921.00	83,558.00	105,349.00
Net FDI (BoP, current $)	-465	217	-72	-1,767	5,098	1,790	8,620
Inward direct investment	2,713.00	2,749.00	3,461.00	7,959.00	15,445.00	14,183.00	21,500.00
Outward direct investment	-3,178.00	-2,532.00	-3,533.00	-9,726.00	-10,347.00	-12,393.00	-12,880.00
Annual change in gross fixed investment (%)	18.10	10.20	2.80	12.80	11.29	10.50	10.70
Annual change in industrial production (%)	11.84	5.05	3.80	7.00	7.30	4.00	4.80
Budget balance/GDP	2.37	3.08	1.66	2.37	4.87	7.52	6.70
Budget revenue/GDP	15.43	17.87	20.52	19.47	20.37	23.79	22.80
Budget expenditure/GDP	13.06	14.80	18.86	17.09	15.51	16.28	16.10
Exchange rate (ruble/$)	28.13	29.17	31.35	30.69	28.81	28.28	27.50
Russian 12.75% government bond of June 24, 2028	16.7	11.5	9.3	7.4	6.5	5.5	5.8

Source: Casewriter compilation of data available from Economist Intelligence Unit, www.eiu.com; World Development Indicators, World Bank, www.worldbank.org; Global Financial Data, www.globalfindata.com, accessed November 8, 2006.

Note: Figures are in US$ million unless otherwise stated.

[a]2006 year—Forecasting.

Exhibit 3   Sakhalin Fact Sheet, September 2005

Name	Sakhalin I	Sakhalin II	Sakhalin III	Sakhalin IV	Sakhalin V	Sakhalin VI
Primary Field/ Block Names	Odoptu [Northern and Southern] (onshore), Chayvo (onshore and offshore), Arkutun-Dagi	Sakhalin Energy Investment Company: Piltun-Astokskoye, Lunskoye	Kirinskii, Vostochno-Odoptu, Aiyashkii	Pogranichny Block, Okruzhnoye fld	Kaigansko-Vasyukansk (active drilling)	Pogranichny
Oil/Gas Reserve Estimate	2.3 billion bbl, 17.1 Tcf	1.0-1.2 billion bbl of oil, 17.6 Tcf of gas	4-5 billion bbl of oil, 27-38 Tcf of natural gas	880 million bbl of oil, 19 Tcf of gas	4.4-5.7 billion bbl of oil, 15.2-17.7 Tcf of gas	600 million bbl of oil
Net Total Investment	$2.6 billion ($12 billion expected)	Phase 1: $4.5 billion, Phase 2: $9-10 billion over next 4-5 yrs.	$13.5 billion expected (ExxonMobil- $80m in geological studies)	$2.6 billion expected	$3-5 billion expected	n/a
Expected & Current Production Level	Chayvo: 250,000 bbl/d (2005); Commercial gas prod'n expected in 2008	Current: 80,000 bbl/d for 6 months, Phase II: 180,000 bbl/d, year-round oil production expected in Dec. 2007, LNG prod'n expected in Summer 2008	n/a	n/a	n/a	n/a
Primary Project Developers	Exxon Neftegaz (30%), in conjunction with consortium members SODECO (30%), ONGC Videsh (20%), Sakhalinmorneftegaz (11.5%), and RN Astra (8.5%)	Sakhalin Energy Investment Company: Shell (55%), Mitsui (25%), Mitsubishi (20%)	Tender awarded to ExxonMobil and Texaco in 1992 annuled in Feb 2004, Developers undetermined.	BP (49%), Rosneft (51%)	BP (49%), Rosneft (51%)	Petrosakh, Alfa Eco
Current Status/Notes	Gas pipeline currently under construction	Oil production began in 1999; Processing terminal under construction which would have cpy of 66,000 bbl/d of oil, 1.8 bcf/d of gas	Lukoil possibly in cooperation with Gazprom would probably take part in new tenders for Kirinskii and Vostochno blocks.	Geological studies of reserves still being carried out	1st exploration well drilling began in July 2004	3 blocks in Sakhalin VI have not been awarded

Source: Project Homepages, Interfax, *Russian Energy Monthly* (www.easternblocenergy.com), *FSU Oil and Gas Monitor, Pipeline & Gas Journal*.

Exhibit 4   World Oil Prices in Three Cases, 1980–2030

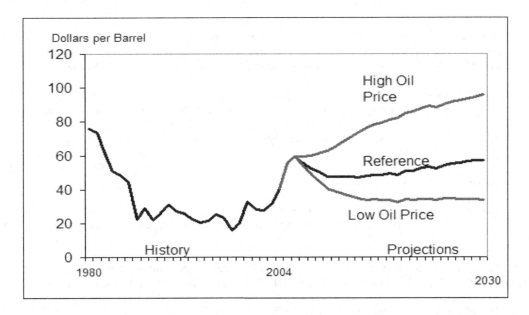

Source: **History:** Energy Information Administration (EIA), *Annual Energy Review 2004*, DOE/EIA-0384 (2004) (Washington, D.C., August 2005), website, www.eia.doe.gov/emeu/aer/. **Projections:** EIA, *Annual Energy Outlook 2006*, DOE/EIA-0383 (2006) (Washington, D.C., February 2006).

Exhibit 5   Changing Equity Shares in SEIC, 2006

Date	Investor	Percentage Ownership
Before December 21, 2006	Shell	55%
	Mitsui	25%
	Mitsubishi	20%
New Agreed Distribution of Shares	Gazprom	50% plus one share
	Shell	27.5%
	Mitsui	12.5%
	Mitsubishi	10%

Source: Casewriter compilation from Royal Dutch/Shell official website, available at www.shell.com, accessed January 16, 2007.

Endnotes

[1] Oleg Mitvol, deputy head of the Federal Service for the Oversight of Natural Resources, Russia, "Inspections do not mean an end to Sakhalin II PSA—Minister," *Russian News and Information Agency Novosty,* September 27, 2006, http://en.rian.ru/business/20060927/54304922.html, accessed October 15, 2006.

[2] "Sakhalin II is one of Russia's top priority projects—Kremlin aide," *Russian News and Information Agency Novosty,* September 5, 2006, http://en.rian.ru/russia/20060905/53546739.html, accessed October 15, 2006.

[3] See "Russia Halts Pipeline, Citing River Damage," *The New York Times,* September 19, 2006.

[4] "Moscow aims green gun at Sakhalin II," *Petroleum Economist,* October 2006, http://www.petroleum-economist.com, accessed December 1, 2006.

[5] "Sakhalin II Phase 2 Environmental Approval Revoked!" *The Sakhalin Times,* September 22, 2006, http://www.thesakhalintimes.com/modules.php?name=News&file=article&sid=2819, accessed October 16, 2006.

[6] "Russian authorities relax pressure on Shell over Sakhalin II," *Russian News and Information Agency Novosty,* October 17, 2006, http://en.rian.ru/russia/20061017/54891192.html, accessed October 25, 2006.

[7] Newsletter *Oil and Gas Journal,* November 6, 2006.

[8] Eric Watkins, senior correspondent, "Sakhalin-2 water-use licenses suspended," *Oil and Gas Journal,* December 7, 2006, http://www.ogj.com/articles/article_display.cfm?article_id=279203&Section=ONART&C= ExplD, accessed December 14, 2006.

[9] "Russia Halts Pipeline, Citing River Damage," *The New York Times,* September 19, 2006.

[10] Official website of Sakhalin Energy Online available at http://www.sakhalinenergy.com/en.

[11] "Sakhalin II pipeline must be closed—ecology official," *Russian News and Information Agency Novosty,* September 28, 2006, http://en.rian.ru/russia/20060928/54344280.html, accessed October 25, 2006.

[12] "Court Proceedings on Sakhalin II to Start in March," *Information and Consulting Agency SeaNews,* December 12, 2006, http://www.seanews.ru/default.asp?l=e&a=l&v=d&g=1&i=29536&n=2, accessed December 15, 2006.

[13] "Kremlin revokes oil project approval," *The New York Times,* September 18, 2006. Also see "Sakhalin I faces delay until '07," *Moscow Times,* Thursday, October 12, 2006, issue 3517, p. 5; and "Sakhalin I oil output reaches 345,000 tons," *RusEnergy,* February 27, 2006, available at http://rusenergy.blogspot.com/2006_02_01_rusenergy_archive.html, accessed October 30, 2006.

[14] "Russia says to honor PSAs, as Sakhalin energy project woes mount," *Russian News and Information Agency Novosty,* September 19, 2006, http://en.rian.ru/russia/20060919/54047254.html, accessed October 25, 2006.

[15] "Gazprom: Ready to join Sakhalin II when disputes settled," November 10, 2006, *The Sakhalin Times,* http://www.thesakhalintimes.com/modules.php?name=News&pagenum=7, accessed November 16, 2006.

[16] "Russia Halts Pipeline, Citing River Damage," *The New York Times,* September 19, 2006.

[17] "Shell CEO in Moscow in search of Gazprom deal," *The Washington Post,* December 15, 2006, http://www.washingtonpost.com/wp-dyn/content/article/2006/12/15/AR2006121500314.html, accessed December 16, 2006.

[18] "Japan seeks guarantees of oil and gas supplies from Sakhalin II," *Russian News and Information Agency Novosty*, December 12, 2006, http://en.rian.ru/russia/20061212/56788467.html, accessed December 15, 2006.

[19] "Gazprom, Shell, Mitsui, Mitsubishi sign Sakhalin II protocol," Royal Dutch/Shell plc, December 21, 2006, http://www.shell.com/home/Framework?siteId=investor-en&FC2=/investor-en/html/iwgen/news_and_library/=/investor-en/html/iwgen/news_and_library/press_releases/2006/sakhalin_protocol_21122006.html, accessed January 15, 2007.

[20] "Debates around Sakhalin II over," *Russian News and Information Agency Novosty*, December 26, 2006, http://en.rian.ru/analysis/20061226/57869771.html, accessed January 15, 2007.

GUNNAR TRUMBULL

LOUISA GAY

Wal-Mart in Europe

"Never resist change… We have to be able to place a store or club side-by-side with the competition and beat them every time."

—David Glass, Director and Chairman of the Board, Wal-Mart[1]

"In Germany, we know how retail is spelled."

—Holger Wenzel, Director, German Retail Federation

Introduction

"What are the 10 worst things we can do to fail?"[2] This was how Lee Scott, CEO of Wal-Mart, summarized Wal-Mart's approach to working in Germany. Wal-Mart had entered the German retail market in 1997, with the acquisition of the failing German retail chain Wertkauf, and had quickly encountered problems. Wal-Mart's EveryDay Low Price (EDLP) guarantee, inventory control, and efficient distribution strategy, so strong in the United States, had each been a source of headaches. Wal-Mart went through protracted struggles with labor unions, with suppliers, and with local zoning boards. It also weathered a major pricing scandal, had been fined for failing to return used bottles to producers, and, in a case that was on appeal at Germany's constitutional court, faced a 330,000 euro fine for failing to release financial data for Wal-Mart Germany.

This was not the first time that Wal-Mart International had run into problems with overseas expansion. It had quickly pulled out of Indonesia after a disappointing 'test project' in the early 1990s. Yet in most cases, time had worked in its favor. In Mexico, where it was now recognized as the country's leading retailer, Wal-Mart had needed five years to post profits. In the United Kingdom, which Wal-Mart had entered by acquiring ASDA in 1999, it was already enjoying double-digit sales growth. Could this success be duplicated in Germany?

Wal-Mart: Brief Background

Founded by Sam Walton in 1962 in Bentonville, Arkansas, Wal-Mart stores offered customers a broad range of goods, including lawn and garden, jewelry, shoes, electronics, family apparel, and toys. In its first year, Wal-Mart Stores garnered $700,000 in sales, which increased to $5.4 million in sales volume by 1974.[3] Throughout the 1970s and 1980s, while other retailers struggled with inflation and recessions, Wal-Mart enjoyed continuous growth.[4] In fiscal 1980, Wal-Mart became the youngest U.S. retail company, and the only regional retailer, to exceed $1 billion in net sales.[5]

During the 1980s, Wal-Mart transformed itself into a national discount retailer, saturating regional markets and forcing the closure of other domestic retailers.[6] It pursued an aggressive diversification strategy, introducing membership-only formats (Sam's Clubs), smaller, more convenient pharmacy/grocery stores (Neighborhood Markets) and Supercenters (food/general merchandise) in addition to its original Wal-Mart Stores. Some ventures in the 1980s failed, but overall Wal-Mart experienced dramatic growth in net sales volume and in-store surface area.

In 1991, with net sales of $43.9 billion, Wal-Mart became the world's largest retailer, and maintained this status through 2003. Between 1977 and 1992, Wal-Mart Stores experienced a 35% compound annual growth of both revenue and net profit. Between 1992 and 2003, revenue and net profit grew at 9% annually.[7] In 2002, Wal-Mart's revenue equaled 2.3% of U.S. gross domestic product.[8] Sales of Wal-Mart International alone grew by more than 16.6% in FYE 2004[9], totaling $47.5 billion with an operating profit of $2.3 billion (**See Exhibits 2-5**).[10] Total Wal-Mart sales on 'Black Friday' (the day after Thanksgiving) in 2002 equaled $1.42 billion, larger than the GDP of 36 countries. Wal-Mart was the largest employer in the United States, with more employees in uniform than the U.S. army.[11] In FYE 2003, it had posted net sales of $244.5 billion and had approximately 4,750 stores worldwide (**See Exhibit 6**).

Wal-Mart's Strategy

In the U.S. retail sector, Wal-Mart differentiated itself through its Everyday Low Prices (EDLP), which it achieved through aggressive bargaining with suppliers, its efficient distribution system, and inventory control, as well as its unique culture. According to a 2002 study by UBS Warburg, U.S. Wal-Mart Superstore prices were, on average, 14% lower than its rivals. Throughout its evolution, Wal-Mart adhered strictly to Sam Walton's three key principles: to respect the individual, to provide superior customer service, and to strive for excellence. After seeing employees of a South Korean tennis ball factory complete morning exercises and a company cheer, Walton incorporated his own Wal-Mart cheer for employee solidarity. Walton hoped the cheer would encourage productivity and unity: "It's sort of a 'whistle while you work' philosophy, and we not only have a heck of a good time with it, we work better because of it (**See Exhibit 1**).[12] Other Walton business practices included the Sundown Rule, which dictated that all business concerns be addressed on the day on which they were presented. The Ten Foot Rule encouraged staff to approach and offer assistance to customers within that radius. Frugality in buildings, offices, and warehouses kept costs low. Only 2% of sales went to support the general offices in Bentonville, Arkansas.[13]

Wal-Mart saved an average of 3% per item in purchasing costs due to its sophisticated logistics system. Its Retail Link satellite/computer system, the result of a four billion dollar investment, controlled the entire inventory of all domestic U.S. Wal-Mart stores.[14] Using Retail Link, Wal-Mart managers and suppliers could track products through a 65-week rolling inventory. Vendors could access point-of-purchase information. Wal-Mart store managers were able to use Retail Link to assess margins, sales, and profits in their own store, and to compare those to other stores and departments.

Wal-Mart's distribution system was regarded as among the most efficient in the world.[15] Each store was located within a day's drive of a distribution center, which supplied an average of 85% of inventory (compared to 50%-60% for competitors).[16] By January 2003, Wal-Mart Stores, Inc. had asked its suppliers to implement Radio Frequency Identification (RFID) technology by 2006. RFID uses radio frequency chips and small antennae attached to cases of products (and, ultimately, to individual products) to transmit a signal to RFID readers in order to track shipments. With RFID, Wal-Mart would be able directly to track its inventory as it moved through distribution centers to stores, creating new efficiencies.

What was good for Wal-Mart appeared to be good for the United States. The U.S. economy had experienced a significant boost in productivity in the late 1990s. Whereas US labor productivity grew approximately 1% per year from 1987 to 1995, it grew at 2.3% from 1995 to 1999 (**See Exhibits 13-14**). Coupled with increased employment, this allowed real output per capita to grow at nearly 4% a year.[17] While managerial and technological innovations were thought to be the most important factors in this labor productivity growth,[18] the McKinsey Global Institute found that 99% of the increase in productivity growth could be attributed to just six sectors, with retail among the most important. Indeed the study found that Wal-Mart, through its affect on the American retail market, was responsible for fully one quarter of the late-1990s productivity boom. With its focus on large discount stores and low prices, unmatched efficiency, and superior information technology, Wal-Mart not only increased U.S. productivity, but also forced other retailers to follow suit. "By making goods cheap and available, Wal-Mart has raised the standard of living of average Americans."[19]

Wal-Mart's success also drew public attention to its business practices. Criticism focused on the low salaries of its employees, who earned an estimated average salary of $18,000 per year.[20] It also faced a series of highly publicized legal suits concerning its hiring practices, including charges of failing to pay overtime, underpaying hourly workers, sexual discrimination (women make up 70% of store workers but 10% of management), and non-compliance with the Americans with Disabilities Act. Recent class-action lawsuits had focused on the company's policy of 'locking in' overnight workers, and on allegations of conspiring with cleaning contractors to underpay immigrant workers.[21] Wal-Mart was also increasingly cited in justifying other retailers' employment practices. In the fall of 2003, when the unionized California employees of the Albertsons, Kroger, and Safeway supermarket chains went on strike for better health benefits, their employers argued that impending competition from non-union Wal-Mart forced them to keep such benefits low.[22]

Not every community was interested in having a Wal-Mart open nearby. Local zoning struggles often became litigious. In Ithaca, NY, the city council unanimously voted to block Wal-Mart's entry in the early 1990s. In response, Wal-Mart employed a development company from South Carolina to secure a zoning variance to build an unidentified retail store. The application ultimately failed. Though Wal-Mart had five stores within a 35-mile radius of Ithaca, they have persisted in their goal to place a store within the city. In 2002, they gained approval to construct a store that will open in late 2004. In another case, in Warrenton, Virginia, Wal-Mart announced plans to construct a 120,000ft² Supercenter. Town law required special permission for retail stores of 50,000 ft² or more. Fauquier County, the area surrounding Warrenton, allowed construction of stores of up to 75,000 ft² without special permits. Wal-Mart opened a Supercenter on a piece of land that overlapped the town of Warrenton and the adjacent Fauquier County, placing less than 50,000 ft² in Warrenton and 75,000 ft² in Fauquier County.

Globalization of Retail

U.S. retail chains had attempted global expansion with varying degrees of success since the early 1900s. Woolworth's extended its operations into Canada in 1897, was present in the United Kingdom by the end of 1909, and in Germany by 1926.[23] By the 1950s, Woolworth's was a household name worldwide.[24] Sears Roebuck and Company began its international expansion in 1942, when it entered Cuba; it moved into Mexico in 1947.[25]

European retailers led a second wave of international retail expansion. Germany's Metro Group began acquiring other European retailers beginning in the 1960s. By 2003, Metro made 47% of sales through affiliates in 27 foreign countries, including China, India, Japan, Morocco, Russia, Turkey, Ukraine, and Vietnam.[26] Dutch food retailer Royal Ahold became an early mover in the globalization of food retailing with its purchase of the US BI-LO supermarket chain in 1977. It proceeded to acquire Giant Food Stores (1981), Finast (1988), Tops Markets (1991), Stop & Shop (1996), Giant Food Inc. (1998), and the on-line supermarket Peapod (2001).[27] In 2003, US operations accounted for nearly 75% of Ahold sales (**See Exhibit 10**).[28]

Wal-Mart was a relative latecomer to international retailing. Wal-Mart's International Division formed in 1993, after opening two stores through a joint venture in Mexico in 1991. The move overseas was driven in part by flagging domestic growth. In late 1996, Wal-Mart's growth started to mirror that of the U.S. retail sector, with annual sales growth of 11%. Same-store sales were growing at 4.6%. Its stock price had lingered in the low 20s since 1993.[29] Wal-Mart believed rapid international expansion was crucial; that the company's culture and stock price rested on an expectation of double-digit sales and profit gains each year. In 2003, analysts believed that the company's expanding chain of U.S. Supercenters would carry the profit burden for a maximum of eight more years.[30] In 2003, Wal-Mart International employed over 330,000 associates in nine countries, and accounted for 18% of total sales (**See Exhibit 2**).[31]

By 1997, Wal-Mart possessed 41 Wal-Mart and Sam's Club stores within Mexico and also had 89 retail outlets (under various names) within its control.[32] During the next few years, Wal-Mart expanded into Puerto Rico (1992), and Canada (1994). The Canadian venture experienced heavy losses for three years, but as of 2003 Wal-Mart was the number one retailer both in Canada and in Mexico. It developed its presence in Argentina (1995), Brazil (1996), China (1996), Germany (1997), Korea (1998), the United Kingdom (1999), and Japan (2002). The company also attempted a 'test' in Indonesia in the early 1990s, but cancelled its plans by the mid-1990s. In FYE 2003, Wal-Mart's International Division achieved sales of almost $41 billion with an operating profit of $2 billion. By August 2003, Wal-Mart International sales increased, above expectations, to 18.8% due to strong performances in Mexico, Brazil, and the United Kingdom. It had 1,288 international stores.[33]

Wal-Mart's competitors were also looking abroad. K-mart entered the European market, in 1992, purchasing 13 stores in the Czech Republic and Slovakia. It sold them to U.K. retailer Tesco in 1996.[34] In 1994, Kmart also embarked upon joint ventures in Mexico and in Singapore. These were dissolved in 1996 and 1997 respectively.[35] Another Wal-Mart competitor, Costco, had by 2003 opened 422 warehouses worldwide, including in 36 U.S. states, nine Canadian provinces, Puerto Rico, the United Kingdom, Taiwan, Korea, Japan, and Mexico. Globally, Costco had 42 million cardholders.[36] Costco Wholesale FYE 2003 sales equaled $41.69 billion with warehouse club operations in eight countries.[37] Costco has sought to maintain operating control and majority ownership of its international stores by using joint ventures with a local partner that understood the local retail climate.[38] Planned international expansion for 2003 included one store in Japan, two in Mexico, and one in Canada. Like Wal-Mart, Costco in 2003 achieved 16% to 18% of sales from its international operations.[39]

Wal-Mart into Europe

Germany

With the largest economy in Europe, Germany accounted for approximately 15% of the continent's $2 trillion annual retail market in 2001.[40] In 1997, Wal-Mart entered the German retail market, acquiring the Wertkauf chain (24 stores) from the Mann Family and the unprofitable Interspar chain (74 stores) in 1998 for a combined $1.6 billion. At the time, both Wertkauf and Interspar equaled less than 3% of the market.[41] The Interspar stores were in poor repair and in poor locations. The leading German retailer was Metro Group, followed by the Rewe Group (**See Exhibit 7**). Germany's top ten retailers generated 30% of total retail sales in 2001.

Wal-Mart's strategy upon entering Germany included the refurbishment of stores to improve their appearance and the maintenance of price leadership through cost leadership, as they had done in the U.S. market. They would achieve these goals through an overhaul of the supply chain systems, implementation of new scanning systems, centralized distribution, and high quality customer service to act as a 'market spoiler'.[42] In doing this, Wal-Mart created the fiercest price war in Germany's recent history.

Retail sector analysts, such as Keith Wills with Goldman Sachs in Frankfurt, praised Wal-Mart's decision to enter Germany, trusting the company's efficiency, low prices, and inventory control system to propel the "underdeveloped, old-fashioned"[43] German market into the future. However, some analysts and prominent figures in the retail industry doubted the U.S. retailer's ability to succeed in Germany: Tengelmann head Erivan Haub stated that Wal-Mart was in for its "blaues Wunder"—the shock of its life.[44] Frankfurt-based A.C. Nielsen analyst Thomas Roeb stated that the German retail market was unique: he explained it through the "Frank Sinatra principle: If you can make it there, you can make it anywhere. . . . The German retail landscape is virtually littered with the carcasses of foreign retailers trying to conquer the country. There is no example of a foreign retailer ever having managed to penetrate the German market to any reasonable extent. And it's not for lack of trying."[45]

Herbert Sturm, senior vice president of the retail and consumer goods section at DG Bank, warned that Wal-Mart's entrance into Germany was a "mistake," as he believed that it would take 20 years before Wal-Mart could dominate the German retail market. Moreover, Sturm stated that market dominance could only be achieved through two options, buying existing stores from 'companies that don't want to sell' or building new hypermarkets 'in the most land-use-restrictive country in Europe.'[46] Further, Wal-Mart's competitors around the world have found fault with Wal-Mart's international strategy. A marketing director for Samsung Tesco Co. in South Korea noted: "I get the impression that Wal-Mart is insisting on American-style layouts and business approach. It's good to introduce global standards, but you also need to adapt to local practice."[47]

Britain

In 1999, Wal-Mart acquired the U.K ASDA retail chain, at a cost of $10.8 billion (**See Exhibit 8**). Considered the leader of the UK superstore segment, ASDA was already thriving in the UK, with an 8.4% market share at the time of acquisition.[48] Prior to the purchase, ASDA management had already incorporated hallmark Wal-Mart strategies, including price rollback campaigns, greeters at the entrances of stores, and even a company cheer. By FYE 2000, under new Wal-Mart management, ASDA accounted for 35-40% of Wal-Mart's International sales.[49]

By the end of 2001, Wal-Mart had expanded the ASDA chain to include 3 supercenters and 247 stores. Overall, the takeover appeared to be a success: ". . . to Wal-Mart's eternal credit . . . they did not send in the troops from Bentonville and change the way everything was done," comments a former ASDA executive.[50] ASDA has since introduced Wal-Mart's IT systems, investment resources and buying power, and made inroads into the non-food business. Wal-Mart also kept the ASDA name on its stores and helped the chain to focus on everyday low prices, to which British consumers responded well. Prior to the deal, ASDA presented its goods for 7% (on average) less than its competitors; since Wal-Mart's acquisition, its price margin over competitors increased to 13%, helping to advance ASDA's total market share from 8.4% to 10.5%.[51]

Since the acquisition by Wal-Mart, ASDA had grown at approximately 10% per annum, nearly twice its pre-acquisition level.[52] Wal-Mart introduced the low-cost George apparel line developed by ASDA to Wal-Mart stores in the U.S., Canada, and Germany. Wal-Mart also began experimenting in Britain with a new format of stand-alone high street clothing shops called George.

German Rules

Unlike its British experience, Wal-Mart faced unexpected obstacles when it entered the German retail market. Germany's regulatory environment included limited store hours, price regulations, and stringent zoning requirements. Unions were also more influential than their U.S. counterparts, and Wal-Mart, typically a non-union employer, had rarely had to negotiate with an organized work force.

Zoning

When Wal-Mart entered the market in 1997, Germany had approximately 2,000 large-surface-area "green field" retail sites, including hypermarkets, furniture stores, and home goods suppliers. Nearly all of these, however, had been built before 1977. Indeed, by the close of 2001, after four years in Germany, Wal-Mart had only managed to open two new stores, and enlargement of existing stores met with government red tape.[53] Despite earlier plans to build 50 new stores by the end of FYE 2003, John Menzer, the head of Wal-Mart International, announced to the press in 2003 that Wal-Mart had no plans for further German expansion.

In 1977, Germany had enacted strict planning and zoning regulations (the *Building Use Code*) designed to protect traditional retailers.[54] The planning legislation prohibited the construction of stores with more than 800m² (8,610 ft²) sales area in locations not designated for retailing.[55] This resulted in large-store development being restricted to town/city centers. As one zoning official explained, "The objective is to locate retail close to the consumers and to the working areas of city centers."[56] Even within cities, where retail restrictions were less onerous, the approval process for a new store could require from 1 to 4 years (**See Exhibits 11a-11d**).

While opening a new large-surface-area store outside of an urban center was technically possible, it required clearing several difficult hurdles. First, a neighboring city or town was required to create a "building use plan" for the area being considered for development. The plan had to present a comprehensive development "concept" that would take into account environmental and conservation concerns, as well as potential private legal conflicts. For example, retailers in the new site could not sell products that would compete directly with stores located in nearby towns. Any failure to demonstrate that the project embodied this kind of "balanced approach to development" could be grounds for private legal challenges.

Once a new plan passed these steps and was approved by the town or city council, it then came under review by regional planning boards at the state and national level.[57] Such regional plans rested on a system of retail categories for cities and towns that specified target levels of retailing based on population. The retail categories provided guidelines—without setting specific limits—for the numbers of new stores that could be approved. As one observer noted of large-surface-area retail sites outside of cities: "it is basically not allowed." Almost no new extra-urban hypermarkets were opened in Germany since 1977.[58]

The retail experience of Germany's five eastern states following reunification served as a reminder of what might happen in the absence of zoning policy. With the fall of the Berlin Wall in 1991, West German retailers flocked to the East to meet pent-up demand for western products. As property rights within Eastern cities were still disputed, and because new building codes imported from the West were not yet being enforced, retail development occurred primarily in the form of new suburban shopping centers. Downtown areas were left underdeveloped. One retail expert noted: "Cities in the East were hurt by this early development strategy. They are trying to change now, but it is already too late."[59]

The scorn of German planners was not reserved for the former East Germany. They also looked to foreign retail experience as an example of what they hoped to avoid. "What Germany fears is the experience of cities like Bordeaux, which has lost retail business to green field sites outside of town. All that is left is old buildings and monuments in the city center."[60] Worst was the situation in the United States. As the head of Germany's retail association explained: "We don't want cities that look like the United States."[61] Another observer noted: "Germany has a different urban culture than in the United States. Cities are arranged in concentric circles, not on the grid format of the Roman city. The concentric circles have created a culture of 'urbanity'. We value that."

Price Setting

Wal-Mart's pricing policies regularly placed it in conflict with Germany's Federal Cartel Office. In September 2000, a state court found that Wal-Mart's price guarantee—which offered to refund the price difference between the Wal-Mart price and any competitor advertising a lower price—violated Germany's Rebate Law. The Law prohibited any retailer from selling a product more than 5 percent below its posted price.[62] Wal-Mart appealed to the *Bundesgerichthof*, which upheld the lower court decision. They found that the policy would only be legal if Wal-Mart lowered the cost of the product for everyone at the time of the first claim.[63] Under pressure from the EU, the Rebate Law was repealed in 2001.

A new amendment to Germany's Cartel Law, voted in 1998, gave Wal-Mart additional pricing concerns. The amendment stated: "Selling below cost is forbidden except with good justification." The practice of selling below cost had been disputed in Germany for 30 years, but was only restricted where such practice was intended to put other companies out of business. The new law appeared to be more general in scope, although it remained unclear how it would be interpreted. As one ministry official noted: "It was the signal that mattered, the signal that we wouldn't accept just anything."

In June of 2000, a pricing scandal broke out, in which Wal-Mart and competitors Lidl, Aldi, Plus, and Norma were implicated under the new law for selling goods below cost. Three months later, after a protracted investigation, the Cartel Office ruled against Wal-Mart, Aldi, and Lidl, citing violations in the pricing of milk, sugar, and vegetable oils. Wal-Mart was fined $308,000 for non-compliance with Germany's competition law.[64] Shortly thereafter, Wal-Mart raised the cost of these items, but also filed an appeal.[65] In December, the appellate court in Dusseldorf cleared Wal-Mart, ruling that the below-cost prices were temporary, insignificant to the overall market, or adopted in response to other competitors as well as suppliers. The Cartel Office then appealed to the Federal Court (*Bundesgerichtshof*), which upheld the Cartel Office's original decision, and in November 2002 ruled against Wal-Mart. Pending EU regulations could yet override Germany's existing pricing legislation, allowing companies to sell below cost, but as of January 2004, Wal-Mart had to tread carefully as it attempted to build a reputation for low prices.

Labor Relations

In late May 2002, Germany's service sector union Ver.di, the largest union in the world, filed a lawsuit against the company, citing Wal-Mart Germany's violation of *Handelsgesetzbuch* (HGB) for not releasing year-end figures for 1999 and 2000. The Register Court (*Registergericht*) requires that all businesses make public their sales and revenue figures. Ver.di argued that the knowledge of this information was crucial to its own attempts to negotiate wages and ensure job security for its workers. Wal-Mart objected that Ver.di was not a legitimate plaintiff. In April 2003, an appeal by Wal-Mart was dismissed and a fine of 330,000 euro assessed. As of February 2004, a second appeal to the Federal Constitutional Court was still pending.

In July 2002, Ver.di organized 2,000 Wal-Mart employees for a two-day strike. Their goal was to get Wal-Mart to join Germany's retail sector employers' association, the HDE (*Hauptverband Deutscher Einzelhandel*). At stake was the way in which Wal-Mart employee wages would be set. Germany has no legal minimum wage. Wage levels are set instead through a process of "coordinated" bargaining, in which state-level retail unions negotiate with employers' associations over the terms of employment contracts. Retailers who are members of the employers' associations are bound to the negotiated wages. Negotiations occur every two years. In the retail sector, the core negotiation concerns the salary of a sales staff with seven year's experience. During the 2002 negotiations, Ver.di and HDE agreed on a salary of 19.51 euros per hour, amounting to an annual raise of 1.35%. Wal-Mart declined to join HDE, announcing that it would determine wages based on "compatibility with the economic situation of the firm."[66] It nevertheless conceded to a salary increase that was 0.5% over negotiated retail-sector levels.

Store Hours

In 1956, German legislators introduced a Store Closing Law (*Ladenschlußgesetz*) that limited store hours to a 6:30pm closing on weeknights and a 2pm closing on Saturdays. Stores could not open at all on Sundays, although each state was allowed to grant four exceptions each year, and certain 'essential' retailers such as pharmacies and tobacconists were given general exceptions. The law was designed to protect workers for exploitative working hours. It also had the effect of protecting traditional retailers from larger competitors, who could afford to keep their stores open longer with lower expenses.[67] At 64.5 hours a week, Germany stores had the shortest opening hours in Europe.[68] While public surveys beginning the 1960s showed that German consumers favored longer store hours, politicians on the left and right opposed liberalization. On the left, Germany's unions argued that it was unfair for retailers to work later than other workers. On the right, religious groups worried longer shopping hours would hurt family life. Even Germany's consumer groups, fearing longer hours would mean higher prices, opposed liberalization.

Beginning in the 1980s, Germany's store hours were gradually liberalized. In 1989, stores were allowed to stay open until 8pm on Thursdays. The proposed reform led 200 retail companies and 30,000 retail workers to strike, but was eventually passed.[69] Several retail unions renegotiated their labor contracts to explicitly limit working hours to a 6:30pm closing. They also called for a reduction in the workweek to 37.5 hours by 1991.[70] In 1996, Germany extended store closing times to 8:00pm for all weeknights. Unemployment had become a serious problem in Germany, and the increased store hours were expected to create 50,000 new positions in retailing.[71] Yet a study conducted by the Ifo Institut showed that the retailing sector had in fact shed 6,000 jobs between 1996 and 1999. The study also found that 71 percent of retailers opposed longer opening hours on weekdays; 64 percent of consumers indicated that they did not need longer weekday shopping hours.

The most recent store hour liberalization came in June, 2003, extending Saturday store hours to 8pm. Wal-Mart reported to the German Economics Ministry that the sales had increased significantly for the first two Saturdays following the longer hours.[72]

Some groups argued for further liberalization. Germany's second-largest retail association and rival to HDE, the *Bundesarbeitsgemeinschaft der Mittel- und Großbetriebe des Enzelhandels* (BAG), felt that retailers located within urban centers should enjoy longer opening hours than those located outside. One retailer, the department store Kaufhof, brought a case before Germany's high constitutional court asserting that the Store Opening Law was unconstitutional – as of April 2004, no decision had yet been taken. Germany's liberal Free Democratic Party (FDP) had also pushed for full store-hour liberalization. Germany's two main political parties, the left Social Democratic Party (SPD) and the right Christian Democratic Union (CDU), agreed that longer hours could hurt both workers and their families. Even Germany's main retail employers' association, HDE, recognized the logic of limited shopping hours. "For culture and lifestyle, it is not so bad to have one day quieter than the others. A lot of retailers, politicians, unions, and churches share this view."[73]

German Markets

The 1990s had been difficult years for German retailing. Retail market growth rates had averaged 0.3% per year.[74] Compared to other European countries, profit margins in Germany were low, particularly in retail food, lingering between one and two percent. Wal-Mart's entry into Germany led many of its competitors to further reduce net margins, to less than one per cent (**See Exhibit 11a-d**).[75] In 2002, overall retail sales in Germany actually diminished by 3.5%,[76] making it what some analysts considered to be the worst year for retailing since World War II (**See Exhibits 15-16**). According to the German retailers' association, 10,000 stores had filed for bankruptcy in 2002—almost twice the 5,500 bankruptcies in 2001—and 30,000 retail workers lost their jobs.[77] Until the mid-1990s, small, private retailers produced roughly half of Germany's retail turnover. In recent years that number had decreased. Independent retailers accounted for 40% of sales in 2002, and were expected to continue declining to overall European levels of 20-30% of sales.[78] Germany's larger hypermarkets were typically located on the outer fringes of cities, with bus service that concluded at approximately 7:30 pm.

Price was another problem. Wal-Mart's German competitors possessed greater penetration within Germany and utilized "zone pricing strategies," matching Wal-Mart's prices in areas where it was a direct competitor. One study found that certain products sold at Wal-Mart in Germany were 11%–25% more expensive than those of its competitors.[79] Wal-Mart disputed these statistics, but did not offer alternative numbers. On the August 8, 2001 opening of a supercenter in Germany, Bloomberg News stated that prices were significantly higher at Wal-Mart as compared to the neighboring Aldi. While an 18-ounce loaf of bread sold for 34 cents at Aldi, the same loaf sold for $1.13 at Wal-Mart.[80] Four months later, prices were still slightly lower at Aldi—although Wal-Mart maintained a much larger selection of American and German goods.

Customers

Unlike many of its German rivals, Wal-Mart offered credit card payment and free bags for goods purchased, improved store interiors, and friendly customer service. At first, it appeared that German consumers responded positively, though they were also skeptical. "When someone puts things in the bag for them, Germans are confused. They think: 'I just bought this. Why are they handling it? It's mine.'"[81] Particularly puzzling was the hallmark Wal-Mart greeter, generally an older employee who is stationed by the entrance to welcome shoppers. German shoppers quickly complained of a stranger approaching them when they entered the store. As one industry observer noted: "The shopping culture is different. The Germans say that it can't be real – the friendly atmosphere. The service-orientation is new. Germans don't want this. They think it costs more. The service culture in Germany is not well developed."[82]

Wal-Mart tried to run the German stores the Bentonville way, using American managers who followed the Wal-Mart's U.S. business model. Wal-Mart employees were encouraged to give the Wal-Mart chant at the beginning of the workday. Initially, they also stocked mainly American brands.[83] They also tried to incorporate elements of German culture into its German stores. They offered soft baked pretzels and Wurstbrot, a traditional German sandwich with sausage and butter, and gave customers the option of packing their own items.[84] Still, Wal-Mart faced a negative perception based on its roots in the American business model. One retail expert noted: "The Wal-Mart brand is the problem. For Germans it sounds like 'hire and fire.' . . . Wal-Mart should adopt a different name."[85] On May 16, 2002, the Wal-Mart in Neukoeln, Berlin, was evacuated when two bombs were discovered in the store, one week before a visit by US President George W. Bush.[86]

Suppliers

Wal-Mart encountered difficulties setting up supplier contracts upon its entry into Germany. Part of the problem was the lack of infrastructure. In the United States, Wal-Mart relied on information provided by suppliers; in Germany, these relationships were not mature. Wal-Mart lacked leverage with suppliers to buy goods at low cost and did not have a reputation of low prices with customers in Germany.[87]

Wal-Mart also sought to structure its supply chain in a manner different from other German retailers. Instead of the traditional direct store delivery model, Wal-Mart implemented a centralized distribution system with new warehouses in Kempen and Hockenheim. But German suppliers were slow to adjust to Wal-Mart's system. Initially, for example, discrepancies in product numbers led to delivery mistakes. In some instances, the out-of-supply rate soared to 20%, compared to a 7% industry average.[88] In August 2001, Wal-Mart addressed its supplier difficulties by hiring Alli Distributors to handle its dried food distribution through Alli's distribution center. This allowed Wal-Mart to focus on its non-food distribution through its Kempen center. Wal-Mart also implemented new scanning systems in its stores so as to better control inventory.

Competitors

German retailers such as Metro, Aldi, Lidl, and Rewe were deeply entrenched, with a loyal customer base, and were not willing to give in easily to a foreign competitor.[89] With low overheads, the advantage of enduring relationships with suppliers, and an understanding of the retail regulatory environment, these retailers proved stiff competition for Wal-Mart. Wealthy families or co-operatives have historically owned the majority of retail companies in the German market.[90]

Typical of the challenge Wal-Mart faced in Germany was the Aldi chain of hard-discounters. Aldi, a 40-year-old retail chain owned by Europe's wealthiest family, the Albrecht brothers (net worth of $13.6 billion), proved to be an especially tough competitor. Aldi was privately held, so it experienced no stock market pressure. A hard discounter, Aldi kept costs low by employing a limited number of cashiers and stockroom workers, by displaying goods on their shipping pallets, and by spending little on store presentation and upkeep. Every aspect of the store focused on keeping costs down. Retail sites had no telephones; cashiers were paid based on the number of items they checked out; the stores accepted only cash. Aldi focused primarily on food, but they also had weekly sales of non-food items. They were, for example, the seventh largest clothing retailer in Germany. As of 2001, Aldi had 3,100 stores throughout Germany, compared to Wal-Mart's 94.[91] Theo Albrecht, owner of Aldi Nord, also owned the U.S. retailer Trader Joe's.

The key to their success was the trust German's placed in them. "Many Germans count their money, even if they are not poor. This has become part of the national culture. Aldi has become important in Germany, not just in economic terms."[92] Aldi had a dedicated customer base, and could extract extremely low prices from suppliers. "Aldi's business model is simple," describes Matthias Goppelt in the German Economics Ministry. "The boss says: 'We will sell only 200 items, at very low cost. We will pay no attention to looks. The atmosphere will be dull. And when I deal with the suppliers, I will be bargaining hard'."[93] Suppliers were occasionally required to wait a full year to receive payment for goods delivered to Aldi. Nor did they always accept Aldi's pressure passively. At the end of March 2004, dairy farmers in Essen poured milked onto the roads in protest against efforts by Aldi to reduce their milk price by 10%.[94]

German hard discounters increasingly came under scrutiny for their labor practices. Ver.di accused the hard discounter Schlecker of operating with a single sales person its stores, forcing them to close the store in order to use the restroom.[95] Another of Germany's hard discounters, Lidl, was particularly aggressive in restricting labor organization. In Germany, workers in firms with more than five employees have the right to organize into works councils (*Betriebsrats*), giving worker representatives access to management decision-making over hiring, firing, and worker training. This process of "codetermination" was protected under Germany's basic law. Lidl regularly blocked store employees from forming works councils, either by actively discouraging workers from voting for codetermination, or by establishing the stores at which they worked as independent companies with less than 5 full-time employees. In 2003, Lidl had 6400 stores, 80,000 employees, and sales of 9.5 billion euros.

Wal-Mart had also palpably changed Germany's retail environment. Prior to Wal-Mart's entry, high labor costs and an overall concern with keeping prices low had kept German retailers from investing in store design, IT systems or merchandising.[96] With Wal-Mart's presence, an increasing number of German retailers implemented advanced scanner systems. Many also altered their business practice. The German chain Metro opened a "Future Store," in which new RFID, intelligent grocery carts, and automated checkout technologies were showcased. German retailers also increased their pressure in dealings with suppliers, resulting in lower shelf prices. Some German retailers had recently expanded into Eastern and Central Europe.[97]

The Way Forward

With plans to increase international sales to 33% of Wal-Mart revenue, Europe was likely to be an important part of this development. Germany offered the largest consumer market in Europe and the third largest in the world. Yet the German retail environment seemed to pose particular challenges. Higher costs, lower margins, smaller stores, undeveloped supply chain relationships, and price sensitive customers loyal to German chains forced Wal-Mart's German stores to operate on a gross margin estimated at 1% or less, compared to a 6%–8% margin for ASDA in the United Kingdom.[98]

The problem appeared not to be unique to Wal-Mart. GAP, the world's largest clothing retailer, had just announced that it was selling its German stores after eight years of disappointing sales (its stock rose on the announcement). A number of large European retailers, including Marks & Spencer, Oviesse and Giacomelli, had also recently abandoned the German market.[99] For Germany, and for

Europe more generally, the challenges confronting these retailers raised broader issues of economic efficiency and social order. One observer writes:

> "80% of the entire difference in productivity growth rates between Europe and the US is located in retailing and wholesaling [and] all of the productivity growth in US retailing in the 1990s is attributable to the new entry of new, more efficient retailing establishments…. Big new stores on green field sites achieved huge productivity improvements. In Europe this doesn't seem to have happened, and… that fact alone explains the vast majority of Europe's widening productivity gap versus the US."[100]

By FYE 2003, Wal-Mart Germany had 9,202,224 total square footage, 94 stores, with estimated sales of $2.6 billion.[101] Wal-Mart's German stores had not turned a profit, though losses were estimated to be less than in previous years. Despite persistent rumors of further German acquisitions, Wal-Mart management continued to insist that it could make a profit with the stores it had. "You do not have to have 400 stores to be successful in Germany," said CEO Lee Scott in 2000. "We have enough stores. The core issue we face is running the stores the way they should be run."[102]

Exhibit 1   The Wal-Mart Cheer

Give me a W!
Give me an A!
Give me an L!
Give me a Squiggly!
Give me an M!
Give me an A!
Give me an R!
Give me a T!
What does that spell?
Wal-Mart!
Whose Wal-Mart is it?
My Wal-Mart!
Who's number one?
The Customer! Always!

Source: <www.walmartstores.com>.

Exhibit 2   Wal-Mart International Stores by Country, 2003

| Country | Wal-Mart International Stores | | | |
	Discount Stores	Supercenters	Sam's Clubs	Neighborhood Markets
Argentina	0	11	0	0
Brazil	0	12	8	2[a]
Canada	213	0	0	0
China	0	20	4	2
Germany	0	94	0	0
Korea	0	94	0	0
Mexico	472[b]	75	50	0
Puerto Rico	9	1	9	33[c]
United Kingdom	248[d]	10	0	0
International Totals	942	238	71	37
Grand Totals	2,510	1,496	596	86

Source: Wal-Mart Annual Report FYE 2003.

[a]Brazil includes Todo Dias.

[b]Mexico includes 118 Bodegas, 50 Suburbias, 44 Superamas, 260 Vips.

[c]Puerto Rico includes 33 Amigos.

[d]United Kingdom includes 248 Asda stores.

Exhibit 3   Wal-Mart Stores, Inc.: Country Value Shares by Retail Subsector 2001

Country	Fascia	% Value
Argentina	Wal-Mart Supercenter	15.4
Brazil	Sam's Club	6.7
	Wal-Mart Supercenter	36.1
Mexico	Suburbia	8.1
	Bodega Aurrera	42.1
	Superama	9.5
	Aurrera	7.5
	Wal-Mart Supercenter	7.5
United States	Sam's Club	20.1
	Wal-Mart/Wal-Mart Supercenter	39.8
Canada	Wal-Mart/Wal-Mart Supercenter	66.0
Germany	Wal-Mart Supercenter	8.1
United Kingdom	Asda/Asda-Wal-Mart	82.0
China	Wal-Mart Supercenter	9.6
Taiwan (Hypermarkets)	Asiaworld	2.0

Source: Copyright and Database Right *Euromonitor* 2003.

Exhibit 4   Wal-Mart Fiscal 2005 Store Opening Program

	Actual Fiscal 2003	Expected Store Openings Fiscal 2004	Fiscal 2005 Guidance
United States	**3,400**	**+308**	**+330 to +355**
Discount Stores	1,568	+ 45	+ 50 to + 55
Supercenters	1,258	+213[a]	+220 to +230
Sam's Club	525	+ 34	+ 35 to + 40
Neighborhood Market	49	+ 16	+ 25 to + 30
International	**1,288**	**+124**	**+130 to +140**

Source: <www.walmartstores.com>.

[a]Including 140 Discount Store conversions.

Exhibit 5   Wal-Mart Sales: Fiscal Year 2001–2003 (thousands)

Fiscal Year	Wal-Mart Stores	Sam's Clubs	International	Other	Total Company	Total Company Increase from Prior Fiscal Year[a]
2003	$157,121	$31,702	$40,794	$14,907	$244,524	12%
2002	139,131	29,395	35,485	13,788	217,799	14%
2001	121,889	26,798	32,100	10,542	191,329	16%

Source: Wal-Mart Annual Report 2003.

Exhibit 6   Wal-Mart Stores, Inc.: Retail Sales and Performance Indicators—1998–2002 (US$ million)

	1998	1999	2000	2001	2002	2003
Net sales	117,958	137,634	165,013	191,329	217,799	244,524
% growth	12.5	16.7	19.9	15.9	13.8	12.3
Operating profits	6,503	8,061	10,105	11,490	12,077	13,671
% growth	13.6	24.0	25.4	13.7	5.1	14.3
% operating margin	5.5	5.9	6.1	6.0	5.5	5.5
Net margin (%)	3	2	3	3	3	3
Shareholders' equity	18,503	21,112	25,834	31,343	35,102	39,337
Long-term debt	7,191	6,908	13,672	12,501	15,687	16,607
Debt/equity ratio (%)	38.9	32.7	52.9	39.9	44.7	49.8
Earnings per share (US$)[a]	0.78	0.99	1.21	1.41	1.49	1.81
Number of employees	825,000	910,000	1,140,000	1,244,000	1,383,000	1,440,350
Sales per employee (US$)	142,979	151,246	144,748	153,801	157,483	

Source: *Euromonitor* from company reports and Wal-Mart Annual Report 2003.

Note: Year-end January.

[a]Wal-Mart Annual Report 2003.

Exhibit 7   Metro AG: Retail Sales and Performance Indicators—1997–2001 (€ million)

	1997	1998	1999	2000	2001
Net sales	24,993	41,730	39,888	50,684	55,464
% growth	-	61.3	-6.5	7.1	5.5
Operating profits	417	706	910	1107	1265
% growth	486	63.4	25.9	2.5	10.2
Operating margin (%)	1.7	1.7	2,3	2.2	2.3
Net margin (%)	1.1	0.8	0.7	0.9	0.9
Shareholders' equity	2,181	3,678	3,660	4,477	4,751
Long-term debt	2,181	3,678	7,855	8,338	8,435
Debt/Equity ratio (%)	0.0	0.0	214.6	186.2	177.6
Earnings per share ( )	N/A	N/A	0.65	1.18	1.37
No. of employees	134,019	181,282	171,440	184,257	193,249
Net sales per employee ( )		192,996	235,368	276,129	285,262

Source: Euromonitor from company reports.

Note: Year-end December. Includes restaurants and catering services.

Exhibit 8 ASDA Retail Sales: 1997–2003 ($millions)

	1997	1998	1999	2001[a,b]	2002	2003
Revenue ($ mil.)	11,318.2	12,729.4	13,208.3	14,500	15,300	18,100
Net income ($ mil.)	501.9	512.1	510.7	--	--	-
Net Profit Margin	4.4%	4.0%	3.9%	--	--	-
Employees	76,619	78,450	--	100,000	109,00	122,000

Source: Hoover's <www.hoovers.com>

[a]Fiscal Year-End Change. ASDA fiscal year (1997-1999) ends in April. Wal-Mart fiscal year ends January 31.

[b]Irregular reporting interval.

Exhibit 9 Retail Store Formats

Store Type	Size	No. employees	Number of products	Merchandise	Characteristics
Hypermarket Concept created by Carrefour (French retailer) in 1963	50,000–200,000+ sq. ft.	Approximately 200-500	70,000 items (average)	Food, general merchandise, specific shops for certain items (furniture, etc).	The Original "big box" store. Location: city limits, bus service provided, close at 7p.m. Some Carrefour hypermarkets have cinemas/restaurants
Supercenter Wal-Mart's version of the hypermarket	109,000–200,000 sq. ft.	220-550 associates	100,000 items (30,000 grocery)	Food, general merchandise, apparel	Tire & Lube Express, restaurants, portrait studios, one-hour photo, vision centers. Open 24 hrs/day in the U.S.
Wal-Mart Discount Store Wal-Mart's first store format, established 1962.	40,000 –125,000 sq. ft.	~ 150 associates	80,000 items	Apparel/general merchandise	Home furnishings, electronics, hardware, automotive products, sporting goods, jewelry, pet supplies
Wal-Mart Neighborhood Market Established 1998	42,000–55,000 sq. ft.	80–100 associates	~28,000 items	Grocery, one hour photo, pharmacy, household & pet supplies	Convenient shopping experience,
Wal-Mart SAM'S Club Established 1983	110,000–130,000 sq. ft.	~125 associates	4,000 products	Food, general merchandise. Products sold in bulk, discount prices.	Members only. Serves small businesses and individuals. Annual membership fee: $35, individual; $30, businesses
Hard Discounter/ Limited Line Discounter (e.g., Aldi)	Less than 12,000 sq. ft. in city center; 40,000–60,000 sq. ft outside of city center	Limited number of staff	~700 items, approximately 85% private label	Dry groceries, staple items	German retailers dominate this market in Europe. Operating costs kept under 10%. Customers pack own bags

Source: <www.walmartstores.com>; <www.carrefour.com>; <www.igd.org.uk>, <www.careerchoices.org.uk> "Fact Sheets: New European Discount Retailing" (IGD Research).

Exhibit 10   Top 20 Global Retailers

Country of Origin	Name of Company	2002 Retail Sales (US$M)	Countries of Operation	Formats	Five-year Retail Sales CAGR % (local currency)	Five-Year Net Income CAGR % (local currency)
United States	Wal-Mart	229,617	Argentina, Brazil, Canada, China, Germany, Japan, South Korea, Mexico, Puerto Rico, United Kingdom, United States	Discount, Hypermarket, Supermarket, Superstore, Warehouse	14.2%	17.9%
France	Carrefour	65,011	Argentina, Belgium, Brazil, Chile, China, Columbia, Czech Republic, Dominican republic, Egypt, France, Greece, Indonesia, Italy, Japan, Malaysia, Mexico, Oman, Poland, Portugal, Qatar, Romania, Singapore, Slovakia, Spain, South Korea, Switzerland, Taiwan, Thailand, Tunisia, Turkey, UAE	Cash & Carry, Convenience, Discount, Hypermarket, Specialty, Supermarket	18.7%	20.5%
United States	Home Depot	58,247	Canada, Mexico, Puerto Rico, United States	DIY, Specialty	19.2%	25.9%
United States	Kroger	51,760	United States	Convenience, Discount, Specialty, Supermarket, Warehouse	14.3%	23.9%
Germany	Metro	48,349	Austria, Belgium, Bulgaria, China, Croatia, Czech Republic, Denmark, France, Germany, Greece, Hungary, Italy, Japan, Luxembourg, Morocco, Netherlands, Poland, Portugal, Romania, Russia, Slovakia, Spain, Switzerland, Turkey, United Kingdom, Vietnam	Cash & Carry, Department, DIY, Hypermarket, Specialty, Superstore	12.4%	9.6%
United States	Target	42,722	United States	Department, Discount, Superstore	9.0%	17.1%
Netherlands	Ahold	40,755	Argentina, Brazil, Chile, Costa Rica, Czech Republic, Denmark, Ecuador, El Salvador, Estonia, Guatemala, Honduras, Indonesia, Latvia, Lithuania, Malaysia, Netherlands, Nicaragua, Norway, Paraguay, Peru, Poland, Portugal, Slovakia, Spain, Sweden, Thailand, United States	Cash & Carry, Convenience, Discount, Drug, Hypermarket, Specialty, Supermarket	12.5%	NM
United Kingdom	Tesco	40,071	Czech Republic, Hungary, Republic of Ireland, Malaysia, Poland, South Korea, Slovakia, Taiwan, Thailand, United States	Convenience, Department, Hypermarket, Supermarket, Superstore	9.7%	13.4%
United States	Costco	37,993	Canada, Japan, South Korea, Mexico, Puerto Rico, Taiwan, United Kingdom, United States	Warehouse	9.8%	72.4%
United States	Sears	35,698	Canada, Puerto Rico, United States	Department, Mail Order, Specialty, E-Commerce	-2.9%	3.0%
United States	Albertsons	35,626	United States	Drug, Supermarket, Warehouse	19.4%	-1.3%
Germany	Aldi Einkauf	33,837E	Australia, Austria, Belgium, Denmark, France, Germany, Luxembourg, Netherlands, Republic of Ireland, Spain, United Kingdom, United States	Discount, Supermarket	15.2%	NA
United States	Safeway, Inc.	32,399	Canada, Mexico, United States	Supermarket	7.6%	NM
United States	JC Penney	32,347	Brazil, Puerto Rico, United States	Department, Drug, Mail Order	1.8%	-6.5%
France	Intermarché	31,688E	Belgium, France, Germany, Poland, Portugal, Romania, Spain	Cash & Carry, Convenience, Discount, DIY, Food Service, Specialty, Supermarket, Superstore	9.2%	NA
Germany	Rewe	31,404	Austria, Bulgaria, Croatia, Czech Republic, France, Germany, Hungary, Italy, Poland, Romania, Slovakia, Ukraine	Cash & Carry, Discount, DIY, Drug, Hypermarket, Specialty, Supermarket, Superstore	7.4%	NA
United States	Kmart	30,762	United States	Discount, Superstore	-0.9%	NM
United States	Walgreens	28,681	United States, Puerto Rico	Drug	16.5%	18.5%
Germany	Edeka/AVA	26,514E	Austria, Czech Republic, Denmark, France, Germany, Poland	Cash & Carry, Discount, DIY, Supermarket, Hypermarket, Superstore	17.2%	NA
United States	Lowe's	26,491	United States	DIY	21.2%	32.7%

Source: "2003 Global Powers of Retailing," *Stores*, January 2004, pp. G12–G13.

Notes: CAGR = Compound Annual Growth Rate. Name after forward slash is retail segment of parent company.   NA = not available; NM = not meaningful; E = Estimate.

Exhibit 11a   Retail Data for Germany, United Kingdom, and United States, 1996–2001: Sales

	Germany						United Kingdom						United States					
	1996	1997	1998	1999	2000	2001	1996	1997	1998	1999	2000	2001	1996	1997	1998	1999	2000	2001
Constant 1996 dollars (billions)	497.4	437.6	421.2	394.9	355.6	318.1	267.5	285.2	283.1	283.7	266.7	259.2	1796.5	1867.3	1964.4	2076.6	2167.1	2242.4
% growth		-1.4	-0.3	-0.9	-0.6	-2.4		0.7	-0.1	2	0.3	2.7		3.9	5.2	5.7	4.4	3.5
% of GDP	21.6	21.1	20.4	20	19.7	9.5	35.3	36.6	35.4	34.4	31.5	30.1	23.4	23.6	24	23.8	23.6	24.8

Exhibit 11b   Employment

	Germany						United Kingdom						United States					
	1996	1997	1998	1999	2000	2001	1996	1997	1998	1999	2000	2001	1996	1997	1998	1999	2000	2001
Retail workers (millions)	2.9	2.9	2.9	2.8	2.8	2.8	2.3	2.4	2.4	2.5	2.6	2.6	21.9	22.1	22.5	22.9	23.3	23.5
% growth		-0.5	-0.5	-1.1	0	0.2		3.9	-1.8	5.1	2.4	2.4		1.3	1.6	1.9	1.4	1.1
% of all workers	8.1	8.1	8.1	7.9	7.9	7.9	8.9	9.1	8.8	9.2	9.3	9.6	16.3	16.1	16.3	16.4	16.4	17.4

Exhibit 11c   Earnings, by Employee Type

($ thousands)		Germany						United Kingdom						United States					
		1996	1997	1998	1999	2000	2001	1996	1997	1998	1999	2000	2001	1996	1997	1998	1999	2000	2001
Full Time:	Floor staff	24.05	22.62	22.96	22.79	21.12	19.88	15.03	16.72	16.95	17.92	17.25	16.70	17.00	17.70	18.5	19.3	20.1	20.8
	Management	37.05	34.22	34.16	33.94	32.16	30.97	26.60	30.01	29.30	30.72	29.55	28.68	38.90	41.2	43.7	46.3	48.9	50.9
Part Time:	Floor staff	9.81	9.28	9.24	9.54	8.64	8.14	6.20	7.05	7.38	7.20	6.90	6.67	12.30	12.8	13.4	14	14.6	15
	Management	..	..	..	..	..	..	8.53	10.0	9.34	10.24	9.90	9.51	28.10	29.8	31.7	33.5	35.6	36.8

Exhibit 11d   Number of Stores

	Germany						United Kingdom						United States					
	1996	1997	1998	1999	2000	2001	1996	1997	1998	1999	2000	2001	1996	1997	1998	1999	2000	2001
Retail businesses (no. of units)	344,999	329,613	314,208	300,068	288,664	268,458	209,017	214,728	211,503	218,843	226,603	231,544	554,800	524,900	502,100	482,800	463,00	444,500
% growth		-4.5	-4.7	-4.5	-3.8	-7		2.7	-1.5	3.5	3.5	2.2		-5.4	-4.3	-3.8	-4.1	-4
Population per retail unit	237	249	261	274	285	307	279	272	277	268	259	254	483	518	548	577	610	642

Sources: Adapted from *Euromonitor* (Official Statistics, Trade Associations, Trade Press, Company Research, Store Checks, Trade Interviews), World Development Indicators

Exhibit 12   German Economic Indicators (billions of 1995 Euros)

Year	1992	1993	1994	1995	1996	1997	1998	1999	2000	2001	2002
GDP	1,749	1,730	1,771	1,801	1,815	1,840	1,876	1,911	1,969	1,980	1,983
Household final consumption expenditure	992	994	1,004	1,025	1,035	1,041	1,060	1,092	1,108	1,121	
Gross capital formation	405	384	405	408	396	398	419	428	445	407	
General government final consumption expenditure	343	343	351	357	363	365	369	375	379	386	
Exports of goods and services	410	388	417	441	463	516	551	582	659	690	
Imports of goods and services	401	379	407	429	443	479	522	566	623	623	
(percentage of GDP)											
Household final consumption expenditure, etc.	56.7	57.5	56.8	56.9	57.4	57.7	57.6	58.2	58.4	59.0	..
Gross capital formation	23.8	22.5	23.2	22.7	21.6	21.5	21.8	21.8	22.2	20.0	..
General government final consumption expenditure	19.8	19.9	19.7	19.8	19.9	19.5	19.2	19.2	19.0	19.1	..
Exports of goods and services	24.5	22.8	23.6	24.5	25.3	27.9	29.0	29.7	33.7	35.0	..
Imports of goods and services	24.8	22.6	23.3	23.8	24.3	26.5	27.6	28.9	33.3	33.1	..
Inflation, consumer prices (annual %)	5.1	4.4	2.8	1.7	1.4	1.9	0.9	0.6	1.9	2.5	1.3

Source: World Development Indicators.

Exhibit 13   Changes in Labor Productivity Growth: 1995–1999 Relative to 1989–1995

	United States	United Kingdom	France	Germany[a]
Agriculture, Forestry and Fishing	7.44	-1.83	-0.79	-0.37
Mining	0.92	-19.28	-14.89	-6.37
Gas, electricity and water	0.11	-1.9	0.73	1.05
Manufacturing	1.33	-2.48	-0.04	-2.4
Construction	-0.17	-1.7	-3.86	1.19
Transport and communications	2.48	0.16	0.8	2.47
Distributive trades	**4.16**	**0.37**	**0.59**	**-2.69**
Financial and business services	1.97	0.59	1.9	0.42
Personal services	-0.13	-2.2	0.05	-2.39
Total market economy	1.9	-1.32	0	-1.16

Source: Adapted from Mary O'Mahoney and Willem de Boer, "Britain's Relative Productivity Performance: Has Anything Changed?" *National Institute Economic Review* (London: National Institute of Social and Economic Research, No. 179, January 2002): 43.

Note: Annual average growth rates from 1995-1999 minus annual average growth rates from 1989-1995.

[a] Growth rates for 1989–1991 refer to West Germany.

Exhibit 14 Evolution of German Retail Sales: Real Annual Change (%)

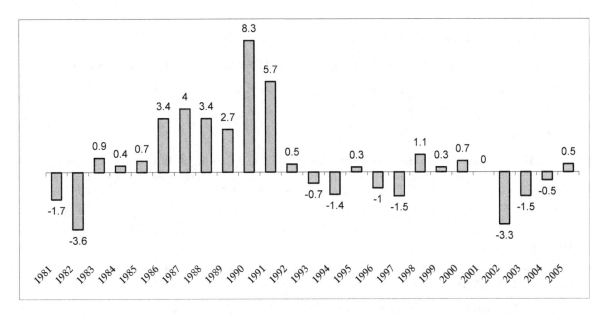

Source: FERI.

Exhibit 15 Germany: Share of Consumer Spending of Private Households by Type of Purchase

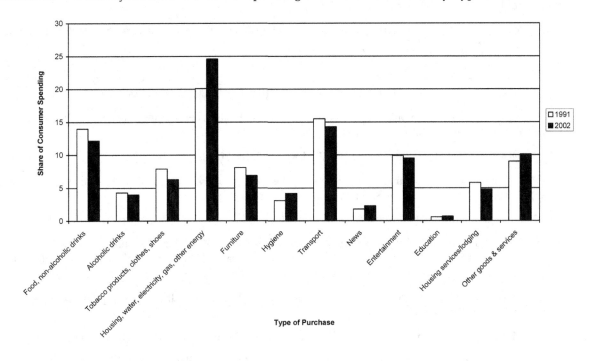

Source: Statistisches Bundesamt.

Endnotes

[1] Wal-Mart Stores, Inc, Annual Report 2000.

[2] Emily Scardino, "Scott speaks out on India and issues," *DSN Retailing Today*, January 26, 2004.

[3] Sam Walton with John Huey, *Sam Walton, Made in America: My Story* (New York: Doubleday, 1992).

[4] *Fortune* , (92: July 1975): 122.

[5] Wal-Mart Stores, Inc, Annual Report 1980, 2, 7.

[6] In 1995/6, "nine regional full-line discounters closed," and, starting in 1998, "three large chains folded a year, first Venture, then Caldor, and finally Bradlees." "1992-2002: The Supercenter Era," *DSN Retailing Today*, (New York: August 2002, Vol. 41, Iss.15, 40th Anniversary), pp27-31; Sandra S. Vance and Roy V. Scott, *Wal*Mart: A History of Sam Walton's Retail Phenomenon* (New York: Twayne Publishers, 1994): 81.

[7] Stephen J. Hoch, "Can Wal-Mart Beat History?" *Advertising Age* (Midwest Region edition, Chicago: Oct. 6, 2003, Vol. 74, Iss.40):.23.

[8] Stephen J. Hoch, "Can Wal-Mart Beat History?" *Advertising Age* (Midwest Region edition, Chicago: Oct. 6, 2003, Vol. 74, Iss.40): 23.

[9] Each Wal-Mart fiscal year ends on the 31st of January (e.g.: FYE 2004 ended Jan 31, 2004).

[10] Wal-Mart Stores, Inc., Annual Report 2003.

[11] Jerry Useem, "One Nation Under Wal-Mart," *Fortune* (New York: Mar. 3, 2003, Vol. 147, Iss.4): 65.

[12] Sam Walton as quoted on the Wal-Mart Stores, Inc, website: <www.walmartstores>.

[13] Wal-Mart Stores, Inc., Annual Report 1997.

[14] Neil Buckley, "Can Wal-Mart Conquer Markets Outside the US?" <www.FT.com>. (London: Jan. 7, 2003).

[15] "The Retail Revolution" *McLean's* (March 1, 1999).

[16] John Fernie and Stephen J. Arnold, "Wal-Mart in Europe: Prospects for Germany, the UK and France," *International Journal of Retail and Distribution Management* (Bradford, 2002, Vol. 30, Iss. 2/3): 92–102.

[17] Virginia Postrel, "Economic Scene: Lessons in Keeping Business Humming, Courtesy of Wal-Mart U," *The New York Times Business Day* (Feb 28, 2002).

[18] "McKinsey Global Institute Report 1999," *McKinsey Quarterly*.

[19] Virginia Postrel, "Economic Scene: Lessons in keeping business humming, courtesy of Wal-Mart U," *The New York Times Business Day* (Feb 28, 2002).

[20] Steven Greenhouse, "Wal-Mart, A Nation Unto Itself," *The New York Times*, April 17, 2004, p B8.

[21] Steven Greenhouse, "Workers Assail Night Lock-Ins by Wal-Mart," January 18, 2004, p 1; Steven Greenhouse, " Suit by Wal-Mart Cleaners Asserts Rackets Violation," *The New York Times*, November 11, 2003, p. A12.

[22] Charlie LeDuff and Steven Greenhouse, "Grocery Workers Relieved, if Not Happy, at Strike's End," *The New York Times*, February 28, 2004, p A8.

[23] F. W. Woolworth Company, *Woolworth's First 75 Years: The Story of Everybody's Store* [New York: 1954].

[24] Nicholas Alexander, *International Retailing* (Malden, MA: Blackwell Publishers, 1997): 6.

[25] D. Sun, Sears Roebuck and Co. A. Hast, D. Pascal et al, eds, *International Directory of Company Histories*, Vol. V (Detroit: St. James Press), pp. 33-35.

[26] Hoover's Online <www.hoovers.com>.

[27] *OneSource*. Giant Food Inc. was not related to Giant Food Stores. An accounting scandal in 2003, in which Ahold acknowledged overstating earnings by $500 million, caused it stock price to fall 60%.

[28] Hoover's Online <www.hoovers.com>.

[29] Source: "Wal-Mart, 1997," by Professor David Yoffie and Research Associate Anthony St. George. Harvard Business School Case No. 797-099 (Boston: Harvard Business School Publishing, 1997).

[30] Wendy Zellner [et al] "How Well Does Wal-Mart Travel?" *Business Week* (New York, Iss. 3747, Sept. 3, 2001): 82.

[31] Wal-Mart Stores, Inc, Annual Report 2002.

[32] Source: "Wal-Mart, 1997," by Professor David Yoffie and Research Associate Anthony St. George. Harvard Business School Case No. 797-099 (Boston: Harvard Business School Publishing, 1997).

[33] "Asda's Picture of Ongoing Success" *Grocer* (Crawley, Aug. 12, 2003, Vol. 226, Iss. 7617): 7.

[34] Brenda Sternquist, "International Expansion of US Retailers," *International Journal of Retail and Distribution* (Bradford: 1997, Vol. 25, Iss. 8,): 262.

[35] <www.kmartcorp.com>, "Corporate history."

[36] <www.costco.com>.

[37] <www.costco.com>.

[38] Brenda Sternquist, "International Expansion of US retailers," *International Journal of Retail and Distribution Management*, (Bradford: 1997, Vol. 25, Iss. 8): 262.

[39] A.T. Kearney, *2003 Global Retail Development Index*, <www.atkearney.com>; 14.

[40] Bill Bowden, "Behind the Berlin Wal-Mart," *Arkansas Business* (Little Rock, AK: Jan 22, 2001, Vol. 18, Iss. 4): 1. See also Uta Harnischfeger, "Wal-Mart Shakes Up Germany's Food Shopping Sector: US retailer may struggler to expand further in Europe," *Financial Times*, (London: June 23, 1999): 32.

[41] David Fairlamb, "A Bumpy Ride in Europe," *Business Week International* (Oct. 8, 2003).

[42] "Wal-Mart: The European Story So Far," *Strategic Direction* (Bradford. New York: June 2002, Vol. 18, Iss. 7): 8.

[43] *Sueddeutsche Zeitung*, Dec. 27, 1997.

[44] *Sueddeutsche Zeitung*, Dec. 27, 1997.

[45] *Chain Store Age Executive*, March 1998.

[46] Bill Bowden, "Behind the Berlin Wal-Mart," *Arkansas Business* (Little Rock, AK: Jan. 22, 2001, Vol. 18, Iss. 4): 1.

[47] Wendy Zellner [et al] "How Well Does Wal-Mart Travel?" *Business Week* (New York, Iss. 3747, Sept. 3, 2001): 82.

[48] David Fairlamb, "A Bumpy Ride in Europe."

[49] "Behind the Berlin Wal-Mart" Arkansas Business, January 22, 2001, Vol. 18, Iss.4.

[50] Susanna Voyle, "Mixed Fortunes in Britain and Germany,"<www.Ft.com>; London, January 7, 2003.

[51] Susanna Voyle, "Mixed Fortunes in Britain and Germany,"<www.Ft.com>; London, January 7, 2003 "

[52] Susanna Voyle, "Mixed Fortunes in Britain and Germany,"<www.Ft.com>; London, January 7, 2003.

[53] Robert Slater, *The Wal-Mart Decade: How a New Generation of Leaders Turned Sam Walton's Legacy into the World's #1 Company* (New York: Portfolio, 2003): 140.

[54] Peter McGoldrick and Gary Davies, eds, *International Retailing: Trends and Strategies* (London: Pitman Publishing, 1995): 90.

[55] Cliff Guy, "Internationlisation of Large-Format Retailers and Leisure Providers in Western Europe: Planning and Property Impacts," *International Journal of Retail & Distribution Management* (Bradford, 2001).

[56] Söfker interview.

[57] The legal basis for state planning is provided in another piece of legislation, the *Raumordnungsgesetz*.

[58] Peter J. McGoldrick and Gary Davies, eds, *International Retailing: Trends and Strategies* (London: Pitman Publishing, 1995): 23.

[59] Ulrich Martinius interview, BAG.

[60] Interview with Söfker, BMVBW.

[61] Holger Wenzel, HDE.

[62] The law also banned the use of frequent customer cards, volume discounts, and in-kind gifts.

[63] *Lebensmittelzeitung*, December 1, 2004.

[64] *Retail Week* 2000, as quoted in John Fernie & Stephen J. Arnold, "Wal-Mart in Europe: Prospects for Germany, the UK and France," *International Journal of Retail & Distribution Management* (Bradford, 2002, Vol. 30, Iss. 2/3): pp. 92–102.

[65] Wendy Zellner [et al] "How Well Does Wal-Mart Travel?" *Business Week* (New York, Iss. 3747, Sept. 3, 2001): 82.

[66] *Lebensmittel Zeitung* (Oct. 20, 2000).

[67] J. Gunnar Trumbull, "Government Support for Traditional Retailing in France and Germany," (Cambridge, MA: Massachusetts Institute of Technology, 1998): 4.

[68] J. Gunnar Trumbull, "Government Support for Traditional Retailing in France and Germany," (Cambridge, MA: Massachusetts Institute of Technology, 1998): 9.

[69] J. Gunnar Trumbull, "Government Support for Traditional Retailing in France and Germany," (Cambridge, MA: Massachusetts Institute of Technology, 1998), pp.14-15.

[70] J. Gunnar Trumbull, "Government Support for Traditional Retailing in France and Germany," (Cambridge, MA: Massachusetts Institute of Technology, 1998): 15.

[71] See J. Gunnar Trumbull, "Government Support for Traditional Retailing in France and Germany," (Cambridge, MA: Massachusetts Institute of Technology, 1998): 16; Interview with Sophia Hein, BMWA, Bonn.

[72] Interview with Sophia Hein, BMWA, Bonn, February 2, 2004.

[73] Interview with Holger Wenzel, Director, HDE, 4 February 2004.

[74] *Retail Intelligence*, 2000 as quoted in John Fernie and Stephen J. Arnold, "Wal-Mart in Europe: Prospects for Germany, the UK and France" *International Journal of Retail & Distribution Management* (Bradford: 2002, Vol. 30, Iss. 2/3), pp. 92–102.

[75] John Fernie and Stephen J. Arnold, "Wal-Mart in Europe: Prospects for Germany, the UK and France," *International Journal of Retail & Distribution Management* (New York: Bradford, 2002, Vol. 30, Iss. 2/3), pp. 92–102.

[76] Uta Harnischfeger, "Sudden Zeitung: German Retail Sector Register Sales Drop" *Financial Times World Media Abstracts,* (London: Jan. 31, 2003): 1.

[77] Uta Harnischfeger, "Germany's Chains Tighten Their Grip: Retailing: Europe's last outpost of small, family-run shops is succumbing to market pressure and an ageing clientele" *Financial Times* (London: Dec. 23, 2002): 9.

[78] Uta Harnischfeger, "Germany's Chains Tighten Their Grip: Retailing: Europe's last outpost of small, family-run shops is succumbing to market pressure and an ageing clientele" *Financial Times* (London: Dec. 23, 2002): 9.

[79] Ursula Wenzl, "Wal-Mart: Doch kein Preisbecher" *Focus Magazin,* (June 13, 2002).

[80] Bill Bowden, "Behind the Berlin Wal-Mart," *Arkansas Business* (Little Rock, AK: Jan 22, 2001, Vol. 18, Iss. 4): 1.

[81] Interview with Holger Wenzel, Director, HDE, 4 February 2004.

[82] Interview with Ingeborg Erdman, BMWA.

[83] "Wal-Mart: Wunderbar in Weisbaden," *Home Textiles Today* (Feb. 7, 2000, Vol. 21, Iss. 22): 8.

[84] Robert Slater, *The Wal-Mart Decade: How a New Generation of Leaders Turned Sam Walton's Legacy into the World's #1 Company* (New York: Portfolio, 2003): 140.

[85] Ulrich Martinius, BAG, Berlin.

[86] *DPA – AFX,* May 17, 2002.

[87] Wendy Zellner [et al] "How Well Does Wal-Mart Travel?" *Business Week* (New York: Iss. 3747, Sept. 3, 2001).

[88] *Financial Times* (London: October 2000).

[89] "Wal-Mart: The European Story So Far," *Strategic Direction* (New York: Bradford, June 2002, Vol. 18, Iss. 7): 8.

[90] John Fernie and Stephen J. Arnold, "Wal-Mart in Europe: Prospects for Germany, the UK and France," *International Journal of Retail & Distribution Management* (New York: Bradford, 2002, Vol. 30, Iss. 2/3), pp. 92–102.

[91] Uta Harnischfeger, "Wal-Mart Shakes Up Germany's Food Shopping Sector: US retailer may struggle to expand further in Europe," *Financial Times* (London Edition: June 23, 1999).

[92] Matthias Goppelt, BMWA.

[93] Interview with Mathias Goppelt, BMWA, 3 February 2004.

[94] "Bauern schütten Milch auf die Straße und in die Gülle-Grube," *Frankfurter Rundschau,* 30 March, 2004, p. 11.

[95] "Das neue Proletariat," *Süddeutsche Zeitung,* March 9, 2004, p 7.

[96] John Fernie and Stephen J. Arnold, "Wal-Mart in Europe: Prospects for Germany, the UK and France," *International Journal of Retail & Distribution Management* (New York: Bradford, 2002, Vol. 30, Iss. 2/3), pp. 92-102.

[97] Uta Harnischfeger, "Wal-Mart Shakes Up Germany's Food Shopping Sector: U.S. retailer may struggle to expand further in Europe," *Financial Times* (London: June 23, 1999): 32.

[98] Robert Slater, *The Wal-Mart Decade* (New York: Portfolio, 2003): 139.

[99] Jürgen Müller, "Gap gibt auf," *Textil Wirtschaft* 7 (February 12, 2004), p 18.

[100] Adair Turner, "What's Wrong With Europe's Economy?," London School of Economics, February 5, 2003 < cep.lse.ac.uk/queens/Adair_Turner_Transcript.pdf>.

[101] Source: Company reports, DSN Retailing Today and analysts' estimates, U.S. Census Bureau and World Bank, as quoted in "Doldrums in Deutschland," *Chain Store Age* (New York: June 2001, Vol. 77, Iss. 6), pp. 62–64.

[102] Bertrand Benoit, "Wal-Mart finds German failures hard to swallow," *The Financial Times*, October 12, 2000, p 25.

9-706-040

REV: AUGUST 16, 2006

DEBORA SPAR

CHRIS BEBENEK

deCODE Genetics: Hunting for Genes to Develop Drugs

Kári asked, "What do you foretell for me?"

"They will find it hard to cope with your good luck," said Njal. "You will prove more than a match for all of them."

— Njal's Saga[1]

In 1996, Kári Stefánsson launched an improbable business from an unlikely spot. After 13 years of working in the United States, the neurologist resigned his positions at Boston's Beth Israel Hospital and Harvard Medical School and returned to his native Iceland. There, he announced, on a rocky island of 270,000 people, he would create a new kind of biotechnology company and a whole new way of attacking disease.

More specifically, Stefánsson had come to Iceland to hunt for genes. Using insights from the exploding fields of genomics and bioinformatics, he planned to identify individual genetic variations, the tiny mutations that lead to disease. Already, scientists had revealed the genetic bases of some of society's most crippling diseases. The inheritance of two faulty genes that control an enzyme called Hex-A, for example, condemned its host to a childhood death from Tay-Sachs disease. The excess repetition of a simple three-nucleotide sequence on chromosome 4 meant the harrowing dementia of Huntington's chorea. Similar genetic abnormalities had been identified for cystic fibrosis and for blood diseases such as sickle-cell anemia and thalassemia. But these were actually the easy culprits— "Mendelian" diseases that stemmed from a single mutation and occurred only when, depending on the particular disorder, one or both parents passed the defective gene to their offspring.

Stefánsson was looking for harder prey. Indeed, upon his return to Iceland he announced his intent to find genes for diseases that were not purely genetic in nature. In other words, while Mendelian diseases such as Tay-Sachs or Huntington's are caused by genes alone, many of society's more common diseases—heart disease, cancer, or asthma—result from a complex interplay of genes and environment. One smoker gets lung cancer, for example, while another remains healthy. One sibling suffers from schizophrenia, but the other does not. Genes in these cases seem to predispose people to certain medical outcomes, but they do not guarantee them. What Stefánsson sought to do, therefore, was to identify these genetic predispositions, searching for the mutations that led, over time and in large populations, to a higher likelihood of a particular disease. If he could identify the

---

Professor Debora Spar and Research Associate Chris Bebenek prepared this case. HBS cases are developed solely as the basis for class discussion. Cases are not intended to serve as endorsements, sources of primary data, or illustrations of effective or ineffective management.

gene, the logic ran, he could also reveal the biological pathway through which it operated. And if he could reveal the pathway, he could theoretically develop a remedy to control its activity.

By the end of 2004, Stefánsson's firm, deCODE Genetics, had made great strides. The firm employed some 400 people, including 100 world-class researchers—geneticists, statisticians, epidemiologists—and a host of technicians, ensconced in an office building near the center of Reykjavik and at facilities in the United States. DeCODE had raised an initial $12 million in venture capital and nearly $200 million from an initial public offering in 2000. Its share price stood at $7.81 (down from a 2000 high of $31.50), and its market capitalization was around $426 million. Most importantly, the firm had already identified more than a dozen disease genes, including those that appeared linked to some of society's most destructive and commonplace illnesses: asthma, schizophrenia, cardiovascular disorders, stroke, osteoarthritis, prostate cancer, and diabetes. In the cardiovascular area, it had also identified a compound—DG031—that lowered the activity of a particular gene and could potentially prevent recurrent heart attacks. Results of its Phase II drug trials were promising, and Phase III was set to begin early in 2006. Company officials reported that they had more than 50 projects under way, some in partnership with the world's major pharmaceutical firms. And analysts repeatedly listed deCODE among the most promising genetically focused biotech firms.

The company's success, however, had been marked by twists and setbacks. Before 2003, for instance, a centerpiece of its strategy was an ambitious and unprecedented plan to create a population-wide database of medical, genealogical, and genetic information unrivalled anywhere in the world. This database would draw jointly from Iceland's well-maintained genealogical records, its modern health statistics, and blood samples donated for research by Icelanders. By combining the genealogy, which for many families stretched back nearly 1,000 years, with contemporary data on each Icelander's medical history, the company planned to assemble a pool of knowledge that was simply unheard of anywhere else in the world. It was the promise of this database that had drawn many investors to deCODE during the firm's early years. As plans for a population-wide medical database unfolded, however, they unleashed a maelstrom of criticism. Even in tiny Iceland, where most people were at least distantly related and Stefánsson was something of a rock star, the medical and scientific communities were deeply concerned about releasing personal information to a private firm, and many felt a sense of grievance that the firm stood to reap great profits, essentially, from Icelanders' flesh and blood. And so the core of deCODE's initial plan fell by the wayside in 2002, victim of a concerted opposition movement and deCODE's own attempts at streamlining the firm.

Rather than give up, however, deCODE simply changed the structure of its assault.

The Promise of Genes

On June 26, 2000, in the East Room of the White House, President Bill Clinton announced the completion of a decade-long effort to document the genetic code that governs human life. The Human Genome Project (HGP), Clinton said, had yielded "the most important, most wondrous map ever produced by humankind."[2] That map, which plotted, for the first time, the intricate directions that prompted individual cells to produce the chemical compounds that together form the human body, was still a rough draft. In time, however, researchers felt confident that it would offer insights into treating some of the world's deadliest illnesses. "I truly feel this is going to revolutionize medicine," said Dr. Stephen T. Warren, a geneticist and editor of the *American Journal of Human Genetics*.[3] The genome, said John Sulston, director of a genomics lab near Cambridge, England, would become "the foundation of biology for decades, centuries, or millennia to come."[4]

From the start, the HGP was a vastly ambitious undertaking, so much so, in fact, that when the project was first proposed by the U.S. Department of Energy in 1986, the scientific community largely dismissed it as a waste of time and effort: the technology for such a project had not yet been perfected, critics argued, and most geneticists and molecular biologists felt other lines of inquiry could bring more immediate benefits. But the necessary technology gradually improved, and, perhaps because of the project's very ambition, many prominent scientists slowly came around to the idea. The HGP was finally launched in 1990, now under the auspices of the National Institutes of Health and headed by James Watson, the biologist who some 40 years earlier had codiscovered the structure of DNA.[5]

The task was every bit the challenge that many had predicted. The genome is a set of instructions contained inside practically every human cell. These instructions are grouped into some 25,000 units called genes, each of which controls a protein or proteins that govern a specific bodily process—everything from replenishing the blood to fighting off infections to maintaining the body's temperature at 98.6° F. If any one of these proteins is missing, defective, or too plentiful, it can trigger a wide array of disorders, from Mendelian diseases like Huntington's to more complex afflictions such as cancer, heart disease, and diabetes. By identifying the genes involved in these diseases and the protein pathways through which they act, scientists hoped to reveal new ways of correcting harmful imbalances and fighting or preventing illness.

The product of the HGP was a sequence of 3 billion letters—an unbroken string of As, Ts, Cs, and Gs. These letters stand for the four nucleotides—adenine, thymine, cytosine, and guanine—which join together the twin strands of DNA that lie coiled inside each cell.[6] The difficulty of the HGP lay in reading back the order of the nucleotides and translating chemicals into letters, a painstaking and expensive process called sequencing. The initial five years of the project were devoted to laying the groundwork, but even accounting for this, progress was slow: by 1998 the HGP had sequenced only 3% of the genome.[7]

That same year, however, a maverick geneticist named Craig Venter stunned the scientific community with an announcement. With $300 million in venture capital from the Perkin Elmer Corporation, Venter had founded Celera Genomics, a biotech firm that would use a new sequencing technology to complete the genome by 2001, four years ahead of schedule. Many doubted that Celera was up to the task, and most scientists deeply resented the intrusion of commerce into a project intended for social benefit. While Celera, like the HGP, planned on making its findings freely available, the company's business model was based on selling access to an enhanced database that contained additional information on the human genome, as well as the complete genomes of many common laboratory animals. By the summer of 2000, both teams had finished their work.

For the next five years, scientists around the world tweaked and refined the "wondrous map." But they did not provide the shower of miracles that some had expected. This gap, though, came as no great surprise to those involved with the project. For while sequencing the genome was a crucial first step, the road to the clinic remained long and uncertain. The map of the genome did not include labels indicating where genes responsible for causing or warding off diseases were found, so even with the complete genome at one's disposal, locating these genes and identifying their function remained slow and difficult work. Celera found itself with few subscribers, and shortly after the genome was completed, Venter parted ways with the firm.[8]

Stefánsson's Vision

Even before Celera's announcement touched off a race to complete the genome, Stefánsson's interest had been piqued by another avenue of genetic inquiry. In the mid-1990s, Stefánsson was professor of neurology, neuropathology, and neuroscience at Harvard and director of neuropathology at Boston's Beth Israel Hospital. Trained initially in Iceland, he had left for the United States in 1983, where he joined the faculty of neurology and neuroscience at the University of Chicago. He moved to Harvard in 1993 but soon grew weary of academia's constraints. An iconoclast who reveled in his bluntness, Stefánsson had long chafed at the lack of incentives to create value in academic medicine, and he harbored a long-standing interest in genetics, which he believed could be brought to bear on some of neurology's most challenging problems. The NIH, however, did not share his enthusiasm and twice rejected his application for a grant to study the genetic bases of multiple sclerosis. Undaunted, Stefánsson decided to seek private funding in 1996 and pursue his research through a biotech start-up. He did not stay in Boston, though, an industry hub, or go to other bustling sites such as San Diego or North Carolina's Research Triangle Park. Instead, Stefánsson returned to Iceland, the tiny island nation he had left some 13 years earlier.

It was not an obvious spot. Iceland at the time had only 270,292 inhabitants—some 300,000 fewer than Boston—and an economy that remained largely dependent on fish. Its medical school graduated 50 doctors a year, and the entire country boasted only a handful of research scientists, all working in academic or clinical settings. The country's gross domestic product (GDP) was a respectable $26,617 per capita, but it ran persistent trade deficits, and much of its industry and banking sector remained under government control.[9] Stefánsson was not returning to Iceland for its rustic charms, however, or to escape the pressures of city life. Instead, he had realized that scale and isolation had blessed Iceland with an intriguing genetic advantage. Iceland's populace, most of whom were descended from the same small band of settlers who had moved to the island between 874 and 1000, was relatively homogeneous, and genealogy was a kind of national obsession.[10] The country's national health system, moreover, had kept meticulous medical histories for patients since 1915. Together, these data sources contained a trove of extremely valuable information on the heredity of disease—"a gift from heaven," in the words of one prominent geneticist.[11]

Discovering a mutation responsible for a particular disease can be an extraordinarily complex process, akin to searching for a single "typo" in the 3 billion letter sequence of the genome. It took scientists 10 years to discover the gene responsible for Huntington's, and a similar amount of time for that responsible for cystic fibrosis. And these, recall, are the "easy" genetic diseases, traceable to a single inherited mutation. When researchers look for the source of more common, non-Mendelian diseases, both time and complexity increase: to find BRCA1, for example, one of the genes that plays a role in breast cancer, geneticists needed 17 years. This is because human DNA contains so many mutations, only a fraction of which manifest themselves as diseases. To discover the culprits behind more complicated diseases, therefore, scientists have to start by comparing patients' genetic material, or genotypes, with their physical traits and symptoms, or phenotypes. If a particular mutation is found to correlate in a statistically significant way with a particular set of symptoms, and if the same mutation is absent from the majority of people who are not afflicted with the disease, that mutation is strongly implicated in the disorder.

At the time of Stefánsson's departure, such studies had been carried out for the most part in extended families, where the similarity of DNA among patients who were related to one another made differences between genetic material of the sick and the well easier to detect. Moreover, researchers could rely on the so-called founder effect, whereby every case of a particular disease in the family could be assumed to stem from the same mutation and be traced back to a common ancestor. Iceland's homogeneous population promised these same advantages on a much larger scale:

in effect, Stefánsson was proposing to conduct genetic studies using an extended family of 270,000. But the country's population was only part of the advantage. As a perfect complement, Iceland's fastidious medical and genealogical records offered a ready index of phenotypes and genotypes for Icelanders living and dead, as well as charts tracing relations among them.

Together, the information amounted to nothing less than a map showing how mutations and disease moved through the generations. It was a powerful combination, one that would allow Stefánsson to correlate mutations quickly with symptoms, thus identifying the genetic underpinnings of common diseases. By comparing the frequency of mutations with the frequency of a specific disease, Stefánsson reasoned that he would also be able to draw inferences about the relative contribution of genes (as opposed to environment or lifestyle) to the genesis of the disorder. From the gene, Stefánsson could then move to its protein pathway—and, eventually, to treatment. This was the logic behind deCODE Genetics.

Building deCODE

From the start, Stefánsson knew he would need powerful data-mining technology and a talented pool of scientists to unleash the possibilities of genes and pedigrees. More critically, he also needed access to the data, because while Iceland's wealth of medical, genetic, and genealogical information was clearly valuable, not all of it was ripe for the taking.

Iceland's genealogical records would be the easiest to collect. They were already in the public domain, and so Stefánsson hired a team of historians, anthropologists, and programmers to compile the raw data and organize them into a searchable database. (When completed it encompassed over half of all the Icelanders who ever lived.) But the most valuable information, the medical records and the Icelanders' DNA, was not as easy to access, since many of the people concerned were still living, and the information was highly personal.

Geneticists had conducted research in Iceland before, recruiting patients with particular diseases as volunteers, but Stefánsson's plans were more ambitious. First he sought to gather the country's medical data into a comprehensive health-sector database. Then he planned to gather DNA samples from as much of the population as possible, combining this information with the country's genealogical records to create a bioinformatics platform that could unearth correlations among the medical, genetic, and genealogical data in a matter of seconds. In order to proceed with a project of this scope, Stefánsson realized that he would need the assistance of Iceland's government. A law sanctioning the endeavor could allow for the blanket release of medical data on all Icelanders living and dead, saving deCODE considerable time and expense. While the firm would still have to collect the DNA itself, obtaining permission from every patient, it could simply rely on the country's doctors to feed their patients' health histories directly into the database. Moreover, Stefánsson believed that deCODE deserved compensation for the time and funds it would devote to the project and needed legal protection for its investment. So he embarked upon a series of meetings with lawmakers and ministers, pitching the idea. Under his proposal, deCODE would invest some $200 million in compiling the database, helping in the process to computerize Iceland's system of medical records. In exchange, it would receive an exclusive 12-year license to sell access to the database, as well as findings from it, to interested parties. While government officials were enthusiastic about deCODE initially, few saw the need for a law. But Stefánsson proved a relentless salesman, and many, including Iceland's prime minister, David Oddsson, soon warmed to the idea.[12]

First, however, the firm had to raise the needed capital. Despite the market's lack of enthusiasm for genetics at the time, Stefánsson's tales of miracle cures from Viking blood quickly won over potential investors, and in just three months he managed to raise $12 million from seven U.S. venture capital firms. Stefánsson resigned his posts at Harvard, moved back to Reykjavik, and set about building deCODE. As the firm was to be Iceland's first-ever biotech, this was no easy task. In order to gather a team of qualified gene hunters, Stefánsson had to engineer a reverse brain drain, luring home Iceland's best and brightest geneticists, statisticians, epidemiologists, and computer programmers, most of whom had long ago decamped for the United States and Europe. By 1997, deCODE had a staff of 55 and had already garnered considerable publicity. *The Economist* heralded the promise of "Norse Code," while many Icelanders believed that Stefánsson and deCODE would help to finally put their tiny country on the map.

DeCODE also caught the eye of the world's pharmaceutical giants. In 1998, before agreement on the structure and nature of the database had even been reached, the company signed a $200 million deal with Swiss pharmaceutical firm Hoffman-La Roche to find the genetic targets for some dozen diseases. Roche agreed to provide investment and research funding in exchange for the right to develop drugs based on the targets deCODE identified. The firm would have to pay deCODE royalties from sales of any products developed, either for 10 years from the first sale or until the patent on the product expired—whichever came later. DeCODE, meanwhile, would be allowed to develop and commercialize any gene-therapy applications resulting from the research. Roche also agreed to provide any drugs it developed free of charge to Iceland's population.[13] The deal allowed deCODE to expand its operations significantly, with 250 new employees joining the firm. By the end of the year, deCODE's scientists were at work searching for targets (early efforts focused on stroke and osteoarthritis, among others), while the Althingi, Iceland's parliament, had approved the database project. The early successes did not take Stefánsson by surprise. "This idea," he quietly explained, "is fantastically good."[14]

Mannvernd: Fighting over Privacy

Not everyone agreed. In March 1998, Iceland's Ministry of Health and Social Security submitted its Bill on a Health Sector Database to the Althingi. Although the bill did not mention any companies by name, it laid out a plan that all Icelanders knew was deCODE's. Specifically, it authorized "those who have an operating license by the terms of this legislation" to create a database of information collected from the country's health-care system and to market it for 12 years.[15] The anonymous licensee would have to work with the country's Data Protection Authority to ensure that no patient's medical records could be identified. Management of the database would also be subject to oversight by an independent ethics committee.[16] Prior to the bill's pronouncement, it had seemed as if most Icelanders were essentially in favor of what deCODE wanted to do. But after the actual bill appeared before the Althingi, the world's oldest parliament, a vocal group of opponents began lobbying stridently against it.

Petur Hauksson, a Reykjavik psychiatrist, was particularly concerned about being compelled to turn over his patients' medical histories to deCODE. (While doctors in private practices would be able to withhold their patients' records, Hauksson worked in a public hospital, where discretion would be left to the board of directors.) "Many of my psychiatric patients and their relatives were very concerned about this from the beginning," he said. "They're used to discrimination, and their health information is very sensitive."[17] Together with Sigmundur Gudbjarnason, a biochemist from the University of Iceland, Hauksson began to rally the country's medical and scientific community against the proposed legislation. Their efforts were successful, and a month after it had first presented its bill, the Ministry of Health withdrew it for revisions. But when a revised bill appeared that summer, featuring additional provisions for privacy and information security, Hauksson and Gudbjarnason were still not satisfied. Together with other doctors and scientists, they founded a group called Mannvernd, or "human protection." While continuing to assail the legislation at home, Mannvernd also took its battle overseas, alerting legal scholars, ethicists, and scientists in the United States and Europe to what Hauksson termed the greatest exploitation of Iceland's people since the nation broke free from Danish rule in 1944.[18]

Mannvernd's critique of deCODE and the government's actions was thoroughgoing and anything but subtle: "Mannvernd believes that this Act infringes on human rights, personal privacy, and on accepted medical, scientific, and commercial standards," proclaimed a statement on the group's Web site.[19] At issue, above all, was privacy. The database bill presumed that all patients consented to the release of their medical records. Those who did not wish to be part of the database were expected to sign a form opting out of the project, and they had to move quickly: once their records were in the database, patients would not be able to remove them. Moreover, children and the mentally disabled would have no say at all. If their legal guardians did not opt out for them, their records would be part of the database. And no one would be allowed to opt out on behalf of deceased relatives. "The parliament is really making a decision on behalf of Icelanders, and we think that's wrong," said Hauksson.[20]

Such an arrangement, Mannvernd and its supporters argued, would undermine the confidence and trust fundamental to the relationship between doctor and patient. It constituted nothing less than a breach of the Hippocratic oath, which deemed patient privacy sacrosanct. Uncertain of who would have access to their records, patients would be less than forthcoming with their physicians about sensitive medical issues such as mental health problems, substance abuse, or sexually transmitted diseases. For the same reason, doctors might also be reluctant to maintain candid records. The inaccurate information that would result would erode the quality of health care and could very well jeopardize patients' lives. The database bill contained strict provisions for data security designed to allay these fears, but Mannvernd dismissed such measures as irrelevant in a country of Iceland's size. "While identity will be encrypted after the data have been entered," wrote two Icelandic scientists opposed to the database, "individuals will be easily identifiable in our small society."[21]

The infringement upon privacy grew deeper, deCODE's critics argued, when the medical records were married with genetic and genealogical information. Many patients would have a difficult enough time envisioning all of the possible studies for which their health histories alone could be used when deciding whether or not to opt out. No one, however, said the firm's critics, could imagine to what use the DNA samples could be put as biotechnology continued to evolve. The uncertainty brought to mind scenarios like the genetic dystopia of the film *GATTACA*, where one's DNA determined one's standing in society. "When you put genealogical information into the data bank and also genetic data, then the data bank knows more about you than you know about yourself," said Tomas Zoega, chairman of the Icelandic Medical Association's ethics council. "I think the idea is a scary one."[22] Given these unknowns, Mannverd reasoned, it was practically impossible for patients to grant deCODE informed consent when turning over samples of their genetic material. Moreover, as the group insisted, deCODE was not only abusing Icelanders' privacy but also—and even worse—profiting from it. From this viewpoint, a 12-year license for deCODE to reap profits on resources that Iceland's people had literally carried inside themselves seemed particularly unjust. Many critics sought to portray the firm as a band of outsiders, referring to it as a "Delaware-based" biotech.

Stefánsson was at first taken aback by the fevered pitch of the opposition. "Why would you not want to support the generation of knowledge?" he demanded. "You'd have to be rather twisted."[23] To deCODE, the potential medical benefits of the database, for the people of Iceland and the world, far outweighed any of the critics' arguments. Stefánsson and his supporters maintained that expecting patients to opt out of research was standard practice in epidemiological studies. In such projects, scientists were interested in aggregate rather than individual data, and deCODE's work, the firm argued, would be no different. "In the United States you have enormous databases containing the health records of millions of individuals," Stefánsson said. "They're also based on presumed consent."[24] Moreover, where DNA samples were concerned, all donors would have to grant deCODE written permission—a fact the firm believed its opponents purposely obscured. Stefánsson also professed that deCODE's critics did not give Iceland's people enough credit, that the Icelandic public was intelligent enough to make reasonable and well-informed decisions about participating in the studies.

Nor was the firm apologetic about the commercial aspects of its project. "The government has no idea how to create value from an enterprise like this," said Stefánsson. "That is my assumption—after all, I did not spend fifteen years at Milton Friedman's university for nothing."[25] The firm maintained that its investment in creating the database would more than warrant the exclusivity granted to it by the legislation and that Iceland's people would be repaid many times over. DeCODE's achievements would bring the tiny island the kind of international prestige that had long eluded it, the company predicted, and deCODE would be the vanguard of a high-tech revolution that would finally diversify Iceland's economy away from fish. DeCODE also promised benefits in the realm of health care, which would stem largely from its investment in computerizing the nation's health-care system, a project the government had long planned on but could not afford. And under an arrangement like the one with Roche, deCODE insisted that any drugs developed using the database would be substantially cheaper for citizens. This was not an insignificant prospect, because although Icelanders enjoyed socialized health care, prescription drugs on the small and remote island were substantially more expensive than in western Europe.[26]

Some critics, however, maintained that deCODE's plan would not be judged on its merits and would instead win approval from the Althingi thanks to Stefánsson's connections and deCODE's political donations. Iceland's prime minister, Oddsson, a major deCODE booster, had been a classmate of Stefánsson's, though the latter recalled that, at the time, the two were on opposite sides of the political spectrum. A former Icelandic president, Vigdis Finnbogadottir, also sat on deCODE's board. Stefánsson defended himself, pointing out that the firm made donations to all political parties that requested them, including those unequivocally opposed to the database.[27] He also campaigned tirelessly on deCODE's behalf, attempting to win over opponents and the undecided, meeting with anyone who would listen: journalists, politicians, activists, and hospital patients. Given the country's size, the ensuing battle could not help but be personal. The same people who squared off against one another in the press were often relatives, acquaintances—or, in one case, squash partners. Many of the physicians opposed to the project had been classmates of Stefánsson's in Iceland's medical school and remembered him for his brash and arrogant style, or "sharp elbows," in the words of one top health official.[28] Stefánsson countered with accusations of professional jealousy; his critics' arguments, he said, were "a horrendous crock of shit."[29]

On December 17, 1998, the Althingi approved the HSD bill. Thirty-seven deputies voted in favor and 20 against, with six abstentions. DeCODE celebrated its victory and pointed to increasing numbers in Gallup polls it had commissioned to show that the ruling reflected the will of Iceland's people. (When the HSD bill first appeared, 57% of Icelanders supported it; by the time of the parliamentary vote, that number had risen to 75%.) Mannvernd, for its part, paid little heed to these results, arguing that few Icelanders understood the full ramifications of the government's actions. "I think that those are the people who have not been ill, who do not have medical records lying about," said Hauksson. These arguments were echoed by Mannvernd supporter and Harvard geneticist Richard Lewontin, who wrote in *The New York Times* that as a result of the parliament's decision and the public's compliance, "the great bulk of the population will be tools of deCODE and its backers."[30]

To avoid such an outcome, nearly a third of Iceland's doctors threatened to defy the law and refuse to turn over medical records without express written permission from their patients.[31] Mannvernd, meanwhile, began a campaign to discourage participation in the database, leaving opt-out forms at clinics and hospitals. The group's critique of deCODE's endeavors grew more fundamental, charging that the very premises of the firm's project were flawed. Einar Arnason, for instance, a geneticist from the University of Iceland and member of Mannvernd, argued that deCODE had repeatedly overstated Iceland's genetic homogeneity, a keystone of the firm's approach.[32] Other critics thought Iceland's population too unique and wondered whether discoveries made on the island would be applicable in other parts of the world. Stefánsson conceded that "the proof of the pudding is in the eating,"[33] but his confidence did not flag. "You walk around here and you see that most people have two legs, two arms, and a head," he said. "It's outrageous to believe that the biological pathways involved in common diseases in Iceland are different than the biological pathways involved with the common diseases elsewhere."[34]

With the database law on the books, the challenge to deCODE also moved into the courts. Early in 2000, Ragnhildur Gudmundsdottir, then 15 years old, requested that her late father's records not be made part of the database. When the Directorate of Public Health refused her request, she filed suit against the government, charging that the Directorate's refusal meant her family had no way to prevent information about its living members, which could be inferred based on her father's medical history, from being included in the database. After a number of unfavorable rulings and appeals, the case was heard in 2003 by Iceland's Supreme Court. In November of that year, the court found in favor of Gudmundsdottir. It argued that even though subsequent regulatory documents issued by the Ministry of Health made specific privacy provisions governing how the data could be used, in order for the database legislation to comply with the Icelandic Constitution's rules on privacy protection, these provisions would have to be part of the legislation. As this was not the case, the database law failed to "[prevent] health information in the database from being traceable to individuals." Gudmundsdottir was thus allowed to remove her father's records from the database.[35]

The Saga Continues

While the battle with Mannvernd raged and the database sat empty, plans for similar databases began to sprout around the world. Some of these projects were intended to be in the public sector; others, like deCODE, would be run by private companies. In 2002, a Swedish firm called UmanGenomics secured access to a database of blood samples and health information from some 100,000 individuals that researchers at Umea University had been collecting since 1987. Around the same time, the Estonian Genome Project launched a pilot database of 10,000 donors. Researchers predicted that with the help of its own commercial wing, EGeen, the database would grow over time to encompass some 1 million samples. In the United Kingdom, the Medical Research Council and the Wellcome Trust earmarked $66 million for a database of 500,000 samples that would be open, in the words of the council, to "any bona fide researcher with a good idea."[36] And in the United States, the initiative came from health-care providers, which already had access to millions of computerized medical records. In 2002, Wisconsin's Marshfield Clinic launched its Marshfield Personalized Medicine Research Project with $2 million in state funding and planned to build an initial database of 40,000 patients.

While none of these projects could boast of access to a population as homogeneous as Iceland's or to the kind of genealogical data at deCODE's disposal, all of the firms and institutions had learned an important lesson from the deCODE controversy. To avoid the storm deCODE was forced to weather, all of them decided early on to use an explicit opt-in model and seek written permission from every participant who would be included in their database, for both DNA samples and medical records. Indeed, Sweden's UmanGenomics was compelled to obtain permission every time it used a patient's sample in a new research project. Estonia's EGeen offered participants another incentive—it would give them access to their genetic profiles.

Meanwhile, in spite of the opponents at home and competition abroad, deCODE had been making progress on the research and development (R&D) front, identifying genetic targets for a range of diseases. The firm could not, for the time being, get its hands on *all* of Iceland's health information. At the same time, though, it could scarcely afford to wait, seemingly indefinitely, until the database was complete. So deCODE scientists continued to follow an older research strategy, the more traditional method employed by population geneticists studying families, which Stefánsson and his team had adapted to deCODE's needs in the firm's early days. Even without the health-sector database, the logic went, the firm still had access to Iceland's genealogical records and its population. In other words, it had enough information at its disposal to make statistically significant discoveries. Rather than querying a computerized system, however, deCODE scientists would first have to gather the samples and information from medical records they needed for each disease they planned to study.

Accordingly, deCODE's researchers began by establishing partnerships with physicians specializing in particular conditions. (Given the country's size, this could be a group of as few as three doctors.) At the same time, the firm applied for a license to carry out the study from the national Science Ethics Committee and the Personal Protection Authority (PPA), a division of the Ministry of Justice. Once the requisite permissions had been granted, collaborating physicians drew up lists of patients suffering from a given disease. The PPA encrypted the lists, replacing patients' names with code numbers, and turned them over to deCODE. DeCODE scientists then fed the encrypted lists into the company's genealogical database, which used the same code, and analyzed the relationships among patients. When they had identified families that interested them, the firm asked physicians to obtain blood samples from these patients, as well as from their healthy relatives. The families in question could, of course, refuse. Moreover, if they agreed, they had the option of giving broad permission, which allowed the company to keep their blood sample on hand for future studies, or narrow permission, allowing deCODE to use their blood only for a specific current project. Patients proved, on the whole, eager to cooperate. "More than 90% of those asked to participate in our research are willing to do so," said the firm's director of information, Eirikur Sigurdsson. "Of those who participate, more than 90% sign the broader form of consent."[37]

Though obtaining the information was more painstaking than with the health-sector database, the underlying science remained the same. Once they had the samples they needed, deCODE's scientists set about comparing the genetic material of sick and healthy relatives to unearth correlations between genotypes and phenotypes. The firm offered participating doctors nominal compensation for the time they spent compiling data and obtaining permission from their patients, as well as coauthor credit on any publications resulting from the research. Patients received a deCODE T-shirt. It was through these channels that deCODE's scientists made their first discovery in 1997, mapping the gene responsible for familial essential tremor, a nonfatal disorder that causes progressive shaking of the limbs. With the health-sector database nowhere in sight, it was also the method responsible for all of the firm's subsequent breakthroughs, which grew more numerous each year.

By 2002, deCODE had isolated genes linked to schizophrenia, stroke, heart attack, hypertension, peripheral arterial disease, osteoarthritis, and adult-onset diabetes. It had also vastly extended its range of strategic partnerships. It expanded its collaboration with Roche, signing two new agreements: a three-year continuation of its original contract aimed at bringing discoveries made under its auspices closer to the clinic, and a five-year alliance aimed at developing DNA-based diagnostic products. It formed similar collaborations with Affymetrix, a bioinformatics firm, and Genmab, a Danish biotech company. For both, deCODE was to use its expertise to help predict genetically determined patient response to drugs. The work was undertaken in exchange for research funding and potential royalty sharing should the research result in a product.[38]

The year 2002 was also the one that saw the final blow dealt to the health-sector database. This time, however, it came from inside deCODE. In September of that year, the firm undertook a financial review. In order to preserve cash reserves and establish a positive cash flow by the following year, it decided to cut 200 jobs, bringing its total staff from 650 to 450. With the health-sector database project sitting idle, pending yet another review by Icelandic data-security authorities, many of those let go were staff who were to be involved in the project's implementation. DeCODE maintained that the database remained an option, noting that the firm still had permission from the government to undertake its originally planned initiative. But as Mark Gurney, senior vice president for drug discovery and development, explained, the firm had already worked around the obstacles to obtain the information it needed: "The database now exists inside deCODE."[39]

By 2003, the firm had gathered some 100,000 samples in 50 different disease programs—enough, Gurney said, to keep the company attractive to those interested in its bioinformatics resources. On the same day that it announced layoffs, deCODE also publicized a three-year collaboration with Merck on treatments for obesity. The firm would use its data and an analytical computer system it had developed called Clinical Genome Miner (CGM) to assess the usefulness of targets that Merck had identified in its own labs. The deal was worth up to $90 million in milestone payments, plus potential future royalties. CGM, the data-mining software, also attracted its share of attention, and in early 2003, deCODE teamed up with IBM to develop and commercialize the product.

A Viking Pipeline?

While such informatics deals remained important sources of funding for the firm's research activities, increasingly, deCODE kept its sights fixed on the clinic. "We've quite swiftly become a pharmaceutical company with lots of drugs in development," said Sigurdsson.[40] The logic of the transformation, according to Gurney, was obvious. "If you hit big with a drug, you get to have $1 billion in sales," he said. "You'll never see that revenue with an information product."[41] By 2005, development was progressing at a nearly feverish pace, including, most recently, genes implicated in such conditions as asthma, heart attack, obesity, osteoporosis, and peripheral arterial occlusive disease (PAOD), a degenerative disorder of blood vessels in the extremities. Seven of these targets had already pointed to potential treatments, and the company was investigating compounds that held the promise of a cure. Three of these compounds were making their way through clinical trials.

DG031 was the most advanced of the firm's compounds and, according to many at deCODE, the most exciting. Targeting a gene that controlled inflammation mechanisms, the compound promised to bring patients with average to high risk of a heart attack to far lower risk levels. In 2003 the firm had in-licensed DG031 from Bayer, which had developed the compound years earlier for another purpose. The deal required deCODE to pay Bayer a license fee, milestone payments, and royalties should DG031 reach the market. In addition, Bayer gained the right of first refusal to manufacture the compound. In exchange, deCODE was granted not only exclusive worldwide license to develop, manufacture, and sell DG031 but also records of Bayer's prior research on the compound, which allowed the firm to move directly into Phase II clinical trials. The compound performed impressively in that stage, and a large-scale, international Phase III trial—the last major hurdle before clinical adoption—was set to begin at the start of 2006. Other compounds were close behind. A compound designed to treat asthma was in a Phase II trial in partnership with another major pharmaceutical firm, for example, and DG041, which had shown promise in halting the progress of PAOD, was in Phase I trials.

DG041 marked another milestone in deCODE's development—it was the first therapeutic compound the firm had developed on its own. The chemical was synthesized by a drug-discovery team that had joined deCODE's ranks in 2002, when the firm acquired MediChem Life Sciences, a U.S. company specializing in medicinal chemistry and biostructure services. DeCODE carried out the merger through a stock-for-stock transaction valued at $83.6 million, acquiring significant downstream capabilities for drug discovery. With 90 employees working in a facility surrounded by warehouses in Chicago's southern suburbs and another 30 in laboratories outside Seattle, deCODE Chemistry and deCODE Biostructures became an essential part of the firm's operations, working to synthesize compounds aimed at targets identified by scientists in Reykjavik. The Chicago facility included a laboratory capable of producing one to five kilograms of a drug—suitable amounts for preclinical and clinical trials. Gurney, who managed the group's operations, hoped to have a pilot plant capable of producing 50 to 100 kilograms within several years. Although the group was busy in 2005 preparing drugs for deCODE's clinical trials, the majority of its work consisted of medicinal chemistry services for outside clients. This kind of service work brought in enough money for the drug-discovery group to sustain itself.[42]

In the summer of 2005, deCODE further expanded its downstream work by adding a team to design and manage its clinical trials. This time the firm expanded not through acquisition but by hiring nine scientists from Pfizer and establishing offices for them outside Ann Arbor, Michigan. Headed by Daniel Hartman, senior vice president of product development, the team took an innovative approach to clinical trials. Using sophisticated mathematical modeling, it sought to design trials with an eye on efficiency, testing drugs in such a way as to weed out ineffective therapies as early as possible. The group had also begun integrating deCODE's genetic data into its trial design, determining not only proper substances and dosage for treatment but also the patient populations genetically predisposed to benefit most from the drug. In the case of DG031, this approach led to a startling discovery. Though it had been identified in Iceland, the variation in the biological pathway targeted by the compound increased the risk of heart attack most drastically in African-Americans. Where Europeans and Americans of European origin who carried the gene bore a slightly increased risk of heart attack, in African-American carriers, risk increased threefold. In late 2005, the group set about integrating this finding into the design of Phase III trials.[43]

Though the team's primary task was demonstrating drug safety and efficacy, it was also the closest part of deCODE to the market, a fact not lost on Hartman. His group's work, he explained, was animated by a fundamental question. "The science coming out of Iceland is second to none," he said. "How do we translate this science into something that makes money for the company?"[44] The answer might be reflected in the structure of deCODE, which by the end of 2005 had come to look more and more like that of a pharmaceutical multinational—albeit on a tiny scale. "DeCODE is a small company thinking it's a big company," explained corporate counsel Tanya Zharov. "Like Iceland, a small country thinking it's a big one."[45] To Stefánsson, that balance seemed a difficult one to maintain. "We have to continue to be entrepreneurial," he said. "But if we succeed, we will have to conform to the standards of the industry."[46]

Exhibit 1   deCODE Genetics Financials, 2000–2004

			Year Ended December 31			
(US$ thousands, except per share data)	2004	2003	2002	2001	2000	
Revenue	42,127	46,811	41,065	26,099	21,545	
Operating expenses:						
R&D, including cost of revenue	68,349	63,466	89,612	70,954	45,742	
Selling, general and administrative	20,187	17,178	18,685	12,402	15,373	
Impairment, employee termination, and other charges	0	951	64,790	0	0	
Total operating expenses	88,536	81,595	173,087	83,356	61,115	
Operating loss	(46,409)	(34,784)	(132,022)	(57,257)	(39,570)	
Interest income	2,903	1,151	2,954	6,925	7,378	
Interest expense	(8,983)	(3,478)	(3,079)	(440)	(495)	
Other non-operating income and (expense), net	(4,766)	1,988	(72)	(1,675)	1,568	
Loss before cumulative effect of change in accounting principle	(57,255)	(35,123)	(132,219)	(52,447)	(31,119)	
Cumulative effect of change in milestone revenue recognition	0	0	333	0	0	
Net loss	(57,255)	(35,123)	(131,886)	(52,447)	(38,119)	
Accrued dividends and amortized discount on preferred stock	0	0	0	0	(7,541)	
Net loss available to common stockholders	(57,255)	(35,123)	(131,886)	(52,447)	(38,660)	
Basic and diluted net loss per share:						
Loss before cumulative effect of change in accounting principle	(1.07)	(0.68)	(2.69)	(1.26)	(1.81)	
Cumulative effect of change in milestone revenue recognition	0.00	0.00	0.01	0.00	0.00	
Net loss	(1.07)	(0.68)	(2.68)	(1.26)	(1.81)	

Source: deCODE Genetics 10K.

Exhibit 2   Seven-Generation Pedigree of Kári Stefánsson, deCODE Founder and CEO

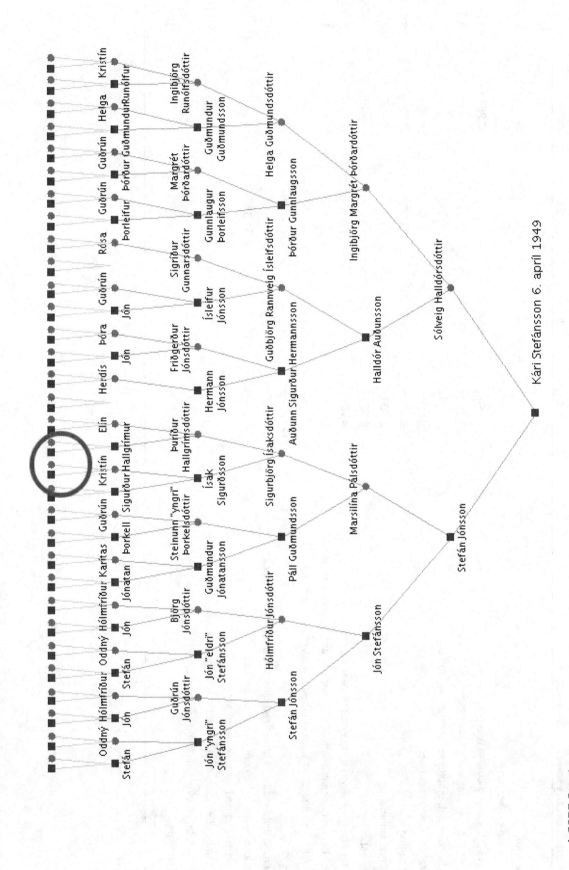

Source: deCODE Genetics.

Exhibit 3   Pedigree of Asthma Patients Descended from a Seventeenth-Century Couple

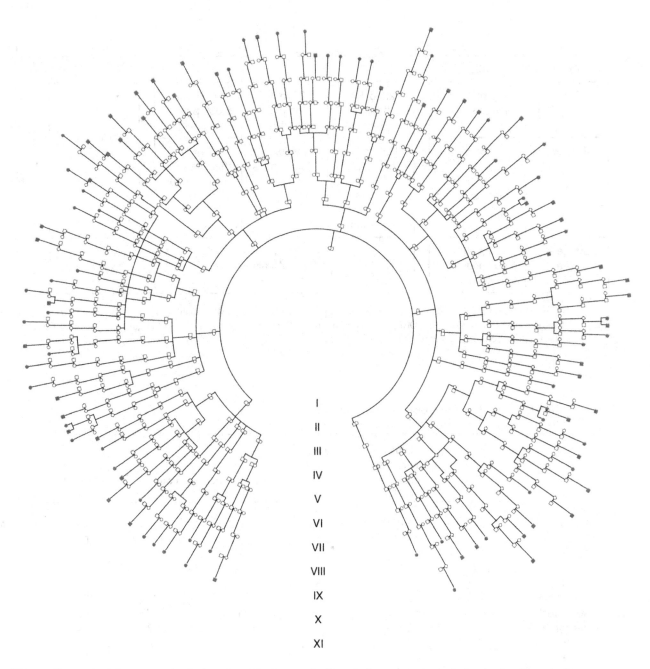

This pedigree combines genealogical and medical records. The dark squares and circles on the figure's fringe represent 107 living asthma patients. The pedigree traces their ancestry back 11 generations, to the innermost circle and square in the diagram. This represents the seventeenth-century "founder" couple responsible for passing down genes predisposing their entire lineage to asthma.

Source: deCODE Genetics.

Exhibit 4   The Drug Development and Approval Process

	Discovery	Clinical Trials			FDA	Phase IV
		Phase I	Phase II	Phase III		
Years	6.5	1.5	2	3.5	1.5	
Test population	Laboratory and animal studies	20 to 100 healthy volunteers	100 to 500 patient volunteers	1,000 to 5,000 patient volunteers	Review of all data from trials; approval	Additional post-marketing testing required by FDA
Purpose	Assess absorption, metabolism, and toxicity	Determine biological activity, proper dosage, and side effects	Evaluate effectiveness, side effects, and potential risks	Confirm effectiveness, safety, and overall benefits of drug		
Success rate	5,000 compounds evaluated	5 enter trials			1 approved	

Source: Compiled from PhRMA, "New Medicines in Development for Women, 2004" (Washington: PhRMA, 2004); U.S. FDA Center for Drug Evaluation and Research, "New Drug Development and Review Process," http://www.fda.gov/cder/handbook dev_rev.htm, accessed February 2006.

Exhibit 5   deCODE in Comparative Perspective

	2004 Revenues (millions US$)	2004 Profit/Loss (millions US$)	Number of Employees	Patents Held	Current Clinical Trials	Drugs on Market
Affymetrix	346	48	900	277	NA[a]	NA
Amgen	10,550	2,33	12,800	414	65	8
Bayer Group AG	40,470	820	93,300	13,382	47	26[b]
Celera Genomics Group	60	(58)	497	263[c]	3	-
deCODE Genetics	42	(57)	429	12	3	-
F. Hoffmann-La Roche	27,645	5,871	65,357	3,621	120	51
Genentech	4,621	785	7,500	987	92	13
Genzyme	2,201	147	6,300	283	24	10
Geron	1	(80)	87	79	2	-
Merck	22,939	5,813	60,000	6,834	96	42
Novartis	28,247	5,767	81,400	1,052	173	49
Pfizer	52,516	11,361	122,000	3,229	191	43

Source: BioScan Directory, 2005; U.S. Patent and Trademark Office; http://www.clinicaltrials.gov, accessed February 2006.

[a]The firm's leading product, GeneChip, is not a pharmaceutical but a bioinformatics tool.

[b]These are only the firm's pharmaceutical products; overall, Bayer has over 10,000 products on the market.

[c]Patents held by Celera's parent corporation, Applera, which also owns Applied Biosystems.

Exhibit 6   Iceland's National Income Accounts, 1990–2004 (billions of constant 2000 Icelandic kronur)

	1990	1995	2000	2001	2002	2003	2004
Government consumption	121.4	134.5	157.9	162.8	169.3	174.3	178.4
Private consumption	285.1	282.2	389.1	375.5	370.4	394.9	430.2
Gross capital formation	93.7	80.8	161.9	145.4	125.0	148.3	173.1[a]
Exports	170.9	179.6	231.6	249.5	258.5	256.7	281.2
Imports	161.8	159.7	278.6	253.6	247.1	271.0	312.0
GDP	509.3	517.4	661.9	679.6	676.0	703.2	750.9
GDP (billions US$)	6.2	6.9	8.4	7.6	8.5	10.5	12.6

Source: Compiled from World Bank World Development Indicators and the Economist Intelligence Unit Country Data, http://www.eiu.com.

[a]Estimated.

Exhibit 7   Iceland's Major Exports, 2002–2004 (as a percentage of total)

	2002	2003	2004
Fish, crustaceans, mollusks, etc.	53.0	53.6	53.3
Aluminum	18.9	18.8	18.1
Other food and live animals	9.5	7.4	7.1
Machinery and transportation equipment	4.4	4.0	4.7
Medical and pharmaceutical products	3.0	2.8	4.4
Iron and steel	2.4	3.3	3.0
Animal and vegetable oils and fats	1.8	3.1	1.7
Miscellaneous manufactured goods	1.6	2.1	2.5
Other	5.4	4.9	5.2
Total (billions US$)	3.2	3.6	4.6

Source: Statistics Iceland, http://www.statice.is.

Endnotes

[1] *Njal's Saga* (New York: Penguin Books, 1960), p. 233.

[2] "Reading the Book of Life; White House Remarks on Decoding of Genome," *The New York Times*, June 27, 2000, p. F8.

[3] Nicholas Wade, "Now the Hard Part: Putting the Genome to Work," *The New York Times*, June 27, 2000, p. F1.

[4] Sharon Begley, "Decoding the Human Body," *Newsweek*, April 10, 2000, p. 50.

[5] James Shreeve, *The Genome War: How Craig Venter Tried to Capture the Code of Life and Save the World* (New York: Alfred A. Knopf, 2004), pp. 40–42.

[6] Ibid., pp. 14–16, 362; Matt Ridley, *Genome: The Autobiography of a Species in 23 Chapters* (New York: Harper Collins, 1999), pp. 4–10.

[7] Shreeve, *The Genome War*, pp. 13–26.

[8] Ibid., p. 369.

[9] Organization for Economic Cooperation and Development, "OECD Economic Surveys: Iceland, 1998" (Paris: OECD, 1998), pp. 1–10.

[10] Karen Van Kampen, *The Golden Cell: Gene Therapy, Stem Cells, and the Quest for the Next Great Medical Breakthrough* (Toronto: HarperCollins Publishers Ltd., 2005), p. 59.

[11] Michael Specter, "Decoding Iceland," *The New Yorker*, January 18, 1999.

[12] Ingrid Wickelgren, *The Gene Masters: How a New Breed of Scientific Entrepreneurs Raced for the Biggest Prize in Biology* (New York: Henry Holt and Co., 2002), pp. 113–128.

[13] deCODE Genetics 2000 10K (Reykjavik: deCODE Genetics, 2000), http://www.decode.com, accessed January 2006.

[14] Kári Stefánsson, author interview, Reykjavik, October 21, 2004.

[15] *Act on a Health Sector Database no. 139/1998* (Reykjavik: Ministry of Health and Social Security, 1998), http://eng.heilbrigdisraduneyti.is/laws-and-regulations/nr/65, accessed January 2006.

[16] Wickelgren, *The Gene Masters*, p. 128.

[17] Stephanie Overby, "Iceland's Dilemma: Privacy vs. Progress," *CIO Magazine*, July 15, 2001.

[18] Ibid.

[19] Mannvernd, "What Is Mannvernd?" http://www.mannvernd.is/english/aboutmv.html, accessed November 3, 2005.

[20] Andy Coghlan, "Selling the Family Secrets," *New Scientist*, December 5, 1998.

[21] Bogi Andersen and Einar Arnason, "Iceland's Database is Ethically Questionable," *British Medical Journal* 318 (June 5, 1999): 1565.

[22] John Schwartz, "With Gene Plan, Iceland Dives into a Controversy," *International Herald Tribune*, January 13, 1999.

[23] Kári Stefánsson, author interview, Reykjavik, October 21, 2004.

[24] Colin Woodard, "Putting a Price on Icelanders," *San Francisco Chronicle*, October 23, 2000, p. A6.

[25] Specter, "Decoding Iceland."

[26] Icelandic health official, author interview, Reykjavik, September 30, 2005.

[27] Ehsan Masood, "Gene Warrior," *New Scientist*, July 15, 2000, p. 42.

[28] Author interview, Reykjavik, September 30, 2005.

[29] Specter, "Decoding Iceland."

[30] Richard Lewontin, "People Are Not Commodities," *The New York Times*, January 23, 1999.

[31] Andy Coghlan, "Viking Wars," *New Scientist*, January 9, 1999.

[32] Alison Abbott, "DNA Study Deepens Rift over Iceland's Genetic Heritage," *Nature* 421 (February 13, 2003): 678.

[33] Alison Abbott, "Manhattan Versus Reykjavik," *Nature* 406 (July 27, 2000): 340–342.

[34] Corie Lok, "Translating Iceland's Genes into Medicine," *Technology Review*, September 2004, pp. 58–64.

[35] Icelandic Supreme Court, "Ragnhildur Gudmundsdottir vs. The State of Iceland. No 151/2003," http://www.mannvernd.is/english/lawsuits/Icelandic_Supreme_Court_Verdict_151_2003.pdf, accessed January 2006.

[36] Jocelyn Kaiser, "Population Databases Boom, from Iceland to the U.S.," *Science* 282 (November 8, 2002): 1158–1161.

[37] Eirikur Sigurdsson, author interview, Reykjavik, September 29, 2005.

[38] deCODE Genetics 2002 10K (Reykjavik: deCODE Genetics, 2002); deCODE Genetics 2003 10K (Reykjavik: deCODE Genetics, 2003); http://www.decode.com, accessed January 2006.

[39] Mark Gurney, author interview, Woodridge, IL, December 13, 2005.

[40] Eirikur Sigurdsson, author interview, Reykjavik, September 29, 2005.

[41] Mark Gurney, author interview, Woodridge, IL, December 13, 2005.

[42] Ibid.

[43] Daniel Hartman, author interview, Brighton, MI, December 19, 2005.

[44] Ibid.

[45] Tanya Zharov, author interview, Reykjavik, September 29, 2005.

[46] Kári Stefánsson, author interview, Reykjavik, September 29, 2005.

9-707-030

REV: JANUARY 23, 2007

RAWI ABDELAL

RAFAEL DI TELLA

PRABAKAR KOTHANDARAMAN

Infosys in India: Building a Software Giant in a Corrupt Environment

That land hath store of such. All men are there,
Except Bonturo, barterers: of 'no'
For lucre there an 'ay' is quickly made.

—Dante Alighieri, *The Divine Comedy*, Canto XXI

On July 31, 2006, 3,000 enthusiastic Infosys employees—Infoscions, as they called themselves—waited anxiously for the coming of 7:00 p.m. The Infoscions had gathered in the main quadrangle of the 400-acre Infosys campus in Mysore, a sleepy town in Karnataka. The opening bell of NASDAQ was to be rung remotely from Mysore at the moment that Narayana Murthy, one of the company's founders, and Nandan Nilakeni, the CEO and cofounder, sent their signatures electronically to New York, some 9,000 miles away. NASDAQ's opening bell had been rung remotely only a few times outside of the United States and then amidst the wealth and opulence of London and Davos in the West; not once had the honor been bestowed in the Asia Pacific, much less in a modest town almost halfway around the world. The Infosys website proudly announced, "The World is Flat."[1]

Infosys had indeed come a long way. But it had not always been a smooth ride. Shortly after the firm was founded in 1981, for example, its managers faced a major turning point when they decided to operate without giving in to the petty corruption rife in the Indian economy. To enter the software development business in 1984, Infosys required a mainframe system so that the first line of code could be written and tested. That mainframe system would have to be imported, and the prevailing customs duty on imported hardware was a prohibitive 135%. Fortunately for Infosys, a legal recourse existed: if Infosys guaranteed that the hardware would be used exclusively to generate export revenues, the government would certify the import under its export-guarantee system. Such certified imports were subject to only a 25% duty, and Infosys's managers were happy to confirm that the mainframe qualified. Soon the imported computer arrived at the bonded customs warehouse. The Infosys employee sent to collect the computer submitted the necessary documents and the money for the 25% duty.

The customs official refused to clear the computer, however, until Infosys "took care of him." Any delay would halt the firm's progress completely, and, after all, Infosys had already paid for the computer, a significant expense for the start-up. "Taking care" of the customs official was a typical nuisance, for civil servants were paid poorly. In the past 25 years, while the salaries the Indian government paid to its civil servants rose 10-fold, private-sector compensation increased 100 times. Consequently, a government official's pay was 20 to 40 times lower than that of private-sector employees at comparable levels.[2] Most supplemented their income by extorting money from those who needed their approval. The cost of taking care of such officials tended to be small, although sometimes there were many palms extended. As many Indian executives knew, these costs could eventually add up. Unsure of what to do next, the employee took the problem to his boss, and eventually the matter reached Murthy himself. His decision would define the company.

Corruption in India

To define and identify corruption is not a straightforward task. Corrupt practices promoted by private firms and individuals, for example, are difficult to identify in black and white; as with much else, the world is mostly gray, and the lines between lobbying, relationships, and network, on the one hand, and corruption, on the other, tend to be finely drawn. The demand for corruption, so to speak, is subject to ambiguity and interpretation.

The task is easier when it comes to supply. The World Bank, for example, defines corruption as "the use of public office for private profit."[3] Public officials, who literally represent the people in their roles in governments, are supposed to enforce and interpret a society's legal rules. When those officials seek to extort payments from those private firms and individuals who expect laws and regulations to be enforced, the very legitimacy of the state and its economic system are called into question.

This kind of corruption—the use of public office for private profit—was endemic to the Indian economy throughout the end of the twentieth and beginning of the twenty-first century. Although everyone knew about it, still, corruption in India was not easy to define or measure.

Transparency International, a nongovernmental organization that had taken on the unenviable, almost hopeless, task of combating world corruption, published measures of corruption in each country derived from surveys of business managers and other people with local institutional knowledge. Alas, India ranked 88th in a recent Transparency International survey. Another study that evaluated 159 countries found that India scored 2.9 out of a possible 10 on its standard of cleanliness.[4] At the top of the list were Sweden, Finland, and New Zealand. At the bottom were countries such as Myanmar, Turkmenistan, Bangladesh, and Chad (see **Exhibit 1**). Karnataka, the Indian state where Infosys was headquartered, was 17th on a list of 20 (20 being the most corrupt) that were taken up for detailed study by the local Transparency International chapter (see **Exhibit 2**). India's judiciary, tax authority, and land administration were regularly included among the more corrupt branches of government. This was particularly true for Karnataka (see **Exhibit 3**).

The sources of India's problem with corruption were, of course, the subject of vigorous, almost endless debate. Some observers, and many Indians, preferred to blame colonial rule.[5] Others pointed to corrupt practices dating to centuries earlier.[6] Others pointed to the lack of competition in the economy or the lack of monetary incentives for good behavior through low bureaucratic wages.[7] Regardless of the source, widespread corruption was simply a fact of life for firms operating in India.

Some firms in India sought, perhaps inevitably, not simply to abide India's corruption but to use its susceptibility to corruption to their advantage. The variety of corrupt practices was, therefore, extraordinary. While some managers simply accepted these practices, thereby implicitly condoning and perpetuating them, others actually caused more corruption by taking advantage of their ability to buy influence over laws, regulations, and their interpretation. This kind of capture was altogether another league of corruption, by design rather than acquiescence. One manager's pragmatism and realism was another manager's soul being sold to Mephistopheles. A few firms, like Infosys, tried to find some space in the Indian economy in which they might be allowed to flourish apart from all of the difficult trade-offs to which executives usually had to concede one principle here, another there. Among the other firms that had cultivated a reputation for cleanliness and for never paying bribes were the venerable Tata Group, including Tata Consulting Services, and Wipro, which, like Infosys, also exported software.[8]

The Story of Infosys

Like many start-up companies, Infosys began modestly. In 1981, Narayana Murthy and six other professionals founded Infosys Consultants Pvt. Ltd. in Pune, 120 miles southeast of Mumbai. Murthy had just quit as general manager of a computer company in Mumbai and was getting ready to embrace his entrepreneurial dreams for the second time in his life. He had done it once previously, chucking his career as a researcher without much success. This time, Murthy's lack of capital was acute. Eventually he turned to Sudha Murthy, who enjoyed a flourishing career in the leading Indian industrial house of Tata and had managed to save a significant amount of money, certainly by middle-class Indian standards. Sudha Murthy was interested in the success of the new firm, and the investment would be her first, a sort of venture capitalism.

Sudha Murthy was an ideal investor, not least because she was Narayana Murthy's wife. Sudha loaned Narayana 10,000 rupees (Rs.) (about $250) and gave him three years to succeed and repay the loan. Like any good venture capitalist, Sudha Murthy played a variety of roles in the new firm— making administrative decisions, writing code, and, in the hard-working late nights of those early years, feeding people with her fine, and much appreciated, cooking.[9] The family members of the other founders also supported these early, challenging efforts. With no infrastructure, no clients, and very little money, Infosys got by on determination during those years. Almost every failed start-up company began with that same determination, and so Infosys would ultimately need something else to help it succeed. Infosys needed a strategy, tactics, corporate values, and, of course, a break.

The break came in 1983 when a Bangalore-based sparkplug manufacturer, Motor Industries Co. Ltd. (MICO), a member of the Bosch Group in Germany, signed them up for its computing needs. In the same year, Infosys moved to Bangalore. The rest of the decade saw the company try out several businesses and business models that included a foray into software product development for bank automation, manufacturing on electronic private automatic exchange (EPABX, a telephone system for an office environment), and manufacturing automation solutions. By the end of the 1980s, the founders began to realize that their promising venture was losing its primary focus—software development. Consequently, the company sold its non-software-related business. During the same period, the company also began to use an innovative way to develop and deliver software for its clients cost-efficiently. Until then, other Indian software companies executed the bulk of their software projects end-to-end at overseas locations. Infosys attacked this value chain and creatively disaggregated it to enable the bulk of code writing to be carried out in Bangalore. The company had pioneered a "global delivery model" with a mix of on-site and offshore technical professionals numbering approximately 100. In an era of unsophisticated communication where wait time for a land-line telephone connection in India ran into several months, Infosys even delivered source code on magnetic computer storage tape to on-site professionals using courier. Later it also used fax for the same purpose.

For many firms, the serious challenges of the Indian institutional environment were compounded during the early 1990s by one of the country's worst-ever economic crises. With a fiscal deficit of 8.5% of gross domestic product (GDP), a current account deficit of 3.1%, and enough foreign exchange reserves to cover only two weeks' worth of imports, the Indian government was forced to abandon its development strategy of import substitution.[10] Perhaps paradoxically, a policy package designed to insulate the economy from balance-of-payments crises seemed often to produce precisely those crises. And this disaster led to a fundamental break with the past.[11]

Prime Minister PV Narasimha Rao turned to Manmohan Singh to head the finance ministry and find a new path for economic development. Singh accepted the mandate and undertook an extraordinarily far-reaching collection of policies to liberalize the economy both domestically and internationally. The plan entailed, in many ways, a radical break with the previous state-led development strategy based on the Soviet model, with planned production in many sectors, import substitution, and an extensive system of permits for production. He did away with licensing in many sectors and announced policies designed to encourage Indian companies to export and thus earn foreign exchange. The software industry was identified as a priority, and the government established well-defined, exclusive software parks with duty-free imports. A liberal tax holiday for export revenues was also established. Foreign exchange restrictions were eased. And a major devaluation of the currency—22% against the U.S. dollar—was a boon to exporters.

Although the crisis and liberalization wreaked havoc on those firms that had become steadily less efficient behind the myriad protections of the import-substitution regime, for Infosys both the devaluation and the liberalization presented an excellent opportunity. Indeed, the Infosys that the world has come to know—immensely profitable, highly globalized—was made possible by this fundamental break with the past. Infosys expanded its market presence in the United States and entered the European market. The company quickly opened its first overseas sales office in Boston in 1992. Infosys grew rapidly, indeed at a pace that was twice the industry average. Infosys managers took the company public in 1993 and resolved to continue the business practices that had made the firm so distinctive. Among those practices was the commitment of Infosys management to refuse any transaction that even hinted at corruption.

By the turn of the century, everything had, it seemed, gone even better than the original plan. Infosys had done astonishingly well (see **Exhibits 4a** and **4b** for comparative performance vis-à-vis competitors), and its managers believed that they had also been good: transparency and fairness remained the foundations of its corporate governance. The Indian government agreed, awarding its own corporate governance award to Murthy in 2000. Infosys had shown to the rest of the world that no matter where one's country sits in corruption ratings, it is possible to build a profitable, respectable, transparent, and socially responsible global business. By the time Murthy stepped down as chairman on August 17, 2006, the company employed 62,000 people of over 50 different nationalities and had revenue of over $2 billion with a market capitalization of over $21 billion.[12]

Managing Around Corruption

Before all that, indeed before Infosys was really Infosys, the start-up was faced with the challenge of reconciling its commitment to transparency, honesty, and fairness to an environment that rewarded opacity and expediency. The very entry of Infosys into the software development business was challenged by an eager customs official, and Murthy had to decide how to proceed. This first, and serious, test was threatening both financially and politically.

Murthy spoke with near total recall of the situation that was to set the firm on a path of great consequence. "My first and only question to this executive," Murthy noted, "was: What is the alternative to paying a bribe?" The manager replied, "Clear the consignment at the full level of 135% duty and go on appeal." Murthy did not hesitate. Then, he announced, "We will do just that."[13]

Doing just that was, alas, easier said than done, for the financial impact was huge. The start-up was obliged to pay for the mainframe, itself a significant capital expenditure, and then another 135% of the cost, with only the slimmest of chances of recovering that additional cash. It was as though it had bought a mainframe for more than double what its competitors paid. Still, Infosys paid the duty, cleared the consignment, and simultaneously appealed the decision.

Three arduous years later, the company finally received a settlement in its favor in New Delhi. Although the appeal was settled behind closed doors in the upper echelons of the Indian judiciary, Infosys knew that its embrace of transparency would be vindicated by a potentially harassment-free political and bureaucratic environment. For the fledgling company, the financial effect had been significant indeed. With litigation costs and the opportunity cost of the duty paid sitting for three years in government coffers, the effective result was that Infosys paid substantially for its principles in that one case. That initial stance turned into a policy. CFO V. Balakrishnan observed, "Whenever there is a dispute regarding payments to the government, our policy is to pay up and fight hard in appeal."[14]

Infosys managers were convinced that their steadfastness would benefit them in the longer term, however. The first benefit was a reputation for intransigence that preceded Infosys managers' visits to customs officials. Murthy noted, "We have had zero trouble with customs since then."[15] The episode also represented a powerful signal to employees; when in doubt, Murthy himself would back them when they chose, per company policy, the hard way. Even when it would be easier, even when everyone else did it, Infosys would just "say no to bribes."[16]

According to Infosys executives, who regularly repeated the company mantra, the prospect of losses or cost disadvantage vis-à-vis competitors did not deter their enthusiasm and proselytizing. K. Dinesh, another cofounder, argued, "For us, having clean transactions is more important than revenue per se. Further, sticking to values at relevant difficult times, we believe, is the ultimate test of integrity." Dinesh highlighted this idea by referring to another episode that tested not the anti-bribery principle but rather the Infosys commitment to transparency at any cost:

> In 1993 we went public with an IPO. It fetched about Rs. 90–100 Cr [approximately $25 million]. We were holding on to the funds pending approval from the government. As was the practice, we were advised by our financial experts to invest a part of the IPO money in stocks. Unfortunately, within weeks, there was a huge stock market scam, and our invested portfolio suffered heavy losses. When the time came to write the annual report, a look at the law revealed that we were not required to disclose our stock market misadventure. However, the leadership argued that we had taken money from the public and lost it in the stock market, and therefore, in our view, we were ethically bound to disclose it. We refused to buy the argument that it was enough to be merely legally compliant. Many pundits warned us that the investors would punish us heavily if we made a full disclosure at that time. We went ahead anyway and disclosed the entire transaction. To our delight the shareholders took our disclosure as a strong signal of transparency and supported us. To us the message was, "If you disclose this much during difficult times, you would do much better during better times." We have always followed the motto—"when in doubt, disclose."

Although Murthy believed that his example was one to be followed throughout India, he was, typically, reluctant to praise Infosys overmuch. "If at all any credit is due," Murthy observed, "it is only to the extent that we were the first ones to do it and bring it to focus so that the society can understand that it is good for everyone."[17] Other Infosys executives reflected on the initial challenges of such an approach. CEO Nilekani explained, "This approach of putting values first has a high cycle time when it comes to positive business gains and short-term pains; there is invariably a 'hump' in the path. Once you cross it you begin to enjoy lower transaction costs in many of your dealings with all stakeholders; the long-term gains start to kick in."[18]

These so-called humps might manifest themselves in the form of lost opportunity, wasted time, and even measurable financial loss. One experience suggested that not every sector would allow the Infosys model to flourish. Dinesh recalled that the Infosys insistence on going by the book made the company uncompetitive in the market for imported shrink-wrapped software, a market that the firm eventually exited. As Dinesh argued:

> In the 1980s we were importing and distributing Turbo C and other software from Borland International. The prevailing duty structure at that time required us to pay 135% customs duty on software. Some of the players, in order to circumvent the duty burden, used to get split invoices—one for the software, accounting for a mere 5% of the price, and the balance of 95% invoiced as manuals for software. As the duty on books was 0%, duty was levied only on the 5% component. Vendors could substantially reduce the landed cost for the buyer. We refused to follow this practice and stood our ground. Eventually we had to leave that segment.[19]

Although the marketing group, citing competitors' practices at that time and the lack of clarity in the law covering the import of packaged software, worried that it was a mistake to forgo this lucrative market, Murthy and Dinesh won the day.

For Murthy, the underlying principle was that simply following the law was not enough. Even the guiding case, the first experience at the customs office, was not so straightforward in terms of the law. The law in most countries, and indeed the apparently restrictive Foreign Corrupt Practices Act of the United States, did not forbid managers from giving in to extortion when public officials refused to fulfill their duties without extra payment. That is, it was generally not illegal in the United States or in other countries to pay public officials to do what they were already supposed to do.[20] Thus, Murthy argued, neither the laws themselves, nor the probability of detection, were useful guides. "Let's take," Murthy noted playfully, "a hypothetical case":

> I am traveling in a train through Siberia where no one knows me. I see an attractive lady co-traveler in the same compartment. She is open to have a consensual relationship with me. There is no one around. No one gets hurt. However, if I agree [to having a relationship], I would have violated the marital vows that I took with my wife. I don't give in. That to me is a value—something that always stays with you.[21]

The challenge became even more acute when it came to dealing with customers, who, after all, had many choices among Infosys competitors in a cutthroat industry. It was common for kickbacks to accrue to the manager who decided on such contracts. Often, significant amounts of money were at stake. Infosys always promised heartfelt thanks and deep commitment—but nothing else, according to Murthy. Murthy recalled an incident involving the CIO of an overseas company from a developed country:

> This person invited me for dinner to discuss some of the issues related to our bid, which was for over $1 million. During the course of the evening he kept expressing his interest in a particular model of car and said how nice it would be if he got his car. He also followed it up by saying that it would be nice if Infosys got that contract. I said that while it is relatively easy for him to buy his car, it is not so straightforward for me to make sure that my wish for getting that contract is fulfilled, as it involved several unknowns. Twice he repeated his wish by saying how nice it will be if he got his car and Infosys got its contract! I once again wished him the very best. Finally, he decided to be direct and said, "Why don't you pay for that car and I

give you the contract?" Then it dawned on me that he was asking for a bribe. I politely told him we simply didn't do such things. He didn't get his car, but I got my business.[22]

Although some of these episodes did not present clear trade-offs between performance and corruption—after all, the Infosys product was good enough in that case that the contract was won despite Murthy's admirable stubbornness—others highlighted not only the cost of opportunities forgone and funds held up in legal disputes but also that being clean sometimes just cost more. The new Infosys campus was a case in point, as Murthy remembered:

> In 1997 we wanted to expand our campus to match our business growth and were looking for land nearby. Just then we learnt that a buyer was pulling out after agreeing to buy 10 acres of land adjoining our campus from a state government organization. The deal was for Rs. 9.9 lacs/acre, and we approached the organization and offered to buy the land at Rs. 10 lacs/acre.[23] Infosys had by then built a good and clean reputation, and the government was happy to sell the land to us. However, we hit a roadblock when an official that needed to sign the dotted line from the seller's side refused to do so without some personal gratification to the tune of about Rs. 40,000 [about $1,000] per acre. We said no and were promptly threatened with action that would make things difficult for us. The difficulty came in the form of the official whipping up trade union sentiment against the deal by propagating that the organization was undervaluing the land by Rs. 4 lacs/acre [about $10,000] and trying to sell it to Infosys. We explained our offer by pointing to the offer made by a buyer (and agreed to by the seller) barely a week or two prior to our proposal. The official wouldn't give up and continued the accusation. It became a sensitive issue for the government, and we couldn't keep waiting. We decided to end the matter once for all and made a counter offer for Rs. 14 lacs/acre [about $35,000] that took the wind out of the vindictive official's campaign. We lost about Rs. 40 lacs [about $100,000] in the deal but did the deal our way without compromising our values. Later, the official tried to play up the matter in a shareholder meeting, accusing the leadership of squandering away shareholder wealth by agreeing to a 40% premium over market rate for this land deal. That none took the accusation seriously was gratifying to us.[24]

The Infosys strategy created a variety of benefits over the longer term. First, it was believed that corrupt officials tended to approach Infosys managers less frequently, as shown by their later dealings with customs officials subsequent to their initial run-in. Second, the challenge of ensuring that these values permeated the entire organization lessened as the repetition and examples set by senior executives became almost second nature. According to Murthy:

> We have somehow managed to capture a slot of being the poster child of good governance and ethical values. I see that there is widespread acceptance in dealing with us in a clean way, and people tend not to expect any bribes from us. We have paid our price in charting a course that was against prevalent practices. It has been worth it. Our value system has inoculated us from any expectations of bribes, and today our brand is our vaccine against corruption.[25]

And third, the company's image provided cover to firms that sought to prove their cleanliness. According to Nilekani, "Decision makers who want to appear fair find it safe to award contracts to Infosys, as the company is never known to bribe its way through. The individual buyer may also see us as his vaccine against malpractice accusation, and it works in our favor."[26]

The globalization of production had empowered Infosys, but the rise of China, which also benefited handsomely from this process, presented the firm with a significant new challenge. Though it was not often discussed, most executives who did business in China knew that corruption was prevalent. And although the Infosys reputation preceded it in London, New York, and Boston, Beijing and Shanghai were, at least for the moment, indifferent. The company's first foray into China was not encouraging. The decades Infosys had spent on its reputation would have to be repeated. "We will invest in building our reputation as straight shooters as we did in India," argued Srinath Batni, a member of the Infosys Board. "In China, investing companies are often provided with automobile registration plates for their use. Issue of plates is regulated, and hence many companies use them as goodwill currency to curry favor from local officials. We said nothing doing and returned the unused ones to the Chinese government."[27]

The decision essentially to service only its multinational companies' clients' operations in China as part of global delivery contracts with them and refrain from going after business on its own in China was not so dissimilar to the decision to forgo the market for servicing the Indian government. "Our strategy map begins with a different set of factors at the top," explained Sanjay Purohit, head of corporate planning at Infosys (see **Exhibit 5** for Infosys's strategic-planning algorithm). "In our scheme of things, financial goals are subservient to values and ethics. We do not enter global markets or customer segments that are not likely to be in synch with our value system. For instance, we have stayed clear of directly servicing government accounts. This is forgoing approximately 30% of the top line. In China, we only execute jobs for other multinational companies' clients that do business there."[28] Infosys planned to wait until the Chinese environment was compatible with the firm's ethos before investing or competing directly.[29] Similarly, Murthy argued: "Ninety-eight percent of our markets lie outside the country. We don't go to the government for business. In many cases it is the buying power of the government that breeds corruption. We have no manufacturing and hence are outside the purview of domestic duties. Predominantly overseas sales exclude us from paying local sales tax."[30]

Throughout the developing world the difficulties multiplied. Increasingly Infosys was obliged to deal with distributors from the host countries. Still, the company stayed clear of so-called influence peddlers, a common species in international business, whose only ware was the "influence" they exercised in their own domestic markets.

Finally, the central challenge early in the years of the new century was to pass on these values to a new generation of Infosys leaders and managers. This was not an easy task. In 1998, the company charged its top managers to spell the value system out for employees and new recruits. The exercise resulted in a codebook called "C-Life" (see **Exhibit 6**). According to Dinesh, who regularly conducted "value workshops" for managers and new trainees, "C-Life was the result of the recognition that the world is not perfect. People join us from different backgrounds, and we need to not only induct them into a shared world view on ethics and values but also provide them an action path to achieve that world view." This handholding appeared to be critical, as behaviors contrary to the value system were dealt with immediately and visibly. "We believe in compliance both in spirit and in letter," declared Mohandas Pai, a member of the Infosys Board, who pointed out that even a technical violation of insider trading rules by one of the members of the board was punished immediately with a fine of Rs. 500,000 (approximately $11,000). "We even fired a project head for fudging a taxi bill to the tune of 100 Swiss francs [$82]. It was his first offense, and he was crucial for the project, but our policy was one of zero tolerance and he had to go," explained Chandrashekar Kakal, senior vice president and global head of enterprise solutions. In the Indian corporate sector practices such as falsifying medical claims with the connivance of medical practitioners and pharmacists, submitting fake bills to claim a travel allowance with the help of travel agents, and cooking bills to show payment of salaries to drivers were not uncommon, and the government too had taken note of their implications on potential tax revenue losses. Many companies had not taken this malpractice seriously, and only recently had some of the multinational companies begun to crack down on these corrupt practices.[31]

The Future of Corruption in India, the Future of Infosys

The Indian government, for its part, faced an enormous challenge, historically insurmountable, to uproot corruption from its political and economic institutions. "Indians," Transparency International recently concluded, "seemed to be ready to do business by paying bribes or extra payments."[32] To combat the problem, in 2003 the government passed the Central Vigilance Commission Act, which considerably enhanced the status of the commission, theretofore a mere consultative body that had been in existence since 1964. The improved version was headed by a central vigilance commissioner who answered only to the parliament and incorporated a strong "whistle-blower" provision to encourage people to come forward with information on corrupt practices.

The proposal to create anticorruption watchdogs was inspired by Hong Kong's experience with the Independent Commission Against Corruption (ICAC). The creation of such institutions has been supported explicitly by the World Bank, the International Monetary Fund, and the U.S. government. Sometimes, it has even been suggested that some sort of financial conditionality should apply to the creation of these institutions, just as countries unwilling to undertake privatization programs in the past were restricted in their access to lending from the main international organizations. Unfortunately, it was not obvious that such an approach was likely to be effective in other country contexts. The experience of Hong Kong's ICAC, for example, unfolded amidst a variety of other anticorruption policies existing in Hong Kong for decades. Another concern was that the ICAC's effectiveness depended crucially on the amount of power it was given. In the words of one of the ICAC's biggest advocates:

> The new organization was given sweeping powers. All the ICAC needed to arrest someone suspected of corruption was to say that the commissioner had reasons to believe that the suspect had committed an offense. For exceptional cases, ICAC officers had powers of search and seizure without need of a warrant. The ICAC could require any person to provide any information that the commissioner deemed necessary. And the ICAC could issue a restraining order to freeze assets and properties.[33]

The commission had also been increasingly using technology to combat corruption. For instance, it regularly published on its website lists of government functionaries that had been found to be corrupt. It also encouraged affected parties to register complaints of corruption through its website. Its jurisdiction, however, was limited to government functionaries, departments, and corporations. Further, the commission could only investigate and render advice. It was then left to the government to penalize or prosecute the concerned individual, a duty that it did not always perform.[34] Thus, it was much inferior to the more effective ones such as in Singapore and Hong Kong where the implementation machinery was backed by strong political will.[35] In fact, the ICAC was located in the prime minister's office complex in Singapore, which underscored the seriousness accorded to corruption by the Singapore government.[36] More recently, in 2005, the parliament of India passed the Right to Information Act (similar to the U.S.'s Freedom of Information Act), which gives the common man the right to access information of public interest. The act laid down the process by which to obtain information and had a chief oversight officer for each of the state governments as well as the central government. Although nine Indian states had already enacted such laws in the past, the public had little faith in them, since the penalty for noncompliance was not specified. For instance, since 2001 there were only 14,000 applications for information filed with the government in Delhi, as opposed to 2.3 million filed in the United States during 2003–2004 alone. The law in India specified he penalty for noncompliance and required that the fines (about $7 per day) for noncompliance be recovered from the personal pay of the designated information official. Appointments to the head of the commission were from the bureaucracy, and early indications were that corrupt bureaucrats did not covet the position. Although it was too early to say whether those appointed to implement the act were being seen as politically biased, the government had come under criticism from all quarters of society in its recent attempts to exclude recommendations by bureaucrats known as "file notings" associated with government records from the ambit of public scrutiny.

Early indications were that the act had helped to reduce corruption.[37] Supplementing the government's efforts were many nongovernmental organizations that engage in fighting corruption.[38] TI India (the local chapter of Transparency International) was one such entity. Alas, these seemed to be only first steps toward a more comprehensive management of the problem. Indians paid out Rs. 210 billion ($4.64 billion), or 1% of the country's GDP, in bribes in 2004, a figure Murthy often quoted.[39]

Murthy hoped that Indian managers might be able to combat corruption by changing their own practices. Murthy urged upon India's new business leaders the appropriate mind-set. Upon their graduation, Murthy told a group of seniors in a management school in Bangalore that differing circumstances might require different tactics but not different ethics. "Set your compass in the direction of fairness," Murthy urged.[40]

Within Infosys itself, Murthy and his colleagues sought to institutionalize their practices, to make them second nature to the firm's increasingly far-flung, diverse enterprise. And the challenge was magnified by the *ad hoc* evolution of the plan itself. "We didn't set out to build Infosys in such a way that it will fight corruption and excel in transparency and corporate governance. It just turned out that way. It has evolved into more than what we anticipated," explained Nilekani.[41] For Murthy, the Infosys stance could not be merely a matter of choice. Authenticity was required. "It cannot be part of strategy," argued Murthy, "it has to be second nature."[42] Authenticity had its personal rewards. "To me," Murthy suggested, "a clear conscience is the softest pillow that one can hope for to get a good night's sleep."[43]

Exhibit 1 Transparency International Country Corruption Index, 2005

Country Rank	Country	2005 CPI Score[a]	Confidence Range[b]	Surveys Used[c]
1	Iceland	9.7	9.5 - 9.7	8
2	Finland	9.6	9.5 - 9.7	9
	New Zealand	9.6	9.5 - 9.7	9
4	Denmark	9.5	9.3 - 9.6	10
5	Singapore	9.4	9.3 - 9.5	12
6	Sweden	9.2	9.0 - 9.3	10
7	Switzerland	9.1	8.9 - 9.2	9
8	Norway	8.9	8.5 - 9.1	9
9	Australia	8.8	8.4 - 9.1	13
10	Austria	8.7	8.4 - 9.0	9
11	Netherlands	8.6	8.3 - 8.9	9
	United Kingdom	8.6	8.3 - 8.8	11
13	Luxembourg	8.5	8.1 - 8.9	8
14	Canada	8.4	7.9 - 8.8	11
15	Hong Kong	8.3	7.7 - 8.7	12
16	Germany	8.2	7.9 - 8.5	10
17	United States	7.6	7.0 - 8.0	12
18	France	7.5	7.0 - 7.8	11
19	Belgium	7.4	6.9 - 7.9	9
	Ireland	7.4	6.9 - 7.9	10
21	Chile	7.3	6.8 - 7.7	10
	Japan	7.3	6.7 - 7.8	14
23	Spain	7.0	6.6 - 7.4	10
24	Barbados	6.9	5.7 - 7.3	3
25	Malta	6.6	5.4 - 7.7	5

Country Rank	Country	2005 CPI Score[a]	Confidence Range[b]	Surveys Used[c]
26	Portugal	6.5	5.9 - 7.1	9
27	Estonia	6.4	6.0 - 7.0	11
28	Israel	6.3	5.7 - 6.9	10
	Oman	6.3	5.2 - 7.3	5
30	United Arab Emirates	6.2	5.3 - 7.1	6
31	Slovenia	6.1	5.7 - 6.8	11
32	Botswana	5.9	5.1 - 6.7	8
	Qatar	5.9	5.6 - 6.4	5
	Taiwan	5.9	5.4 - 6.3	14
	Uruguay	5.9	5.6 - 6.4	6
36	Bahrain	5.8	5.3 - 6.3	6
37	Cyprus	5.7	5.3 - 6.0	5
	Jordan	5.7	5.1 - 6.1	10
39	Malaysia	5.1	4.6 - 5.6	14
40	Hungary	5.0	4.7 - 5.2	11
	Italy	5.0	4.6 - 5.4	9
	South Korea	5.0	4.6 - 5.3	12
43	Tunisia	4.9	4.4 - 5.6	7
44	Lithuania	4.8	4.5 - 5.1	8
45	Kuwait	4.7	4.0 - 5.2	6
46	South Africa	4.5	4.2 - 4.8	11
47	Czech Republic	4.3	3.7 - 5.1	10
	Greece	4.3	3.9 - 4.7	9
	Namibia	4.3	3.8 - 4.9	8
	Slovakia	4.3	3.8 - 4.8	10
51	Costa Rica	4.2	3.7 - 4.7	7

Country Rank	Country	2005 CPI Score[a]	Confidence Range[b]	Surveys Used[c]
	El Salvador	4.2	3.5 - 4.8	6
	Latvia	4.2	3.8 - 4.6	7
	Mauritius	4.2	3.4 - 5.0	6
55	Bulgaria	4.0	3.4 - 4.6	8
	Colombia	4.0	3.6 - 4.4	9
	Fiji	4.0	3.4 - 4.6	3
	Seychelles	4.0	3.5 - 4.2	3
59	Cuba	3.8	2.3 - 4.7	4
	Thailand	3.8	3.5 - 4.1	13
	Trinidad and Tobago	3.8	3.3 - 4.5	6
62	Belize	3.7	3.4 - 4.1	3
	Brazil	3.7	3.5 - 3.9	10
64	Jamaica	3.6	3.4 - 3.8	6
65	Ghana	3.5	3.2 - 4.0	8
	Mexico	3.5	3.3 - 3.7	10
	Panama	3.5	3.1 - 4.1	7
	Peru	3.5	3.1 - 3.8	7
	Turkey	3.5	3.1 - 4.0	11
70	Burkina Faso	3.4	2.7 - 3.9	3
	Croatia	3.4	3.2 - 3.7	7
	Egypt	3.4	3.0 - 3.9	9
	Lesotho	3.4	2.6 - 3.9	3
	Poland	3.4	3.0 - 3.9	11
	Saudi Arabia	3.4	2.7 - 4.1	5
	Syria	3.4	2.8 - 4.2	5
77	Laos	3.3	2.1 - 4.4	3

Country Rank	Country	2005 CPI Score[a]	Confidence Range[b]	Surveys Used[c]
78	China	3.2	2.9 - 3.5	14
	Morocco	3.2	2.8 - 3.6	8
	Senegal	3.2	2.8 - 3.6	6
	Sri Lanka	3.2	2.7 - 3.6	7
	Suriname	3.2	2.2 - 3.6	3
83	Lebanon	3.1	2.7 - 3.3	4
	Rwanda	3.1	2.1 - 4.1	3
85	Dominican Republic	3.0	2.5 - 3.6	6
	Mongolia	3.0	2.4 - 3.6	4
	Romania	3.0	2.6 - 3.5	11
88	Armenia	2.9	2.5 - 3.2	4
	Benin	2.9	2.1 - 4.0	5
	Bosnia and Herzegovina	2.9	2.7 - 3.1	6
	Gabon	2.9	2.1 - 3.6	4
	India	2.9	2.7 - 3.1	14
	Iran	2.9	2.3 - 3.3	5
	Mali	2.9	2.3 - 3.6	8
	Moldova	2.9	2.3 - 3.7	5
	Tanzania	2.9	2.6 - 3.1	8
97	Algeria	2.8	2.5 - 3.3	7
	Argentina	2.8	2.5 - 3.1	10
	Madagascar	2.8	1.9 - 3.7	5
	Malawi	2.8	2.3 - 3.4	7
	Mozambique	2.8	2.4 - 3.1	8
	Serbia and Montenegro	2.8	2.5 - 3.3	7
103	Gambia	2.7	2.3 - 3.1	7

Country Rank	Country	2005 CPI Score[a]	Confidence Range[b]	Surveys Used[c]
	Macedonia	2.7	2.4 - 3.2	7
	Swaziland	2.7	2.0 - 3.1	3
	Yemen	2.7	2.4 - 3.2	5
107	Belarus	2.6	1.9 - 3.8	5
	Eritrea	2.6	1.7 - 3.5	3
	Honduras	2.6	2.2 - 3.0	7
	Kazakhstan	2.6	2.2 - 3.2	6
	Nicaragua	2.6	2.4 - 2.8	7
	Palestine	2.6	2.1 - 2.8	3
	Ukraine	2.6	2.4 - 2.8	8
	Vietnam	2.6	2.3 - 2.9	10
	Zambia	2.6	2.3 - 2.9	7
	Zimbabwe	2.6	2.1 - 3.0	7
117	Afghanistan	2.5	1.6 - 3.2	3
	Bolivia	2.5	2.3 - 2.9	6
	Ecuador	2.5	2.2 - 2.9	6
	Guatemala	2.5	2.1 - 2.8	7
	Guyana	2.5	2.0 - 2.7	3
	Libya	2.5	2.0 - 3.0	4
	Nepal	2.5	1.9 - 3.0	4
	Philippines	2.5	2.3 - 2.8	13
	Uganda	2.5	2.2 - 2.8	8
126	Albania	2.4	2.1 - 2.7	3
	Niger	2.4	2.2 - 2.6	4
	Russia	2.4	2.3 - 2.6	12
	Sierra Leone	2.4	2.1 - 2.7	3

Country Rank	Country	2005 CPI Score[a]	Confidence Range[b]	Surveys Used[c]
130	Burundi	2.3	2.1 - 2.5	3
	Cambodia	2.3	1.9 - 2.5	4
	Congo, Republic of	2.3	2.1 - 2.6	4
	Georgia	2.3	2.0 - 2.6	6
	Kyrgyzstan	2.3	2.1 - 2.5	5
	Papua New Guinea	2.3	1.9 - 2.6	4
	Venezuela	2.3	2.2 -2.4	10
137	Azerbaijan	2.2	1.9 - 2.5	6
	Cameroon	2.2	2.0 - 2.5	6
	Ethiopia	2.2	2.0 - 2.5	8
	Indonesia	2.2	2.1 - 2.5	13
	Iraq	2.2	1.5 - 2.9	4
	Liberia	2.2	2.1 - 2.3	3
	Uzbekistan	2.2	2.1 - 2.4	5
144	Congo, Democratic Republic	2.1	1.8 - 2.3	4
	Kenya	2.1	1.8 - 2.4	8
	Pakistan	2.1	1.7 - 2.6	7
	Paraguay	2.1	1.9 - 2.3	7
	Somalia	2.1	1.6 - 2.2	3
	Sudan	2.1	1.9 - 2.2	5
	Tajikistan	2.1	1.9 - 2.4	5
151	Angola	2.0	1.8 - 2.1	5
152	Cote d'Ivoire	1.9	1.7 - 2.1	4
	Equatorial Guinea	1.9	1.6 - 2.1	3
	Nigeria	1.9	1.7 - 2.0	9
155	Haiti	1.8	1.5 - 2.1	4

Country Rank	Country	2005 CPI Score[a]	Confidence Range[b]	Surveys Used[c]
	Myanmar	1.8	1.7 - 2.0	4
	Turkmenistan	1.8	1.7 - 2.0	4
158	Bangladesh	1.7	1.4 - 2.0	7
	Chad	1.7	1.3 - 2.1	6

Explanatory notes

[a]**CPI score** relates to perceptions of the degree of corruption as seen by businesspeople and country analysts and ranges between 10 (highly clean) and 0 (highly corrupt).

[b]**Confidence range** provides a range of possible values of the CPI score. This reflects how a country's score may vary, depending on measurement precision. Nominally, with 5% probability the score is above this range, and with another 5% it is below. However, particularly when only a few sources (n) are available, an unbiased estimate of the mean coverage probability is lower than the nominal value of 90%.

[c]**Surveys used** refer to the number of surveys that assessed a country's performance. Sixteen surveys and expert assessments were used, and at least three were required for a country to be included in the CPI.

Source: Compiled from Transparency International, www.transparency.org.

Exhibit 2   Corruption Ranking of States in India

RANKING OF STATES

STATE	COMPOSITE INDEX	RANK
Kerela	240	1
Himachal Pradesh	301	2
Gujarat	417	3
Andhra Pradesh	421	4
Maharashtra	433	5
Chattisgarh	445	6
Punjab	459	7
West Bengal	461	8
Orrisa	475	9
Uttal Pradesh	491	10
Delhi	496	11
Tamil Nadu	509	12
Haryana	516	13
Jharkhand	520	14
Assam	542	15
Rajasthan	543	16
Karnataka	576	17
MP	584	18
J & K	655	19
Bihar	695	20

Source: Compiled from Transparency International—CMS Study 2005.

Note: Higher score = more corruption.

Exhibit 3   Ranking of Corruption Index of Basic Services in India

NATURE OF INTERFACE	COMPOSITE INDEX	RANK
NEED BASED		
RFI[a] (Farmers)	22	1
Income Tax (Individual Assessors)	35	2
Municipal Services	47	3
Judiciary	59	4
Land administration	59	5
Police (Crime/Traffic)	77	6
BASIC		
Schools (Up to 12th)	26	1
Water supply	29	2
PDS (Ration Card/Supplies)	37	3
Electricity (Consumers)	39	4
Govt. Hospitals	42	5

Source: Compiled from Transparency International—CMS Study 2005.

Note: Higher score = more corruption.

[a] RFI = rural financial institution.

Exhibit 4a Infosys's Comparative Performance with an Indian Peer Group

Return on Equity					
Company Name	2001	2002	2003	2004	2005
Cognizant Tech Solutions	22.43	20.89	20.93	22.10	23.28
Infosys Technologies -ADR	38.84	31.13	28.35	33.44	30.21
Satyam Computer Svc Ltd -ADR	7.00	17.32	17.65	20.02	25.08
Wipro Ltd -ADR	34.20	23.92	27.47	30.83	34.76
HCL Technologies Ltd	25.99	19.25	10.78	26.07	17.97
Return on Assets					
Company Name	2001	2002	2003	2004	2005
Cognizant Tech Solutions	15.29	14.93	15.91	17.50	19.11
Infosys Technologies -ADR	31.81	27.67	23.87	28.82	26.86
Satyam Computer Svc Ltd -ADR	5.02	14.02	15.67	17.39	21.11
Wipro Ltd -ADR	27.41	19.81	18.31	22.61	24.66
HCL Technologies Ltd	22.82	16.40	8.80	19.59	14.31

Source: Standard & Poor's Research Insight and Bloomberg, accessed January 5, 2007.

Exhibit 4b Infosys's Comparative Performance with a Global Peer Group

Return on Equity					
Company Name	2001	2002	2003	2004	2005
Accenture Ltd	308.103	55.832	62.734	46.937	55.423
Computer Sciences Corp	9.469	9.556	9.437	7.643	8.521
Electronic Data Systems Corp	21.517	14.341	-4.41	-3.965	3.807
Infosys Technologies -ADR	38.838	31.129	28.345	33.44	30.212
Return on Assets					
Company Name	2001	2002	2003	2004	2005
Accenture Ltd	14.344	4.47	7.714	8.649	10.499
Computer Sciences Corp	3.966	4.219	4.4	3.929	4.458
Electronic Data Systems Corp	8.482	5.334	-1.379	-1.663	1.674
Infosys Technologies -ADR	31.813	27.668	23.873	28.817	26.864

Source: Standard & Poor's Research Insight, accessed January 5, 2007.

Exhibit 5   Infosys Strategic-Planning Algorithm

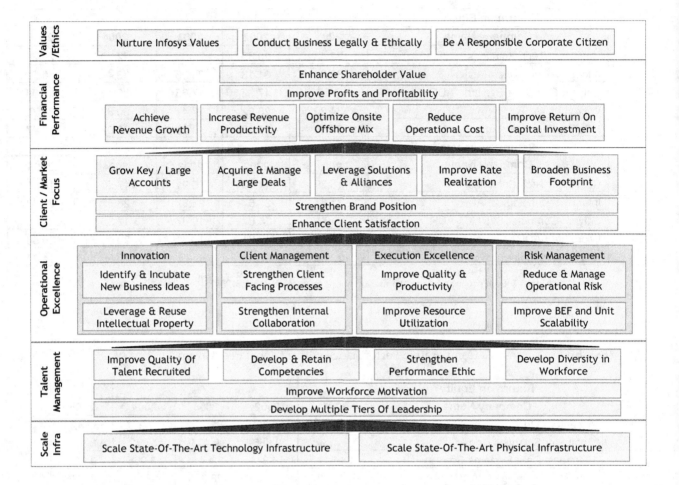

Source: Infosys.

Exhibit 6   C-Life @ Infosys

C-Life @ Infosys	Values	Vision	Definitions	Business Conduct
C	Customer Delight	A commitment to surpassing our customers' expectations	We will surpass our customers' expectations of competence, performance, delivery schedules and value for money such that they take pride in ownership of Infosys products and Infosys becomes their 'natural choice' for repeat business.	Delight moves beyond customer satisfaction and it is important that our commitment to customer delight be demonstrated in our interactions with our customers. At Infosys, we believe that the ambition to surpass expectations requires the courage to change acceptable norms, redefine boundaries, and the will to go the extra mile. It calls for sustained effort throughout the relationship, it needs a certain obstinate perseverance to excel and surprise, sometimes in the face of scarce resources, or stretch goals.
			We will endeavor to raise our level of service to our internal as well as external customers to an extent whereby we continuously set standards for others in the areas we work in and the industry as a whole.	Customer Delight becomes a core value when all of us involved in every aspect of the business become active contributors to the process. It begins with you and the standard for customer service excellence that you set for yourself and others. Over time, our level of service will raise the bar and what was once "Delight" will become "Norm" and the exciting adventure will begin all over again.
L	Leadership by Example	A commitment to set standards in our business and transactions and be an exemplar for the industry and our own teams	We will be a role model for our stakeholders by continuously striving to raise and set benchmarks in our area of business, in our commitment to society and in the growth of our people.	Leadership is both: action and being. Leadership empowers, motivates and organizes people to achieve a common objective. Leaders are able to show the way for many - in principle rather than in detail - by a consistent and creative interpretation of situations, actions, information and by example. We hope Infosys can be continually transformed by each one's commitment. We know that each Infoscion can earn trust and commitment from their peers, teams and managers by setting an example, by ensuring our words and our actions are congruent.
			We will encourage an environment where we walk-the-talk and we achieve our objectives through discipline, commitment and fair play so that personal accountability and credibility become paramount features in any transactions.	Accountability for achieving the task, taking risks, accepting bottom-line responsibility for success or failure can motivate our teams, enhance trust, boost credibility and can prepare the ground for fresh ideas and path-breaking work. Discipline, fair play and dogged commitment can hone our leadership skills and these are the tools to enthuse, organize, achieve and show the way. " To show the way by going first" captures the courage expressed in action that is essential to leadership.
I	Integrity and Transparency	A commitment to be ethical, sincere and open in our dealings	We will transact with our stakeholders with integrity, honesty and appropriate levels of transparency and our actions will stand the test of society we operate within.	The word integrity comes from the word integer, meaning "one" or wholeness. Integrity and transparency are essential building blocks of trust and respect. Integrity is the inner voice, the source of self-control. When a person has integrity, his/her actions match his/her words. Transparency is the action that indicates trust and sharing. Life presents us with difficult choices and sometimes there is great gain in taking the easy, convenient or dishonest road. Our sense of honor, our conscience and our sense of right have to be nurtured to be able to put up a spirited fight at these times.
			We will demonstrate our ethical standards in the information that we disseminate, the practices and conduct that we adopt.	Each time we fail to do what we know is right, our self-respect diminishes. Each time we compromise in a situation to be "agreeable and go along" to fit in or choose a path that will not stand up to scrutiny, we have given up some of our freedom and honor. At Infosys, we feel that it is important to demonstrate our commitment to this value through what we say and what we do - whether it is in our interactions with each

C-Life @ Infosys	Values	Vision	Definitions	Business Conduct
				other or with society. We hope that each Infoscion will provide him/herself and the team enough support to be able to take the right decisions or make the right choice.
F	Fairness	A commitment to be objective and transaction-oriented, thereby earning trust and respect	We will be impartial, rational and unbiased in our dealings with our stakeholders and society such that we earn their trust and respect to enable us to foster a long-term relationship.	While some situations and decisions are clearly unfair, fairness usually refers to a range of morally justifiable outcomes. Disagreeing parties tend to maintain that there is only one fair position (their own, naturally). Fairness begins with the suspension of personal prejudice (whether towards a person or issue). Once done, we move towards the exploration of data and facts to arrive at a decision.
			We will be transaction-oriented in our dealings to ensure that we are unprejudiced and our disagreements and perceptions do not blind us to facts.	In Infosys, this translates to approaching each transaction with a fresh perspective and not let disagreements and gossip spill over and threaten the basis of collaboration or decision making. Every level of work calls for this astute practice, be it a fresh engineer who is required to work in a team consisting of people who have differing views and life experiences or a manager who is required to take people decisions with relation to rewards, ESOP, recognition, promotions and resources. The reliance of data, objective reasoning and rationale are weapons that can be used towards being fair and appearing so.
E	Pursuit of Excellence	A commitment to strive relentlessly to constantly improve ourselves, our teams, our services and products so as to become the best	We will inculcate the spirit and will to excel in all spheres of our business and interactions with people by fostering continuous learning and leveraging this knowledge.	The pursuit of excellence has an evolving dimension. It supposes that the pursuit is continuous and any level attained forms the building block for the next. At Infosys, we hope we have the courage to leap into space with conviction, explore uncharted territory, take risks boldly, learn from failure, get up and dust ourselves each time we fall and fail, and persist with the quest for bigger, better, faster, more.
			We will promote an ongoing effort to excel by providing an atmosphere where innovation, initiative, change and result-orientation are encouraged and lauded.	We hope each of us has the strength to seize change by the horns and expose ourselves to ambiguity, chaos, structure, order or any uncertainty that it might bring. We hope we have the vision to learn and teach others through our successes as well as failure. The pursuit of excellence requires a brave heart and humility to constantly take stock of one's limitations. Individuals to whom this value is important would have to possess the child-like quality of wonder and the wisdom to put to practice before moving towards a more challenging horizon.

Source: Company records.

Endnotes

[1] "Infosys rings Nasdaq opening bell from Mysore," *Rediff News*, July 31, 2006.

[2] "India must pay for good governance," *The Hindu Business Line,* June 23, 2006.

[3] "Helping countries combat corruption: The role of the World Bank," PREM, World Bank, Washington, D.C., September 1997.

[4] Transparency International website, available at http://www.transparency.org/policy_research/ surveys_indices /cpi/2005.

[5] V. Gangadhar, "Roots of Corruption," *The Hindu, Magazine: Slice of Life,* June 6, 2004.

[6] N.Vittal, "Fighting Corruption: Moral Values Must Prevail," *The Tribune, India: Tasks Ahead,* Special Edition, September 24, 2005.

[7] See Susan Rose-Ackerman, *Corruption and Government: Causes, Consequences, and Reform* (Cambridge, UK: Cambridge University Press, 1999), as well as Jakob Svensson, "Eight Questions about Corruption," *Journal of Economic Perspectives* 19, no. 5 (2005): 19–42. On competition, see Rafael Di Tella and Alberto Ades, "Rents, Competition and Corruption," *American Economic Review* 89, no. 4 (1999): 982–994. On the role of bureaucratic wages, see Rafael Di Tella and Ernesto Schargrodsky, "The Role of Wages and Auditing during a Crackdown on Corruption in the City of Buenos Aires," *Journal of Law and Economics* 46, no. 1 (2003): 269–292.

[8] For an excellent account of the evolution of high-quality corporate governance, including resistance to petty corruption in the Indian software industry, see Tarun Khanna and Krishna G. Palepu, "Globalization and Convergence in Corporate Governance: Evidence from Infosys and the Indian Software Industry," *Journal of International Business Studies* 35, no. 6 (2004): 484–507.

[9] Sudha Pillai, " Interview with Sudha Murthy," *Savvy*, August 2000, pp.26–27.

[10] Indian government website, available at http://indiabudget.nic.in/es2005-06/chapt2006/chap62.pdf.

[11] Richard H.K. Vietor, Waleed J. Iskandar, and Max L. Weston, "India (A)," HBS No. 793-112 (Boston: Harvard Business School Publishing, 1993).

[12] Company website.

[13] Interview with Narayana Murthy.

[14] Interview with V. Balakrishnan.

[15] Interview with Narayana Murthy.

[16] Ibid.

[17] Ibid.

[18] Interview with Nandan Nilekani.

[19] Interview with K. Dinesh.

[20] Robert E. Kennedy and Rafael di Tella, "Corruption in International Business (A)," HBS No. 791–128 (Boston: Harvard Business School Publishing, 1991).

[21] Interview with Narayana Murthy.

[22] Ibid.

[23] Approximately $25,000/acre (10 lacs= 1 million).

[24] Interview with Narayana Murthy.

[25] Interview with Narayana Murthy.

[26] Interview with Nilekani.

[27] Interview with Srinath Batni.

[28] Interview with Sanjay Purohit.

[29] Interview with Batni.

[30] Interview with Narayana Murthy.

[31] Sujit John, "Intel (India) fires 250 employees," *The Times of India*, September 21, 2005.

[32] "India World Leader in Greasing Palms," *The Times of India*, October 5, 2006.

[33] Robert Klitgaard, *Controlling Corruption* (Berkeley: University of California Press, 1988), p. 108.

[34] 2004 Annual Report of the CVC, available at http://www.cvc.nic.in.

[35] John S.T. Quah, "Curbing Asian Corruption: An Impossible Dream?" Stanford University's Asia-Pacific Research Center website, available at http://iis-db.stanford.edu/pubs/21128/Corruption_article_in_CH.pdf.

[36] Jeremy Pope, "The Need for, and the Role of, an Independent Anti-Corruption Agency," Transparency International (TI) Working Paper, August 13, 1999.

[37] "Drive Against Bribe Campaign with RTI," Right to Information website, available at http://www.ndtv.com/rti/genboard/impact.asp.

[38] S.D. Sharma, "Mobilizing Civil Society: NGO Initiatives to Fight Corruption and Promote Good Governance in the Indian Context," *Asian Review of Public Administration* 12, no. 1 (January–June 2000): 57–73.

[39] "Corruption pervades in all institutions," *The Hindu Business Line*, December 12, 2005.

[40] "Graft Robbed 3.2M Children of Education," *The Times of India*, July 10, 2005.

[41] Interview with Nilekani.

[42] Interview with Narayana Murthy.

[43] Ibid.

JULIO J. ROTEMBERG

The Dubai Ports World Debacle and its Aftermath

In September 2006, the House-Senate Conference Committee members charged with the new foreign investment bill were likely to have a profound effect on the international business landscape. After the upheaval caused by DP World's attempt to become the manager of some port terminals in the U.S., the House and Senate had each passed bills governing how foreign investments were supposed to be screened to protect national security. While each bill had passed unanimously, the two bills were quite different. The stakes were captured by Representative Carolyn Maloney (Democrat – New York) who said, "After the Dubai Ports fiasco, the American people demanded a better process for ensuring that foreign investment does not threaten national security. The [House] Bill strengthens the CFIUS process and strengthens our country's protections but does not chill safe foreign investment, which provides American jobs and helps our economy." [1]

The underlying questions were: how much additional scrutiny was required to protect national security and to what extent would this extra scrutiny deter foreign direct investment? The House Bill was regarded as "weaker" than the Senate Bill and had the support of the U.S. Chamber of Commerce and the Business Roundtable. The Senate bill, which involved the possibility of longer reviews and of more congressional oversight of foreign acquisitions, was dubbed "The Don't Invest in America Act" by the *Wall Street Journal*. In crafting a bill that would be sent to both the House and Senate for approval, the Conference Committee members had to consider the positions adopted by House and Senate members in previous debates, the history of foreign investment in the United States and, particularly, the lessons that needed to be drawn from the DP World case.[2]

DP World bids for the U.S. assets of P&O

News that DP World was interested in acquiring London-based Peninsular and Oriental Steam Navigation Company (P&O) first broke in October 2005.[3] P&O had once been a major steamship company and still operated some ferries in the United Kingdom. However, after recent divestitures of a variety of businesses including the Princess Cruise line, it was mainly a ports operator. Its port operations were so vast that this acquisition would lead DP World to move from being the sixth to being the world's fourth largest container port operator measured by throughput (behind Hutchinson Whampoa of Hong Kong, the Port of Singapore Authority (PSA) and APM Terminals, which belonged to Moller-Maersk of Denmark). In 2005, the combined throughput of P&O and DP

World was equal to about 36.6 million TEU (TEU means twenty foot equivalent units - a standard twenty foot container equals 1 TEU while a forty foot container equals 2 TEU) .[4]

P&O's management had recommended that its shareholders approve DP World's initial bid of $5.8 billion. However, the Singapore government-owned PSA also had ambitions to grow further, and made a rival bid of $6.3 billion on January 26, 2006. DP World responded with a $6.8 billion bid that same day and P&O's shareholders agreed to this offer on February 13. In the meantime, DP World secured approval by the Committee on Foreign Investments in the United States (CFIUS). A CFIUS panel chaired by Deputy Treasury Secretary Robert Kimmit had unanimously allowed the deal to proceed on January 17. Among the 12 agencies and departments represented in the panel were members of the Departments of Defense, State, Justice and Homeland Security. [5] If any of the panelists had officially objected, a mandatory 45 day investigation would have been required, and the President of the United States would have had to decide whether to approve the deal or not.

Dubai Ports World and its Owner

DP World was owned by the government of Dubai and was formed in 2005 by the merger of a government-owned company (DPI International) with international operations and the Dubai Ports Authority, which ran the ports in Dubai. The Dubai Ports Authority had been enormously successful in transforming Dubai's two ports into the most important shipping destination in the Arabian Gulf. Dubai's Sheik Rashid had ordered both these ports, Port Rashid and Jebel Ali, to be dredged from the sandy coastline before there was demand for their services. Nonetheless, the ports' efficiency and customer service had ensured spectacular growth in traffic.[6]

The stated mission of DP World was to export its efficiency and customer service know-how to the rest of the world. One transaction that made this intention clear, and catapulted DP World into the sixth largest port operator in the world, was its acquisition in January 2005 of the port operations outside the United States of U.S.-based CSX Corporation. DP World thereby gained operations in China, Australia, Germany, the Dominican Republic and Venezuela. The P&O deal would have complemented these operations because P&O also had a substantial portfolio of ports in China.

In addition, P&O had some container terminals in the five ports of Baltimore, Miami, New Orleans, New York-New Jersey and Philadelphia. Collectively, these P&O terminals had a container throughput of about 2.2 million TEU in 2005 when total container throughput at U.S. ports was about 40 million TEU.[7] The acquisition of these terminals would represent the first foray of DP World in the United States. Their contribution to P&O's bottom line was relatively modest, however. According to the *Wall Street Journal*, these U.S. ports contributed only about 10.2% of the $276 million in profits reported by P&O's port operations in 2004.[8]

After its P&O acquisition, DP World continued its expansion abroad. Its projects under development in the middle of 2006 included large ports in India, Peru and South Korea [see **exhibit 2** for a list of DP World's actual and planned operations at the time].

The operation of ports played a large role in Dubai itself. Dubai was part of the United Arab Emirates (UAE), a fairly loose confederation of seven emirates. The leaders of these emirates had considerable autonomy, particularly because they controlled their own revenue. In the case of the largest and richest of these emirates, Abu Dhabi, this revenue consisted mainly of oil. While Dubai was the second most populous emirate, oil represented only about 6% of its GDP. Its emphasis, instead, was on attracting global businesses and tourism. For this purpose it opened several "free zones" where foreign companies could do business without being subject to the restrictions that applied in the rest of the country. These free zones had attracted both high technology and financial services firms, including many that were based in the United States.

Like Singapore, with which Dubai's development strategy was often compared, Dubai had built a very large and successful airport. The government of Dubai also owned Emirates Airline, which had been instrumental in converting the Dubai airport into an important international hub. In addition, government-owned companies had invested heavily in construction and were responsible for iconic projects like "The Palm Islands" and Burj al-Arab, the world's tallest hotel.

Non-citizens constituted about 80% of Dubai's resident population of 1.2 million. Thus, a large fraction of the managers and technical personnel working inside Dubai's gleaming new buildings as well as of the construction workers erecting these buildings in the scorching heat came from abroad. Similarly, most key executives at DP World were foreigners. Its Chief Operating Officer at the time of the P&O acquisition, Edward H. Bilkey, was born in the United States. The members of DP World's managerial team in mid-2006, along with some of the background, are shown in **Exhibit 3**.

One of the aims of Dubai was to provide a peaceful and safe haven amidst the tension-ravaged Middle East. And, since Iraq's invasion of Kuwait, the UAE had embraced close relations with the United States. A symbol of this relationship was UAE's purchase of 80 F-16 Desert Falcons in 2000.[9] In 2006, the United States government repeatedly declared that Dubai and UAE were staunch allies. For example, a White House news release of February 22, 2006 stated

"The UAE is a key partner in the war on terror. The UAE provides U.S. and Coalition forces unprecedented access to its ports and territory, overflight clearances, and other critical and important logistical assistance. Today, the UAE is providing assistance to the missions in Afghanistan and Iraq...

UAE ports host more U.S. Navy ships than any port outside the United States. The UAE provides outstanding support for the U.S. Navy at the ports of Jebel Ali - which is managed by DP World – and Fujairah and for the U.S. Air Force at al Dhafra Air Base (tankers and surveillance and reconnaissance aircraft). The UAE also hosts the UAE Air Warfare Center, the leading fighter training center in the Middle East.

The UAE is a partner in shutting down terror finance networks. The UAE has worked with us to stop terrorist financing and money laundering, including by freezing accounts, enacting aggressive anti-money-laundering and counter-terrorist financing laws and regulations, and exchanging information on people and entities suspected of being involved in these activities."[10]

President Bush also praised Dubai for its cooperation in efforts to stop the proliferation of nuclear weapons. It had, in particular, recently joined the U.S. sponsored Megaports initiative to install equipment to detect radiation and share the resulting information. Other observers, on the other hand, emphasized that Dubai may have served as a hub for nuclear trades in the past. Abdul Qadeer Khan, a Pakistani scientist who trafficked in nuclear equipment, was said to have used Dubai as an entrepot. There were also accusations that, in 2003, Dubai had refused to intercept a shipment of nuclear material bound for South Africa.[11]

A Furious Reaction Stops the Deal

After P&O shareholders approved the DP World deal, objections were raised in the United States. Senator Charles Schumer (Democrat – New York) was one of the earliest and most vocal critics. On

February 14, 2006, he said, "Foreign control of our ports, which are vital to homeland security, is a risky proposition. Riskier yet is that we are turning it over to a country that has been linked to terrorism previously." Al Qaeda had used Dubai-based intermediaries to funnel funds to the 9/11 terrorists, two of which were from the UAE. Moreover, until September 21, 2001, the UAE has been one of only three countries to recognize the Taliban government in Afghanistan (along with Pakistan and Saudi Arabia).

The deal gained prominence among lawmakers in part due to the lobbying efforts of a Florida firm, Eller & Co. An Eller subsidiary was a partner of P&O in its Florida operations and was involved in a contractual dispute with P&O. Its lobbyists first tried to raise objections to the DP World acquisition in front of CFIUS, on the ground that it would lead Eller to "become involuntarily a business partner with the government of Dubai." When CFIUS ignored these pleas, Eller's lobbyists circulated in Congress a white paper that emphasized security concerns. Here, they were more successful. According to a spokesman for Senator Schumer, Eller "was really the canary in the mineshaft for many people on the Hill and in the media."[12]

In the second half of February, politicians and newspaper editorials extensively criticized the deal. The Port Authority of New York and New Jersey as well as the Port of Newark sought to have the sale blocked and several suits were filed to accomplish this. At a protest against the deal organized by teamsters (the truckers' union) and longshoremen (members of the union of workers engaged in the unloading of ships), Senator Frank Lautenberg (Democrat - New Jersey) said, "Don't let them tell you that it's just a transfer of title. Baloney. We wouldn't transfer the title to the devil, and we're not going to transfer it to Dubai."[13]

The most common complaint about the deal was that it endangered port security, an issue discussed more fully below. In addition, individuals who tended to criticize the business connections of the Bush administration pointed to the relationship between Treasury Secretary John Snow and DP World. Until February 2003, Snow had been CEO of CSX, a company that later sold its foreign terminal operations to DP World.[14]

While on a fact-finding tour of ports, Senate majority leader Bill Frist (Republican – Tennessee) threatened to pass a law to put the deal on hold unless the White House initiated a more thorough 45-day CFIUS "investigation." Meanwhile, the Governors of Maryland and New Jersey sought to scuttle the deal altogether, and several members of Congress introduced legislation to this effect. President Bush, on the other hand, threatened to veto any bill blocking the sale. President Bush had never actually vetoed any act of Congress, but his occasional veto threats had been effective in shaping legislation. The President also sent aides to explain the rationale for the DP World deal to the Republican leadership in Congress. "If there was any chance that this transaction would jeopardize the security of the United States, it would not go forward," he said in a press release. At the same time, DP World sought to sway Congress by retaining former Senator Robert Dole and the lobbying firm belonging to former Secretary of State Madeleine Albright.[15]

On February 27, DP World itself requested a 45-day CFIUS investigation. By then, however, several lawmakers were asking for more. Senator Schumer, in particular, said, "We still believe that the report also has to go to Congress, that as much of it as possible ought to be public and that we would have the right of disapproval."[16]

The strongest opposition, however, came from House Republicans who had heretofore supported most of President Bush's initiatives. On March 7, Jerry Lewis (Republican – California), the chairman of the House Appropriations Committee said, "It is my intention to lay the foundation to block the deal." And the next day, his committee approved by a vote of 62 to 2, an amendment blocking the DP

World transaction. This amendment was attached to an emergency appropriations bill designed to cover the costs of Hurricane Katrina and the war in Iraq.

This lopsided vote among Representatives reflected the attitude of the American public. In a Gallup poll conducted between February 28 and March 1, 66% of Americans opposed the deal, with 45% being strongly opposed. The vast majority of Americans saw the sale as posing a threat to national security, with 39% seeing it as a "major threat," and 36% viewing it as a "minor threat." Only 16% felt that the deal posed "no threat at all". Moreover, awareness of the issue seemed very high, with 73% of respondents saying they had followed the issue either "very closely" or "somewhat closely."[17]

The poll also revealed that Americans cared about the nationality of port operators. Only 26% of respondents thought that "the federal government should not allow companies" from Great Britain "to own cargo operations at U.S. ports," while 71% thought that the government should allow this. In the case of companies from France, from "Arab countries that are friendly to the United States," and companies from China, the fraction wishing to ban foreign ownership was 50%, 56% and 65% respectively.[18]

Many defenders of the deal argued that the opponents were not drawing a sufficiently sharp distinction between Dubai/UAE and other Arab states that were less friendly to the United States. Paul Krugman, on the other hand, blamed the Bush administration for having blurred this type of distinction. He wrote, "The administration successfully linked Iraq and 9/11 in public perceptions through a campaign of constant insinuation and occasional outright lies. In the process, it also created a state of mind in which all Arabs were lumped together in the camp of evildoers."[19]

On March 9, DP World capitulated. It announced that, based on a decision by the ruler of Dubai, Sheikh Mohammed bin Rashid al Maktoum, it would "transfer" its U.S. operations to a "US entity."[20] Several commentators in Dubai deplored this outcome. In a column published in Dubai-base Gulf News, political scientist Abdul Khaleq Abdullah wrote, "People, businesses as well as the government in the UAE are deeply offended as a result of the ports deal fiasco. People across the UAE are angry at the extent to which their open and moderate country has been demonized by the American media and lawmakers in Washington."[21]

Later in March, DP World's director of operations for Europe and Latin America David Sanborn withdrew his nomination to head the U.S. Maritime Administration. Senators Kerry (Democrat – Massachusetts) and Nelson (Democrat – Florida) had planned to hold up the retired Naval officer's nomination by asking about Sanborn's role in the DP World acquisition of P&O.[22]

Port Ownership and Security

U.S. ports usually belonged to local governments or to agencies set up by local governments. In some cases, as in the case of the Port Of Savannah, these agencies also operated the ports. More typically, ports allowed private parties to bid for the right to use the "terminals" that handled cargo. The terms of the resulting leases varied, as did the extent to which the loading and unloading equipment belonged to the government agency that ran the port. Particularly in large ports, different terminals were leased to different lessees. The lessees had to find their own customers and had to hire the personnel to load and unload cargo, though they sometimes engaged stevedoring companies for this purpose. Many of the contracts for port operations had been awarded to foreign-owned firms.

Foreign ownership was particularly prevalent in the case of terminals dedicated to containers. In the case of the largest ports (New York-New Jersey and Los Angeles) the fraction of container terminals operated by foreign firms reached about 80%. Los Angeles terminals were managed in part by firms from China, Denmark, Japan, Singapore and Taiwan. One reason for this preponderance of foreign management was that American firms carried less than 3% of U.S. international cargo and many container terminals were operated by shipping lines. Since they were invented around 1950, containers represented the fastest-growing form of maritime transportation. By 2006, these containers carried about 66% of U.S. international trade by value.[23]

Containers were "intermodal" in the sense that they could easily be fitted in ships, truck or trains. This allowed transit times to be reduced and facilitated just-in-time production. Containers were also difficult to inspect quickly. As of the April 2006, only about 5% of containers bound for the United States were opened and inspected either in the United States or abroad.[24]

This low inspection rate was often mentioned by people who were concerned with port security. Such concerns were widely expressed after the 9/11 Commission recommended that U.S. port security be strengthened. Two particularly terrifying scenarios were the explosion of a "dirty bomb" at a large port and the use of U.S. ports to import a nuclear device that would be exploded elsewhere.

In defending the DP World deal, the Bush Administration reiterated that port security was principally the responsibility of two federal agencies, the Coast Guard and Customs, which were part of the Department of Homeland Security. Customs was nominally in charge of the cargo entering the United States while the Coast Guard was in charge of ships and ports. As part of its responsibility over ports, the Coast Guard was supposed to approve the security plans of individual port operators, who would then be responsible for security within the area in which they operated. In practice, responsibility for security was also shared with local and port authorities. According to the Department of Homeland Security, the resulting confusion over responsibility had delayed the adoption of a cargo security plan.[25]

There were also disputes concerning the funding of Customs and the Coast Guard. While $18 billion had been spent securing airports from September 11, 2001 to April 2006, only $630 million had been spent on enhancing port security. Senator Barbara Mikulski (Democrat – Maryland) and Senator Daniel Inouye (Democrat – Hawaii) were particularly vocal in arguing that funding had been insufficient. Senator Inouye said, "[The Bush administration] has consistently submitted inadequate funding requests and has routinely missed critical security deadlines that were required by law."[26] On the other hand, opponents of increased funding argued that companies involved in shipping as well as local authorities needed to share the burden of paying for these security measures.

The Bureau of Customs hailed two programs aimed at improving U.S. security. The first of these was called the Container Security Initiative (CSI) and involved an arrangement with 42 foreign ports – including ports in Dubai. Ports that were party to this arrangement allowed U.S. Customs inspectors to inspect containers before they boarded ships bound for the United States. U.S. Customs was supposed to receive information about these containers at least 24 hours before they were loaded, so that it could target riskier containers for inspection. The Government Accountability Office (GAO) criticized this program for not being sufficiently thorough. The GAO complained that important foreign ports were not part of CSI and that many containers that were deemed to be risky were not inspected until they reached the United States.[27]

Customs' second program, the Customs-Trade Partnership against Terrorism (C-TPAT), was an arrangement between Customs and importers. Importers that agreed to secure their entire supply chain were promised expedited treatment. About 10,000 importers participated, accounting for about 70% of U.S.-bound cargo. The GAO nonetheless criticized this program as well because the supply chains of only about 1300 importers had been checked. Moreover, the vast majority of the 400,000 importers that brought goods into the United States did not participate.[28]

One source of trepidation concerning container security was that stowaways had been discovered on several occasions, and at least one stowaway had been linked to terrorism. An aspect of containers that may have facilitated this practice is that containers routinely included cargo belonging to more than one customer. In any event, both defenders and attackers of existing security procedures used an episode in which stowaways were apprehended in Seattle to illustrate their point of view.[29]

On April 4, 2006, 22 Chinese stowaways were in a container at the Seattle harbor. On the basis of information in the container's manifest, the container had been set aside for inspection (but not inspected at Shanghai, which was a CSI port). Since the container was scheduled to be inspected only days after its arrival, the stowaways had time to leave it. A private security guard nonetheless saw them at the terminal and arrested them.[30]

Several new technologies were being pursued to speed up and reduce the costs of inspections. One of these technologies involved the use of tracking devices in containers to ensure that they were not tampered with. In 2002, Hutchinson Whampoa and PSA financed an experimental deployment of these devices in the sea lanes between Singapore, Hong Kong and Seattle. Another technological effort, this one pioneered by the Port of Hong Kong, tried to screen all containers for nuclear materials. At one point, Senator Schumer sought to introduce legislation demanding that all cargo bound for the U.S. be inspected with this type of equipment. The Hong Kong technology had been developed by DP World which, along with Hutchinson Whampoa was seeking to become a supplier of these services.[31]

Technological solutions did seem to have their limitations, however. In 2006, the GAO reported two tests in which disguised GAO agents had succeeded in importing nontrivial quantities of nuclear material into the United States. In both cases, Customs recognized the material to be radioactive, but nonetheless allowed it to go through on the basis of fraudulent manifests.[32]

A Brief History of Security Concerns with Investment in the United States

The Effect of World War I

In 1914, at the peak of the first wave of industrialized globalization, assets owned by foreigners were equal to about 20% of U.S. GDP in 1914. The stock of foreign investment fell in the early War years (1915-1916) although some new investment – including investment by Germans in the chemical industry – arrived in the United States to make up for the difficulties in importing goods by sea. In 1917, the United States entered the War on the Allied side and passed the Trading with the Enemy Act (TWEA).[33]

It did not take long for President Wilson to make use of the provisions of the law that gave the President broad powers to regulate businesses owned by foreigners. That same year, he nationalized the assets of every business that was owned by Germans or deemed to be indirectly controlled by Germans. These businesses were initially held by a government entity, but were transferred to private U.S. firms after the War ended in 1919. One important beneficiary of this was the U.S. chemical industry, which obtained not only the physical assets of firms such as Bayer but also intellectual property rights over patents previously held by German firms.[34]

Other pieces of legislation also reflected national security concerns with foreign investment. Under the influence of the Navy, Congress passed a series of laws forbidding foreigners from holding certain assets. The Navy's fear that wireless communication devices could be used to pass secrets to enemies was reflected in the Radio Act of 1927. This law specified that radio licenses (and thus telecommunications assets)

> "shall not be transferred in any manner, either voluntarily or involuntarily, to (a) any alien [non-U.S. citizen] or the representative of any alien; (b) to any foreign government, or the representative thereof; (c) to any company, corporation, or association organized under the laws of any foreign government; (d) to any company, corporation, or association of which any officer or director is an alien, or of which more than one-fifth of the capital stock may be voted by aliens or their representatives or by a foreign government or representative thereof, or by any company, corporation, or association organized under the laws of a foreign country."

The Navy, concerned with ensuring that the United States would have access to a sufficient number of civilian ships and airplanes in case of war., also pushed for the "Jones Act." This required that American-built and American-owned ships be used for transportation between U.S. ports. It also lobbied for a law requiring that flights between points in the United States be the exclusive province of U.S.-registered airplanes. And, to register a plane in the United States, one had to be either a United States citizen or a corporation that was controlled by Americans. In this case, such control was deemed to be present if the president and two thirds of the corporations' officers were American citizens and if no more than 25% of the corporation's voting stock was held by foreigners.[35]

The Exon-Florio Amendment

In spite of these restrictions, and in spite of further nationalizations of German assets during World War II, foreign direct investment (FDI) both into and out of the United States grew in the second half of the 20th century (see **Exhibit 4**). Comfort with FDI did not grow apace. Unease over FDI into the United States became particularly marked in the second half of the 1980s, when a weak dollar encouraged substantial Japanese acquisitions of U.S. assets. The proposed acquisition of Fairchild Semiconductor by Fujitsu was even compared to "selling Mount Vernon to the Redcoats". While Fujitsu relented in the face of political opposition, Congressional leaders wished to create a mechanism that would facilitate the blocking of problematic transactions.

Senator Jim Exon (Democrat – Nebraska) thus proposed legislation that would allow multiple federal agencies to request a 45-day investigation by the Secretary of Commerce. This investigation would study whether a foreign acquisition would affect "national security" or "essential commerce" and allow the President to block such acquisitions. The "essential commerce" criterion was attacked as too broad and as endangering FDI into the United States. What survived, after much wrangling, was the Exon-Florio amendment to the Defense Procurement Act of 1950. This amendment, which was passed in 1988, instituted a review process for foreign acquisitions with potentially negative national security implications.[36]

The Exon-Florio Amendment allowed either firms or government agencies to request that CFIUS initiate a 30-day "review" of the national security implications of any acquisition that would give foreigners control over U.S. assets. Since the amendment offered no definition of what constituted a national security threat, a broad reading was possible. The CFIUS panel that carried out these reviews consisted of members of the 12 government agencies listed in **Exhibit 5**, and was chaired by the Department of the Treasury. If any of the panelists found the transaction troublesome, the law required CFIUS to conduct a 45-day "investigation" and write a report containing its conclusions. After receiving this report, the President had 15 days in which to decide whether to block the transaction (or force a divestment).[37]

In October 1992, the "Byrd Amendment" further strengthened these requirements by directing "the President (or his designee) to make an investigation in any instance in which an entity controlled by or acting on behalf of a foreign government seeks to engage in any merger, acquisition, or takeover which could result in the control of a person engaged in interstate commerce in the United States that could affect U.S. national security." Several lawmakers felt that this provision compelled an investigation in the DP World case since this transaction "could affect national security."[38]

In the period from 1988 to 2005, nearly 1600 transactions (representing about 10% of foreign acquisitions) had been reviewed by CFIUS. Of these, 25 transactions had been investigated, and the President blocked just one transaction. Critics argued that this showed the ineffectiveness of CFIUS, with journalist Lou Dobbs calling it "a remarkable rubberstamp organization."[39]

The single negative Presidential decision was made by President George Bush in 1990. He forced government owned China National Aero-Technology Import and Export Company (Catic) to divest itself of aircraft parts manufacturer Mamco, which it had recently acquired. Mamco's president had expected this transaction to pass muster because Catic already did considerable work on Boeing planes that were assembled in China.[40]

The impact of CFIUS's went beyond the number of transactions blocked by the President. Twelve transactions were withdrawn after CFIUS initiated an investigation and an unknown number of additional transactions were dropped during the review stage (CFIUS did not officially keep track of withdrawals that occurred at this stage). There was also some evidence that CFIUS had grown tougher since 9/11, and particularly since the Department of Homeland Security was added to the panel in 2003. A disproportionate fraction of the investigations through 2005 (6 out of 25) and of the withdrawals (5 out of 13) took place in the period 2003-2005.[41]

One prominent bidder who dropped out in 2003 as a result of trouble with CFIUS was Hutchinson Whampoa, which was seeking to acquire Global Crossing in association with Singapore Technology Telemedia. However, Hutchinson Whampoa faced insistent questions about the closeness of the relationship between its owner, billionaire Li Ka-shing, and the government of China. Rather than face the prospect of having its bid turned down, Hutchinson Whampoa bowed out in favor of its partner.[42]

Nonetheless, critics of CFIUS took issue with some approved transactions. In a press release, Senator Bayh (Democrat – Indiana) complained, "Another example of CFIUS failing to prevent the takeover of a company with national security interests took place in 1995, when the Committee approved the sale of Magnequench, an Indiana-based company responsible for making 80 percent of the magnets used to guide U.S. smart bombs, to a Chinese consortium."[43]

Even when 30-day reviews allowed transactions to go forward, CFIUS often extracted concessions from foreign acquirers and these where recorded in secret "mitigation agreements." In the case of telecommunications acquisitions, these agreements were enforced by being incorporated in FCC licenses. This allowed Edward Graham and David Marchik to study telecommunications agreements in their book *U.S. National Security and Foreign Direct Investment*. They concluded that these agreements varied from acquisition to acquisition and that, in general, foreign acquirers of U.S. telecommunications assets had to comply with tougher conditions after 9/11. In some cases, acquirers were required to place U.S. citizens in key security positions and/or were forbidden from using equipment located outside the United States for communications whose origin and destination was in the United States. Both of these requirements were presumed to help U.S. agencies conduct surveillance activities and to make it harder for foreign governments to learn about these surveillance activities.[44]

A mitigation agreement was also signed between CFIUS and DP World. According to Homeland Security Secretary Michael Chertoff, this agreement actually increased security at U.S. ports and provided a "template" for future security arrangements. According to Chertoff, DP World had agreed to "assist and support federal, state and local law-enforcement agencies" while also being willing to "provide federal agencies with any records in the U.S. involving its foreign operations."[45]

CNOOC's Attempt to Buy Unocal

Even before the DP World deal, Congress had helped stop another foreign acquisition, namely CNOOC's attempted takeover of Unocal. In late June, 2005, CNOOC (the China National Offshore Oil Corporation) had made an unsolicited all-cash offer for Unocal for $18.5 billion. This topped the $16.8 billion cash and shares offer that Chevron had made in April. After PetroChina and Sinopec, CNOOC was the third largest government-owned Chinese company in the energy sector. Like the other two, CNOOC had sought international acquisitions for some time, though none of these companies had scored any major successes.[46]

Unocal's most valuable oil and gas fields were in Thailand, Myanmar and Indonesia, and it also had deep underwater wells in the Gulf of Mexico. Nonetheless, it was not among the top 40 oil and gas producers by size. Even before CNOOC announced its bid, Republican Congressmen from California Richard Pombo (whose district included Chevron's headquarters) and Duncan Hunter wrote a letter in protest to President Bush. "The United States increasingly needs to view meeting its energy requirements within the context of our foreign policy, national security and economic security agenda. This is especially the case with China," they said.[47]

CNOOC quickly sought a CFIUS review and, while it started its campaign for approval by promising to increase its supply of gas to the U.S. market, it also declared that it was willing to give up Unocal's U.S. assets. Unfortunately for CNOOC, CFIUS declined to review the transaction until they felt that Unocal and CNOOC were ready to strike a deal. Meanwhile, opponents seized on SEC filings showing that CNOOC was financing the acquistion with subsidized loans from the Chinese government.[48]

Congressional opposition increased further after the Chinese Foreign Ministry said, "We demand that the U.S. Congress correct its mistaken ways of politicizing economic and trade issues and stop interfering in the normal commercial exchanges between enterprises of the two countries." With polls suggesting that 73% of Americans were opposed to the deal, Congress amended an energy bill to require a 120-day study of Chinese energy needs before the CNOOC purchase could proceed. This led CNOOC to bow out, and Unocal accepted Chevron slightly sweetened bid of $17 billion.[49]

The Changes in the Law Proposed by the House and Senate

By March 15, 2006, the DP World purchase had already inspired lawmakers to introduce 21 bills in Congress. Some of these were narrowly targeted at preventing the acquisition of P&O's U.S. assets but most were considerably broader. Several House and Senate Bills made it illegal for foreign governments to own, lease, manage or operate any U.S. ports. A House Bill introduced by Congressman Duncan Hunter and signed by 13 other Representatives went much further. It did not allow foreigner to own, manage or operate any asset that was deemed to be part of the U.S. "critical infrastructure." In this bill, critical infrastructure was defined as "any system or asset, whether physical or virtual, that is so vital to the United States that the incapacity or destruction of such system or asset would have a debilitating effect on national security, on national economic security, on national public health or safety, or on any combination of those matters."[50]

Rather than legislating new prohibitions, most proposed bills were modifications of the Exon-Florio amendment. In this regard, there were three broad areas of reform. These were changes in the CFIUS process within the departments of the executive; changes in the aims that were given to CFIUS in its deliberations; and changes in the transparency of the process.

Several of the proposed changes in the process were designed to ensure that there would be more "investigations." A GAO report had found that, because firms saw "investigations" as a negative signal and because it was sometimes difficult to complete "reviews" in 30 days, CFIUS had been content to allow firms to withdraw in the middle of the 30-day review period and then reapply later for a new review. Some of the proposed Bills would have made this "stopping of the clock" more difficult and more visible.

Other bills took aim at the central role of the Treasury Department, which chaired the CFIUS process. A GAO report accused Treasury of having an inherent conflict with Exon-Florio because it was both the Department that sought foreign investment in the United States and the Department charged with trying to convince other countries to welcome U.S. investment. While the Secretary of the Treasury kept his chairmanship under both the House and Senate bills, the Secretary of Defense was added as a vice chairman in the latter while both the Secretary of Homeland Security and the Secretary of Commerce became vice chairmen in the former. Because lawmakers were perturbed that the Secretary of the Treasury and the Secretary of Homeland Security claimed to be unaware of the DP World transaction until after it erupted in the media, the House bill required their signatures as well as that of the Secretary of Commerce before any CFIUS review was deemed to be complete.[51]

Several bills sought to clarify what constituted a national security threat. Aside from explicit mention of the importance of protecting "critical infrastructure," some bills also mentioned economic considerations. The Bill approved by the Senate, for example, instructed the Committee to consider "the long term projection of United States requirements for sources of energy and other critical resources and materials" in determining whether a transaction should be stopped.

Lastly, many lawmakers complained that the CFIUS process was not sufficiently transparent. One source of this frustration was that the President had only made reports to Congress when he reached a decision. This meant that Congress had not been given details about the vast majority of transactions. Observers also complained that the President had simply disobeyed the law in failing to submit a report every four years describing, "whether foreign companies or governments have coordinated strategy to acquire U.S. critical technology companies"[52]

While acknowledging that firms were concerned with assuring the confidentiality of the information they provided to CFIUS, lawmakers felt that Congress had a long record of handling confidential information concerning national defense and intelligence activities. They thus felt that they should be entrusted with some CFIUS information as well.

On July 26, 2006, both the House and the Senate unanimously passed their bills to change section 721 of the Defense and Production Act of 1950. The House Bill was called "National Security Foreign Investment Reform and Strengthened Transparency Act of 2006" (or "National Security FIRST") while the Senate's went under the simpler title of "Foreign Investment and National Security Act of 2006". While their aims were similar, they differed in many details.

Both the House and the Senate Bill added the requirement that the Director of National Intelligence (DNI) write a report to CFIUS about every transaction subject to review, but only the

Senate version made the DNI a member of the CFIUS Committee. A controversial aspect of the Senate Bill was that it allowed high-ranking officials to prolong the 30-day "review" for an additional 30 days if more time was needed to complete a review. Many observers feared that these delays would become routine and would have a substantial negative effect on investment.

One aspect of the Senate Bill that was opposed by the administration was that it required that CFIUS reviews be based on an "assessment" of the countries in which acquiring companies were based. The government would be required to develop a system to assess countries on their adherence to nonproliferation controls, on their relationship with the United States (and specifically on their cooperation with counter-terrorism efforts) and on their potential for exporting technologies with military applications to third countries. The Department of State worried that the existence of such a system could hurt diplomatic relations and, in response, the Senate Bill stipulated that this system of country classification should be kept confidential.[53]

The most discussed difference between the House and Senate Bills concerned the extent to which Congress had to be apprised of CFIUS activities. The House required CFIUS to provide Congress with a report at the end of its 45-day investigations. It also demanded extensive semi-annual reports with complete lists of reviews. These reports also had to include discussions of trends and of the mitigation agreements signed by acquiring firms. Extensive reports only needed to be filed annually according to the Senate Bill. On the other hand, the Senate version required that Congress be notified whenever a review was either initiated or completed and whenever an investigation either started or ended.[54]

In *U.S. National Security and Foreign Direct Investment*, Graham and Marchik made three arguments against increasing the information provided to Congress by CFIUS. First, they worried that lawmakers might reveal information to competitors located in their own district. Second, they felt that these disclosures could imperil national security by revealing the concerns of security agencies. Lastly, they feared an increased "politicization" of CFIUS reviews in which "domestic competitors dream up fallacious national security arguments against a foreign acquisition of a U.S. company."[55]

Todd Malan of the Organization for International Investment, an association of U.S. subsidiaries of foreign firms that supported the House Bill complained about the Senate Bill and said "The extra 30-day extension and the really broad congressional notification don't do anything for national security and would have a negative impact on foreign investors." On the other hand, Senate majority leader Bill Frist said the Senate Bill "strikes a careful balance between continuing to welcome this investment and ensuring that Congress has an appropriate role in reviewing transactions that impact our nation's homeland security."[56]

Conclusion

Given the large differences between the House and Senate Bills, the Conference Committee would have to work very hard to reach a consensus. The alternative, of course, was for the Exon-Florio process to remain unchanged. Representative Joseph Crowley (Democrat – New York) seemed to contemplate this prospect with equanimity when he said, "the House wants a good bill, or we will take no bill at all." There was a question, however, whether Congress could face the November 2006 elections without having responded in any way to the DP World debacle.

Exhibit 1   Persian Gulf Region

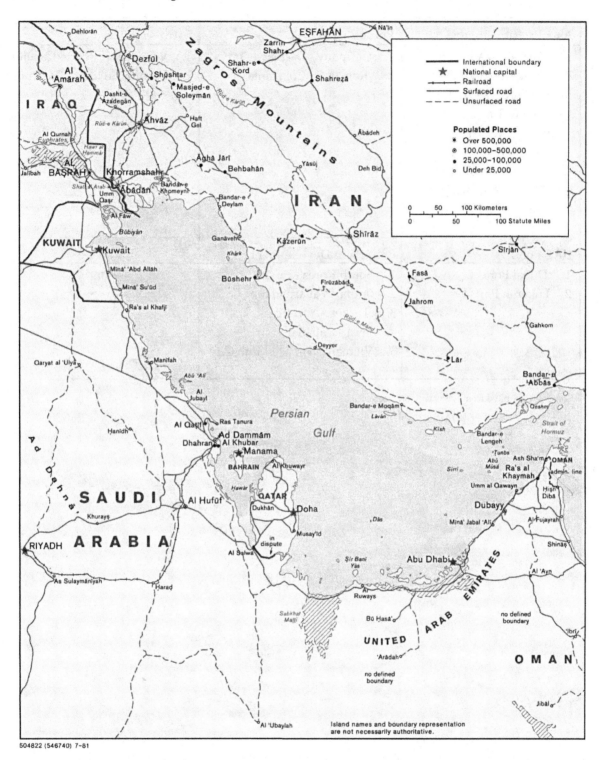

504822 (546740) 7-81

Source: University of Texas.

Exhibit 2   DP World — Operations and Projects in Development as of July, 2006

Asia Pacific	Europe	Latin America
1. Australia - Adelaide 2. Hong Kong - CT3 3. Hong Kong - ACT 4. China - Tianjin 5. China - Yantai 6. Hong Kong - ATL 7. China - ATL Yantian 8. China - Shanghai Ji Fa 9. China - Yantian	1. Germany - Germersheim 2. Romania - Constanta	1. Venezuela - Puerto Cabello 2. Dominican Republic - Puerto Caucedo
UAE Ports	**Projects in Development**	
1. Dubai Port 2. Fujairah Port	1. South Korea - Pusan 2. India - Vallarpadam 3. Turkey - Yarmica 4. Peru - Callao 5. Vietnam - Ho Chi Minh City	

Source: Compiled from www.dpworld.com.

Exhibit 3   DP World Management Team, July 2006 (With information from DP World website)

Mohammed Sharaf - Chief Executive Officer Has worked at the company since 1992, has Executive Degree in Business Administration from the University of Arizona, Tucson.
Anil Wats - Executive Vice President & Chief Operating Officer Before joining DP World in 2003, was CEO for the A.P. Moller group activities for Indonesia. At DP World, was Senior Vice President & Managing Director for the Asia Pacific region.
George Dalton - Senior Vice President - Legal & General Counsel Has JD from Fordham University. Founding partner of Maddy, Dalton & Lion, joined Sea-Land in 1995 as counsel to the North America Terminal Operating Group. Joined CSX World Terminals in 1999 as Vice President and General Counsel.
Matt Leech - Senior Vice President - Business Development MBA from the University of Maryland. Joined Sea-Land in 1995 and was Vice President for Operations and Development at CSX World Terminals.
Michael Moore - Senior Vice President - Sales, Marketing, and Public Relations Joined Sea-Land in 1984. Was Vice President of Global Sales in Europe for 6 years at Maersk.
Yuvraj Narayan - Chief Financial Officer Worked for ANZ group between 1984 and 1997. Was Chief Financial Officer of Salalah Port Services Co.

Source: Compiled from www.dpworld.com.

Exhibit 4   Trends in U.S. Foreign Investment

	Total U.S. owned assets outside the U.S.	Total Foreign holdings of U.S. assets	U.S. owned FDI outside the U.S.	Foreign owned FDI in the U.S.	U.S. GDP
	% of US GDP	% of US GDP	% of US GDP	% of US GDP	billions
1976	25.0%	16.0%	12.2%	2.6%	1,825.3
1977	25.2%	16.8%	12.1%	2.7%	2,030.9
1978	27.1%	18.1%	12.4%	3.0%	2,294.7
1979	30.7%	18.3%	13.1%	3.5%	2,563.3
1980	33.3%	20.4%	13.9%	4.6%	2,789.5
1981	32.0%	21.2%	13.0%	5.3%	3,128.4
1982	34.1%	23.9%	11.5%	5.7%	3,255.0
1983	34.2%	25.8%	10.1%	5.5%	3,536.7
1984	30.6%	26.5%	8.9%	5.7%	3,933.2
1985	30.5%	29.2%	8.8%	5.9%	4,220.3
1986	32.9%	33.7%	9.1%	6.4%	4,462.8
1987	34.7%	36.4%	10.1%	7.1%	4,739.5
1988	35.8%	39.3%	10.1%	7.9%	5,103.8
1989	37.8%	42.5%	10.1%	8.5%	5,484.4
1990	37.5%	41.8%	10.6%	8.7%	5,803.1
1991	38.1%	43.3%	10.7%	8.9%	5,995.9
1992	36.8%	43.6%	10.5%	8.5%	6,337.7
1993	41.4%	46.0%	10.9%	8.9%	6,657.4
1994	42.2%	46.8%	11.1%	8.7%	7,072.2
1995	47.1%	53.3%	12.0%	9.2%	7,397.7
1996	51.6%	57.9%	12.7%	9.5%	7,816.9
1997	55.0%	64.9%	12.9%	9.9%	8,304.3
1998	58.3%	68.5%	13.7%	10.5%	8,747.0
1999	64.5%	72.7%	15.3%	11.9%	9,268.4
2000	63.6%	77.6%	15.6%	14.5%	9,817.0
2001	62.3%	81.2%	16.7%	15.0%	10,128.0
2002	63.5%	83.5%	17.8%	14.3%	10,469.6
2003	69.8%	89.2%	18.8%	14.4%	10,960.8
2004	78.4%	98.6%	20.5%	14.7%	11,712.5
2005	80.4%	102.0%	19.7%	15.0%	12,455.8

Source: U.S. Bureau of Economic Analysis.

Note: investments are valued at cost rather than at market value.

Exhibit 5   Members of CFIUS as of June 2006

The Secretary of the Treasury (chair)
The Secretary of Commerce.
The Secretary of Defense.
The Secretary of Homeland Security.
The Secretary of State.
The Attorney General.
The Chairman of the Council of Economic Advisors.
The United States Trade Representative.
The Director of the Office of Management and Budget.
The Director of the Office of Science and Technology Policy.
The President's Assistant for Economic Policy
The President's Assistant for National Security Affairs.

Exhibit 6   Fraction of responses to the question: "Is your opinion of George W. Bush favorable, not favorable, undecided, or haven't you heard enough about George W. Bush yet to have an opinion?"

	Favorable	Not Favorable	Undecided	No opinion
7/21-25/06	32	50	15	3
5/4-8/06	29	55	13	3
2/22-26/06	29	53	14	4
1/20-25/06	37	48	13	2
12/2-6/05	38	46	11	5
10/30 - 11/1/05	33	51	12	4
1/14-18/05	44	40	14	2
11/18-21/04 *	48	39	10	3
10/28-30/04 *	48	42	8	2
10/14-17/04 *	43	45	11	1
10/9-11/04 *	45	42	12	1
10/9-11/04 *	45	42	12	1
10/1-3/04 *	44	44	10	2
9/20-22/04 *	46	38	14	2
9/12-16/04 *	47	38	14	1
9/6-8/04 *	47	39	12	2
8/15-18/04 *	43	44	11	2
7/30 - 8/1/04 *	40	43	14	3
7/11-15/04 *	41	45	12	2
6/23-27/04 *	39	45	15	1
5/20-23/04 *	36	47	15	2
4/23-27/04 *	38	43	18	1
3/30 - 4/1/04 *	39	42	16	3
3/10-14/04 *	43	39	15	3
2/24-27/04	40	36	18	6
2/12-15/04	44	36	14	6
1/12-15/04	41	38	16	5
12/14-15/03	48	31	17	4
12/10-13/03	44	35	17	4
9/28 - 10/1/03	43	34	13	10
8/26-28/03	46	32	16	6
7/03	46	32	17	5
7/13-16/02	64	21	13	2
8/28-31/01	40	29	17	14
6/14-18/01	37	29	16	18
4/23-25/01	41	26	18	15
4/4-5/01	40	29	13	18
3/8-12/01	42	19	17	22
2/10-12/01	42	24	16	18
12/9-10/00 *	51	35	11	3
11/27-28/00 *	48	37	11	4
11/19/00 *	48	39	10	3

* Indicates poll was conducted among registered voters only.

Source: Adapted from: http://www.pollingreport.com/BushFav.htm.

Based on CBS News/New York Times Poll.

Endnotes

[1] "House Overwhelmingly Approves CFIUS Reform Bill, 424-0," US Fed News, July 26, 2006.

[2] Wall Street Journal, July 19, 2006, p. A12.

[3] Financial Times, FT.com, October 30, 2005.

[4] "Ports in a Storm", Wall Street Journal, February 23, 2006, p. A12., Pedal to the metal, Peter Leach, Journal of Commerce, July 31, 2006; American Association of port Authorities, 2005.

[5] Hot topic, Panel Saw No Security Issue In Port Contract, Officials Say, The New York Times, 23 February 2006.

[6] See HBS Case # 9-603-061: Dubai Ports Authority.

[7] Dewry Shipping Consultants – personal communication.

[8] "Ports in a Storm", Wall Street Journal, February 23, 2006, p. A12.

[9] Hot Topic: Dubai: Business Partner or Terrorist Hotbed?, Wall Street Journal, February 25, 2006, A9, Political Gulf: In Ports Furor, a Clash Over Dubai, Wall Street Journal, February 23, 2006.

[10] White House press release of February 22, 2006 on The United States – UAE Bilateral Relationship.

[11] White House press release of February 22, 2006 on The CFIUS Process and the D World Transaction; Political Gulf: In Ports Furor, a Clash Over Dubai , Wall Street Journal, February 23, 2006.

[12] Small Florida Firm Sowed Seed of Port Dispute, Wall Street Journal, February 28, 2006.

[13] Senators, teamsters and longshoremen protest port takeover by Arab company, Associated Press Newswires, 27 February 2006.

[14] Trouble on the waterfront, The Economist, February 23, 2006.

[15] Frist wants P&O buy blocked, Journal of Commerce, February 21, 2006; Fact Sheet: The CFIUS Process And The DP World Transaction, White House, February 22, 2006; Panel Saw No Security Issue In Port Contract, Officials Say, New York Times, February 23, 2006.

[16] Dubai Deal Will Undergo Deeper Inquiry Security, New York Times, February 27, 2006.

[17] Americans Opposed to Ports Sale to Dubai, Gallup Poll News Service, March 03, 2006.

[18] Americans Opposed to Ports Sale to Dubai, Gallup Poll News Service, March 03, 2006.

[19] Krugman, Paul, Osama, Saddam and The Ports, New York Times, February, 24, 2006.

[20] Under Pressure, Dubai Company Drops Port Deal, The New York Times, March 10, 2006.

[21] Ports Deal: A UAE Perspective, Gulf News, March 17, 2006.

[22] DP World executive's nomination to federal post is withdrawn, Associate Press Newswires, March 27, 2006.

[23] Port Deal: Not a Foreign Idea, Wall Street Journal, March 9, 2006, Port and Maritime Security, Congressional Research Service Report RS31733, May 27, 2005, p. 3.

[24] Democrats Want All Ship Containers Inspected, New York Times, April 26, 2006.

[25] Difficult to Discern Who Runs U.S. Ports, Associated Press Newswires, February 23, 2006.

[26] Senator Mikulski responds to Bush speech at Port of Baltimore, US Fed News, July 20, 2005; Difficult to Discern Who Runs U.S. Ports, Associated Press Newswires, February 23, 2006. One program that was delayed

beyond its planned launch date was the issuance of biometric security cards to all individuals who were allowed to work in ports. The Maritime Transportation Security Act of 2002 mandated these cards.

[27] Port and Maritime Security, Congressional Research Service Report RS31733, May 27, 2005, p. 11, Seattle case shows port security risk, The Seattle Times, April 24, 2006.

[28] Seattle case shows port security risk, The Seattle Times, April 24, 2006.

[29] Ibid.

[30] Ibid.

[31] Seattle, Tacoma to test port-security program, The Seattle Times, July 12, 2002; Schumer's Dubai Deal, The Washington Times, May 11, 2006.

[32] United States Government Accountability Office, Report 06-939T, Border Security: Investigators Transported Radioactive Sources Across Our Nation's Borders at Two Locations, July 2006.

[33] Graham, Edward M. and David M. Marchick, US National Security and Foreign Direct Investment, Institute for International Economics, p. 1-4.

[34] Ibid, p. 5-6.

[35] Graham, Edward M. and David M. Marchick, US National Security and Foreign Direct Investment, Institute for International Economics, p. 12.

[36] Amendment to Increase Presidential Power Sen. Exon, Baldrige Disagree on Foreign Takeover Limits, The Omaha World-Herald, June 11, 1987; Graham, Edward M. and David M. Marchick, US National Security and Foreign Direct Investment, Institute for International Economics, p. 42-46.

[37] US Code of Federal Regulations, Section 31 Chapter 8.

[38] For Byrd amendment, see http://thomas.loc.gov/cgi-bin/bdquery/z?d102:HR05006:@@@D&summ2=m&

[39] CNN: Lou Dobbs Tonight, March 2, 2006.

[40] Bush says block on Chinese investment was issue of security, Financial Times, February 6, 1990, Government Eyes Purchase of Mamco by China's Catic, Metalworking News, December 18, 1989.

[41] Graham, Edward M. and David M. Marchick, US National Security and Foreign Direct Investment, Institute for International Economics, p. 56-57.

[42] Keeping out Li Ka-shing, The Economist, May 3, 2003.

[43] Senator Bayh Introduces Legislation to Make Security a Top Priority in Future Business Deals, US Fed News, February 28, 2006.

[44] Graham, Edward M. and David M. Marchick, US National Security and Foreign Direct Investment, Institute for International Economics, p. 59-66.

[45] Chertoff Says U.S. Ports Takeover Would Tighten Grip on Security, Wall Street Journal, March 7, 2006.

[46] Chinese firm drops bid to buy U.S. oil concern, New York Times, August 3, 2005; Politics & Economics: Could Asian Oil Firms' Demand Be Overstated? Wall Street Journal, June 9, 2006.

[47] The dragon tucks in, The Economist, June 30, 2005; Unocal Becomes a Hot Property, Wall Street Journal, June 27, 2005; Congressmen Are Seeking Review Of CNOOC's Potential Unocal Bid, Wall Street Journal, June 20, 2005.

[48] CNOOC Bid Review Is Dealt Setback, Wall Street Journal, July 13, 2005; CNOOC Pressured Unocal on Deal, Wall Street Journal, July 26, 2005.

[49] China's Tough Talk On Unocal Bid Could Backfire, Dow Jones Business News, July 6, 2005; U.S. Public Is Hostile to CNOOC Bid, Wall Street Journal, July 14, 2005; Congress Raises New Roadblock In CNOOC's Path to Unocal Deal, Wall Street Journal, July 27, 2005.

[50] The Exon-Florio National Security Test for Foreign Investment, Congressional research Service Report RL 33312, March 16, 2006, 109th Congress: House Bill 4881.

[51] Enhancements to the Implementation of Exon-Florio Could Strengthen the Law's Effectiveness, GAO report GAO-05-686, September 2005, The Exon-Florio National Security Test for Foreign Investment, Congressional Research Service Report RL33312, March 2006, Senate Bill S3549, House Bill HR 5337.

[52] Graham, Edward M. and David M. Marchick, US National Security and Foreign Direct Investment, Institute for International Economics, p. 152-153.

[53] Report of the Senate Committee on Banking, Housing and Urban Affairs on the Foreign Investment and national Security Act of 2006, June 21, 2006.

[54] 109th Congress: Senate Bill S3549, 109th Congress: House Bill HR 5337.

[55] Graham, Edward M. and David M. Marchick, US National Security and Foreign Direct Investment, Institute for International Economics, p. 155-156.

[56] House and Senate Respond to Dubai Ports Deal, The Washington Post, July 27, 2006.

Part III

THE INTERNATIONAL FINANCIAL ARCHITECTURE

HARVARD | BUSINESS | SCHOOL

9-705-026
REV: OCTOBER 27, 2005

RAWI ABDELAL

CHRISTOPHER M. BRUNER

Private Capital and Public Policy: Standard & Poor's Sovereign Credit Ratings

For emerging market ministers of finance in the contemporary world, an important visitor in any given year might be a private-sector credit-rating agency—in many cases, Standard & Poor's (S&P),[1] a global firm with headquarters in New York. Through its opinions on the creditworthiness of sovereign governments and the risk of default for specific debt issues, S&P exercises influence over the capacity of sovereign nations to access private international capital and the opinions of the investment community on a broad range of political and economic risks. Even major industrialized countries, with their relatively greater stability and economic clout, may be affected by the views of rating agencies like S&P on fundamental issues of governmental policy, especially when it comes to spending or borrowing.

As the power and prominence of S&P and other agencies have increased, particularly through the 1990s, awareness of their history, ratings methodologies, regulatory significance, and performance as predictors of default has become increasingly central to a nuanced understanding of modern capital markets, and particularly international capital flows. David Beers, S&P's global head of sovereign and international public finance ratings and a managing director based in London, expressed justifiable pride in the role that S&P has played in the capital markets, built at least in part on a "common language of credit risk that we at S&P helped to invent."[2] That history, however, and the market role played by agencies like S&P, are as complex—and as much of a lightning rod for controversy—as any aspect of the market machinery. In the experience of Marie Cavanaugh, a managing director of sovereign ratings, a visit by S&P can be a "high-profile" event,[3] with finance ministers endeavoring to impress S&P and, through it, international investors. In the words of Laura Feinland Katz, S&P's chief criteria officer for Central and Latin America and a managing director, "Sovereign rating changes usually draw much attention."[4]

And yet for all of the criticisms of the rating agencies' performance following financial crises like those in Mexico and east Asia in the 1990s, given the rating agencies' independence from governments and track record in predicting default, investors continue to look to them for guidance, and regulators around the world continue to employ credit ratings in banking and other financial regulations aimed at measuring financial institutions' exposure to credit risk. The roots of this complex relationship with financial regulators, and the unique role that agencies like S&P play in capital markets, are integrally bound up with the history of America's industrial expansion, use of debt financing, and evolving domestic and global efforts to improve market efficiency.

The Rise of Rating Agencies

Historical Origins

The advent of credit-rating agencies in the early twentieth century reflected the emergence of highly capital-intensive industries in the United States and the corresponding expansion of capital markets to finance them. The U.S. economy at the time had grown to "continental proportions," with "development projects grand in scale, and its individual enterprises larger than elsewhere."[5] Principal among these were the railroads. Credit-rating agencies initially issued ratings solely for such railroad debt.[6]

Though ratings as such were an innovation, the first rating agencies (the precursors of Moody's and Standard & Poor's, entering the business in 1909 and 1916, respectively)[7] were actually built on a substantial historical foundation. In particular, they took over and built upon the roles of precursor institutions of the nineteenth century. So-called credit-reporting agencies emerged by the 1830s, such as that of Lewis Tappan, who in 1841 used his substantial records on customer creditworthiness (accumulated as a dry goods and silk merchant) to found the Mercantile Agency, which "gathered through a network of agents and sold to subscribers information on the business standing and creditworthiness of businesses all over the United States."[8] Around the same time a specialized financial press developed, focusing on railroads. Henry Poor edited one such railroad publication and went on to found his *Manual of the Railroads of the United States* in 1868.[9]

Credit ratings performed well in the early decades of the twentieth century; the ratings market was generally competitive, the agencies endeavoring "to acquire their respective reputations for independence, integrity, and reliability" through ratings financed solely by investors' subscription fees. Demand for credit ratings increased following the 1929 stock market crash, reflecting increased investor concern about credit risk and the prominence of the U.S. bond market. In the decades following World War II, however, the agencies "experienced austerity and contraction," as "bond prices were not volatile, the economy was healthy, and few corporations defaulted." By the early 1970s, the agencies employed few ratings analysts and generated revenues principally through research reports.[10]

Since then, however, the agencies have experienced spectacular growth in size and prominence, for reasons very similar to those prompting their emergence and early development. From 1909 until about 1930, agencies grew as railroads, followed by utilities and manufacturers, entered the U.S. bond market. This development was reinforced by rising income levels and the "mass-marketing of bonds" during World War I, both of which expanded the investor base, while the development of the Federal Reserve System reinforced investor confidence. Investors, then, looked to ratings "to sort out the great variety of issues with which they were presented," an informational need that the investment banks were poorly positioned to meet. The period since the 1970s has seen growth in the credit-rating industry for similar reasons, though at the global level.[11] (See **Exhibit 1** for historical data on S&P sovereign ratings.)

At the same time, aspects of the contemporary ratings business differ markedly from those during the period of the agencies' emergence. First, the major agencies now derive their revenue almost exclusively from fees charged to issuers rather than investors. This development has generally been explained as a response to the cost of maintaining a deep, global bench of trained credit analysts and appropriate research and editing support,[12] as well as the "public good" characteristics of ratings— principally that once a rating is publicized, it is impossible and unfair to exclude nonpaying users from this information and insight; having issuers pay the fees and pass them along to investors in the form of lower returns should, in theory, solve the "free-rider" problem.[13] Although issuers technically need not pay the fees, insofar as the agencies might rate them anyway, they typically pay in order to have "the opportunity provided by the formal ratings process to put their best case before the agencies."[14] Though creating potential conflicts of interest, the agencies have responded that their internal codes of practices, procedures, and ethics as well as their ratings methodologies, committee structures, merit-based pay system, and need to preserve their reputations in the capital markets have sufficiently addressed these concerns.[15] One study of corporate bond credit-rating changes conducted by researchers at the Federal Reserve Board found that "rating changes do not appear to be importantly influenced by rating agency conflicts of interest," suggesting rather that "rating agencies are motivated primarily by reputation-related incentives."[16]

Another fundamental change in the ratings business has resulted from the trend of "disintermediation," which led to the growth of securitization and other complex financial engineering mechanisms such as off-balance sheet financing. Historically, banks served as intermediaries between lenders and borrowers, obtaining funds from depositors and then lending them. Starting in the 1980s, however, other institutions began to replace banks as allocators of capital, a process occurring "on both sides of the balance sheet" (e.g., through institutional investors).[17]

Standard & Poor's

Henry Poor's company entered the credit-rating business in 1916, "a natural outgrowth of the financial and operating information it compiled and sold."[18] In 1941, Poor's Publishing Company merged with Standard Statistics to form Standard & Poor's,[19] and in 1966, S&P was acquired by The McGraw-Hill Companies, Inc., of which S&P would become the financial services operating segment.[20] S&P rated corporate bonds from the outset, with sovereign debt ratings "following shortly thereafter" and municipal bond ratings appearing in 1940.[21] Over time S&P would be the first to introduce a number of additional ratings products, including securitized financings, bond-insured transactions, letters of credit, non-U.S. insurance companies, bank holding companies, and financial guaranty companies.[22] Its business has grown far beyond ratings over the years. Today, S&P comprises, essentially, three separate and fire-walled divisions that focus on corporate and government ratings and securitized or structured finance ratings; equity research, corporate fundamental data, fund data, portfolio analysis, and index calculation; and corporate valuation and consulting, respectively.[23] By mid-2003, S&P Ratings Services had ratings outstanding on "approximately 150,000 securities issues of obligors in more than 100 countries," with a U.S. staff of approximately 1,250 credit analysts issuing ratings opinions on "more than 99.2% of the debt obligations and preferred stock issues publicly traded in the United States."[24] As of December 2004, they did business with over 42,000 issuers and rated over $6 trillion in debt, employing approximately 6,000 people in 21 countries.[25]

While S&P's financials are consolidated with McGraw-Hill's and little ratings-specific information has been made publicly available, both the ratings business and S&P's broader business have clearly generated substantial profits. According to its 2003 annual report, S&P was "a key growth driver" for McGraw-Hill, due particularly to the ratings business, and in fact McGraw-Hill's "revenue and operating profit increase [was] primarily attributable" to S&P.[26] (See **Exhibit 2** for selected McGraw-Hill financial data by operating segment.)

S&P Sovereign Credit Ratings

S&P first assigned credit ratings to sovereign debt issues in 1927.[27] By 1929, S&P's sovereign ratings "covered most European nations, several Latin American republics, Australia, Canada, Japan, and China."[28] Sovereign ratings were largely suspended during World War II, with the exception of Canada's Yankee bonds and a handful of non-investment grade Latin American bonds.[29]

After World War II, S&P's Yankee bond ratings picked up as industrialized nations sought to tap the U.S. capital market, but access was effectively cut off by the Interest Equalization Tax (IET), a U.S. tax on foreign investment,[30] and S&P suspended all sovereign ratings in 1968 (with the exception of Canada, which was exempt from this tax),[31] not to resume until the IET was repealed in 1974.[32] As of early 1975, S&P rated only Canada and the United States (both receiving its highest rating of "AAA"), but from there the sovereign ratings business grew phenomenally. The number of rated sovereigns increased to 11 in 1980 (all AAA), hit 30 in 1990 (all but one investment grade), and by the beginning of 1998 had reached 74.[33] Over the course of the 1990s, numerous emerging market sovereigns sought ratings for debt issues denominated in foreign currencies, catalyzed in part by the emergence of Brady bonds (essentially bonds exchanged for defaulted commercial bank debt of certain emerging market sovereigns), which "whetted investor appetites for high-yielding emerging markets securities just as developing countries coming out of their 1980s recessions sought lower-cost, longer-term alternatives to bank loans."[34] As Beers put it, "Globalization helped our business more than anything else."[35] (See **Exhibit 3** for S&P's sovereign ratings as of January 12, 2005.)

By March 2004, S&P rated "virtually all cross-border bonds in the sector" and had reached its 100th sovereign rating (Burkina Faso),[36] a milestone achieved in part through an innovative partnership with the United Nations Development Programme (UNDP), under which the UNDP has paid for ratings of African sovereigns in order to help them demonstrate transparency and facilitate their integration into global private capital markets. [37] This reflects a broader trend, starting in the early 1990s, of sovereigns seeking ratings not because they contemplated debt offerings, but in order to communicate their financial status to capital markets.[38]

With respect to staff composition, the sovereign ratings group at S&P embodies, in Beers's words, an "eclectic mix of skills." Beers himself is an economist, Cavanaugh is a graduate of Harvard's Kennedy School of Government, while another senior member of the group is a former investment banker with a CFA degree. In Beers's view, "It's about how you synthesize all these skills"; in the sovereign ratings group, they "tend to take a holistic view" in recruiting, though ultimately they are "training everyone to be credit analysts."[39] Beers added that sovereign rating is definitely "a business" with its own profit metrics and that it is not a loss leader for subsequent private-sector ratings in a given country.[40]

Sovereign Ratings, Methodology, and Policy

Sovereign credit ratings reflect S&P's "opinions on the ability and willingness of sovereign governments to service their commercial financial obligations in full and on time."[41] At least since the late 1980s, when more and more sovereigns began to seek ratings, S&P's methodological statements have become increasingly detailed and explicit.[42] Beers observed that some credit analysis involves subjectivity and judgment; whether the issuer is a corporation, a bank, or a sovereign, it is "all about uncertainty and risk."[43]

S&P puts out both "issuer" and "issue" ratings, the former providing "a current opinion of an obligor's overall financial capacity (its creditworthiness) to pay its financial obligations," and the latter providing "a current opinion of the creditworthiness of an obligor with respect to a specific financial obligation, a specific class of financial obligations, or a specific financial program."[44] Distinct ratings are also assigned to debt denominated in local and foreign currencies, respectively (the former typically equaling or exceeding the latter, given the sovereign's domestic taxation and monetary powers).[45] S&P has noted that a rating "is not a recommendation to purchase, sell, or hold a financial obligation issued by an obligor, as it does not comment on market price or suitability for a particular investor."[46]

S&P's rating scales are essentially letter-grade hierarchies ranging from "AAA," the highest long-term credit rating, or "A-1+," the highest short-term rating, down to "D," meaning default.[47] Long-term ratings of "BBB-" and above are considered "investment grade" by the investment community, while ratings of "BB" and below are viewed as non-investment, or "speculative," grade (sometimes more pejoratively referred to as "junk"), meaning they have "significant speculative characteristics."[48] S&P also provides "Outlook" and "CreditWatch" services, the former indicating "the potential direction of a long-term credit rating" over the next two years, and the latter indicating that a noteworthy event has occurred and that more information is required to determine its impact.[49]

The rating process itself centers on the "rating committee," a group of senior sovereign analysts who assess various issues relating to the sovereign's political and economic affairs and then vote on the rating to be assigned.[50] The team of analysts who have visited the country and reviewed the information made available to them by various public- and private-sector entities (including the ministry of finance and central bank) present a ratings report in draft form to the full committee,[51] which proceeds to evaluate the sovereign across a number of analytical categories broadly reflective of "economic risk" (that is, the sovereign's "ability to repay") and "political risk" (the sovereign's "willingness to repay").[52] If the sovereign does not agree with the rating determined by the committee, it can appeal the decision, particularly if it feels it has additional information to provide. The committee will then make a final decision at which time the rating, in most cases, will be made public.[53]

Rating Changes

While S&P "seeks to look through economic, commodity, and political cycles"[54] when issuing ratings, and while committees "consider reasonable 'worst-case' scenarios" over five-year periods as part of the standard rating process, changing circumstances do sometimes require that a rating be raised or lowered; in general, rating changes "occur whenever new information significantly alters Standard & Poor's view of likely future developments,"[55] which "usually results from the policy response or degree of latitude in a given area being different from what was expected."[56] Cavanaugh added that while no issuer has ever questioned an upgrade, an abbreviated appeals process is available in the case of downgrades.[57] Beers noted that "changes in our ratings, in general, are not the destabilizing factor claimed by some critics," often changing little when market spreads have been volatile.[58] As a matter of policy, S&P has ongoing surveillance and meets most sovereigns "at least annually," through face-to-face meetings in the country, in S&P's offices, or at "various development bank gatherings." The primary analyst for a given sovereign also communicates with them regularly, and any of the foregoing sources of information "may be the basis for a committee at any time it is deemed necessary."[59]

Default Patterns

S&P defines "default" as "the failure to meet a principal or interest payment on the due date (or within the specified grace period) contained in the original terms of the debt issue." S&P considers a sovereign default to have occurred, for instance, when "an exchange offer of new debt contains terms less favorable than the original issue," when central bank notes are "converted into new currency of less than equivalent face value," and when a bank loan is rescheduled "at less favorable terms than the original loan."[60]

According to S&P, the "number of sovereign governments . . . increased to 202 in 2003 from 39 in 1824," greatly expanding the universe of potential sovereign issuers since the early nineteenth century. S&P data show that defaults on foreign currency bonds "took place repeatedly, and on a substantial scale," from the nineteenth century until the 1940s, falling off after World War II "when cross-border bond issuance was also minimal." While defaults on foreign currency bonds remained infrequent in the 1970s and 1980s, this primarily reflected the fact that less creditworthy borrowers at that time tended to rely more heavily on bank debt (upon which defaults were more common). The market for speculative-grade sovereign bonds took off following the introduction of Brady bonds in the early 1990s, upon which the default rate on sovereign bonds predictably increased (though not reaching default rates equivalent to those on sovereign bank debt in the 1980s). While defaults in the nineteenth and early twentieth centuries "reflected a variety of factors, including wars, revolutions, lax fiscal and monetary policies, and external economic shocks," more recent defaults have tended, in S&P's view, to reflect challenges of "fiscal discipline, debt management, and the contingent liabilities arising from weak banking systems."[61]

Over time, S&P "expects sovereign default rates to gradually rise," especially in light of the "number of speculative-grade ratings assigned since 1991, together with the below-average credit quality of most unrated sovereigns."[62] As Cavanaugh pointed out, part of S&P's "value-added is that an A is an A is an A" across sectors and regions, so if the sovereign default rate for a given letter grade were to remain below the equivalent for corporations over time, S&P would likely "recalibrate" the sovereign ratings criteria accordingly.[63] This issue highlights the challenge of applying the same ratings scales across different sectors; as Cavanaugh puts it, "It's hard to compare Ford and Mexico, both of which have ratings in the BBB category, but over time we monitor the behavior of BBB corporates and sovereigns to ensure comparable creditworthiness."[64]

The "Sovereign Ceiling"

Though it has often been said that private-sector issuers within a given country cannot have foreign-currency credit ratings higher than their sovereign's—the so-called sovereign ceiling—S&P has emphasized that there is no hard-and-fast rule. While sovereign risk "comes into play in analyzing nonsovereign creditworthiness because the unique, wide-ranging powers and resources of each national government affect the financial and operating environments of entities under its jurisdiction" (e.g., given the sovereign's capacity to impose exchange controls), it remains possible (if uncommon) for a corporation or other subnational issuer to have a higher rating than its sovereign if, for example, it has substantial corporate assets outside the country.[65]

Ratings Criteria and Economic Development

Sovereign ratings are, in S&P's words, not just a "quantitative" exercise but a "qualitative" one as well. As a consequence, there is a subjective component to the rating process, which is readily perceptible in the agency's methodological statements. With respect to political risk, for instance, S&P considers not simply the "stability, predictability, and transparency of a country's political institutions" in the abstract, but more specifically whether the "separation of powers" and the "development of civil institutions, particularly an independent press" have developed to the point that "policy errors" can be quickly "identified and corrected."[66] Likewise, with respect to economic structure, S&P has favored "a market economy with legally enforceable property rights" as "less prone to policy error."[67]

Similarly contentious issues are highlighted by S&P's description of the "characteristics" exhibited by sovereigns at particular rating levels. Higher-rated sovereigns, for instance, demonstrate "[o]penness to trade and integration into the global financial system," with economic policies that are "generally cautious, flexible, and market-oriented"; "orthodox market-oriented economic programs are generally well established."[68] Lower-rated sovereigns, on the other hand, tend to impose "more restrictions" with respect to trade and investment; "[o]rthodox economic policies are usually not well established."[69]

In Cavanaugh's experience, there is broad adherence among committee members to what she described as "basic economic orthodoxy." There is, for instance, a general consensus that "openness is better, but not openness no matter what"; there is "a lot of gray" and substantial debate among committee members within these broad parameters, with special attention paid to the "sequencing of reforms." At the end of the day, a ratings report is "not saying these are good or bad policies"; the question to which all analysis returns is whether the country can service its debt.[70]

S&P's emphasis on policy has been felt in practice. The "proximate cause" of sovereign downgrades in the wake of the Asian financial crisis, for instance, was described by S&P as "policy mistakes that were inconsistent with Standard & Poor's rating levels."[71] Short of default, such errors included "imposing capital controls, jawboning banks to lend imprudently, establishing dual currency rates, managing reserves imprudently, intervening in equity markets, or taking timid fiscal adjustment measures."[72] Such assessments of policy are often offered prospectively, as well, and are not limited to emerging markets.[73]

Certain policy prescriptions have, over time, fallen out of favor, leading S&P to revise its methodology and policy stances. For instance, imposition of capital controls was identified as a contributing factor in Malaysia's downgrade during the Asian financial crisis.[74] Subsequent methodological statements, however, have taken a much softer position on this issue, observing that "[p]ast economic crises, particularly in Asia in the late 1990s, suggest capital account liberalization should take place in conjunction with current account liberalization, but at an orderly pace that meshes with transparent progress in other areas."[75] Beers has observed that "occasionally there are big events with a credit impact that take almost everyone by surprise, and the Asian financial crisis was one such event. At Standard & Poor's, we certainly learn from these episodes, and we incorporate what we learn into our credit analysis."[76]

The Nature of the Ratings Market and Competitive Issues

S&P and Moody's—the agencies that introduced credit ratings, sometimes called the "Big Two"— "dominate the contemporary market," each issuing ratings on approximately US$30 trillion worth of securities.[77] Both are based in New York with branch offices throughout the world.[78] By the end of the 1990s, these two agencies accounted for 90% of the sovereign ratings market.[79] Fitch is typically viewed as a "distant third" behind S&P and Moody's.[80] Beyond these three primary players there are numerous smaller, local rating agencies throughout the world (bringing the total to an estimated 130 to 150 agencies worldwide).[81]

Perhaps not surprisingly, the agencies themselves express differing views on the market for credit ratings and their relative positions within it. Fitch, for instance, has sought to draw regulators' attention to "Moody's and S&P's power in the current market," characterizing them as "a dual monopoly, each possessing separate monopoly power in a market that has grown to demand two ratings."[82] (Empirical research has suggested that Fitch ratings, which have tended to be somewhat higher, are sought as a tiebreaker when S&P's and Moody's ratings differ.)[83] Fitch has also charged that each has "engage[d] in practices designed to perpetuate its market dominance" in areas of comparative strength for Fitch, such as structured finance ratings.[84]

The dominant agencies, on the other hand, have tended to characterize the market as competitive, emphasizing the confidence the market places in their ratings, earned through a track record of strong performance as predictors of default. In S&P's view, for instance, "[u]nderlying the credibility and reliability" of S&P's ratings "is the market's recognition of the independence, integrity, objectivity and quality of S&P Ratings Services' credit ratings, rating process and reputation, as evidenced by its excellent track record."[85]

Why Sovereigns Seek Ratings

In general, sovereign governments have sought credit ratings in order to gain access to international capital markets. Credit-rating agencies effectively facilitate this process by addressing "the information problem between those with funds and those seeking them,"[86] providing a simplified language "condensing the highly complex contingencies of credit risk into a single measure" and thereby reducing transaction costs between borrowers and lenders.[87] Additionally, as discussed further below, the incorporation of credit ratings into banking and other financial regulations, both domestically and internationally, greatly influences—and in some cases may determine—investors' buy/sell decisions. Credit ratings are expected to gain greater prominence once the so-called "Basel II" capital-adequacy framework for banks comes into effect, incorporating credit ratings for purposes of determining whether bank capital reserves are sufficient in light of the riskiness of their loan portfolios.[88]

Over the course of the 1990s, however, sovereigns with no immediate plans to issue debt began to seek credit ratings in order to communicate their financial status to capital markets. Under its contract with the UNDP, for instance, S&P has issued ratings for seven sub-Saharan African sovereigns.[89] Beers explained that under the initiative the UNDP played a "quasi-advisory" role (similar to that played by the investment banks typically hired by sovereigns going through the ratings process), providing "technical and financial support" and helping to "explain to the sovereign how it works and what it means."[90]

The hope, as expressed by the UNDP, is that credit ratings will help these sovereigns to achieve "'stamps of approval'" from capital markets and to negotiate "better and more favorable contracts"; that countries will learn about ratings criteria and the expectations of capital markets; and that the process will "improve transparency in the credit rating processes, increase investor education, and protect the independence and quality of credit ratings."[91] S&P has likewise observed that advantages offered by credit ratings include "[d]emonstrating greater public-sector financial transparency, attracting foreign direct investment, providing access for private-sector borrowers to the global financial markets, and developing deeper domestic capital markets."[92] As Beers put it, for these sovereigns "it was never about the rating received" so much as the recognition that "a rating is useful."[93] Cavanaugh added that the UNDP initiative is "part of a process" of financial integration, observing that S&P has already received calls from potential foreign direct investors who view the rating as an "independent opinion" on various risks they have to consider.[94]

Reputational Capital or Regulatory Licensing?

Credit ratings have been incorporated into regulation at both the domestic and international level, serving as a benchmark for default risk. In the United States, credit ratings have been used in banking and other financial regulation substantially longer than elsewhere, dating back to 1931.[95] Ratings-dependent regulation in the United States took on far greater significance in 1975, however, when the Securities and Exchange Commission (SEC) introduced the concept of "nationally recognized statistical rating organizations," or NRSROs, for purposes of regulation incorporating credit ratings as a means of limiting exposure to credit risk.[96] The SEC recognizes credit-rating agencies as NRSROs based on various criteria, the most important of which is whether the agency is "nationally recognized" in the United States "as an issuer of credible and reliable ratings by the predominant users of securities ratings."[97] Since 1975, the NRSRO concept has been incorporated into a wide range of federal and state laws and regulations and has even been incorporated into regulations in some foreign countries.[98] For instance, investments by money market funds are limited to short-term securities of highly creditworthy issuers, and a downgrade could thus require sale of the security.[99] As of September 2004, there were only four NRSROs—S&P, Moody's, Fitch, and Dominion Bond Rating Service Ltd.[100] (See **Exhibit 4** for selected data on the NRSROs.)

This regulatory use of credit ratings has led critics such as Frank Partnoy to question whether dominant agencies like S&P really rely on their reputation in the marketplace, or whether their success is more a reflection of artificial demand for their ratings created by their status as NRSROs. It has been argued, for instance, that "credit ratings are valuable, not because they contain valuable information, but because they grant 'regulatory licenses'" guaranteeing compliance with ratings-dependent regulation.[101] This has led some to advocate eliminating regulatory use of credit ratings altogether, replacing them with credit spreads, which are "determined by the market as a whole, not by any individual entity or entities."[102] Others, however, have observed potential benefits of ratings-dependent regulation (and investment policies), suggesting that they lend "'bite'" to negative credit-watch announcements, thereby strengthening an issuer's incentive to undertake reforms.[103]

In Beers's view, NRSRO status has not had "any influence at all" on S&P's discussions with sovereigns, and the regulatory environment was "not decisive" in the growth of the ratings business.[104] Feinland Katz similarly felt that NRSRO status had not historically had a great effect on S&P internationally.[105]

Similar concerns have been expressed about the incorporation of ratings into the Basel II capital-adequacy framework for banks. The Basel II framework was prepared by the Basel Committee on Banking Supervision, "a group of central banks and bank supervisory authorities in the G10 countries, which developed the first standard in 1988."[106] The primary purpose behind Basel II was to make the framework more risk sensitive, "aligning capital requirements more closely to the risk of credit loss"[107] while "retaining key elements of the 1988 capital adequacy framework, including the general requirement for banks to hold total capital equivalent to at least 8% of their risk-weighted assets."[108] Essentially Basel II permits banks a choice between the so-called standardized approach incorporating credit ratings, aimed at banks with simpler loans and control structures, and an alternative based on internally generated ratings for banks engaging in "more sophisticated risk-taking and that have developed advanced risk measurement systems."[109] (The Basel I approach, under which "it was not necessary for banks to set aside capital against bonds issued by member countries of the Organization for Economic Cooperation and Development [OECD]," fell out of favor when South Korea was admitted to the OECD and subsequently fell below investment grade during the Asian financial crisis.)[110] Under the standard approach, claims on sovereigns are risk weighted according to their credit rating, ranging from 0% (for issues rated AAA to AA-) up to 150% (for issues rated B- and lower).[111] National supervisors are responsible for designating "external credit assessment institutions (ECAIs)," according to criteria roughly similar to the NRSRO criteria (objectivity, independence, international access/transparency, disclosure, resources, and credibility demonstrated by "reliance on an ECAI's external credit assessments by independent parties").[112]

Critics such as Michael King and Timothy Sinclair have observed that Basel II is likely to increase the influence of credit-rating agencies and have argued that such reliance on credit ratings can be expected to "produce perverse outcomes for the financial markets and global public policy."[113] These same critics worried that capital would flow more cyclically.[114] This system can also be expected to result, according to its critics, in "ratings shopping" as banks look from agency to agency for the highest possible ratings to reduce their capital charges and to "undermine the reputational constraint otherwise enforced by the capital market."[115] S&P has itself expressed concern that Basel II could in many instances result in an imprudent reduction in regulatory capital relative to potential losses.[116]

Others, such as Lawrence White, have argued that the system further solidifies the position of the incumbent firms through ECAI designation criteria focusing on "inputs" (i.e., the resources devoted to the ratings process) as opposed to "output" (i.e., the historical efficacy of the agency's method).[117] S&P has itself observed that, with respect to sovereigns in particular, Basel II "likely will increase reliance of bank counterparties on sovereign credit ratings in the future and could disadvantage those jurisdictions that do not have credit ratings."[118] Beers felt, however, that while "of course it's helpful," Basel II would not in his view have "a decisive impact" for S&P, nor would it "dramatically help or hinder" the sovereign rating business.[119] By way of alternatives, critics have suggested greater reliance on price and yield spreads, more forward-looking forms of accounting emphasizing market value (supplemented by stress tests),[120] or some combination of internal and external risk measures (for those unable to rely solely on internal measures).[121]

Another criticism common to both the NRSRO and Basel II frameworks emphasizes the lack of economic and political accountability that results from incorporation of ratings into regulation. As Dieter Kerwer has observed, agencies like S&P "seldom have to justify their decisions," a result following from the government's effective enforcement of what the agencies insist constitutes only nonbinding opinions.[122]

To all of this S&P has responded that neither the NRSRO designation nor inclusion in Basel II were sought out by S&P; such regulatory use of ratings reflects not the actions of S&P but of the SEC, Congress, and other G10 governments.[123] While the SEC "can, and should, increase the transparency of the NRSRO designation process" and reduce barriers to entry, the NRSRO designation should be based on a number of factors, including track record and recognition or acceptance by market participants. S&P has also maintained steadfastly that "the essence of the rating process is the gathering of information about a particular issuer or security from a variety of sources, the analysis of that information, the forming of opinions about that issuer or security and the broad dissemination of those opinions to the public"—activities "highly akin to those regularly performed by professional journalists," underscoring that any intrusive form of regulation or accountability under U.S. law would be strenuously resisted by S&P on First Amendment grounds.[124] In general, S&P has advocated continuation of the NRSRO regulatory concept[125] and broadly supported the Basel II framework.[126] S&P has also argued that price and yield spreads are more volatile and questioned their utility as a regulatory alternative to credit ratings.[127]

Challenges and Opportunities for S&P Moving Forward

Objectivity and Effectiveness

The "qualitative" element of credit rating—a factor of particular salience in sovereign rating, where much turns on an analyst's assessment of policy responses to economic challenges—inevitably opens rating agencies like S&P to charges that they lack objectivity and that their ratings do not provide information that the market did not already possess (i.e., that was not already reflected in sovereign bond prices). While historical default data demonstrate that "sovereign ratings are robust predictors of default risk,"[128] some scholars have argued that they are nevertheless a lagging indicator of creditworthiness (often preceded by price movements in the market). For instance, sovereign ratings upgrades by S&P, Moody's, and Fitch during the 1990s appear to have followed "market rallies," while downgrades followed "market downturns."[129]

Cavanaugh pointed out that while sovereign analysts "try to be forward looking," there is inevitably a reinterpretation of the information that is available whenever rating changes occur,[130] as they did following financial meltdowns in Mexico, east Asia, Russia, and Argentina. Emphasizing that "these are opinions," Cavanaugh observed that they are based on "what we have at the time" and that many of the sovereigns hit by crises in the 1990s, such as Argentina, Mexico, and Russia, were "never investment grade prior to their crises."[131]

Crises and Calls for Regulation

The appearance of not always being able to predict sovereign financial crises and major corporate bankruptcies has prompted critics in the United States and elsewhere to question whether regulatory use of credit ratings makes sense and whether some degree of direct regulation of rating agencies should be instituted. Agencies including S&P were widely criticized following the Asian financial crisis, though as one emerging market observer has noted, it required a crisis closer to home for U.S. lawmakers and regulators to take these criticisms more seriously.[132] Following the bankruptcy of Enron and similar corporate scandals, Congress held hearings to examine the role of credit-rating agencies in capital markets (noting particularly that Enron was rated investment grade until just four days before its bankruptcy was announced), and the Sarbanes-Oxley Act of 2002 directed the SEC to conduct a more thorough review of the credit-rating industry.[133] The SEC subsequently issued a concept release requesting comments regarding whether the NRSRO designation should be eliminated or modified, as well as "the appropriate degree of regulatory oversight that should be applied to credit rating agencies."[134] As to whether the NRSRO concept should be maintained at all, the Big Two came out on opposite sides, with S&P recommending that it be kept and Moody's prepared to let it go,[135] perhaps underscoring the mixed blessing such status constitutes—greater demand for ratings at the cost of greater scrutiny.

Lawmakers in Europe have posed similar questions, though with the additional concern that rating agencies like S&P have perpetuated U.S. economic and financial hegemony. In a February 2004 resolution, the European Parliament observed, among other things, that "the ratings industry is heavily concentrated"; that "the ownership and business orientation of rating agencies is predominantly centred on the United States"; that the U.S.'s NRSRO designation has "established among agencies a hierarchy fraught with serious regulatory implications and protectionist overtones"; and that "European capital markets are faced with the prospect of an ever-increasing use of rating assessments for business and for regulatory purposes."[136] The resolution directed the European Commission to assess the possible creation of a "European Registration Scheme" for rating agencies, including "a cost-benefit analysis of the effects on European capital markets," and suggested the possibility of a "voluntary industry body that would determine best practice, encourage training and provide a disputes and arbitration procedure for [aggrieved] issuers or investors." The resolution further called on the commission to report back to the parliament by July 31, 2005 with "its assessment of the need for appropriate legislative proposals to deal with the issues in the . . . Resolution."[137]

Noting that most witnesses testifying before the parliament questioned the usefulness of a predominantly regulatory solution, the resolution "rejected any attempt at regulatory intervention into the substance of [rating] opinions" and, among other things, called upon rating agencies to take steps to enhance transparency in their operations.[138] The European Parliament further "stresse[d] the need for total freedom of expression and for the agencies' independence from political and business influence." The resolution also acknowledged "that the line between the regulation of process and the regulation of content and opinion may prove hard to draw," considering this "an important consideration to take into account in reaching any regulatory solution. In addition, [the resolution noted] that the debt of sovereign governments is rated, and that administrative requirements of regulatory agencies may be used to exert indirect pressure for higher ratings of government debt."[139]

The European Parliament also considered international consistency in the approach to rating agencies to be of vital importance, calling for work of the Financial Stability Forum, the International Organization of Securities Commissions (IOSCO), and the SEC to be taken into account,[140] as urged by influential market participants such as the European Banking Federation and S&P.[141] In a public response to a draft report (by rapporteur Giorgis Katiforis) to the parliament, S&P had emphasized that "any approach to these issues must be global in nature"; that regulation would undermine the independence of ratings; that S&P was confident it had not violated EU competition rules; and that there was no evidence of any U.S.-centrism leading to such an "imbalance" through credit ratings.[142]

The actions of the European Parliament reflect the complex dynamics of this debate. On the one hand there is discontent in some quarters that "Europe doesn't have a major rating agency that would take into account the special characteristics of European accounting or the prevailing differences in financial ratios as they evolved in a bank-based financial system,"[143] while at the same time there is recognition of the important role that rating agencies play and widespread scepticism regarding regulatory oversight over the agencies.[144]

Following the European Parliament, other regulatory authorities have also called for an international approach to rating agencies. In September 2003, IOSCO produced a Statement of Principles on Rating Agencies setting out general principles for rating agencies to adopt.[145] Further work toward the development of code-of-conduct fundamentals for rating agencies was finalized in December 2004, calling on rating agencies to implement these fundamentals into their firm-specific codes of conduct.[146]

Mixed Signals

The foregoing criticisms of the rating agencies, and the Big Two in particular, present very real challenges to S&P as it moves forward, creating substantial uncertainty regarding the regulatory environment it can expect to face in years to come. As S&P has emphasized, however:

> ... over the last century credit ratings have served the U.S. securities markets extremely well, providing an effective, independent and objective tool in the market's evaluation and assessment of credit risk. S&P Ratings Services believes that the availability of credit ratings that are credible and, as demonstrated by their performance, reliable is a principal factor in the U.S. debt markets' depth, breadth, efficiency and cost effectiveness. Moreover, the widespread acceptance of the NRSRO regulatory framework by market participants and its adoption in other federal and state regulations and legislation evidences the success of the NRSRO designation. Key to preserving the valuable role of credit rating agencies in the U.S. capital markets is the continuation of a regulatory framework that recognizes the market as the best judge of the credibility and reliability of a credit rating agency's rating opinions.[147]

Regardless of criticism, the fact remains that while legislative bodies and securities regulators on both sides of the Atlantic query the wisdom of incorporating ratings into regulation, these very same governments have—through their central bankers and finance ministries—simultaneously laid the groundwork for a vast extension of ratings-dependent regulation through the Basel II capital-adequacy framework.

S&P thus finds itself at a very complex point in its history, marked both by widespread skepticism about, and by increasing reliance upon, credit ratings. At the end of the day, even critics of the agencies have acknowledged that tearing them down would be far easier than filling the void left behind in international capital markets.[148] Contradictory signals from some of the world's most powerful governments reflect that, for all of the criticisms and arguable imperfections in the credit-rating industry, agencies like S&P have for almost a century played a central role and performed well in the functioning of global capital markets, and that any fundamental changes to the industry or its regulatory environment would raise a host of economic and political issues affecting virtually every nation in the world.

S&P also faces a host of concerns arising from technological and financial developments, as well as the myriad sources of instability that continue to threaten the efficient functioning of international capital markets. Advances in financial engineering, and the cost of maintaining a staff of analysts trained to grapple with such advancements, present ongoing challenges, as does the larger issue of what, if anything, might constitute a viable alternative to ratings as a governance mechanism in capital markets. Amidst the ever-expanding complexities of global finance, understanding and, to some degree, predicting factors that might lead to future financial crises and global credit meltdowns—including, in the twenty-first century, international terrorism and other destabilizing developments—demand constant vigilance in defining and refining S&P's credit risk and credit-rating methodologies.

Exhibit 1   Historical Sovereign Credit-Ratings Data

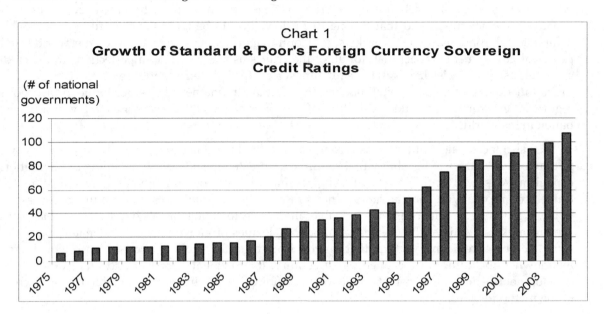

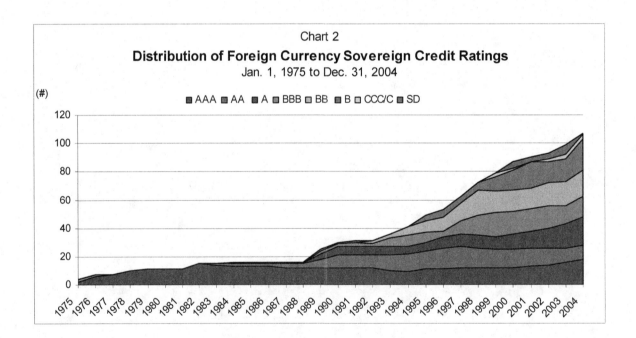

Source: Sovereign Ratings Group Media Relations, Standard & Poor's.

Exhibit 2   McGraw-Hill 2003 Revenue and Profit Data, Consolidated and by Operating Segment

($ in millions)	Consolidated	Financial Services (S&P)	McGraw-Hill Education	Information and Media Services
Operating revenue	$4,827.9	$1,769.1	$2,286.2	$772.6
% increase (decrease)	4.0	13.1	0.5	(4.6)
Operating profit	$1,099.2	$667.6	$321.8	$109.8
% increase (decrease)	8.6	19.0	(3.4)	(7.0)
% operating margin	23	38	14	14

Source: Drawn from The McGraw-Hill Companies, Inc., Annual Report for the year ended December 31, 2003, pp. 32–46, available at http://www.sec.gov/Archives/edgar/data/64040/000095012304002457/y94410exv13.htm.

Exhibit 3   Standard & Poor's Sovereign Ratings

Local and foreign currency credit ratings (long-term, outlook, short-term) of all rated sovereign issuers as of January 12, 2005

Sovereign	Local Currency	Foreign Currency
Andorra	AA/Stable/A-1+	AA/Stable/A-1+
Argentina	SD/NM/SD	SD/NM/SD
Australia	AAA/Stable/A-1+	AAA/Stable/A-1+
Austria	AAA/Stable/A-1+	AAA/Stable/A-1+
Bahamas	A-/Stable/A-2	A-/Stable/A-2
Bahrain	A/Stable/A-1	A-/Positive/A-2
Barbados	A-/Stable/A-2	BBB+/Stable/A-2
Belgium	AA+/Stable/A-1+	AA+/Stable/A-1+
Belize	B/Negative/C	B-/Negative/C
Benin	B+/Stable/B	B+/Stable/B
Bermuda	AA/Stable/A-1+	AA/Stable/A-1+
Bolivia	B-/Stable/C	B-/Stable/C
Botswana	A+/Stable/A-1	A/Stable/A-1
Brazil	BB/Stable/B	BB-/Stable/B
Bulgaria	BBB/Stable/A-3	BBB-/Stable/A-3
Burkina Faso	B/Stable/B	B/Stable/B
Cameroon	CCC/Stable/C	CCC/Stable/C
Canada	AAA/Stable/A-1+	AAA/Stable/A-1+
Chile	AA/Stable/A-1+	A/Stable/A-1
China	BBB+/Positive/A-2	BBB+/Positive/A-2
Colombia	BBB/Stable/A-3	BB/Stable/B
Cook Islands	BB-/Stable/B	BB-/Stable/B
Costa Rica	BB+/Negative/B	BB/Negative/B
Croatia	BBB+/Stable/A-2	BBB/Stable/A-3
Cyprus	A/Stable/A-1	A/Stable/A-1
Czech Republic	A/Stable/A-1	A-/Stable/A-2
Denmark	AAA/Stable/A-1+	AAA/Stable/A-1+
Dominican Republic	CC/Negative/C	CC/Negative/C
Ecuador	CCC+/Stable/C	CCC+/Stable/C
Egypt	BBB-/Negative/A-3	BB+/Negative/B
El Salvador	BB+/Stable/B	BB+/Stable/B
Estonia	A/Stable/A-1	A/Stable/A-1
Finland	AAA/Stable/A-1+	AAA/Stable/A-1+
France	AAA/Stable/A-1+	AAA/Stable/A-1+
Germany	AAA/Stable/A-1+	AAA/Stable/A-1+
Ghana	B+/Stable/B	B+/Stable/B

Exhibit 3 (continued)

Sovereign	Local Currency	Foreign Currency
Greece	A/Stable/A-1	A/Stable/A-1
Grenada	CCC/Negative/C	SD/NM/SD
Guatemala	BB/Stable/B	BB-/Stable/B
Hong Kong	AA-/Stable/A-1+	A+/Stable/A-1
Hungary	A/Stable/A-1	A-/Stable/A-2
Iceland	AA+/Stable/A-1+	A+/Positive/A-1+
India	BB+/Stable/B	BB/Positive/B
Indonesia	BB/Positive/B	B+/Positive/B
Ireland	AAA/Stable/A-1+	AAA/Stable/A-1+
Isle of Man	AAA/Stable/A-1+	AAA/Stable/A-1+
Israel	A+/Stable/A-1	A-/Stable/A-1
Italy	AA-/Stable/A-1+	AA-/Stable/A-1+
Jamaica	B/Stable/B	B/Stable/B
Japan	AA-/Stable/A-1+	AA-/Stable/A-1+
Jordan	BBB/Stable/A-3	BB/Stable/B
Kazakhstan	BBB/Stable/A-3	BBB-/Stable/A-3
Korea	A+/Stable/A-1	A-/Stable/A-2
Kuwait	A+/Stable/A-1+	A+/Stable/A-1+
Latvia	A-/Stable/A-2	A-/Stable/A-2
Lebanon	B-/Stable/C	B-/Stable/C
Liechtenstein	AAA/Stable/A-1+	AAA/Stable/A-1+
Lithuania	A-/Stable/A-2	A-/Stable/A-2
Luxembourg	AAA/Stable/A-1+	AAA/Stable/A-1+
Macedonia	BB+/Positive/B	BB/Positive/B
Madagascar	B/Stable/B	B/Stable/B
Malaysia	A+/Stable/A-1	A-/Stable/A-2
Mali	B/Stable/B	B/Stable/B
Malta	A+/Stable/A-1	A/Stable/A-1
United Mexican States	A-/Stable/A-2	BBB-/Stable/A-3
Mongolia	B/Stable/B	B/Stable/B
Montenegro	BB/Stable/B	BB/Stable/B
Montserrat	BBB-/Positive/A-3	BBB-/Positive/A-3
Morocco	BBB/Stable/A-3	BB/Positive/B
Mozambique	B/Positive/B	B/Positive/B
Netherlands	AAA/Stable/A-1+	AAA/Stable/A-1+
New Zealand	AAA/Stable/A-1+	AA+/Stable/A-1+
Norway	AAA/Stable/A-1+	AAA/Stable/A-1+

Exhibit 3 (continued)

Sovereign	Local Currency	Foreign Currency
Oman	A-/Stable/A-2	BBB+/Stable/A-2
Pakistan	BB/Stable/B	B+/Stable/B
Panama	BB/Negative/---	BB/Negative/B
Papua New Guinea	B+/Positive/B	B/Positive/B
Paraguay	B-/Stable/C	B-/Stable/C
Peru	BB+/Stable/B	BB/Stable/B
Philippines	BBB-/Stable/A-3	BB/Stable/B
Poland	A-/Stable/A-2	BBB+/Stable/A-2
Portugal	AA/Negative/A-1+	AA/Negative/A-1+
Qatar	A+/Positive/A-1	A+/Positive/A-1
Romania	BBB-/Stable/B	BB+/Stable/B
Russian Federation	BBB-/Stable/A-3	BB+/Stable/B
Saudi Arabia	A+/Stable/A-1	A/Stable/A-1
Senegal	B+/Stable/B	B+/Stable/B
Serbia	B+/Stable/B	B+/Stable/B
Singapore	AAA/Stable/A-1+	AAA/Stable/A-1+
Slovakia	A-/Positive/A-2	A-/Positive/A-2
Slovenia	AA/Stable/A-1+	AA-/Stable/A-1+
South Africa	A/Stable/A-1	BBB/Stable/A-3
Spain	AAA/Stable/A-1+	AAA/Stable/A-1+
Suriname	B/Stable/—	B-/Stable/—
Sweden	AAA/Stable/A-1+	AAA/Stable/A-1+
Switzerland	AAA/Stable/A-1+	AAA/Stable/A-1+
Taiwan	AA-/Negative/A-1+	AA-/Negative/A-1+
Thailand	A/Stable/A-1	BBB+/Stable/A-2
Trinidad and Tobago	A/Positive/A-1	BBB+/Positive/A-2
Tunisia	A/Stable/A-1	BBB/Stable/A-3
Turkey	BB/Stable/B	BB-/Stable/B
Ukraine	B+/Stable/B	B+/Stable/B
United Kingdom	AAA/Stable/A-1+	AAA/Stable/A-1+
United States of America	AAA/Stable/A-1+	AAA/Stable/A-1+
Uruguay	B/Stable/B	B/Stable/B
Venezuela	B/Stable/B	B/Stable/B
Vietnam	BB/Stable/B	BB-/Stable/B

Source: Sovereign Ratings Group Media Relations, Standard & Poor's.

CW-Neg.-On CreditWatch with negative implications. SD-Selective default. NM-Not meaningful. Notes: "Very Strong," "Strong," "Satisfactory," and "Only Adequate" are sovereign-assessment ratings. Rating outlooks were introduced by Standard & Poor's in June 1989. In 1981, Standard & Poor's added a plus (+) sign to 'A-1'-rated short-term issuers with extremely strong safety characteristics.

* Only long-term local and foreign currency ratings remain at CW-Neg.; short-term local and foreign currency ratings are removed.

Exhibit 4 Nationally Recognized Statistical Rating Organizations (NRSROs)—Selected Data

NRSRO (headquarters)	Employees (analysts)	Total rated securities, US$	Rated sovereigns	Ownership
Standard & Poor's (New York)	~6,000 (~1,100)	~$30 trillion	107	Operating segment of The McGraw-Hill Companies
Moody's Investors Service (New York)	~1,800 (~1,000)	~$30 trillion	101	Subsidiary of Moody's Corporation
Fitch, Inc. (New York/ London)	~1,250 (~700)	(not available)	89	Subsidiary of Fimalac, S.A.
Dominion Bond Rating Service Limited (Toronto)	65 (45)	(not available)	Not rated	Privately owned

Sources: Securities and Exchange Commission, "Credit Rating Agencies—NRSROs," available at http://www.sec.gov/answers/nrsro.htm; Sovereign Ratings Group Media Relations, Standard & Poor's; Standard & Poor's, "Fact Sheet – At a Glance," March 29, 2004; Michael R. King and Timothy J. Sinclair, "Private Actors and Public Policy: A Requiem for the New Basel Capital Accord," *International Political Science Review* 24:3 (2003): 347; David T. Beers and Marie Cavanaugh, "Sovereign Credit Ratings: A Primer," S&P, March 15, 2004; The McGraw-Hill Companies, Inc., Annual Report for the year ended December 31, 2003, p. 27, available at http://www.sec.gov/Archives/edgar/data/64040/000095012304002457/y94410exv13.htm; Moody's Investors Service, "Introduction to Moody's," available at http://www.moodys.com/moodys/cust/AboutMoodys/AboutMoodys.aspx?topic=intro&redir_url=/cust/AboutMoodys/staticRedirect.asp; Moody's Investors Service, "Sovereign Ratings List," January 7, 2005, pp. 6–15; Moody's Corporation, Annual Report on Form 10-K for the fiscal year ended December 31, 2003, p. 4, available at http://www.sec.gov/Archives/edgar/data/1059556/000095012304003262/y95090e10vk.htm; Fitch, Inc., "About Fitch: Overview," available at http://www.fitchratings.com/corporate/aboutFitch.cfm?detail=1; Charles D. Brown, Response Letter to SEC Concept Release: Rating Agencies and the Use of Credit Ratings under the Federal Securities Laws, July 28, 2003, available at http://www.sec.gov/rules/concept/s71203/cbrown072803.htm; Fitch, Inc., "About Fitch: The History of Fitch Ratings," available at http://www.fitchratings.com/corporate/aboutFitch.cfm?detail=2; Gregory Root, Testimony before the Subcommittee on Capital Markets, Insurance and Government Sponsored Enterprises of the Committee on Financial Services, U.S. House of Representatives, April 2, 2003, available at http://financialservices.house.gov/media/pdf/040203gr.pdf; Dominion Bond Rating Service, "About DBRS," available at http://www.dbrs.com/web/jsp/pub_about.jsp; Dominion Bond Rating Service, "About DBRS: The Industries," available at http://www.dbrs.com/web/jsp/pub_industries.jsp.

Endnotes

[1] The views expressed in this case do not necessarily reflect the views of Standard & Poor's.

[2] Authors' interview with David T. Beers, managing director and global head of sovereign and international public finance ratings, Standard & Poor's, August 11, 2004.

[3] Authors' interview with Marie Cavanaugh, managing director of sovereign ratings, Standard & Poor's, August 11, 2004.

[4] Authors' interview with Laura Feinland Katz, managing director and chief criteria officer for Central and Latin America, Standard & Poor's, August 11, 2004.

[5] Richard Sylla, "An Historical Primer on the Business of Credit Rating," in *Ratings, Rating Agencies and the Global Financial System*, edited by Richard M. Levich et al. (Boston: Kluwer Academic Publishers, 2002), p. 22.

[6] Ibid. Banks at the time were generally regulated by—and confined their business to—individual states. The revolutionary influence of the railroads was felt far beyond the world of finance. See, e.g., Stephen Kern, *The Culture of Time and Space: 1880 – 1918* (with a new preface) (Cambridge, MA: Harvard University Press, 2003) (discussing the impact of railroads on conceptions of time and space in the late nineteenth and early twentieth centuries).

[7] Sylla, pp. 22–24.

[8] Ibid., p. 23. The Mercantile Agency eventually became R.G. Dun and Company in 1859, which merged with John Bradstreet's similar company in 1933, forming Dun & Bradstreet, which acquired Moody's in 1962.

[9] Ibid., pp. 23–24.

[10] Frank Partnoy, "The Siskel and Ebert of Financial Markets?: Two Thumbs Down For the Credit Rating Agencies," *Washington University Law Quarterly* 77 (Fall 1999): 639–641, 646–647.

[11] Sylla, pp. 33–34.

[12] Authors' interview with Michael L. Privitera, vice president, public affairs, Standard & Poor's, December 6, 2004.

[13] See, e.g., Partnoy, p. 653.

[14] Richard Cantor and Frank Packer, "The Credit Rating Industry," *The Journal of Fixed Income* 5:3 (December 1995): 15.

[15] See, e.g., Securities and Exchange Commission, "Report on the Role and Function of Credit Rating Agencies in the Operation of the Securities Markets," January 2003, available at http://www.sec.gov/news/studies/credratingreport0103.pdf.

[16] Daniel M. Covitz and Paul Harrison, "Testing Conflicts of Interest at Bond Ratings Agencies with Market Anticipation: Evidence that Reputation Incentives Dominate," December 2003 (latest draft), available at http://www.federalreserve.gov/pubs/feds/2003/200368/200368pap.pdf. The authors also found "stronger support for the importance of reputation concerns at S&P than at Moody's." Ibid., p. 5.

[17] Timothy J. Sinclair, "Between state and market: Hegemony and institutions of collective action under conditions of international capital mobility," *Policy Sciences* 27 (1994): 448–451.

[18] Sylla, p. 24.

[19] Standard & Poor's, "Company History," available at http://www2.standardandpoors.com/NASApp/cs/ContentServer?pagename=sp/Page/AboutUsMainPg&r=1&l=EN&b=8&s=1. For the sake of clarity, both Standard & Poor's and its precursors will be referred to throughout as "S&P."

[20] See ibid.; The McGraw-Hill Companies, Inc., Annual Report for the year ended December 31, 2003, p. 66, available at http://www.sec.gov/Archives/edgar/data/64040/000095012304002457/y94410exv13.htm.

[21] Standard & Poor's, "Company History."

[22] Ibid.

[23] Authors' interview with Michael L. Privitera.

[24] Leo C. O'Neill, Response Letter to SEC Concept Release: Rating Agencies and the Use of Credit Ratings under the Federal Securities Laws, July 28, 2003, available at http://www.sec.gov/rules/concept/s71203/standard072803.htm; ibid. at Appendix A, response to Question 43.

[25] Authors' interview with Michael L. Privitera.

[26] McGraw-Hill Annual Report, pp. 27, 32.

[27] David T. Beers, "Credit FAQ: The Future of Sovereign Credit Ratings," S&P, March 23, 2004, Table 1.

[28] Standard & Poor's, "Sovereign Ratings Before the Interest Equalization Tax," April 5, 1999.

[29] Standard & Poor's, "Sovereign Ratings Before the Interest Equalization Tax." "Yankee bonds" are dollar-denominated debt issued in the United States by non-U.S. issuers. See Campbell R. Harvey, "Yankee bond," *Forbes* Financial Glossary, "Yankee bond," available at http://www.forbes.com/tools/glossary/search.jhtml?term=yankee_bonds. Similarly, "samurai bonds" are yen-denominated debt issued in the Tokyo market by non-Japanese issuers. See Harvey, "Samurai bond," available at http://www.forbes.com/tools/glossary/search.jhtml?term=samurai_bond. Confusingly, however, "Eurobonds" have nothing to do with euros or Europe; they are internationally syndicated debt issued in a number of countries, and outside the jurisdiction of any single country, such as "Euroyen" bonds, which are denominated in yen. See Harvey, "Eurobond" and "Euroyen bonds," available at http://www.forbes.com/tools/glossary/glossary.jhtml?letter=e.

[30] See Harvey, "Interest equalization tax," available at http://www.forbes.com/tools/glossary/glossary.jhtml?letter=I.

[31] Standard & Poor's, "Sovereign Ratings Before the Interest Equalization Tax."

[32] John Chambers and David T. Beers, "Sovereign Ratings Display Stability Over Two Decades," S&P, April 5, 1999.

[33] Ibid.

[34] Brendan Murphy, "Credit ratings and emerging economies," *Friedrich Ebert Stiftung Digitale Bibliothek* (2000), Section II, "The Emerging Markets Challenge to Credit Rating Agencies," available at http://www.fes.de/fulltext/iez/00767toc.htm. The "Brady Plan" was a debt restructuring plan named for U.S. Treasury Secretary Nicholas Brady, who sponsored it. Under the Brady Plan, defaulted commercial bank debt was "converted into marketable securities," typically involving forgiveness of part of the principal and interest in exchange for bonds, some of which were collateralized by U.S. Treasury bonds. Initially traded among the banks themselves, Brady bonds "soon found their way into speculative and institutional portfolios" throughout the world.

[35] Authors' interview with David T. Beers.

[36] Beers, "Credit FAQ."

[37] Jan Vandemoortele, "Credit Quality Moves Center Stage as African Countries Seek to Improve their Economic Performance," in *Sovereign Ratings in Africa*, June 2004 (New York: Standard & Poor's), p. 7 (commentary of the principal adviser and group leader, UNDP Poverty Group, New York). Ghana, Cameroon, Benin, Burkina Faso, Mali, Madagascar, and Mozambique participated in the program. "Mozambique Sovereign

Credit Rated 'B' by Standard & Poor's under UNDP Credit Initiative for Africa," July 8, 2004, available at http://www.undp.org/dpa/pressrelease/releases/2004/july/prMoz8July04.html.

[38] Beers, "Credit FAQ."

[39] Authors' interview with David T. Beers.

[40] Ibid.

[41] David T. Beers and Marie Cavanaugh, "Sovereign Credit Ratings: A Primer," S&P, March 15, 2004. Except where otherwise noted, references below refer to the March 2004 version of this document.

[42] Beers and Cavanaugh, "Sovereign Credit Ratings: A Primer." The trend toward more explicit methodological detail is evident in comparison with previous iterations. See, e.g., David T. Beers and Marie Cavanaugh, "Sovereign Credit Ratings: A Primer," *Standard & Poor's Sovereign Ratings Service*, December 1998 (New York: Standard & Poor's), p. 1; Philip Bates, "Rating criteria overview," *Standard & Poor's CreditWeek*, May 25, 1987 (New York: Standard & Poor's), p. 6.

[43] Authors' interview with David T. Beers.

[44] Standard & Poor's, "Ratings Definitions," March 4, 2003.

[45] Marie Cavanaugh, "Credit FAQ: Foreign/Local Currency and Sovereign/Nonsovereign Ratings Differentials," S&P, September 22, 2003.

[46] Standard & Poor's, "S&P Long-Term Issuer Credit Ratings Definitions," May 17, 2002.

[47] Standard & Poor's, "S&P Long-Term Issuer Credit Ratings Definitions"; "S&P Short-Term Issuer Credit Ratings Definitions," May 17, 2002.

[48] See Marie Cavanaugh, "Sovereign Credit Characteristics by Rating Category," S&P, November 19, 2003; Standard & Poor's, "S&P Long-Term Issuer Credit Ratings Definitions." So-called "junk bonds" are also sometimes referred to as "high-yield" bonds. See, e.g., Harvey, "Junk bond," available at http://www.forbes.com/tools/glossary/glossary.jhtml?letter=j.

[49] Standard & Poor's, "Ratings Definitions"; authors' interview with Michael L. Privitera.

[50] Standard & Poor's, "Sovereign Ratings," on file with the authors.

[51] Ibid.

[52] Beers and Cavanaugh, "Sovereign Credit Ratings: A Primer."

[53] Authors' interview with Marie Cavanaugh.

[54] Cavanaugh, "Sovereign Credit Characteristics by Rating Category."

[55] Beers and Cavanaugh, "Sovereign Credit Ratings: A Primer."

[56] Cavanaugh, "Sovereign Credit Characteristics by Rating Category."

[57] Authors' interview with Marie Cavanaugh.

[58] Authors' interview with David T. Beers.

[59] Cavanaugh, "Sovereign Credit Characteristics by Rating Category."

[60] David T. Beers and John Chambers, "Sovereign Defaults: Heading Lower Into 2004," S&P, September 18, 2003.

[61] Ibid.

[62] Ibid.

[63] Authors' interview with Marie Cavanaugh.

[64] Ibid.

[65] Beers and Cavanaugh, "Sovereign Credit Ratings: A Primer."

[66] Ibid.

[67] Ibid.

[68] Cavanaugh, "Sovereign Credit Characteristics by Rating Category."

[69] Ibid.; see also Dieter Kerwer, "Rating Agencies: Setting a Standard for Global Financial Markets," *Economic Sociology (European Electronic Newsletter)* 3:3 (June 2002): 43; Sinclair, "Between state and market," pp. 454–455 (arguing that the credit-rating process essentially advocates—or enforces—a neoliberal ideology).

[70] Authors' interview with Marie Cavanaugh.

[71] John Chambers and David T. Beers, "S&P's Sovereign Ratings Focus on Fundamentals," S&P, May 26, 1999.

[72] Ibid.

[73] Moritz Kraemer and Luc Marchand, "Western Europe Past Its Prime – Sovereign Rating Perspectives in the Context of Aging Populations," S&P, January 9, 2002, p. 1. Cf. Todd Milbourn, Arnoud Boot, and Anjolein Schmeits, "Credit Ratings as Coordination Mechanisms," July 2, 2004, pp. 1–2, manuscript on file with the authors (arguing that credit ratings, through the "credit watch" structure, result in "a 'deal' (implicit contract) between the firm and the credit rating agency where the former promises to undertake specific actions … to mitigate the possible deterioration of its credit standing," a process that is given "'bite'" by the fact that "institutional investors condition their investment decisions on the rating").

[74] See, e.g., David T. Beers et al., "Government Policy Responses Key To Ratings In Emerging Markets Says S&P," S&P, September 24, 1998.

[75] Beers and Cavanaugh, "Sovereign Credit Ratings: A Primer."

[76] Beers, "Credit FAQ: The Future of Sovereign Credit Ratings."

[77] Michael R. King and Timothy J. Sinclair, "Private Actors and Public Policy: A Requiem for the New Basel Capital Accord," *International Political Science Review* 24:3 (2003): 347.

[78] Ibid.

[79] Partnoy, p. 650 at n. 149.

[80] King and Sinclair, p. 347.

[81] Bank for International Settlements (BIS), "Credit Ratings and Complementary Sources of Credit Quality Information," Basel Committee on Banking Supervision Working Paper No. 3, August 2000, pp. 14–15, available at http://www.bis.org/publ/bcbs_wp3.htm.

[82] Charles D. Brown, Response Letter to SEC Concept Release: Rating Agencies and the Use of Credit Ratings under the Federal Securities Laws, July 28, 2003, available at http://www.sec.gov/rules/concept/s71203/cbrown072803.htm.

[83] Jeff Jewell and Miles Livingston, "A Comparison of Bond Ratings from Moody's S&P and Fitch," *Financial Markets, Institutions & Instruments* 8:4 (August 1999): 42.

[84] Brown, Response Letter to SEC Concept Release.

[85] O'Neill, Response Letter to SEC Concept Release.

[86] Timothy J. Sinclair, "Bond-Rating Agencies and Coordination in the Global Political Economy," in *Private Authority and International Affairs*, edited by A. Claire Cutler et al. (Albany, NY: State University of New York Press, 1999), p. 161; see also Kerwer, p. 43.

[87] Kerwer, p. 43.

[88] See generally Bank for International Settlements (BIS), "Basel II: International Convergence of Capital Measurement and Capital Standards: a Revised Framework," Basel Committee Publications No. 107, June 2004, available at http://www.bis.org/publ/bcbs107.htm; Bank for International Settlements (BIS), "G10 central bank governors and heads of supervision endorse the publication of the revised capital framework," June 26, 2004, available at http://www.bis.org/press/p040626.htm.

[89] See generally Standard & Poor's, *Sovereign Ratings in Africa*.

[90] Authors' interview with David T. Beers.

[91] Vandemoortele, in *Sovereign Ratings in Africa*, p. 7.

[92] Konrad Reuss and David Beers, "Sovereign Ratings Gain Momentum in Africa," in *Sovereign Ratings in Africa*, p. 8.

[93] Authors' interview with David T. Beers.

[94] Authors' interview with Marie Cavanaugh.

[95] See Bank for International Settlements (BIS), "Credit Ratings and Complementary Sources of Credit Quality Information," p. 54 (providing a partial listing of U.S. regulation incorporating credit ratings).

[96] Securities and Exchange Commission, "Report on the Role and Function of Credit Rating Agencies in the Operation of the Securities Markets," pp. 5–6. The first use of the NRSRO concept occurred in the net capital rule for broker-dealers, which essentially "requires broker-dealers, when computing net capital, to deduct from their net worth certain percentages of the market value of their proprietary securities positions," with a lower deduction required for securities rated investment grade by NRSROs (reflecting the lower risk of loss). Ibid., p. 6 (summarizing Rule 15c3-1 under the Securities and Exchange Act of 1934).

[97] Other factors include the agency's organizational structure; its financial resources; the adequacy of its staff; its "independence from the companies it rates"; its rating procedures; and whether it has effective procedures "to prevent the misuse of nonpublic information." Ibid., pp. 9–10.

[98] Ibid., p. 6.

[99] Ibid., p. 7 (discussing Rule 2a-7 under the Investment Company Act of 1940).

[100] Securities and Exchange Commission, "Credit Rating Agencies – NRSROs," available at http://www.sec.gov/answers/nrsro.htm.

[101] Partnoy, pp. 681–682. According to Partnoy, while rating agencies did rely on their "reputational capital" during the 1920s, when barriers to entry were low and ratings were financed by investors (639–640), the reputational capital hypothesis does not explain the current state of affairs—the "recent dominance and growth of a small number of rating agencies"; an issuer-based fee structure; the "dramatic changes in the [information] value of ratings over time"; and that periods in which credit ratings "increased in importance" (i.e., through incorporation into regulation in the 1930s and since the 1970s) were "followed by a series of bond defaults" suggestive of rating errors. Ibid., pp. 651–654. Others have made similar arguments. See, e.g., Lawrence J. White, "The Credit Rating Industry: An Industrial Organization Analysis," in *Ratings, Rating Agencies and the Global Financial System*.

Evidence on the accuracy of the regulatory license hypothesis has been mixed. One study, examining eurobond returns after watchlistings and rating changes by S&P and Moody's, found that the announcement effects of downgrades were "significantly stronger for downgrades into speculative grade," and speculated that such announcement effects "can in part be explained by price pressure effects due to regulatory constraints rather than original information content of rating changes." Manfred Steiner and Volker G. Heinke, "Event Study Concerning International Bond Price Effects of Credit Rating Actions," International Journal of Finance and Economics 6 (2001): 139. Another study, however, found "no evidence that firms seek third ratings [beyond S&P and Moody's] specifically to help meet regulatory requirements" (Richard Cantor and Frank Packer, "Differences of opinion and selection bias in the credit rating industry," Journal of Banking & Finance 21 (1997): 1409), contrary to what the regulatory license hypothesis might have led one to expect.

[102] Partnoy, pp. 704–705.

[103] Milbourn, Boot, and Schmeits, pp. 1–2.

[104] Authors' interview with David T. Beers.

[105] Authors' interview with Laura Feinland Katz.

[106] Bank for International Settlements (BIS), "G10 central bank governors and heads of supervision endorse the publication of the revised capital framework" (Note to Editors). The "Group of Ten" actually includes 11 countries (Belgium, Canada, France, Germany, Italy, Japan, the Netherlands, Sweden, Switzerland, the United Kingdom, and the United States), which "consult and co-operate on economic, monetary and financial matters," including through periodic meetings of their finance ministers and central bank governors. See "Group of Ten," May 2004, available at http://www.bis.org/cgi-bin/print.cgi. For further background on Basel II and a discussion of its anticipated impact on German-style relationship banking, see Jeffrey Fear, "Banking on Germany?" HBS Case No. 703-028 (Boston: Harvard Business School Publishing, Rev. 2003).

[107] Ibid.

[108] Bank for International Settlements (BIS), "Basel II: International Convergence of Capital Measurement and Capital Standards: a Revised Framework," Introduction, para. 5.

[109] Bank for International Settlements (BIS), "G10 central bank governors and heads of supervision endorse the publication of the revised capital framework" (Note to Editors).

[110] Murphy, Section III.

[111] Bank for International Settlements (BIS), "Basel II: International Convergence of Capital Measurement and Capital Standards: a Revised Framework," p. 15, para. 53. Interestingly, unrated claims on sovereigns receive a risk weighting of 100%, or 50% less than the risk weighting for the lowest-rated sovereign issues.

[112] Ibid., p. 23, para. 91. Note also that S&P's rating scale is used as the example in the framework (p. 15, para. 53), leaving little doubt that S&P should qualify as an ECAI. ECAI status is not, however, limited exclusively to credit-rating agencies. See, e.g., ibid., p. 15, para. 55 (regarding use of export credit agencies' assessments in "risk weighting claims on sovereigns").

[113] King and Sinclair, p. 351.

[114] Ibid., pp. 351–352; see also Edward I. Altman and Anthony Saunders, "The Role of Credit Ratings in Bank Capital," in Ratings, Rating Agencies and the Global Financial System, pp. 102–103.

[115] King and Sinclair, pp. 353–354.

[116] See Scott Bugie et al., "Basel II: Evolution not Revolution for Banks," S&P, October 21, 2004; see also Scott Bugie et al., "The Essentials of Basel II," S&P, October 21, 2004.

[117] White, "The Credit Rating Industry: An Industrial Organization Analysis," pp. 55–56.

[118] Standard & Poor's, "Sovereign Ratings."

[119] Authors' interview with David T. Beers.

[120] White, "The Credit Rating Industry: An Industrial Organization Analysis," pp. 56–57; see also Partnoy, p. 704 (advocating use of credit spreads).

[121] Altman and Saunders, p. 113.

[122] Kerwer, pp. 43–45.

[123] O'Neill, Response Letter to SEC Concept Release; authors' interview with Michael L. Privitera.

[124] Ibid.

[125] O'Neill, Response Letter to SEC Concept Release.

[126] Standard & Poor's, "Basel Committee on Banking Supervision Third Consultation Paper: Standard & Poor's Response," S&P, August 22, 2003.

[127] Authors' interview with Michael L. Privitera.

[128] Beers, "Credit FAQ: The Future of Sovereign Credit Ratings."

[129] Graciela Kaminsky and Sergio Schmukler, "Rating Agencies and Financial Markets," in *Ratings, Rating Agencies and the Global Financial System*, p. 229; see also Helmut Reisen and Julia von Maltzan, "Boom and Bust and Sovereign Ratings," *International Finance* 2:2 (July 1999): 289 (finding "suggests that sovereign ratings by the three leading agencies do not independently lead the market, but that they are interdependent with bond yield spreads once ratings and spreads"). At the same time, "a highly significant announcement effect" has been found when "emerging-market sovereign bonds are put on review with negative outlook," suggesting that credit rating agencies have "the potential to help dampen excessive private capital inflows into the emerging markets" – provided announcements are made "in time." Gillermo Larraín, Helmut Reisen, and Julia von Maltzan, "Emerging Market Risk and Sovereign Credit Ratings," OECD Development Centre, Technical Papers No. 124, April 1997, p. 21.

Joseph Stiglitz, in particular, has been a vocal critic of credit-rating agencies and the role they played in emerging market crises in the 1990s. In a paper with G. Ferri and L.-G. Liu, Stiglitz sought to demonstrate that "rating agencies attached higher weights to their qualitative judgment than they gave to the economic fundamentals." G. Ferri, L.-G. Liu, and J.E. Stiglitz, "The Procyclical Role of Rating Agencies: Evidence from the East Asian Crisis," *Economic Notes* 28:3 (1999): 349.

[130] Authors' interview with Marie Cavanaugh.

[131] Ibid.

[132] K. Subramanian, "The fall of rating agencies," The Hindu Business Line (Internet Edition), July 17, 2002, available at http://www.blonnet.com/2002/07/17/stories/2002071700060800.htm. ("The failings of rating agencies [during the Asian crisis] did not worry the US public or the Congress as long as they occurred in foreign jurisdictions and promoted US interests. They were alerted only when those methods were re-exported to its homeland and brought about a major crisis – Enron.")

[133] Securities and Exchange Commission, "Report on the Role and Function of Credit Rating Agencies in the Operation of the Securities Markets," pp. 3–4. The SEC had in fact attempted to impose greater regulatory oversight upon credit-rating agencies through a proposed rule in 1997 that, among other things, would have required that the agencies register with the SEC as investment advisers. Securities and Exchange Commission, "Proposed Rule: Capital Requirements for Brokers or Dealers Under the Securities Exchange Act of 1934," Release No. 34-39457; File No. S7-33-97, December 17, 1997, available at http://www.sec.gov/rules/proposed/34-39457.txt. The proposal was not acted upon, due in part to concerns regarding regulatory oversight of the agencies. Securities and Exchange Commission, "Report on the Role and Function of Credit Rating Agencies in the Operation of the Securities Markets," pp. 5–6.

[134] Securities and Exchange Commission, "Concept Release: Rating Agencies and the Use of Credit Ratings under the Federal Securities Laws," Release Nos. 33-8236; 34-47972; IC-26066; File No. S7-12-03, June 4, 2003, available at http://www.sec.gov/rules/concept/33-8236.htm.

[135] O'Neill, Response Letter to SEC Concept Release; Raymond W. McDaniel, Response Letter to SEC Concept Release: Rating Agencies and the Use of Credit Ratings under the Federal Securities Laws, July 28, 2003, available at http://www.sec.gov/rules/concept/s71203/moodys072803.htm.

[136] European Parliament resolution on role and methods of rating agencies (2003/2081(INI), February 10, 2004, available at http://www2.europarl.eu.int/omk/sipade2?PUBREF=-//EP//NONSGML+TA+P5-TA-2004-0080+0+DOC+PDF+V0//EN&L=EN&LEVEL=3&NAV=S&LSTDOC=Y.

[137] Ibid.

[138] Ibid.; see also Sergio Beristain, "EU's Plan To Regulate Is Fiercely Opposed," *The Banker*, December 1, 2004, available at http://www.thebanker.com/news/fullstory.php/aid/2370/EU%92s_plan_to_regulate_is_fiercely_opposed.html .

[139] European Parliament resolution on role and methods of rating agencies.

[140] Ibid.

[141] European Banking Federation, "Draft Report on the role and method of credit rating agencies," January 8, 2004 (letter responding to a draft report by Giorgis Katiforis, rapporteur), available at http://212.3.246.149/1/JOFJLJFAGABFEMDMKALIPCNJY9V6U6498DULQD6CBK9YBDG3BYB3A3BY9LTE4Q /EBF/docs/DLS/rating_agencies_04-2004-02073-01-E.pdf; Standard & Poor's, "Maintaining Transparency in European Financial Markets: Position on Draft Katiforis Report on: Role and Methods of Rating Agencies," S&P, December 2003; authors' interview with Michael L. Privitera.

[142] Standard & Poor's, "Maintaining Transparency in European Financial Markets: Position on Draft Katiforis Report on: Role and Methods of Rating Agencies."

[143] Klaus C. Engelen, "Das empire strikes back: German banks have had enough of Standard & Poor's and other agencies, and they're not going to take it anymore," *International Economy* (Winter 2004), available at http://www.findarticles.com/p/articles/mi_m2633/is_1_18/ai_113564065.

[144] See, e.g., European Parliament resolution on role and methods of rating agencies; Theresa Villiers, MEP, "Credit rating agencies," February 9, 2004, available at http://www2.europarl.eu.int/omk/sipade2?PUBREF=-//EP//TEXT+CRE+20040209+ITEM-004+DOC+XML+V0//EN&L=EN&LEVEL=3&NAV=S&LSTDOC=Y&MODE-CRE=SEARCH&DETAIL=1-055 (speech during European Parliament debate). ("[I]t is difficult to see how changing the scheme or regulation for rating agencies could have prevented the Parmalat scandal.")

[145] IOSCO, "Statement of Principles Regarding the Activities of Credit Rating Agencies," September 25, 2003, available at http://www.iosco.org/pubdocs/pdf/IOSCOPD151.pdf (statement of the Technical Committee).

[146] IOSCO, "Press Release: Task Force of Securities Regulators from Major Markets Agrees on Code of Conduct Fundamentals for Credit Rating Agencies," December 3, 2004, available at http://www.iosco.org/news/pdf/IOSCONEWS78.pdf; see also Liz Rappaport, "IOSCO Brings Light Touch To Ratings Agencies Oversight," Dow Jones Newswires, December 8, 2004; Union of Industrial and Employers' Confederations of Europe, Letter to Phillippe Richard, IOSCO Secretary General, November 8, 2004, available at http://www.iosco.org/pubdocs/pdf/IOSCOPD177_3.pdf (commenting on the draft Code of Conduct, and arguing that self-regulation of credit-rating agencies "should be given priority over formal regulation at this point").

[147] O'Neill, Response Letter to SEC Concept Release.

[148] See, e.g., Subramanian. ("It is easy to demolish the rating agencies. It is not as easy to establish a new structure in their place.")

RAWI ABDELAL

CHRISTOPHER M. BRUNER

Standard & Poor's Sovereign Credit Ratings: Scales and Process

This note provides a brief overview of rating scales and related announcements to credit markets (such as "Outlook" and "CreditWatch" actions) employed by Standard & Poor's Ratings Services in its opinions on the creditworthiness of sovereign governments and the risk of default for specific debt issues. It also provides background on the rating process, including communications with the sovereign and the role and function of the "rating committee," and briefly discusses analytical categories and key risks substantially impacting S&P's analysis.

Standard & Poor's Rating Scales

S&P's long-term credit-rating scale establishes a letter-grade hierarchy. Ratings include "AAA" ("extremely strong" repayment capacity); "AA" ("very strong"); "A" ("strong"); "BBB" ("adequate"); "BB" ("less vulnerable"); "B" ("more vulnerable"); "CCC" ("currently vulnerable"); "CC" ("currently highly vulnerable"); "R" ("under regulatory supervision owing to its financial condition"); "SD" ("selective default"); "D" ("default"); and "NR" ("not rated"). Ratings of BBB and above are considered investment grade, while ratings of BB and below are non-investment grade, or "speculative" grade, meaning that they have "significant speculative characteristics" including "large uncertainties or major exposures to adverse conditions."[1]

Short-term credit ratings also consist of letter grades, but according to a simpler scale including "A-1" ("strong" repayment capacity); "A-2" ("satisfactory"); "A-3" ("adequate"); "B" ("more vulnerable"); "C" ("currently highly vulnerable"); "R" ("under regulatory supervision"); "SD" ("selective default"); "D" ("default"); and "NR" ("not rated").[2]

A rating Outlook "assesses the potential direction of a long-term credit rating over the intermediate to longer term," addressing "any changes in the economic and/or fundamental business conditions." Outlook categories include "Positive" (rating "may be raised"); "Negative" ("may be lowered"); "Stable" ("not likely to change"); "Developing" ("may be raised or lowered"); and "NM" ("not meaningful"). However, an Outlook "is not necessarily a precursor of a rating change or future CreditWatch action."[3]

The CreditWatch service "highlights the potential direction of a short- or long-term rating," addressing "identifiable events and short-term trends" resulting in "special surveillance," which in the case of sovereigns might include referenda or regulatory actions. Essentially, a CreditWatch

---

Professor Rawi Abdelal and Research Associate Christopher M. Bruner, J.D., prepared this note as the basis for class discussion.

listing means that a noteworthy event has occurred and "additional information is necessary to evaluate the current rating." CreditWatch designations include "positive" (rating "may be raised"); "negative" ("may be lowered"); and "developing" ("may be raised, lowered, or affirmed"). As with a rating Outlook, a CreditWatch listing "does not mean a rating change is inevitable," and conversely, "rating changes may occur without the ratings having first appeared on CreditWatch."[4]

Standard & Poor's Rating Process

A sovereign seeking a rating establishes a formal relationship with S&P by executing a written agreement governing the rating process.[5] S&P sends information regarding its ratings criteria and requests a preliminary set of information from the sovereign.[6] The analysts review the various economic and financial data made available to them (at least five years' worth), budget and economic projections, and any available longer-term projections, as well as any analyses on the country "by organizations such as the IMF [International Monetary Fund] and the World Bank."[7] (Marie Cavanaugh, a managing director of sovereign ratings, noted that S&P often visits the IMF office within a given country and that it often has more "in country" contact with the IMF than through its headquarters in Washington, D.C.)[8] S&P then forwards "an outline of discussion points and a suggested meeting schedule." Typically, a team of two analysts (possibly more if language presents an issue, or if private-sector ratings are being done simultaneously)[9] visits a country for three to four days, meeting with representatives of the finance ministry, central bank, and other governmental agencies, as well as "individuals and organizations outside the government who are well informed about economic and political trends in the country."[10]

Such a visit from S&P, in Cavanaugh's experience, "tends to be fairly high profile," involving meetings with high-level officials, as well as more midlevel staff closer to the numbers.[11] "Outside" meetings might include representatives of banks, trade unions, the press, academia, and embassies.[12] Cavanaugh emphasized that they "always meet with the opposition," the effort being "to get as many opinions as possible" and to generate a range of potential future scenarios, adding that analysts might speak with foreign "observers" when a country's debt-service capacity is greatly affected by external relations (e.g., "China risk" in Hong Kong), though a formal visit to a neighboring country would be unusual.[13] Topics of discussion include economic strategy (particularly fiscal and monetary policies), privatization and "other microeconomic reforms," and "other factors likely to influence trends in government debt and the balance of payments," as well as "political trends in the country and how they may affect the predictability and sustainability of government policies over time."[14] Though the process relies heavily on government statistics, Cavanaugh observed that it is sometimes necessary to discount the officials' numbers, as where there is significant off-budget spending or a substantial "gray economy"[15] (sometimes called a "shadow economy," consisting of "business activities that are not accounted for by official statistics").[16]

Upon completion of their meetings and analyses, the analysts prepare a report for submission to the "rating committee," which discusses the report and votes on the eventual rating. This report generally includes all of the components of the eventual rating package in draft form—a rationale, an Outlook, a comparative section, and a suggested letter rating, as well as analysis of political risk, economic prospects, fiscal and monetary policy, and external factors. Committee meetings typically convene at 8 a.m. New York time and involve up to 12 individuals from two or three offices in order to ensure coordination and "global comparability." Meetings often include nonvoting observers from other groups to which the rating is relevant (e.g., corporates) and typically last about two hours. Cavanaugh explained that while there is "no set method of voting," analysts with more experience in the country or region, or with similar sovereigns, generally vote first (a method she does not believe affects the more junior analysts' votes, as it is "more about the reasoning," and they "don't hire shy people"). While more extensive debate typically ensues when the committee is considering an emerging market rating, it is "not common for votes to vary much," and Cavanaugh does not believe that the greater relative impact of ratings in emerging markets affects the process.[17]

Once the committee has arrived at a rating the sovereign is notified of the decision, and if the government accepts the rating, then S&P issues it to the public (effectively the committee report with confidential information removed).[18] The sovereign can appeal the rating once, typically providing new information or arguing that certain factors should be weighted differently, in which case the committee process is repeated for a final, unappealable decision (which the sovereign may nevertheless choose not to make public).[19] In Cavanaugh's experience, explanation of and "dialogue" regarding the process and outcome are particularly important with first-time ratings.[20]

The rating committee considers both "quantitative and qualitative" factors in arriving at a rating decision.[21] The process involves ranking the sovereign by a one-to-six scale (one being the best) with respect to each of 10 "analytical categories," though there is "no exact formula for combining the scores to determine ratings."[22] As Cavanaugh put it, they "don't use the same statistics to rate Canada and Cameroon," as the process involves weighing the interaction of policy choices in a particular environment.[23] The 10 analytical categories are broadly intended to address "economic risk" (that is, the sovereign's "ability to repay") and "political risk" (the sovereign's "willingness to repay").

Specific analytical categories include political risk; income and economic structure; economic growth prospects; fiscal flexibility; general government debt burden; off-budget and contingent liabilities; monetary flexibility; external liquidity; public-sector external debt burden; and private-sector external debt burden. Somewhat different considerations apply in the case of debt denominated in a foreign currency, insofar as foreign exchange must be secured to repay the debt; local currency debt ratings tend to be either the same or higher, since they are "supported by [the sovereign's] taxation powers and its ability to control the domestic financial system, which give it potentially unlimited access to local currency resources." The issue of political risk, a fundamentally qualitative issue, "distinguishes sovereigns from most other types of issuers"; unlike a corporation or a municipality, a sovereign has significant latitude simply to choose not to repay even when able, leaving creditors with "limited legal redress."[24] (Indeed, as Cavanaugh observed, sovereign defaults are, in a manner of speaking, almost always a matter of willingness to repay, insofar as a sovereign's policy choices determine its ability to meet its obligations.)[25]

S&P has identified certain "[k]ey economic and political risks" that weigh heavily on the analysis: (1) political institutions and trends, and particularly "their impact on the effectiveness and transparency of the policy environment"; (2) economic structure and growth prospects; (3) government revenue flexibility and expenditure pressures, deficits and the debt burden, and contingent liabilities; (4) monetary flexibility; and (5) external liquidity and "trends in public and private sector liabilities to nonresidents."[26]

Endnotes

[1] Standard & Poor's, "S&P Long-Term Issuer Credit Ratings Definitions," May 17, 2002.

[2] Ibid.

[3] Standard & Poor's, "Ratings Definitions," March 4, 2003.

[4] Ibid.

[5] Standard & Poor's, "Sovereign Ratings," on file with the authors.

[6] Authors' interview with Marie Cavanaugh, managing director of sovereign ratings, Standard & Poor's, August 11, 2004.

[7] Standard & Poor's, "Sovereign Ratings."

[8] Authors' interview with Marie Cavanaugh.

[9] Ibid.

[10] Standard & Poor's, "Sovereign Ratings."

[11] Authors' interview with Marie Cavanaugh.

[12] Ibid.

[13] Ibid.

[14] Standard & Poor's, "Sovereign Ratings."

[15] Authors' interview with Marie Cavanaugh.

[16] World Bank, "Gray economy (shadow economy)," in *Beyond Economic Growth* Student Book, available at http://www.worldbank.org/depweb /english/beyond/global/glossary.html#31 . The gray economy "includes illegal activities (or the so-called black market) and activities that are in themselves legal but go unreported or under-reported for purposes of tax evasion."

[17] Authors' interview with Marie Cavanaugh.

[18] Standard & Poor's, "Sovereign Ratings."

[19] Authors' interview with Marie Cavanaugh.

[20] Ibid.

[21] David T. Beers and Marie Cavanaugh, "Sovereign Credit Ratings: A Primer," March 15, 2004.

[22] Ibid.

[23] Authors' interview with Marie Cavanaugh.

[24] Beers and Cavanaugh, "Sovereign Credit Ratings: A Primer."

[25] Authors' interview with Marie Cavanaugh.

[26] Beers and Cavanaugh, "Sovereign Credit Ratings: A Primer."

9-705-007
REV: MAY 30, 2006

RAWI ABDELAL

VINCENT DESSAIN

MONIKA STACHOWIAK

Bohemian Crowns: Československá Obchodní Banka (A)

Isn't it the moment of most profound doubt that gives birth to new certainties?
—Václav Havel, Czech dissident, dramatist, and politician

On Tuesday, June 13, 2000, Pavel Kavánek, CEO of Československá Obchodní Banka (ČSOB), the fourth-largest bank in the Czech Republic, received an unexpected phone call from the Czech National Bank (CNB). The central bank was in charge of stabilizing and potentially selling off Investiční a Poštovní Banka (IPB), a retail bank experiencing liquidity problems. ČSOB had already expressed its interest in acquiring the retail bank but had been turned down by the central bank only two weeks earlier. As Kavánek now understood it from the phone call, however, it seemed as if ČSOB were being reconsidered.[1]

Traditionally, ČSOB's focus was corporate banking. However, given the low growth in corporate lending over the last three years, Kavánek had started to plan a strategic move for ČSOB toward retail banking. Rather than growing internally, he preferred acquiring a commercial bank. One potential target that Kavánek had studied was IPB, the country's third-largest retail bank with approximately 3 million personal savings accounts. With IPB, ČSOB could gain a huge retail network, as well as strong subsidiaries in insurance, fund management, and pensions.

On the other hand, Kavánek knew that there were many risks associated with acquiring the troubled IPB. For instance, IPB's asset structure was not completely known. Also, rumors about asset stripping and forged financial reporting at IPB continued to fill the local press. The retail bank struggled with a mountain of bad debt on its balance sheet, and it was under investigation by the central bank for letting reserves fall to unacceptable levels. Outflows of bank deposits had started in February and, according to analysts, about 34 billion Czech Republic crowns (US$881.1 million)[2] had so far been withdrawn by the bank's customers. That very week, the withdrawals had increased dangerously, and if they kept up, they could very well lead to the bank's insolvency.[3]

An external audit of IPB was due in two weeks.[4] Kavánek would have preferred to make up his mind after reading that audit, but chances were that the bank might already be bankrupt by then. He had to decide right away if ČSOB should apply to the central bank to acquire IPB, and if so under what conditions.[5]

Czech Economy and Financial System (1990–1994)

The Velvet Revolution and First Economic Reforms

Before ČSOB became a purely Czech bank, it had served both the Czech and Slovak territories when the two were joined to form the nation of Czechoslovakia. Czechoslovakia was founded in October 1918 as one of the successor states of the Austro-Hungarian Empire. After World War II, Czechoslovakia found itself within the Soviet sphere of influence—a fact that dramatically altered the country's economic trajectory. Communist governments nationalized industries and set up a planned economy. In 1968, Alexander Dubček, first secretary of the Communist Party, instituted a series of democratic reforms. These changes, known as the "Prague Spring," showed signs of increasing political independence for Czechoslovakia. Soviet leadership saw its control over Eastern Europe waning, and on August 20, 1968, the armies of the Eastern Bloc invaded Czechoslovakia, thus bringing an end to a period of political liberalization.

Over 20 years later, however, in November 1989, with communist regimes falling in other Central and East European countries, the communist government was overthrown in Czechoslovakia. The relatively bloodless Czech revolt was commonly referred to as the "Velvet Revolution." The country's first democratic elections since 1948 were held in June 1990 and brought to power the first completely noncommunist government. The former dissident Václav Havel was elected Czechoslovakia's first president.[6]

Like its neighboring countries, Czechoslovakia embarked on a transition from a centrally planned to a free-market economy. The strategy built on rapid liberalization and privatization to create a quickly emerging private sector.[7] Finance Minister Václav Klaus introduced the main reform package in 1990, and several measures followed quickly. The Czech crown was devalued three times in 1990 alone, for a total devaluation of over 110%. Foreign trade restrictions were substantially reduced during 1991. The majority of all price controls were eliminated, leading to a jump in price levels in early 1991 and average yearly inflation of 57%. A restrictive monetary policy was put in place to avoid further price rises and an inflationary spiral. The macroeconomic stabilization was based on a fixed exchange rate, kept in a narrow band of ±0.5% against a basket of currencies.[8] The monetary policy was successful, and inflation stabilized just above 10% in 1992.[9]

Also in January 1991, the formerly nonconvertible crown was declared internally convertible. The primary goal of internal convertibility was to make it easier for domestic corporations to access convertible currencies for trade-related transactions. In paying for imported goods and services, companies were constrained only by their balances of crowns, while the authorities guaranteed the conversion—at the prevailing exchange rate—of those balances into a foreign currency without any limit. Free access to foreign exchange on the demand side was combined with a surrender duty on the supply side.[10] For the household sector, the internal convertibility meant that citizens could buy a limited but guaranteed amount of convertible currencies for foreign travel.[11] Overall, the currency reform sought to stimulate the inflow of foreign direct investment as well as portfolio investment to further the restructuring and privatization of the Czech corporate sector.[12]

Creation of a Banking System

One of the first sectors to experience radical reforms was the banking sector. A first banking reform included the breakup of the monobank system[13] into two tiers—a central bank responsible for the country's monetary policy, and state-owned commercial and specialized banks responsible for deposits, lending, and other commercial banking activities.[14]

The previous monobank, the socialist Czechoslovakian State Bank, ceased to exist. The National Bank of Czechoslovakia was created to be the new central bank. For commercial banking activities, Komerční Banka of Prague and General Credit Bank of Bratislava (the current capital of Slovakia) were created simultaneously to take over the old state bank's commercial functions and its loan portfolio. In 1991, the old state bank's long-term assets were transferred to Investiční Banka (Investment Bank), and the savings function was given to separate Czech and Slovak savings banks (Česka Sporitelna and Slovenska Sporitelna). Československá Obchodní Banka (ČSOB, or the Czechoslovak Trade Bank), which had existed since 1964, was kept intact and retained its market-leader position in foreign trade and foreign exchange.[15]

One of the legacies of the monobank system was a large portfolio of worrisome loans to state-owned firms. Since Komerční Banka received the biggest share of the former central bank's loans, it had the most serious nonperforming loan portfolio among all the newly created commercial banks. In order to establish a healthy banking industry, a state-owned consolidation bank (Konsolidační Banka) was founded in 1991 to take over the worst-performing loans of Komerční Banka and other banks.[16]

Voucher Privatization

In the early 1990s, Czechoslovakia had virtually no private sector. Several steps were taken to privatize different business sectors gradually. First, restaurants and stores were sold to private owners in 1991. Simultaneously, a separate method—the so-called voucher privatization method—was devised to accelerate the sale of small and medium-sized enterprises and of some large-scale state-owned firms.[17] The method involved offering the population at large the opportunity to buy vouchers (denominated in points) for a nominal fee of 1,000 Czech Republic crowns (US$34). Vouchers could then be exchanged for shares in state-owned companies about to be privatized. Two such waves of "voucher privatization" were carried out between 1991 and 1994. The voucher scheme succeeded in privatizing companies representing 30% of the country's gross domestic product (GDP). The state then used the proceeds from the voucher sales to help finance economic reforms.

Although the voucher system was considered a success by some analysts, it resulted in significant cross-ownership patterns. Most Czech citizens did not participate directly in the voucher privatization but indirectly through investment privatization funds (IPFs),[18] which, in turn, were sponsored by the state-owned banks.[19] In essence, about two-thirds of all individuals exchanged their vouchers for shares of these investment funds. Investment funds then used those points to acquire shares of privatized companies.[20] This method strengthened the relationships between the banks and their company clients. However, since banks often were simultaneously shareholders (through their IPFs) as well as creditors (through corporate lending) of the same company, conflicts of interest arose in cases where restructuring would entail writing off loans and creating provisions. In such events, banks gained more from protecting their interests as creditors (by rolling over nonperforming loans) than by acting as shareholders promoting rapid restructuring. This troubled corporate governance system was further strained by the fact that the largest banks remained majority held by the state.[21] The Czech state was unwilling to privatize large banks as fast as industrial companies in order to keep control of the financing of the privatization process.[22]

Further complicating the situation was that the Czech regulatory environment lacked an adequate legal and institutional basis to protect minority shareholders and a functioning bankruptcy process.[23] Corporate executives, many of whom remained from communist days, were allowed therefore to use a flexible regulatory and legal framework to "tunnel" assets out of the formerly state-owned sector.[24] ("Tunneling" was commonly used as a generic term for misappropriation of assets.)[25]

The Velvet Divorce

For almost 80 years, since the end of World War I, Czechs and Slovaks had lived together in one country, Czechoslovakia. However, growing polarization concerning economic and political reforms, in addition to a Slovak separatist movement, resulted in a deadlock in the 1992 parliamentary elections. In the end, it led to the breakup of the country into two separate nations. On January 1, 1993, the "Velvet Divorce" split Czechoslovakia into the Czech Republic and Slovakia. Václav Klaus, former minister of finance, of the Civic Democratic Party, became prime minister of the Czech Republic. (See **Exhibit 1** for a map of the Czech Republic.)

After the breakup, the Czechoslovakian central bank split into two independent central banks, one for each country. The new Czech central bank gradually amended and improved the regulatory framework governing all bank activities that had been established before the Velvet Divorce.[26] For instance, the central bank set a series of rules for the behavior of commercial banks. These provisions included the control of banks' solvency and liquidity and the limitation of risk exposure to individual borrowers. Further, a required minimum risk-weighted capital/assets ratio, the so-called capital adequacy ratio (CAR), was set at 8%.[27] Should a bank's CAR fall below one-third of the required threshold, the central bank was allowed to revoke its banking license.[28]

The Czech Banking Sector after the Velvet Divorce

By mid-1994, 55 banks were operating in the Czech Republic. However, the industry was highly concentrated, with the four largest banks—Komerční Banka, Česka Sporitelna, Československá Obchodní Banka, and Investiční a Poštovní Banka—accounting for 55% of bank capital and controlling 85% of banking activity, 83% of loans, and 87% of deposits. (**Exhibit 2** summarizes banking sector indicators, and **Exhibit 3** provides financials for the four largest banks.)

Komerční Banka benefited from its extensive relationships with the domestic corporate world and was the biggest bank, measured by assets. Česka Sporitelna, on the other hand, could rely on a dense retail branch network. Both banks diversified their banking activities in order to become more universal banks.

Československá Obchodní Banka (ČSOB) was the only bank in the former communist Czechoslovakia that had provided foreign trade services. After the Velvet Divorce, ČSOB remained under the combined control of the Czech and Slovak states (65.7% and 24.13% of the bank's shares, respectively). In the early 1990s, ČSOB embarked on a transformation into a general commercial bank specializing in foreign-currency transactions as well as in various types of trade finance. The bank mainly expanded its corporate client base with a limited branch network.

Investiční a Poštovní Banka (IPB) had been created from the merger of the Investment Bank and the Post Bank in 1993. At the time, the former Investment Bank had had an unclear future, carrying a large portfolio of loans on large investment projects from the communist era and only a small customer base. The Investment Bank had expanded by collecting primary deposits and acquiring strategic stakes in Czech enterprises during the voucher privatization. After the merger with Post Bank, the new combined entity controlled a large deposit base and an extensive retail network.[29]

The Golden Years of Czech Transformation (1994–1997)

After a temporary stagnation in 1993, the Czech economy accelerated from 1994 through 1996. The inflation rate fell below 10%. Unemployment was kept low, hovering at 3% annually. Foreign exchange reserves growth was strong, and privatizations of the corporate sphere progressed at a steady pace. (See **Exhibit 4**.)

The regime of internal convertibility, regulated by the Foreign Exchange Act, triggered an increasing mobility of capital. In 1995, capital account liberalization had reached a higher degree than the Foreign Exchange Act described. Together with other favorable economic indicators, it seemed as if the Czech economy was ready to open up more. A belief that it was time for a higher status of convertibility for the Czech currency resulted in the adoption of a new Foreign Exchange Act. The new act removed all existing restrictions on current account transactions. In doing so, it met International Monetary Fund Article VIII requirements on currency external convertibility[30] and brought Czech currency law in line with the European Union currency regulations. The revised act paved the way for the Czech Republic to become the first state in eastern Europe to be accepted as a member of the Organization for Economic Cooperation and Development (OECD), in November 1995.[31] This prestigious membership was seen as recognition for the success of the transformation and catalyzed liberalization efforts.[32]

The fixed exchange rate regime, in place since the Velvet Revolution, together with the full liberalization of balance-of-payments transactions[33] stimulated massive inflows of foreign investments into Czech banks and companies. Additionally, foreign capital was attracted by the high Czech interest rates, in comparison with those of Western European countries. Capital inflows accelerated from 1993 to 1995, peaking at 15% of GDP.[34]

The capital inflows were largely driven by a strong borrowing demand from the Czech corporate sector. Corporations looking to restructure and modernize had only banks to turn to for investment capital, given the embryonic Czech capital markets.[35] The banks were also motivated to grant loans through their role as principal owner of many companies (via the investment privatization funds). Analysts commonly talked about this as the Czech Republic's "credit boom" years. (For credit growth statistics, see **Exhibit 5**.) However, the loan situation was at times complicated by the fact that requiring collateral from the borrowers was still not common practice.[36] Since bankruptcy laws were virtually nonfunctional, repayments on loans were frequently difficult to obtain.

Between 1994 and 1996, Czech banks generally lacked a strong domestic deposit base. They therefore had to look for capital abroad. With the ongoing liberalization of capital flows and the positive interest yield differential mentioned above, banks were also making profits by borrowing abroad in foreign currencies at lower interest rates and lending domestically at higher ones.[37]

The foreign borrowing of Czech banks peaked at 6% of GDP at the end of 1995. The inflow of foreign short-term capital resulted in Czech banks accumulating a negative position toward nonresidents of about 100 billion Czech Republic crowns (US$3.68 billion) in 1996.[38] (See **Exhibit 6**.) Banks took advantage of lower foreign interest rates relative to domestic rates. The foreign loans increased their disposable resources but at the same time left them exposed to foreign exchange risk. If the banks lent in crowns and the crown lost its value relative to the foreign currency, the banks would bear high losses. The central bank, however, anticipated the problem and put in place prudential regulation[39] under which domestic banks had to limit their borrowing in foreign currencies to equal their lending in foreign currencies. As a result, the banks lent much of their foreign borrowing to the domestic companies as foreign currency loans, which meant that they did not open their foreign exchange balance sheet position much more than their total position toward nonresidents. Whatever small exposure was left on the balance sheet, the banks would hedge with off-balance sheet operations. As a result, the total open foreign exchange position of the Czech banks remained close to zero. In fact, by passing on their foreign exchange borrowing to domestic companies, the banks transformed foreign exchange risk into credit risk.[40]

Of the "Big Four" banks, ČSOB was the only one that stayed away from the credit boom. Influenced by its extensive foreign trade track record, and unlike its peers, ČSOB paid great attention to its credit-making decisions and applied a conservative approach in credit classification. It particularly shied away from enterprises with a dubious and unpromising future. Milan Tomanek, the bank's spokesman, explained that "ČSOB protected itself from customers with low credit worthiness through two efficient measures. The first was the four eyes principle when discussing the loan and centralized decision-making on credits."[41] Second, ČSOB charged higher interest rates than remaining large banks, making borrowing more expensive for businesses. The bank's prudential regulations were orchestrated by two members of the board of directors, Kavánek and Petr Knapp. Kavánek explained:

> My executive committee colleagues and I asked ourselves, "Should we call this a credit boom?" Several of us had significant experience working abroad and knew clearly that this was not a normal market situation. We had a reasonable understanding of risks and certainly did not want to play the crony debt/equity state-organized game, nor get involved in politicking. We were aiming for a business proposition that would create sustainable value, and as we were thinking of migrating into retail, it was important for us to maintain a solid reputation in order to justify our fiduciary responsibility. We were also lucky to have a structured supervisory board, a combination of a number of ministerial positions, both Czech and Slovak, where Czechs were supporting Czech interests and Slovaks the Slovak ones, a sort of quasi-corporate governance unwritten rule.[42]

Not all shared this view of the ČSOB risk-averse corporate-lending strategy. As an industry observer put it, "When the conservative management finally realized that they could benefit from cheap foreign capital funds, the credit boom was already over." Kavánek commented, "Analysts could interpret our strategy as either too cautious or wise."[43]

By contrast, IPB's growth strategy was based on extensive credit granting. "IPB would even regularly grant loans to enterprises whose business plans had been previously turned down by us. Sometimes we thought, 'Are they demented?'" explained Marek Ditz, a ČSOB senior executive. As for the other two large banks, the retail-specialized Česka Sporitelna also was inexperienced in corporate-lending risk management, and Komerční Banka operated under political pressure from the Czech state and frequently lent to companies on the brink of bankruptcy.[44]

Problems in the Banking Sector

By 1997, unwanted effects from the credit boom started to emerge. Above all, the banks' exposure to unpaid loans was growing. In addition, a liberal bank-licensing policy had resulted in numerous new small banks during the early 1990s. Most were undercapitalized and lacked experienced staff. Incidents of fraud were frequent, such as founding retail and savings banks only to lend the deposits to companies belonging to the bank's shareholders. Not surprisingly, the central bank considered 5% to 7% of the Czech banking system insolvent by the mid-1990s—mainly small banks.[45]

The central bank's authority had been strengthened in a 1994 amendment to the Act on Banks. Among other things, the amendment detailed the principle of conservatorship, whereby an individual or legal entity unable to take care of legal matters was appointed a guardian or conservator. Another amendment, in 1996, laid down banks' obligations regarding banking secrecy and introduced an anti-money laundering reporting duty. It also tightened up licensing conditions, restricted banks' links with the corporate sector, and introduced tougher measures against shareholders who demonstrably acted to the financial detriment of the bank.

Growing Macroeconomic Imbalances

At the same time, the central bank also faced problems on a macroeconomic level. A growing capital account surplus led to inflationary pressures, as some of the foreign borrowing financed consumption.[46] Money-supply growth exceeded the central bank's targets between 1993 and 1995.[47] From 1993 to 1996, the central bank accumulated large amounts of foreign exchange reserves that were sterilized by issuing central bank treasury bills, which logically paid a higher interest rate than the foreign exchange reserves were earning.[48] The total sum of these costs since 1993 was estimated at 105 billion Czech Republic crowns (US$3.87 billion), about 6.7% of GDP.[49] Observers criticized the central bank, believing it targeted two different objectives with one policy—a fixed exchange rate and an appropriate rate of money-supply growth.[50]

The country's economic development was further undermined by other macroeconomic weaknesses. High wage growth outpaced productivity gains, domestic demand grew much faster than GDP, the trade balance deteriorated sharply, and the current account deficit reached almost 8% of GDP in 1996. According to analysts, all of these developments were hallmarks of an overheating economy.[51] (See **Exhibit 7** for the Czech balance of payments from 1993 to 1999.)

A Fading Image of a Successful Transformation (1997–1999)

Currency Turmoil and Economic Recession

In February 1996, the central bank concluded that its foreign exchange sterilized operations had not stemmed the inflow of speculative capital. As a new countermeasure, it widened the exchange rate's fluctuation band to ±7.5%. With a now higher exchange risk, it was expected that both foreign and domestic investors would be less keen to profit from the high interest rate differential. In effect, this measure led to an outflow of short-term speculative capital, returning the money supply to the target band. However, in the absence of fiscal restrictive measures, monetary policy remained confronted with high inflationary pressures. The central bank decided therefore to tighten its monetary policy in the second half of 1996. The discount rate was raised from 9.5% to 10.5%, and the required-reserves ratio increased by 3% to 11.5%. These restrictive measures, however, did not succeed in reversing the tendency of deficits in the current account.[52]

A sharp slowdown in the country's growth, a high budget deficit, and a further deterioration of the trade balance triggered an attack on the Czech Republic crown in May 1997. On May 26, the central bank had to abandon the fixed exchange rate. The crown depreciated quickly. This, combined with already increased interest rates and higher reserve needs, stabilized capital flows, and reduced the current account deficit by about one-third. Lower domestic aggregate demand and the delayed effect of the devaluation kept inflation in check in the 10% range. In addition, measures to restrain and freeze wages in the budgetary sector were introduced in the spring of 1997.

Once the currency crisis was overcome, a period of economic recession followed in 1997–1999, marked by a dramatic GDP drop and sharply rising unemployment. Structural and institutional reforms were unavoidable, including speeding up banking-sector privatizations. Tighter regulation of the banking sector and a strengthening of creditors' protections followed in 1998. The new rules requiring banks to make provisions against unsecured loans made loans harder to obtain for borrowers. These changes brought the regulatory framework closer in line with European Union norms in preparation for the Czech Republic's accession to the European Union, scheduled for 2004.[53]

In June 1998, facing slumping foreign direct investment, the Czech government started implementing a policy of granting incentives to foreign investors.

Banking-Sector Hardships

From 1996 through 1997, capital inflows slowed due to the widened fluctuation band of the Czech Republic crown, weakening investor confidence in the Czech economy, and the growing current account deficit. The situation got even worse after the currency turbulence in May 1997. Throughout the second half of the 1990s, domestic firms, which had been weakened by the economic recession and subsequent stabilization measures, struggled to improve their performance and repay loans. A credit crunch in the banking sector replaced the preceding credit euphoria.[54]

The Czech banks, which had previously transformed foreign exchange risk into credit risk, suffered indirectly from the currency turmoil. The number of nonperforming loans in the banking sector increased dramatically the banks' ratio of classified loans to total loans, exceeding 32% in 1999.[55] The bad loans undermined the profitability of the banking sector, as they required higher bad-loan provisions and reserves. Overall, bank net profits were very poor in 1997–1999. Several smaller banks with liquidity troubles had their operations suspended by the central bank. With the exception of ČSOB, which had stayed away from the credit boom, all the Big Four banks registered net losses in 1998 and 1999. The bad-loan problem forced the government to again engage in extensive cleanups of the banks' balance sheets, similar to those undertaken in 1991. The ultimate public costs of these operations were estimated at 15% to 20% of GDP.[56]

The Gradual Economic Recovery (1999–2000)

By 1999, the Czech economy was still stagnant. However, GDP in 2000 was expected to grow by 3%, and analysts saw an upcoming economic upswing. In 1999, fixed direct investment reached a record high of 11.5% of GDP. With rapidly falling inflation—down from 10.7% in 1998 to 2.1% in 1999—the central bank could also reduce interest rates.[57]

Completion of Bank Privatizations

Although the Velvet Revolution had brought privatization to most sectors of the Czech economy, the Czech state had remained the majority shareholder of all major Czech banks. The banking sector was considered so vital that the state wanted to maintain direct control. However, by the end of 1996, state officials started to agree that this ownership situation hindered the stability and growth of the Czech economy. Privatization of the banking sector should therefore be accelerated.

Before privatizations could take place, however, the banks' capital had to be increased and their portfolios cleansed of bad debt, which was transferred to the consolidation bank. The aggregate net costs of these measures ran close to 85 billion Czech Republic crowns (US$2.46 billion).[58]

The sale of the state's stakes in the four large banks had been planned to start in 1997, but it was not until the first quarter of 1998 that the first stake was sold. Japanese investment bank Nomura Europe plc paid 2.9 billion Czech Republic crowns (US$90 million) for the state's 36% holding in IPB.

Parliamentary elections in June 1998 slowed the pace of privatization. However, the newly elected government announced its intention to sell off its majority stake in ČSOB later in the fall by publishing a tender offer soon after taking office. An exception among the Big Four banks, ČSOB was owned by both the Czech and Slovak governments. The Slovaks now pressured the Czech government for a combined sale. Unable to reach a compromise, the two sides ultimately agreed that both stakes would be offered separately. In June 1999, the Czech 65.7% stake was sold to KBC Bank and Insurance Company NV for 40 billion Czech Republic crowns (US$1.16 billion). At the same time, International Finance Corporation of the World Bank Group acquired a 4.4% share in ČSOB. At the end of 1999, the European Bank for Reconstruction and Development took an additional 7.47% that Slovakia had held, while KBC acquired a further 16.66% stake from Slovakia. In total, KBC acquired just over 82% of ČSOB. (See **Exhibit 8** for ČSOB's ownership structure in 2000.)

Belgian-based KBC was a financial services company engaged in retail banking and insurance. The group was committed to developing Central Europe into a second home market through acquisition. Patrick Daems, KBC's senior executive, explained the bank's strategy that led to the ČSOB takeover:

> Apart from the price, our hands-off acquisition style was another decisive factor that influenced the Czech government and made us win the ČSOB tender. Even though we did not intend to replace all senior management upon our arrival, we certainly made sure we got a majority interest. We already got badly burned elsewhere in Central Europe only because we did not have a controlling interest and management control of a firm. You do not take a minority interest in a transition country; you take control. We learned our lesson. The entrance of the International Finance Corporation and the European Bank for Reconstruction and Development capital in ČSOB also increased our confidence in the bank and confirmed the relevance of our acquisition target.[59]

The sale of another bank, Česka Sporitelna, followed in February 2000. Erste Bank of Austria acquired the state's 52% for 19.9 billion Czech Republic crowns (US$515 million). Preparations for the sell-off of Komerční Banka were already under way, and the transaction was expected to take place by mid-2001.

ČSOB's Retail Expansion

One of the Big Four banks in the Czech Republic, ČSOB had been in existence since 1964. It had been founded by the Czechoslovak government to handle the country's foreign trade and foreign exchange operations. In addition to foreign trade, the bank had extensive experience in corporate lending. However, by 2000, with easy and cheap foreign capital drying up and corporate lending activities shrinking, the bank turned its attention to retail banking as an area of future growth.

ČSOB started to prepare the strategic shift before KBC stepped in as majority owner. Management considered growing both organically and by acquiring another bank with a strong retail foothold. They established an expansion strategy for the next several years, including a rollout of a new information system, new retail products, and new retail outlets. "We even hired a western retail banking specialist to lead us successfully through these changes," explained Geert de Kegel, ČSOB's distribution director.[60]

ČSOB's and KBC's managers jointly reviewed the retail plans after the bank had been privatized. ČSOB benefited from KBC's experience and realized synergies from its new owner. A number of new products complemented the old range of retail services. Managers of both banks also agreed that a further development of the ČSOB branch network would be the priority of the next few years.

Despite these efforts (see **Exhibit 9** for the bank volume of primary deposits), ČSOB continued to lag behind its peer banks in the retail segment. (See **Exhibit 10** for a comparison of banks' positions in the retail sector.) The bank management started favoring making a "strategic jump" by acquiring a bank with a strong retail presence over slowly growing internally. After the recent privatization of Česka Sporitelna, Komerčni Banka or IPB emerged as the two most likely candidates for a takeover.

Komerčni Banka was the country's largest commercial bank, with an extensive branch network. However, the bank had suffered severely from the recent economic downturn. Its bottom line had been hit hard by continued provisioning for risky loans and a deteriorating real estate portfolio. The Czech government had initiated several bailout operations and did not intend to privatize Komerčni Banka until mid-2001.

By contrast, IPB, the third-largest Czech bank, was available. IPB had an excellent retail distribution network based on the combination of its own branches and access to the Post Office network. (See **Exhibit 11** for IPB retail information.) IPB's Post Savings Bank was a separate business line operating on a contract basis with the Czech Post, including over 3,300 postal outlets around the country. An acquisition of IPB would boost ČSOB's market position, particularly in the retail segment. Its share in the country's primary-deposit market would rise from 9.7% to 23.4%, and the number of its customers would rise from 400,000 to about 3.4 million. By purchasing IPB, ČSOB would also become the largest bank in the Czech Republic. (For retail market-positioning information if ČSOB were to acquire IPB, see **Exhibit 12**.)

The Situation at IPB

IPB had benefited a great deal from the interest rate differential between 1994 and 1996, considerably expanding its loan portfolio. By mid-1997, though, IPB began to experience problems with nonperforming loans. The bank's financial situation seemed to be temporarily stabilized when Nomura acquired the state's minority share and increased its equity capital by 6 billion Czech Republic crowns (US$185.9 million) as well as issued 6 billion Czech Republic crowns (US$185.9 million) in subordinated bonds.[61] Following Nomura's investment, IPB began to offer higher deposit interest rates than its competitors in order to increase rapidly its retail market share. A significant rise in client deposits did follow, with deposits amounting to 227.2 billion Czech Republic crowns (US$5.9 billion) by March 2000.[62] Still, the bank's portfolio of nonperforming loans, securities, and other classified receivables continued to worsen. IPB resorted to various short-term solutions, such as sales of receivables or transfers of securities.

Nomura had never actively participated in IPB's restructuring and appeared to regard this acquisition as a portfolio investment hedged by Pilsner Urquell shares that IPB held on its balance sheet.[63] It was even rumored that IPB's management, which indirectly controlled a considerable number of shares in the bank, had arranged the transaction with Nomura in order to continue its ownership control.[64] (See **Exhibit 13** for IPB's ownership structure.)

Concerned by IPB's problems, the central bank sent a supervisory group to clarify the bank's financial situation. The group carried out a series of visits between 1998 and 1999 and revealed some serious shortcomings, especially in the area of classified receivables and asset valuation. The group calculated a need for additional provisions of 40 billion Czech Republic crowns (US$1.16 billion) for the examined asset sample only. In October 1999, IPB was requested to increase its equity capital to provide sufficient credit-risk provisions.

This attempt was blocked, however, by a minority shareholder.[65] And in any event, IPB disagreed with the findings of the supervisory group. The bank argued that the group had not analyzed all documents and that IPB in fact had already reduced credit risk and created provisions. In March and April 2000, IPB submitted a number of written appeals against individual parts of the supervisor's report. However, some analysts believed that IPB was providing the central bank with distorted data. Others noted that an IPB bankruptcy would threaten the banking system and, more importantly, have a substantial impact on the Czech economy, resulting in a GDP drop of 2% to 4%.[66] Given the potential adverse effects on the Czech economy, finding a solution for IPB's problems was becoming vital.[67]

Whatever the central bank decided with regard to IPB would depend on the audit to be carried out by the international audit firm Ernst & Young, which was due on June 26, 2000. It was clear that if the audit showed that the bank's capital adequacy ratio had dropped below one-third of the required threshold, the central bank would revoke IPB's banking license.[68]

After the earlier investigation, parallel discussions had already been held among the central bank, IPB, Ernst & Young, the Ministry of Finance, and shareholder Nomura to find a "cooperative solution" whereby the bank could be sold to a strategic investor in cooperation with the current shareholders. Nomura agreed to participate, provided that the government guarantee the return of Nomura's investment in the bank. The central bank also prepared a crisis scenario should the agreement with Nomura fail. This "noncooperative solution" meant the state would impose a conservatorship on the bank and then sell it.

For the cooperative solution, ČSOB and jointly bidding Italian bank Unicredito and German insurer Allianz were seen as the leading potential acquirors of IPB. However, they differed in terms of the manner and speed of a potential takeover. Allianz-Unicredito wanted an immediate takeover of the bank's management but did not want to formally agree to take ownership of the bank until a few months later, once IPB's true financial situation had been determined. By contrast, ČSOB wanted an immediate takeover of the bank's ownership and management. These different approaches also stemmed from the fact that only a Czech bank with the relevant banking license could immediately purchase IPB and carry on banking activities.[69]

However, for some reason, ČSOB's interest was not considered in depth by the central bank. Explained Marek Ditz, a ČSOB senior executive, "We were really surprised that ČSOB did not receive any response from the central bank to its analysis on how to solve the IPB insolvency. No one even explained why to us."[70]

On June 7, 2000, about two weeks before its official report, Ernst & Young informed the central bank that IPB would have to create provisions of at least 21 billion Czech Republic crowns (US$544.2 million) and perhaps as much as 40 billion Czech Republic crowns (US$1.16 billion). Creating large provisions meant that IPB would face a large loss and would not be able to maintain the capital adequacy ratio without external support. Some analysts predicted that this indicator would fall below zero even if the auditor's minimum requirement of 21 billion Czech Republic crowns (US$544.2 million) was fulfilled.[71]

Kavánek's Decision

Pavel Kavánek, CEO and chairman of ČSOB, was a business and economics graduate of the Prague School of Economics and Georgetown University. A longtime employee of ČSOB, Kavánek had joined the bank in 1972. In 1991, he was made a member of the executive board responsible for the bank's capital and money market operations, and two years later, in 1993, he was appointed chairman and chief executive.

A strong advocate of growing ČSOB's retail activities through acquisition, Kavánek was astonished when ČSOB was rejected as a potential acquirer of IPB. Now, on June 13, 2000, he was again surprised when the central bank called him to say that ČSOB was after all being considered. ČSOB would, however, need to submit a proposal very quickly if it wanted to stay in the running. Kavánek suspected that the talks between the state, Nomura, and Allianz-Unicredito had not yielded concrete results, yet he would have preferred more time, since the Ernst & Young report would not be out for another 10 days.

Adding further urgency was that there was a large run on the bank since the day before, June 12. Clients of IPB were withdrawing their money to a degree never experienced before in the Czech banking sector. On one day alone, deposits of 4.5 billion Czech Republic crowns (US$116.6 million) had been withdrawn, and analysts predicted that the bank would end up insolvent if the trend continued for a few days.[72] Given the crisis, Kavánek assumed that the central bank was seriously considering conservatorship of the bank without the consent of Nomura.

Although it seemed as if Allianz-Unicredito had been favored before, Kavánek knew that ČSOB was in a better position to move in quickly and save IPB from bankruptcy, simply because ČSOB already had a banking license in the Czech Republic.

Kavánek realized that he did not have time for a proper due-diligence phase. (See **Exhibit 14** for the recent auditor's net asset value statement of IPB.) The phone call from the central bank meant he had to make a very quick decision: "We understood the market, we were one of the important market players, and so we had a very good bird's-eye view of IPB's profile. We knew that IPB was a good strategic fit. With public information and 'gut feeling,' it would be enough to estimate the IPB franchise."

Kavánek went through the pros and cons of the acquisition one more time. On the positive side, acquiring IPB's franchise network would immediately give ČSOB a leading position in the market in terms of deposits. The acquisition would also enhance ČSOB's position in the bancassurance sector[73]—IPB Pojistovna, one of IPB's numerous subsidiaries, was the number three[74] insurance company in the country. ČSOB's strategic investor, KBC, was traditionally strong in insurance and banking, and when it acquired the bank in 1999 it had developed strategic plans for a gradual implementation of a bancassurance operating model. The opportunity for rapid diversification by acquiring IPB was particularly tempting. ČSOB would also benefit from the consolidation with other strong IPB subsidiaries in asset management, building, mortgage banking, pension funds, and leasing.

On the negative side, however, IPB was not only in a problematic situation with its customers, but its general asset structure was completely nontransparent. Kavánek observed: "There was a consensus among the financial community that IPB had a big gap in their books, both in terms of size and transparency of the accounts. Nobody really trusted the IPB financials as reported. Information was simply not available, and ČSOB had to do without it."[75]

Ditz, ČSOB senior executive and Kavánek's advisor, insisted: "No rational and informed investor would spend a crown on IPB. There was a certain amount of nonstandard behavior, if not outright crime. The bank will go bust, and we should recover its market share in primary deposits."[76]

ČSOB's lawyers were also opposed to the transaction, saying, "We cannot do a deal like that, we cannot work a contract strong enough under such pressure, they are not heaven, we should jump out, not even try."[77]

Kavánek realized that he would need a well-structured state guarantee for IPB's nonperforming assets to go through with an acquisition. The central bank would likely be open to this, however, since even the price of a state guarantee would be a less costly option for the government than letting the bank go bankrupt, given the effect this would have on the Czech economy as a whole.[78]

He was also worried whether ČSOB had the capacity and capability to deal with such a sizable and complex merger. "And how would IPB staff react to such a sudden takeover?" he wondered. His main objective was to create value, and if he decided to go for the acquisition, the main difficulty might be determining the appropriate structure for the deal.

Kavánek knew he had to figure out the pros and cons quickly so that he could make his decision in time.

Exhibit 1   Map of the Czech Republic

Source: http://www.lib.utexas.edu/maps/cia03/czech_republic_sm03.gif, accessed April 14, 2004.

Exhibit 2   Czech Republic, Summary Banking-Sector Indicators, 1992–1999

	1992	1993	1994	1995	1996	1997	1998	1999
Number of banks	37	52	55	55	53	50	45	42
Number of employees	n.a.	n.a.	n.a.	n.a.	54,461	50,233	51,076	48,924
Interest rate on loans	14.1	13.1	12.8	12.5	13.2	12.8	8.7	7.2
Interest rate on deposits	7	7.1	7	6.8	7.7	8.1	4.5	3.4
M2 (%)	n.a.	n.a.	20.4	29.3	6.4	1.7	3.4	2.6
Capital adequacy ratio (%)	n.a.	n.a.	n.a.	10.2	9.8	10.6	12.1	13.6
Operating income/assets	n.a.	n.a.	n.a.	n.a.	4.19	4.58	4.55	3.9
Operating costs/assets	n.a.	n.a.	n.a.	n.a.	2.14	2.2	2.25	2.21
ROA	n.a.	n.a.	n.a.	n.a.	0.63	-0.07	-0.39	-0.24
ROE	n.a.	n.a.	n.a.	n.a.	19.61	-1.2	-5.74	-4.32
Operating income/employee[a]	n.a.	n.a.	n.a.	n.a.	1291	1735	1889	1845
Banks net foreign assets ($ mn)	n.a.	1,343	738	-2,645	-3,281	-539	994	3,624
Foreign exchange reserves	n.a.	3,789.4	6,144.5	13,843	12,352	9,734	12,542	12,806
Total assets (CZK bn)	n.a.	1,259	1,531	1,951	2,153	2,423	2,576	2,695
Clients' deposits (CZK bn)	580	696	845	956	1,025	1,136	1,167	1,173
Classified loans (% of total loans)	n.a.	20.0	38.0	30.0	29.3	27.0	26.5	32.2

Source: Compiled from the Economist Intelligence Unit, www.eiu.com, and from the Czech National Bank, www.cnb.cz, accessed April 13, 2004.

[a]CZK thousand per employee.

Exhibit 3　　Big Four Financials, 1994–1999

a) ČSOB's Consolidated Six-Year Financial Summary

	1999	1998	1997	1996	1995	1994
Results for the year (CZKm)						
Net profit	2,823	3,159	2,798	2,845	2,663	570
At year-end (CZKm)						
Shareholders' equity	31,478	27,501	24,670	21,853	19,018	16,616
Due to customers	126,498	113,328	115,639	90,632	83,376	64,323
Due to banks	45,363	67,255	61,708	59,331	53,372	54,671
Debt securities in issue	38,750	22,329	15,353	15,535	15,880	9,718
Loans and leases	97,046	116,505	112,171	85,325	79,839	81,585
Due from banks	115,257	83,883	62,199	49,391	48,191	36,751
Total assets	257,698	251,166	237,451	209,802	194,141	164,399
Ratios (%)						
Return on average shareholders' equity (ROAE)	9.57	12.11	12.03	13.92	14.95	3.46
Return on average total assets (ROAA)	1.11	1.29	1.25	1.41	1.49	0.39
Bank capital adequacy ratio	20.24	18.16	13.33	12.21	10.02	7.25
Total shareholders' equity to total assets	12.22	10.95	10.39	10.42	9.80	10.11

Source: ČSOB, 1994–2000 annual reports.

b) Komerční Banka's Consolidated Six-Year Financial Summary

	1999	1998	1997	1996	1995	1994
Results for the year (CZKm)						
Net profit/loss	-9,782	-9,546	528	5,299	5,111	4,827
At year-end (CZKm)						
Shareholders' equity	17,776	20,458	30,005	31,456	31,624	27,653
Due to customers	259,191	273,698	296,882	280,457	234,340	254,465
Due to banks						51,875
Debt securities in issue	27,742	31,646	37,046	33,938	33,294	17,985
Loans and leases	181,754	214,018	249,989	236,779	217,187	212,383
Due from banks	n.a.	n.a.	n.a.	n.a.	n.a.	342
Total assets	390,122	422,084	466,517	445,954	387,137	333,033
Ratios (%)						
Return on average shareholders' equity (ROAE)	x	x	1.61	17.81	17.24	n.a.
Return on average total assets (ROAA)	x	x	0.12	1.28	1.46	n.a.
Bank capital adequacy ratio	10.69	9.56	8.31	10.68	10.73	9.08

Source: Komerční Banka, 1994–2000 annual reports.

Exhibit 3 (continued)

c) IPB's Consolidated Six-Year Financial Summary

	1999	1998	1997	1996	1995	1994
Results for the year (CZKm)						
Net profit/loss	1,030	474	-11,122	882	1,007	675
At year-end (CZKm)						
Shareholders' equity	n.a.	n.a.	6,958	18,103	13,103	n.a.
Due to customers	243,898	197,611	150,435	127,370	105,694	78,187
Due to banks	29,242	33,469	47,225	52,079	57,716	53,463
Debt securities in issue	2,000	2,550	12,760	1,000	5,000	6,380
Loans and leases to customers	164,273	154,454	139,665	139,645	119,200	103,511
Due from banks	33,170	57,600	33,924	29,856	23,465	15,364
Total assets	354,781	278,014	227,080	219,348	190,080	149,011
Ratios (%)						
Return on average shareholders' equity (ROAE)	n.a.	n.a.	n.a.	n.a.	n.a.	n.a.
Return on average total assets (ROAA)	n.a.	n.a.	n.a.	n.a.	n.a.	n.a.
Bank capital adequacy ratio	n.a.	n.a.	8.80	8.23	8.47	8.41
Classified loan share of bank's total loans	27.2	36.54	31.7	26.03	25.24	16.39

Source: IPB, 1994–2000 annual reports.

d) Česka Sporitelna's Consolidated Six-Year Financial Summary

	1999	1998	1997	1996	1995	1994
Results for the year (CZKm)						
Net profit/loss	-6,040	-3,944	2,597	2,739	1,442	757
At year-end (CZKm)						
Shareholders' equity	22,844	21,466	26,779	20,958	18,983	17,704
Due to customers	317,327	330,536	312,678	300,320	296,802	300,543
Due to banks	10,877	27,442	30,698	26,103	21,730	10,948
Debt securities in issue	5,165	5,165	5,000	0	0	0
Loans to customers	124,210	146,584	168,274	143,533	118,715	105,914
Loans to financial institutions	133,143	103,483	99,485	77,036	128,783	128,853
Total assets	377,868	407,372	390,788	357,581	351,568	342,638
Ratios (%)						
Return on average shareholders' equity (ROAE)	X	X	11.02	13.88	7.91	5.25
Return on average total assets (ROAA)	X	X	0.69	0.77	0.42	0.23
Bank capital adequacy ratio	17.7	14.2	12.5	11.4	10.98	n.a.
Classified loan share pf bank's total loans	n.a	16	24	24.7	20.9	n.a.

Source: Česka Sporitelna, 1994–2000 annual reports.

Exhibit 4   Czech Republic, Summary Economic Indicators, 1991–1999

	1991	1992	1993	1994	1995	1996	1997	1998	1999
GDP (current $ billion)	26.04	30.68	31.22	41.09	52.04	57.72	53.00	56.97	55.03
Annual GDP growth (%)	-11.5	-3.3	0.6	3.6	5.9	4.3	-0.8	-1	0.5
Population (mn)	10.3	10.32	10.33	10.33	10.32	10.31	10.3	10.29	10.28
GDP per head ($ at PPP)	10,247	10,128	10,409	11,010	11,909	12,671	12,797	12,817	13,076
Annual CPI (%)	n.a.	11.1	20.8	9.9	9.2	8.8	8.4	10.6	2.1
Unemployment rate (%)	2.8	3.0	3.0	3.3	3	3.1	4.3	6.1	8.6
Current account balance	n.a.	n.a.	466	-820	-1,374	-4,127	-3,622	-1,308	-1,466
Current account (% of GDP)	n.a	n.a	1.49	-2	-2.64	-7.15	-6.83	-2.3	-2.7
Net direct investment flows (mn)	n.a.	n.a.	564	762	2,531	1,280	1,261	3,574	6,223
Foreign direct investment (mn)	n.a.	n.a.	653	868	2,562	1,428	1,300	3,718	6,324
Foreign direct Investment (% of GDP)	n.a.	n.a.	2.09	2.13	4.93	2.49	2.43	6.5	11.47
Outward direct investment (mn)	n.a.	n.a.	-89	-116	-37	-155	-26	-125	-90
Annual change in gross fixed investment (%)	22.5	27.9	29.3	28.7	32	31.9	30.6	29.1	27.8
Annual change in industrial production (%)	n.a.	-5.7	-7.5	-0.0	7.1	5.0	4.6	1.6	-3.1
Budget balance (% of GDP)	n.a.	n.a.	n.a.	0.8	0.2	-0.4	-1.3	-1.6	-0.6
Budget revenue (% of GDP)	n.a.	n.a.	n.a.	43.6	43.1	41.6	40.7	39.5	40.1
Budget expenditure (% of GDP)	n.a.	n.a.	n.a.	42.8	42.9	41.9	42	41.1	40.8
Trade balance	n.a.	n.a.	n.a.	-1,408	-3,685	-5,878	-4,938	-2,647	-1,902
Exchange rate (CZK/$)	29.48	28.26	29.15	28.78	26.54	27.14	31.7	32.28	34.57

Source: Compiled from the Economist Intelligence Unit, www.eiu.com, accessed April 13, 2004.

Note: Figures are in US$ million unless otherwise stated.

Exhibit 5   Credit Growth in the Czech Republic

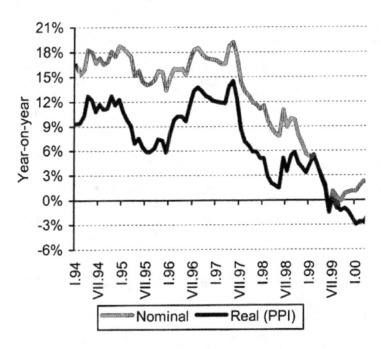

Source: Adapted by casewriters from the Czech National Bank in Tomas Holub and Zdeněk Túma, eds., *Managing Capital Inflows in the Czech Republic: Experiences, Problems and Questions,* CNC working paper, fig. 10, p. 15, www.cnb.cz, accessed April 5, 2004.

Exhibit 6   Banks' Net Position toward Nonresidents

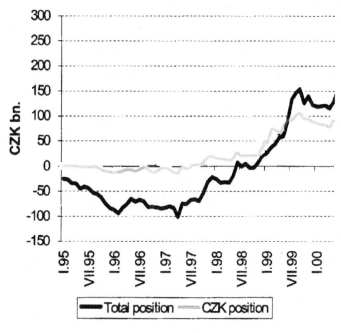

Source: Adapted by casewriters from the Czech National Bank in Tomas Holub and Zdeněk Túma, eds., *Managing Capital Inflows in the Czech Republic: Experiences, Problems and Questions,* CNC working paper, fig. 11, p. 16, www.cnb.cz, accessed April 5, 2004.

Exhibit 7   Balance of Payments

USD billion	1993	1994	1995	1996	1997	1998	1999
Current Account	**2.48**	**-0.75**	**-2.76**	**-9.04**	**-9.79**	**-2.25**	**-3.07**
Trade balance	0.07	-2.48	-8.38	-13.17	-12.73	-5.74	-3.70
Balance of services	2.41	1.45	4.39	4.76	3.91	4.80	2.67
Income balance	-0.20	-0.01	-0.29	-1.64	-1.99	-2.58	-3.52
Current transfers	0.20	0.29	1.52	1.01	1.02	1.27	1.48
Capital Account	-1.67	0.0	0.02	0.0	0.04	0.0	-0.01
Financial Account	**7.80**	**7.30**	**18.57**	**7.97**	**4.11**	**7.65**	**5.65**
Foreign direct investment	1.67	1.31	4.99	2.84	2.82	9.28	13.53
Portfolio investment	3.81	2.46	2.45	1.28	1.35	2.17	-0.84
Other investment	2.32	3.53	11.13	3.85	-0.06	-3.80	-7.04
Net errors and omissions, valuation changes	**-1.29**	**-0.65**	**0.84**	**-1.79**	**2.09**	**0.37**	**-0.24**
Change in reserves[a]	**-7.32**	**-5.91**	**-16.67**	**2.86**	**3.56**	**-5.78**	**-2.33**

Source: Compiled from the Czech National Bank, Statistics, www.cnb.cz, accessed May 11, 2004.

[a]Minus sign means an increase in reserves.

Exhibit 8   ČSOB's Ownership Structure in 2000

Shareholder	Stake
KBC Bank and Insurance Company NV	82.36%
European Bank for Reconstruction and Development	7.47%
International Finance Corporation	4.39%
Others	5.78%
Total	100%

Source: ČSOB 1999 annual report.

Exhibit 9   ČSOB's Volume of Primary Deposits

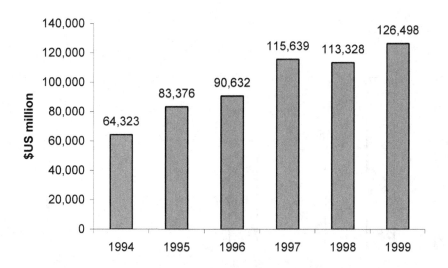

Source: ČSOB, 1994–2000 annual reports.

Exhibit 10   Big Four Deposits and Loans (1999)

a) Big Four Primary Customer Deposits (1999)

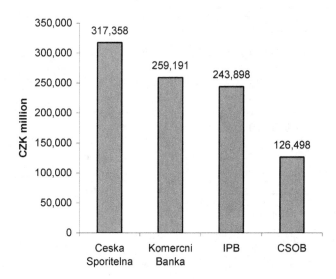

Exhibit 10 (continued)

b) Big Four Customer Loan Volume (1999)

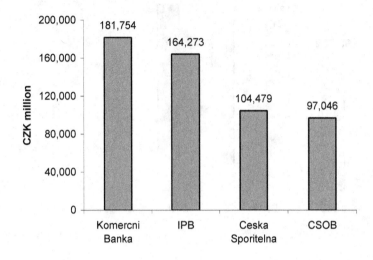

Source: Česka Sporitelna 1999 annual report, Komerční Banka 1999 annual report,
        IPB 1999 annual report, ČSOB 1999 annual report.

Exhibit 11   IPB's Financials, March 31, 2000

Item	
Total assets (CZK billion)	316.7
Volume of primary deposits (CZK billion)	227.2
Market share in total primary deposits	20%
Volume of loans (CZK billion)	193.2
Number of employees	5,057
Number of clients	2,938,979
Number of accounts	3,497,197
Number of outlets	3,532
Number of post offices	3,340

Source: "Report for the Session of the Chamber of Deputies of the
         Parliament of the Czech Republic," available from the Czech
         National Bank, www.cnb.cz, accessed April 28, 2004.

Exhibit 12   Situation in Retail Market If ČSOB Acquired IPB

| | Market Share (%) | | | | Number | | |
	Total Assets in CZK bn	Client Deposits	Loans (net)	Assets	Branch Network	Clients (in million)	Employees
SOB/IPB	524	23.4	12.9	19.5	240[a]	3.4	9,200
KB	477	20.9	14.1	17.7	334	1.3	10,700
S	451	23.9	11.3	16.7	707	3.9	14,100

Source: ČSOB information, compiled by casewriters.

[a]Plus 3,336 points of sale at the counters of the Czech Post.

Exhibit 13   IPB Ownership Structure in December 1999

Shareholder	Stake
Owners under the control of Nomura	46.2%
Owners clearly under the control of IPB management	25.2%
Owners related to IPB management and/or co-owned by IPB	12.3%
Others	16.3%
Total	100%

Source: Adapted from Zdeněk Kudrna, Eva Kreuzbergová, and Pavel Streblov, "The Rise
          and Fall of IPB," Charles and Georgetown Universities, p. 43,
          http://www.historieipb.cz/doc/study-en.pdf.

Exhibit 14   IPB Net Asset Value Statement in June 2000

Assets	CZK millions
Cash and balances with central bank	16,741
Treasury bills	12,465
Loans and advances to banks	18,256
Loans and advances to customers	62,041
Debt securities—trading	880
Debt securities—nontrading	6,878
Equity shares—trading	1,870
Equity shares—nontrading	2,514
Equity shares—special investment structures	0
Shares in group companies and the joint venture	3,938
Interest in associated companies	33
Property and equipment	4,522
Other assets	4,011
Total assets	**134,149**
Liabilities	
Amounts owed to banks	44,237
Amounts owed to customers	186,256
Debt securities in issue	17,286
Other liabilities	25,437
Provisions	18,962
Total liabilities	**292,178**
Net liabilities	**-158,029**

Source: Andersen, "Special Purpose Net Asset Value Statement of Investiční a Poštovní Banka on June 19, 2000," www.csob.cz, accessed April 5, 2004.

Endnotes

[1] Authors' interview with Marek Ditz, director, Banking Operations Support, ČSOB, Prague, March 26, 2004.

[2] "Report for the session of the Chamber of Deputies of the Parliament of the Czech Republic on the situation and the course of action for stabilizing Investiční a Poštovní Banka, a.s.," June 2000, p. 5, available at http://www.cnb.cz, accessed April 4, 2004.

[3] "Statement of the Czech National Bank on the 'Concluding Report of the Chamber of Deputies Fact-finding Commission for Clarification of Decision-Making by the State in IPB from the Time of its Founding until the Imposing of Receivership and its Sale to CSOB, for the Purposes of Deliberation by the CD PCR,'" available at http://www.cnb.cz/en/pdf/a_ipb_reakcecnb_13_7_01.pdf.

[4] "Report for the session of the Chamber of Deputies of the Parliament of the Czech Republic on the situation and the course of action for stabilizing Investiční a Poštovní Banka, a.s.," p. 5.

[5] Authors' interview with Marek Ditz.

[6] Paul A. Gompers, "The Prague Post," HBS No. 299-033 (Boston: Harvard Business School Publishing, 1999), pp. 1–2; Nationmaster.com, available at http://www.nationmaster.com/encyclopedia/Velvet-Revolution, accessed April 24, 2004.

[7] Thomas S. Mondschean and Bruce R. Scott, "Economic Reform in the Czech Republic: Velvet Revolution or Velvet Blanket," HBS No. 700-100 (Boston: Harvard Business School Publishing, 2000), pp. 1–7.

[8] The crown was pegged to the basket of German Deutsche marks (DEMs) and U.S. dollars with no change in central parity despite fluctuations in DEM/U.S. dollar rates. DEMs were weighted approximately 65%, and U.S. dollars were weighted approximately 35% in the basket.

[9] Tomas Holub and Zdeněk Túma, "Managing Capital Inflows in the Czech Republic: Experiences, Problems and Questions," CNB working paper, available at www.cnb.cz, accessed April 5, 2004.

[10] All export earnings of convertible currency had to be sold—at the prevailing exchange rate—to authorized domestic banks. Holding foreign exchange accounts was not permitted.

[11] Oldřich Dědek, "Capital Account Liberalization in the Czech Republic," in Zdeněk Drábek and Stephany Griffith-Jones, eds., *Managing Capital Flows in Turbulent Times: The Experience of Europe's Emerging Market Economies in Global Perspective* (London: M.E. Sharpe, 1999), pp. 98–114.

[12] Oldřich Dědek, "The Currency Shake-up in 1997: A Case Study of the Czech Economy," in Stephany Griffith-Jones, Ricardo Gottschalk, and Jacques Cailoux, eds., *International Capital Flows in Calm and Turbulent Times: The Need for New International Architecture* (Ann Arbor, MI: University of Michigan Press, 2003).

[13] In the centrally planned economies, the state bank performed all banking functions. Private banks did not exist.

[14] Ali M. Kutan and Josef C. Brada, "The evolution of monetary policy in transition economies," *Federal Reserve Bank of St. Louis Review*, 82 (March 1, 2000): 2.

[15] Michael Borish et al., "The evolution of the state-owned banking sector during transition in Central Europe," *Europe-Asia Studies*, 49 (November 1, 1997): 7.

[16] Česka Konsolidacni Agentura, available at http://www.kobp.cz/ckaen.htm, accessed April 27, 2004.

[17] Antonín Rusek, "The Czech Economic Crisis: Policy Revenge?" *International Advances in Economic Research*, 5 (May 1, 1999): 2.

[18] IPFs were investment companies that managed the equivalent of mutual funds.

[19] Gerald A. McDermott, *Embedded Politics: Industrial Networks & Institutional Change in Postcommunism* (Ann Arbor, MI: The University of Michigan Press, 2003), p. 86.

[20] Oldřich Bures, "Czech Banking Reform—Biggest Free Lunch Ever?" *10th International Anti-Corruption Conference*, Prague 2001, available at http://www.10iacc.org/download/w2-01.pdf.

[21] John Bonin and Paul Wachtel, "Lessons from Bank Privatization in Central Europe," working paper for World Bank and Federal Reserve Bank of Dallas Conference on Bank Privatization, Dallas, November 19–20, 1998, available from Stern School of Business, New York University, available at http://pages.stern.nyu.edu/~pwachtel /WBpaperrev.pdf.

[22] Kalman Mizsei, "Privatization of individual banks or of the banking system?" Organization for Economic Cooperation and Development, 11th Plenary Session of the OECD Advisory Group on Privatization, Rome, September 18 and 19, 1997; see also McDermott, pp. 64–94, for an insightful discussion on how the prudent adherence by the Czechs to the standard reform approaches of depoliticization during 1990–1992 failed to initiate the restructuring of banks and industrial firms and produced a financial stalemate.

[23] World Bank, *Czech Republic: Completing the Transformation of Banks and Enterprises* (Washington, DC: World Bank, 2000), available at http://www-wds.worldbank.org/servlet/WDSContentServer WDSP/IB/2001/01/06/000094946_00121906020354/Rendered/PDF/multi_page.pdf. For an empirical study analyzing the impact of past industrial networks on the way the post-communist Czech Republic built new institutions to govern the restructuring of their economies, see generally McDermott.

[24] Mihir A. Desai and Alberto Moel, "Czech Mate: CME and Vladimir Zelezny (A)," HBS No. 204-118 (Boston: Harvard Business School Publishing, 2004). Desai and Moel provide an interesting insight into how insiders can expropriate value from shareholders in emerging markets when property rights are ill-defined.

[25] World Bank, Czech Republic: Completing the Transformation of Banks and Enterprises, p. vii.

[26] Acts on banks and on the central bank were issued in February 1992. The act on the central bank stated that the central bank's primary objective was to maintain the stability of the Czech currency.

[27] CAR is a measure of a bank's capital. It is expressed as a percentage of a bank's risk-weighted credit exposures. This ratio is used to protect depositors and promote the stability and efficiency of financial systems around the world.

[28] "The Czech National Bank 1993–2003," CNB working paper, p. 14, available at http://www.cnb.cz/en/pdf/CNB_1993-2003_EN.pdf.

[29] Zdeněk Kudrna et al., "The Rise and Fall of IPB," Charles and Georgetown Universities, available at http://www.historieipb.cz/default_en.htm.

[30] The full liberalization of international transactions enabled the use of the Czech currency in payments directed abroad and formed offshore markets.

[31] See Rawi Abdelal, *Capital Rules: The Construction of Global Finance* (Cambridge, Mass.: Harvard University Press, 2007), chapter 5. OECD accession required full liberalization of capital accounts. The OECD code of liberalization of capital movements came into existence in its current format with the formation of the OECD in 1961. It is worth noting that the very rapid capital account liberalization in the Czech Republic contrasts with the gradual process in original OECD member countries. The use of initial reservations or the application of a general derogation at the time of adherence to the code extended the adaptation period to over 25 years for some of these countries. Stephany Griffith-Jones et al., "The OECD Experience with Capital Account Liberalization," preliminary paper for the Institute of Development Studies, University of Sussex, November 2000.

[32] Dědek, "The Currency Shake-up in 1997," pp. 7–12.

[33] Balance of payments is a record of all transactions made by one particular country during a certain period of time. It compares the amount of economic activity between a country and all other countries. This includes trade balance and foreign investments, among other things.

[34] *Forty Years' Experience with the OECD Code of Liberalization of Capital Movements*, Organization for Economic Cooperation and Development (OECD) (Paris: OECD, 2002), pp. 126–133.

[35] Josef Tosovsky, "The Czech Experience with Asset Bubbles and Financial Crises," *Proceedings*, Journal of the Federal Reserve Bank of Kansas City, August 1999, pp. 155–170, available at http://www.kc.frb.org/PUBLICAT/SYMPOS /1999/S99toso.pdf.

[36] *The Czech National Bank 1993–2003*, CNB, p. 12.

[37] Dědek, "Capital Account Liberalization in the Czech Republic," pp. 98–114.

[38] *Forty Years' Experience with the OECD Code of Liberalization of Capital Movements*, OECD.

[39] CNB, Foreign Exchange Act No. 219/1995, September 1995, available at http://www.cnb.cz/en/search_en.php?hledat=foreign+exchange+act.

[40] Holub and Túma.

[41] "CSOB safe from Corruption," *CTK Business News*, January 25, 1995.

[42] Authors' phone interview with Pavel Kavánek, chief executive officer, ČSOB, July 28, 2004.

[43] Authors' phone interview with Pavel Kavánek.

[44] Authors' interview with Vit Hruška and Karel Nechmač, managers, Structural Risk Management, ČSOB, March 26, 2004.

[45] *The Czech National Bank 1993–2003*, CNB, p. 13.

[46] A sterilized intervention is any foreign exchange market activity by which the central bank buys or sells foreign currency in an attempt to influence the exchange rate value. Purchases of foreign exchange usually are intended to push down the home currency value of the exchange rate, and sales usually are intended to push it up.

[47] Holub and Túma.

[48] Jan Klacek, "Economic Transformation, Exchange Rate, and Capital Inflows in the Czech Republic," in Zdenek Drabek and Stephany Griffith-Jones, eds., *Managing Capital Flows in Turbulent Times: The Experience of Europe's Emerging Market Economies in Global Perspective* (London: M.E. Sharpe), pp. 78–97.

[49] Holub and Túma.

[50] *The Czech National Bank 1993–2003*, CNB, p. 16.

[51] *Forty Years' Experience with the OECD Code of Liberalization of Capital Movements*, OECD, pp. 126–133.

[52] *The Czech National Bank 1993–2003*, CNB, pp. 16–17.

[53] Roman Matusek, "The Czech Banking System in the Light of Regulation and Supervision: Selected Issues," CNB Working Paper No. 5, available at http://www.cnb.cz/ en/pdf/a-wp5-98.pdf.

[54] Dědek, "The Currency Shake-up in 1997," pp. 37–39.

[55] Banks classify their loan portfolio into standard, watch, substandard, doubtful, and loss loans. Classified loans or nonperforming loans encompass all positions mentioned above apart from standard.

[56] Holub and Túma.

[57] *The Czech National Bank 1993–2003*, CNB, p. 23.

[58] Ibid., p. 25.

[59] Authors' interview with Patrick Daems, member of board and senior executive officer, ČSOB, March 26, 2004.

[60] Authors' interview with Geert de Kegel, distribution director, ČSOB, March 26, 2004.

[61] Kudrna et al., pp. 44–47.

[62] "Report for the session of the Chamber of Deputies of the Parliament of the Czech Republic on the situation and the course of action for stabilizing Investiční a Poštovní Banka, a.s.," p. 29.

[63] *Czech Republic: Financial System Stability Assessment*, International Monetary Fund (Washington, DC: June 25, 2001) available at http://www.imf.org/external/pubs/ft/scr/2001/cr01113.pdf, accessed April 28, 2004.

[64] Kudrna et al.

[65] "Czech IPB bank says new suit holding up issue, " *Reuters*, March 31, 2000.

[66] "Report for the session of the Chamber of Deputies of the Parliament of the Czech Republic on the situation and the course of action for stabilizing Investiční a Poštovní Banka, a.s.," p. 4.

[67] Some analysts maintained that the bankruptcy of a bank of the stature of IPB, which was generally considered as "too big to fail," would negatively affect confidence in all banks, as well as in other financial institutions. The state needed to pay compensation for the IPB-insured deposits from the Deposit Insurance Fund, which was likely to experience deficit. These compensation payments would also hurt other banks due to the automatic and statutory twofold increase in the percentage rate of obligatory contributions to the fund. This rate would remain effective until the final repayment of the financial assistance. Higher costs for the banks would be passed on in higher interest rates and reduced accessibility of credit in the economy and would ultimately affect the development of GDP.

[68] Kudrna et al., p. 58.

[69] Ibid., pp. 52–54.

[70] Authors' interview with Marek Ditz.

[71] "Report for the session of the Chamber of Deputies of the Parliament of the Czech Republic on the situation and the course of action for stabilizing Investiční a Poštovní Banka, a.s.," p. 29.

[72] Ibid., p. 30.

[73] Refers to the selling of insurance through a bank's established distribution channels.

[74] "Forming an Allianz," *Prague Business Journal*, May 6, 2000.

[75] Authors' phone interview with Pavel Kavánek.

[76] Authors' interview with Marek Ditz.

[77] Authors' phone interview with Pavel Kavánek.

[78] Kudrna et al., p. 51.

RAWI ABDELAL

VINCENT DESSAIN

MONIKA STACHOWIAK

Bohemian Crowns: Československá Obchodní Banka (B)

Československá Obchodní Banka (ČSOB) acquired Investiční a Poštovní Banka (IPB) on Monday, June 19, 2000, after a weekend of intense negotiations. A week earlier, on Monday, June 12, IPB had come under increasing liquidity pressure, and by Wednesday night about 50% of the bank's liquid assets, or 17 billion Czech Republic crowns (US$430 million),[1] were withdrawn. By Thursday, fearing insolvency, IPB applied to the central bank for a loan. The next day, the central bank, having lost trust in IPB management, instead imposed conservatorship. An interim IPB administrator had to stop the run on the bank and ensure that IPB was quickly taken over by a reliable investor.[2] Later that same day, the central bank opened negotiations with ČSOB, which had already expressed interest in taking over IPB. ČSOB was also the only potential acquirer with a Czech banking license. The state authorities drew up transaction documents by Saturday. As Marek Ditz, ČSOB senior executive, explained: "No one slept over the weekend. Several members on the supervisory board of KBC, the bank's foreign strategic investor, even flew to Prague on Sunday to oversee the acquisition. . . . Still, we had a tremendous fear of new risks, which we were discovering by the hour."[3]

The parties reached an agreement on Sunday night, and the contract documents were signed at 6 a.m. the next morning. Since there had not been enough time for due diligence and separation of potentially nonperforming assets, the central bank and the Ministry of Finance agreed to cover ČSOB's future losses stemming from the transaction. All IPB's business, assets, and liabilities, both known and potential, were transferred to ČSOB. A deferred compensation, based on the difference between the real value of the IPB assets and liabilities, was established later by three international investment banks.[4] Pavel Kavánek, ČSOB CEO, recalled:

> We expected that IPB would be in disastrous shape and that the employees would resist the takeover. That did not prove correct. Once we entered the bank, we were applauded by the staff. In fact, top management were so disconnected in their dealings with the staff that when we arrived, the employees were confident that their situation could only change for the better. It was a great relief.

> When it came to the financials, losses estimated by the media, which in the end triggered the run on IPB, were of 12 billion crowns. I thought it would be more than twice that, but it proved to be on the order of 100 rather than 12 billion crowns. But after all, it did not make much of a difference in terms of the transaction structure and the cleanup on the loan side.

Professor Rawi Abdelal, Director of HBS Europe Research Center Vincent Dessain, and Research Associate Monika Stachowiak prepared this supplement. HBS cases are developed solely as the basis for class discussion. Cases are not intended to serve as endorsements, sources of primary data, or illustrations of effective or ineffective management.

Obviously, moving in so quickly helped us to stop the run on the bank and at least mitigate the liquidity risk.[5]

In August 2001, ČSOB signed an agreement to restructure IPB with the consolidation bank Konsolidační Banka and the Czech Ministry of Finance. The ex-IPB assets and liabilities were put into three groups—those retained by ČSOB, those transferred to Konsolidační Banka, and so-called other items. ČSOB retained the right to transfer any "other item" to Konsolidační Banka by June 19, 2002.[6] After a series of transfers to the Czech Consolidation Agency, which replaced the Konsolidační Banka in September 2001, an audit valued the IPB assets that ČSOB chose to keep at 3.7 billion Czech Republic crowns (US$131.5 million). This amount, plus the associated interest, was paid to the Czech state in 2003.[7]

Integration Challenges

The IPB acquisition made ČSOB the largest bank in the Czech Republic in terms of assets and client deposits. (See **Exhibit 1** for the retail market situation.) The bank obtained a solid retail market foothold, as well as leading subsidiaries in mortgages, building savings, construction loans, and leasing. ČSOB's primary-deposit market share rose from 9.7% to 23.4%, and its customer base from 400,000 to 3.4 million.[8] (See **Exhibit 2** for ČSOB's and peer banks' 2000–2003 financials.)

ČSOB immediately acted to stabilize IPB's deposit base. ČSOB then focused on merging the two banks. Kavánek recalled: "KBC helped us to mobilize retail expertise. It had been a year since KBC focused their assistance and attention on transforming ČSOB into a retail bank, and many colleagues from KBC's headquarters came to support us."

Restoring consumer faith in IPB was one of the larger challenges ČSOB had to face. The bank outlined marketing actions to retain customers or to attract them back. In fact, ČSOB quickly realized that its good reputation was at stake in the regions where IPB previously exploited its customers. Geert de Kegel, ČSOB's distribution director, explained: "Some of the branches had really good value, but others were just a nuisance. A branch did not necessarily mean customers. Many of the former IPB branches were not even located in the cities. We had to rationalize the branch network and adopt a new regional structure."[9]

In the end, the number of branches was brought down from 240 to 176. The integration concluded after 22 months in March 2002 at a total cost of 1.5 billion Czech Republic crowns (US$45.8 million).[10] Cost synergies came mostly from a reduction in headcount (1,500 employees—18% of total staff—were dismissed).

Finding IPB's Skeletons in the Closet: Cayman Funds and Nomura

As ČSOB began evaluating IPB after the acquisition, several abnormalities were uncovered. For one, ČSOB found assets of 42 billion Czech Republic crowns (US$1.3 billion)[11] to be participation certificates in funds in the Cayman Islands established by IPB in 1999. The funds had enabled IPB to evade regulations concerning capital adequacy. By removing poorly performing assets from its portfolio, IPB could maintain lower reserves than otherwise would have been required. IPB did not hold any voting rights controlling those assets.[12]

Another surprise that ČSOB found was the overall management of the bank by the Japanese securities firm Nomura. The 1998 IPB sale to Nomura had initially been considered the first successful privatization of a large bank to a foreign buyer. In hindsight, it now seemed to some analysts as though Nomura had not pushed for a thorough IPB restructuring. It further seemed to those analysts as though Nomura's main motivation to acquire IPB was to obtain the Pilsner Urquell breweries, which IPB held on its balance sheet.[13] In February 1998, IPB had transferred Pilsner Urquell shares worth 7 billion Czech Republic crowns (US$216.8 million) to the Česke Pivo (Czech Beer) holding company. Česke Pivo was owned by companies closely related to IPB management. IPB granted Česke Pivo a loan that made the whole transaction possible. In June 1999, Nomura, via its subsidiary Pembridge, acquired a 100% stake in Česke Pivo for 1.6 billion Czech Republic crowns (US$49.6 million). Later on, Nomura, together with some members of IPB management, carried out several complex operations involving the Cayman funds resulting in Nomura obtaining the right to repay IPB for the Pilsner Urquell stake with IPB's own shares. In November 1999, Nomura merged its stake in Radegast, another Czech brewery, with Pilsner Urquell and sold the new entity to South African Breweries for 23 billion Czech Republic crowns (US$629 million).[14]

As ČSOB learned about those deals in 2000, it worked to reclaim assets that were either spirited away to the Cayman funds or sold to the South African investor. In October 2001, after several months of struggling with Nomura and MeesPierson, an investment company that served as administrator to the Cayman funds, ČSOB finally gained control over the Caribbean activities. The Cayman assets, regarded by ČSOB as the property of the Czech state, were taken back to the Czech Consolidation Agency for a controlled liquidation. At the same time, ČSOB filed a lawsuit against Nomura in the courts of Prague and London for damages to IPB in the Česke Pivo transaction.[15]

Exhibit 1   Retail Market Positions at December 2000

| | Market Share (%) | | | | Number | | |
	Total Assets in CZK bn	Client Deposits	Loans (net)	Assets	Branch Network	Clients (in million)	Employees
SOB/IPB	524	23.4	12.9	19.5	240[a]	3.4	9,200
KB	477	20.9	14.1	17.7	334	1.3	10,700
S	451	23.9	11.3	16.7	707	3.9	14,100

Source: ČSOB 2000 Annual Report.

Exhibit 2   Big Three Financials, 2000–2003

a) ČSOB

	2000	2001	2002	2003
Results for the year (CZKm)				
Net profit/loss	4,691	5,952	6,591	6,240
At year-end (CZKm)				
Shareholders' equity	34,336	37,853	41,275	46,001
Due to customers	348,820	417,743	418,143	439,999
Loans and leases	164,501	181,476	213,682	230,100
Total assets	535,544	586,426	597,044	606,480
Ratios (%)				
Return on average shareholders' equity (ROAE)	14.26	16.49	16.65	14.3
Return on average total assets (ROAA)	1.18	1.05	1.11	1.04
Bank capital adequacy ratio	13.70	15.04	13.99	15.36

Source: ČSOB 2000–2003 annual reports.

b) Komerční Banka

	2000	2001	2002	2003
Results for the year (CZKm)				
Net profit/loss	-19	2,532	8,763	9,262
At year-end (CZKm)				
Shareholders' equity	20,211	23,598	33,758	40,399
Due to customers	287,624	316,791	341,114	349,505
Loans and leases	126,943	135,197	121,154	130,900
Total assets	402,205	421,720	439,753	447,565
Ratios (%)				
Return on average shareholders' equity (ROAE)	x	11.56	30.56	11.60
Return on average total assets (ROAA)	x	0.61	2.03	0.60
Bank capital adequacy ratio	14.38	15.18	13.35	15.20

Source: Komerční Banka 2000–2003 annual reports.

Exhibit 2 (continued)

c) Česka Sporitelna

	2000	2001	2002	2003
Results for the year (CZKm)				
Net profit/loss	41	1,798	5,805	7,615
At year-end (CZKm)				
Shareholders' equity	22,655	24,455	29,831	34,408
Due to customers	n.a.	388,252	402,728	428,572
Loans and leases	n.a.	165,010	169,766	205,878
Total assets	438,055	491,605	519,691	554,048
Ratios (%)				
Return on average shareholders' equity (ROAE)	0.2	7.6	21.4	23.7
Return on average total assets (ROAA)	0.01	0.37	1.12	1.37
Bank capital adequacy ratio	16	16.5	16.8	14.6
Classified loan share of bank's total loans	25.5	14.7	9.5	3.5

Source: Česka Sporitelna 2000–2003 annual reports.

Exhibit 3   Czech Republic, Summary Economic Indicators, 2000–2003

	2000	2001	2002	2003
GDP (current $ billion)	51	57	70	85
Annual GDP growth (%)	3.3	3.1	2	2.9
Population (mn)	10.3	10.2	10.2	10.3
GDP per head ($ at PPP)	13,808	14,646	15,190	15,800
Annual CPI (%)	3.9	4.7	1.8	0.1
Unemployment rate (%)	9	8.6	9.2	9.9
Current account balance	-2,688	-3,272	-4,484	-5,570
Current account (% of GDP)	-5.2	-5.7	-6.5	-6.5
Net direct investment flows	4,944	4,829	9,096	2,351
Foreign direct investment	4,984	5,639	9,319	2,550
Foreign direct investment (% of GDP)	9.7	8.6	13.4	3
Outward direct investment	-42	-94	-209	-232
Annual change in gross fixed investment (%)	28.3	27.7	26.3	26
Annual change in industrial production (%)	5.4	6.7	3.8	3.3
Budget balance (% of GDP)	-3.1	-2.4	-6.3	-6.6
Budget revenue (% of GDP)	40.4	40.1	39.5	38.9
Budget expenditure (% of GDP)	43.6	42.5	45.8	45.5
Trade balance	-3,093	-3,077	-2,239	-2,458
Exchange rate (CZK/$)	38.59	38.04	32.74	28.21

Source: Compiled from the Economist Intelligence Unit, www.eiu.com, accessed May 28, 2004.

Note: Figures are in US$ million unless otherwise stated.

Endnotes

1 David Shirreff, "Grand masters of opacity," *Euromoney*, September 2000, available at http://www.euromoney.com/default.asp?Page=14&S=S&PUB=20&ISS=1192&SID=86959&Country=&SM=ALL&SearchStr=masters%20of%20opacity, accessed May 12, 2004.

2 Zdeněk Kudrna et al., "The Rise and Fall of IPB," Charles and Georgetown Universities, available at http://www.historieipb.cz/default_en.htm.

3 Authors' interview with Marek Ditz, director, Banking Operations Support, ČSOB, Prague, March 26, 2004.

4 Kudrna et al.

5 Authors' phone interview with Pavel Kavánek, chief executive officer, ČSOB, July 28, 2004.

6 ČSOB 2001 Annual Report, available at http://www.csob.cz/pb/slozka.asp?prmKod=PB5.1.5&prmMenu=1, accessed May 28, 2004.

7 ČSOB 2003 Annual Report, available at http://www.csob.cz/data/pb/pdf/ CSOB_AR_2003.pdf, accessed May 28, 2004.

8 ČSOB 2000 Annual Report, available at http://www.csob.cz/pb/ slozka.asp?prmKod=PB5.1.4&a=0, accessed May 28, 2004.

9 Authors' interview with Geert de Kegel, distribution director, ČSOB, Prague, March 26, 2004.

10 ČSOB 2001 Annual Report.

11 The later ČSOB estimation valued those assets at only 18 billion Czech Republic crowns (US$557.6 million).

12 "Caribbean Funds and ČSOB," April 2002, available at http://www.csob.cz/pb/ slozka.asp?prmKod=PB6&a=0, accessed June 7, 2004.

13 Kudrna et al.

14 Stefan Wagstyl and Robert Anderson, "Nomura Faces Breweries Action," *The Financial Times*, September 8, 2000; Rick Jervis, "Beer Brawl is Spilling Into Europe Civil Courts -- CSOB Pursues Claim Against Nomura," *The Financial Times*, February 28, 2002; Robert Anderson and Stefan Wagstyl, "Nomura Case to Start Today," *The Financial Times*, December 9, 2002; and "Czech Beer at Caymans," April 25, 2002, available from Kajmany, Global Access, http://www.kajmany.cz/english.php?clanekid=80, accessed June 7, 2004.

15 "Transactions Pursued by ČSOB with Respect to Stabilizing Caribbean Funds – key moments," April 2002, available at http://www.csob.cz/pb/slozka.asp?prmKod=PB6&a=0, accessed June 7, 2004; "Ten Myths about Caymans," April 2002, available at http://www.csob.cz/pb/slozka.asp?prmKod=PB6&a=0, accessed June 7, 2004.

HARVARD | **BUSINESS** | **SCHOOL**

9-706-009
REV: MARCH 8, 2007

RAWI ABDELAL

CHRISTOPHER M. BRUNER

Politics and Prudential Supervision: ABN Amro's Bid for Antonveneta (A)

Give me control of a nation's money and I care not who makes her laws.

—Mayer Amschel Rothschild[1]

By early 2005, the decades-old common market project in Europe had achieved substantial successes in many sectors of the economy, though far less so in banking, which remained subject to the substantial discretionary authority of national bank regulators to approve—or rather, to disapprove—cross-border mergers and acquisitions among banks. For many, Italy exemplified this reality perhaps better than any other country, as central bank head Antonio Fazio had never, since assuming the position in 1993, approved a foreign takeover of an Italian bank—a stance for which there was widespread political support in Italy.

Indeed, skepticism regarding European economic and financial integration was on the rise in Italy, reflected particularly in growing dissatisfaction with the realities of membership in Europe's common currency, the euro. As the value of the euro against the U.S. dollar continued to climb, Italian businesses dependent on exports to the U.S. market found themselves pinched by increasingly potent competition from elsewhere, notably China, which pegged its currency to the U.S. dollar, insulating its businesses from such currency effects. In past times Italy might simply have devalued its national currency, the lira, to maintain competitiveness, but such action was precluded by euro-zone membership (monetary authority having been ceded to the European Central Bank). Some Italian leaders increasingly called upon the government to withdraw from the common currency, with "anti-euro backlash . . . ricocheting up and down the peninsula as the country [sank] deeper into a recession."[2]

It was against this backdrop that ABN Amro, the Dutch bank, made its bid on March 30, 2005, to purchase all shares of Padua-based Banca Antoniana Popolare Veneta S.p.A.—popularly known as Antonveneta. Though ABN Amro was already a substantial shareholder, with holdings dating to 1995, and held four of Antonveneta's 15 board seats, ABN Amro's effort to solidify its presence in the Italian retail market by achieving control over the much smaller Italian bank was to encounter concerted political opposition and substantial regulatory obstacles. For many, ABN Amro's bid for Antonveneta was to become an important test of Italy's commitment to the creation of a single European market for financial services and of the openness of the Italian retail banking market.

Rijkman Groenink, the chairman of ABN Amro's managing board, recognized the large stakes for the Dutch bank as well: "We had set our minds on Italy; we wanted to buy a bank in Italy. But we

---

were also defending some things: the integrity of Antonveneta, our own financial interest, and of course, our pride."[3] Failure would, according to Richard Bruens, ABN Amro's head of Investor Relations, entail "serious downside risks to our strategic and managerial credibility."[4] The episode was to be one of the defining moments of the European integration project.

The Common Market and Financial Integration in Europe

A common market had been an important goal of the European Union's member states since the founding treaty took effect in 1957. By the first decade of the new millennium, however, the substantial level of integration reached in many sectors of the European economy over intervening decades—particularly during the 1990s—had not been achieved in the financial services sector. Most mergers and acquisitions (M&A) activity in financial services since the 1990s had reflected domestic consolidation, not cross-border integration. [5] National diversity continued to be the norm and the rule. ABN Amro board member Tom de Swaan described the "three trends in European banking consolidation" succinctly. There were those countries with "substantial domestic consolidation to produce a few national champions that can then engage with the wider world: Spain, France, and the Netherlands, for example." Another, contradictory pattern prevailed in "those countries whose banking systems consolidated during the process of becoming almost completely foreign owned: central and eastern Europe, for example." Finally, there were the "banking systems that have done neither: Germany and Italy."[6]

The banking sector remained highly fragmented, particularly on the retail side. While many eastern European banks had ended up under foreign control through privatization programs initiated in the 1990s, the picture was very different in western Europe, where 90% of the total value of banking M&A in the 1990s took the form of domestic consolidation. Aside from the purchase by Spain's Banco Santander Central Hispano of the U.K.'s Abbey National, substantial cross-border retail banking mergers were essentially unkown.[7] (See **Exhibit 1** for data on domestic M&A activity involving European banks, **Exhibits 2a** and **2b** for data on cross-border M&A activity involving European banks, and **Exhibit 3** for cross-border M&A data for various sectors across the Organization for Economic Cooperation and Development [OECD].)

By 2004 the European Commission, as it reviewed the ongoing implementation of its 1999 Financial Services Action Plan, was actively evaluating impediments to cross-border banking integration in Europe and looking particularly closely at the role of national banking supervisors. Under the EU Banking Directive, which had taken effect in 2000, central bankers had substantial discretionary authority to veto banking mergers and acquisitions—including cross-border deals— where they deemed it necessary to "ensure sound and prudent management" of the bank in question. (The EU's 2004 merger regulation likewise included an exception for prudential rules, significantly curtailing the commission's effective jurisdiction over cross-border banking mergers and acquisitions in Europe.) The crucial standard of "sound and prudent management" had never been defined, a shortcoming—in the commission's view—that left the regime open to political interference and economic protectionism. An "Expert Group on Banking" assembled to report to the commission seemed to agree, while national banking supervisors (through the Committee of European Banking Supervisors, or CEBS) emphasized other impediments to cross-border retail banking integration— notably lack of consumer "confidence" in foreign banks.[8]

In January 2005, the commission requested CEBS's views on impediments to cross-border banking deals, with an explicit "focus on the criteria used by national authorities to block the acquisition of a qualifying shareholding when they believe that the acquisition could threaten the 'sound and prudent management' of the target institution." Noting that "[o]bviously, only prudential criteria may be taken into account when reviewing applications," the commission expressed the view that there would "be benefits in clarifying the scope of any supervisory review and identifying a set of relevant criteria." Among other things the commission wondered whether, upon exercise of the supervisory veto, it might make sense to "requir[e] the relevant national authority to post a public notification of the refusal and to provide a detailed reasoning for its decision." The commission further asked whether there should be "an objective redress mechanism that would allow [shareholders] to challenge negative decisions taken by national authorities," introducing "an element of accountability."[9]

Banking in Italy

Banking and prudential regulation in Italy exemplified, perhaps better than anywhere else in Europe, both the promise of integration and the entrenchment of domestic impediments to it.

Though Italy had the sixth-largest economy in the world, it was largely built on small to medium-size, family-controlled firms traditionally reliant on bank financing (with only a few larger standouts, such as the auto manufacturer Fiat).[10] Average firm size, measured by employees, was smaller in Italy than in other major European economies (4.4 employees, as compared with 10.3, 7.1, and 9.6 in Germany, France, and the United Kingdom, respectively), and "firms with more than 500 employees (conventionally taken as the threshold for defining 'large' businesses) account[ed] for only 15 percent of employment in Italy whereas firms of this size contribute[d] to at least 40 percent of employment in many other countries."[11] (See **Exhibits 4, 5a,** and **5b** for data illustrating reliance on bank debt.)

Italy had taken substantial measures to privatize its banks in the 1990s, principally to raise money and reduce public debt to qualify for membership in the euro zone, leading in turn to widespread consolidation among Italian banks.[12] Relative to the rest of Europe, however, Italy's banks remained small (none making Europe's top 10 by market capitalization), and with "800 different banks . . . the sector [was] one of the most fragmented in Europe."[13] (See **Exhibit 6.**)

While Italian retail consumers—"strong savers" in the past—had begun "to embrace consumer finance products such as leases, mortgages and insurance," the "penetration of more sophisticated finance products [was] still low."[14] Banking fees for retail customers in Italy were higher than anywhere else in Europe, with the annual weighted price of core banking services totaling €252, as compared with a European average of €108, and a low of €34 in the Netherlands.[15] (See **Exhibit 7** for retail banking price data for selected European and other countries.) Still, profits (and market capitalizations) remained lower than elsewhere due to poor historical levels of demand for more lucrative services (i.e., beyond deposit accounts), leading some to conclude that "the largest groups could easily be swallowed by outsiders with stronger share prices and more capital." According to the chief executive of Banca Intesa, Italy's largest bank, "[T]he first 10 banks in Italy are all interesting targets. They make money, they have significant potential for growth. Given that there are European banks with lots of free capital and a lack of other opportunities, Italy is a strong target." Consumer groups in Italy thought that "households would benefit from more outsiders potentially freeing them from what one group call[ed] 'feudal' bank charges."[16]

Italy proved a tough market to crack, however, for foreign banks. The "popolari"—small banks with "less of an eye on profits but good relations with local business"—were very well connected within Italy. "Through political parties, the Roman Catholic Church, business associations and even football clubs, intricate networks of friendship link[ed] local bankers to politicians, business people and trade unionists in a way that contribute[d] to the distinctive identity of almost every Italian region or municipal area." Carlo Giovanardi, the parliamentary affairs minister, "liken[ed] foreign takeovers to 'colonization'" and "argued that foreign banks 'would care less about the state of the nation's firms.'"[17] (See **Exhibits 8** and **9** for data on the loan composition of Italian banks by size category and data reflecting Italian manufacturing firms' banking relationships.)

At the top of the Italian banking world sat Antonio Fazio, the governor of the Bank of Italy. Fazio first joined the Bank of Italy's economic research department through a scholarship as a young man, before leaving in the 1960s to study in the United States at Northwestern University and the Massachusetts Institute of Technology. He later returned to the Bank of Italy, eventually becoming governor in 1993.[18] As *The Economist* observed, his "power over what can or cannot be done in Italian banking [was] legendary." He had "control over competition issues as well as prudential supervision" and "seem[ed] to be bulletproof" politically.[19]

Italy's banking law gave Fazio the full measure of discretion permitted under the EU Banking Directive—requiring Bank of Italy authorization unless "in conflict with the principle of sound and prudent management"[20]—and Fazio exercised his veto power readily in the cross-border context. Since taking over in 1993, Fazio had never approved a foreign takeover of an Italian bank, a track record rumored in the Italian press to reflect a *quid pro quo* for the life tenure as Bank of Italy governor granted him by the Italian government.[21] The degree of power that Fazio seemed to enjoy in Italian political circles puzzled many observers, as he generally declined interviews, was "not overtly political," and in his annual addresses had vocally criticized the center-right government's economic policies. Some pointed to his devout Catholicism, one observer noting that "[m]any banks, particularly at a local level, have strong Catholic links." In any event, the Italian press had come to refer to Italian bankers, with whom Fazio maintained close ties, as "Fazio's boys."[22]

Fazio's intentions for Italy's banking system were thus the subject of both controversy and speculation. Those intentions created a variety of informal rules for Italy's banks. According to Francesco Spinelli, ABN Amro's country head for Italy, "In Italy there was an informal rule—Fazio's rule, which was known by all—that in general foreign banks could not own more than 15% of an Italian bank. Because most Italian banks are run by syndicate pacts of only 30%, this prevented foreign owners from acquiring a majority of a syndicate pact."[23] According to Spinelli, "Fazio did not want banks to become part of a distribution network. He wanted them to be committed to the local economies in which they had traditionally been embedded."[24] ABN Amro's head of Group Risk Management, David Cole, recognized that "Italian banks traditionally have played a cohesion role in the economy. The internationalization of banking will lead to a review of many cozy relationships. But over the next five to seven years, much has to change to make Italy more efficient."[25] Thus, one important part of the transformation of the Italian model of capitalism would involve profound changes in banking practices.

ABN Amro's Groenink recognized that foreign ownership remained "a legitimate concern for regulators, who naturally want the local economy to be served by a strong local banking infrastructure. A domestic-owned bank has a natural inclination to serve the local economy. A foreign-owned bank considers the local economy within the context of an international portfolio. The answer, in my view, is to have a mix of foreign and domestic ownership."[26] Because Italy had no foreign ownership at all, ABN Amro's executives did not recognize the threat that Fazio apparently interpreted.

Fazio had also discouraged domestic consolidation of Italy's banking sector, which remained intensely localized. Thus, the Italian central bank governor, according to Spinelli, "seemed to propose two contradictory goals. Fazio sought to prevent foreign control of the Italian banking system until domestic banks were stronger, but then he also refused to allow mergers among the top 15 Italian banks."[27] As ABN Amro's managing director of the Alliance Solutions Group, Leonard Stolk, observed, "Local consolidation must precede the Europeanization of banking. And that local consolidation will take some time due to the ownership complexities and socioeconomic atmosphere."[28]

And finally, according to Groenink, there was the simplest rule of all, one that practically defines cross-border banking in general: "the unspoken rule that within the four walls of the Bank of Italy you listen to the governor and follow his preferences."[29]

"In the Commission's eyes," the effective insulation of Italy's banking sector from cross-border takeovers made it Europe's "worst offender" in terms of perceived misuse of prudential supervisory authority.[30] In February 2005, Charlie McCreevy, the European Commissioner for Internal Market and Services, had written to Fazio requesting that he "clarify that his policy was not to block foreign-led takeover bids."[31] Fazio publicly "rejected the commission's charges, pointing out that while foreigners own[ed] just 7% of Germany's top four banks and 3% of France's, foreigners own[ed] 17% of Italy's top four institutions."[32] In a speech on March 22, McCreevy observed that the debate was in fact "about whether national supervisors use solely prudential criteria"—and not about the level of foreign ownership. He identified "enabl[ing] cross-border consolidation in the European banking sector" as a priority, adding that "what we politely call 'political intervention mechanisms' . . . have not disappeared." He further noted that the commission planned to "review the application of the EC Treaty freedom of capital movements in the area of cross-border bank mergers and acquisitions."[33]

Testing the Italian Banking Market

By March 2005, the landscape of European retail banking was heavily fragmented along the boundaries of domestic markets subject to substantial discretionary authority of national bank supervisors to block cross-border banking M&A. The European Commission had begun to consider how to address what it considered illegitimate political obstacles to banking integration and had particularly trained its eye on the actions of Italy's top central banker.

Later that month, the Dutch bank ABN Amro would enter these uncertain waters with a cash-tender offer for shares of Banca Antoniana Popolare Veneta S.p.A.—known generally as Antonveneta. The offer was "conditional on ABN Amro achieving at least 50% plus one share"—that is, complete control. In ABN Amro's view, Italy represented "'an attractive and large market with strong growth opportunities,'" and Antonveneta would "expand its presence in the mid-market segment."[34] The offer was widely perceived as a test of the openness of Italy's banking sector, and perhaps more pertinently, of Fazio's power to keep foreigners out.[35] Meanwhile, within a matter of days, Banca Popolare di Lodi—known as Lodi—"a small mutual bank," would "quickly and controversially amass a large rival shareholding," with "talk of defending the autonomy of Antonveneta."[36]

ABN Amro

The Netherlands' ABN Amro described itself as "an international bank with European roots and a clear focus on consumer and commercial banking, strongly supported by an international wholesale business." The bank's business lines were consumer and commercial clients, wholesale clients, and private clients and asset management.[37] Its "strategic focus [was] on the mid-market segment." On the consumer side this meant "clients who require more than a basic banking package (mass affluent and private clients), but who don't yet fall into the small category of our top-end private clients." On the commercial side it "range[d] from mid-sized companies in our home markets [the Netherlands,

Brazil, and the U.S. Midwest] to a smaller number of large multinational clients and financial institutions."[38]

Dating back to 1824, ABN Amro was the 11th-largest bank in Europe and the 20th-largest in the world, "with over 3,000 branches in more than 60 countries, a staff of more than 97,000 full-time equivalents and total assets of EUR 742.9 billion."[39] (See **Exhibit 10** for ABN Amro's consolidated balance sheet as of March 31, 2005.)

Antonveneta

Based in the northern Italian city of Padua, Antonveneta was much smaller than ABN Amro, though its €50 billion in total assets made it Italy's ninth-largest bank. It had approximately 1,000 branches concentrated in northern Italy (though present throughout the country) and 10,000 employees, and its products and services included retail banking, private banking, asset management, "bancassurance," and merchant banking.[40] Antonveneta was itself the result of a 1996 merger of two Padua-based banks and a number of subsequent smaller acquisitions.[41] (See **Exhibit 11** for Antonveneta's consolidated balance sheet as of March 31, 2005.)

Although ABN Amro had ended up with 0.5% of Antonveneta's shares in 1995 "by accident," according to Groenink, over time the Dutch bank's executives had recognized an excellent opportunity to enter the Italian market, which they predicted would open more quickly than Germany's. Groenink also argued that, over time, ABN Amro's "strategy evolved such that Antonveneta fit perfectly, for its customer base was exactly what we were trying to cultivate: mid-market commercial and retail with some investment-banking advisory services. We were in the process of moving from a wholesale to a midmarket retail banking strategy."[42]

Lodi

Lodi itself was actually smaller than Antonveneta. Though it stood just one spot behind as the 10th-largest bank in Italy, Lodi's market value was in fact only about one-third that of Antonveneta.[43] Described as "tiny" and "debt-laden" by financial analysts, Lodi was "straining under the weight of a $12 billion debt load from [an] earlier mergers and acquisitions spree." With a "debt-to-consumer deposits ratio of 1.09—nearly triple the Italian average," Lodi's CEO Gianpiero Fiorani had just months earlier, in late 2004, "assured analysts . . . that his bank would not be making any more near-term acquisitions."[44] Also concentrated in the north of Italy (but with branches elsewhere), Lodi took pride in its "social importance" as "the first cooperative bank to be created in Italy" (1864). Lodi had over 3 million clients and total assets of €45 billion.[45]

Competing Bids, the Bank of Italy, and the European Commission

On March 21 ABN Amro announced that it had filed a "pre-notification" with the Bank of Italy regarding a potential bid for Antonveneta[46] and on March 30 announced "a cash offer for all ordinary shares." Once required approvals were secured from Italian, Dutch, and European regulators, ABN Amro would launch the offer of €25 per share, valuing all shares at €6.3 billion and providing a premium of about 7% over the previous day's share price (30% over the average price for the prior six months). The bank stated that it would "support local decision making and . . . safeguard Banca Antonveneta's continued support of the local economy, while at the same time extracting the benefits of being one group." Antonveneta would "remain headquartered in Padua and . . . maintain its brand and its role as a bank with historically strong ties to the local community." According to ABN Amro's

Cole, the Dutch bank had "much to offer in terms of modernization—leveraging our AA rating, employing our IT infrastructure, offering new products, and more effectively managing NPLs [nonperforming loans]."[47] As of the announcement, ABN Amro held 12.676% of outstanding shares (as well as certain convertible bonds representing another 6.996% on conversion, totaling 18.747% of fully diluted shares), and the offer was conditional on reaching 50% of shares plus one. The offer would be funded through "a combination of new equity, debt and hybrid capital" structured to keep ABN Amro's capital ratios "at a level . . . expected to preserve its current credit ratings" and within its Tier 1 capital ratio targets.[48] (Tier 1 capital, under bank capital adequacy rules, "refers to core capital, the sum of equity capital and disclosed reserves as adjusted." In contrast, Tier 2 capital "refers to undisclosed reserves, revaluation reserves, general provisions and loan loss reserves, hybrid debt-equity instruments, and subordinated long-term debt.")[49]

Meanwhile, however, Lodi's shareholdings were already starting to grow. As of March 16, Lodi owned "shares equivalent to 4.983%," the bank affirming that its "dealing in Banca Antonveneta's shares on behalf of third parties . . . [had] no connection with the above-mentioned stake . . . nor with alleged agreements with current shareholders." By April 6, Lodi held 10.82% of Antonveneta, a stake intended to "position . . . Lodi as one of Banca Antonveneta's stable shareholders." The bank again affirmed that it had "not entered into agreements . . . in respect of Banca Antonveneta's shares," though it added that "the stake [had] been taken to safeguard the investment made by . . . Lodi" and by others, "whether Italian or not."[50]

Lodi's moves—as well as those of the Bank of Italy—were garnering attention in the press. *The Financial Times* (FT) reported, "Lodi talks of defending the autonomy of Antonveneta," opining that the "openness or otherwise of the Italian market is under the spotlight, while there is also the possibility that successful bids will be followed by a wave of acquisitions from outside." Fazio was "having his every step scrutinised by the European Commission," and FT observed that whereas he had readily deployed his veto in the past "to keep foreign predators at bay," Lodi was "a veteran of domestic acquisitions" with 13 approvals from Fazio in seven years under its belt. Lodi had "been in regular consultation with Mr. Fazio over Antonveneta," and Fazio had not impeded Lodi's Antonveneta share purchases.[51]

On April 14 ABN Amro received approval from Italy's securities regulator, CONSOB, "to publish the offering document for the cash offer for all ordinary shares of Banca Antonveneta."[52] The next day, Antonveneta's board approved the offer, observing in a press release that the board "has deemed that the business purpose at the basis of the offer can be shared, also considering the derivable advantages for Banca Antonveneta S.p.A. and its shareholders" and that it "deemed adequate the consideration offered by ABN Amro."[53] As ABN Amro reported in its own press release, Antonveneta's board "gave a positive recommendation" of the offer, finding the offer price to be a fair one, "subscrib[ing] to the strategic logic of [the] offer," endorsing ABN Amro's plan for the smaller bank, and—from ABN Amro's perspective—showing that its "decision to make a tender offer [was] a friendly step, intended to support the future stability and development" of Antonveneta.[54]

However, the obstacles to a successful acquisition were becoming ever clearer, as Lodi, with Fazio's permission, had "overtaken ABN [Amro] as the largest shareholder in Antonveneta" while Bank of Italy approval for ABN Amro's bid remained in question. Moreover, Antonveneta's board, of which ABN Amro held four of 15 seats, was expected to "be reconstituted" within a matter of weeks and—in light of Lodi's share acquisitions—"it [was] possible that a slate put forward by Lodi [would] become the new board."[55]

Over the coming weeks, the race for control over Antonveneta would take shape and pick up pace. On April 15, the day Antonveneta's board endorsed ABN Amro's bid, Lodi announced the unanimous decision of its own board "to take all steps needed to set up and, where possible, conclude negotiations with ABN Amro for the purchase of shares and convertible bonds [then] held by ABN Amro in Banca Antonveneta."[56] Shortly thereafter, on April 19, the Bank of Italy approved an increase in ABN Amro's stake to 20% while reserving judgment on the offer itself.[57] Lodi, meanwhile, was reportedly "considering buying up to 29.9 per cent" (just short of the threshold at which, in Italy, a takeover bid would have been required), "for which it [was] assumed to have been granted approval."[58] On April 27, ABN Amro received approval from the Bank of Italy "to increase its shareholding in Banca Antonveneta to up to 30%,"[59] though Lodi had by this time announced that its board would—on April 29—"deliberate on the strategy to be implemented" with respect to its Antonveneta shareholding, and particularly whether it should "lead to a de facto control" over Antonveneta.[60]

At the announced meeting, Lodi's board ultimately did approve (unanimously) a takeover bid for Antonveneta and "a complex development plan to create the fifth-largest Italian banking hub by aggregating" Lodi and Antonveneta, "with a view to generating value for investors, shareholders, customers, and the Italian economy in general." The plan, "based on the two banks' common entrepreneurial culture and strong vocation for serving the local community," would, among other things, "enhanc[e] the identity and autonomy of individual local entities, while safeguarding their governance, management and community representation"; "create a new national player able to perform an important function in the revival of Italy's economic and industrial system"; and "help reinforce the Italian banking industry and act as a strong point of reference for other entities of the same category and size." Lodi's bid was to take "the form of a 100%, voluntary public share exchange offer" worth €26 per share, paid principally in the form of Lodi shares and bonds, to be financed through "a complex plan to reinforce the capital structure by a total of 3 billion euro, including a 1.5 billion issue of convertible bonds." At the same time, the Lodi Board approved submission to its shareholders of a proposed name change to "Banca Popolare Italiana."[61]

Having previously "confined its efforts to protect its bid from Italian rivals to lobbying regulators and the European Commission," on April 27 ABN Amro "ask[ed] an Italian administrative court to rule that the central bank had inappropriately allowed a rival to buy shares in Banca Antonveneta." ABN Amro reportedly argued that Fazio's approval of Lodi's share purchases should be suspended because "Lodi's expenditures [had] jeopardised its financial soundness and should not have been allowed without adequate capital." It was a risky move, viewed by observers as "likely to inflame relations with Antonio Fazio," whose decision on ABN Amro's own bid remained open.[62] In any event, the move was unsuccessful, the court refusing "to act immediately against Italy's central bank" to reverse the authorizations.[63]

ABN Amro's European lobbying efforts brought pressure to bear in the form of additional letters to Fazio—the first coming from the European Commission's competition authority, reportedly querying delays in permitting ABN Amro to raise its stake in Antonveneta, and the second being a "similar missive" from McCreevy. "Brussels helped as much as possible," according to Groenink, "but the issue was a nonlevel playing field created by an interpretation of the rules. The Commission was vocal, making clear statements, but in terms of formal powers and actions, it was unable to do much to help our cause."[64]

As *The Financial Times* observed, Fazio's approval for ABN Amro to acquire up to 30% of Antonveneta had come so late that it could not conceivably "buy the shares and register them in time for [the] crucial Antonveneta shareholders' meeting" on April 30. Meanwhile, "Lodi and other Italian groups opposed to the ABN deal" reportedly had "taken their combined stakes in Antonveneta to more than 40 per cent" with the Bank of Italy's blessing[65] (another press account reporting that Lodi itself then held 29.5%, taking the opposition's aggregate stake to 51%).[66] As ABN Amro's CFO Tom de Swaan recognized, "[T]he next 10 days are critical as far as the shareholders' meeting and the decision by the Bank of Italy."[67]

The next day, on April 28, the European Commission approved ABN Amro's bid under its merger regulation, "conclud[ing] that the proposed operations do not impede effective competition." Neelie Kroes, the competition commissioner, commented in connection with the approval that "[t]he proposed operations are a positive sign of movement towards a more integrated internal market for financial services" and that "[i]ntegrated and efficient financial markets play an essential role to support competitiveness, growth and welfare in Europe. Cross-border mergers and acquisitions can increase competition and consumer choice."

ABN Amro could not, however, expect a similar approval from the Bank of Italy before the Antonveneta shareholders' meeting. While the Bank of Italy would normally have had 30 days to rule on a proposed bank takeover, which would have required a decision by April 29, the rules permitted it to stop the clock during periods when it was waiting for information requested from a bank or its home regulator (i.e., the Dutch Central Bank). Because the Bank of Italy had requested information on April 12 that the Dutch Central Bank ultimately provided on April 20, Fazio effectively had until May 8 to render a decision on ABN Amro's bid. In one observer's view, the Bank of Italy had "in effect delayed its decision on the deal by a week."[68]

As ABN Amro had feared, at the April 30 shareholders' meeting, "Lodi and its backers proceeded to oust Antonveneta's entire board . . . replacing its members with friendlier faces."[69] Having already "ousted ABN Amro as the largest shareholder," Lodi had now succeeded in "kick[ing] ABN off the board, taking over 14 of the 15 seats." At the meeting, Lodi's CEO Gianpiero Fiorani expressed his view that "Italian banks must remain in Italian hands."[70]

Assessing the Road Ahead

As things then stood, ABN Amro faced what appeared to be a weak competitor with strong political backing.

Lodi's debt level had, according to Unicredit Banca Mobiliare (the brokerage unit of UniCredito), brought its Tier 1 capital ratio down from 6.4% in late 2004 "to an estimated 3.2% in mid-April" 2005, falling "below the 4% legal limit." The rating agency Fitch, "which [had] a BBB+ rating on Lodi's debt, put the bank on negative watch on April 29." According to a Fitch analyst, "[T]his reflects our concerns over the potential strain on Lodi's capitalization, and over the execution of the plan" to finance its proposed Antonveneta acquisition through additional debt.[71]

It had been speculated in the press that ABN Amro would be "determined to defend its offer by all means at its disposal" and that it would be "likely to take legal action" should a Lodi-friendly Antonveneta Board reverse the prior board's approval of ABN Amro's bid.[72] But law was one thing and politics another. ABN Amro had watched as a much smaller and apparently weak bank had been permitted to amass a significant stake in Antonveneta while its own approvals for further share acquisitions were delayed and consideration of its bid was effectively deferred until after the Antonveneta shareholders' meeting. Its unsuccessful legal challenge of Lodi's share acquisitions could not have improved relations with Fazio, in whose hands the fate of ABN Amro's bid rested, and European Commission pressure on the bank's behalf appeared to have yielded nothing substantial thus far. ABN Amro clearly faced a difficult road ahead if it chose to pursue Antonveneta at all costs.

ABN Amro would also be obliged, according to Spinelli, "to depart from some of our usual practices." Although the Dutch bank usually preferred "not to be in the newspapers," ABN Amro would have to "engage the media enthusiastically to change public opinion." Generally avoiding the imprudence of picking fights with central bank governors, "in order to succeed we recognized that Fazio would have to change his policies or resign." And perhaps most importantly, ABN Amro always sought not to involve itself in politics, "but in Italy our purchase of Antonventa was inescapably political."[73] In such an unfair fight, ABN Amro's executives would also have to decide whether to play by their internal standards or according to apparently more complicated Italian rules. ABN Amro needed a strategy to fit those informal rules or make sure that they changed. As Jeroen Drost, head of Corporate Development at the time, recalled, "Fighting in an environment like that was a tremendous challenge, but we did not stop. We stuck to our own internal norms, not the norms of the fight in which we found ourselves."

Exhibit 1   Domestic M&A Activity Involving Credit Institutions (number of deals)

Country	1997	1998	1999	2000	2001	2002	2003
Belgium	1	6	1	0	1	0	1
Denmark	0	0	2	1	1	1	1
Germany	15	12	22	10	8	6	13
Greece	1	8	3	4	0	2	3
Spain	7	12	9	7	3	3	4
France	17	9	7	10	11	9	8
Ireland	0	0	0	0	0	0	1
Italy	17	16	24	31	21	17	22
Luxembourg	0	0	0	0	0	0	0
Netherlands	3	1	1	0	1	2	1
Austria	5	2	4	4	1	1	0
Portugal	2	3	1	5	2	0	1
Finland	0	0	0	0	0	2	0
Sweden	1	0	1	0	0	1	1
United Kingdom	4	0	0	1	1	6	7

Source: *Report on EU Banking Structure*, European Central Bank, November 2004, p. 46, Table 28.

Exhibit 2a   European Economic Area M&A between Credit Institutions (number of deals)

Country	1997	1998	1999	2000	2001	2002	2003
Belgium	2	1	6	1	2	1	0
Denmark	1	0	4	3	1	1	0
Germany	3	5	9	5	2	3	1
Greece	0	1	1	2	1	2	0
Spain	2	4	10	9	3	4	3
France	3	2	7	8	4	3	1
Ireland	0	0	1	0	1	1	0
Italy	0	4	12	5	2	4	0
Luxembourg	2	4	3	4	4	1	1
Netherlands	2	1	3	3	2	3	2
Austria	0	1	0	0	3	0	0
Portugal	0	0	2	5	2	1	4
Finland	0	0	1	1	1	2	0
Sweden	1	0	5	2	1	3	0
United Kingdom	2	0	3	2	2	2	0

Exhibit 2b   Third-Country M&A between Credit Institutions (number of deals)

Country	1997	1998	1999	2000	2001	2002	2003
Belgium	6	0	5	5	2	6	1
Denmark	0	1	0	1	1	0	0
Germany	5	6	14	11	8	5	2
Greece	0	0	3	4	0	1	2
Spain	6	10	3	8	5	6	3
France	6	7	6	3	8	3	5
Ireland	1	0	2	0	0	0	0
Italy	1	2	2	4	3	3	7
Luxembourg	0	1	0	1	0	0	0
Netherlands	4	4	2	1	5	1	0
Austria	1	3	2	3	4	8	4
Portugal	0	1	1	3	0	0	1
Finland	0	0	2	3	0	0	0
Sweden	1	3	2	4	1	2	0
United Kingdom	4	3	8	3	4	2	6

Source: *Report on EU Banking Structure*, European Central Bank, November 2004, p. 47, Tables 29, 30.

Exhibit 3   Cross-border M&A by Sector across the OECD (number and percentage cross-border)

Sector	1990	1991	1992	1993	1994	1995	1996	1997	1998	1999	Total
Agriculture, forestry, fishing	5 (20.0)	11 (45.5)	11 (9.1)	7 (28.6)	10 (30.0)	16 (12.5)	21 (28.6)	16 (25.0)	24 (33.3)	20 (5.0)	141 (23.4)
Mining	167 (27.5)	232 (25.0)	211 (28.0)	299 (22.1)	252 (27.0)	296 (27.4)	316 (23.7)	249 (24.5)	241 (20.7)	262 (21.8)	2,525 (24.6)
Construction	17 (29.4)	37 (27.0)	34 (35.3)	28 (32.1)	40 (25.0)	39 (25.6)	56 (23.2)	46 (15.2)	62 (14.5)	75 (20.0)	434 (23.0)
Manufacturing	507 (51.1)	599 (37.9)	698 (36.4)	778 (34.1)	832 (33.8)	1,077 (34.4)	1,099 (31.9)	1,061 (35.1)	1,100 (34.4)	1,447 (33.8)	9,198 (35.3)
Transportation	31 (58.1)	52 (23.1)	58 (22.4)	67 (23.9)	73 (23.3)	76 (15.8)	86 (37.2)	70 (32.9)	70 (28.6)	100 (38.0)	683 (29.4)
Public utilities	87 (21.8)	116 (18.1)	117 (18.8)	216 (25.0)	176 (23.9)	269 (23.8)	233 (24.5)	281 (21.4)	303 (29.4)	476 (31.5)	2,274 (25.4)
Wholesale trade	63 (73.0)	80 (45.0)	95 (26.3)	109 (34.9)	145 (32.4)	145 (40.0)	148 (31.8)	146 (28.8)	148 (26.4)	190 (26.3)	1,269 (33.7)
Retail trade	33 (24.2)	64 (25.0)	62 (27.4)	90 (15.6)	100 (12.0)	98 (18.4)	113 (17.7)	109 (20.2)	116 (16.4)	158 (22.2)	943 (19.2)
Banks	193 (21.2)	245 (15.5)	312 (9.3)	428 (9.8)	489 (10.0)	496 (12.7)	460 (10.9)	532 (10.2)	547 (14.1)	530 (19.6)	4,232 (12.9)
Insurance	126 (30.2)	102 (29.4)	116 (25.9)	118 (24.6)	121 (23.1)	131 (30.5)	135 (25.9)	127 (28.3)	123 (37.4)	110 (40.9)	1,209 (29.5)
Other financial	671 (15.1)	785 (13.5)	745 (17.3)	799 (11.4)	985 (12.3)	1,276 (12.2)	1,376 (11.3)	1,030 (13.6)	900 (19.2)	1,228 (21.9)	9,795 (14.7)
Services	113 (30.1)	156 (30.1)	203 (19.7)	274 (13.9)	312 (19.9)	367 (22.6)	467 (23.8)	501 (20.6)	528 (26.3)	656 (27.4)	3,577 (23.4)
Public administration	16 (25.0)	31 (35.5)	20 (15.0)	19 (5.3)	13 (15.4)	12 (16.7)	25 (20.0)	21 (9.5)	26 (34.6)	38 (26.3)	221 (22.2)

Source: Reprinted from *Journal of Banking & Financ,e* 25, Dario Focarelli and Alberto Franco Pozzolo, "The patterns of cross-border bank mergers and shareholdings in OECD countries," 2311, 2001, with permission from Elsevier.

Note: Focarelli and Pozzolo state that the "[n]umber of M&As is the number of operations with both bidder and target companies in an OECD country." Ibid.

Exhibit 4   Reliance on Bank Debt in Selected Countries—Bank Debt as a Percentage of Total Debt

Country	Small, medium-size firms	Large firms
Belgium	46.5	50.1
France	48.8	21.3
Germany	57.4	29.9
Italy	66.4	27.3
Netherlands	54.9	35.9
Spain	66.5	50.4
United Kingdom	n.a.	n.a.
United States	40.9	7.9

Source: Emilia Bonaccorsi di Patti and Giorgio Gobbi, "The changing structure of local credit markets: Are small businesses special?" *Journal of Banking & Finance* 25 (2001): 2210, Table 1. Note: Patti and Gobbi state that data for Belgium, France, and Italy are as of 1998, and data for other countries in Europe are as of 1997. Data for the United States is as of 1995. Small and medium-size firms for European countries "are those with annual turnover below ECU 40 million," while for the United States they are "firms with turnover up to ECU 7 million" (large firms being those "with turnover between ECU 7 million and ECU 40 million").

Exhibit 5a   Capital Structure of Manufacturing Firms in Italy

	Median and (mean), by number of employees				
	<30	30–99	100–249	250–500	> 500
Total debt/ assets	0.448 (0.419)	0.605 (0.555)	0.640 (0.614)	0.611 (0.596)	0.598 (0.575)
Financial debt/assets	0.092 (0.172)	0.245 (0.251)	0.299 (0.297)	0.299 (0.284)	0.248 (0.254)
Financial debt/capital	0.231 (0.322)	0.493 (0.448)	0.562 (0.520)	0.546 (0.491)	0.488 (0.462)
Trade debt/ assets	0.159 (0.188)	0.241 (0.236)	0.237 (0.245)	0.219 (0.235)	0.223 (0.244)
Bank debt/ financial debt	1.000 (0.789)	0.962 (0.789)	0.902 (0.769)	0.838 (0.728)	0.809 (0.691)
Equity/assets	0.198 (0.239)	0.227 (0.228)	0.236 (0.264)	0.241 (0.280)	0.235 (0.278)

Source: Luigi Guiso, "Small business finance in Italy," *EIB Papers* 8:2 (2003): 124, Table 1. Note: Guiso "draw[s] data from the 1999 Survey of Manufacturing Firms (SMF), which *Mediocredito Centrale*, an investment bank, conducts every three years on a sample of over 4,000 mostly small and medium-sized firms and some larger firms (with more than 500 employees) in manufacturing." Total debt includes "all non-equity liabilities of the firm," financial debt "equals total debt minus pension liabilities and trade debt," and capital means "the sum of financial debt and the book value of equity" (pp. 122–123).

Exhibit 5b   Importance of Debt Instruments for Manufacturing Firms in Italy

	Percentage of firms using debt instruments, by number of employees				
	<30	30–99	100–249	250–500	> 500
Financial debt	58.5	85.4	97.5	98.0	99.4
Bank debt	53.1	79.7	93.6	94.1	95.5
Trade debt	60.2	85.6	99.3	100.0	100.0
Bonds	19.3	16.0	25.8	24.8	17.9
Long-term financial debt	33.7	65.5	84.6	87.1	89.3
Long-term bank debt	25.3	51.2	70.3	68.4	74.7

Source: Luigi Guiso, "Small business finance in Italy," *EIB Papers* 8:2 (2003): 125, Table 2. Note: Guiso defines "debt with a maturity of more than 18 months as long term."

Exhibit 6   Selected National Banking Data (2003)

Country	Credit institutions (#)	Share of five largest credit institutions in total assets (%)
Belgium	108	83
Denmark	203	67
Germany	2,225	22
Greece	59	67
Spain	348	44
France	939	47
Ireland	80	44
Italy	801	27
Luxembourg	172	32
Netherlands	481	84
Austria	814	44
Portugal	200	63
Finland	366	81
Sweden	222	54
United Kingdom	426	33

Source: *Report on EU Banking Structure*, European Central Bank, November 2004, pp. 33, 35, Tables 1, 6.

Exhibit 7   Retail Banking Price Data (2005)

Country	Annual weighted prices of core banking services (€)
Italy	252
Germany	223
Switzerland	159
Norway	131
United States	126
Spain	108
Slovakia	106
Poland	101
France	99
Portugal	99
Canada	93
Austria	93
Czech Republic	83
Australia	81
Sweden	80
United Kingdom	64
Belgium	63
China	54
Netherlands	34

Source: *World Retail Banking Report 2005*, Capgemini, European Financial Management & Marketing Association, and ING Group, March 2005, p. 5, available at http://www.capgemini.com. © 2005 Capgemini.

Note: The study included "four main categories of day-to-day banking products and services (account management, means of payment, cash utilization, and exceptions handling)," p. 3.

Exhibit 8 Data on the Loan Composition of Italian Banks by Size Category

	1989	1992	1995	1998
Large banks				
Large non-financial firms	42.9	42.9	43.2	41.6
Small, medium-size nonfinancial firms	26.5	24.1	25.9	23.1
Other borrowers	30.7	33.0	31.5	35.3
Medium-size banks				
Large non-financial firms	42.4	44.9	44.8	47.9
Small, medium-size nonfinancial firms	32.6	30.1	30.4	28.7
Other borrowers	25.0	25.1	24.8	23.4
Small banks				
Large non-financial firms	31.2	32.9	32.1	34.5
Small, medium-size nonfinancial firms	45.5	43.9	46.9	43.5
Other borrowers	23.2	23.2	21.0	22.0
Total banks				
Large non-financial firms	40.6	41.6	41.7	41.8
Small, medium-size nonfinancial firms	31.3	28.8	29.7	27.6
Other borrowers	28.1	29.6	28.5	30.5

Source: Emilia Bonaccorsi di Patti and Giorgio Gobbi, "The changing structure of local credit markets: Are small businesses special?" *Journal of Banking & Finance* 25 (2001): 2222, Table 4. Note: Patti and Gobbi state that loan data "refer to total outstanding loans (inclusive of bad loans) to customers whose total bank debt is greater than ITL 250 million. Medium-sized firms are defined as all the non-financial enterprises with bank debt between ITL 1 billion and ITL 5 billion. Small firms are defined as non-financial firms with bank debt between ITL 0.25 billion and ITL 1 billion."

Exhibit 9　Italian Manufacturing Firms' Banking Relationships

Aspects of manufacturers' banking relationships, by number of employees			
	< 30	**30–100**	**100–250**	**250–500**
Relationships (#)	4.4	6.2	9.3	11.1
Firms with multiple relationships (%)	91	97	98	95
Loans from main bank (%)	32	29	27	25
Length of relationship with main bank (years)	14.8	16.1	17.9	18.9
Firms for which main bank local (%)	67	65	55	60

Source:　Luigi Guiso, "Small business finance in Italy," *EIB Papers* 8:2 (2003): 141, Table B3.

Exhibit 10   ABN Amro Consolidated Balance Sheet as of March 31, 2005 (in € millions)[a]

	March 31, 2005	December 31, 2004	% Change
Assets			
Cash and cash equivalents	10,545	17,896	(41.1)
Financial assets held for trading	169,306	167,035	1.4
Investments	117,696	109,986	7.0
Loans and advances banks	92,224	82,862	11.3
Loans and advances customers	323,898	296,078	9.4
Prepayments and accrued income	5,125	5,740	(10.7)
Investments in associates	2,358	2,214	6.5
Property and equipment	7,480	7,173	4.3
Goodwill and other intangibles	3,536	3,437	2.9
Other assets	10,764	9,355	15.1
	742,932	701,776	5.9
Liabilities			
Financial liabilities held for trading	132,475	129,506	2.3
Due to banks	143,131	133,859	6.9
Due to customers	298,865	284,072	5.2
Issued debt securities	108,416	97,289	11.4
Accruals and deferred income	6,831	8,074	(15.4)
Provisions	10,931	8,897	22.9
Other liabilities	6,649	6,840	(2.8)
Total liabilities excluding subordinated liabilities	707,298	668,537	5.8
Subordinated liabilities	17,996	16,687	7.8
Minority interests	*1,502*	*1,737*	*(13.5)*
Share capital	*954*	*954*	*0.0*
Share premium	*2,564*	*2,564*	*0.0*
Reserves	*11,887*	*10,988*	*8.2*
Net gains / (losses) not recognised in the income statement	*731*	*309*	*136.6*
Shareholders' equity	16,136	14,815	*8.9*
Group equity	17,638	16,552	6.6
Group capital	35,634	33,239	7.2
	742,932	701,776	5.9
Exchange EUR/USD-rate	1.30	1.36	(4.4)

Source: "ABN Amro reports first quarter 2005 results: Net operating profit up 16.1% compared with first quarter 2004," ABN Amro press release, April 27, 2005, p. 29, available at http://www.abnamro.com/pressroom/releases/media/pdf/abnamro_2005q1_en.pdf .

[a]2004 unaudited.

Exhibit 11   Antonveneta Consolidated Balance Sheet as of March 31, 2005

Assets				% Change	
(in thousands of euro)	03/31/2005	03/31/2004	12/31/2004	on 03/2004	on 12/2004
Loans:					
Due from banks	3,048,098	2,500,423	3,834,069	21.9%	-20.5%
Due from customers	34,437,628	36,183,079	35,127,119	-4.8%	-2.0%
Investment and trading securities	1,119,446	1,575,802	1,399,029	-29.0%	-20.0%
Fixed assets:					
Financial (equity investment)	698,141	835,824	710,347	-16.5%	-1.7%
Intangible and tangible	1,183,835	1,473,982	1,230,239	-19.7%	-3.8%
Goodwill arising on consolidation and on application of the equity method	153,253	177,524	160,585	-13.7%	-4.6%
Other assets [a]	2,713,016	3,179,493	2,970,864	-14.7%	-8.7%
Total Assets	**43,353,417**	**45,926,127**	**45,432,252**	**-5.6%**	**-4.6%**

[a] Other assets: Cash, other assets, accrued income and prepaid expenses

Liabilities and Shareholder's Equity				% Change	
(in thousands of euro)	03/31/2005	03/31/2004	12/31/2004	on 03/2004	on 12/2004
Payables:					
Due to banks	2,571,990	2,811,630	3,368,940	-8.5%	-23.7%
Due to customers	18,488,457	19,095,439	19,505,958	-3.2%	-5.2%
Securities issued	14,100,920	15,985,321	14,652,863	-11.8%	-3.8%
Administered third-party funds	13,636	14,783	13,596	-7.8%	0.3%
Specific Provisions	822,307	886,019	791,649	-7.2%	3.9%
Other liabilities [b]	1,758,367	1,857,082	1,605,190	-5.3%	9.5%
Negative goodwill arising on application of the equity method	29	1,164	29	-97.5%	--
Reserves for possible loan losses					
Subordinated liabilities	2,486,277	2,468,601	2,527,417	0.7%	-1.6%
Shareholders' equity pertaining to minority interests	29,464	26,850	28,597	9.7%	3.0%
Shareholders' equity:	2,960,918	2,696,457	2,655,325	9.8%	11.5%
Capital and reserves	2,665,369	3,515,725	2,642,464	-24.2%	0.9%
Reserve for general banking risks	12,861	15,376	12,861	-16.4%	
Retained profit (loss)	282,688	-834,644	--	n.s.	n.s.
Net profit (loss) for the period	121,052	82,781	282,688	46.2%	-57.2%
Total liabilities and shareholders' equity	**43,353,417**	**45,926,127**	**45,432,252**	**-5.6%**	**-4.6%**

[b] Other liabilities: other liabilities, accrued expenses and deferred income

Source: "Antonveneta approves consolidated results as at 31 March 2005," Antonveneta press release, April 26, 2005, p. 5, available at http://investor.antonveneta.it/press/comunicati.jsp?id_categoria=5.

Endnotes

[1] See "Mayer Amschel Rothschild Quotes," available at http://www.brainyquote.com/quotes/ authors/m/ mayer_amschel_rothschild.html.

[2] Gabriel Kahn and Marcus Walker, "Golden Handcuffs: With Italy in the Doldrums, Many Point Fingers at the Euro – Strong Currency Hurts Exports, Causing Some to Want Out; Another Blow to the EU – Buying Baby Formula In Austria," *The Wall Street Journal*, June 13, 2005, p. 1; see also Roger Cohen, "Kicking the Euro When Europe Is Down," *The New York Times*, June 19, 2005, p. 4.

[3] Author's interview with Rijkman Groenink, chairman of the managing board, ABN Amro, Amsterdam, June 12, 2006.

[4] Author's interview with Richard Bruens, executive vice president, head of Investor Relations, ABN Amro, Amsterdam, June 13, 2006.

[5] See generally Rawi Abdelal and Christopher M. Bruner, "European Financial Integration," HBS Case No. 706-010 (Boston: Harvard Business School Publishing, 2005), pp. 1–3.

[6] Author's phone interview with Tom de Swaan, ABN Amro board member, August 28, 2006.

[7] Ibid., p. 4.

[8] Ibid., pp. 4–7; see also Directive 2000/12/EC of the European Parliament and of the Council of 20 March 2000 relating to the taking up and pursuit of the business of credit institutions, Art. 16(1); Council Regulation (EC) No 139/2004 of 20 January 2004 on the control of concentrations between undertakings (the EC Merger Regulation), Arts. 1, 6(1)(b), 21(2)–(4).

[9] See generally "Call for Technical Advice (No. 1) from the Committee of European Banking Supervisors (CEBS)," European Commission, January 18, 2005.

[10] "Country Briefings: Italy: Economic structure," *The Economist*, December 9, 2003, available at http://www.economist.com/countries/Italy/PrinterFriendly.cfm?Story_ID=228067; F. Panetta, F. Schivardi, and M. Shum, "Do mergers improve information? Evidence from the loan market," Bank of Italy discussion paper No. 521, October 2004, p. 8; Tony Barber, Adrian Michaels, and Peter Thal Larsen, "New allure: why foreign banks are battling for Italian assets," *The Financial Times* (London), April 12, 2005, p. 17. For additional background on Italy's domestic economy and politics, as well as its integration into Europe, see Richard H.K. Vietor and Rebecca Evans, "Italy: A New Commitment to Growth," HBS Case No. 703-007 (Boston: Harvard Business School Publishing, Rev. 2003).

[11] Luigi Guiso, "Small business finance in Italy," *EIB Papers* 8:2 (2003): 121.

[12] "Allegro ma non troppo," *The Economist*, May 19, 2005.

[13] "Spaghetti Banking," *The Wall Street Journal* (Europe), April 1, 2005, p. A8.

[14] Barber, Michaels, and Larsen, p. 17.

[15] *World Retail Banking Report 2005*, Capgemini, European Financial Management & Marketing Association, and ING Group, March 25, 2005, p. 5, available at http://www.us.capgemini.com/DownloadLibrary/requestfile .asp?ID=460.

[16] Barber, Michaels, and Larsen, p. 17 (internal quotation marks omitted).

[17] *The Wall Street Journal* (Europe), p. A8.

[18] Robert Galbraith, "Analysis: Fazio plays out a foreign affair," *The Financial News*, July 10, 2005.

[19] "Allegro ma non troppo," *The Economist*.

[20] 1993 Banking Law, Article 57, available at http://wwwbancaditalia.it/vigilanza_tutela/vig_ban/norma/leggi/tub/en_tub_7_2000.pdf (Bank of Italy translation, as amended through July 2000). Fazio's approval was also required for "acquisition of a stake of more than 5 percent in any Italian bank." "Bank of Italy Denies Showing Favoritism," *Associated Press Newswires*, May 31, 2005.

[21] *The Wall Street Journal* (Europe), p. A8.

[22] Galbraith.

[23] Author's interview with Francesco Spinelli, country representative for Italy, ABN Amro, Amsterdam, June 12, 2006.

[24] Ibid.

[25] Author's interview with David Cole, head of Group Risk Management, ABN Amro, Amsterdam, June 13, 2006.

[26] Author's interview with Groenink.

[27] Author's interview with Spinelli.

[28] Author's interview with Leonard Stolk, managing director, Alliance Solutions Group, ABN Amro, Amsterdam, June 13, 2006.

[29] Author's interview with Groenink.

[30] Barber, Michaels, and Larsen, p. 17.

[31] "Banking: EU and Italy square up for a fight," €urActiv.com, March 24, 2005, available at http://www.euractiv.com/Article?tcmuri=tcm:29-137234-16&type=News; see also "Allegro ma non troppo," *The Economist*; "Charlie McCreevy: Member of the European Commission," available at http://europa.eu.int/comm/commission_barroso/mccreevy/index_en.htm (describing McCreevy's biography and position with the commission).

[32] *The Wall Street Journal* (Europe), p. A8.

[33] Charlie McCreevy, "The Future of banking policy in the Union," speech/05/191, March 22, 2005, p. 4 (speech at the "Informal first meeting of the European Banking Committee").

[34] "ABN Amro to offer EUR 25 per share in cash for Banca Antonveneta," ABN Amro press release, March 30, 2005. Unless otherwise noted, ABN Amro press releases and presentations are available at http://www.abnamro.com/pressroom/anton.jsp.

[35] See, e.g., "BBVA bid heralds foreign bank invasion of Italy," *Banker*, April 4, 2005, p. 12; Barber, Michaels, and Larsen, p. 17.

[36] Barber, Michaels, and Larsen, p. 17.

[37] "Profile," available at http://www.abnamro.com/com/about/profile.jsp.

[38] Ibid.; "Profile: Strategy," available at http://www.abnamro.com/com/about/strategy.jsp.

[39] "Profile" (rankings "based on Tier 1 capital").

[40] "Overview," available at http://investor.antonveneta.it/investor/gruppo.jsp?lingua=ENG&id_categoria=39&id_versione=6725&id_contenuto=61; "Machiavellian manoeuvres," *The Economist*, May 7, 2005, p. 70. "Bancassurance" essentially combines banking and insurance services. A bank might, for example, "seal both mortgages and the life insurance policies that must go with them." See "Bancassurance," available at http://www.finance-glossary.com/terms/bancassurance.htm?ginPtrCode=00000&id=1856&PopupMode=false.

[41] See "Overview."

[42] Author's interview with Groenink.

[43] "Machiavellian manoeuvres," *The Economist*, p. 70; Gregory Ruben, "ABN Amro Relies on Judges, Regulators in Bid for Antonveneta," May 2, 2005, available at http://www.bloomberg.com/apps/news?pid= 10000085&sid=adswPileSbpE&refer=europe# (reporting market values of €2.3 billion for Lodi, €7.5 billion for Antonveneta, and €34.6 billion for ABN Amro).

[44] Gail Edmondson and Maureen Kline, "Banking Italian Style: A Dutch bid for Banca Antonveneta may get sidelined – as Lodi steps up to the plate," *BusinessWeek* (Online), May 16, 2005.

[45] "Profile," available at http://www.bancapopolareitaliana.it/index.php?option=com_content&task=view &id=35&Itemid=187; "970 Deeply Rooted Branches," available at http:// www.bancapopola reitaliana.it/images/rete_territoriale_ing.jpg.

[46] "Press statement on Antonveneta," ABN Amro press release, March 21, 2005.

[47] Author's interview with Cole.

[48] "ABN Amro to offer EUR 25 per share in cash for Banca Antonveneta"; see also "ABN Amro launches cash offer for Banca Antonveneta: Fully aligned with mid-market strategy," ABN Amro presentation, March 30, 2005.

[49] John Downes and Jordan Elliot Goodman, "Tier 1 and Tier 2," in *Dictionary of Finance and Investment Terms* (6th ed.) (Hauppauge, NY: Barron's Educational Series, Inc., 2003), pp. 731–732.

[50] "Statement on Reports Appearing in the Press," Lodi press release, March 16, 2005; "Investment in Banca Antonveneta," Lodi press release, April 6, 2005. Unless otherwise noted, Lodi press releases are available at http://www.bancapopolareitaliana.it/index.php?option=com_wrapper&Itemid=229.

[51] Barber, Michaels, and Larsen, p. 17.

[52] "ABN Amro receives approval from CONSOB for its cash offer for Banca Antonveneta," ABN Amro press release, April 14, 2005.

[53] "Banca Antonveneta's Board of Directors' Meeting deemed adequate the consideration offered by ABN Amro Bank N.V.," Antonveneta press release, April 15, 2005. Unless otherwise noted, Antonveneta press releases are available at http://investor.antonveneta.it/press/comunicati.jsp?id_categoria=5.

[54] "Banca Antonveneta board of directors recommends ABN Amro's cash tender offer," ABN Amro press release, April 15, 2005.

[55] Ian Bickerton, Tobias Buck, and Adrian Michaels, "Banca Antonveneta backs ABN bid – Italian Banking," *The Financial Times* (USA), April 16, 2005, p. 9.

[56] "Mandate Conferred on CEO For Negotiations with ABN Amro," Lodi press release, April 15, 2005.

[57] "ABN Amro: Bank of Italy approves increase stake in Banca Antonveneta to 20%," ABN Amro press release, April 19, 2005.

[58] Adrian Michaels, "Bankers weigh up Lodi questions: Small bank has a big role in debates on regulation of Italian market and its openness," *The Financial Times* (London), April 21, 2005, p. 28.

[59] "ABN Amro: Bank of Italy approves increase stake in Banca Antonveneta to 30%," ABN Amro press release, April 27, 2005.

[60] "Banca Popolare Di Lodi's Shareholding in Banca Antonveneta: Importance of the Operation in Terms of Core Business and Profitability," Lodi press release, April 26, 2005.

[61] "New Name: Banca Popolare Italiana – Capital Reinforcement – 100% Public Share Exchange Offer for Banca Antonveneta," Lodi press release, April 29, 2005 (all emphasis removed).

[62] Ian Bickerton, Tobias Buck, and Adrian Michaels, "ABN Amro petitions local court to stop rival buying bigger stake in Antonveneta," *The Financial Times* (Europe), April 28, 2005, p. 1.

[63] "Ruling deals blow to ABN moves on Antonveneta," *The Financial News Online*, April 29, 2005.

[64] Author's interview with Groenink.

[65] Bickerton, Buck, and Michaels, "ABN Amro petitions local court to stop rival buying bigger stake in Antonveneta," p. 1.

[66] Edmondson and Kline.

[67] Bickerton, Buck, and Michaels, "ABN Amro petitions local court to stop rival buying bigger stake in Antonveneta," p. 1.

[68] "Dutch Crtl Bk: Provided Bk Italy With ABN Amro Info Wed," *Dow Jones International News*, April 25, 2005.

[69] Edmondson and Kline; see also "Banca Antonveneta Shareholders Meeting approves 2004 financial accounts, confirming a €0.45 dividend and appoints corporate positions," Antonveneta press release, April 30, 2005.

[70] "Italian banking tussle hots up," €urActiv.com, May 4, 2005, available at http://www.euractiv.com/Article?tcmuri=tcm:29-139098-16&type=News.

[71] Edmondson and Kline.

[72] Ian Bickerton and Adrian Michaels, "ABN's lawyers watch Italian situation," *The Financial Times* (London), April 15, 2005, p. 30.

[73] Author's interview with Spinelli.

RAWI ABDELAL

CHRISTOPHER M. BRUNER

Politics and Prudential Supervision: ABN Amro's Bid for Antonveneta (B)

Ah . . . Tonino. . . . I've got goose bumps. . . . I'd give you a kiss right now, on the forehead.

—Lodi CEO Gianpiero Fiorani, in a wiretapped phone call with Bank of Italy
Governor Antonio Fazio, upon receiving approval of Lodi's takeover bid[1]

When Banca Popolare di Lodi succeeded in ousting the entire board of the much larger Banca Antoniana Popolare Veneta S.p.A. (known generally as Antonveneta) at the latter's shareholder meeting on April 30, 2005,[2] a rational observer might fairly have concluded that Dutch bank ABN Amro's rival bid for control of Antonveneta had little hope of success. Few, however, would have predicted the course of events to follow, including regulatory and criminal investigations uncovering substantial wrongdoing aimed at keeping the foreigners out; fundamental reforms to modernize Italian banking supervision; and the opening of the hitherto closed Italian retail banking sector. Piero Montani, the CEO of Antonveneta, recalls the moment vividly: "When the shareholder meeting in favor of Lodi, I knew that it could happen. It was somehow expected. However, my position as a CEO was very clear: between dying of starvation and working for Lodi, I would rather starve. It was above all a matter of integrity and personal values. On that day, I left the office with a small plastic bag carrying some documents with no idea what the future would bring."[3]

Regulatory and Criminal Investigations

ABN Amro had actually had Antonveneta in its sights since as early as March 2004, but when CEO Rijkman Groenink approached Bank of Italy Governor Antonio Fazio about the matter, Fazio suggested that he contact Gianpiero Fiorani, CEO of Lodi, which was also interested. When Fiorani suggested a mutual deal putting Lodi in control, ABN Amro declined and determined to pursue Antonveneta alone. According to materials that would ultimately land in prosecutors' hands, however, Lodi's own plan was already under way. Lodi apparently had been funding (and would continue to fund) substantial Antonveneta share purchases by various associated entities, with an understanding that Lodi would itself buy the shares when the time was right—while in the meantime appearing to own only a very small stake in the bank.[4] Italy's securities regulator, Consob, "[s]uspicious that information was being withheld from the market . . . decided in mid-March [2005] to investigate all [Lodi's] direct and indirect dealings in Antonveneta shares" over recent months,[5] and the results of that investigation would prove the beginning of the end for Lodi's bid.

Professor Rawi Abdelal and Research Associate Christopher M. Bruner, J.D., prepared this case. HBS cases are developed solely as the basis for class discussion. Cases are not intended to serve as endorsements, sources of primary data, or illustrations of effective or ineffective management.

At that point, perhaps paradoxically, ABN Amro was very nearly obliged to pursue Antonveneta aggressively. To ABN Amro executives it was clear that remaining a minority shareholder in a Lodi-controlled Antonveneta was downright imprudent. The bank thus at least needed to become a large enough shareholder so that Lodi would be obliged to bid for ABN Amro's shares—an exit option, at least. As Richard Bruens, executive vice president and head of Investor Relations, recalled, "It was simply not an option for us to stay a minority investor with Lodi in control. Effectively we were forced into the decision to go for it or not. If we had just let events unfold, our 12.75% share would have been worthless."[6]

Lodi's Share Acquisitions

Lodi could not make the desired Antonveneta share purchases itself because it lacked the core capital, and a plan for Antonveneta sufficiently credible, to vouchsafe Bank of Italy approval, which was required to pass various ownership thresholds.[7] Thus, according to regulatory reports and prosecution materials, Lodi pursued its plan indirectly by lending money for share purchases to others. Loans amounting to "hundreds of millions of euros" were made, often without standard credit checks, at very low interest rates (around 1%) and without collateral.[8] Between December 2004 and February 2005 alone, Lodi lent €552 million to fund share purchases amounting to 9.5% of Antonveneta's shares[9] but nevertheless told Consob in February that it owned less than 3% of Antonveneta.[10] Subsequent loans of €666 million funded purchases amounting to another 11.7% of Antonveneta, which (like the previous purchases) were not disclosed to the Bank of Italy.[11] In a press release dated April 6, Lodi stated that it owned 10.82% of Antonveneta, while denying that any agreements regarding additional Antonveneta shares existed.[12]

While the plan had initially focused on taking control of the board at Antonveneta's April shareholder meeting, "an objective possible with around 30% of the votes," the emergence of ABN Amro's cash-tender offer in March required Lodi to retrain its sights on majority control (in order to block ABN Amro's bid). Aided by the Bank of Italy's swift authorization for acquisition of up to 29.9%, achieved in three days, Lodi raised its stake to 28% in a single week by purchasing shares previously teed up through the aforementioned loans. Meanwhile ABN Amro's authorization to reach 29.9% languished for a month until April 27, by which time Lodi and certain allied parties—it would later be revealed—already held shares amounting to a majority. ABN Amro's tender offer was approved by the Bank of Italy on May 6, but by that time its bid was already effectively hopeless. Lodi's own "paper" tender offer (consisting mainly of Lodi securities) was announced days later, on May 9.[13]

On May 10, however, Consob announced its ruling (based on the investigation under way since March) that Lodi had acted as "part of an illegally undeclared concert party"—that is, a group "acting in concert to acquire shares," though purchasing as individuals to make an end run around the mandatory cash-tender offer required under Italian law upon exceeding 30% ownership. In light of this finding, Consob required the concert party to make a cash-tender offer for Antonveneta (in addition to the paper offer previously commenced). But more consequentially, the report explaining the ruling was published, and "soon after . . . members of the concert party (and most of those who had bought Antonveneta shares with [Lodi] loans) were under criminal investigation for either alleged insider trading or market abuse."[14]

Fiorani and Fazio

As the takeover battle for Antonveneta moved into the summer, so did the criminal investigations. Indeed, for a period of about a month, prosecutors wiretapped phone conversations between Lodi's

Fiorani and the Bank of Italy's Fazio (as well as Fazio's wife), recording conversations that would help establish their close personal ties and the manner in which Bank of Italy approval of Lodi's bid was ultimately secured.[15]

In a conversation on June 24, Fiorani complained to the Fazios about the fact that Consob had "questioned whether [Lodi] could raise the necessary funds" to carry off its tender offer, repeatedly requesting additional information. Fazio was encouraging but added, "You can't make one wrong move now." Consob ultimately approved the tender offer on June 28, leaving Bank of Italy approval—required by July 11 to prevent the bid from lapsing by operation of law—as the last remaining hurdle. In another recorded conversation on July 6, Fiorani described to Mrs. Fazio the plea he had made to her husband for approval. Bank of Italy inspectors, however, reportedly came to the conclusion that the bid could not be approved because, among other things, Lodi lacked sufficient capital. On July 8 the inspectors signed their opinion, locking it in a safe.

The head of the Bank of Italy's regulatory unit requested that the inspectors revisit their opinion, but the request was refused, one inspector reportedly remarking that the opinion was "going to wind up with the prosecutors." This turn of events evidently left Fazio "very upset," but a solution was devised. University professors were invited to opine on Lodi's bid, which they did, approving of the offer, and on July 11—the last day before which the offer would otherwise have lapsed—an employee of the Bank of Italy reportedly "opened a computer file containing [the] negative opinion and pasted in a section with the professors' opinions." The revised opinion was signed by Fazio that night, and Fiorani received the good news in a call from Fazio shortly after midnight on July 12.[16]

"On Friday, July 21," according to ABN Amro's Bruens, "we knew that we had lost."[17] A short time later, on July 22, ABN Amro's tender offer expired, just 2.88% of Antonveneta's shares having been tendered—obviously far short of the 50%-plus-one-share tender condition. ABN Amro, left with a 29.98% stake, "reiterate[d] that it [had] no intention of remaining a minority shareholder"[18]—a statement effectively conceding defeat. That defeat would have been final and complete, Bruens recalled, "were it not for the legal actions" that followed.[19]

Legal Wranglings

That spring, however, ABN Amro had also begun to pursue a separate strategy to engage the Italian legal system and media more directly. "There was no current in favor of the Dutch," recalls Montani. "As a matter of fact, everybody would rather see a merger between two Italian banks. The support was on the side of the regulators and in favor of the ones that were respecting the law. Therefore, it became crucial to use the media to bring transparency and show that ABN Amro was on the right side."[20] Informally surveying its Italian peers, ABN Amro finally found someone who was sympathetic to its plight, someone who also thought that Italy needed to change: Guido Rossi, a Harvard law school graduate and titan of the Italian legal establishment. Rossi, who had himself been Consob's chairman during the early 1980s, was apparently dismayed at the Italian central bank's unwillingness to play by the European rules to which the Italian government had, after all, agreed.[21] Not only did Rossi know the Italian legal system intimately, he also recognized that regardless of the seeming popularity of Fazio's motives, his means would not survive public scrutiny. Rossi helped to expose the behind-the-scenes machinations to Italy's big three newspapers. As ABN Amro's Jeroen Drost, head of Corporate Development at the time, recalled:

> The decision to engage Guido Rossi was critical. Rossi is not only a brilliant legal advisor, he is also a respected member of the establishment in Italy. When Rossi decided to back ABN Amro, the apparent solidarity of Italy against us began to crack. It became clear that we had

supporters in Italy as well. It was a controversial choice for him, and he probably lost money and clients at the beginning. It was a courageous move.[22]

By early August a court had granted requests made by prosecutors that all Antonveneta shares held by Lodi be frozen and that Fiorani be suspended from his post as Lodi's CEO. And once the Italian media "began publishing wiretap excerpts of his late-night talks with Mr. Fiorani, Mr. Fazio . . . faced almost daily calls to resign" (though he was not yet under investigation himself)—which Fazio, who enjoyed a lifetime appointment, steadfastly refused to do.[23] In a press release remarking on the share seizure, Lodi stated that "with all due regard for the legal authorities, [Lodi] is nonetheless convinced that it will be able to demonstrate the legitimacy of its actions."[24] Likewise when Fiorani and Lodi's CFO Gianfranco Boni were suspended on August 2, Lodi stated, again "with all due respect for the work of the magistrates," that it "confirmed the esteem that it has in . . . Fiorani and . . . Boni and is confident that they will be able to provide all the explanations necessary to definitively clarify this incident."[25]

Meanwhile, however, Consob had found another undisclosed shareholder agreement and concluded that certain Cayman mutual funds had acted as "nominees" for Lodi share purchases[26] and issued a precautionary suspension of Lodi's tender offers.[27] Over coming months rumors in the Italian press regarding the solidity of Lodi's assets would persist,[28] and on September 16, Fiorani resigned permanently amidst a criminal probe into false statements, insider trading, market rigging, and regulatory obstruction.[29] In October, Consob finally annulled Lodi's tender offers,[30] and by mid-December, the whole Lodi Board would resign "to allow the total renewal of the administrative body of the Bank."[31]

Sale of Lodi's Stake in Antonveneta

By late August it had become clear that Lodi would have to unload its stake in Antonveneta, given the "legal quagmire" in which it had found itself. Lodi stated that several international banks were showing interest in the shares—among them ABN Amro, with which Lodi's advisors met.[32] By late September ABN Amro was confirmed to be the purchaser, thereby prevailing in the battle for Antonveneta.[33] ABN Amro agreed on September 26 to buy an additional 39.37% of Antonveneta's shares from Lodi (which held 25.885%) and certain other parties, at a price of €26.50 per share (totaling €3.2 billion), pending release of the frozen shares. This would bring ABN Amro's total stake to 69.28%, after which it would launch a tender offer for all remaining shares at the same price. Assurance was offered, once again, that ABN Amro would "safeguard local decision-making" and ensure "Antonveneta's continued support of the local economy." Antonveneta's headquarters would remain in Padua.[34]

Calls for Reform

As the scandal grew, numerous observers began to call for fundamental reforms to Italy's banking supervisory system. Montani reflects, "It was a very difficult period for the Italian legislators, regulators, and magistrates because the laws were not made to accommodate such extraordinary circumstances."[35] Long before the takeover contest was resolved, economists within and without Italy already "urged far-reaching changes at the central bank so that it would not be majority owned by the private sector banks that it regulates." Mario Monti, the former EU competition and internal market commissioner, called for "a change in the ownership structure, more collegial management, a fixed term of office for the governor and changes in the regulatory responsibilities of the bank, the stock market watchdog and the antitrust authority."[36] ABN Amro's chairman of the managing board,

Groenink, upon signing the deal to purchase Lodi's shares, foresaw consolidation among Italy's hitherto fragmented top-tier banks and reported that ABN Amro's relationship with the Bank of Italy was improving. Fazio, however, continued to defy calls that he resign, even as he lost the confidence of Italy's political elite, including Prime Minister Silvio Berlusconi.[37]

The European Commission Acts

In late November, the European Commission (EC) announced that it would soon mount a legal challenge to Italy's supervisory regime for cross-border banking mergers, "accus[ing] the Italian authorities of contravening the free movement of capital and the freedom for businesses to operate in another member state."[38]

Indeed the EC had the previous month issued a communication on "Intra-EU investment in the financial services' sector" that, in retrospect, read like a draft legal brief for just such a case against Italy. The communication generally "aims to remind Member States of the relevant basic Treaty freedoms" and "encourages financial institutions to document instances of what they may consider as unjustified barriers to the integration process."[39] After reciting the EC's understanding of the freedoms of capital movements and establishment and the strictly limited scope of exceptions to those freedoms—including with respect to prudential supervision—the EC ultimately stated that no national supervisory requirements "should be insurmountable tasks for any EU financial institution, which is already subject to similar requirements in its home country, and wishes to acquire a participation (controlling or otherwise) in a financial institution in another Member State."[40] Such parties "need to be given clear indication of the specific, objective circumstances in which prior approval will be granted or withheld," and the bases for such decisions should be disclosed. The EC, for its part, warned that it would "pursue infringement cases vigorously."[41]

The EC's legal challenge was announced formally on December 14 by letter of notice to Italy, charging that Italy's banking laws were essentially opaque, lacking both objective criteria for assessing proposed mergers as well as transparent procedures.[42] The EC's release on the matter specifically identified the Antonveneta affair as a principal impetus for the action and referred back to its October communication on intra-EU investment, emphasizing that "Member States must both respect the basic freedoms guaranteed by the EC Treaty and ensure compliance with the relevant Directive when legislating, creating or enforcing administrative practices."[43]

The Changing Face of Italian Banking Supervision

Following the announcement of the EC's legal action against Italy in mid-December and Fiorani's arrest on embezzlement charges, there was a "renewal of calls for the resignation of Antonio Fazio" from his post as governor of the Bank of Italy.[44] Facing what the *Financial Times* described as "serious allegations never before faced by a governor of a big, modern, western central bank," Fazio now faced multiple investigations for "abuse of office" and "passing on inside information," each arising from the Antonveneta takeover battle. His mode of prudential supervision had come to be viewed as "increasingly out of step with a more open Europe," one Italian banking scholar expressing the view that "this system of no rules, of discretion, is not fashionable any more. It is very 18th century."[45]

On December 19, Fazio finally resigned, by which time investigation of Fiorani's broader business dealings—allegedly amounting to "a large criminal operation for personal enrichment"—was beginning to implicate a number of Italian politicians.[46] Almost immediately after Fazio's resignation, the Italian government "rushed through legislation" that (among other things) capped the bank governor's tenure at six years and gave the government nomination power.[47]

Following these initial reforms, it took little time to identify Fazio's successor—Mario Draghi, a former treasury official who had spearheaded Italy's wave of privatization in the 1990s and who had more recently been a managing director of the investment bank Goldman Sachs. Viewed as more internationally minded, Draghi was "expected to break with one of the most controversial policies of Mr. Fazio"—his opposition to foreign control over Italian banks[48]—and generally to "oversee an opening up of the banking sector."[49] His appointment was broadly welcomed, though "some politicians warned that his investment-banking experience makes him ill-suited to become an arbiter of mergers and acquisitions in Italy."[50]

Epilogue for Italy

Though the Antonveneta affair was a painful episode in the nation's economic and political history, Italy's regulatory reputation appeared to be on the mend by early 2006. Draghi's appointment as governor and concurrent legislative reforms were repairing the image of the Bank of Italy, while Consob and local prosecutors had emerged from the affair as "steely and aggressive" guardians of the public interest.[51]

In any event, on December 22, 2005, Lodi's stake in Antonveneta was unfrozen,[52] and on January 2, 2006, ABN Amro closed its purchase of the Lodi shares. This raised its stake to 55.8%, and the Dutch bank confirmed that it would proceed with the required tender offer for all remaining shares.[53] ABN Amro had become "the first foreign bank to gain majority control over a large Italian lender."[54] "The final victory," Montani observes, "was not with ABN Amro per se, but it was the victory of the legal system as a whole that favored the honest buyer."[55]

Lessons for Europe and the Internationalization of Banking

ABN Amro's executives reflected on the broader implications of the Antonveneta affair with relief, enthusiasm, and pride.

Although few observers expected a wave of cross-border banking acquisitions, the last, more informal barriers were finally breaking down. Still, approaches would have to be welcome, since it was not difficult to ruin a bank over the course of a weekend. "There will be no hostile takeovers in banking in Europe," observed ABN Amro's Groenink, "and certainly not across borders." But there were now possibilities, even in theretofore closed banking systems such as Italy's. "The result for Europe, however," according to Groenink, "is promising. A bank supervisor will think twice about doing anything like this again."[56] Further informal barriers remained, however, even as prudential supervision appeared less and less likely to be the regulatory stumbling block. "Despite the absence of formal barriers," argued Leonard Stolk, ABN Amro managing director, "and despite a European passport for banks, national borders still demarcate the European banking market."[57]

The struggle for Antonveneta, a struggle that consumed vast amounts of managerial attention and literally exhausted some of the bank's important executives, succeeded in part because of what had once seemed like the naïveté of Dutch bankers trying to play by Italian rules. Relying on ABN Amro's internal governance standards and the advice of Rossi, the bank had fought with Lodi as transparently as possible. What was second nature turned out to be prudent strategy. "If you try as a foreigner to play the same dirty game of a local," suggested Groenink, "you will always lose."[58] Thus, what had once appeared as an ongoing embarrassment came to represent for the bank a study of its own best practices. "Throughout the organization," noted Drost, "there was pride that we had accomplished all of this without deviating from our core values and business principles. We had been the good guys, and we had won."[59]

Endnotes

[1] Gabriel Kahn and Sabrina Cohen, "Walled Off: Wiretaps of an Executive in Italy Put Central Banker in Hot Seat—Fazio Appears to Have Helped Compatriot Beat Foreigner In an Acquisition Battle – Share Purchases on the Sly," *The Wall Street Journal*, September 13, 2005, p. A1, available at Factiva.

[2] See Rawi Abdelal and Christopher M. Bruner, "Politics and Prudential Supervision: ABN Amro's Bid for Antonveneta," HBS Case No. 706-009 (Boston: Harvard Business School Publishing, 2005), p. 8. On June 2, 2005, Lodi's shareholders approved the proposed change of the bank's name to "Banca Popolare Italiana." According to a press release, the name change was "consistent with the Gruppo Antonveneta merger project, within which values such as the focus on local realities, the respect for tradition and social sensitivity will continue to coexist with growth in size, operating efficiency and innovation, safeguarding the bank's 'popular' matrix." "Shareholders' Meeting Gives Go-Ahead for Change of Name to Banca Popolare Italiana. Unanimous Approval for the Asset Base Strengthening Plan of Approx. 3 Billion Euro," June 2, 2005 (Lodi press release). For consistency and ease of reference, the bank will nevertheless be referred to as "Lodi" throughout. Lodi press releases are available at http://www.bancapopolareitaliana.it/index.php?option=com_wrapper&Itemid=229.

[3] Interview by Maria Teresa Sallet with Piero Montani, CEO of Antonveneta, March 5, 2007. Maria Teresa Sallet, Senior Vice President, ABN Amro, was instrumental in ensuring that both the A and B cases were written and provided significant logistical support.

[4] Kahn and Cohen, "Walled Off."

[5] "Brothers in arms—Italian banking scandal," *The Economist*, August 13, 2005, available at Factiva.

[6] Author's interview with Richard Bruens, executive vice president, head of Investor Relations, ABN Amro, Amsterdam, June 13, 2006.

[7] Ibid.

[8] Kahn and Cohen, "Walled Off."

[9] Ibid.; "Brothers in arms," *The Economist*.

[10] Kahn and Cohen, "Walled Off."

[11] "Brothers in arms," *The Economist*.

[12] Ibid.; "Investment in Banca Antonveneta," April 6, 2005 (Lodi press release).

[13] "Brothers in arms," *The Economist*; see also Abdelal and Bruner, "Politics and Prudential Supervision: ABN Amro's Bid for Antonveneta (A)," p. 7 (describing the Lodi Board's authorization of an offer consisting principally of Lodi securities). While the Bank of Italy scrutinized ABN Amro's application to pass 20% as "tantamount to one for majority control," Lodi was permitted to reach 29.9% notwithstanding core capital insufficient to pass 20% (through so-called stock borrowing, under which Lodi essentially rented the remaining 10%, deferring purchase until its core capital permitted purchase) ("Brothers in arms," *The Economist*). The Bank of Italy, however, insisted that "[i]t is not true that foreign banks are treated differently from Italian banks" and pointed to the outcome of Antonveneta's April shareholder meeting as indicating that "the majority of the bank's shareholders do not concur with ABN Amro's takeover bid." Angelo De Mattia (central manager for the Governor's Secretariat, Bank of Italy), Letter to the Editor, *The Financial Times* (London), May 4, 2005, p. 18, available at Lexis.

Lodi's share purchases occurred between April 15 and April 22, immediately following expiration of a "shareholders' pact" formed in March 2002 "to provide stability of ownership and ensure autonomy for the bank's management" (*The Economist*). The bulk of the trades were arranged such that "sell orders hit the market at the same time as matching buy orders"—so-called *ordini baciati* (kissing trades). Kahn and Cohen, "Walled Off."

[14] "Brothers," *The Economist*. See also Consob, "Consob's Decision With Regard to Antonveneta," *Weekly Newsletter*, year 11, no. 20, May 16, 2005; Consob, "Tender Offers," *Weekly Newsletter*, year 12, no. 1, January 2,

2006. Consob newsletters are available at http://www.consob.it/mainen/consob/publications/newsletter/search_newsletter.html.

[15] The following account of the events leading to Bank of Italy approval of Lodi's bid on July 12, 2005 is drawn from Kahn and Cohen (internal quotation marks omitted).

[16] Ibid.; see also the opening quote accompanying note 1 (reflecting Fiorani's response to the news).

[17] Author's interview with Richard Bruens, executive vice president, head of Investor Relations, ABN Amro, Amsterdam, June 13, 2006.

[18] "ABN Amro obtains 6,283,038 (2.88%) shares of Banca Antonveneta in tender offer," July 25, 2005 (ABN Amro press release). ABN Amro press releases are available at http://www.abnamro.com/pressroom/anton.jsp.

[19] Author's interview with Bruens.

[20] Sallet's interview with Montani.

[21] See, for example, "The Troubleshooter," *The Economist*, December 9, 2006.

[22] Author's phone interview with Jeroen Drost, CEO, ABN Amro Asia, September 20, 2006. Head of Corporate Development at the time of the acquisition.

[23] Kahn and Cohen, "Walled Off."

[24] "New Member For Shareholders' Agreement Between Banca Antonveneta Shareholders," July 26, 2005 (Lodi press release).

[25] "Board of Directors Appoints Giorgio Olmo As CEO," August 2, 2005 (Lodi press release).

[26] Consob, "New Consob Intervention Concerning Antonveneta," *Weekly Newsletter*, year 11, no. 30, July 25, 2005; Consob, "Tender Offers"; see also "Banca Popolare Italiana Board of Directors: Green Light for Capital Increase With Exclusion of Preemptive Right For €332 Million Reserved For OICR, Banking Institutions and Strategic Partners," July 26, 2005 (Lodi press release).

[27] Consob, "Precautionary Suspension of the BPI Cash and Cash and Exchange Tender Offers," *Weekly Newsletter*, year 11, no. 31, August 1, 2005.

[28] "Board of Directors—11 August 2005—Legal proceedings against the spreading of unfounded rumours regarding the Bank's solidity—Dresdner and Lazard confirmed as Advisors—Giorgio Olmo elected representative of the Steering Committee for the Banca Antonveneta shareholders' agreement—Paolo Landi appointed Coordinator of the Key Divisions," August 11, 2005 (Lodi press release); "Legal Action Taken to Protect the Bank's Image. Consolidated Shareholders' Equity: €4 Billion. Financial Liquidity: €3 Billion," August 25, 2005 (Lodi press release); "Legal Actions," September 19, 2005 (Lodi press release).

[29] "Banca Popolare Says CEO Quits Inquiries Linger," *The Wall Street Journal*, September 19, 2005, p. C9, available at Factiva; see also "Press Release," September 16, 2005 (Lodi press release).

[30] Consob, "Annulment of BPI's Cash and Cash and Exchange Tender Offers for Banca Antonveneta Shares," *Weekly Newsletter*, year 11, no. 41, October 17, 2005; Consob, "Tender Offers."

[31] "Call of the Board of Directors," December 1, 2005 (Lodi press release).

[32] "BPI Cites Interest From Major Banks On Antonveneta," *The Wall Street Journal*, August 26, 2005, p. B5, available at Factiva.

[33] Edward Taylor and Gabriel Kahn, "ABN Amro Wins Fight For Antonveneta Stake—Dutch Bank's Chief Says Italy's Fragmented Market Is Likely to Be Consolidated," *The Wall Street Journal*, September 27, 2005, p. C4, available at Factiva; see also "ABN Amro to acquire controlling stake in Banca Antonveneta," September 26, 2005 (ABN Amro press release); "Press Release With Regard to the News Disclosed Today," September 6, 2005 (Lodi

press release); "Hypothesis of Selling Antonveneta Shares to ABN Amro Considered Final Decision to be Taken At a Board Meeting in the Next Few Days," September 9, 2005 (Lodi press release); "Keeping on With the Sale of Antonveneta Shares. Exclusive Contract To ABN Amro," September 14, 2005 (Lodi press release); "Sale of Antonveneta Shares to ABN Amro," September 21, 2005 (Lodi press release); "Disposal of Banca Antonveneta Holding," September 23, 2005 (Lodi press release); "Sale of Holding in Banca Antonveneta," September 23, 2005 (Lodi press release); "Banca Popolare Italiana Signs the Contract For the Sale of Its Holding in Banca Antonveneta," September 26, 2005 (Lodi press release).

[34] See "ABN Amro to acquire controlling stake in Banca Antonveneta"; "Banca Popolare Italiana Signs the Contract For the Sale of Its Holding in Banca Antonveneta."

[35] Sallet's interview with Montani.

[36] Tony Barber, "Pressure grows on Bank of Italy owner structure," *The Financial Times* (London), August 25, 2005, p. 7, available at Factiva.

[37] See Taylor and Kahn, "ABN Amro."

[38] "Bank of Italy investigated by EU," *BBC News*, November 24, 2005, available at http://news.bbc.co.uk/go/pr/fr/-/1/hi/business/4465668.stm.

[39] European Commission, "Intra-EU investment in the financial services' sector," C/2005/4080, October 21, 2005, part 7 (European Commission communication).

[40] Ibid., part 5.

[41] Ibid., parts 5 and 6. For additional background on the treaty regime and EC actions in response to barriers to cross-border banking mergers, see generally Rawi Abdelal and Christopher M. Bruner, "European Financial Integration," HBS Case No. 706-010 (Boston: Harvard Business School Publishing, 2005).

[42] "Proceedings opened against Italy on merger rules," EurActiv.com, December 15, 2005, available at http://www.euractiv.com/Article?tcmuri=tcm:29-150897-16&type=News.

[43] European Commission, "Free movement of capital: Commission opens an infringement procedure against Italy on the issue of acquisition of stakes in domestic banks," IP/05/1595, December 14, 2005 (European Commission press release).

[44] "Proceedings opened against Italy on merger rules," EurActiv.com.

[45] Adrian Michaels, "Departure is ignominious finale to 45 years at central bank," *The Financial Times* (London), December 20, 2005, p. 6, available at Factiva (quoting Giacomo Vaciago of Catholic University, Milan) (internal quotation marks omitted).

[46] Adrian Michaels, "Italy's banking scandal looks likely to claim further scalps," *The Financial Times* (London), p. 6, available at Factiva; see also Gabriel Kahn and Christopher Emsden, "First Task for Draghi Atop Bank of Italy: Clean Up," *The Wall Street Journal*, December 30, 2005, p. A10, available at Factiva.

[47] "Italy to limit bank boss' tenure," *BBC News*, December 23, 2005, available at http://news.bbc.co.uk/go/pr/fr/-/1/hi/business/4553670.stm; see also Kahn and Emsden, "First Task."

[48] Kahn and Emsden, "First Task"; see also "Italy chooses successor to Fazio," *BBC News*, December 29, 2005, available at http://news.bbc.co.uk/go/pr/fr/-/1/hi/business/4566744.stm.

[49] "New Italian bank boss starts work," *BBC News*, January 16, 2006, available at http://news.bbc.co.uk/go/pr/fr/-/1/hi/business/4617800.stm.

[50] Kahn and Emsden, "First Task."

[51] Tony Barber and Adrian Michaels, "Banking on change: how Italy hopes to salvage good from its corporate wreckage," *The Financial Times* (London), January 18, 2006, p. 17, available at Factiva.

[52] "Unfreezing of Banca Antonveneta Shares," December 22, 2005 (Lodi press release).

[53] "ABN Amro acquires majority stake in Banca Antonveneta," January 2, 2006 (ABN Amro press release); see also "Stake in Banca Antonveneta Sold," December 30, 2005 (Lodi press release) (describing major technical steps involved in bringing about the sale).

[54] Taylor and Kahn (describing prospectively the significance of the agreed upon sale), "ABN Amro."

[55] Sallet's interview with Montani.

[56] Author's interview with Rijkman Groenink, chairman of the managing board, ABN Amro, Amsterdam, June 12, 2006.

[57] Author's interview with Leonard Stolk, managing director, Alliance Solutions Group, ABN Amro, Amsterdam, June 13, 2006.

[58] Author's interview with Rijkman Groenink.

[59] Author's phone interview with Jeroen Drost.

9-706-010
REV: MAY 31, 2006

RAWI ABDELAL

CHRISTOPHER M. BRUNER

European Financial Integration

This note provides a brief overview of the history and status of financial integration in the European Union. It describes the nature and extent of the treaty-based "fundamental freedoms" most pertinent to the development of a common European financial market—the free movement of services and capital. The note then discusses integration in financial services, emphasizing challenges to further cross-border consolidation in the banking sector and including discussion of the European Commission's regulatory role in establishing conditions conducive to financial integration in Europe.

Fundamental Freedoms and the Common Market

Under the Treaty Establishing the European Community (the EC Treaty), the fundamental task of the European Union (so-called, following the expansion of cooperative efforts in the 1992 Treaty of Maastricht)[1] is to promote economic and social harmony in Europe, principally "by establishing a common market and an economic and monetary union." Specific activities toward this end are to include the creation of "an internal market characterised by the abolition, as between Member States, of obstacles to the free movement of goods, persons, services and capital."[2] As this treaty language makes clear, these "fundamental freedoms"[3] represent positive terms for the absence of market impediments, the implication being that the achievement of a single internal market in Europe essentially means the elimination of regulatory and other barriers at the national level.

The fundamental freedoms most centrally implicated by the creation of a single financial market are the free movement of services, together with the closely related freedom of establishment, and the free movement of capital.[4]

Free Movement of Services and Freedom of Establishment

The EC Treaty provides that "restrictions on the freedom of establishment of nationals of a Member State in the territory of another Member State shall be prohibited." This freedom includes "the right to take up and pursue activities as self-employed persons and to set up and manage undertakings, in particular companies or firms" as described in the treaty (as well as "agencies, branches or subsidiaries"), "under the conditions laid down for its own nationals by the law of the country where such establishment is effected."[5] Thus nationals of other EU countries are to have the same rights to set up and run businesses as nationals of the EU country in which the business is to be located.

Professor Rawi Abdelal and Research Associate Christopher M. Bruner, J.D., prepared this note as the basis for class discussion.

Additionally, "restrictions on freedom to provide services within the Community" are "prohibited in respect of nationals of Member States who are established in a State of the Community other than that of the person for whom the services are intended."[6] Though the freedom to establish a business within a given country and the freedom to provide services to residents in that country are technically distinct, they share a conceptual focus on the cross-border conduct of business. Indeed, the freedom of establishment and the free movement of services are frequently considered to be different aspects of the same legal right.[7]

Capital Mobility

Under the original (1957) version of the treaty, the free movement of capital was limited by the vague qualifier that such freedom applied only "to the extent necessary to ensure the proper functioning of the common market."[8] Thus capital mobility was initially limited to what could be agreed upon as "necessary" (i.e., through European Council directives) and, unlike the other three fundamental freedoms, was not deemed to have "direct legal effect," meaning that the provision created rights only as among member states, with no private enforcement rights.[9]

Through the 1970s Germany was alone in advocating the expansion of this freedom, other states such as France, Italy, and the Netherlands preferring to maintain policy autonomy in this area for fear of instability resulting from potentially volatile short-term capital flows. Commission directives in 1960 and 1962 did little to enhance the free movement of capital, essentially categorizing transaction forms by level of necessity to the common market but declining to require that many be liberalized. Another attempt at a directive initiated in 1967 ultimately failed in the face of concerted opposition to expanded capital mobility by France and the Netherlands. Indeed, a 1972 directive took a step backward in requiring countries to maintain the apparatus to apply capital controls.[10]

The prevailing attitude toward capital mobility would change fundamentally, however, with the new policy course adopted by France starting in 1983. Though the French had previously imposed strict capital controls, they eventually found that in reality those controls applied only to the middle classes because the rich had the resources and connections to evade them. Thus the decision was made—by President François Mitterrand's socialist government, ironically enough—to liberalize capital movements. With this came a retraining of French policymakers' focus on Europe as the operative level of government at which policy goals could most efficaciously be pursued. Once former French finance minister Jacques Delors became president of the European Commission in 1985, this perspective took the form of a push for complete capital liberalization in Europe—a goal achieved through a 1988 directive that essentially defined all capital movements as necessary to the common market.[11]

The 1988 directive stated, "Member States shall abolish restrictions on movements of capital taking place between persons resident in Member States" and repealed prior directives that had created a hierarchy of transaction forms and required the apparatus for capital controls, respectively.[12] Effective January 1, 1994, the obsolete treaty language was replaced by a new provision stating that, in general, "all restrictions on the movement of capital between Member States and between Member States and third parties shall be prohibited."[13] Moving the requirement to the treaty itself was symbolically important, confirming the status of this fundamental freedom as equal to the others, and the language further established that the free movement of capital would apply vis-à-vis non-EU countries as well.[14] Notwithstanding the broadly stated principle, however, another provision carved out important exceptions, notably including the right of Member States "to take all requisite measures to prevent infringements of national law and regulations, in particular in the field of taxation and the prudential supervision of financial institutions . . . or to take measures which are justified on grounds of public policy or public security."[15]

The freedom of establishment and the free movement of capital are closely related in practice because both tend to apply to important categories of economic and financial activity—notably cross-border investment,[16] which can often involve both the establishment of a business presence in another member state (e.g., through a merger or acquisition) and, associated with that, the movement of money. "Not surprisingly, an infringement of one [freedom] is often linked with an infringement of the other," and the European Court of Justice (ECJ, the judicial organ of the European Union) "has applied the laws governing the two freedoms in parallel" (though it often chooses to apply one or the other, but not both, even where the second might also logically have applied).[17]

The Acquis Communautaire

The four fundamental freedoms of goods, persons, services, and capital—the latter, since 1988, being equal to the former three, as an integral component of the common market project—constitute part of the *acquis communautaire*. The *acquis* is essentially the complete set of obligations of EU member states, including all treaties, directives, and ECJ opinions—a body of law weighing in at about 80,000 pages, to which existing EU members have agreed to adhere and with which new EU members commit to bring themselves into compliance. The nature of this undertaking "has perhaps been at its most dramatic on each of the occasions that Europe welcomed new members," as preparing for the obligations of membership has tended to require opening up economies and financial markets quite a bit more quickly than was required of the established members that composed the rules.[18]

Financial Integration in the European Union

During the 1990s, substantial economic integration—as reflected by cross-border mergers and acquisitions (M&A) activity—occurred across the industrialized world. However, the degree of integration in the financial sector lagged behind that of other sectors. Across the Organization for Economic Cooperation and Development (OECD, a club of European and other industrialized countries), for example, the percentage of M&A that occurred across borders in nonfinancial sectors during this period was 29.6%. The corresponding figure for banking was only 12.9%.[19] In Europe, between 1999 and 2004, the comparison was just as stark, with cross-border M&A representing 45% of the value of nonfinancial sector M&A activity but just 20% in the financial sector.[20] The relatively slower rate of integration in the financial sector has remained a vexing problem for the European Commission, which—though officially agnostic on the wisdom of "specific business models" or particular cross-border deals—has embraced its role in addressing "unjustified obstacles that would hamper companies in making their own decisions regarding their business organisation in the Internal Market."[21]

Consolidation in European Banking

In Europe, cross-border banking consolidation has tended to involve foreign acquisition of newly privatized east European banks, with M&A activity in western Europe essentially limited to domestic deals. Across the 15 member states predating the May 2004 enlargement (when 10 additional countries joined), the total number of credit institutions dropped 23% between 1997 and 2003 (falling below 7,500 in total). The drop was "mainly attributable to mergers and acquisitions," though largely "confined to domestic consolidation."[22] "Domestic deals constituted 87% in number and 90% in total value of banking M&A activity in Europe in the 90's."[23] In contrast, among the new (2004) member states—predominantly east European countries—bank privatization programs implemented since the 1990s resulted in much higher levels of ownership by foreign banks. Whereas by 2004 only 23% of bank assets in the original 15 member states were under foreign banks' control, the figure among new member states averaged almost 70%, with their own banks tending to have "little or no presence abroad."[24]

By May 2005 there had been "only one significant" cross-border banking merger in Europe, the purchase by Spain's Banco Santander Central Hispano of the U.K.'s Abbey National.[25] What cross-border consolidation has occurred in western Europe has tended to involve wholesale rather than retail banking. As *The Economist* put it, in "retail banking, each national banking system, whether inside or outside the EU, is still an island."[26]

Banking Regulation and Cross-Border Mergers

An EU banking directive that went effective in 2000 (the EU Banking Directive) established a process for the regulation of banking consolidation that placed significant discretionary authority in the hands of national banking supervisors. Among other things, a person proposing to establish (or increase) an ownership stake reaching certain threshold percentages—or otherwise achieving control—must first notify the national supervisory authority, which has three months "to oppose such plan if, in view of the need to ensure sound and prudent management of the credit institution, they are not satisfied as to the suitability of the person."[27] The EU Banking Directive does not define the vague yet crucial standard of "sound and prudent management," thereby leaving to national supervisory authorities significant discretion with respect to approval of banking M&A activity, including potential cross-border deals.

More broadly, cross-border mergers and acquisitions having a "community dimension" (essentially determined by reference to size) are generally subject to European Commission jurisdiction under a 2004 regulation (the Merger Regulation), though this regime similarly accommodates national supervisory authority to ensure the sound functioning of the domestic financial system involved. The Merger Regulation requires that where the commission finds that a potential M&A transaction "does not raise serious doubts as to its compatibility with the common market, it shall decide not to oppose it and shall declare that it is compatible with the common market." However, while the commission has "sole jurisdiction to take the decisions provided for in this Regulation," with contrary application of national competition laws prohibited, an exception to this general rule permits member states to "take appropriate measures to protect legitimate interests other than those taken into consideration by this Regulation and compatible with the general principles and other provisions of Community law," which interests are explicitly deemed to include "prudential rules."[28]

The inherent tension between these policy goals—creating a competitive European financial market, on the one hand, while protecting the safety and soundness of domestic financial institutions, on the other—has, in the view of some, been reinforced by the strong emphasis placed on bank capital adequacy rules since the 1980s. A series of substantial bank failures in the 1970s and 1980s ultimately resulted, in 1988, in a set of global capital adequacy standards for banks called the "Basel Accord" (updated in 2004 by "Basel II"), establishing minimum capital reserve requirements to be implemented through national law and overseen by national banking supervisors.[29] This system has improved the soundness of the global financial system by forcing banks to maintain capital adequate to the risks of their loan portfolios.[30] It has been observed, however, that national banking supervisors, "because of their preoccupation with systemic risk, have tended to be quite tolerant of anti-competitive behaviour by banks,"[31] and that such emphasis has resulted in a myopic focus on the interests of banks, in particular, as opposed to the financial system as a whole. "Regulators' first priority is the safety and soundness of their banks. If pushed by their governments, they might also look at the public-policy function of the banking system and the related capital markets," though they tend to do so reluctantly.[32] Thus while bank capital adequacy rules have undoubtedly lent stability to the global financial system, they may indirectly (and ironically) have reinforced financial market fragmentation within Europe and elsewhere by placing great discretionary power in the hands of national banking regulators and training their eyes squarely on the soundness and survival of the banks under their watch.

Views on Retail Banking Consolidation

As noted above, cross-border consolidation in European retail banking has been extremely rare. There are several potential explanations for this. The European Commission, for example, has outlined an extensive list of potential factors including myriad legal barriers (e.g., company law, privatization measures); tax barriers (e.g., uncertainty regarding applicable regimes); economic barriers (e.g., transaction costs resulting from equity market fragmentation); so-called attitudinal barriers; and barriers resulting from "supervisory rules and requirements."[33] It is perhaps the latter two categories that the commission finds of most concern. Beyond the fact that "[c]onsumers may mistrust foreign entities," supervisors themselves may actually promote "national champions" to "ensure adequate financing of the national economy" and base supervisory decisions on other than "prudential grounds."[34] As the commission has observed, there are so many impediments to such transactions that "it is realistic to think that no cross-border merger can be achieved if there is a strong political opposition."[35]

In any event, viewpoints on the wisdom of permitting—let alone encouraging—European retail banking consolidation differ markedly. The arguments for such consolidation emphasize broad efficiencies—essentially basic economies of scale and scope[36]—including specific advantages to be gained in areas such as technology and compliance with capital adequacy rules.[37] The counterarguments emphasize culture, national market idiosyncrasies, and lending practices of domestic versus national banks.

The European Savings Bank Group, "Europe's main representative of retail, decentralised, local and regional" banks, has emphasized "the importance that cultural preferences and local product and service demand play in Europe's retail banking markets" and argued that "changes in regulations may unfairly tip the balance in favour of internationally active banks wishing to consolidate across borders."[38] One Italian bank has argued that "[m]odern economies can be either 'market-oriented,'" like the United States and the United Kingdom, "or 'banking-oriented,'" like Germany and Italy, and that efficiencies available through wholesale banking consolidation (i.e., among investment banks servicing large securities issuers) are not available on the retail side, where consolidation could result in "a possible decrease of the variety of services and a lesser focus of the large newly formed banking institution on the retail sector."[39] (The broad discretion to veto banking M&A activity afforded by the EU Banking Directive, it is argued, reflects the fact that "there was no plain consensus" on the precise meaning of "sound and prudent management"—hence the "rather generic expression.")[40] It is also feared that "foreign-owned banks . . . may be less inclined than locally owned ones to make business decisions that support the national economy, and perhaps more resistant to moral suasion or political pressure."[41] In light of protectionist supervisory practices and other barriers to entry, many share the view that "pan-European" retail banking is unlikely to coalesce any time soon.[42]

European Commission Actions Challenging Restrictions on Banking Integration

Since the late 1990s the European Commission has taken action on various occasions to challenge political impediments to cross-border banking consolidation and staked out a policy position consistent with those actions. In a series of cases before the ECJ, the commission has successfully challenged restrictive "golden shares"—that is, control rights retained by governments in privatized companies.[43] In one such case the ECJ found that a golden share in a commercial banking group could not be justified by "overriding requirements of the general interest linked to strategic imperatives and the need to ensure continuity in public services," as the Spanish government had argued, because the banks "operate[d] in the traditional banking sector," were "not claimed to carry out any of the functions of a central bank or similar body," and were "not undertakings whose objective [was] to provide public services."[44] The "system of prior administrative approval" involved was found, for lack of adequate justification, to violate the free movement of capital. This finding rendered separate consideration of the commission's freedom of establishment claim unnecessary in the ECJ's view, though it did observe that "in so far as the legislation in issue entails restrictions on the freedom of establishment, such restrictions are a direct consequence of the obstacles to the free movement of capital."[45]

The commission similarly intervened when the Portuguese government attempted to interfere with a Spanish bank's attempted takeover of a Portuguese banking group. The commission expressed its view that the Portuguese government had violated the freedom of establishment and the free movement of capital, principally because its veto was "not justified on prudential grounds" and actions taken (i.e., suspension of voting rights) were "disproportionate to any prudential objectives."[46] The commission threatened to take the case to the ECJ, following which the Portuguese government backed down.[47] Though not adjudicated by the ECJ, the affair came to be viewed as a precedent-setting episode, evidencing the commission's willingness and ability to challenge national political interference with cross-border banking consolidation.[48]

The commission's policy agenda has focused on implementation of the Financial Services Action Plan (FSAP), conceived in 1999 as "an aspirational programme for rapid progress towards a single financial market."[49] The FSAP lays out a number of specific objectives for the integration and liberalization of wholesale and retail financial markets, the improvement of prudential rules and supervision, and other means toward "an optimal single financial market."[50] Among other things, the commission stated that "[e]nsuring a secure and transparent environment for restructuring is of particular importance when it involves the financial services industry." While acknowledging the importance of prudential oversight, the commission took the position that "arriving at configurations that bring about greater efficiency is crucial given the key role that financial services play in ensuring an efficient allocation of resources throughout the EU economy." Thus "the supervisory authorities, while taking prudential considerations fully into account when dealing with the restructuring process (mergers, acquisitions, take-over bids etc.), should do so in full respect of the principles of transparency and non-discrimination." Such evaluations, the commission felt, should "be based on a set of objective and publicly disclosed criteria, stable over time," to "ensure free movement of capital and freedom of investment."[51]

By 2004, progress in the banking sector remained disappointing. An "Expert Group on Banking," in its May 2004 report to the commission, observed that "[c]ross-border [banking] mergers and acquisitions have been relatively limited" beyond Scandinavia and the Benelux countries and that "[d]espite progress in cross-border integration in wholesale markets, domestic consolidation has prevailed in the retail sector where no pan-European bank has yet emerged."[52] The group "felt that the full potential of integration, in particular in the field of cross-border retail activities still remains far from achieved," concluding among other things that "[i]mplementation and enforcement of existing legislation should have overall priority" and that the "focus needs to be on ensuring that fragmented market places are truly open to competitive forces."[53] While acknowledging that the lag in retail integration involved "the inclination of consumers to turn to their local and more familiar institutions," the group also felt that "market structures" and "national legal requirements" were contributing factors, observing that "[i]n some Member States cross-border acquisitions are perceived as hampered by . . . takeover legislation and administrative practices generally protective of domestic interests."[54]

The Committee of European Banking Supervisors (CEBS), in response to the expert group's views, was circumspect: "[A]s regards the overall objective of further market integration, CEBS notes that the report makes some sensible comments about the different levels of integration in wholesale and retail banking markets." CEBS continued, "The report correctly stresses that a single market cannot be created by simply introducing new harmonising measures, as there are several reasons (confidence, practical considerations, different levels of consumer protection, etc.) why retail consumers still prefer to deal with locally established entities."[55] Though not addressing directly the expert group's call for the elimination of politically motivated interference with cross-border retail consolidation by national supervisory authorities—a goal the commission has clearly embraced— CEBS' cool response makes eminently clear that integration along these lines remains a controversial matter and that such tensions will likely attend these issues for the foreseeable future.[56]

Endnotes

[1] See "The History of the European Union," available at http://europa.eu.int/abc/history/index_en.htm.

[2] See "Consolidated Version of the Treaty Establishing the European Community," Official Journal C 325, December 24, 2002 (hereinafter Consolidated EC Treaty), Articles 2–3, available at http://europa.eu.int/eur-lex/en/treaties/dat/EC_consol.html.

[3] These four freedoms are typically described as the "fundamental freedoms." See, e.g., Christine O'Grady Putek, "Comment: Limited But Not Lost: A Comment on the ECJ's Golden Share Decisions," *Fordham Law Review* 72 (April 2004): 2227.

[4] See, e.g., "Financial Services: Commission to send reasoned opinion to Portugal over veto against BSCH participation in Champalimaud group," European Commission, IP/99/773, October 20, 1999 (characterizing the Portuguese government's efforts to impede a cross-border banking acquisition as violating the freedom of establishment and free movement of capital).

[5] Consolidated EC Treaty, Art. 43.

[6] Ibid., Art. 49.

[7] Putek, p. 2227, n. 60.

[8] Treaty Establishing the European Community, March 25, 1957 (hereinafter Unconsolidated EC Treaty), Art. 67, available at http://europa.eu.int/abc/obj/treaties/en/entr6d03.htm#Article_67 (providing the text with later amendments, not reflecting redenomination of section numbers in the consolidated text of December 2002).

[9] See Rawi Abdelal, *Capital Rules: The Construction of Global Finance* (Cambridge, Mass.: Harvard University Press, 2007), chapter 4; and Putek, pp. 2227–2228 and n. 62.

[10] See Abdelal.

[11] Ibid.

[12] Council Directive 88/361/EEC of 24 June 1988 for the implementation of Article 67 of the Treaty, Arts. 1, 9.

[13] Unconsolidated EC Treaty, Art. 73b. Effective December 24, 2002, this provision was redenominated as Article 56. Consolidated EC Treaty, Art. 56. Although the 1988 directive would appear to have been rendered irrelevant when the treaty provision it interpreted was replaced, it remained useful for interpreting related concepts such as "direct investment." See, e.g., Commission of the European Communities v. Kingdom of Spain, Case C-463/00, May 13, 2003, 2003 ECJ CELEX LEXIS 189; Communication of the Commission on Certain Legal Aspects Concerning Intra-EU Investment (97/C 220/06), July 19, 1997.

[14] See Abdelal.

[15] Such measures, however, were "not [to] constitute a means of arbitrary discrimination or a disguised restriction on the free movement of capital and payments." See Unconsolidated EC Treaty, Art. 73d(1)(b), (3); Consolidated EC Treaty Art. 58(1)(b), (3).

[16] See Putek, p. 2235.

[17] Ibid.; see also pp. 2246–2249 (concluding that "some cases infringe both freedoms, and the reason for the Court's application of one body of law over another may be apparent only by considering the development of relevant precedent"); European Commission, "Special rights in privatised companies in the enlarged Union—a decade full of developments" (hereinafter Report on Special Rights), Commission Staff Working Document, July 22, 2005, Annex 1, p. 27, n. 57 (observing that exceptions to the "parallel approach" to application of these freedoms would include cases involving third countries, because "of the two only the freedom of capital movements applies to third countries and Member States alike").

[18] See Abdelal.

[19] Dario Focarelli and Alberto Franco Pozzolo, "The patterns of cross-border bank mergers and shareholdings in OECD countries," *Journal of Banking & Finance* 25 (2001): 2310.

[20] "Background Paper: Obstacles to cross-border mergers and acquisitions in the financial sector," April 2005, p. 1, available at http://europa.eu.int/comm/internal_market/finances/docs/cross-sector/mergers/consultation_en.pdf .

[21] Ibid.

[22] *Report on EU Banking Structure*, European Central Bank, November 2004, pp. 8–9.

[23] "European Banking Consolidation: A Considered Analysis of the Retail Banking Market and the Position of the European Savings Banks Group," European Savings Banks Group (ESBG), December 2004, p. 9.

[24] European Central Bank, pp. 15–16. Exceptions were Cyprus and Slovenia, with much lower levels of foreign ownership, and Hungary and Estonia, which had "a more significant foreign presence" than others. See also, "A blurred Euro-vision," *The Economist*, May 19, 2005.

[25] See "A blurred Euro-vision," *The Economist*. *The Economist* observes that "[a]part from some cross-border bank consolidation in the Benelux and Scandinavian countries, that is as far as integration in western Europe has got."

[26] Ibid.

[27] "Directive 2000/12/EC of the European Parliament and of the Council of 20 March 2000 relating to the taking up and pursuit of the business of credit institutions," Art. 16(1). Indeed the directive states that authorities "shall refuse authorisation" of "the taking-up of the business of credit institutions" if "taking into account the need to ensure the sound and prudent management of a credit institution, they are not satisfied as to the suitability of the . . . shareholders or members," Art. 7(2). Likewise "where the influence exercised" by a person passing a triggering ownership threshold "is likely to operate to the detriment of the prudent and sound management of the institution, the competent authorities shall take appropriate measures to put an end to that situation," which actions might include "injunctions, sanctions against directors and managers, or the suspension of the exercise of the voting rights attaching to the shares held by the shareholders or members in question," Art. 16(5).

Other banking directives include Directive 2000/28/EC of the European Parliament and of the Council of 18 September 2000 amending Directive 2000/12/EC relating to the taking up and pursuit of the business of credit institutions; Directive 2000/46/EC of the European Parliament and of the Council of 18 September 2000 on the taking up, pursuit of and prudential supervision of the business of electronic money institutions; and Directive 2002/87/EC of the European Parliament and of the Council of 16 December 2002 on the supplementary supervision of credit institutions, insurance undertakings and investment firms in a financial conglomerate and amending Council Directives 73/239/EEC, 79/267/EEC, 92/49/EEC, 92/96/EEC, 93/6/EEC and 93/22/EEC, and Directives 98/78/EC and 2000/12/EC of the European Parliament and of the Council.

[28] Council Regulation (EC) No. 139/2004 of 20 January 2004 on the control of concentrations between undertakings (the EC Merger Regulation), Arts. 1, 6(1)(b), 21(2)–(4). A proposed directive implementing a new cross-border merger regime—aimed at eliminating legal barriers to cross-border M&A—would not alter this balance of power. Commission of the European Communities, Proposal for a Directive of the European Parliament and of the Council on cross-border mergers of companies with share capital, COM(2003) 703 final, 2003/0277 (COD), November 18, 2003, p. 4 (noting that the proposal "is without prejudice to the application of the legislation on the control of concentrations between undertakings, both at the Community level and at the level of Member States").

[29] Ethan Kapstein has written extensively on the emergence of the Basel Accord. See Ethan B. Kapstein, *Governing the Global Economy: International Finance and the State* (Cambridge, MA: Harvard University Press, 1994), chapter 5; Ethan B. Kapstein, "Resolving the Regulator's Dilemma: International Coordination of Banking Regulations," *International Organization* 43:2 (Spring 1989): 323–347; Ethan B. Kapstein, "Supervising International Banks: Origins and Implications of the Basel Accord," Essays in International Finance No. 185

(December 1991), International Finance Section, Department of Economics, Princeton University; Ethan Barnaby Kapstein, "Between Power and Purpose: Central Bankers and the Politics of Regulatory Convergence," *International Organization* 46:1 (Winter 1992): 265–287. For background on "Basel II," a substantial revision completed in 2004, see generally "Basel II: revised international capital framework," available at http://www.bis.org/publ/bcbsca.htm.

[30] Ibid.

[31] "Open wider," *The Economist*, May 19, 2005.

[32] "Crusader castles," *The Economist*, May 19, 2005.

[33] See generally "Background Paper: Obstacles to cross-border mergers and acquisitions in the financial sector"; see also "A blurred Euro-vision," *The Economist*. ("When it comes to retail banking, each national banking system, whether inside or outside the EU, is still an island. Tax, ownership, consumer protection and conduct-of-business rules have not been harmonised.")

[34] "Background Paper: Obstacles to cross-border mergers and acquisitions in the financial sector," pp. 7, 9 (all emphasis and internal quotation marks removed).

[35] Ibid., p. 9.

[36] See, e.g., ESBG, pp. 14–17 (summarizing various "drivers of banking consolidation").

[37] "A blurred Euro-vision," *The Economist* (citing a Morgan Stanley study).

[38] ESBG, pp. 7, 10.

[39] "Cross Border Mergers and Acquisitions Among Banks: Memorandum on Existing Legal Barriers and Antitrust Considerations," Banca Intesa, April 29, 2005, pp. 4–5, available at http://www.c-ebs.org/documents/BA_2_MA.pdf.

[40] Banca Intesa, p. 7.

[41] "A blurred Euro-vision," *The Economist*. Empirical data on the effects of banking consolidation on small to medium-size businesses yields results of mixed policy significance. The "most common finding" in the literature on the effects of bank mergers on small businesses has been that "consolidation involving large banking organizations tends to reduce small business lending," but such studies have tended to focus on the United States. Emilia Bonaccorsi di Patti and Giorgio Gobbi, "The changing structure of local credit markets: Are small businesses special?" *Journal of Banking & Finance* 25 (2001): 2214. One study from Italy, where the "economy is mainly composed of small and unlisted firms," found that bank mergers resulted in lower interest rates for lower-risk borrowers and higher rates for higher-risk borrowers, supporting an "interpretation that M&As improve banks' abilities to screen borrowers" and suggesting that "the simple consideration of average price effects might underestimate the welfare effects of mergers, because information improvements should imply a better allocation of resources." F. Panetta, F. Schivardi, and M. Shum, "Do mergers improve information? Evidence from the loan market," Bank of Italy discussion paper No. 521, October 2004, pp. 9–10. Another study, also focused on Italy, similarly found that "mergers are followed by a temporary reduction in credit and by an increase in the share of bad loans, which is consistent with the view that they lead to efficiency improvements in lending policies and a cut in credit to negative present value borrowers" (Bonaccorsi and Gobbi, p. 2234). As noted above, however, very little significant *cross-border* banking M&A has occurred to date. See "A blurred Euro-vision," *The Economist*.

[42] See, e.g., "Market Overview," European Financial Management & Marketing Association, available at http://www.efma.com/retail_market.php4 ; "Crusader castles," *The Economist*.

[43] See Putek, p. 2220. For the commission's assessment of progress made in addressing golden shares retained in privatized companies and for its analysis of the legality of such regimes, see generally "European Commission, Report on Special Rights."

[44] Commission of the European Communities v. Kingdom of Spain, paragraph 70.

[45] Ibid., paragraphs 84–85. In Commission of the European Communities v. Portuguese Republic, Case C-367/98, June 4, 2002, 2002 ECJ CELEX LEXIS 3566, the ECJ similarly struck down a regime involving prior government authorization and maximum shareholdings, which had been applied in the banking sector.

[46] "Financial services: Commission to send reasoned opinion to Portugal over veto against BSCH participation in Champalimaud group," European Commission, IP/99/773, October 20, 1999.

[47] "Commission refers BSCH/Champalimaud case to the Court of Justice," European Commission, November 3, 1999, available at http://europa.eu.int/comm/internal_market/en/finances/infr/99-818.htm; "EU/Competition—Champalimaud/BSCH Affair," *Agence Europe*, November 13, 1999; "Commission authorises the acquisition by Banco Santander Central Hispano (BSCH) of two Portuguese banks belonging to the Champalimaud Group," European Commission, IP/00/21, January 12, 2000; "Champalimaud—EU closes infringement cases against Portugal," European Commission, IP/00/296, March 27, 2000.

[48] See, e.g., Lisa Jucca and Thomas Atkins, "Twin bank bids offer EU chance to spur mergers," *Reuters News*, April 1, 2005; "Background Paper: Obstacles to cross-border mergers and acquisitions in the financial sector," p. 7.

[49] "Financial Services: Implementing the Framework for Financial Markets: Action Plan," European Commission, COM(1999) 232, May 11, 1999, p. 4.

[50] Ibid., pp. 19–31.

[51] Ibid., p. 9.

[52] "Expert Group on Banking, Financial Services Action Plan: Progress and Prospects, Final Report," May 2004, p. 6. The "Benelux" countries are Belgium, the Netherlands, and Luxembourg. Originally "created for the Benelux Economic Union," the name "is now used in a more generic way." See "Benelux," available at http://en.wikipedia.org/wiki/Benelux.

[53] Expert Group on Banking, pp. 8–9.

[54] Ibid., pp. 10, 16.

[55] "Post-FSAP: CEBS' Comments on the Final Report of the Expert Group on Banking," CEBS/04/61, September 2004, p. 5 (emphasis removed).

[56] See, e.g. European Commission Green Paper on Financial Services Policy (2005-2010), COM(2005) 177, pp. 3, 10–11; see also Annex I, pp. 3, 9. In the commission's view the "debate is not about the overall level of 'foreign' participation in individual Member States' financial sectors," but "rather about whether or not national supervisors use solely prudential criteria to assess the merits or demerits of a particular merger or acquisition. Supervision should not be misused for protectionist purposes," Annex I, p. 12; see also Charlie McCreevy, "The Future of banking policy in the Union," speech/05/191, March 22, 2005, and Charlie McCreevy, "European Banking—Challenges and changes ahead," speech/05/294, May 20, 2005 (speeches by the European Commissioner for Internal Market and Services).

Such tensions between European and member state regulators are further reflected in positions on potentially clarifying the M&A approval process outlined in the EU Banking Directive. See, e.g., "Call for Technical Advice (No. 1) from the Committee of European Banking Supervisors (CEBS)," European Commission, January 18, 2005; "Commission consultation on obstacles to cross-border mergers and acquisitions in financial sector—Frequently asked questions," European Commission, memo/05/131, April 18, 2005; "Technical advice to the European Commission on a review of Article 16 of Directive 2000/12/EC," CEBS/05/76, May 31, 2005.

RAWI ABDELAL

DAVID LANE

Chrysanthemum and Dragon: JAFCO Asia in China

The past is a foreign country; they do things differently there.

—L. P. Hartley, The Go-Between

In the autumn of 2002, JAFCO Asia, a subsidiary of JAFCO Co., Ltd., became the first foreign private equity firm to open an office in Beijing's Haidian Science Park. The park, widely known as China's Silicon Valley, was home to China's fastest growing and most promising technology firms. For JAFCO Asia, the decision was important and symbolic.

JAFCO was believed to be the only Japanese private equity firm operating in China. As such, Managing Director Vincent Chan observed, "JAFCO is the bridge between Japan and China."[1] Yet under that bridge the waters appeared increasingly choppy. While the economic relationship between Japan and China had grown close, their political relations had not. In April 2005, anti-Japanese rioting in China lasted nearly two weeks and led to the damage of Japanese department stores in Chengdu and Shenzhen and the removal of Japanese goods from store shelves in northeast China. As usual, contested history was one of the sparks, as Chinese protestors objected to what they considered to be a revisionist history of Japan's wartime experience.[2]

Despite these ongoing "hot economics, cool politics," as they were described in Japan, almost no one benefited from the persistent tensions. Some Japanese firms had begun to reassess their commitment to China. Observed JAFCO's President and CEO, Toshiaki Ito, "The political tensions with China change the instincts of Japanese firms. It is very difficult to divide politics from economics."[3] Much was at stake for Asia. Would capital-rich Japan and capital-poor China find a way to transcend their troubled history? Could JAFCO Asia be a catalyst for cooperation, or would its managers find their own operations affected by the rivalry between Asia's two most important countries?

The mix of formal rules and informal practices that governed foreign private equity firms in China was complex in the extreme. Opening an office in Beijing signified a renewal of JAFCO Asia's efforts to master these challenges, and coincided with an acceleration of the firm's investments. But JAFCO's first years of engagement with China had not been notably successful, and without some fundamental changes there was little reason to believe that the addition of a physical presence there would yield better results now. With its establishment of the Beijing office, however, some wondered if JAFCO had discovered the secret to success in China.

Japan in Asia

For most of the twentieth century, Japan was the preeminent economic power in Asia. Japan's extraordinary post-war economic success created the second largest economy in the world, and as Japan grew, so did the reach of its firms and investors throughout the world. In Asia, Japanese corporations created regional production networks that spurred growth in and helped integrate the economies of neighboring countries. In contrast to post-war European regionalism, which was deeply institutionalized and codified, Asian regionalism primarily reflected the impact of Japanese firms' technology and capital. Networks of overseas Chinese also connected the national economies of Asia, but primarily on a commercial rather than technological basis.[4]

As the dollar declined in value following the 1985 Plaza Accord, Japanese firms began to relocate manufacturing and assembly facilities to low-cost production centers overseas. At home, these factors combined with low yen interest rates, which promoted domestic asset inflation and heavy buying of foreign assets throughout the late 1980s. Land prices in Tokyo and Osaka, as well as the Nikkei stock market average, more than tripled in less than a decade. The party came to a sudden end, however, when the central Bank of Japan in 1989 moved to constrain speculation by raising interest rates, deflating Japan's asset bubble and ushering in over a decade of anemic performance.[5]

The stagnant decade changed interpretations of the Japanese model at home and abroad. In Asia, the model was admired less, and the fears of the U.S. in the 1980s of being overtaken completely appeared in retrospect quaint and over-hyped. Japan's economy languished in recession as banks sought to recover from huge loan losses in the bubble's aftermath.[6] Consumer spending withered, despite several years of deflation in the late 1990s. Even as the Bank of Japan pushed the real interest rate toward zero, corporations focused on reducing costs, and sharply curtailed new investment at home (see **Exhibits 1** and **2**). Instead, firms and financial institutions both looked overseas for better returns.

Japanese Investment in China

Japanese firms weathered the prolonged downturn of the 1990s in part by moving manufacturing to China. During this time, Japan and other emerging market economies in East Asia became the primary source of China's annual $64 billion inflows of foreign direct investment (FDI), most of which was invested in manufacturing for export (see **Exhibit 3**).[7] Japan accounted for about 9% of China's annual FDI in the mid-2000s, though this relatively humble slice of the whole masked the fact that Japan's investments tended to be in manufactures—autos, photocopiers, and a broad array of consumer electronics over time—that were sophisticated relative to the products made by the average FDI plant in China.

Wherever a leading Japanese manufacturer set up shop in China, its main subcontractors and the emergence of local supply chains soon followed. Japanese government statistics for 2004 put the number of Japanese firms operating in China at 31,855 and the cumulative stock of Japanese direct investment in China at $54.5 billion. Japanese companies had created an estimated 9.2 million local jobs and paid RMB 49 billion in Chinese taxes in 2004.[8] Together with the complementarity of their economies—China imported Japanese high technology while exporting foodstuffs and commodities—Japanese investment helped China replace the United States as Japan's leading trade partner in 2004 (see **Exhibit 4**).

Financing the Rise of China

The rise of China since the reform process initiated by Deng Xiaoping in the late 1970s was extraordinary. In the following 30 years China became the fastest growing economy in the world in almost every single year (see **Exhibits 5** and **6**).[9] China's embrace of foreign capital played an important part in its development strategy. Over the decade ending in 2005, foreigners invested half a trillion dollars in FDI in China.[10] In 2004, FDI accounted for over 70% of China's total capital inflows, and foreign-invested firms produced about half of China's exports.[11]

Foreign Direct Investment

For most of two decades beginning in 1980, FDI dominated foreign investment in China, at first strictly through joint ventures with state-owned enterprises (SOEs). Export performance and foreign exchange balance requirements initially were imposed on foreign-invested firms, but as such restrictions gradually eased, FDI grew from a trickle in the early 1980s to a flood in the middle of the 1990s (see **Exhibits 7** and **8**).[12] A mix of tax and other incentives encouraged the trend: no corporate income tax was levied on the first two years of a foreign-invested firm's profits, and the firm paid only 15% in subsequent years, "less than half the normal rate of 33% paid by Chinese companies."[13] By the late 1990s, the growing complexity of China's economy, the experience of two decades of FDI, government concern over its weak banks and SOEs, and preparation for China's WTO accession all combined to loosen the central government's grip on FDI, not least as provincial and local governments rushed to solicit foreign investors and foreign exchange restrictions were eased. In the early 1990s, the central government allowed the creation of wholly owned foreign enterprises (WOFEs), a move that encouraged further FDI by foreign firms previously deterred by the management effort required of joint ventures and the intellectual property rights issues they sometimes created. By 1998, WOFEs had displaced joint ventures as the typical vehicle for new direct investments in China.

Confronting China's SOEs, Property Rights, and Banks

Throughout this period, China's SOEs and banks remained nagging hobbles on the economy. More than two-thirds of SOEs incurred losses in 1998, and the government estimated that one-third of them were effectively bankrupt.[14] Although the state did its best to rationalize underperforming SOEs, it was constrained both by their size and scope—the largest SOEs employed hundreds of thousands and included dedicated housing, medical, and educational facilities—and by the potential social and political impact of mass unemployment for a regime officially dedicated to the well-being of its workers. Despite these constraints, the state successfully shed 26 million SOE employees between 1998 and 2001. These competed for new positions with the 15 million new workers joining the labor market each year for an estimated 11–12 million additional jobs being generated annually in China.[15]

More dramatic than the challenge of urban unemployment was the plight of China's rural workers, large numbers of whom migrated illegally to the cities in search of alternatives to farming. In many cases, farmers were thrown off the land by local government officials who enriched themselves by transferring land rights to developers interested in building housing, shopping complexes, or factories. China's farmers typically found themselves illegally dispossessed of the means of earning a living and unqualified to live or work at the premises that replaced their fields. These developments prompted increasingly frequent popular protests at the local level, some resulting in violent clashes. Official sources reported 74,000 incidents in 2004.[16]

Sustaining the SOEs were China's four state banks, which, in doing so, held back Joseph Schumpeter's "creative destruction" and at the same time left many of China's more viable potential borrowers out of the formal market for capital. By the mid-1990s, loans to SOEs accounted for more than 70% of the total loans made by China's state banks. Significant numbers of these loans eventually went unpaid, and became non-performing (NPLs). At year-end 2001, official estimates put the share of NPLs in total loans of the four banks at more than 30%. Although the state in 1999 moved to reduce NPLs, improving bank balance sheets and bringing their capital adequacy ratios into line with international standards, NPLs in mid-2005 remained at $122 billion, 10% of the state banks' total loans. NPLs elsewhere in the banking system and those already transferred off bank balance sheets combined with these to yield a total of $304 billion, equivalent to 18% of GDP. Unofficial estimates were much higher.[17] Moreover, persistent low interest rates fueled a continuing boom in fixed asset investment. As banks added $1 trillion in new loans to their books between 2003 and 2005, NPLs as a share of GDP was forecast to rise, even in the face of growing GDP.[18]

To reduce the pressures to lend cheaply to SOEs that would likely never repay, China's central bank liberalized bank lending rates in October 2004 to more closely reflect the risk of lending to newer or smaller private sector firms. The central bank also linked required reserve ratios to bank asset quality and capital adequacy: weaker banks faced higher reserve ratios and, therefore, limits on business expansion. Foreign financial institutions for the first time were allowed to take ownership of Chinese banks, up to 20% of equity as of 2003.[19]

Capital Markets

China's stock markets, which opened in Shanghai and Shenzhen in late 1990, existed primarily to raise capital for China's state-owned enterprises. Although the government in 2000 proposed establishing a new NASDAQ-style organization in Shenzhen—the Growth Enterprise Market, to fund small and medium non-state firms—no action had been taken to do so by the time of the case, and private or quasi-private firms that in some cases were becoming among China's most competitive and well-known (see **Exhibit 9**) looked instead to the Shanghai market or abroad for capital. By 2002, over 1,200 companies were listed on the Shanghai and Shenzhen stock exchanges, up more than 60% from five years earlier.[20] At the end of 2005, 1,520 Chinese firms were listed domestically and abroad. Of this total, only 40 firms were not state-owned enterprises.[21]

Because of the division of SOE shares into tradable and nontradable categories, observers estimated that in 2005 only 40% of the shares of publicly listed firms were tradable. The ownership dilution potentially created by any eventual conversion of nontradable to tradable shares placed downward pressure on China's stock markets; share prices had fallen every year since 2001. Poor performance and a government effort to reform the shareholding structure of listed firms had virtually closed the markets to new IPOs since mid-2004. In late December 2005, even a leading government official publicly advised Chinese firms to put overseas listing ahead of an IPO in Shanghai or Shenzhen.[22]

Capital Controls

From the start, China's reforms sought foreign capital to the extent that it helped transfer technology. This favored FDI over foreign borrowing and portfolio inflows. Over time, the government began to relax restrictions on foreign borrowing by corporations, and expanded the market for all share classes.[a] The government declared in the mid-1990s that it intended to make the capital account convertible by 2000. In early 2006, however, this remained undone due to continuing pressures on the renminbi.

After maintaining a peg to the U. S. dollar at RMB 8.28 since 1994, the Chinese government in July 2005 permitted a 2.1% revaluation of the currency, the first and thus far only direct change to its foreign exchange regime.[23] However, most observers believed that China was seeking to broaden currency convertibility, initially by allowing the RMB to trade in a wider band against a trade-weighted portfolio of currencies. As early as 1996, the RMB had been made fully convertible for current account transactions, allowing importers to purchase foreign exchange without restriction and exporters to retain all export earnings.[24] As state spokespeople repeatedly pointed out, however, any such developments would follow China's own timetable. February 2006 saw additional slight movement, as China's four largest banks signed on with Reuters to begin trading 40 non-RMB spot currency pairs, but it remained to be seen how easily Chinese banks and exporters could manage a freer-floating currency.[25]

Despite current account liberalization and slight adjustments to the exchange rate, China kept in force capital controls on capital market securities, money market instruments, derivatives, commercial and financial credit, financial guarantees, direct investment, real estate, and personal capital (see **Exhibit 10**).[26] China's capital control regime and its sluggish liberalization ensured that all foreign capital allowed into China would remain tightly restricted unless explicitly freed from review. Additional regulations continued to limit foreign portfolio flows, and strict international loan ceilings limited external borrowing.[27] Reflecting the state's cautious stance, China's ratio of external debt to GDP remained around 15% since the early 1990s.[28]

Capitalism with Socialist Characteristics or Market Socialism?

As China continued to grow and liberalize, the contrast between the official Marxist ideology of China's ruling Communist Party and the capitalist business practices that had led to the economic boom grew more obvious. Increasingly the Party derived its legitimacy from economic growth rather than Marxism. JAFCO's Toshiaki Ito noted that the paradox was even higher for his industry: "China is a socialist country, but private equity is an extreme form of capitalism."[29]

The Party reacted to the potential for a crisis of legitimacy in a variety of ways. The Party first encouraged greater nationalist sentiment, to the extent that anti-Japanese nationalists appeared to operate beyond state control.[30] In early 2006, the Party sought also to revive its traditional basis of legitimacy by investing $25 million to "modernize Marxism and make it relevant to the contradictions of today's China." A new Marxism Institute was created and allocated $25 million to bring together several hundred Marxist scholars to reinterpret the classics of socialism and communism and produce more than 100 new textbooks.[31]

---

[a] A-shares (and B-shares) were shares in Chinese firms listed in Shanghai and Shenzhen available for purchase only with renminbi (foreign exchange), initially for Chinese (non-Chinese) buyers only. H-shares were China-domiciled companies listed in Hong Kong, and N-shares were China-domiciled companies listed in New York (and elsewhere outside China and Hong Kong). Eswar Prasad and Shang-Jin Wei, "The Chinese Approach to Capital Inflows: Patterns and Possible Explanations," NBER Working Paper 11306, April 2005, p. 18.

Venture Capital and Private Equity in China

Though venture capital in China was given the green light in March 1998, it was not until September 2001 that the Chinese Ministry of Commerce (MOFCOM) issued regulations allowing foreign-invested venture capital firms and inviting their comment on its provisions.[32] Moving quickly, foreign venture capitalists found opportunities in China's private sector starting in early 2002. According to JAFCO Asia's Chan, "We hear of four or five deals being invested in a single month, but a clear division is appearing. You have local companies being invested by local, onshore venture capitalists, then you have the offshore companies. There are a lot of deals being closed, but there are really two markets."[33] A vice president at Walden International concurred with Chan's caution: "It has always been difficult to close deals in China despite the overall level of deals being done. There might be four or five deals per month, but there are more than 200 venture capital firms in Hong Kong and China. It is not every firm closing a deal every month."[34] The competition for deals was compounded by the increasing presence of Taiwanese venture capitalists (VCs) in China supporting local firms that moved to the mainland to lower their labor costs. Nearly 200 venture capital firms were registered in Taiwan.[35]

New rules amending the 2001 MOFCOM regulations, the Rules on Administration of Foreign-Invested Venture Capital Investment Enterprises (FIVCIE), were issued in January 2003. The revised regulations reduced the capital requirement for foreign investors to $10 million and relaxed requirements on the organizational structure of FIVCIEs. Although the new rules made it easier for foreigners to invest in Chinese start-ups, there remained, in the words of one report:

> No proper exit mechanism because of the stock market's inability to attract and serve high-technology companies and the delay in setting up a NASDAQ-style exchange in Shenzhen. Consequently, venture capitalists exit their investments by listing them on an overseas exchange or by transferring shares to other investors. Another problem is that venture capitalists have to use their own capital in their investments; they are not allowed to borrow the funds.[36]

By March 2004, China had by some estimates 300 venture capital firms of its own, with assets worth a combined RMB 50 billion (see **Exhibit 11** for a ranking of the top domestic and foreign VCs operating in China),[37] and official data put mergers and acquisitions at 5% of China's FDI as of mid-2004.[38] Venture capital firms raised $4.1 billion worldwide in 2005 for investment in China, nearly five times the average of the previous three years.[39]

The Entry Solution

Part of the challenge for VC firms in China was regulatory. Most foreign VCs did not invest directly in Chinese companies before 2003 because of foreign exchange regulations and the inconvertibility of the renminbi, corporate and tax laws, and the young domestic IPO and merger markets. Rather, they invested in the Chinese start-up's offshore holding company. This allowed both the investment and the exit to occur offshore. Onshore, the VC firm had a representative office that managed the investment in the portfolio's onshore entity. A more complex situation arose when a foreign VC wanted to invest in a restricted sector of the economy, such as Internet services or broadband applications. In this case, the start-up established a licensing and service revenue-generating vehicle (the PRC vehicle) to bypass the legal and regulatory constraints. The offshore entity and the PRC entity would route the revenue generated by the PRC entity back to the offshore holding company.[40]

This structure facilitated exits by allowing companies to list on non-domestic exchanges. In the first half of 2004, foreign VC firms operating in China had achieved 36 exits, 15 of them by foreign firms. Nine VC-backed companies went public outside China: four on the Hong Kong main exchange, three on NASDAQ, and one each on the Hong Kong GEM (Growth Enterprise Market) and the NYSE. The other 27 exits occurred via management buyout, merger, and, most frequently, trade sale (sale to another industry player). Management buyout was much less frequent, though on the rise by 2005.

The practice of investing in Chinese firms through their offshore holding companies created some managerial challenges around the shareholding control of the local PRC companies and the appointment of local legal representatives. Still, Hiroshi Yamada, President and CEO of JAFCO Asia, argued that the "investments had to be in U.S. dollars. Otherwise the foreign private equity market would not exist. Without these offshore vehicles we never would have invested this much money in China."[41] Often foreign private equity and venture capital firms found it necessary to educate their Chinese partners about the process. "Particularly with early-stage investments," Yamada noted, "it is necessary for us to teach the managers in whose firms we invest how to create firms in the Cayman Islands."[42]

As JAFCO Asia's Michael Chow[b] added, "Everyone does it this way."[43] For these reasons, most foreign venture capital firms did not have a dedicated presence in China, but instead ran their China investments out of Hong Kong or set up funds (many listed on the London and New York Stock Exchanges) to invest in foreign firms that themselves operated in China.[44] Such direct investment funds effectively served as venture capital funds for joint ventures in China.[45]

The Exit Problem

If you ask VCs in China what is their No. 1 issue, 99 out of 100 will say "exit." The other one just hasn't been in China for long.

—Wu Xin, Shanghai NewMargin Venture Capital partner46

Exiting China investments was problematic for several reasons, said JAFCO Asia's legal director, Xiaoning Liu: (1) strategic foreign investors are required to hold A-shares for at least three years after acquiring them, and (2) initial shareholders in a foreign invested company limited by shares (CLS) cannot transfer their shares within three years of its establishment. Those willing to wait that long to see a return also faced market risk created by the overhang of state-owned shares. Rarely did VC firms exit through listings on the two Chinese exchanges in Shanghai and Shenzhen, as the listing requirements, such as three consecutive profitable years, were virtually prohibitive for young companies. The new SME board also presented challenges, as it shared the larger exchanges' three-year-profit requirement along with other burdensome strictures. Bankruptcy laws, under discussion since at least 1991, had yet to be formalized, though optimistic sentiment in September 2004 was that they at last would be introduced sometime in the following two years.[47] Legislation of a new property rights law was shelved in early 2006 by the need for the state to be seen to be addressing the growing rural-urban income divide.[48]

Venture capitalists faced additional constraints. Unlisted Chinese companies usually took a corporate form that made it difficult for investors to be involved in management. Among other restrictions, China banned the granting of stock options and the issuance of stock other than common shares, and companies were allowed to issue new shares only after being profitable and paying dividends for three consecutive years. Similarly, China's rules for stock market listing required all

[b] Director and Chief Representative of JAFCO Asia.

applicants to be profitable for three consecutive years and have more than 1,000 pre-existing shareholders. Furthermore, PRC company law banned venture capital companies from selling their shares in firms for one year after a listing, and any subsequent sale could not occur in the open market, but only through direct negotiations with potential purchasers. And, unlike the United States or Japan, China levied capital gains taxes on venture capital firms.[49]

Beginning in April 2004, China allowed foreign investors to take stakes in its publicly listed companies. Financial institutions, such as HSBC Holdings, Citigroup, and Newbridge Capital, all moved quickly to take highly publicized stakes in Chinese financial institutions, and U.S. Internet giants Amazon, eBay, Google, and Yahoo made similar acquisitions in the Chinese Internet sector. For the VCs that had entered China several years before, such trade sales to foreign firms created an opportunity to exit earlier investments.[50] Google's $10 million commitment in June 2004 to Chinese search engine Baidu was welcome news to the foreign investors who committed $11.2 million to its first three rounds of financing.[51] Yahoo completed its purchase of Beijing-based 3721 Network Software, conferring internal rates of return of 224% and 84% to early venture investors JAFCO Asia and IDG Technology, respectively.[52] Ebay's purchase of online auctioneer Eachnet for $180 million gave AsiaTech Ventures—which had invested in Chinese start-ups—a good exit opportunity too.[53]

Local versus Foreign Approaches

The increasing dominance of foreign venture capitalists in start-up financing led Chinese private equity firms to move toward buyout strategies in 2004 and 2005. The bet was that local consortia could capitalize on their local knowledge to turn around state-owned assets. This approach required less capital than early-stage financing, and local firms presumably were advantaged by superior local knowledge.

Legend Hony Capital, for example, had helped bring a former state-owned glass maker to market in a Hong Kong listing within two years. Hony held two rounds of fundraising since 2003, raising over $148 million from such backers as Goldman Sachs and its parent, Legend Holdings. While Legend Hony Capital focused on buyouts, another Legend Holdings investment vehicle, Legend Capital, had attracted $105 million in funds to invest in emerging technology companies.

In a bid to foster domestic private equity firms, China's National Development and Reform Commission—China's chief economic planning body— in late 2005 announced Measure No. 39, rules that offered domestic venture capitalists better tax treatment and easier exit routes than those available to foreign rivals. Firms eligible for domestic treatment were required to have exclusively Chinese nationals among top management and investors. Domestic firms would need capitalization of RMB 30 million ($3.7 million) rather than the RMB 40 million ($4.9 million) required of foreign firms. The minimum investment for each investor in domestic firms would be RMB 1 million ($122,000), not the RMB 8 million ($1 million) required of investors in foreign funds. Domestic firms would also benefit from more streamlined government approvals and less strict regulations.[54]

In addition to straight venture capital, SOE privatization and the growing strength of the private economy created increasing opportunities for venture capitalists to fund management buyouts. As JAFCO Asia's Chan noted, "Naturally people believe there will be more opportunities in collective enterprises and privately held enterprises. And there will be more state assets being privatized or disposed of, following in the footsteps of other Asian nations such as South Korea and Japan. There will be great opportunities both for venture capitalists and investment bankers."[55]

Supply and Demand

Despite the challenging environment, China's rapid growth and the sheer number of firms and dollars chasing venture investments there quickly drove up deal pricing. Chan gave the example of a Chinese firm that demanded a valuation equal to that of a South Korean competitor with triple the annual revenue: "It's because China is hot. There's a China premium."[56] "You make more money in the bear market," he added.[57] In May 2004, Carlyle Group opened a Shanghai office and said it planned to invest $1 billion in China over the next 18 months. Smaller players such as Colony Capital also set up a presence in China.[58]

At least it could be argued that the premium was appropriate given the newly found profitability of numerous Chinese Internet firms, the growing probability that technology companies would be granted public listings, and growing foreign interest in acquiring Chinese market leaders in lieu of building a local presence from scratch. The argument was that China's rapid growth would boost the sales of local market leaders and create a high P/E (price-to-earnings) multiple for the acquirer.

Said one Hong Kong-based venture capitalist, "We've got people willing to commit dollars. Two years ago, it was all capital-raising" for Chinese companies.[59] By mid-2004, around 40% of inquiries of his firm were potential foreign buyers of Chinese companies rather than mainlanders trying to raise capital.[60] Despite the ready supply of funds for investment, IDG Technology Venture Investment, one of the biggest venture capital firms in China, projected annual returns on investments in high tech Chinese companies to range between 45%–65% in the period 2000–2010, compared with projected 25%–35% annual returns in comparable U.S. firms.[61]

JAFCO and JAFCO Asia's Experience in China

Founded in April 1973 with capital of ¥500 million, JAFCO was Japan's dominant venture capital investment company by the start of 2006 (and the eighth-largest in the world in 2002), with ¥460 billion ($4 billion) in assets under management worldwide.[62] Over its 32 years of operations, JAFCO had invested in some 2,000 companies in Japan, of which 30% had gone public. Through JAFCO's overseas operations, the company had invested in another 600 companies globally. JAFCO was 35% owned by the Nomura Group (as of March 2006), which provided a source of capital and marketing to JAFCO, but otherwise left management to JAFCO.

JAFCO articulated its value to potential portfolio companies as "comprehensive business development services to accelerate expansion across Asian markets, especially Japan." Beyond its VC roles, therefore, JAFCO offered market research to assess opportunities in the region; advice to management teams on local and regional strategy; strategic meetings with potential customers, distributors, and partners; and assistance in identifying, negotiating, and structuring joint ventures, OEM partnerships, and distributorships (see **Exhibit 12**).

JAFCO Asia was set up in Singapore in 1990, initially as a joint venture between Nomura Securities and JAFCO, to invest primarily Japanese funds in Southeast Asian economies. Over time, and as a result of poor early results and the Asian financial crisis of 1997–98, the locus of investment shifted to Hong Kong and an interest in emerging regional opportunities, emphasizing high technology firms located in greater China. Most of the investments in Thailand, Indonesia, and the Philippines were written down. As Ito recalled, "In Southeast Asia we had covered too wide an industry area without focus, and our activities were opportunistic. The financial crisis was, for us, an important lesson, as well as a turning point."[63]

Another important decision was for JAFCO Asia to acquire local knowledge through human capital. During the 1990s, JAFCO field offices were staffed primarily by Japanese managers dispatched from Tokyo and chosen by JAFCO and Nomura. By the end of the decade, the decision was made to hire local managers and give them a great deal of autonomy from Tokyo. According to Ito, "Venture capital is above all a local business. So we need local executives with local, non-public knowledge."[64] This decision was symbolized and codified when JAFCO Asia became a wholly owned unit of JAFCO in 1999. JAFCO Asia's local management team acquired control of the investment decision-making process as well. "The field offices have complete autonomy from Tokyo," observed JAFCO's Munetsugu Wakamatsu.[c] "In Tokyo, we just receive progress reports. The decisions are made there."[65]

Since that time, JAFCO Asia had focused on technology-related companies, investing around $200 million (as of March 2006) in Asia, mostly in China, Taiwan, and Korea. In China, JAFCO's favorite technology sectors included service platform infrastructure providers, content providers, integrated circuit chip designers, billing or payment software creators, makers of firewalls and other security products, and storage and data managers. The firm's main criteria in selecting venture capital investments included the quality of the management team, the company's sales and marketing capability, and the available and potential markets for the company's products or services.[66]

JAFCO Asia opened its first representative office in China in Beijing on October 7, 2002, initially working in cooperation with the administrative office of Haidian Science Park and VCs such as Legend Capital, a local venture capital firm affiliated with Legend Holdings, owners of China's dominant computer maker, Lenovo.[67] Legend Holdings was 65% owned by the Chinese Academy of Sciences, the state-run research organization that had spawned a number of China's other high technology leaders. As Yamada observed, "Legend Capital speaks the same language as we do."[68] While continuing to meet with Legend Capital regularly, after five years JAFCO Asia had co-invested with Legend just once.

The JAFCO Asia office represented the first foothold in China by any Japanese venture capital firm, though Nippon Technology Venture Partners—run by a former JAFCO VC—was expected to follow, and IDG Technology had set up a representative office in Beijing as early as 1990.[69] The JAFCO Asia Beijing office sought out and managed investments in Beijing, Tianjin, Chengdu, Xian, and Dalian (north China); JAFCO Asia's investments in companies located in south China were managed by its Hong Kong office.

As of November 2002, JAFCO Asia had committed approximately ¥3 billion to seven companies operating in China. Because FIVCIEs at this time were not yet permitted in China, each of JAFCO Asia's portfolio companies was registered in either Hong Kong or the Cayman Islands.[70] By May 2004, JAFCO Asia had invested in 12 Chinese companies, including China Grentech, a maker of wireless communication system that listed on the NASDAQ in March 2006, and China Wireless, a wireless solution provider that listed on the HK Stock Exchange in December 2004 (see **Exhibit 14** for a list of JAFCO investments in China).[71] JAFCO Asia was also the second-largest shareholder and the largest institutional investor in 3721, a keyword search provider that was sold subsequently to Yahoo China for $120 million in late 2003. In September 2004, JAFCO was reportedly one of several foreign venture capitalists along with the Carlyle Group and Colony Capital to have earmarked over $100 million to China.[72] The same year, Japan's Shinsei Bank set up a $196 million China fund with China's CITIC Capital Markets Holdings, another instance of a Japanese financial organization working with a strong Chinese partner.[73] At the end of 2004, Zero2ipo, a Chinese private equity research and

---

[c] Managing Director of JAFCO Tokyo.

advisory firm, cited JAFCO Asia as the 13th most active venture capital firm in China; JAFCO Asia's Chan was named 10th most active venture capitalist.[74]

By 2006, JAFCO Asia had offices in Beijing, Hong Kong, Seoul, Singapore, and Taipei employing a total of 17 investment professionals. These 17 included an investment committee of four, headed by CEO and President Yamada. Four of the remaining professionals focused on opportunities in China, three focused on Southeast Asia, three on South Korea, and three on Taiwan. China had seen a decade of economic growth at levels approximating 10% a year and was expected to continue growing into the future, with strong demand for IT infrastructure. Korea had a strong electronics industry and offered many opportunities for technology ventures with major electronics makers. Taiwan remained the world leader in semiconductor industries and the source of many opportunities from related ventures and spin-offs.

At the start of 2006, JAFCO Asia had invested in various stages and sectors in eight countries, typically entrusting $2 million to $6 million in early to middle-stage technology-related companies, with a strong emphasis on facilitating Japan-Asia collaboration. JAFCO Asia was lead investor for between two-thirds and three-quarters of its deals and co-led another 15%. The company had board representation about 75% of the time, and observer status another 15% of the time. Deal flow came from JAFCO Asia's own network as well as from JAFCO, Nomura, portfolio companies, fellow VCs, research organizations, and other intermediaries. Between November 2000 and September 2005, the JAFCO Asia team reviewed 2,948 companies on a preliminary basis, conducted due diligence on 720 of these, and ultimately invested in 75.

The JAFCO Asia Technology Fund I (JATF I) focused on early and middle-stage investments, but had already seen 10 listings and five trade sales within its first five years ending March 2006. As of October 1, 2005, JATF I had invested $136 million in 49 companies since raising $178 million in November 2000. JATF II had invested $60 million in 29 companies after raising $100 million in February 2004 (see **Exhibit 13**).[75]

The JAFCO Asia Business Model

Local Knowledge   The empowerment of local knowledge was a critical part of the JAFCO Asia business model. Although most Western venture capital firms in China had hired local managers, for almost all of them, decision-making authority was at home. JAFCO Asia operated autonomously from Tokyo, however. "In terms of decision making, we are much more localized, and much quicker, than the Americans," observed Yamada.[76]

In practice, such local knowledge required an understanding of the practices of Chinese managers and the idiosyncrasies of the Chinese market. "In China," argued Chan, "we are not looking for firms that created a disruptive technology. We are trying to discern those firms that have a disruptive business model that can succeed in the Chinese market." Chan also suggested that change was the rule. Reflecting on a missed opportunity to invest in a firm with an apparently unworkable business model, Chan suggested that, in China, "you cannot use history as your guide. You must understand China-specific business and social practices that can make otherwise impractical business models successful."[77]

Incubation and Business Development   Compared with its Western competitors, JAFCO Asia tended to invest in firms at a much earlier stage of development. This practice implied that JAFCO Asia would have more influence on the development of the business itself, and executives prided themselves on the fact that, as Chow put it, "When the entrepreneur needs advice, he calls us first."[78]

JAFCO Asia's model required patience, of course, as well as a tolerance for failure. Chan described his colleagues' thinking: "We are much better than the Americans at building companies. This is a patient exercise, inconsistent with the late-stage, quick-turnaround, I-banker mentality."[79] This approach permeated the organization. In Tokyo, Ito argued that JAFCO's "value added is as a bridge—between Chinese and Japanese firms, between Chinese firms and Western and Japanese capital. We make introductions, cultivate new relationships, and help to construct partnerships and alliances. American VCs are the investment banking type: they are interested in a fast turnaround. We incubate. We never take a majority position and try to run or turn around a firm. Ours is a different style."[80]

Relationships and Bridges   Chinese firms eyeing the Japanese market found JAFCO Asia an especially useful partner. "Our value-added is to help build companies, enable their expansion overseas, and, because of our dominant position in Japan, connect them with Japanese buyers, suppliers, and partners," argued Chan. "We help them go to the Japanese market, and we are the only ones who can do that."[81]

JAFCO Asia's executives also encouraged the firms with which they worked to ultimately list in Tokyo. Indeed, as Yamada argued, "At this moment, the Tokyo market can provide better valuations than NASDAQ."[82] Moreover, another manager pointed out, few China technology companies could command even in Hong Kong the P/E ratios they could receive on NASDAQ.

Improving Corporate Governance   What most concerned JAFCO Asia's executives was not deal flow, which, as Chow observed, was "not the big challenge." Rather, "many Chinese managers do not yet have a fully developed concept of corporate governance."[83] For both monitoring and exit purposes, JAFCO Asia insisted on educating its portfolio companies about the importance of raising their corporate governance standards in order to meet future listing and trade sale requirements. Notably, accounting treatments for Chinese companies differed substantially from international norms, and portfolio companies typically devoted significant resources to bring them into alignment before a public listing. Virtually all ventures required restructuring before venture funding or an IPO.

The Huachang Investment

In early 2004, JAFCO Asia invested in Wuhan-based Huachang Corporation, receiving board representation and becoming Huachang's sole institutional investor. Huachang was an innovative wireless application provider, delivering integrated software and hardware wireless solutions to China's mobile sector, including back-end wireless value-added platforms and front-end smart terminals. Huachang developed smart terminals and related wireless data applications around its own, self-developed operating system for both corporate customers and telecom carriers. The operating system eliminated the need to pay licensing fees to third-party technology providers and gave Huachang the autonomy to design and refine smartphone functions and to develop applications and technical innovations that met the market's changing requirements in a timely manner.

In 1990s and early 2000s, Huachang supplied wireless coverage solutions for the paging networks of China's telecom carriers. As this market matured and demand waned, JAFCO Asia used its board position to recommend that Huachang discontinue active marketing of this product line, advocating instead that Huachang concentrate its R&D spending on smartphone technology and wireless value-added services. The board agreed, and decided to position Huachang as the preferred wireless system solution provider to China's telecom carriers.

At the time of JAFCO Asia's investment in 2004, Huachang was well positioned to capitalize on the opportunities arising from deregulation in China's telecom industry, the growing popularity of wireless applications, and its own technological advances. The 2003 restructuring of China's telecommunications sector allowed carriers to provide new value-added and data services, and tolerated their build-out of localized mobile service on the back of existing fixed-line networks (smartphones). Competition among telecom carriers intensified. To enhance competitiveness and tap new revenue streams, the carriers sought to provide more comprehensive value-added services and to develop innovative industry applications of wireless services on top of basic voice services. These developments created opportunities for solution and equipment providers such as Huachang with technical expertise, a track record, and a nationwide service network.

JAFCO Asia managers believed that Huachang's success was due in no small part to its understanding of wireless communications and the unique requirements of China's market. Through years of experience of offering wireless telecom solutions, Huachang developed and accumulated core technologies in the areas of telecommunication protocol software development, RF system design, embedded real-time control, and its proprietary operating system for wireless terminals.

With Huachang, JAFCO Asia spent a considerable amount of time highlighting the role of the board of directors in driving corporate governance and, thereby, the prosperity and integrity of the company. Said Chan, "In particular, we stressed the importance of integrity. Directors and shareholders should avoid conflicts of interest. Before our investment, therefore, all possible related party transactions and potential conflicts were tabled and ironed out. To meet the good-practice standard, full and prior disclosure of any or potential conflicts was made to the board."

On the basis of JAFCO Asia's efforts and recommendations, Huachang ultimately listed on the Hong Kong Main Board in mid-2005, attracting a broader shareholder base and greater liquidity than its initial plan of listing on the Hong Kong GEM. JAFCO Asia did not appoint an independent board of directors at the time of investment. This was subsequently built in preparation for the IPO.

SAFE and Sound

With increasing offshore financing activities by Chinese individuals and firms, China's State Administration of Foreign Exchange (SAFE) laid the basis for new regulations in early 2005. Two documents were particularly important. On January 24, SAFE issued "Notice of the SAFE on Issues Concerning Improvement in the Administration of Foreign Exchange in Connection with Mergers and Acquisitions by Foreign Investors" (commonly known as Circular #11), which was followed on April 5 by "Notice of the SAFE on Issues Concerning Registration of Offshore Investment by Chinese Domestic Individuals and Foreign Exchange Registration of M&A Transactions by Foreign Investors" (commonly known as Circular #29). The purpose of the circulars was to propose regulations that would establish a reporting system of cross-border financing so that SAFE could effectively monitor foreign exchange flows, protect state-owned assets, and avoid the abuse of tax benefits offered to legitimate foreign investors.[84]

SAFE officials had not intended to deter legitimate, and legal, offshore venture capital and private equity financing of Chinese firms. Foreign investors reacted with alarm, however, and within just a few months, foreign venture capital and private equity flows had fallen by more than half. Because the business model of nearly all such foreign investors involved offshore holding companies, so-called "special purpose vehicles" (SPVs), uncertainty about the new regulations created serious concern within the investment community.

In response to its members' requests, the China Venture Capital Association (CVCA), a venture capital industry organization consisting primarily of foreign venture capital and private fund management companies active in China, formed a special committee, the Public Policies Action Committee (PPAC), to initiate a dialogue with SAFE.

Over the next six months, the CVCA, under the leadership of its PPAC, sought to emphasize to SAFE officials the negative impact of the SAFE circulars. Ultimately the CVCA hoped that SAFE would revise its proposed new rules in a way that would be mutually acceptable. SAFE, the CVCA urged, could still fulfill its regulatory objectives but avoid deterring the legitimate investment of the venture capital/private equity community. The PPAC successfully coordinated a series of productive meetings with SAFE officials, and indeed the CVCA was surprised at the receptiveness of SAFE to its views and recommendations.

On October 21, 2005, SAFE issued Circular #75, "Notice Regarding Certain Administrative Measures on Financing and Inbound Investments by PRC Residents Through Offshore Special Purpose Vehicles." The new circular superseded the previous two (#11 and #29). Circular #75 was largely consistent with the goals set forth in the earlier documents, but it also reopened the door for genuine venture capital and private equity funds to invest with an offshore holding structure in which PRC individual residents were also shareholders. Moreover, the policy regime created by the new circular was, according to the investment community, significantly improved in several other important ways:

- Offshore activities had to be registered with SAFE, but they did not require specific SAFE approval. That registration could be at local SAFE branches, rather than central SAFE, as well.

- Offshore companies were allowed to use funds according to their business plans, whereas the previous circulars mandated the repatriation of funds raised at the offshore SPV level.

- The domestic PRC firm was no longer required to conduct an asset appraisal if it was privately owned.

- SAFE offered greater clarification on the key concepts of "PRC Residents" and "SPVs."

The new circular was warmly welcomed by the venture capital and private equity community, and members of the community suggested that it reflected China's increasingly business-friendly stance in its rule-making process. A number of prominent foreign investors regularly referred to the policy change and the CVCA's lobbying achievement as one of the most significant events of the past decade of foreign investment in China. Financial flows resumed apace.

Past, Prologue, and Promise

In the wake of the April 2005 riots, Japan's External Trade Organization (JETRO) moved quickly to assess their potential damage to economic ties, reporting in June that 37% of the 414 surveyed Japanese firms operating in China expected that their businesses would see an impact of the riots within the fiscal year. Almost 10% of respondents stated that the riots had already affected their business development in China.[85]

Despite its Japanese parent, JAFCO Asia had so far continued to fly under the radar of China's more aggressively anti-Japanese activists and policy makers. The success or failure of private equity was measured at exit, not entry, and JAFCO's few exits had yet to attract much attention. Yet some observers worried that the harvest season for foreign private equity would provoke Chinese complaints about the "excessive returns" enjoyed by foreign investors at the expense of local entrepreneurs. Foreign financial and manufacturing firms had already run into trouble over buyouts of troubled Chinese assets. MOFCOM in 2005 objected to Carlyle's proposed buyout of a major construction equipment maker on the grounds that Carlyle might ultimately sell its stake to a foreign construction equipment group in a trade sale. Similarly, Caterpillar had made little headway in acquiring a presence in China, although no barrier to buyouts in the sector supposedly existed. In the finance sector, Citigroup, JPMorgan, Merrill Lynch, and UBS had all seen deals stalled due to Chinese debate over price and control.[86]

Early in 2006, JAFCO Asia was looking forward to closing a third Asia Technology Fund of $200 million, at least 40% of which would be invested by JAFCO Asia and JAFCO Co., Ltd., and the balance by limited partners contributing at least $1 million each. Would JAFCO's engagement with China be a strategy or a hedge? "We are not necessarily optimistic about our China investments," observed Wakamatsu, "but we would never exclude China from our portfolio."[87] In view of the continuing challenges of investing there, however, was JAFCO Asia justified in devoting a major chunk of JATF III to China? Should JATF III focus exclusively on China? Or was it necessary to continue to wait for the market and the rules to stabilize further?

Exhibit 1 Japan's National Income Accounts, 1995–2005

	1995	1996	1997	1998	1999	2000	2001	2002	2003	2004	2005
JAPAN—GROSS DOMESTIC PRODUCT											
Key indicators											
GDP (% real change pa)	1.87	2.65	1.39	-1.86	-0.11	2.90	0.37	0.14	1.82	2.26	2.60
Nominal GDP (US$ at PPP billions)	2,810.15	2,943.10	3,038.67	3,018.79	3,058.75	3,238.11	3,329.78	3,408.86	3,526.95	3,721.98	3,913.66
National savings											
Gross national savings rate (%)	30.54	30.31	30.46	29.23	27.36	27.79	26.95	25.89	26.26	26.43	27.30
Structure of GDP											
Private consumption (% of GDP)	55.04	55.24	55.30	56.00	57.09	56.38	57.04	57.67	57.35	57.45	57.50
Government consumption (% of GDP)	15.14	15.38	15.40	15.97	16.59	16.93	17.51	18.01	18.00	17.94	17.80
Gross fixed investment (% of GDP)	28.00	28.46	27.67	25.83	25.54	25.26	24.67	23.29	22.95	22.85	23.20
Stockbuilding (% of GDP)	0.43	0.43	0.51	0.31	-0.81	-0.04	0.13	-0.28	0.09	-0.18	0.10
Exports of G&S (% of GDP)	9.16	9.85	10.94	10.96	10.32	11.03	10.59	11.40	11.99	13.35	14.70
Imports of G&S (% of GDP)	7.76	9.35	9.82	9.07	8.72	9.56	9.94	10.09	10.37	11.42	13.20
Domestic demand (% of GDP)	98.59	99.50	98.88	98.11	98.40	98.53	99.36	98.69	98.38	98.06	98.50
Ratios, GDP at factor cost											
Agriculture/GDP	1.88	1.84	1.61	1.60	1.50	1.39	1.34	1.34	1.30	1.30	1.30
Industry/GDP	30.37	30.32	29.80	28.69	28.34	28.66	27.27	26.14	26.08	25.70	25.30
Services/GDP	67.75	67.84	68.59	69.71	70.17	69.95	71.39	72.52	72.61	73.00	73.50
FISCAL AND MONETARY INDICATORS											
Inflation and wages											
Consumer prices (% change pa; av)	-0.13	0.14	1.73	0.66	-0.34	-0.67	-0.73	-0.92	-0.25	-0.01	-0.29
Budgetary indicators											
Budget balance (% of GDP)	-4.71	-5.07	-3.79	-5.53	-7.22	-7.47	-6.12	-7.94	-7.68	-6.46	-6.10
DEMOGRAPHICS AND INCOME											
Income											
GDP per head (US$)	41,828.10	36,792.70	33,633.60	30,421.30	34,397.90	36,717.50	32,219.80	30,737.70	33,274.10	36,008.70	35,880.00
GDP per head ($ at PPP)	22,420.00	23,423.90	24,124.70	23,912.00	24,180.90	25,557.30	26,241.10	26,827.50	27,724.50	29,230.30	30,720.00
Real GDP growth per head (% pa)	1.60	2.40	1.14	-2.09	-0.31	2.74	0.21	0.00	1.70	2.17	2.50

Source: Economist Intelligence Unit.

Exhibit 2   Japan's Balance of Payments, 1995–2004

	1995	1996	1997	1998	1999	2000	2001	2002	2003	2004
Current account balance	111.0	65.8	96.8	118.8	114.6	119.7	87.8	112.5	136.2	172.1
Merchandise trade balance	131.8	83.6	101.6	122.4	123.3	116.7	70.2	93.8	106.4	132.1
Services trade balance	-57.4	-62.3	-54.2	-49.4	-54.2	-47.6	-43.7	-42.2	-33.9	-37.9
Capital account balance	-2.23	-3.29	-4.05	-14.45	-16.47	-9.26	-2.87	-3.32	-4	-4.79
FDI, net	-22.5	-23.2	-22.9	-21.4	-10.0	-23.3	-32.3	-22.9	-22.5	-23.2
Portfolio investment, net	-26.3	-33.8	32.1	-39.2	-27.5	-36.0	-46.3	-106.0	-95.1	23.0
Other investment, net	-4.9	36.3	-123.9	-55.4	1.2	-14.4	29.0	63.0	184.0	20.3
Errors and omissions, net	13.8	0.7	34.3	4.4	17.0	16.9	3.7	0.4	-17.0	-28.9
Gross international reserves	-58.6	-35.1	-6.6	6.2	-76.3	-49.0	-40.5	-46.1	-187.2	-160.9

Source: Casewriter calculation from International Monetary Fund, "International Financial Statistics."

Exhibit 3 Sources of Utilized FDI in China, 1978–2004

Country	Cumulative Utilized FDI: 1978–2004		Annual Utilized FDI by Country (as % of total)					Annual Utilized FDI by Country (in US$bn)
	Amount (US$bn)	% of Total	2000	2001	2002	2003	2004	2004
Hong Kong	242	43%	38%	36%	34%	33%	30%	19.0
United States	48	9%	11%	10%	10%	8%	6%	3.9
Japan	47	8%	7%	9%	8%	9%	9%	5.5
Taiwan	40	7%	6%	6%	8%	6%	5%	3.1
Virgin Islands	37	7%	9%	11%	12%	11%	11%	6.7
South Korea	26	5%	4%	5%	5%	8%	10%	6.2
European Union	--	--	11%	9%	7%	7%	7%	4.7
Total	**564**	**100%**	**100%**	**100%**	**100%**	**100%**	**100%**	**64.0**

Source: Eswar Prasad and Shang-Jin Wei, "The Chinese Approach to Capital Inflows: Patterns and Possible Explanations," NBER Working Paper 11306, April 2005, p. 41; and Wayne M. Morrison, "China's Economic Conditions," CRS Issue Brief for Congress, April 25, 2005, available at http://fpc.state.gov/documents/organization/45465.pdf, accessed September 28, 2005, as presented in Laura Alfaro and Rafael Di Tella, "China: To Float or Not To Float? (A)," HBS No. 706-021, February 3, 2006, p. 19.

Note: Some FDI from Hong Kong is thought to represent round-tripping of funds to take advantage of the favorable tax treatment of foreign investment in China. While shares from Hong Kong have fallen over recent years, shares of small economies like the Virgin Islands and Western Samoa have risen. It is thought that these smaller economies could now be accounting for some of the round-tripping flows.

Exhibit 4 Trade between China and Japan, 1995–2005

	1995	1996	1997	1998	1999	2000	2001	2002	2003	2004	2005
Exports for Japan (as % total exports)	18.8	20.4	17.4	14.5	16.6	16.6	16.9	14.9	13.6	12.4	11.0
Imports from Japan (as % total imports)	22.0	21.0	20.4	20.1	20.4	18.5	17.6	18.1	18.0	16.8	15.2
Exports destined for Japan ($ bn)	28.463	24.539	22.600	26.700	32.400	37.700	45.000	48.437	59.423	73.514	83.992
Imports from Japan($ bn)	29.005	22.168	20.000	28.200	33.800	37.600	42.800	53.468	74.151	94.372	100.452

Source: Economist Intelligence Unit Country Reports.

Exhibit 5   China's National Income Accounts, 1995–2005

	1995	1996	1997	1998	1999	2000	2001	2002	2003	2004	2005
CHINA—GROSS DOMESTIC PRODUCT											
Key Indicators											
GDP (% real change pa)	10.93	10.01	9.28	7.83	7.63	8.42	8.30	9.09	10.03	10.08	9.90
Nominal GDP (US$ at PPP billions)	2,998.13	3,343.13	3,686.92	4,040.49	4,376.56	4,824.69	5,324.82	5,828.61	6,446.03	7,282.54	8,203.25
National savings											
Gross national savings rate (%)		41.00	40.20	41.90	40.50	39.10	38.10	39.30	41.60	45.10	47.70
Structure of GDP											
Private consumption (% of GDP)	46.10	47.10	46.50	46.70	47.60	48.00	46.60	45.30	43.30	41.40	39.90
Government consumption (% of GDP)	11.40	11.50	11.60	12.00	12.60	13.10	13.20	12.90	12.20	11.50	10.60
Gross fixed investment (% of GDP)	34.70	34.20	33.60	35.00	35.70	36.50	37.30	38.90	42.10	43.80	44.40
Stockbuilding (% of GDP)	6.10	5.20	4.40	2.40	1.50	-0.10	0.70	0.40	0.20	0.40	0.10
Exports of G&S (% of GDP)	20.20	20.10	21.80	20.30	20.40	23.30	22.60	25.10	29.60	34.00	36.80
Imports of G&S (% of GDP)	18.60	18.00	18.10	16.70	17.90	21.10	20.60	22.80	27.60	31.40	33.40
Domestic demand (% of GDP)	98.30	97.90	96.20	96.10	97.30	97.50	97.80	97.40	97.80	97.10	95.10
Ratios, GDP at factor cost											
Agriculture/GDP	19.77	19.51	18.06	17.32	16.22	14.83	14.15	13.50	12.57	13.11	12.46
Industry/GDP	47.17	47.54	47.54	46.21	45.76	45.92	45.15	44.79	45.97	46.23	47.28
Services/GDP	33.05	32.95	34.40	36.47	38.02	39.25	40.70	41.72	41.46	40.67	40.26
FISCAL AND MONETARY INDICATORS											
Inflation and wages											
Consumer prices (% change pa; av)	17.07	8.33	2.81	-0.78	-1.48	0.35	0.73	-0.77	1.17	3.90	1.82
Budgetary indicators											
Budget balance (% of GDP)	-1.56	-1.48	-1.74	-2.82	-3.70	-3.28	-2.74	-2.96	-2.70	-2.10	-1.60
DEMOGRAPHICS AND INCOME											
Income											
GDP per head (US$)	601.00	699.50	770.60	817.10	861.20	945.60	1,038.00	1,131.80	1,269.80	1,486.00	1,700.00
GDP per head ($ at PPP)	2,475.30	2,731.60	2,982.30	3,238.60	3,479.40	3,806.70	4,172.20	4,537.50	4,988.10	5,600.00	6,270.00
Real GDP growth per head (% pa)	9.77	8.87	8.19	6.85	6.76	7.60	7.55	8.39	9.37	9.44	9.30

Source: Economist Intelligence Unit.

Exhibit 6   China's Balance of Payments, 1995–2004 (in $ billion)

	1995	1996	1997	1998	1999	2000	2001	2002	2003	2004
Current account balance	1.6	7.2	29.7	29.3	21.1	20.5	17.4	35.4	45.9	70.0
Merchandise trade balance	18.1	19.5	46.2	46.6	36.0	34.5	34.0	44.2	44.7	
Service trade balance	-6.1	-2.0	-5.7	-4.9	-5.3	-5.6	-5.9	-6.8	-8.6	
Capital account balance	38.7	40.0	23.0	-6.3	5.2	2.0	34.8	32.3	97.8	112.0
FDI, net	33.8	38.1	41.7	41.1	37.0	37.5	37.4	46.8	47.2	55.0
Portfolio, net	0.8	1.7	6.8	-3.7	-11.2	-4.0	-19.4	-10.3	11.4	
Other investment, net	4.0	0.2	-25.5	-43.7	-20.5	-31.5	16.9	-4.1	39.1	
Errors and omissions, net	-17.8	-15.6	-17.0	-16.6	-17.8	-11.9	-4.9	7.8	18.4	24.3
Non-FDI capital account balance (including errors and omissions)	-13.7	-35.6	-64.0	-49.6	-47.4	-7.4	-6.7	69.0	81.3	
Gross international reserves	76.0	107.7	143.4	149.8	158.3	168.9	218.7	295.2	457.2	663.6
Foreign exchange reserves	73.6	105.0	139.9	145.0	154.7	165.6	212.2	286.4	448.3	654.9

Source: Prasad and Wei 2005, p. 46.

Exhibit 7 Level and Composition of China's Gross Capital Inflows, 1982–2003 (in $ billions)

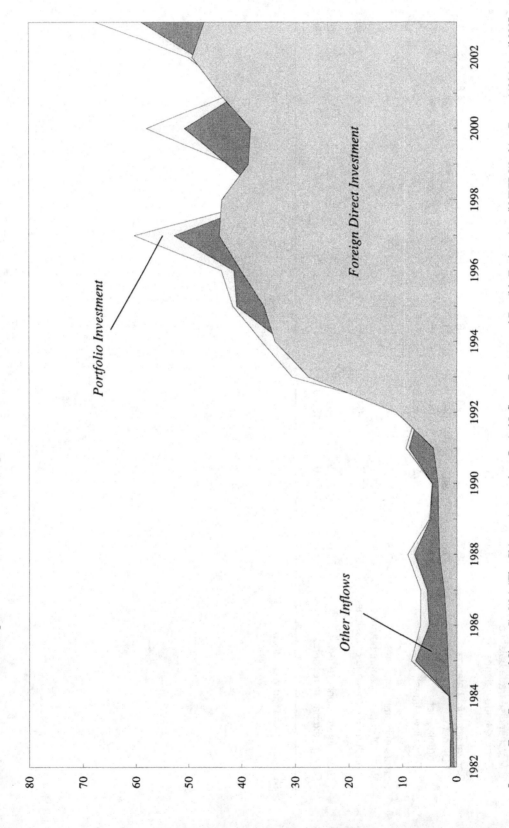

Source: Eswar Prasad and Shang-Jin Wei, "The Chinese Approach to Capital Inflows: Patterns and Possible Explanations," NBER Working Paper 11306, April 2005, p. 51.

Exhibit 8   China's Gross Capital Flows by Component, 1982–2003 (in $ billion)

Figure 2. Gross Capital Flows by Component
(In billions of U.S. dollars)

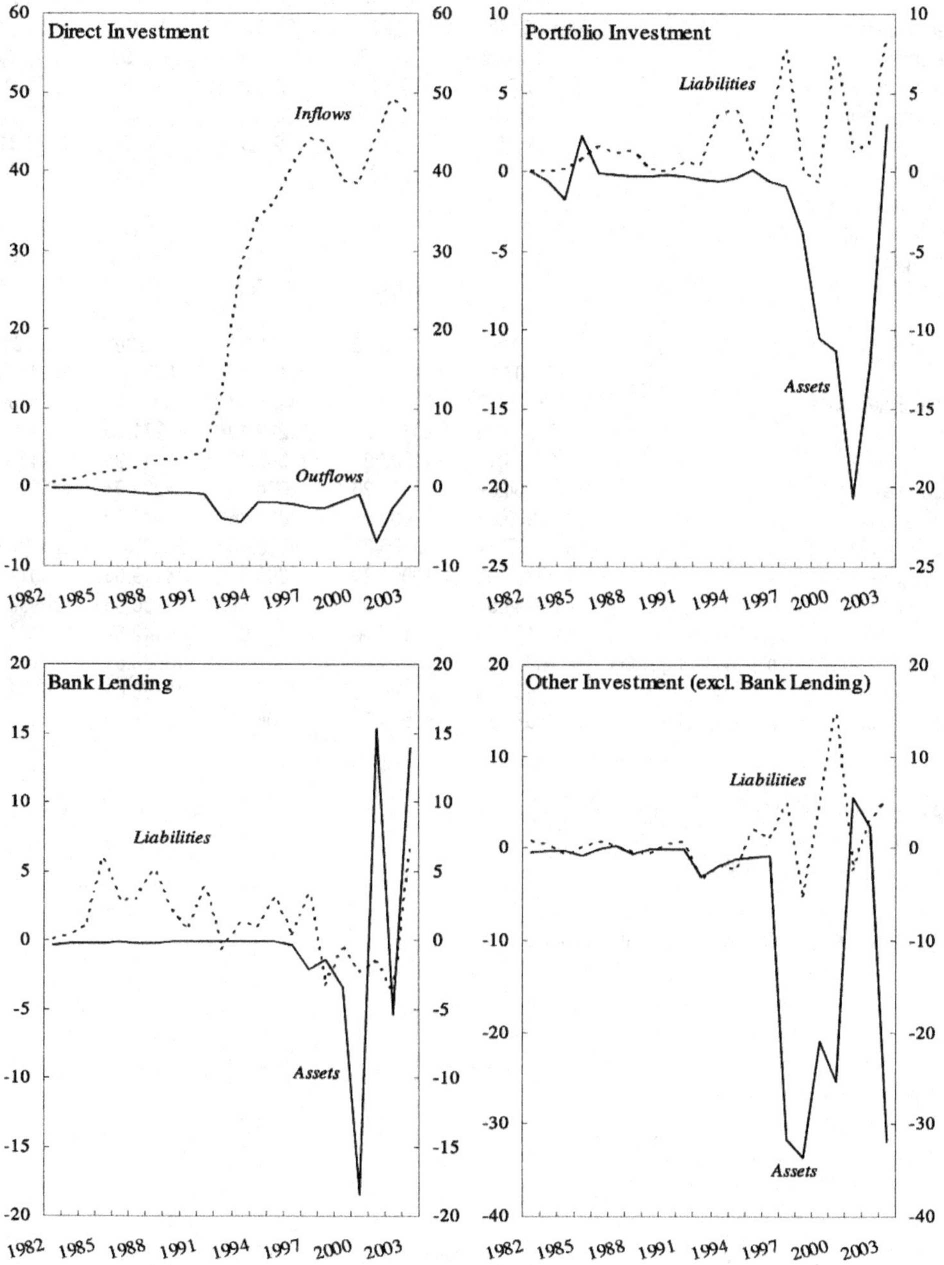

Source: CEIC database.
Note: Scales differ across the four panels of this figure.

Source: Eswar Prasad and Shang-Jin Wei, "The Chinese Approach to Capital Inflows: Patterns and Possible Explanations,"
          NBER Working Paper 11306, April 2005, p. 52.

Exhibit 9   Enterprise Numbers and Output by Firm Type, 1999–2003

Number of Industrial Enterprises	1999	2000	2001	2002	2003
National Total	162,033	162,885	171,256	181,557	196,222
'Domestically Funded Enterprises	135,196	134,440	139,833	147,091	157,641
'State-Owned Industry	50,651	42,426	34,530	29,449	23,228
'Collective-Owned Industry	42,585	37,841	31,018	27,477	22,478
Cooperative Enterprises	10,149	10,852	10,864	10,193	9,283
Joint Ownership Enterprises	2,771	2,510	2,234	1,964	1,689
Limited Liability Corporations	9,714	13,215	18,956	22,486	26,606
Share-Holding Enterprises	4,480	5,086	5,692	5,998	6,313
Private Enterprises	14,601	22,128	36,218	49,176	67,607
Other Enterprises	245	382	321	348	437
Enterprises Funded by Foreigners (including Hong Kong,	15,783	16,490	18,257	19,546	21,152
Foreign Funded Enterprises	11,054	11,955	13,166	14,920	17,429
State-owned or State Holding Majority Shares Enterprises	61,301	53,489	46,767	41,125	34,280

Gross Industrial Output Value (100 million yuan)	1999	2000	2001	2002	2003
National Total	72707.04	85673.66	95448.98	110776.48	142271.22
'Domestically Funded Enterprises	53752.81	62209.11	68228.08	78317.20	97913.42
'State-Owned Industry	22215.89	20156.29	17229.19	17271.09	18479.40
'Collective-Owned Industry	12414.11	11907.92	10052.49	9618.95	9458.43
Cooperative Enterprises	2594.62	2897.26	2994.96	3202.94	3250.90
Joint Ownership Enterprises	903.65	900.55	850.76	941.90	948.67
Limited Liability Corporations	7027.24	10926.38	15535.43	20069.77	26583.94
Share-Holding Enterprises	5247.08	10090.29	12698.34	14119.03	18017.06
Private Enterprises	3244.56	5220.36	8760.89	12950.86	20980.23
Other Enterprises	105.67	110.06	106.01	142.64	194.79
Enterprises Funded by Foreigners (including Hong Kong,	8994.00	10574.30	11847.18	13668.81	17425.62
Foreign Funded Enterprises	9960.23	12890.25	15373.72	18790.47	26932.18
State-owned or State Holding Majority Shares Enterprises	35571.18	40554.37	42408.49	45178.96	53407.90

a) All state-owned and non-state-owned industrial enterprises above designated size refer to all state-owned industrial enterprises and the non owned industrial enterprises with an annual sales income of over 5 million yuan.
b) The gross industrial output value is calculated at current prices.

Source: China Data Online database – China Statistical Yearbook.

Exhibit 10   Summary of China's Capital Controls, 1997–2005

On Capital and Money Market Instruments	
Nonresident purchases	Nonresidents may purchase only RMB-denominated B shares; purchases of money market instruments were not allowed. Beginning in 2004, domestic purchase of A shares was allowed for "Qualified Foreign Institutional Investors," the largest and longest established banks, insurance, and securities firms. QFIIs must set up RMB accounts with domestic banks and use domestic securities companies. No single QFII could own more than 10% of any firm listed in Shanghai or Shenzhen, total QFII ownership of any firm could not exceed 20%. QFII(closed end QFII) capital remittance was permitted after 1(3) year(s) in increments of 20% at 3(1) month intervals.
Nonresident sale or issuance	Not allowed
Resident purchase abroad	Not allowed, except for financial institutions approved by SAFE and authorized enterprises
Resident sale abroad	Sales or issue abroad of securities other than stocks requires PBC and SAFE approval
On Derivatives and Other Instruments	
Nonresident purchases	Not allowed
Nonresident sale or issuance	Not allowed
Resident purchase abroad	Activity by financial institutions subject to review of qualifications and limits on open forex positions (no more than 20% of forex working capital)
On Commercial and Financial Credits	
By residents to nonresidents	Not allowed for industrial and commercial enterprises; Lending by financial institutions subject to SAFE review and a forex asset-liability ratio
To residents from nonresidents	Except for foreign-funded enterprises, external borrowing of commercial credit may only occur through SAFE-approved financial institutions. All transaction amounts must be registered with SAFE and are subject to forex balance requirements except for maturities less than 90 days.
On Direct Investment	
Inward direct investment	All MOFTEC approved nonresidents are free to invest in China, with no foreign exchange restrictions on inward remittances. Some sectors are off limits, however. Beginning in 2004, the ceiling on foreign bank ownership of a Chinese bank was raised from 20% to 25%, and the ceiling for any one bank was raised from 15% to 20%.
Outward direct investment	MOFTEC approval, SAFE registration and review of investment risks and the source of foreign exchange assets required
Nonresident Deposit Accounts/Foreign Currency Deposit Accounts	
Reserve requirements	13% for RMB deposits, 5% for foreign currency deposits in domestic banks, and 3%(5%) for foreign currency deposits in foreign funded enterprises for over(under) 3 months. As of January 2005, reserve requirements on accounts domestic- and foreign-currency denominated domestic were unified at 3%.
Liquid asset requirements	Bank (nonbank) forex liquid assets must be 60% or more of liquid liabilities and 30%(25%) of total foreign exchange assets. Total deposits with 90 day maturity, deposits in both domestic and foreign banks, funds used for purchasing foreign currency denominated securities, deposits with the central bank, and cash holdings, should be 15%(10%) or more of total foreign exchange assets.

Source: Adapted from Qing Wang, "Appendix II. Evolution of Capital Controls in China," in Eswar Prasad and Shang-Jin Wei, "The Chinese Approach to Capital Inflows: Patterns and Possible Explanations," NBER Working Paper 11306, April 2005, pp. 34–40.

Notes: PBC: People's Bank of China, the central bank
SAFE: State Administration for Foreign Exchange
MOFTEC: Ministry of Foreign Trade and Economic Construction

Exhibit 11   Leading Venture Capital Firms in China, End 2003

Domestic Firms		Foreign Firms	
Company	Funds under Management ($ million)	Company	Funds under Management ($ million)
1. First Company[a] Investment Group	412	1. Newbridge Capital[b]	1,221
2. Shenzhen Capital Group	299	2. H&Q Asia Pacific[b]	1,187
3. China Merchants China Investment Mgt.[a]	134	3. Walden International[b]	1,153
4. NewMargin Investments	133	4. Softbank Asia Infrastructure Fund[b]	1,050
5. Beijing Venture Capital	121	5. AsiaVest Partners, TCW/YFY[b]	710
6. Legend Capital	95	6. IDG Technology Venture Investment	500
7. CDH China Holding Mgt.	89	7. Sycamore Ventures[b]	488
8. DragonTech Ventures Mgt.[a]	88	8. ChinaVest	311
9. Jiangsu Hi-Tech Venture Capital	79	9. Gateway International Investment	230
10. Nanjing Creation Capital Mgt.	79	10. AIG Investment Group Asia	186

Source: Casewriter presentation of Asian Venture Capital Journal data quoted in Economist Intelligence Unit, "2.6 Venture Capital and Private Equity Firms," *Country Finance*, August 31, 2004, p. 17, available from Factiva, www.factiva.com, accessed August 25, 2005.

[a] Based in Hong Kong.

[b] Includes funds invested throughout Asia, but not funds that clearly exclude China.

Exhibit 12   Selected JAFCO Value Added Activities in Japan

Company	Activity
HiSoft	Introduced potential acquisition opportunities in Japan and supported the business with a major systems integrator, resulting in a significant contract
PentaMicro	Introduced the company to Japan's major electronics firms, resulting in orders for digital video recorders
Reakosys	Introduced the company to game developers in Japan, leading to codevelopment of game software for Sony Playstation 2.
SmartAnt	Introduced the company to three peripheral makers in Japan, all of which led to orders.
SoftRun	Introduced the Korean company to over 10 systems integrators in Japan and advised the company on Japan market strategy

Source: JAFCO Asia, "Introduction to JAFCO Investment (Asia/Pacific) Ltd., October 2005, p. 15.

Exhibit 13   JATF I and II, Investments by Country, Sector, and Stage

Investments	JATF I	JATF II
By Country (%)		
Australia	5%	
China	35%	41%
India		5%
Israel	3%	
Korea	21%	30%
Philippines	1%	
Singapore	9%	9%
Taiwan	26%	15%
Total	100%	100%
By Sector		
Life Sciences	1%	4%
Optical Fiber/Photonics	15%	
Peripherals	14%	18%
Semiconductor	35%	30%
Software/E-commerce	13%	22%
Storage	4%	
Wireless/Telco applications	18%	26%
Total	100%	100%
By Stage		
Early	27%	30%
Middle	45%	54%
Late	28%	16%

Source: JAFCO Asia, "Introduction to JAFCO Investment (Asia/Pacific) Ltd., October 2005, pp. 20–21.

Exhibit 14   JAFCO's Selected Investments in China

Company	Sector	Business
InterChina Network Software	Software/ e-commerce	Software research developer: backend high speed database search management
Odysys International	Storage	Development and sales of SAN and NAS systems and solutions based on proprietary unified file system
BCD Semiconductor	Semiconductor	Analog IC design and open foundry
Photonic Bridges Holdings	Optical fiber/ photonics	Optical system manufacturer and distributor
Sinosun Holding Corp	Software/ e-commerce	R&D and manufacturing of information security products
China Wireless Technologies	Wireless/telco	Leading wireless data communications and information solution provider
China Grentech Corp	Wireless/telco	Development of wireless communication system based on RF technology, and provision of wireless network optimization solutions
Fiberxon	Optical fiber/ photonics	Design and manufacture of high performance optical transceivers
MicroTech International	Semiconductor	Fabless IC design company for Smart Card
Hisoft Technology International	Software/ e-commerce	Software and outsourcing services
Agape Package Manufacturing	Semiconductor	IC packaging services
Arkmicro Technologies	Semiconductor	Fabless semiconductor design focusing on the TV/video industry
Pollex Mobile	Wireless/telco	Software solutions for mobile handsets and devices
Cgogo Technologies	Wireless/telco	Developer of search engines for mobile phones
Chinacache	Software/ e-commerce	Content delivery network provider

Source: JAFCO Asia, "Introduction to JAFCO Investment (Asia/Pacific) Ltd., October 2005, pp. 32–33, 36.

Endnotes

[1] Author's interview with Vincent Chan, Managing Director for North Asia, JAFCO Asia, Hong Kong, December 7, 2005.

[2] See Kent E. Calder, "China and Japan's Simmering Rivalry," *Foreign Affairs*, vol. 85, no. 2 (2006), pp. 129-139. Many controversies had worsened the political relationship between Japan and China. They included: simmering territorial disputes, the labeling of China as a security threat in Japanese defense guidelines, and Japan's support for the United States against China's anti-secession law aimed at corralling Taiwan. For its part, China continued to view Japan as insufficiently contrite for its wartime occupation of China. See Chua Chin Hon and Kwan Weng Kin, "China-Japan Ties Become More Tense," *Straits Times* (Singapore), April 7, 2005, available from Factiva, www.factiva.com, accessed February 21, 2006; Gerald Curtis, "A Bargain that Could End Japan-China Bickering," *Financial Times*, February 21, 2006, p. 13. On China's reaction to the possibility of a permanent seat for Japan on the U.N. Security Council, see Antoaneta Bezlova, "China: Regime Facing Tough Decision on Japan's Bid for U.N. Seat," Inter Press Service/Global Information Network, April 5, 2005, available from Factiva, www.factiva.com, accessed February 21, 2006. Also see Geoffrey York, "Nationalist Fervor Runs Amok," *The Globe and Mail* (Toronto), October 25, 2004, p. A1, available from Factiva, www.factiva.com, accessed February 24, 2006. Also see "Army to Ensure Order during China-Japan Soccer Match," BBC Monitoring Newsfile, August 6, 2004, 6:10am, which reports a figure of "over 6,000 police officers and People's Liberation Army troops."

[3] Authors' interview with Toshiaki Ito, President and CEO, JAFCO, Tokyo, December 5, 2005.

[4] See Peter J. Katzenstein, *A World of Regions: Asia and Europe in the American Imperium* (Ithaca, N.Y.: Cornell University Press, 2005). See also Peter J. Katzenstein and Takashi Shiraishi, eds., *Network Power: Japan and Asia* (Ithaca, N.Y.: Cornell University Press, 1997); and Peter J. Katzenstein and Takashi Shiraishi, eds., *Beyond Japan: The Dynamics of East Asian Regionalism* (Ithaca, N.Y.: Cornell University Press, 2006).

[5] Richard H. K. Vietor, "Japan: Deficits, Demography, and Deflation," Harvard Business School No. 706-004, revised January 9, 2006, p. 3.

[6] Loan loss charges for Japan's banks eventually exceeded $1 trillion. Vietor, p. 3.

[7] Laura Alfaro, Rafael Di Tella, and Ingrid Vogel, "China: To Float or Not To Float? (A)," Harvard Business School No. 706-021, February 3, 2006, p. 8.

[8] Japanese Ministry of Foreign Affairs, "Japan China Statistics," mimeo, December 5, 2005.

[9] For an excellent survey of China's economic growth and related policy developments, see Debora Spar, Jean Oi, and Chris Bebenek, "China: Building 'Capitalism with Socialist Characteristics,'" HBS No. 706-041, February 14, 2006.

[10] James T. Areddy, "Venture Capital Swarms China," *The Wall Street Journal*, March 14, 2006, p. C1.

[11] Eswar Prasad, Thomas Rumbaugh, and Qing Wang, "Putting the Cart before the Horse? Capital Account Liberalization and Exchange Rate Flexibility in China," IMF Policy Discussion Paper, January 2005, and Economist Intelligence Unit China Country Report 2005, cited in Laura Alfaro, Rafael Di Tella, and Ingrid Vogel, "China: To Float or Not To Float? (A)," Harvard Business School No. 706-021, February 3, 2006, p. 7.

[12] Eswar Prasad and Shang-Jin Wei, "The Chinese Approach to Capital Inflows: Patterns and Possible Explanations," NBER Working Paper 11306, April 2005, p. 18.

[13] Ibid., p. 19.

[14] Robert E. Kennedy, "China: Facing the 21st Century," Harvard Business School No. 798-066, January 14, 2002, quoted in Laura Alfaro, Rafael Di Tella, and Ingrid Vogel, "China: To Float or Not To Float? (A)," p. 3.

[15] U.S. Department of State, Bureau of East Asian and Pacific Affairs, "Background Note: China," March 2005, available from www.state.gov/r/pa/ei/bgn/18902.htm, cited in Laura Alfaro, Rafael Di Tella, and Ingrid Vogel, "China: To Float or Not To Float? (A)," p. 4.

[16] See Howard W. French, "Land of 74,000 Protests (But Little Is Ever Fixed)," *The New York Times*, August 4, 2005, p. 4, cited in Debora Spar, Jean Oi, and Chris Bebenek, "China: Building 'Capitalism with Socialist Characteristics,'" p. 14.

[17] Laura Alfaro, Rafael Di Tella, and Ingrid Vogel, "China: To Float or Not To Float? (A)," p. 4.

[18] Laura Alfaro, Rafael Di Tella, and Ingrid Vogel, "China: To Float or Not To Float? (A),"p. 5, citing Eswar Prasad, Thomas Rumbaugh, and Qing Wang, "Putting the Cart before the Horse? Capital Account Liberalization and Exchange Rate Flexibility in China," IMF Policy Discussion Paper, January 2005; and Morris Goldstein and Nicholas R. Lardy, "China's Revaluation Shows Size Really Matters," *Financial Times*, July 22, 2005.

[19] Laura Alfaro, Rafael Di Tella, and Ingrid Vogel, "China: To Float or Not To Float? (A),"p. 5.

[20] Takashi Ueda, "Venture Capital: China Begins to Attract Funds," *Nikkei Report*, November 22, 2002, available from Factiva, www.factiva.com, accessed August 25, 2005.

[21] Minxin Pei, "The Dark Side of China's Rise," *Foreign Policy*, March/April 2006, available from www.foreignpolicy.com, accessed February 27, 2006.

[22] Rongrong Li, chairman of China's State-owned Assets Supervision and Administration Commission, quoted in Geoff Dyer, "HK Is China's Preferred Stock Market," *Financial Times*, December 23, 2005, p. 2.

[23] For a discussion of the revaluation issue, see Laura Alfaro, Rafael Di Tella, and Ingrid Vogel, "China: To Float or Not To Float? (A)."

[24] Nicholas Lardy, "Trade Liberalization and Its Role in Chinese Economic Growth," paper prepared for an International Monetary Fund and National Council of Applied Economic Research conference, "A Tale of Two Giants: India's and China's Experience with Reform and Growth," New Delhi, November 14-16, 2003, quoted in Laura Alfaro, Rafael Di Tella, and Ingrid Vogel, "China: To Float or Not To Float? (A)," p. 9.

[25] Steve Johnson, "Chinese Banks in Forex Trade Link," *Financial Times*, February 21, 2006, p. 1.

[26] See Laura Alfaro, Rafael Di Tella, and Ingrid Vogel, "China: To Float or Not To Float? (A)," Exhibit 12, p. 20.

[27] Laura Alfaro, Rafael Di Tella, and Ingrid Vogel, "China: To Float or Not To Float? (A)," p. 8.

[28] Eswar Prasad and Shang-Jin Wei, "The Chinese Approach to Capital Inflows: Patterns and Possible Explanations," p. 7.

[29] Authors' interview with Toshiaki Ito.

[30] See Peter Hays Gries, "China's 'New Thinking' on Japan," *China Quarterly*, vol. 184 (2005), pp. 831-850; and Gries, "Chinese Nationalism: Challenging the State?" *Current History*, (2005), pp. 251-256. Also see Gries, *China's New Nationalism: Pride, Politics, and Diplomacy* (Berkeley: University of California Press, 2004); and Allen Whiting, *China Eyes Japan* (Berkeley: University of California Press, 1989).

[31] See Geoffrey York, "Making Marx Relevant Again: Under Siege from Cynicism and Greed," *Globe and Mail*, February 15, 2006, available from Factiva, www.factiva.com, accessed March 3, 2006.

[32] Takashi Ueda, "Venture Capital: China Begins to Attract Funds."

[33] "Reform Progress Keeps Mainland under Spotlight," *South China Morning Post*, September 12, 2002, p. 9, available from Factiva, www.factiva.com, accessed August 25, 2005.

[34] S. C. Mak, quoted in "Reform Progress Keeps Mainland under Spotlight."

[35] Anthony Fan, cited in "Reform Progress Keeps Mainland under Spotlight."

[36] Economist Intelligence Unit, "2.6 Venture Capital and Private Equity Firms," *Country Finance*, August 31, 2004, p. 17, available from Factiva, www.factiva.com, accessed August 25, 2005.

[37] Ministry of Science and Technology figures cited in Economist Intelligence Unit, "2.6 Venture Capital and Private Equity Firms."

[38] "On the Sino Shore," *Asia Private Equity Review*, September 1, 2004, available from Factiva, www.factiva.com, accessed August 25, 2005.

[39] Zero2IPO, cited in James T. Areddy, "Venture Capital Swarms China," *The Wall Street Journal*, March 14, 2006, p. C1.

[40] This and the following paragraph come from Felda Hardymon and Ann Leamon, "Gobi Partners: October 2004," HBS No. 805-090, March 8, 2005, pp. 3-4.

[41] Authors' interview with Hiroshi Yamada, President and CEO, JAFCO Asia, Hong Kong, December 7, 2005.

[42] Ibid.

[43] Authors' interview with Michael Chow, Director and Chief Representative, JAFCO Asia, Hong Kong, December 7, 2005.

[44] "Sino-Japan Gestures," Asia Private Equity Review, January 1, 2003, available from Factiva, www.factiva.com, accessed August 25, 2005.

[45] Economist Intelligence Unit, "2.6 Venture Capital and Private Equity Firms."

[46] Quoted in Paul Waide, "Job-hopping VCs in China," TheDeal.com, September 27, 2004, available from Factiva, www.factiva.com, accessed August 25, 2005.

[47] "On the Sino Shore," *Asia Private Equity Review*, September 1, 2004.

[48] See "Planning the New Socialist Countryside," *The Economist*, March 11, 2006, pp. 37-38.

[49] Takashi Ueda, "Venture Capital: China Begins to Attract Funds."

[50] See "On the Sino Shore," *Asia Private Equity Review*.

[51] Ibid.

[52] Ibid.

[53] "Venture Capitalists Catch China Fever," *South China Morning Post*, May 3, 2004, p. 3, available from Factiva, www.factiva.com, accessed August 25, 2005.

[54] Francesco Guerrera, "China Planning to Nurture Domestic Venture Capitalists," *Financial Times*, November 23, 2005, p. 1.

[55] "Reform Progress Keeps Mainland under Spotlight," *South China Morning Post*.

[56] "Venture Capitalists Catch China Fever," *South China Morning Post*.

[57] Authors' interview with Vincent Chan, Managing Director for North Asia, JAFCO Asia, December 7, 2005.

[58] "Venture Capitalists Catch China Fever," *South China Morning Post*, p. 3.

[59] Ibid.

[60] Ibid.

[61] Economist Intelligence Unit, "2.6 Venture Capital and Private Equity Firms."

[62] Like the Japanese government and many Japanese firms, JAFCO's fiscal year-end was March 31.

[63] Authors' interview with Toshiaki Ito, President and CEO, JAFCO, Tokyo, December 5, 2005.

[64] Authors' interview with Ito.

[65] Authors' interview with Munetsugu Wakamatsu, Managing Director, JAFCO, Tokyo, December 5, 2005.

[66] Rita Raages De Ramos, "Asia Fund View: JAFCO Asia Focuses on China Investments," Dow Jones Australia and New Zealand Report, May 6, 2002, available from Factiva, www.factiva.com, accessed August 25, 2005.

[67] Takashi Ueda, "Venture Capital: China Begins to Attract Funds."

[68] Author's interview with Hiroshi Yamada, President and CEO, JAFCO Asia, Hong Kong, December 7, 2005.

[69] "Sino-Japan Gestures," Asia Private Equity Review, January 1, 2003, available from Factiva, www.factiva.com, accessed August 25, 2005.

[70] Takashi Ueda, "Venture Capital: China Begins to Attract Funds."

[71] "Venture Capitalists Catch China Fever," South China Morning Post.

[72] Paul Waide, "Job-hopping VCs in China," TheDeal.com, September 27, 2004, available from Factiva, www.factiva.com, accessed August 25, 2005.

[73] "The Sino Allure," Asia Private Equity Review, January 1, 2005, available from Factiva, www.factiva.com, accessed August 25, 2005.

[74] "SAIF Won Two Laurels of China Venture Capital Annual Ranking 2004," PR Newswire, December 17, 2004, 11:24am, available from Factiva, www.factiva.com, accessed August 25, 2005.

[75] JAFCO Asia, "Introduction to JAFCO Investment (Asia/Pacific) Ltd., October 2005, p. 9.

[76] Authors' interview with Hiroshi Yamada.

[77] Authors' interview with Vincent Chan, Managing Director for North Asia, JAFCO Asia, December 7, 2005.

[78] Authors' interview with Michael Chow, Director and Chief Representative, JAFCO Asia, Hong Kong, December 7, 2005.

[79] Authors' interview with Vincent Chan.

[80] Authors' interview with Toshiaki Ito.

[81] Authors' interview with Vincent Chan.

[82] Authors' interview with Hiroshi Yamada.

[83] Authors' interview with Michael Chow.

[84] The authors are grateful for the input of Jasmine Lin of the China Venture Capital Association in drafting this section.

[85] Japan External Trade Organization, "Special Survey of Japanese Business in China—Impact of the April Anti-Japan Demonstrations," June 2005, pp. 2-4.

[86] Doug Cameron, Francesco Guerrera, and Richard McGregor, "Foreign Buyouts in China Face Backlash from Volatile Mix of Nationalists and Leftwingers," Financial Times, March 30, 2006, p. 2, available from Factiva, www.factiva.com, accessed March 30, 2006.

[87] Authors' interview with Munetsugu Wakamatsu, Managing Director, JAFCO, Tokyo, December 5, 2005.

Part IV

THE POLITICS AND RULES OF INTERNATIONAL TRADE

HARVARD | BUSINESS | SCHOOL

9-706-003

NOVEMBER 22, 2005

REGINA ABRAMI

The Delta Blues: U.S.–Vietnam Catfish Trade Dispute (A)

The catfish is a plenty good enough fish for anybody.

—Mark Twain, *Life on the Mississippi*

If Vietnam ever got around to declaring a national fish, the catfish would be it.

—Andrew X. Pham, *Catfish and Mandala*

On June 28, 2002, the Vietnamese government received worrying news. The Catfish Farmers of America (CFA) had just filed a petition with the U.S. government. It accused 53 Vietnamese firms of dumping "certain frozen fish fillets" on the U.S. market. Suddenly, one of Vietnam's most promising export industries found itself under serious threat. The livelihoods of thousands were at stake. By 2002, aquatic products had ranked third among Vietnamese exports, with total sales reaching $1.5 billion.[1] Was it now about to end?

Without question, Vietnam's footprint on the global economy had widened considerably since the introduction of economic reforms in 1986 (see **Exhibit 1**). Within a decade, the country went from being one of the world's major rice importers to being one of the major exporters. In other commodities as well, including coffee, crude oil, cinnamon, pepper, and later shoes and textiles, Vietnam quickly established an international reputation. But trade with the United States was a relatively new phenomenon (see **Exhibit 16**).

After its failed conflict with North Vietnam, the U.S. aimed to prevent Communism's spread throughout the region. Vietnam's 1979 decision to send troops into Cambodia only furthered the U.S. objective. Occurring just months after the Vietnamese government granted the Soviet Union access to its naval bases, it sparked fears of growing Soviet influence in the Pacific. The U.S., in turn, quickly persuaded a number of noncommunist Asian and Western European countries to impose a political and economic embargo against Vietnam, transforming the country into an international pariah. Lacking good relations with China and denied access to World Bank and International Monetary Fund (IMF) funds until 1993, Vietnam only grew more dependent on Soviet financial and military assistance.

Finally, in 1994, President Bill Clinton lifted the U.S. trade embargo. Almost immediately, U.S. business interest in Vietnam picked up. But without the benefit of a bilateral trade agreement (BTA), and the lower tariffs that it would bring, the cost of doing business remained high for both sides. A year later, in July 1995, diplomatic relations were restored, and trade negotiations got underway. Conservatives within the ruling Vietnamese Communist Party worried about the impact of greater foreign access to Vietnam's economy, leading to a sudden cancellation of the BTA signing ceremony in summer 1999. A year later, Vietnamese government officials finally sat down to sign the historic accord. A few months later, throngs of people lined Hanoi's streets to celebrate Clinton's historic visit to the ancient city.

Filled with considerable faith in their new ally, the Vietnamese were deeply dismayed by the catfish-dumping accusation. It occurred just months after the BTA had been implemented. The general secretary of the Vietnam Association of Seafood Exporters and Producers (VASEP) was prompted to reflect on prior U.S.-Vietnam relations, saying, "We try to forget it, try something new, based on a spirit of cooperation and free trade, but now we are made to wonder whether you wish us ill, as much in the present as you did in the past."[2]

For American catfish farmers, the dumping charge was not about the political past but about the economic present. Their livelihoods were also at stake, and in an industry methodically built up over the past 20 years (see **Exhibit 4**).

Until "certain frozen fish fillets" from Vietnam began to appear in the late 1990s, U.S. producers held 95% of the domestic catfish market (see **Exhibit 13**).[3] By the end of 2001, the Vietnamese product captured 20% of the U.S. domestic frozen fillet market.[4] It seemed as if the trend was set to continue. The volume of "certain frozen fish fillet" imports had jumped from 575,000 to nearly 20 million pounds between 1998 and 2002, and at prices well below what U.S. producers could offer.[5] In fact, both U.S. and Vietnamese prices showed steady decline over this period. U.S. domestic producers received $2.70 per pound of frozen fish fillets in 1999. In 2001, they only received $2.57 for commercial shipments. Vietnamese frozen fish fillet imports had an average unit value of $1.99 per pound in 1999, which declined to $1.41 in 2001.[6]

Surveying the evidence, Vietnam's supporters argued that increasing volume and declining prices only reflected working markets. American catfish producers did not agree. They pointed instead to a range of practices, including subsidies, mislabeling, and low wages, to account for Vietnam's success. But whether these practices led to prices at *less than fair or normal value* and thus constituted dumping was another matter entirely.

At issue was nothing less than the right of government to aid in national development. At what point did it become a form of unfair trade? When was it simply responsible government? Had Vietnam's catfish industry been the benefactor of too much government support? Or was it, as advocates claimed, just another victim of U.S. protectionism? The answers affected not only the definition of legitimate business-government relations but also what constituted "fair" prices.

From Farms to River Fields: The Growth of Catfish as a Vietnamese Industry

With its long, snaking coastline and extensive network of rivers, Vietnam's geography had long encouraged households to sustain themselves through fishery activities. Nowhere was this more the case than in the south of Vietnam where the Mekong River melds with the South China Sea and the Gulf of Thailand (see **Exhibit 2**). This region, known as the Mekong Delta, was a key source of Vietnam's food security, continuing to provide the bulk of rice and aquatic products to this day.

For over 50 years, catfish was an important part of this economic landscape. Its cultivation in private ponds supplemented small family farms, providing rural households with an important source of protein and income, with exports mostly to Hong Kong, Singapore, and Taiwan.[7] After the U.S.-Vietnam War ended in 1973, the industry faced a number of challenges. Socialist transformation deeply unsettled agriculture and manufacturing in the south. Private businesses were nationalized. Land was collectivized, and thousands of boats were lost to Vietnamese seeking asylum in other countries. Roads and other infrastructure were also severely damaged during the war, disrupting transport channels even further. By the late 1970s, Vietnam also faced new and costly battles on two fronts: China in the north and Cambodia in the south. As a result, the government was unable to manage fully the economic recovery of the fishery sector.

Initial improvements instead took hold through grass-roots efforts. Restrictions on free market exchange, for example, led people to turn directly to state-owned enterprises to sell their catch. This development integrated private producers and publicly owned processors in new, if unintended, ways. Farmers were nonetheless still dependent on catching fingerlings (young fish) in nature for their brood stocks. But uncertain supply, including risks associated with transport and possible disease and death, made aquaculture a prohibitive venture for many households.

The situation began to change in the late 1980s with a shift toward river-based farming, an innovation that drew on the experience of catfish farmers in Cambodia.[8] Housed in large cages below river houseboats, catfish remained in their accustomed environment, and yields increased dramatically (see **Exhibit 9**). In 1995, breeding technology was also introduced to the catfish sector, resulting in a significant drop in the price of fingerlings.[9] Industrial feed was also introduced around this time, allowing farmers greater predictability over growing times and expected yields. Catfish farming, in turn, became an ever more attractive option to rural households, especially for those with insufficient land and in need of alternative sources of income.

The Vietnamese government recognized the potential of catfish farming. In 1995, it approved a national strategy for the development of fishery exports up to 2010. In 1999, the program was linked to the "National Hunger Eradication and Poverty Reduction" strategy. The combination positioned aquaculture as both a major export sector and source of employment creation. Supporting this effort were two new associations, the Humanity Fund of Vietnam's Fisheries, created in 1996, and VASEP, created in 1998. In addition, the Ministry of Fisheries operated a number of extension centers around the country to allow farmers and others to share their experiences and cultivation techniques with others.

The growing number of people employed in the industry suggested that the government's aquaculture and poverty alleviation plans had worked. For 2000, estimates were as high as 400,000 people variously processing, cultivating, breeding, and trading catfish in the Mekong region.[10] They included casual laborers on river houseboats, newly minted factory workers, and company executives (see **Exhibit 9**). Overwhelmingly, factory workers were rural women 18–30 years of age, while houseboat laborers tended to be male. Houseboat and hatchery owners also relied on unpaid family members to assist with work.[11]

An Giang province, located in the Mekong Delta, was the center of catfish production, responsible for the bulk of "basa" (*pangasius bocourti*) and "tra" (*pangasius hypophthalmus*) cultivation, two catfish species common to Asia (see **Exhibit 15**). Two state-owned enterprises, Agifish and Afiex, were initially responsible for the province's success.[12] Founded in 1986 and 1999, respectively, these firms were managed by the An Giang Provincial People's Committee, the highest provincial-level Communist Party organization. The catfish industry was also active in other provinces, taking off especially after 1995.

By the late 1990s, half of all Vietnamese frozen catfish fillets were headed to the United States.[13] The most dramatic increase occurred between 2000 and 2001, when Vietnamese frozen fish fillet imports jumped from 8.4 million pounds to 16.4 million pounds (see **Exhibit 13**). In 2001, the year in which the BTA was finally implemented, U.S. tariffs on Vietnamese fish fillets went to zero, only encouraging further shipments to the U.S.[14]

Still, this trend was hardly unusual. Developing countries increasingly relied on aquaculture as a development strategy and source of export earnings (see **Exhibit 5** and **Exhibit 17**). The U.S. played an important role in this global shift. For over two decades, it had been the world's largest importer of fishery products, second only to Japan. In fact, the value of fishery products entering the U.S. jumped 79% between 1985 and 1994, reaching an astonishing $12 billion in 1994. At the same time, U.S. aquaculture was also booming. The number of pounds produced jumped 116% between 1983 and 1994.[15] Over 84% of the increase was due to a single species—the catfish (see **Exhibit 4**).[16]

Something Wicked This Way Comes? The Vietnamese Catfish in the United States

An Industry Caught Off Guard?

Similar to its Vietnamese cousin, the U.S. catfish was a staple of southern culture. Once abundantly found in the fresh waters of Mississippi, Alabama, Louisiana, and Arkansas, catfish was a cheap and easy source of food for people in the Mississippi Delta region (see **Exhibit 3**). But thought to have a musky taste and negatively portrayed as a "river rat" or "bottom feeder," the catfish was regarded as poor people's food in some parts. For this reason, the development of the U.S. catfish industry depended on not only increasing production but also changing the image of a much maligned fish. As a first step, catfish farmers established a national industry association, the Catfish Farmers of America, in 1968.

A move to raise U.S. catfish in commercial quantities also got underway around the same time, but in a decidedly different direction than its Vietnamese counterpart.[17] Instead of river cultivation, the U.S. catfish industry relied on clay ponds, some as wide as 20 acres, to raise one species of catfish in particular—the U.S. channel catfish (*ictalurus punctatus*) (see **Exhibit 15**). Forged out of soil whose clay base was too heavy to grow cotton or soybean, these catfish ponds were viewed as a new path to economic development in the South.[18] Initially catfish farmers were only able to attract buyers in regional markets. But business was good enough that a number of them banded together to form cooperatives and build processing plants in the 1970s. As the industry grew, bigger players, such as ConAgra and Hormel, joined in, building their own ponds and processing plants (see **Exhibit 9**).

By the 1980s, the economic landscape of the Delta was changed. But for some observers, it was still far too much of the same. The poorest of the region remained overwhelmingly African-American. The catfish industry also did not escape the region's legacy of slavery, with some critics describing it as a new plantation system.[19] While more than 13,000 people found work in the catfish industry, critics noted that whites for the most part owned the farms and processing plants. In other respects, however, the division of labor was quite similar to Vietnam's. In the Mississippi Delta, women mostly worked in the factories, while men assisted with catfish cultivation.

Industry supporters also observed that grinding poverty had driven both black and white into the catfish business. The region was, after all, among the poorest in the country, with teenage pregnancy and infant mortality rates above the national average (see **Exhibit 14**). In some counties, less than

25% of the adult population had completed high school. Other counties struggled, with more than 50% of households living below the poverty line.[20]

Mississippi, last on so many of these socioeconomic measures, was first in the U.S. catfish business.[21] By 2001, it was responsible for 72% of national catfish production.[22] In fact, of the 190,000 acres of U.S. catfish ponds operating in 2001, 110,000 of them were in the state.[23] The majority were located in Humphreys County, self-declared catfish capital of the world. The small city of Belzoni was its soul. In 1985, the Catfish Institute was established there to increase public awareness and improve the image of farm-raised catfish.

Coining the phrase "you don't have to fry it to love it," the Catfish Institute spent upwards of $60 million in its first decade to market catfish as low in fat, cholesterol, and calories. A special effort was also made to distinguish farm-raised catfish as lighter tasting than its muskier river-based counterpart.[24] The effort paid off: Between 1985 and 2001, annual catfish consumption in the U.S. had more than doubled, from 0.41 pounds to one pound per person.[25] U.S. catfish production also became one of the world's largest aquaculture industries.[26]

The U.S. government played an important role in the transformation and growth of the catfish industry, beginning with the National Aquaculture Act of 1980. It established an interagency sub-committee on aquaculture whose first task was to prepare a national aquaculture development plan. The act also included provisions for budget appropriations and grants programs.[27] Two examples included subsidies for catfish feed and market guarantees through the U.S. Department of Agriculture's surplus-removal purchase program. The latter program made it possible for industry advocates to appeal to the U.S. government to purchase its product during times of market downturn. Catfish industry employers were also given tax credits for hiring low-skilled labor transitioning out of social welfare programs.

In no time, single mothers, many in their first jobs, made up nearly 75% of employees in the catfish-processing sector.[28] Standing along the "kill line," they processed live fish, one after another, for minimum wage. The fish, once stunned by electric shock, were deheaded, gutted, vacuumed out, and passed through the skinning station minutes before final inspection and flash freezing (see **Exhibit 9**).[29] Low pay and poor working conditions prompted labor unrest in the mid-1980s, with the biggest processing plant eventually unionized.[30] Others followed suit, but the livelihood of workers was no more secure as a result.

Instead trouble came in the form of "certain frozen fish fillets" from Vietnam. Selling for more than $1 a pound less than its U.S. counterpart, the Vietnamese product was popular with the biggest buyers—restaurants and supermarkets.[31] Fear of closed factories and declining profits spread throughout the region. The CFA leadership wondered if one of the brightest spots in U.S. agricultural commodities was about to dim.[32]

A Market Made by Misrepresentation? Mississippi vs. the Mekong

With Americans long prejudiced against the catfish, how its "foreign" counterpart became so widely accepted in the late 1990s puzzled U.S. catfish industry insiders. Initial suspicions were that American consumers simply did not know what they were buying. In response, the CFA teamed up with the well-known public relations firm Fleishman-Hillard.[33] Together they set out to distinguish the U.S. and Vietnamese product on taste and hygiene.

A particularly notorious ad was placed in the trade weekly *Supermarket News*. It played on xenophobic sentiment, warning consumers to "never trust a fish with a foreign accent!" CFA-funded ads also joked that "those other guys [the Vietnamese] probably couldn't spell U.S. even if they tried." Instead, consumers were encouraged to look for "U.S. born and raised" catfish, described as "farm-raised . . . in pure, fresh waters [on] a diet of natural grains and proteins." The Vietnamese catfish, in contrast, were depicted as "flapping around in third world rivers and dining on whatever they can get their fins on."[34]

Arkansas Congressman Marion Berry took matters a step further, suggesting that Vietnamese catfish were contaminated with Agent Orange, a defoliant used by the United States during the Vietnam-American War. "That stuff doesn't break down," he warned.[35] Research by Japanese and Vietnamese experts also raised concerns. In their small sample of caged and noncaged catfish in Can Tho province, they found significant levels of chlorine pesticides, including DDT.[36] But to counter these charges, Vietnamese producers amassed a diverse set of allies on their side.

First among them was the U.S. embassy in Hanoi. Its own study found no "substance to claims that catfish raised in Vietnam were less healthy than [those raised] in other countries."[37] If anything, there were a good number of similarities in food safety and hygienic standards, supporters noted. Both the Vietnamese and the U.S. catfish, for example, were fed Cargill-manufactured food pellets.[38] The pellets were light and floated on the water's surface, disputing claims that either country's farm-raised fish were "bottom feeders." The VASEP general secretary also added that Vietnamese catfish routinely underwent quality control evaluations as set by the U.S. Food and Drug Administration.[39]

A more intractable problem facing the Vietnamese industry was the charge of deliberately misleading customers through packaging and marketing strategies. Their product entered the U.S. under brand names such as "Delta Fresh," "Harvest Fresh," and "Farm Select." For U.S. catfish industry advocates, the similarity to the U.S. brands "Delta Pride," "Harvest Select," and "Farm Fresh" was far too close for coincidence.[40] They argued that Vietnamese exporters were trying to mislead consumers into thinking that they were buying Mississippi Delta products.

Indeed, regional press reports and other research suggested that the practice was working. Surveys found that buyers associated the phrase "farm raised" with U.S. products, overlooking small letters at the bottom of frozen catfish fillet boxes that read "Product of Vietnam." In its own telephone survey, the CFA found similar results. "Every restaurant we contacted swore they were using nothing but American farm-raised catfish," bemoaned Hugh Warren, CFA president. "But two million pounds of Vietnamese catfish are coming into this country every month. You tell me where it's going," he complained.[41]

In February 2001, a coalition of southern U.S. senators and congressmen wrote to U.S. Trade Representative Robert Zoellick to express their concerns, but little was done. In summer 2001, they instead proposed a bill requiring country-of-origin labeling on all fish at point of sale. U.S. restaurant owners strongly opposed having to list on menus and buffet lines where food items originated. In the end, the measure failed even to come up for a vote on technical grounds.

The Vietnamese government nonetheless took heed. It insisted that exporters identify their product as belonging either to the "basa" or "tra" species of catfish.[42] It already required exporters to label their product as "Made in Vietnam." But tra and basa still sold under a wide variety of names in the United States.[43] For basa, they included "basa," "bocourti," "pacific basa," "mekong basa," "basa catfish," and "bocourti catfish." Tra was sold as "tra," "swai," "sutchi," "striped catfish," and "tra catfish." Other names included "mekong catfish," "china sole," "river cobbler," "white ruffy," "shortbarbel," "grouper," and of course, "catfish."[44]

This diverse nomenclature lent credibility to the complaint that Vietnamese exporters were using the word "catfish" only to gain U.S. market share. But "fair trade," argued Alabama U.S. Senator Jeff

Sessions, "is not importing 'basa' fish, labeling them as catfish and passing them to American consumers as American catfish. The Vietnamese," he said, "need to play by the rules."[45] With a good deal less diplomacy, the CFA simply described tra and basa as "slippery catfish wannabes" that were "probably not even sporting real whiskers" (see **Exhibit 15**).[46]

Science Weighs In

Growing attention to the issue of nomenclature encouraged both sides to turn toward the scientific community. To Vietnam's favor, Ed Wiley, an ichthyologist from the University of Kansas, said that "to think that [basa] is not a catfish is hooey. . . . It is not a North American catfish. It is an Asian catfish. But to say it is not a catfish is wrong."[47] In fact, of the 2,500 different kinds of catfish, ichthyologists explained, all belonged to the *Siluriformes* order. But U.S. industry advocates rejected this line of reasoning, arguing that only catfish belonging to the *Ictaluridae* family of the *Siluriformes* order could rightly be labeled and sold as "catfish" in the U.S. To make their argument stronger, they pointed to the example of cattle and yak, both of which belonged to the *Eutheria* order. "I can't imagine if a country wanted to export yak to the United States and label it as beef that it would be readily acceptable to American consumers," said one advocate.[48]

The Catfish Becomes American

In the end, law, not scientific evidence, decided the identity of basa and tra in the United States. An amendment to the 2002 Agriculture Appropriations Bill (also known as the "Farm Bill") passed in autumn 2001. It stated that any fish sold in the United States as catfish must belong to the *Ictaluridae* family. Vietnamese "catfish," as such, ceased to exist legally in the U.S. Senator John McCain, former prisoner of war and longtime advocate of normalized U.S.-Vietnam relations, derided the amendment as "a clever trick of Latin phraseology" promising to do more harm than good.[49] Others in the business and nongovernmental organization (NGO) communities were also dismayed. Successive efforts to overturn the amendment nonetheless failed. Instead, all incoming product from Vietnam had to be relabeled immediately. Subsequent Vietnamese products were increasingly imported and sold under the names of "basa fish" and "tra fish."

Like Fish in a Barrel? The Dumping Case against Vietnam

The U.S. catfish industry expected the new labeling policy to work to its advantage. It did not. U.S. market share instead continued to decline, despite the U.S. product's selling at increasingly lower prices. In June 2002, the CFA sought remedy through an antidumping petition. If the petition were successful, importers would have to pay additional, possibly hefty tariffs on the Vietnamese product. The investigation took place in stages and primarily involved the U.S. Department of Commerce (DOC) and the U.S. International Trade Commission (ITC).

The CFA petition was jointly submitted to the DOC and the ITC. It charged Vietnamese producers of frozen basa and tra fillets with selling their product at *less than fair value (or normal value)* on the U.S. market. As a first step, the U.S. government had to decide whether to pursue the antidumping petition further. Toward this end, both government agencies embarked on their preliminary research, each with different responsibilities in the investigation.[50]

The U.S. Antidumping Investigation Process

The ITC had up to 45 days to make its preliminary determination. At this early stage, it needed only "reasonable indication" of "material injury or threat of material injury" to rule in the petitioner's favor and thus allow the investigation to continue. Before deciding, however, the ITC had to rule on the petitioner's definition of "like product" and "like industry." It was, after all, within these parameters that the degree of injury had to be assessed.

To no one's surprise, the ITC ruled that all frozen fish fillets processed from Vietnamese basa and tra were "interchangeable" with U.S. frozen catfish fillets, thus constituting a "like product." But the ITC rejected the inclusion of other Vietnamese whitefish, such as tilapia, as a "like product." It also rejected the petitioner's request that U.S. catfish farmers and catfish processors both be considered part of the U.S. industry. Instead, for the purposes of investigation, the U.S. industry was ruled to include processors alone.[51] The implication of the more narrow definition was huge. Under the rules of the Byrd Amendment, passed in 2000, injured U.S. parties were entitled to redistribution of levies obtained from antidumping penalties. Now catfish farmers in their own right would see none of it, even if the U.S. government ruled against Vietnam. Nonetheless, they continued to support the case, with some farmers having shares as well in the processing plants.

With the parameters of "like product" and "like industry" defined, the ITC next had to assess whether "material injury or the threat of material injury" had occurred to U.S. firms from the import of the Vietnamese product.[52] On August 9, 2002, the ITC announced its preliminary determination. It found that the frozen fish fillets from Vietnam were entering the U.S. at prices that had a "depressing or suppressing" effect on domestic prices.[53] For example, the average unit value (selling price) for the Vietnamese product had declined from $1.99 per pound in 1999 to $1.69 per pound in 2000 and to $1.41 per pound in 2001. This occurred when the average unit value (selling price) for domestically produced U.S. frozen catfish fillets increased from $2.70 per pound in 1999 to $2.75 per pound in 2000 and then sharply declined to $2.57 per pound in 2001.

The report also noted, however, that these indications of present material injury were far weaker than those of "imminent threat of material injury" by reason of the Vietnamese imports.[54] U.S. catfish industry operating profits, for example, increased from $6.7 million in 1999 to $8.5 million in 2001. Income margins were also up, increasing from 3% in 1999 to 4.2% in 2001.

The ITC preliminary ruling nonetheless signaled the DOC to begin its own preliminary inquiry. The DOC had a different role to play. It was responsible for determining whether dumping had occurred, and if so, to what degree. The DOC had several months to complete its research. If its preliminary determination were positive, there would be immediate consequences. Specifically, importers would have to post cash, bond, or other security with U.S. Customs to cover the cost of expected antidumping duties, a penalty refundable only if the petition was rejected at the final determination stage of the investigation.

The Dumping-Margin Calculation

The entire antidumping investigation from preliminary to final determination normally lasted no more than 14 months. But the Vietnamese and their supporters were rightly worried from the start. Of greatest concern was the preliminary calculation of the *dumping margin*. To obtain this number, the DOC had to consider a number of factors.

First, the DOC had to derive the Vietnamese product's *net export price*. This adjustment was a necessary first step toward determining whether the Vietnamese product was selling below production costs on the U.S. market. Drawing on data provided by exporters, the DOC derived the net export price by subtracting selling costs (e.g., insurance, freight, U.S. Customs duties) from the exporter's gross price so as to obtain factory-gate prices.

Second, the DOC had to determine the product's *normal or fair value*, meaning the price at which the good sold in its home market. The normal value was also a net price, meaning that it was adjusted to reflect costs at the factory gate. This adjustment allowed the DOC to compare export and home-market factory-gate prices of the same product.

Pulling these variables together, the DOC calculated the dumping margin as *the percentage of difference between the normal value and the net export price divided by the net export price*. For example, if Vietnam's normal value was \$135 per pound of basa and its net export price was \$90 per pound of basa, then the difference attributed to dumping would be \$45. The dumping margin was this difference divided by net export price multiplied by 100, or (\$45/\$90 * 100), which equalled a 50% dumping margin.

Exceptions to the Rule

Sometimes, the U.S. DOC did not use the product's home-market price to obtain the product's fair or normal value. Three conditions typically precluded using home-market prices.[55] First, whenever a product's home market was either nonexistent or its sales were less than 5% of the product's export volume, the DOC used the net price of the product as exported to a third country. Second, in cases where there were no home-market sales above production costs, then the DOC relied on a "constructed value" of the home-market price. To do so, it combined home-market production costs with overhead and selling and administrative costs, as well as some margin for profits. The DOC then derived the normal value from this constructed aggregate figure. Finally, in cases where the home market was deemed to be a "nonmarket economy," prices or costs of production from a "surrogate" market economy were used instead to construct the fair or normal value.

The DOC's criteria for finding an appropriate surrogate were comparability in terms of the country's level of development and its production of a like product at a comparable volume. In cases where specific data were missing, another surrogate country could be used. This allowed the U.S. government considerable discretion in the construction of the normal value and ultimately in the calculation of dumping margins.

The decision to use surrogate prices for nonmarket economies was based on the assumption that items had to be compared with like items for a claim of goods being sold "at less than fair value" to be established. It began with the identity of like ("interchangeable") products, then of like industry, and finally of like economic systems. Under market conditions, and assuming similarities in production process, if like products sold for less in the export market than in the home market, then the DOC assumed that the goods had been sold below the cost of production and, perhaps, as a result of government subsidies or other distortionary measures favoring exporters.

To ascertain whether an economy was "nonmarket," the DOC considered a number of factors. They included (1) whether the country had a convertible currency; (2) whether wages were freely set through bargaining between labor and management; (3) whether capital, especially foreign capital, was free to enter, leave, and be invested in the country; (4) the degree to which the government owned the means of production and directed national output decisions; and finally (5) the extent to which the government controlled the allocation of credit, prices, and other resources.

The Petitioner's Claim: Vietnam as a Nonmarket Economy

U.S. catfish farmers and producers were disappointed that the ITC excluded all but basa and tra from its category of "like products." But they heralded its preliminary determination that threats of material injury to the U.S. industry existed. The decision opened the way for a harder fight ahead over the nature of Vietnam's economy. For the purposes of antidumping investigations, it had yet to be classified. But whatever the DOC decided would apply to subsequent antidumping cases against Vietnam as well. As such, the stakes were high. A nonmarket economy classification was especially worrisome for an export-oriented country such as Vietnam, as it tended to result in higher dumping margins through the use of constructed values.

Given this, few were surprised that the CFA argued that Vietnam was a nonmarket economy. As was customary, however, CFA included dumping-margin calculations under both market and non-market scenarios in its petition (see **Exhibit 18**).

For the market economy scenario, it used a constructed value approach, claiming that Vietnam's domestic frozen fish market was too insignificant to allow the petitioner to derive the normal value. The petition also noted that data from Vietnamese exports to a third country were unavailable. As a result, the CFA argued that it had to use a combination of Vietnamese and U.S. prices to derive the normal value.

For the nonmarket economy scenario, the CFA chose India as a proxy, claiming that it shared a similar level of development with Vietnam (see **Exhibit 12**). Indian prices, as such, were set against Vietnamese factors of production and input quantities. These prices, however, were not based on either the U.S. or Vietnamese catfish species in dispute. Instead, the CFA derived the normal value and net export price from the production of the torpedo-shaped catfish (*clarias spp.*) common to south Asia (see **Exhibit 15**). There were other adjustments made as well. Most notably, whenever the petitioner was unable to obtain production input quantities for Vietnam, it relied on information provided from a U.S. processor.

Building on the above adjustments, the petitioners determined that the dumping margin was 143.7% under market economy conditions. But under the nonmarket economy conditions, the petitioners determined that the dumping margin was 190.2%, an increase of 47.2%. The 190.2% tariff implied that Vietnamese producers were selling catfish to U.S. distributors for 190.2% less than they were selling it to Vietnamese distributors. That meant in 2001, when U.S. distributors paid $1.41 a pound for frozen fish fillets from Vietnam, distributors in Vietnam would have had to pay $4.10.

The CFA argued that features of Vietnam's political economic system allowed its producers to sell frozen fish fillets on the U.S. market at less than fair value. To make their case, lawyers for the petitioner pointed to Vietnam's currency nonconvertibility, absence of free labor bargaining, Communist Party rule, limited privatization, and soft loans to state-owned enterprises. They also included a list of major Vietnamese processing plants exporting to the U.S., the bulk of which were state-owned enterprises (see **Exhibit 10**). To the petitioner, the absence of a viable private sector to counterbalance the state sector also implied that Vietnamese fish farmers were not able to sell their product at true market value.

In hopes of drawing the DOC toward a speedy conclusion, the CFA also included in its petition references to other U.S. government agencies that already had depicted Vietnam as a nonmarket economy. Most significantly, it noted that Congress had described the recently implemented U.S.-Vietnam Bilateral Trade Agreement as "the most comprehensive trade agreement ever negotiated with a non-market economy."[56]

The CFA did acknowledge that important economic reforms were underway in Vietnam. But lawyers for the petitioner also warned that "the relevant inquiry is not whether laws have been or may be passed but, rather, whether, in fact, the current economic conditions in Vietnam are such that the Department [of Commerce] may rely on prices and costs in Vietnam in order to conduct meaningful analyses under the U.S. trade laws."[57]   The CFA thought it was impossible.

The Respondent's Defense: Designing for Development, Not Dumping

Vietnam's supporters did not agree. If anything, they wondered how it was possible for one branch of the U.S. government to establish tra and basa as not being catfish, while another could claim that they were "like products." Equally troubling was that an antidumping petition was filed over practices the Vietnamese government claimed were allowed under the terms of its BTA with the U.S. (see **Appendix**).[58] Vietnam was, after all, not the only country with a national development strategy.

U.S. government-funded export promotion programs, investment credits, and indirect subsidies, such as the relatively weak enforcement of labor laws in farming, aided U.S. industrial development and export competitiveness as well.[59]   In fact, the very same year that Vietnam was accused of dumping, the U.S. Department of Agriculture bought $6 million worth of U.S. farm-raised catfish under its surplus-removal purchase program. Congressman Mike Ross of Arkansas pushed for the deal, citing national food security and the potential "rippling effect on Middle America" (see **Exhibit 14**).[60] Senator Blanche Lincoln of Arkansas also warned that the cycle of poverty in the Delta states was doomed to continue if the U.S. catfish industry faltered.[61]

Vietnam's deputy minister of fisheries saw the benefactors of U.S. support in less positive terms. She described the petitioners as a "relatively small group of wealthy catfish industrialists" who were seeking protection "at the expense of the free trade spirit and the best interests of the United States consumer."[62]   For Vietnam to win its case, however, vocal charges of hypocrisy and trickery had to be replaced with counterarguments within the confines of investigation procedures.

First among these counterarguments was the claim that U.S. catfish industry problems had little to do with Vietnamese imports. It had to do instead with the industry's own economic and organizational challenges. Real prices paid to U.S. catfish farmers, for example, were in decline years before the Vietnamese fish hit American shores (see **Exhibit 6**). One study linked the decline to an oligopsony-like dependence on a narrow set of processors and the limited ability of farmers to diversify their businesses.[63] There were also counterarguments to declining fillet prices as well. They included changes in supply resulting from efficiencies gained from automating much of the processing line and increasing pond acreage over the past decade (see **Exhibit 7**).[64] The catfish industry also engaged in price fixing in the late 1980s, leading to a downturn in the 1990s.[65] In fact, the largest U.S. processors were found guilty of violating antitrust laws and had to pay over $30 million in damages to buyers in the mid-1990s.[66]

U.S. catfish farmers were also thought to have a higher loss ratio than their Vietnamese counterparts.[67] To begin, the U.S. growing season was shorter than Vietnam's. Ambitious birds also routinely plucked catfish from ponds. In Mississippi alone, one study found that cormorants ate more than $5 million worth of catfish.[68] Equally difficult was the problem of pond algae. It gave the fish a muddy smell and "off-flavor" that kept them off the market and delayed pond harvesting. Vietnam's farmers, in contrast, benefited from the fast-flowing and highly aerated waters of the Mekong River, which shortened growing times, eliminated the cost of monitoring oxygen levels, and allowed for year-round harvesting.[69] The VASEP general secretary summed up the differences in market terms, arguing that Vietnam had the comparative advantage over the U.S. "You [the U.S.] can produce Boeing, but you cannot produce catfish very well," he said, adding that the U.S. industry would do well to invest instead in Vietnamese catfish farmers.[70]

Sal Piazza, a leading New Orleans-based importer of Vietnamese basa, agreed. He made much of these intra-industry differences in his marketing strategy. The Piazza Seafood World webpage, for example, reminded customers that U.S. farmers used "the pesticide diuron" to manage algae and off-flavor problems.[71] Caged Vietnamese basa fish, in contrast, were described as "consistently sweet [and] mild tasting." Rapid growth in U.S. basa imports and sales also suggested that American consumers agreed with the portrayal. In fact, Piazza deliberately sought out a "substitute for catfish in the United States" when he identified the fish on a research trip to Vietnam some years ago.[72] He later sold it under his company brand, "Cajun Delight" (see **Exhibit 8**). The decision made it possible for the Vietnamese to argue that they could not be held responsible for product misrepresentation, as they had no control over what brand names U.S. buyers chose to use.

Efforts to identify a market and industry basis for Vietnam's competitiveness were matched with evidence aimed to counter depictions of its economy as "nonmarket." Among them were letters addressed to the DOC from major U.S. corporations, including Cargill, Citibank, and New York Life International. The latter wrote, "With regard to the domestic labor market, we have been free to choose our employees in our office, and to establish wage rates by mutual agreement with our candidates."[73] Vietnam's own Chamber of Commerce and Industry also wrote to the DOC, explaining that significant reforms were underway. Farmers, for example, had long-term land-use rights that included a right of sale. In addition, they had autonomy in decision making about production and sales, as did Vietnam's catfish farmers. The number of state-owned enterprises also declined sharply in the early 1990s, going from around 13,000 firms to 6,000.[74] The U.S.-ASEAN Business Council subsequently concluded in its own letter to the DOC that "the Communist label attached to Vietnam has very little to do with economic reality."[75]

If anything, Vietnam's supporters were worried about what the market impact would be if the catfish industry lost access to the U.S. market. One international NGO warned that farmers would not be able to sustain employment levels.[76] Its survey also revealed that Vietnamese farmers did not enjoy government subsidies. Instead, they had to rely on loans from local financial institutions and family members to develop their businesses.[77] Given this, farmers were likely to go bankrupt if the export market collapsed.

The impact promised to be especially severe if Vietnam was subject to the higher dumping margins associated with nonmarket economy classification. An industry-specific exception could be made under U.S. antidumping law if it proved to operate according to market principles. But this option was unlikely for Vietnam, given the prevalence of state-owned enterprises in the processing sector. These firms had easier access than private-sector competitors to large state bank loans. In fact, so long as the political leadership advocated the "state sector as the leading sector" of the economy, a case for market economy classification was unlikely.

Instead, the Vietnamese had to begin immediately to consider the implications of India as a proxy for Vietnam. Shortly after hearing the CFA proposal, they raised objections. Foremost among them was concern that India's costs of production were far higher than Vietnam's, promising to result in higher dumping margins. Its industry also looked nothing like what was underway in Vietnam, even at the most basic level. To begin, the catfish exported to the U.S was different (see **Exhibit 15**). Catfish farming in India also was done primarily in ponds, not rivers. Finally, the state sector in India played a far greater direct role in fish farming than was the case in Vietnam, even with carp, a cheap fish found throughout Asia that was easily cultivated at the household level in combination with rice farming (see **Exhibit 11**).[78]

For all of these reasons, Vietnam preferred that the DOC consider Bangladesh as a proxy instead. Not only were its levels of development more comparable, argued Vietnam's supporters, but the private sector played a greater role in Bangladesh's fish farming sector as compared to India. The Bangladesh economy also was more "open" to trade than India's if average tariff rates were used as a measure (see **Exhibit 19**). Vietnam was the most open of all, yet it alone had the fight ahead over the status of its economy.

Conclusion

On September 30, 2002, a team of DOC investigators boarded a plane for Vietnam. On arrival, they began to survey exporters, gather data on production costs, and interview government officials and others familiar with the catfish industry. Some companies refused to cooperate. Others were eager, hoping that the investigation ended in their industry's favor. It was, after all, just a matter of weeks before the DOC had to announce its decision on the status of Vietnam's economy, after which preliminary findings on the antidumping charge against Vietnam would follow. The work was front page news in Vietnam. Its fate again, it seemed, was left to how Americans saw Vietnam.

Exhibit 1 Vietnam's Direction of Trade, 1985–2003 (in millions of U.S. dollars)[a]

	1985	1995	1999	2000	2001	2002	2003
Total Exports	693	5,621	11,541	14,482	15,014	15,714	20,679
Japan	32	1,461	1,461	2,575	2,510	2,300	2,897
United States	...	170	170	733	1,066	2,350	4,463
China	...	362	362	1,536	1,417	1,013	1,324
Australia	2	55	55	1,273	1,042	1,172	1,545
Singapore	36	690	690	886	1,044	853	931
Germany	2	218	218	730	722	1,001	1,202
United Kingdom	1	75	75	479	512	667	903
South Korea	16	235	235	353	406	428	488
Total Imports	1,842	8,359	11,741	15,636	16,216	20,014	24,864
Singapore	24	1,425	1,879	2,694	2,478	2,290	2,653
Japan	142	916	1,618	2,301	2,183	2,349	2,689
South Korea	3	1,254	1,486	1,754	1,887	2,464	2,810
China	...	330	673	1,401	1,606	2,365	3,496
Thailand	...	440	562	811	792	1,042	1,395
Hong Kong	29	419	505	598	538	845	1,077
United States	1	130	323	364	411	638	1,457
Malaysia	...	191	305	389	464	731	834

Source: Asian Development Bank, *Key Indicators*.

[a] "..." indicates data unavailable.

Exhibit 2 Mekong Delta Map

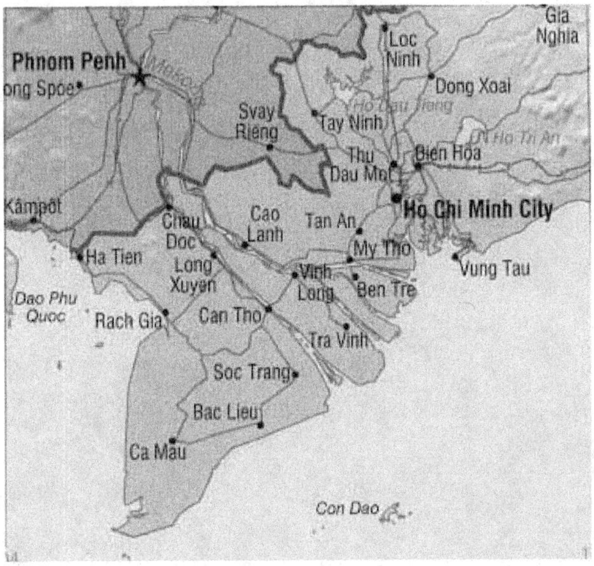

Exhibit 3 Mississippi Delta Map

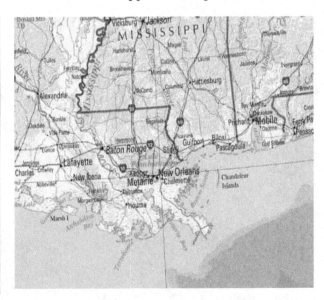

Source: The University of Texas at Austin, University of Texas Libraries, *Perry-Castaneda Library Map Collection*.

Source: The University of Texas at Austin, University of Texas Libraries, *Perry-Castaneda Library Map Collection*.

Exhibit 4　Catfish Production as Share of U.S. Aquaculture Production, 1983–2001

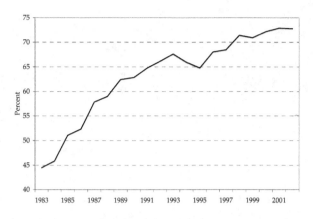

Source: Fisheries Statistics and Economics Division of the National Marine Fisheries Service.

Exhibit 5　World Fish Production, Developed and Developing Countries, 1961–2001

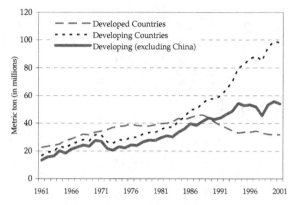

Source: Food and Agriculture Organization, FAOSTAT (2005).

Exhibit 6　Real Prices Paid to U.S. Catfish Farmers, 1970–1998

Source: U.S. Department of Agriculture, National Agricultural Statistics Service.

Exhibit 7　U.S. Pond Acreage, 1988–1998

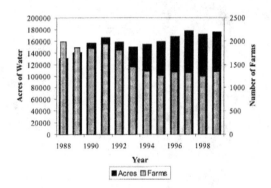

Source: U.S. Department of Agriculture, National Agricultural Statistics Service.

Exhibit 8　"Cajun Delight" Brand Product Label

Source: Helene Cooper, "Catfish Case Muddies Waters For Bush 'Fast Track' Plans," *The Wall Street Journal*, July 13, 2001.

Exhibit 9   Stages of Catfish Processing, Vietnam and United States Compared

Vietnam

4. Fillets being prepared for packaging.

3. Fish deheading and evisceration station.

2. Farmers gathering fish.

1. Fish farm houses.

Source: Photos courtesy of Vietnam Net.

United States

2. Stunned fish enter production line.

3. Automatic deheading station.

6. Fillets are quick frozen, glazed, and packaged.

1. Farmers gathering fish.

5. Mechanical skinning and fillet trimming.

4. Evisceration (vacuum) station.

Sources: Richard F. Kaxmierczak and Patricia Soto, "The Impact of Price and Yield Variability on Southeastern United States Catfish Producer Operations," LSU AgCenter: Research & Extension, September 2000. See also Juan L. Silva, Gale R. Ammerman, and Stuart Dean, "Processing Channel Catfish," Southern Regional Aquaculture Center, SRAC Publication No. 183, August 2001.

Exhibit 10   Ownership Form, Selected Vietnamese Catfish Processing Firms

Company Name	Ownership Status During Period of Investigation [a]
Nam Viet	Nonstate
Agifish[b]	State
Vinh Long	State
CATACO	State
Mekonimex	State
Afiex	State
CAFATEX	State
Da Nang	State

Source: "[A-552-801] Certain Frozen Fish Fillets Final Antidumping Duty Determination of Sales at Less Than Fair Value and Affirmative Critical Circumstances: Memorandum to Joseph A. Spetrini, Acting Assistant Secretary for Import Administration," United States Commerce, International Trade Administration, Import Administration, June 16, 2003.

[a]Period of investigation is October 1, 2001 to March 31, 2002.

[b]Agifish became a publicly listed company on Vietnam's stock exchange after the period of investigation.

Exhibit 11   Asian Carp Production, Ownership Forms, 1998–1999 Survey[a]

	Bangladesh	China	India	Vietnam Total	North	South
Fish farm area by tenure (%)						
Privately owned	100	41.1	62.6	90.1	35	95.7
State owned	0	29.6	29.3	0.7	45	0.57
Collective	0	29.3	2.2	8.5	17.8	0
Leased/ Rented	0	0	6.8	0.7	0	3.73
Others	0	0	1.2	0	2.2	0

Source: WorldFish Center Field Survey (1998–1999).

[a]Due to rounding, numbers may not add up to 100.

Exhibit 12   Socioeconomic Statistics, 2002

	Bangladesh	India	Vietnam
GDP (in current millions of U.S. dollars)	47,563	596,543	35,058
GDP per capita, PPP (current international dollars)	1,696	2,674	2,304
GDP by sector composition (%)			
Agriculture	23	23	23
Industry	26	27	38
Manufacturing	16	16	21
Service	51	51	38
Gini Index[a]	32	33	37
Aid per capita (in current U.S. dollars)	7	1	16
Health expenditure per capita (in current U.S. dollars)	11	30	23
Infant mortality rate per 1,000 live births, under 1 (2003)	46	63	19
Population (in millions)	136	1,049	80
Urban (%)	26	28	25
Total adult literacy rate (%) (2000)	40	57	93
Total labor force (in millions)	69	464	43
Females as share of total labor force (%)	43	33	49
No. of phones per 100 people	1	5	7
No. of television sets per 100 people (2001)	5	8	19

Source: World Bank, *World Development Indicators*.

[a] "Gini Index" measures inequality over the entire distribution of income or consumption. A value of 0 represents perfect equality, and a value of 100 represents perfect inequality.

Exhibit 13   U.S. Imports and Consumption of Frozen Catfish Fillets, 2000–2001

	2000	2001
U.S. Consumption Quantity (in millions of pounds)	148.4	158.6
U.S. producer market share (%)	90.7	83.0
Vietnam market share (%)	8.4	16.4
Other countries market share (%)	0.8	0.6
U.S. Consumption Value (in millions of U.S. dollars)	395.6	380.7
U.S. producer market share (%)	93.6	88.9
Vietnam market share (%)	5.9	10.8
Other countries market share (%)	0.4	0.3
U.S. Import Quantity (in millions of pounds)	13.7	27.0
Vietnam share of U.S. import quanitity (%)	91.2	96.4
Other countries share of U.S. import quantity (%)	8.8	3.6
U.S. Import Value (in millions of U.S. dollars)	25.3	42.3
Vietnam share of U.S. import value (%)	92.9	96.9
Other countries share of U.S. import value (%)	7.1	3.1

Source: "Certain Frozen Fish Fillets from Vietnam: Investigation No. 731-TA-1012 (Final)," U.S. International Trade Commission, Publication 3617, August 2003.

Exhibit 14   Mississippi Delta Socioeconomic Statistics, 2002

	Per capita income (in U.S. dollars)	Percent below poverty level[a]	Unemployment rate (%)	Infant Mortality (per 1,000 births)[b]	Education		
					People 5-17 years old, Enrollment rate (%)	Completed High School or more (%)	Completed College or more (%)
United States	30,906	11.7	5.8	6.8	89.6	84.1	26.7
Mississippi Delta	24,238	16.8	6.1	9.4	87.7	79.5	21.0
Alabama	25,548	14.6	5.9	9.4	90.3	78.9	22.7
Arkansas	23,556	18.0	5.4	8.3	90.4	81.0	18.3
Mississippi	22,550	17.6	6.8	10.5	87.2	79.1	20.9
Louisiana	25,296	17.0	6.1	9.8	83.0	78.8	22.1

Source: U.S. Census Bureau, Statistical Abstract of the United States.

[a]Data for the United States and its subcategories are the average of 2000–2002.

[b]Data for the United States and its subcategories are for 2001.

Exhibit 15   Illustrations of Different Catfish Species

U.S. Channel Catfish (U.S.)   **Basa Catfish** (Vietnam)   **Torpedo (Walking) Catfish** (India)

Sources: "Fishing Identification," Nevada Department of Wildlife; Manfred Klinkhardt, "FISH INFOnetwork Market Report on Basa," EUROFISH, February 2004; and Robert H. Robins, "Biological Profiles," Florida Museum of Natural History.

Exhibit 16   U.S.-Vietnam Trade, Key Items, 1998–2004[a]

U.S. Exports to Vietnam (in millions of U.S. dollars)

	1998	1999	2000	2001	2002	2003	2004
Rice	0.0	0.0	0.0	0.0	0.1	0.0	0.0
Coffee, Roasted	0.0	0.0	0.0	0.2	0.0	0.0	0.0
Farmed fish and related products	...	...	...	...	...	...	...
Fish, fresh, chilled or frozen and other marine products	0.7	1.3	2.2	6.8	8.6	3.4	6.1
Frozen fish fillets	0.1	0.0	0.1	0.0	0.1	0.3	1.3
Footwear	0.0	0.3	0.0	0.0	0.0	0.2	0.1
Apparel	0.2	0.4	0.1	0.8	0.2	1.0	1.0

U.S. Imports from Vietnam (in millions of U.S. dollars)

	1998	1999	2000	2001	2002	2003	2004
Rice	5.7	0.0	0.1	0.0	0.1	0.0	0.1
Coffee, Roasted	0.3	0.2	0.7	0.3	0.7	1.9	1.8
Farmed fish and related products	0.2	0.2	0.2	0.3	0.3	0.5	0.6
Fish, fresh, chilled or frozen and other marine products	95.7	146.0	311.6	491.5	626.7	734.1	549.9
Frozen fish fillets	8.8	16.0	33.3	43.1	70.1	57.2	77.9
Footwear	121.1	155.8	131.8	140.0	239.1	346.4	505.2
Apparel	24.2	34.1	45.9	45.9	943.1	2,498.0	2,655.2

Source: U.S. International Trade Commission, *USITC Interactive Tariff and Trade Dataweb.*

[a] "..." indicates data unavailable.

Exhibit 17   World Fish Production and Exports, 1990–2001

	1990		1995		1999		2000		2001	
	Production (in metric tons)	Exports (in millions of U.S. dollars)	Production (in metric tons)	Exports (in millions of U.S. dollars)	Production (in metric tons)	Exports (in millions of U.S. dollars)	Production (in metric tons)	Exports (in millions of U.S. dollars)	Production (in metric tons)	Exports (in millions of U.S. dollars)
World Total Value	98,590,481	6,336	116,685,883	9,315	127,082,153	10,230	130,782,342	10,396	129,942,647	9,910
					Region/Country's Percent Share of World Total Value					
Africa	5.2	4.5	5.1	5.5	5.2	4.9	5.4	6.3	5.6	4.4
Asia	47.4	23.3	53.2	25.5	59.3	20.8	58.9	21.9	60.6	24.2
Bangladesh	0.9	0.0	1.0	0.0	1.2	0.0	1.3	0.0	1.3	0.0
China	15.0	11.3	25.6	12.3	32.7	7.0	32.9	6.9	33.9	7.6
India	3.9	0.0	4.2	0.6	4.4	0.8	4.3	0.7	4.6	0.8
Japan	10.5	0.8	5.8	0.7	4.7	1.1	4.4	1.4	4.2	1.3
Vietnam	1.0	0.1	1.3	0.3	1.5	1.2	1.5	2.1	1.5	3.3
Central America	1.6	1.0	1.4	1.4	1.2	1.4	1.4	1.4	1.4	1.4
European Union	7.2	38.0	7.1	31.4	5.9	37.2	5.6	35.0	5.7	35.2
Latin America and Caribbean	16.5	3.6	18.7	4.7	14.9	4.0	15.9	3.9	13.8	4.1
Peru	7.0	0.0	7.7	0.0	6.6	0.2	8.2	0.1	6.2	0.2
Other	22.1	29.5	14.5	31.5	13.5	31.9	12.9	31.5	12.9	30.8
Canada	1.7	7.1	0.8	7.8	0.9	8.0	0.9	8.4	0.9	9.0
United States	6.0	5.5	4.8	5.0	4.1	5.5	4.0	4.8	4.2	4.3

Source: Food and Agriculture Organization, *World Fishery Statistics.*

Exhibit 18   Petitioner's Estimated Cost of Producing a Pound of Frozen Fish Fillet in Vietnam, Author's Calculation[a]

Catfish Farmers of America's estimated dumping margins of Vietnam

CFA: Market Economy	Cost per pound	CFA: Nonmarket Economy	Cost per pound
Cost of live fish	0.62	Cost of live fish	0.53
Cost of fish used	2.37	Cost of fish used	1.83
Value of fish waste	0.21	Value of fish waste	0.17
Labor	0.18	Labor	0.15
Electricity, water, chemicals, packing materials	0.03	Electricity, water, chemicals, packing materials	0.03
Cost of goods sold	2.58	Cost of goods sold	2.01
Overhead costs	0.02	Overhead costs	0.40
Selling, general, & administrative cost plus interest	0.09	Selling, general, & administrative cost plus interest	0.91
Total costs	2.68	Total costs	3.32
Profit (before exporting)	0.10	Profit (before exporting)	0.03
Normal value	2.78	Normal value	3.35
FOB plant price	1.14	FOB plant price	1.15
Dumping margin	143.86	Dumping margin	191.30

Sources: "Petition for the Imposition of Antidumping Duties: Certain Frozen Fish Fillets from the Socialist Republic of Vietnam," Catfish Farmers of America (CFA), June 28, 2002; Thanh Tung Nguyen, Van Thanh Nguyen, and Michael Phillips, "Policy Research – Implications of Liberalization of Fish Trade for Developing Countries: A Case Study of Vietnam," Food and Agriculture Organization (FAO) of the United Nations, July 2004; and Xuan Thanh Nguyen, "Catfish Fight: Vietnam's Tra and Basa Fish Exports to the U.S," Fulbright Economics Teaching Program, March 2003.

[a] The original dumping margins calculated by the CFA were 143.7% if Vietnam had a market economy and 190.2% if Vietnam had a nonmarket economy. The estimated dumping margins in this exhibit differ from the CFA's because variables such as "cost of fish used," "value of fish waste," and "labor" were estimated by using comparable multiples acquired from Thanh Tung Nguyen, Van Thanh Nguyen, and Michael Phillips (2004), Xuan Thanh Nguyen (2003), and CFA (2002). This led to a difference in the "normal value" and thus the dumping margin. "Live fish" is the cost per pound of live fish. "Cost of fish used" refers to the total cost of the amount of fish used to produce a pound of fillet.

Exhibit 19   Openness to Trade, Various Countries, 1990–2004

Country	Openness Ratio (%)[a]			Average Tariff (%)[b]
	1995	2002	2004	1990-1999
Bangladesh	18.9	23.1	36.2	43.7
China	38.3	49.7	75.1	31.1
France	43.5	40.0	51.5	6.9
India	17.2	20.0	33.7	48.7
Japan	18.3	16.0	24.3	6.0
United Kingdom	47.4	52.0	53.1	6.9
United States	20.5	20.8	25.2	6.0
Vietnam	66.9	66.2	138.0	14.6

Source: World Bank, *World Development Indicators*; *The Economist*, Economist Intelligence Unit; and Steve Parker, "Vietnam's Road to International Economic Integration (Draft)," January 10, 2005.

[a] The ratio is calculated as the value of imports plus exports divided by the gross domestic product; the following value is then multiplied by 100.
[b] For Vietnam, the average tariff rate for 1996–2001 is used.

Appendix

Agreement between the United States of America
and the Socialist Republic of Vietnam on Trade Relations

Signed in Washington July 13, 2000; Entered into force December 10, 2001

Article 2 National Treatment

1. Each Party shall administer tariff and non-tariff measures affecting trade in a manner which affords meaningful competitive opportunities for products of the other Party with respect to domestic competitors.

2. Accordingly, neither Party shall impose, directly or indirectly, on the products of the other Party imported into its territory, internal taxes or charges of any kind in excess of those applied, directly or indirectly, to like domestic products.

3. Each Party shall accord to products originating in the territory of the other Party treatment no less favorable than that accorded to like domestic products in respect of all laws, regulations and other requirements affecting their internal sale, offering for sale, purchase, transportation, distribution, storage or use.

6. Consistent with the provisions of GATT 1994, the Parties shall ensure technical regulations and standards are not prepared, adopted or applied with a view to creating obstacles to international trade or to protect domestic production…Accordingly the Parties shall:

A. ensure that any sanitary or phytosanitary measure which is not inconsistent with the provisions of the GATT 1994, is applied only to the extent necessary to protect human, animal or plant life or health, is based on scientific principles and is not maintained without sufficient evidence (i.e., a risk assessment), taking into account the availability of relevant scientific information and regional conditions, such as pest free zones;

B. ensure that technical regulations are not prepared, adopted or applied with a view to or with the effect of creating unnecessary obstacles to international trade. For this purpose, technical regulations shall not be more trade-restrictive than necessary to fulfill a legitimate objective, taking into account the risks non-fulfillment would create. Such legitimate objectives include national security requirements; the prevention of deceptive practices; protection of human health or safety, animal or plant life or health, or the environment…

Article 6 Emergency Action on Imports

4. The Parties acknowledge that the elaboration of the market disruption safeguard provisions in this Article is without prejudice to the right of either Party to apply its laws and regulations applicable to trade in textiles and textile products, and its laws and regulations applicable to unfair trade, including antidumping and countervailing duty laws....

CHAPTER IV DEVELOPMENT OF INVESTMENT RELATIONS

Article 2 National Treatment and Most-Favored Nation Treatment

1. With respect to the establishment, acquisition, expansion, management, conduct, operation and sale or other disposition of covered investments, each Party shall accord treatment no less favorable than that it accords, in like situations, to investments in its territory of its own nationals or companies (herinafter "national treatment") or to investments in its territory of nationals or companies of a third country (herinafter "most favored nation treatment"), whichever is most favorable (herinafter

"national and most favored nation treatment"). Each Party shall ensure that its state enterprises, in the provision of their goods or services, accord national and most favored nation treatment to covered investments, subject to the provisions of paragraph 4.3 of Annex H.

2. A Party may adopt or maintain exceptions to the obligations of paragraph 1 in the sectors or with respect to the matters specified in Annex H to this Agreement. In adopting such an exception, a Party may not require the divestment, in whole or in part, of covered investments existing at the time the exception becomes effective.

ANNEX H VIETNAM

In accordance with the provisions in Article 2 of Chapter IV, the Government of the Socialist Republic of Vietnam reserves the right to adopt or maintain exceptions to national treatment in the following sectors and matters:

1. Vietnam may adopt or maintain exceptions to the obligation to accord national treatment to covered investments in the sectors or with respect to the matters specified below:

> Broadcasting, television; production, publication and distribution of cultural products; investment in insurance; banking; brokerage, dealership in securities and currency values, and other related services; mineral exploration and exploitation; construction, installation, operation and maintenance of telecommunication facility; construction and operation of inland water, sea and airports; cargo and passenger transportation by railway, airway, road, sea and inland water-way transportation; fishing and fish catching; real estate business....

4.4 Government subsidies and supports:

> Government subsidies and supports granted to domestic enterprises, which include land allocation for investment projects, preferential credits, research and development and education assistance programs and other forms of Government supports, may not be made available to nationals or companies of the United States....

ANNEX H UNITED STATES

1. The Government of the United States of America may adopt or maintain exceptions to the obligation to accord national treatment to covered investments in the sectors or with respect to the matters specified below:

> Atomic energy; customhouse brokers; licenses for broadcast, common carrier, or aeronautical radio stations; COMSAT; subsidies or grants, including government-supported loans, guarantees and insurance; landing of submarine cables; ...

2. The Government of the United States of America may adopt or maintain exceptions to the obligation to accord national and most favored nation treatment to covered investments in the sectors or with respect to the matters specified below:

> Fisheries; air and maritime transport, and related activities; banking, insurance, securities, and other financial services; leasing of minerals and pipeline rights-of-way on government lands; and one-way satellite transmissions of direct-to-home (DTH) and direct broadcast satellite (DBS) television services and of digital audio services....

Endnotes

[1] "'Free' Trade with the U.S. can be Fishy Business, Aquaculture Industry Finds," *InternationalReports.net*, 2003, www.internationalreports.net/asiapacific/vietnam/2003/freetrade.html.

[2] Paul Blustein, "Free Trade's Muddy Waters; Vietnamese 'Catfish' Spawn a Story of Diplomacy and Domestic Priorities Clashing at the Dinner Table," *The Washington Post*, July 13, 2003.

[3] Greg Rushford, "Catfishing for Sympathy," *The Rushford Report*, July 2003.

[4] Ibid.

[5] Seth Mydans, "Americans and Vietnamese Fighting Over Catfish," *The New York Times*, November 5, 2002.

[6] "Certain Frozen Fish Fillets from Vietnam: Investigation No. 731-TA-1012 (Preliminary)," U.S. International Trade Commission, Publication 3533, August 2002, pp. 14–15.

[7] Thanh Tung Nguyen, Van Thanh Nguyen, and Michael Phillips, "Policy Research – Implications of Liberalization of Fish Trade for Developing Countries: A Case Study of Vietnam," Food and Agriculture Organization (FAO) of the United Nations, July 2004.

[8] Dr. Nguyen Huu Dung, general secretary of VASEP, disputes this claim, noting that commercial fish cages had been used in Vietnam since at least the 1920s. See www.internationalreports.net /asiapacific/vietnam/2003/uscatfish.html.

[9] Xuan Thanh Nguyen, "Catfish Fight: Vietnam's Tra and Basa Fish Exports to the U.S," Fulbright Economics Teaching Program, March 2003, p. 2.

[10] Seth Mydans, "Americans and Vietnamese Fighting Over Catfish," *The New York Times*, November 5, 2002.

[11] Thanh Tung Nguyen, Van Thanh Nguyen, and Michael Phillips, "Policy Research – Implications of Liberalization of Fish Trade for Developing Countries: A Case Study of Vietnam," Food and Agriculture Organization (FAO) of the United Nations, July 2004, p. 32. See also "What Do the Catfish Farmers Say? Report of an Interaction with Catfish Farmers in the Mekong Delta of Vietnam," ActionAid, August 2002, p. 14.

[12] Thanh Tung Nguyen, Van Thanh Nguyen, and Michael Phillips, "Policy Research – Implications of Liberalization of Fish Trade for Developing Countries: A Case Study of Vietnam," Food and Agriculture Organization (FAO) of the United Nations, July 2004, p. 32. Agifish is an acronym for the An Giang Fish Import-Export Company. Afiex is an acronym for the An Giang Agricultural Import-Export Company.

[13] Thanh Tung Nguyen, Van Thanh Nguyen, and Michael Phillips, "Policy Research – Implications of Liberalization of Fish Trade for Developing Countries: A Case Study of Vietnam," Food and Agriculture Organization (FAO) of the United Nations, July 2004, p. 21.

[14] "Certain Frozen Fish Fillets from Vietnam: Investigation No. 731-TA-1012 (Preliminary)," U.S. International Trade Commission, Publication 3533, August 2002, p. 13.

[15] "Draft Aquaculture Development Plan of 1996," Joint Subcommittee on Aquaculture National Science and Technology Council.

[16] Ibid.

[17] Randy Ziegenhorn, "A River Full of Fish: Industrial Catfish Production and the Decline of Commercial Fishing on the Upper Mississippi River," *Human Organization*, Vol. 59, Issue 2 (Summer 2000): 165.

[18] Bonnie Coblentz, "State Catfish Grow Under Tight Watch," Mississippi State University, Office of Agricultural Communication, July 2, 2001, http://msucares.com/news/print/agnews/an01/010702.htm.

[19] Molly Ivans and Lou DuBose, "The Blues in Belzoni," *The Texas Observer*, October 10, 2003. See also Danna Harman, "The New Plantation?" *The Christian Science Monitor*, November 26, 2003.

[20] Robert E. Pierre, "Poverty Tightens Grip on Mississippi Delta," *The Washington Post*, July 17, 2004. See also "Racial and Ethnic Tensions in American Communities: Poverty, Inequality, and Discrimination Volume VII, The Mississippi Delta Report," The U.S. Commission on Civil Rights, February 2001.

[21] Danna Harman, "The New Plantation?" *The Christian Science Monitor*, November 26, 2003.

[22] "Pickering's Amendment to Stop Vietnamese Fish from Misleading Consumers Approved by U.S. House," October 3, 2001, http://www.house.gov/pickering/Misleading.htm.

[23] Bonnie Coblentz, "State Catfish Grow Under Tight Watch," Mississippi State University, Office of Agricultural Communication, July 2, 2001, http://msucares.com/news/print/agnews/an01/010702.htm.

[24] Robyn Hearn, "Catfish Producers Stand to Win Big in Industry Promotion Campaign," Alabama Agricultural Experiment Station, Office of Communications, July 21, 1995, http://www.ag.auburn.edu/aaes/webpress/1995/catfishproducers.htm.

[25] Xuan Thanh Nguyen, "Catfish Fight: Vietnam's Tra and Basa Fish Exports to the U.S," Fulbright Economics Teaching Program, March 2003, p. 7.

[26] Ibid. See also Brenda Jo Narog, "Past – Present – Future: Catfish in Vietnam and the U.S.," *Aquaculture Magazine*, May/June 2003, p. 1. See also "Catfish Row Mars Vietnam," *BBC News*, December 20, 2001.

[27] Act available online at http://www.nmfs.noaa.gov/sfa/sfweb/aqua_act.htm.

[28] "Imports & Lackluster Demand Pressure Catfish Prices," *Agricultural Outlook*, April 2002, p. 7. See also "Letter to Robert Zoellick," various members of the Congress of the United States, February 9, 2001.

[29] "Quick Catfish Facts: From the Pond to the Plate," The Catfish Institute, http://www.catfishinstitute.com/About/Fact.asp. See also Juan L. Silva, Gale R. Ammerman, and Stuart Dean, "Processing Channel Catfish," Southern Regional Aquaculture Center, SRAC Publication No. 183 (August 2001, Revised).

[30] Kristal Brent Zook, "Catfish and Courage: A Struggling Mother Becomes a Labor Organizer in a Mississippi Factory," *Essence Magazine*, April 2003; for more details, see the documentary *Standing Tall: Women Unionize the Catfish Industry* (1999).

[31] "Certain Frozen Fish Fillets from Vietnam: Investigation No. 731-TA-1012 (Final)," U.S. International Trade Commission, Publication 3617, August 2003, p. III-3 and p. IV-2.

[32] Dan Chapman, "Catfish Tangle. U.S., Vietnam Fight Trade War Over Down-home Delicacy," *The Atlanta Journal-Constitution*, December 11, 2002.

[33] "Raised in the U.S.A.: The Catfish Institute Addresses Fishy Issue with Strategic Marketing Campaign," *Agri Marketing*, April 2002.

[34] Margot Cohen and Murray Heibert, "Muddying the Waters," *Far Eastern Economic Review*, December 6, 2001.

[35] Dan Morgan, "Vietnamese Catfish Rile Southern Lawmakers," *The Washington Post*, September 10, 2001.

[36] Hung Minh Nguyen, Binh Minh Tu, Natsuko Kajiwara et al., "Persistent Organic Pollutants (POPs) in Catfish and Sediment from the Mekong River: Sources, Occurrences, and Risk Assessment," Center for Marine Environmental Studies, Ehime University, Japan, 2001.

[37] Shalmali Guttal, "The Mississippi-Mekong Catfish Wars," *People's Food Sovereignty*, October 8, 2002.

[38] Greg Rushford, "Never Trust a Catfish with a Foreign Accent," *The Rushford Report*, December 2001.

[39] "'Free' Trade with U.S. can be Fishy Business, Aquaculture Industry Finds," *InternationalReports.net*, 2003.

[40] "Petition for the Imposition of Antidumping Duties: Certain Frozen Fish Fillets from the Socialist Republic of Vietnam," Catfish Farmers of America, June 28, 2002, p. 39.

[41] Robb Walsh, "Fish Fraud," *Houston Press,* November 1, 2001.

[42] David Bennet, "Producers Charge Labels Improper: Fish Imports Hurt U.S. Catfish Prices," *Delta Farm Press,* August 3, 2001. See also Ronette King, "A Fine Kettle of Catfish," *The Times-Picayune* (New Orleans), September 9, 2001.

[43] "Vietnam Agrees to Use New Names for Catfish Exports," U.S. House of Representatives press release, July 31, 2001.

[44] "Petition for the Imposition of Antidumping Duties: Certain Frozen Fish Fillets from the Socialist Republic of Vietnam," Catfish Farmers of America, June 28, 2002, p. 8. See also Xuan Thanh Nguyen, "Catfish Fight: Vietnam's Tra and Basa Fish Exports to the U.S," Fulbright Economics Teaching Program, March 2003, p. 9.

[45] "Senator Sessions Opposes U.S.-Vietnam Bilateral Trade Pact, Cites Concerns with Mislabeled Vietnamese Fish Displacing American Catfish," press release of Senator Sessions, October 3, 2001, http://sessions.senate.gov/pressapp/record.cfm?id=178959.

[46] "The Great Catfish War," *The New York Times,* July 22, 2003.

[47] Eric Palmer, "Catfish at the Center of U.S.-Vietnam Trade Battle," *The Kansas City Star,* April 22, 2002.

[48] Forrest Laws, "House Acts on Mislabeled Fish Imports," *Delta Farm Press,* October 12, 2001. See also Elton Robinson, "Senate: Catfish Uniquely American," *Delta Farm Press,* November 9, 2001.

[49] "McCain: Catfish Import Barrier Puts International Trade Agreements at Risk," press release, Office of U.S. Senator John McCain, December 18, 2001.

[50] "Import Administration Antidumping Manual," Import Administration, 1997. See also "Antidumping and Countervailing Duty Handbook," U.S. International Trade Commission, January 2005.

[51] "Certain Frozen Fish Fillets from Vietnam: Investigation No. 731-TA-1012 (Preliminary)," U.S. International Trade Commission, Publication 3533, August 2002, pp. 9–10.

[52] "Trade Remedy Investigations," U.S. International Trade Commission, http://www.usitc.gov/trade_remedy/.

[53] "Certain Frozen Fish Fillets from Vietnam: Investigation No. 731-TA-1012 (Preliminary)," U.S. International Trade Commission, Publication 3533, August 2002, p. 14.

[54] Ibid., pp. 20 and 21.

[55] "Antidumping and Countervailing Duty Handbook," U.S. International Trade Commission, January 2005.

[56] H.R. REP. No. 107-198, at 2, September 5, 2001.

[57] "Re: Antidumping Duty Investigation of Certain Frozen Fish Fillets from the Socialist Republic of Vietnam," Akin Gump Strauss Hauer & Feld LLP, October 2, 2002, p. 6.

[58] "Vietnam Protests U.S. Ban on Foreign Catfish," *Associated Press,* May 15, 2002.

[59] Dan Danielsen and Karl Klare, "Trade, Labor & Catfish: A Case Study (Draft)," Northeastern University, School of Law, May 2003, p. 4. There are many U.S. government social welfare and private-sector development programs. Of those geared explicitly to enhance international competitiveness, see http://www.export.gov/comm_svc/; http://www.wusata.org/; http://www.exim.gov/index.cfm; http://www.sbaonline. sba.gov/financing/ loanprog/tradeloans.html; http://www.fas.usda.gov/ excredits/ scgp.html; http://www.miatco.org/noflash_ miatco_home.htm; http://www.foodexportusa.org/.

[60] Michael Ross, "Congressman Ross's Letter to Secretary Veneman," press release from Office of U.S. Congressman Michael Ross, September 7, 2001.

[61] Paul Blustein, "Free Trade's Muddy Waters; Vietnamese 'Catfish' Spawn a Story of Diplomacy and Domestic Priorities Clashing at the Dinner Table," *The Washington Post*, July 13, 2003.

[62] Seth Mydans, "Americans and Vietnamese Fighting over Catfish," *The New York Times*, November 3, 2002.

[63] Richard F. Kaxmierczak and Patricia Soto, "The Impact of Price and Yield Variability on Southeastern United States Catfish Producer Operations," LSU AgCenter: Research & Extension, September 2000, p. 6.

[64] Ibid., p. 7.

[65] For more information see *"In Supreme Court of Mississippi: No. 95-CA-00116-SCT,"* June 26, 1997, http://lw.bna.com/lw/19970722/9500116.htm.

[66] John M. Sullivan, "Harvesting Cooperatives and U.S. Antitrust Law: Recent Developments and Implications," unpublished paper, 2000. See also Randy Ziegenhorn, "A River Full of Fish: Industrial Catfish Production and the Decline of Commercial Fishing on the Upper Mississippi River," *Human Organization*, Vol. 59, Issue 2 (Summer 2000): 166.

[67] "What Do the Catfish Farmers Say? Report of an Interaction with Catfish Farmers in the Mekong Delta of Vietnam," ActionAid, August 2002, p. 13. See also Thanh Tung Nguyen, Van Thanh Nguyen, and Michael Phillips, "Policy Research – Implications of Liberalization of Fish Trade for Developing Countries: A Case Study of Vietnam," Food and Agriculture Organization (FAO) of the United Nations, July 2004, pp. 28–29.

[68] See "Economic Impact and Management of Bird Predation at Aquaculture Facilities in the Southeastern U.S," U.S. Department of Agriculture, Animal & Plant Health Inspection Service, Wildlife Services, National Wildlife Research Center, http://www.aphis.usda.gov/ws/nwrc/research/aquaculture.

[69] Thanh Tung Nguyen, Van Thanh Nguyen, and Michael Phillips, "Policy Research – Implications of Liberalization of Fish Trade for Developing Countries: A Case Study of Vietnam," Food and Agriculture Organization (FAO) of the United Nations, July 2004, p. 29. See also "What Do the Catfish Farmers Say? Report of an Interaction with Catfish Farmers in the Mekong Delta of Vietnam," ActionAid, August 2002, pp. 13–14.

[70] "U.S. Catfish Decision Hurts Poorest," *InternationalReports.net*, 2003.

[71] See Piazza's Seafood World webpage, http://cajunboy.net/basa.htm. For more information on the use of diuron in the U.S. catfish industry, see "Impact of Diuron Usage on the U.S. Catfish Industry," Mississippi Agricultural and Forestry Experiment Station, Bulletin 1101, March 2001. See also Doreen Muzzi, "EPA Approves Diuron for Catfish Ponds," *Delta Farm Press*, April 12, 2002.

[72] Steve Bradshaw, "Unfair Meal Gives Taste of Global Trade Pitfalls," *Landline*, April 13, 2003, http://www.abc. net.au /landline/stories/s828402.htm.

[73] "RE: Comments on Non-market Economy Status for Vietnam (Case Number A-552-801)," New York Life International, September 24, 2002.

[74] "Re: Request for Comments on Vietnam's Status as a Market or Non-market Economy," Vietnam Chamber of Commerce and Industry, September 30, 2002, p. 3.

[75] "Re: Case No. A-552-801," US-ASEAN Business Council, October 2, 2002.

[76] "What Do the Catfish Farmers Say? Report of an Interaction with Catfish Farmers in the Mekong Delta of Vietnam," ActionAid, August 2002, p. 15.

[77] Ibid., p. 9. See also Thanh Tung Nguyen, Van Thanh Nguyen, and Michael Phillips, "Policy Research – Implications of Liberalization of Fish Trade for Developing Countries: A Case Study of Vietnam," Food and Agriculture Organization (FAO) of the United Nations, July 2004, p. 41.

[78] David J. Penman, Modadugu V. Gupta, and Madan M. Dey, eds., "Carp Genetic Resources for Aquaculture in Asia," WorldFish Center, 2005.

REGINA ABRAMI

ALAN W. TU

The Delta Blues: U.S.–Vietnam Catfish Trade Dispute (B)

Divide a river to prevent a market (ngan song cam cho).

—Vietnamese saying

On November 8, 2002, the U.S. Department of Commerce (DOC) made its decision public. Vietnam was not a market economy, at least not for the purpose of U.S. antidumping investigations. As such, the dumping margin had to be calculated with the assistance of a proxy country.

The Vietnamese were deeply disappointed by this decision, having already mustered considerable international support for their position. In fact, the DOC acknowledged the recent growth of small and medium-sized private enterprises in Vietnam. But limited amounts of privatization in such critical areas as banking and industry also allowed government economic control to remain considerable, the U.S. government agency concluded.

Hearing that Vietnam was declared a nonmarket economy, members of the Catfish Farmers of America (CFA) celebrated another victory for their side. Only some months ago, the organization had submitted its antidumping petition against "certain frozen fish fillets" from Vietnam. Now the CFA had only to wait for the U.S. government to make its final determination.

Things were certainly looking up. Few nonmarket economies were able to evade dumping charges. The CFA was also convinced that if the Vietnamese product were "fairly priced" on the U.S. market, American catfish could regain lost market share. The Vietnamese also expected defeat, but for different reasons. Antidumping tariffs, they argued, promised to drive their growing aquaculture industry into the ground. As both sides watched the next stage of the investigation unfold, they were filled with expectations about what lay ahead.

The DOC Investigation: Bad Math or Good Politics?

With the classification of Vietnam's economy completed, the battle over which country to use as a proxy intensified. The proxy, after all, was going to be used to construct "market" prices for Vietnam.   Once this information was gathered, the dumping margin could be determined. Calculated as *the percentage of difference between the normal value (that is, net home-market price) and the*

---

net export price divided by the net export price, the margin need only be 2% above the export price for a company to be found guilty of dumping under U.S. trade law. Given this, only a slight difference in input costs from one country to another could result in an unfavorable decision for Vietnam. The CFA pushed for India. Vietnam's supporters argued that Bangladesh was more appropriate.

Picking Proxy Countries

After considerable lobbying on both sides, the DOC chose to use Bangladesh. The country was not only at a comparable level of development but also a significant producer of the *Pangasius* catfish species.[1] Bangladesh costs of production were then used to calculate costs within the Vietnamese industry. But whenever prices were unavailable for Bangladesh, the DOC used prices from India.

Preliminary Determination

After months of gathering input costs on everything from electricity to plastic bags used to ship frozen fillets, the DOC constructed its estimated dumping margin for Vietnam. It fell well above the 2% minimum and was thus "unfair" according to U.S. trade law. On January 31, 2003, the DOC made its preliminary determination public. It announced that Vietnamese producers were selling their product at less than normal value on the U.S. market. Immediately thereafter, the DOC imposed preliminary tariffs on "certain frozen fish fillets" from Vietnam.[2]

Going forward, importers had to post a cash deposit or a bond equal to the preliminary dumping margin, which ranged from 38% to 64% of the total shipment value of the frozen Vietnamese fish fillets. Vietnamese firms demonstrating operational independence from the government enjoyed the lowest tariff rates. For example, state-owned companies such as Agifish and Vinh Hoan and a non-state-owned company, Nam Viet, were given separate rates corresponding to data they had provided to the DOC. Vietnamese companies that either failed to respond to the DOC's request for information or to meet the DOC's standard of operational independence were given the highest tariff rate. In effect, the DOC aimed to assign tariff rates on the basis of a firm's proximity to market costs.

Vietnamese producers argued, however, that the U.S. government got its math wrong, counting as product what they treated as waste. Specifically, fins, fish heads, and other parts, although resold, were part of the costs, not the profits of fillet production. And if counted as such, then the dumping margin was lowered considerably for Vietnamese processors. The DOC agreed, and new preliminary dumping margins were announced in March 2003.[3]

The DOC also agreed that it had incorrectly relied on a gross export price instead of net export price, leading to an improper comparison between the home market (that is, "normal value") and the export price of frozen fish fillets. Both were supposed to be net prices. The error resulted in considerably higher dumping margins for producers who ice-"glazed" more heavily than others. Specifically, the gross export price included the additional weight of a fillet frozen in water, making it seem as if a bigger fish was being produced at a lower cost than was actually the case. The tariff adjustment that came from the DOC correction was significant. Agifish, for example, saw its preliminary tariff rate drop from 61.88% to 31% after the DOC conceded to the mistake.

The DOC nonetheless maintained that the CFA's initial charge of "critical circumstances" was correct. The phrase implied that Vietnamese companies were aware of the dumping petition in advance of the CFA's filing and deliberately exported as much as possible beforehand. To discourage such behavior, the DOC had the right to apply the preliminary tariffs retroactively to the time when a surge first began, rather than to the later date of its preliminary determination. In May 2003, the

DOC did so, citing critical circumstances existed for a number of Vietnamese firms. These included Nam Viet, Afiex, Cafatex, QVD, Da Nang, as well as all other firms already subject to the country-wide highest tariff. Immediately, U.S. importers had to post deposits equal to the preliminary dumping margins for certain frozen fillets retroactive to November 2, 2002.

Final Determination

Given this, it seemed that the DOC's final determination could not possibly go in Vietnam's favor. The Vietnamese government jumped in to offer a voluntary export restraint program in May 2003. But disputes over quota amounts quickly shelved the strategy.

A few weeks later, on June 17, 2003, the DOC did issue its final determination. It found that "certain frozen fish fillets" from Vietnam were dumped on the U.S. market. Proposed final tariffs changed only slightly, ranging from 36% to 64%. In addition, another firm had critical circumstances applied to it. Still, until the International Trade Commission (ITC) signed off, no official antidumping order was issued.

Coming Full Circle: Back to the ITC

As a last stage, the ITC had to affirm material injury to the petitioners. If not, despite all the months of hard work, the case would be dropped. In July 2003, the ITC made its decision public, announcing that the petitioners were materially injured from "certain frozen fish fillets" from Vietnam. But in a surprising move, the ITC ruled against critical circumstances. As a result, antidumping tariffs were only to begin once the antidumping order was issued on August 7, 2003.

Sink or Swim? After the U.S. Government Decision

For Vietnamese producers, the decision was a bittersweet victory tempered by fear of what lay ahead. Before the final ruling, 40,000 farmers from An Giang province had tried to sway matters. In their own signed appeal, they argued that the DOC's decision was not only "unjust" but promised to thrust them into "major difficulties in both production and daily life."[4] U.S. petitioners, in contrast, were ecstatic. Hugh Warren, the CFA executive director, predicted "much-needed relief to catfish farmers, processors, and thousands of workers who felt the impact of [an] unfairly traded product."[5]

The Vietnamese Catfish Industry: Building New Roads, Battling Old Barriers

The late 2001 requirement that exporters relabel their product had caused shipments to plunge. By the end of 2002, the export value of frozen catfish fillets to the U.S. dropped 42%.[6] By late 2003, and in the wake of the U.S. decision, nearly 10% of basa and tra went without buyers.[7] The economic damage seemed irreparable, with the value of frozen fish fillets to the U.S. dropping precipitously, from $23.1 million to $595,000.[8]

Vietnam's share of U.S. frozen catfish fillet imports also shrunk 74% between 2001 and 2004 (see **Exhibit 1**). But at the same time, Vietnamese exporters were able to secure higher prices for their product. Export prices to the U.S. jumped from $1.36 per pound in 2002 to around $1.65 per pound in 2004.[9] At the lower end of the supply chain, however, Vietnamese catfish farmers nonetheless suffered considerably. In response to oversupply and additional tariff costs, processors offered them 10%–30% less per kilogram of live fish.[10] More job losses were expected as a result.[11]

To prevent an industry meltdown, both provincial and national-level Vietnamese government bodies stepped in, offering suggestions on product and market diversification. Even the prime minister helped out, directly asking local traders to offer farmers higher purchase prices.[12] The Vietnam Association of Seafood Exporters and Producers (VASEP) also established a committee to coordinate activities among these various government bodies, catfish farmers, and processors.[13]

These efforts appeared to have paid off. By August 2004, tra and basa were exported to 40 foreign markets.[14] Besides Southeast Asia, the biggest new market for Vietnam was the European Union (see **Exhibit 6**). Vietnamese catfish imports into the EU jumped 523% between 2002 and 2004, reaching $51.1 million between January and August 2004 alone. EU buyers were not discouraged by increasing import prices, either. They jumped from $1.10 to $1.80 per pound between 2002 and 2004.[15]

Helping Vietnam along was the German wholesaler Metro Cash & Carry. It agreed to offer Vietnamese basa worldwide through its shops.[16] The Vietnamese also began their own international marketing campaign.[17] And as the industry began its recovery, new processors, including some private firms, entered the market, while some existing firms upgraded their operations.[18] The government also initiated privatization efforts in the seafood industry.[19]

Still, the Vietnamese industry was not without challengers. Over the past decade, more and more developing countries had entered into the international trade of fish products. Increasing international competition led some of the biggest Vietnamese firms to develop the domestic market in response, and with considerable success. Vietnam also had to contend with the United States.

Despite all the wrangling of recent years, the U.S. remained one of the biggest importers of Vietnamese basa and tra catfish.[20] But the nature of the relationship had changed. Looking back, the VASEP general secretary concluded, "[Vietnam's] error in the past few years was to focus too much on the U.S. market. The Bilateral Trade Agreement made us look through rose-colored lenses and forget [about] the ill-fated side of that giant [U.S.] market. We should have studied the market thoroughly and known the rules of the game better."[21]

Just a year later, in August 2004, VASEP had its first opportunity to show how much it had learned. It requested administrative review of the U.S. antidumping order. Companies (or their representatives) affected by antidumping duties were allowed to make this request each year until an antidumping order came up for its sunset review, usually five years after the initial decision. Now, nearly a year later, the VASEP request still remained under review at the DOC. But the prospects of Vietnam securing World Trade Organization accession within a year were brighter than ever. If successful, Vietnam would never again have to stand alone in its trade disputes with the U.S.

The U.S. Catfish Industry: No Quick Fix

As much as the Vietnamese industry had changed, the U.S. industry seemed to stay the same after the antidumping case ended. Instead of diversification, signs of consolidation emerged. The average water-surface acres devoted to catfish farming, for example, declined 10% between 2001 and 2004, from 188,050 to 169,650 acres in Alabama, Arkansas, Louisiana, and Mississippi.[22] To everyone's dismay, total U.S.-bred catfish fillet sales increased only slightly after the antidumping order was issued in 2003.

Part of the reason had to do with the rising cost of the U.S. product, a reflection of processors paying more for live catfish owing to higher feed and fuel costs (see **Exhibit 2**).[23] In fact, U.S. catfish farmers raised prices 22% between 2002 and 2004. But U.S. catfish processors dared not raise fillet prices so high, when lower-priced foreign competitors remained on the U.S. market.

China was especially worrisome to U.S. industry advocates as it began to produce and export the same species of catfish found in the U.S. As such, it was not subject to the same labeling restrictions that other catfish species faced. Instead, Chinese catfish could be sold and labeled in the U.S. as catfish. Importers certainly did not fail to notice the opportunity, especially Sal Piazza. Lambasted for selling basa as catfish under his "Cajun Boy" brand, he began to import the Chinese product in 2003.[24]

In fact, the well-publicized U.S.-Vietnam trade dispute did little to dampen U.S. seafood imports (see **Exhibit 5**). All signs indicated instead that the developing world was increasingly relying on aquaculture as a means of export earnings (see **Exhibit 4**). Part of the reason had to do with limited opportunities in the home market and global economic integration. But no less significant were U.S. and other foreign aid programs geared to alleviate poverty and improve trade capacity in the developing world.[25] The latter program included courses in standards harmonization, dispute-settlement procedures, and customs facilitation.

In combination with weather-related financial losses in 2001 and 2002, U.S. catfish farmers felt increasingly vulnerable. They had been ruled out of the U.S.-Vietnam trade dispute, meaning that they were ineligible for proceeds from the antidumping order. Their only option was to apply for compensation, technical assistance, and retraining under the U.S. Trade Adjustment Assistance (TAA) Program. In November 2003, catfish farmers were declared eligible for the program on the grounds that increased imports of Vietnamese basa and tra fish had led to a decline in domestic catfish prices in 2002. Over 375 catfish farmers, not all in the Mississippi Delta, received benefits of over $500,000 for fiscal year 2003–2004.[26] Just a year later, they were on their own again, having failed to meet program requirements for continued financial support in 2003. To do so, the price of catfish had to be 80% or less than the previous five-year average price, but under terms whereby similar imports did not increase in the previous year and imports did not contribute to a price decline.[27] TAA support, in other words, was not intended to be a response to dumping.

Declining government support and the continued competitiveness of non-U.S. products encouraged the U.S. industry to continue with earlier marketing tactics. First among them was the campaign to depict catfish as a distinctly American product. One promotional flier, for example, appealed for an official declaration of a national fish, noting how the United States had "a national tree, a national bird, and a national pastime, [and] now we need a national fish! Catfish, an American original," it continued.[28] Posters meant for distribution in shops and restaurants also described U.S. farm-raised catfish as part of the "All American Meal" (see **Exhibit 7**). More dramatic was the "Pride Ride," a 2002 Volkswagen remade to look like a U.S. channel catfish (see **Exhibit 10**). Sponsored by the Alabama Catfish Producers Association and the Southern Pride Catfish Company, the "Pride Ride" continued to tour parts of the U.S. in 2005.[29]

The U.S. industry also tried to shape the consumer market through partnerships with high-profile firms. Wal-Mart, for example, agreed to distribute only U.S. farm-raised catfish in its Mississippi stores.[30] Piccadilly Restaurants LLC, which operated 130 cafeterias in 15 states, also began to serve only U.S. catfish products as of April 2003.[31] In addition, restaurants began to affix decals to entryways informing customers that they served only U.S. farm-raised catfish.

Nonetheless, the idea of Vietnamese basa as the better tasting fish continued to haunt the industry. Indeed, some blind taste tests indicated that consumers preferred the Vietnamese product, while in other cases the margin of preference was too close to call. But in one way, the U.S. catfish was way ahead. It did not test positive for fluoroquinolones, a class of antibiotics banned in the

U.S.[32] The winning Vietnamese basa fillet at a recent Louisiana competition did. According to the San Jose-based *Mercury News*, the importer, LA Fish Company, was based in Milpitas, California, but had only a post office box and no known telephone number.[33] In fact, no one even knew who ordered the drug test on that day.

The impact nonetheless was immediate. The Louisiana government issued a "stop sale" order against all Vietnamese seafood products in the state.[34] Alabama followed days later with its own ban, leading some to question whether the issue was consumer health or local industry protection. Mississippi promised to act likewise if contaminated products were found in its market.

Still, U.S. social welfare advocates did not think that economic development was possible through the provision of fair trade and consumer protection alone. The Mississippi Delta was, by many accounts, a "third world country in the heart of America," a place where rural poverty, weak infrastructure, and inequality remained a huge problem (see **Exhibits 8** and **9**).[35] Both government help and private-sector development was desperately needed. One returned resident, now working with the poor, reflected how in the past she used to wonder, "What's wrong with these people? Why can't they do better?" only to realize that today there were simply too few jobs.

Conclusion

On June 19, 2005, the airplane carrying the prime minister of Vietnam, Pham Van Khai, landed in the United States. It was the first visit of its kind since the end of the U.S.-Vietnam War. Although brief, the trip was closely watched on both sides of the Pacific. A chorus of protesting Vietnamese-Americans, human rights activists, and veterans tried to derail discussions, but U.S. and Vietnamese government representatives forged ahead, agreeing to closer economic and military ties.

In contrast, U.S. federal support for the Mississippi Delta was in decline. Budget allocations for the Mississippi Delta Regional Authority had dropped precipitously, from $20 million in 2001 to $6 million in 2005.[36] But this joint federal-local agency was still responsible for "stimulating economic development and fostering [economic and social] partnerships" in the region. But now, it had considerably less money with which to do so.[37] Given this, the question of how to alleviate poverty and enhance international competitiveness seemed to loom all the larger.

Exhibit 2   U.S. Producers and Processors' Catfish Prices, 1995–2004

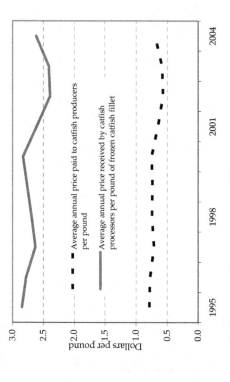

Source: National Agricultural Statistics Service, U.S. Department of Agriculture.

Exhibit 4   Net Exports of Selected Commodities of Developing Countries, 1981–2001

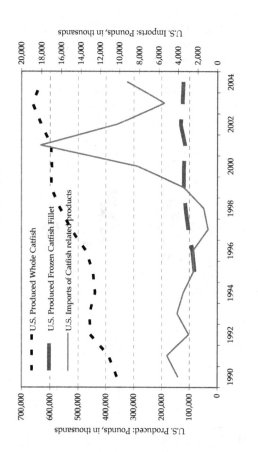

Source: "Medium Term Plan 2005–2007," WorldFish Center.

Exhibit 1   Vietnam's Share of Selected U.S. Fish Imports, 1995–2004

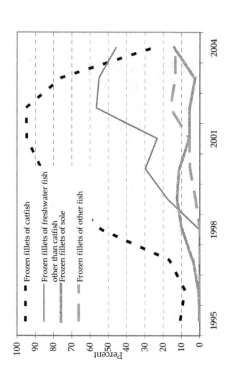

Source: U.S. Trade Internet System, Foreign Agriculture Services.

Exhibit 3   Pounds of U.S Catfish, 1990–2004

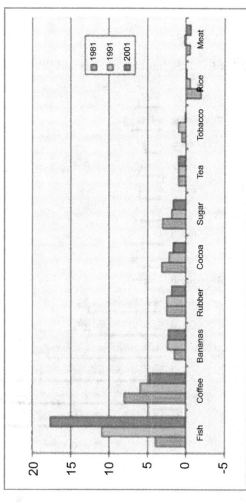

Source: National Agricultural Statistics Service, U.S. Department of Agriculture.

Exhibit 5   U.S. Imports of Fish and Shellfish, 2002–2004

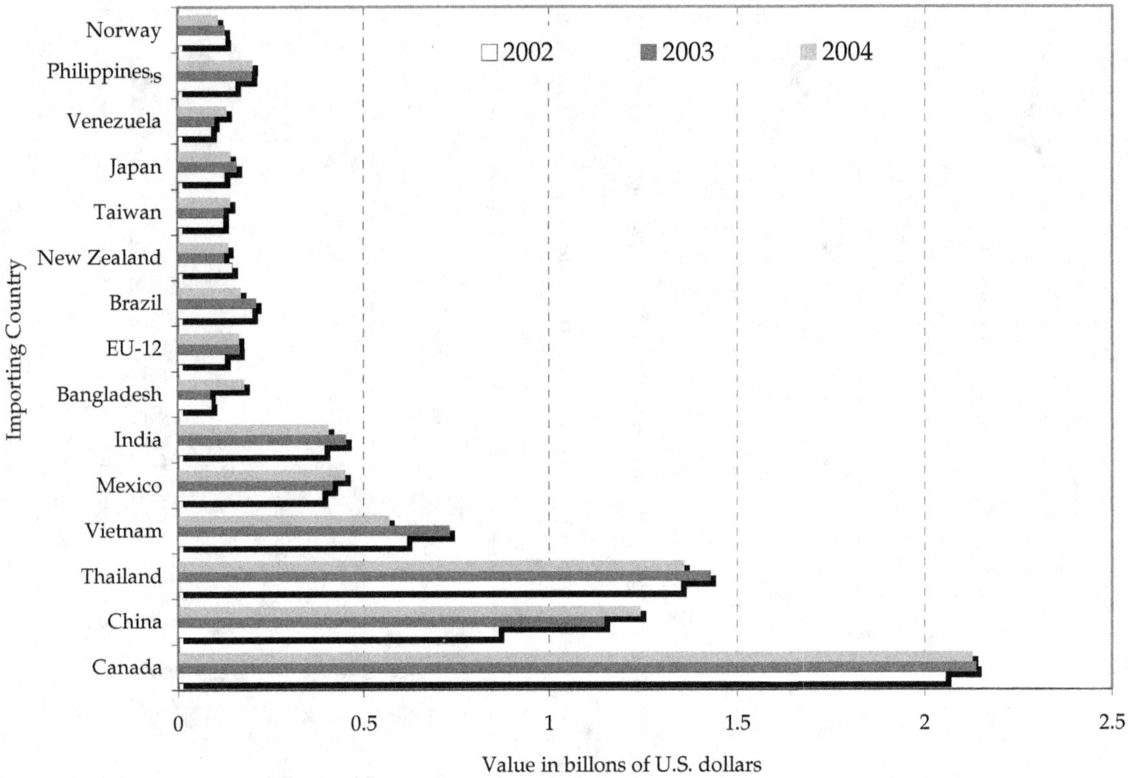

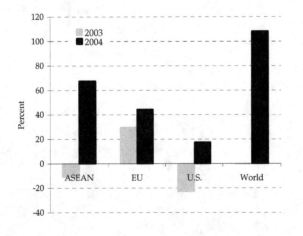

Source: Foreign Agricultural Service, U.S. Department of Agriculture.

Exhibit 6   Vietnam's Growth in Share of Country/
                 Region's Frozen Fish Fillet Imports,
                 2003–2004

Exhibit 7   U.S. Catfish Marketing Poster

Source: UN Comtrade, United Nations.

Source: Courtesy of American Pride Seafoods, a division of
American Seafoods Group LLC.

Exhibit 8   U.S. Counties with Persistent Poverty, 1970–2000 [a]

Exhibit 9   U.S. Nonmetro Counties with High Poverty, 2000[a]

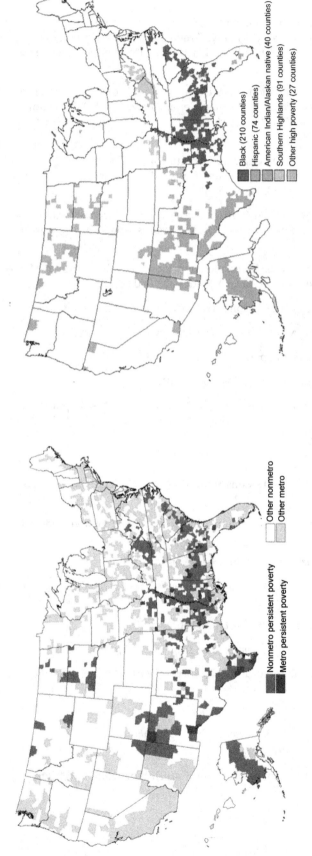

Black (210 counties)
Hispanic (74 counties)
American Indian/Alaskan native (40 counties)
Southern Highlands (91 counties)
Other high poverty (27 counties)

Nonmetro persistent poverty
Metro persistent poverty

Other nonmetro
Other metro

Source: Economic Research Service, Department of Agriculture.

[a] 20% or more of residents were poor in persistent poverty counties according to the last four censuses, 1970, 1980, 1990, and 2000.

Source: Economic Research Service, U.S. Department of Agriculture.

[a] The Economic Research Service calculated the data using the 2000 census. Poverty rate of 20% or more is considered "high poverty."

Exhibit 10   U.S. Channel Catfish Car, "The Pride Ride"

The Pride Ride

Source: Courtesy of American Pride Seafoods, a division of American Seafoods Group LLC. See http://www.southernpride.net/the%20pride%20ride.htm.

Endnotes

[1] Import Administration, International Trade Commission, and Department of Commerce, "Notice of Preliminary Determination of Sales at Less Than Fair Value, Affirmative Preliminary Determination of Critical Circumstances and Postponement of Final Determination: Certain Frozen Fish Fillets from the Socialist Republic of Vietnam," *Federal Register*, Vol. 68, No. 21, January 31, 2003.

[2] Import Administration, International Trade Commission, and Department of Commerce, "Notice of Amended Preliminary Determination of Sales at Less Than Fair Value: Certain Frozen Fish Fillets from the Socialist Republic of Vietnam," *Federal Register*, Vol. 68, No. 43, March 5, 2003. See also Greg Rushford, "The Unmentionable Fish," *The Rushford Report*, February 2003.

[3] Import Administration, International Trade Commission, and Department of Commerce, "Notice of Amended Preliminary Determination of Sales at Less Than Fair Value: Certain Frozen Fish Fillets from the Socialist Republic of Vietnam," *Federal Register*, Vol. 68, No. 43, March 5, 2003.

[4] "Vietnamese Public Opinion Condemns U.S. Decision on Catfish Lawsuit," *BBC Monitoring International Reports*, June 28, 2003; Tran Dinh Thanh Lam, "Vietnamese Exporters Draw Lessons from 'Catfish War' with U.S.," Interpress Service, July 31, 2003.

[5] "Stiff Tariffs Recommended for Catfish Imports into U.S.; Vietnamese Producers Illegally Captured Market Share, Commerce Department says," *The Times-Picayune* (New Orleans), January 28, 2003.

[6] "USITC Interactive Tariff and Trade DataWeb," U.S. International Trade Commission, 2005.

[7] Manfred Klinkhardt, "Basa Market Report- February 2004," *Globefish*, February 2004.

[8] "USITC Interactive Tariff and Trade DataWeb," U.S. International Trade Commission, 2005.

[9] Hong Ngoc, "Catfish export prices rebound," *The Saigon Times*, March 6, 2004, p. 3.

[10] Thanh Tung Nguyen, Van Thanh Nguyen, and Michael Phillips, "Policy Research – Implications of Liberalization of Fish Trade for Developing Countries: A Case Study of Vietnam," *Food and Agriculture Organization (FAO) of the United Nations*, July 2004, p. 39.

[11] Ibid., p. 42.

[12] Tran Dinh Thanh Lam, "Vietnamese Exporters Draw Lessons from 'Catfish War' with U.S.," Interpress Service, July 31, 2003.

[13] "VASEP Freshwater Fish Committee established," *VNA*, June 15, 2005, http://www.vietrade.gov.vn /news.asp?cate=18&article=4257&lang=en.

[14] "Trade: Vietnam Catfish Nets New Markets," *Vietnam News Brief Service*, June 21, 2004.

[15] "Vietnamese Pangasius Production and Trade," *Globefish*, November 2004. See also "Vietnam Catfish Selling Well in EU," *Asia Pulse*, March 9, 2004.

[16] Manfred Klinkhardt, "Basa Market Report- February 2004," *Globefish*, February 2004.

[17] "Belgium to Showcase Vietnamese Aquatic Products," *Financial Times Information*, April 14, 2005.

[18] "Agriculture: Navico Begins Work on Vietnam's Biggest Catfish Factory," *Vietnam News Briefs*, March 24, 2005.

[19] Manfred Klinkhardt, "Basa Market Report," *Globefish.org*, February 2004.

[20] "Catfish Exports Hit by Global Slowdown," *VNECONOMY*, August 12, 2005, http://www.vneconomy. com.vn /eng/index.php?param=article&catid=07&id=2cc977ac612899.

[21] Tran Dinh Thanh Lam, "Vietnamese Exporters Draw Lessons from 'Catfish War' with U.S.," Interpress Service, July 31, 2003.

[22] "Catfish Production," National Agricultural Statistics Service, U.S. Department of Agriculture, July 27, 2005; February 3, 2002; February 7, 2002; July 29, 2002.

[23] Terry Hanson, "U.S. Farm-Raised Catfish Industry: 2004 Review and 2005 Outlook," *National Warmwater Aquaculture Center*, Vol. 8, No. 1 (April 2005): 10.

[24] See Piazza's Seafood World webpage, http://www.cajunboy.net/completeproductlist.htm.

[25] See, for example, the Trade Capacity Building Project webpage, http://www.tcb-project.com/tcb/level1.php.

[26] Terry Hanson and Dave Sites, "2004 U.S. Catfish Database," Department of Agricultural Economics, Mississippi State University, March 2005, p. 4.

[27] For more information see Forrest Laws, "Catfish Producers Eligible for Trade Assistance," *Southwest Farm Press*, January 22, 2004. Also see "Trade Adjustment Program," Cooperative State Research, Education, and Extension Service, http://www.csrees.usda.gov/nea/economics/in_focus/farm_if_trade.html.

[28] Vote for Catfish campaign, see http://www.americanprideseafoods.com/Promotions/Catfish%20 Month %2004/Cat%20month%20promo.pdf.

[29] Further information on the "Pride Ride" and its image can be found at http://www.southernpride.net/the%20pride%20ride.htm.

[30] "There is no place like home," *The Saigon Times Magazine*, August 21, 2003.

[31] Brenda Jo Narog, "Past-Present-Future: Catfish in Vietnam," *Aquaculture Magazine*, May/June 2003.

[32] Used to treat tuberculosis and other infections, the antibiotic has been banned from use in U.S. consumer products out of fear that germs might grow resistant to the medicine. For more information see http://2theadvocate.com/stories/081205/new_vietnamese001.shtml; http://www.etaiwannews.com/World/2005/07/20/1121827417.htm; and http://www.sanluisobispo.com/mld/sanluisobispo/news/politics/12370696.htm.

[33] Janet McConnaughey, "La. Stops Sales of Vietnamese Seafood: Banned Antibiotic Found," *Associated Press*, August 12, 2005,

http://www.mercurynews.com/mld/mercurynews/news/local/states/california/northern_california/12370696.htm. See also Louisiana Department of Agriculture and Forestry, "Declaration of Emergency – Fluoroquinolones," press release from the Office of the Commissioner, Louisiana, August 12, 2005, http://www.ldaf.state.la.us/aboutldaf/presscenter/pressreleases/pressrelease.asp?id=499.

[34] "Detention Without Physical Examination of Aquaculture Seafood Products Due to Unapproved Drugs; Attachment Revised 8/8/05," Food and Drug Administration, August 8, 2005,

http://www.fda.gov/ora/fiars/ora_import_ia16124.html.

[35] Michael Parfit, "And What Words Shall Describe the Mississippi, Great Father of Rivers," *Smithsonian*, February 1993, p. 36; Robert E. Pierre, "Poverty Tightens Grip on Mississippi Delta," *The Washington Post*, July 17, 2004; and Hilary Roxe, "Mississippi Delta Advocates Push for More Money, Attention," *Associated Press*, May 19, 2005, http://www.kentucky.com/mld/kentucky/news/local/11688873.htm.

[36] Hilary Roxe, "Mississippi Delta Advocates Push for More Money, Attention," *Associated Press*, May 19, 2005, http://www.kentucky.com/mld/kentucky/news/local/11688873.htm.

[37] A more detailed description can be found at http://www.dra.gov/about.php.

9-706-043

REV: NOVEMBER 9, 2006

RAWI ABDELAL, REGINA ABRAMI

NOEL MAURER, ALDO MUSACCHIO

The Market and the Mountain Kingdom: Change in Lesotho's Textile Industry

If you can meet with Triumph and Disaster
And treat those two impostors just the same
　　　—Rudyard Kipling

Maseru, the capital of the Kingdom of Lesotho, was a place of unlikely contrasts. Hundreds of miles from the sea, high in the mountains, and surrounded on all sides by South Africa, Lesotho was not an especially convenient destination for even the most intrepid traveler. Maseru was not famous for its cosmopolitanism, and yet foreign influences had made their way to the city. Although there were no Chinese restaurants in rural South Africa, Maseru had one on every corner. The restaurants were there to serve the large Taiwanese and Chinese expatriate communities, whose members owned and managed almost all of the local apparel factories. Some of those factories were supplied by the Formosa denim mill, one of the largest and most sophisticated in the world. The stirrings of industrialization and modernization were promising, and more than 50,000 workers, mostly women, were employed in the textile sector; the figure reflected more than a three-fold increase in just a few years. Just outside Maseru, however, life was pastoral. Of Lesotho's 1.9 million citizens, 86% were engaged in subsistence agriculture. It was little exaggeration to say that the men of Lesotho worked in South African mines, the women worked in the apparel factories, and the country's formal economy consisted of almost nothing else. The country's hopes for progress rested with the Taiwanese and Chinese firms and the jobs they created.

In early 2006, however, the survival of the nascent industry hung in the balance. Everything seemed to have gone wrong all at once. The appreciation of Lesotho's currency, the loti, made life difficult for the apparel firms, which exported almost all of their production to the United States. Although the firms enjoyed duty-free access to an otherwise protected U.S. clothing market through the African Growth and Opportunity Act (AGOA), the provisions that most benefited Lesotho were set to expire in 2007. A few large buyers—Levi's and the Gap Inc.—would be making decisions about sourcing that could make or break Lesotho's industry. Local union leaders were upset with the government's handling of the textile boom and its putatively impending bust.

The end of the story was still to be written. Certainly the government would play an important role in formulating a strategy and adjusting the institutional context, but decisions made by the unions, foreign investors, foreign buyers, and the American government would also be critical.[1] How would posterity judge Lesotho's first encounter with world markets—as a triumph or a disaster?

Basutoland to Lesotho

The mountain kingdom had not traditionally been an easy place to govern. Fearful of violent conquest by the Afrikaner settlers of the Orange Free State, King Moshoeshoe of what was then known as Basutoland sought security for his subjects by allying with the United Kingdom. In 1868 the United Kingdom annexed Basutoland and incorporated the kingdom into the Cape Colony.[2] The Cape Colony's ill-fated attempt to ban indigenous Africans, predominantly of the Basotho ethnic group, from owning firearms, however, led to the Gun War of 1880–81. With the Cape Colony unable to impose order, the Colonial Office decided to govern Basutoland directly from London. Thus was a quasi-autonomous existence restored.

London protected some of the traditional privileges of the local Basotho chiefs. Particularly consequential was the decision to prohibit the sale of land to non-Basotho.[3] The ban was permanently codified in the South Africa Act of 1909, which created the Union of South Africa. Basutoland was a founding member of the South African Customs Union (SACU) in 1910.

The Basotho vigorously resisted incorporation into South Africa for more than 50 years. Not only did the Basotho lobby actively in London, they contributed financially to further British goals as a way to signify their loyalty. In 1916, for example, the Basotho contributed £50,000 to the British effort in World War I—a sum equal to 42% of the colony's 1910 annual revenue.[4] The U.K. government continued to protect Basutoland's autonomy from the entreaties of the South Africans.[5] After World War II, the rise of the National Party and adoption of apartheid made union with South Africa less and less probable. When South Africa withdrew from the Commonwealth in 1961, the possibility of union all but disappeared.

The Basutoland economy stagnated under British rule. The country's primary export remained workers for the Witwatersrand gold mines near Johannesburg.[6] Although a Basutoland Factory Estate Development Company was established, the restriction on non-Basotho ownership of land hindered investment from abroad.[7]

The United Kingdom granted Basutoland independence as the Kingdom of Lesotho on October 4, 1966. The Kingdom was created as a constitutional monarchy on the U.K. model, with a popularly elected lower house that selected the prime minister, and an upper house (with limited power) that represented the traditional tribal chiefs.

Lesotho did not maintain its democracy, however, and the new country remained extraordinarily difficult to govern peacefully. Contested electoral results in 1970 initiated 30 years of intermittent violence, political assassinations, coups and counter-coups, and interventions by the South African government. When the results of the 1998 election were again violently contested, the country experienced escalating protests until junior army officers revolted in September. Six hundred South African troops, who were later joined by 200 soldiers from Botswana, entered Lesotho to restore order. The pitched battle in Maseru left nearly 100 dead and physical damage worth 159 million rand, or 3% of Lesotho's GDP.[8]

The civilian government returned to power, and over the next several years the government made remarkable progress in improving the governance of Lesotho. Lesotho's democracy appeared increasingly consolidated by 2006, and the country earned an international reputation for political and macroeconomic stability. Inflation was modest, and, with 53% of tax revenues deriving from SACU duties, the government enjoyed a budget surplus of approximately 4% of national income. (See **Exhibits 1, 2,** and **3.**)

South African Gold and Highlands Water: The Economy Before Textiles

The remittances of Basotho migrant laborers in South Africa were for many years the main driver of the local economy. At the peak in 1987, more than 125,000 Basotho worked in South Africa; 112,722 worked in the mines. Basotho workers made up 19% of South Africa's entire mining labor force, and one out of every five Basotho workers made his living in the mines.[9] South Africa's mines proved, however, to be a fickle source of income for the miners and an unreliable growth engine for Lesotho's economy. A combination of mechanization, mine closures, and efforts to replace Basotho workers with South Africans drove Basotho mining employment down to 60,000 by 2003.[10] (See **Exhibit 4**.) As of 2005 many South Africans hoped that their country's mining output would soon recover and expand, but it was widely recognized that Basotho employment in the mines was unlikely to return to previous levels.

Water exports provided Lesotho another major source of income. South Africa and Lesotho signed the Lesotho Highlands Water Project Treaty in 1986. The Treaty established a binational committee to run the project, the first phase of which consisted of a dam at Katse, in the central Maluti mountains, a second 475-foot high dam on the Senqunyane river, a 20-mile-long transfer tunnel between the two dams, 51 additional miles of water tunnels reaching to the Ash river in South Africa, and a hydropower station. South Africa paid an average of 180 million rand annually for the water, and the Water Project generated approximately 4,000 jobs.[11] (See **Exhibit 5**.)

Although the ambitious project was envisioned to have five phases, a variety of problems stalled development at the first.[12] Several side effects of the project worried planners. The dam displaced 27,000 people and contaminated downstream supplies.[13] The construction camps spread HIV in surrounding villages with incredible speed.[14] The rural electrification program that would have created critical infrastructure for development proved uneconomical, and electricity rates in Lesotho remained persistently high even after the dam's construction.[15] Further delays resulted from the finding in a Lesotho court that Acres International, a Toronto-based firm, had passed a $260,000 bribe to the chief executive of the project.[16] Although the construction sector had boomed when the Water Project was initiated, many observers worried that the delays would reduce construction by more than half.[17]

International Politics and the Arrival of the Industrial Revolution

The international condemnation of the evils of South African apartheid indirectly, and unexpectedly, created Lesotho's garment industry during the 1980s. American and European sanctions on South African exports led textile firms to move across the border to Lesotho to maintain access to the American and European markets. The government in Maseru welcomed the firms as harbingers of private sector development.[18] The Lesotho National Development Corporation (LNDC) was charged with facilitating the influx of firms from South Africa by providing pre-constructed factory shells and a five-year tax holiday.[19] Many of these firms were Taiwanese, and their business model consisted of importing cloth from China, assembling the garments in Lesotho, and then exporting the final product.[20]

European trade policy, facilitated by good diplomacy on the part of Lesotho, provided a further boost to the textile industry. Exports from Lesotho enjoyed preferential access to the European market under the Lomé Convention, which applied to former European colonies. Lomé rules at first required garments merely to be assembled by factories in former colonies to enter Europe duty-free. By the 1980s, however, Europeans required that the cloth from which garments were assembled must also be from a former colony to be eligible for duty-free access. Active lobbying by Lesotho prompted the Europeans to grant the country in 1990 an eight-year exemption from the new rule, which—together with a decision by the Lesotho government to continue its tax subsidies to the industry—drew in a wave of new garment investment aimed at the European market.[21] When Lesotho's exemption from the Lomé rules on the origins of cloth expired in 1998, however, exporters faced roughly a 17% tariff in European markets.[22] Their competitiveness in Europe thus all but disappeared in 1998.

Access to the U.S. market was defined by a series of country quotas established under the rules of the Multi-Fiber Arrangement (MFA).[23] The MFA, which lasted from 1974 until 1994, was a multilateral agreement that legitimized a system of quantitative restrictions to govern the international textile and garment trade. The MFA allowed importing countries, including those in Europe, to establish import quotas on a country-by-country basis. The dominant effect of the MFA was to give countries unequal access to export markets, with some having no quota restrictions on particular items and others effectively barred from producing certain goods owing to small quota allowances and prohibitive tariff rates. Manufacturers and buyers, in turn, were driven to distribute their production facilities and supply sources around the world based on the export quotas established under the MFA. Some argued that the MFA served as an engine of economic development, spurring industrialization in the world's poorest nations, while others argued that the MFA system was not only unfair and protectionist, but distorted the international market by shielding uncompetitive exporting nations from more efficient producers.[24] The MFA was replaced in 1995 by the World Trade Organization (WTO) Agreement on Textiles and Clothing (ATC). When the ATC expired in 2005, observers expected prices for textiles and apparel to decline significantly, with the lowest-cost producers, and especially China, gaining unrestricted access to export markets in the United States and Europe.

In the era of the MFA and ATC, although Lesotho received a quota for access to the American market, the quantitative ceiling did not exempt Lesotho's apparel exports from an average 17% tariff.[25] As a result, firms in Maseru had generally found greater success in the duty-free European market. By 1998, however, Lesotho faced a dire situation: it no longer enjoyed duty-free access to any major export market.

Trade, Not Aid: AGOA

Lesotho's industry might have vanished at the turn of the century, had it not been for AGOA. Originally conceived by Representative Jim McDermott, a Democratic congressman from the state of Washington, AGOA represented an emerging political consensus in favor of replacing development aid with the incentives of market access. The consensus was forged by connecting the traditional concerns of the American Right, such as economic incentives and responsibility, with those of the Left, including the prioritization of the poor. AGOA thus enjoyed political support from conservative Republicans like John Sununu of New Hampshire and leftist Democrats like McDermott, informally known as the "father of AGOA." Even U2's lead singer Bono spoke out in support of AGOA.

In 2000, the U.S. Congress passed AGOA, which authorized the U.S. President to provide duty-free treatment for any article from any African countries, as long as the President determined that they "have established, or were making continual progress toward establishing the following: market-based economies; the rule of law and political pluralism; elimination of barriers to U.S. trade and investment; protection of intellectual property; efforts to combat corruption; policies to reduce poverty, increasing availability of health care and educational opportunities; protection of human rights and worker rights; and elimination of certain child labor practices."[26] AGOA, scheduled to last until 2015, provided for an extension and expansion of duty-free treatment for the vast majority of products, excluding apparel and agricultural goods. AGOA countries could export textiles and apparel free of duty and quantitative restrictions only if the yarn, fabric, or thread originated in Sub-Saharan Africa or the United States. Thirty-seven African countries were identified as AGOA beneficiaries.

Of greatest relevance to Lesotho, however, was AGOA's so-called "Special Rule." The Special Rule allowed the 33 AGOA beneficiaries with least-developed country (LDC) status to export apparel both duty- and quota-free, regardless of the origin of the textile inputs. This feature was vitally important for Lesotho, since its garment industry initially relied on cloth from China. "We did not have fabric and yarn here," explained Daniel Maraisane, General Secretary of LECAWU, Lesotho's second-largest labor union. "Without the MFA and AGOA quotas there would have been no industry in Lesotho."[27] The Special Rule would provide for duty-free access to the American market as long as AGOA exports did not exceed 3% of overall U.S. apparel imports. This ceiling would eventually grow to 7% of total imports.

The Special Rule was originally scheduled to expire in September 2004, but it was subsequently extended, after a desperate lobbying effort and at the very last moment, to September 2007.[28] The implicit bargain of the extension was that the U.S. Congress would not again reconsider the Special Rule, and the least-developed countries that benefited would not request another extension.

As a result of AGOA, Lesotho's garment exports to the United States boomed. (See **Exhibit 6.**) In fact, Lesotho alone accounted for more than one-third of Africa's total garment exports under AGOA. (See **Exhibit 7.**) Employment similarly grew, from about 17,000 in 1999 to a peak of 53,467 in 2004. (See **Exhibit 8.**) By 2005 Lesotho had completely reoriented its exports to the United States, which imported almost all of Lesotho's production.

In addition to AGOA, which virtually saved the industry, the reorientation to the American market held other advantages. Whereas the European market was fragmented, country-wide chain stores in the United States allowed for bulk orders of homogenous garments. The European market generally required faster turnaround times than did the American market. And SACU's entire market (which included South Africa, Namibia, Botswana, Swaziland, and Lesotho) was smaller than any one of Europe's fragmented markets, save Luxembourg. Finally, South Africa possessed its own economically-beleaguered and politically-influential garment industry. Lesotho factories were competitive with South Africa—according to LECAWU, "our wages are one-quarter of South Africa's, and our productivity is four times higher"[29]—but South African firms took steps to improve their competitiveness. One factory, for example, cut wages 25%, and several others moved to piece work.[30] More importantly, Lesotho was wary of promoting exports to South Africa for fear of an adverse political response. In the words of the head of the LECAWU labor union, "when you have a big brother, you do what he wants."[31]

Although the benefits of the textile boom were significant, they did not include higher prices for the exporters or higher wages for workers. AGOA, according to the government of Lesotho, had the opposite effect: duty-free access primarily benefited the buyers, who received lower prices.[32] For the manufacturers, the benefits were simply market access and vastly increased volumes. Wages in the garment industry, meanwhile, remained quite low and grew only slowly. As of July 2005, the average wage in the Lesotho textile industry was only 47¢ per hour—roughly similar to wage levels in the rest of the country's urban formal sector. (See **Exhibit 9.**) The benefit to Lesotho came from the generation of jobs that provided living standards far above those available in the country's rural areas. In 1999, only 22.3% of Basotho households (or 83,860 families) had access to wage labor.[33] According to the Lesotho government, garment and textile industry wages in 2004 amounted to $65 million.[34]

Rules and Responses

Garment manufacturers responded aggressively to the possibilities created by AGOA's Special Rule. Dozens of firms set up shop between 2000 and 2004, by which time 46 firms operated in Lesotho. The LNDC had seized on the opportunity created by market access to encourage as many apparel manufacturers as possible to invest in Lesotho.

The LNDC offered, first, incentives for foreign textile manufacturers to locate in Lesotho. These included a permanent maximum profit tax rate of 15%, no withholding tax on dividends, and unrestricted repatriation of profits. The government offered duty-free access to machinery, and the cost of imported raw materials could be credited to the firms' tax burdens. The LNDC also facilitated the establishment of new firms by providing subsidized long-term loans and factory shells (sometimes with machinery included) ready for production. Although non-Basotho still could not own land, the LNDC implemented a program of subsidized rent.[35]

Lesotho's garment industry consisted almost exclusively of so-called "Cut, Make, and Trim" (CMT) operations. That is, the factories in Lesotho physically manufactured the garments, but they were concerned neither with downstream operations such as design, sampling, finance, or raw material purchasing, nor were they concerned with upstream marketing.

The only exception to this rule was the Formosa textile mill, which imported raw cotton from elsewhere in Africa and spun it into yarn. The yarn was then woven into denim, which was sold to the eight local jeans manufacturers or exported to other SACU countries.[36] The experience of the Formosa mill revealed one of the central challenges facing both the U.S. and Lesotho governments. A subsidiary of the Taiwanese Nien Hsing Group, Formosa invested $100 million to create a denim mill that would supply the jeans manufacturers. The mill was timed to begin operations in the autumn of 2004, just as the Special Rule was expected to expire, so that Lesotho's jeans manufacturers could continue to take advantage of AGOA-created access to the U.S. market by using local fabric. The mill that would save the local jeans manufacturers from extinction after the end of the Special Rule was, however, rendered irrelevant by the extension to 2007. With higher costs than fabric imported from Asia, denim from the Formosa mill would be attractive to local manufacturers only if its African origin were critical to market access. Upon extension of the Special Rule, Formosa managers decided to scale back the plant by installing only 70% of the planned machinery, and in 2006 the mill was operating at only 40% capacity and, according to knowledgeable observers, barely breaking even.[37]

The non-denim factories generally obtained their fabric from East Asia. The fabric was imported into East London and then traveled by truck to Maseru or by railroad to Bloemfontein, South Africa, or the Maseru Container Terminal (Mascon). Trucks then transported the containers to the factories. The containers arrived not only with fabric, but also with markers, trims, thread, swing tickets, hangers, and plastic bags—in short, all the materials necessary to process the order and ship it to the United States.[38] Workers unloaded the fabric manually and laid it out on cutting tables. Other employees used mechanical cutters to cut the fabric into garment parts. The cut pieces were then manually grouped in large bins according to the garments in which they were to be used. Lines of seated sewers drew the pieces up a row of seated sewing machine operators and assembled the garments. The sewn garments were washed, pressed, packed, and loaded into containers, where they were carried by road or rail to Durban or Port Elizabeth for export.[39]

Textile producers organized into two large employer associations after Lesotho's Congress passed the Labor Code (Amendment) Act, in 2000.[40] This Act created the Industrial Relations Council, a negotiation venue for labor, employers, and the government. The main objective of the law was to negotiate labor conditions and minimum wages in an orderly fashion. As a consequence, 10 textile manufacturers joined the Lesotho Employer's Association, an established organization representing the largest employers across various business sectors. Most of the Chinese and Taiwanese textile manufacturers created the Lesotho Textile Exporters Association (LTEA) (which had a total of 28 members in 2006). Both employer organizations were designed to improve employer-employee relations and had limited capacity to mobilize employers for other purposes. Taiwanese managers who had been in Lesotho for as many as 20 years saw their influence on the local economy as positive in a variety of ways. "The Chinese work ethic," argued Jennifer Chen, the Managing Director of Shining Century, "is being transferred to the Lesotho nation."[41]

The End of the Beginning

By the summer of 2005, it was clear that Lesotho's emergent industrialization was faltering. Six factories had closed down, and nearly 20,000 textile workers had lost their jobs. According to LECAWU, one fleeing investor had an overdraft from a Lesotho bank for $10 million: "The government was left holding the bag."[42] Some firms had literally closed shop and left the country overnight, leaving without paying workers their final paychecks, much less some sort of termination package. Workers told stories of showing up one morning at an empty factory. With employment in the sector at 38,000, many in Lesotho worried that the boom had ended and would never return. The concatenation of events that had saved the industry in 2000 seemed to have given way to the worst possible scenario.

Dollars, Rand, Maloti, and Wages

The loti was pegged 1:1 to the South African rand. Considering Lesotho's size, porous borders, fragile financial system, and dependence on imports from South Africa, the peg had long been seen as sensible. The rand's value relative to the U.S. dollar had almost doubled between 2002 and 2005, however. (See **Exhibit 10**.) The massive exchange-rate swing had been disastrous for the apparel exporters, who were even more dependent on the American market for sales than Lesotho as a country was dependent on South Africa for purchases. And although wages had increased only modestly, the appreciation increased the dollar value of local wages. Finally, although the long-standing peg seemed to many to be firm, interest rates were more than 100 basis points higher than in South Africa.[43]

The End of Rules, Multilateral and Special

The international and domestic rules that governed the textile trade also were in a period of flux and, indeed, some uncertainty as well. Especially worrying was the end of the WTO's ATC on January 1, 2005, at which point all WTO members ended textile and apparel quotas, although countries could still impose "safeguard measures" against surges in Chinese exports.[44] Even more consequential for Lesotho would be the expiration of AGOA's Special Rule in September 2007, at which point Lesotho manufacturers would be required to source all their fabric inputs from the United States, other AGOA countries, or Lesotho itself. Otherwise, full U.S. tariffs would apply.

The essence of the problem was that both the ATC and the Special Rule had protected Lesotho, among many other textile-exporting countries, from head-to-head competition with China. There was some hope, however. The more "safeguard measures" imposed by American and European policy makers, the easier life would be for Lesotho's textile industry. And if the Special Rule were to be extended again, then Lesotho's exporters could continue to benefit from preferential access. But neither investors nor buyers could bet on an extension, which would, if the previous pattern held, be granted by the U.S. Congress at the last minute.

Without these rules, Lesotho's manufacturers could not possibly compete with China in the context of the prevailing levels of wages, productivity, and exchange rates. Chinese wages were rising quickly, however.[45] (See **Exhibit 11**.) Several southern Chinese cities had developed labor shortages, and Chinese labor costs were expected to continue rising in the future.[46] A World Bank study projected that the Chinese yuan would be valued around 5.8 to the dollar by 2010, and 2.8 to the dollar by 2020.[47] If Chinese wages were to rise, for example, to Mexican levels, it was not clear that China would be able to maintain its dominance in low-value-added manufacturing activities.

Unfortunately for Lesotho, other low-cost garment producers were poised to take China's place. Vietnamese wages in the garment and textile industry, for example, had historically been very low— just $40 per month, less than 40% of Lesotho's, until 2005. In January 2006, following several wildcat strikes in Ho Chi Minh City, the Vietnamese government raised the wages of workers in foreign-owned firms to $55 per month.[48] (See **Exhibit 12**.) In addition, the poorer Central American nations were to enjoy duty-free access to the U.S. market under the Central American Free Trade Agreement (CAFTA). CAFTA required its signatories either to produce yarns and fabrics domestically or to source them from Canada, Mexico, or the United States in order to enjoy duty-free access to the U.S. market. Nicaragua, however, had negotiated a 10-year phase-in that would allow Nicaraguan producers to continue to import yarns and fabrics from third countries. Levi's, Liz Claiborne, Dickey's, AMC, and Wal-Mart—some of them major buyers of Lesotho's exports—all sourced in Nicaragua as well. Nicaraguan wages, however, were still higher (at 70¢ per hour) than Lesotho's (47¢ per hour).[49] Lesotho's policy makers were debating whether to try to negotiate a similar phase-in as part of the free trade agreement being negotiated between SACU and the United States.[50] (See **Exhibit 13** for statistics on U.S. trade with Sub-Saharan Africa.)

Unresolved Challenges

A number of other unresolved challenges threatened the existence of the textile industry. Lesotho's manufacturers continued to face high transportation costs, low labor productivity, and a looming HIV/AIDS pandemic.

The middle of nowhere Transportation costs were very high. Rail transport was inadequate. The Mascon terminal had only one siding capable of handling containers. Neither the siding nor the container storage area was paved. Mascon also lacked storage areas for containers, a fact that obliged importers to store their containers in Bloemfontein and prioritize which ones they wanted brought to Maseru.[51] Mascon was owned by Spoornet, the South African rail company. Spoornet, however, did not own the land, and did not want to modernize the container station unless it received some form of land tenure.[52] As a result, the garment companies considered rail service unreliable and generally preferred to import raw materials and move their finished product by road.[53]

Road transport, however, was very expensive. Transporting a single 40-foot container by road from port to factory cost one apparel producer 15,326 rand ($2,584) in 2005, while moving a similarly-sized container in the opposite direction cost 7,530 rand ($1,270).[54] The latter price was more than 80% higher than the $700 cost of moving a container from Vientiane, Laos to Bangkok Port.[55] In fact, it cost more to import a container to Lesotho than it did to Outer Mongolia: the U.N. estimated that the total cost of moving a container from Port Tianjin, China, to Ulaan Bataar was only $1,712, including the cost of returning the empty container to China.[56] Chen considered transportation costs a major obstacle for Lesotho's exporters. Transportation costs represented "between 7%–10% of total cost, including all export expenses." From Maseru "it takes 28 days to get a shipment of clothes to New York City. It takes two days alone to get the merchandise to a South African port."[57]

Productivity   Productivity was acknowledged to be a major problem for the Lesotho textile industry. A 2003 report based on three representative factories (with a total of 8,600 employees) found overmanning in excess of 15% in all parts of the production process.[58] Many factors contributed to low productivity levels. In some cases, companies were hesitant to use specialized machinery—for example, automatic laying-up machines in the cutting rooms to replace workers laying out fabric on cutting room tables by hand—because of worries about the availability of spare parts. (Manual laying was inefficient because the layers tended to lay out the cloth in a way that left unusable excess fabric.[59]) In other cases, the problem was inadequate training. Larger inefficiencies were noted in the sewing process, due to "poor operator skills, inconsistent work flow, or the lines not being properly balanced by the supervisors."[60] The laying-out problem, for example, could also be resolved by better training of those laying the fabric; this might reduce fabric use by 0.5%.[61]

Gender and HIV   The expansion of the textile industry created greater economic opportunities for women and drew them into the formal, urban sector from the informal, rural sector. At the same time, however, according to the Behavioral Surveillance Survey, some female migrant laborers engaged in risky sexual practices, often connected to commercial sex work during slack times at the factory.[62] As a result, the incidence of HIV among factory workers was high. Ten percent of garment workers reported knowing someone who had died of AIDS in the last 12 months.[63]

HIV was a serious problem in Lesotho. The pandemic reached Lesotho relatively late, in the early 1990s, but then spread with shocking rapidity. The first cases of seropositive women appeared among urban antenatal clinic attendees in 1992, yet by 2001 roughly 42% of clinic attendees tested positive. UNAIDS estimated that 31% of adults aged 15–49 lived with HIV by the end of 2001, and reported that 25,000 adults and children died of AIDS-related causes that year. As a result, life expectancy in Lesotho fell from 60 years in 1991 to 52 in 2001, and was projected to fall to 35 by the year 2015.[64] Natural population growth in the country had almost ground to a halt, with the 2005 birth rate of 26.5 per thousand barely exceeding the death rate of 25.0 per thousand.[65] Given such trends, the population would begin to shrink over the next few years.

The HIV epidemic in Lesotho had a significant impact on private enterprise. HIV-infected workers were less productive, especially once they developed AIDS. "HIV is the opposite of investment in skills; it destroys productive labor," reflected finance minister Timothy T. Thahane.[66] Unfortunately, the resources that the Lesotho government could bring to bear on the problem were limited. In a promising move, in December 2005 Lesotho's health minister announced an initiative to test every Basotho citizen for HIV/AIDS.

Chen, who was also president of the Lesotho Textile Exporters Association (LTEA), tried to persuade employers "to face their workers' HIV problems." Shining Century, the company she managed and partly owned, was "plastered with AIDS-awareness posters." Chen observed that "about a third of the 1,200 employees have taken HIV tests" and that infection rates had turned out to be lower than expected. However, Chen's factory seemed to be the exception rather than the rule.[67] Her factory provided HIV-positive workers with a special vitamin-enriched porridge to help them keep their jobs.[68]

Big Buyers: New Heroes for an Old Problem?

Lesotho's rise in apparel production coincided with a dramatic shift in how international buyers approached labor, environmental, and other issues occurring in their supply chains. A good deal of the change came about by way of a number of well-publicized cases. No longer was it possible for international buyers to ignore how their suppliers treated labor. Instead, famous-maker buyers' demands for increasingly shorter lead times were being blamed for the unwillingness of suppliers to eliminate compulsory overtime and provide greater security to labor. "The buyers are the key determinant," according to Christopher Maloney, "of Lesotho's sustainability in apparel manufacturing."[69]

Nonetheless, vocal criticism by student groups, non-governmental organizations, and organized labor threatened the reputation of a number of well-known brands. It also gave power to workers in the developing world, and Lesotho was no exception. In 2002, an international campaign against Nien Hsing, the Taiwanese multinational, gained momentum. Its Lesotho-based factories, C & Y Garments and Nien Hsing International, were accused of anti-union activities. Restricted from organizing at the factories, LECAWU union leaders turned to the international community.

UNITE, the U.S. textile and garment workers union, the Maquila Solidarity Network, and other groups mobilized on LECAWU's behalf.[70] A number of LECAWU organizers also traveled to New York to protest outside big brand stores.[71] The Gap Inc. and Canadian-based Hudson Bay Company came under considerable pressure. In response, Hudson Bay ceased relations with the famous supplier, while the Gap Inc. earned praise for engaging both labor and management in a dialogue that eventually led to a memorandum of understanding and union representation in Nien Hsing factories.

According to Sean Ansett, Gap Inc.'s Director for Global Partnerships, the events of 2002 "were a fundamental step for us in evolving our stakeholder strategy," though he cautioned that Gap Inc.'s relation with management and labor remained one of "facilitating, but not engaging in direct negotiations." Toward this end, the Gap Inc. supported a number of in-country initiatives, including human resource training for factory managers, collaboration with the non-governmental organization CARE on HIV/AIDS education in the workplace, as well as productivity training by way of its partnership with ComMark, an NGO that promoted pro-poor industrialization. Such efforts were, he said, about getting some managers away from "seeing labor as a cost, rather than as a resource."[72]

Still, it remained unclear whether the demand from the Gap Inc. and other big buyers would be substantial enough to sustain the industry in the face of foreign competition and increasingly unfavorable exchange rates. As of 2006, the Gap Inc. was responsible for approximately 30% of Lesotho's garment exports, an amount that had remained fairly stable since it began sourcing there in 1998.[73] Industrial relations had also improved, making the country an attractive site for the sourcing of "replenishment goods," such as t-shirts and jeans. For these products, long lead times were less of a problem.

Maraisane said that along with Levi's, the Gap Inc.'s continued sourcing would guarantee employment of at least "20,000 people in the sector."[74] Ansett also affirmed that the Gap Inc. was "committed to Lesotho," but warned that if "other industrial players don't stay, it becomes hard for us to stay."[75]

A number of manufacturers heard the message, taking steps to remain competitive. Taiwan-owned Lesotho Fancy Garments, for example, announced in 2003 that it would change its strategy in order to cope with a post-AGOA world. First, in anticipation of the new rules regarding the origin of the fabrics, they planned to invest $60 million to expand operations to include a fully integrated factory with in-house cotton weaving.[76] This would allow them to expand their sales of t-shirts to the Gap Inc., JC Penney, Target, Wal-Mart, and Sears.[77] Second, they planned to develop an "elaborate training and incentives system aimed at increasing productivity and quality."[78] As a result, LECAWU officials predicted that "denims might stay because cotton can be purchased in southern Africa."[79]

Growing signs of uncertainty were nonetheless on the horizon. Without the special provisions of AGOA, it was feared that only a few companies would stay in Lesotho. Moreover, Lesotho's benefit of special preference as a less-developed country under AGOA's rules had been deeply diminished by the insistence of the Mauritian government that its apparel industry be granted the same privilege to use fabric from outside the United States and Mauritius without penalty. Otherwise, various Mauritian stakeholders, including labor, threatened to continue vocal opposition to AGOA's renewal. The change in the Mauritian apparel industry's status went into effect in December 2004 as part of the U.S. "Miscellaneous Trade and Technical Corrections Act."

Crisis and Coordination

The way out of the crisis was unclear. Indeed, it was not even certain that there were any decisions to be made in Maseru that might improve the long-term prospects for Lesotho's only real export industry. The government, the manufacturers, and the unions and workers considered their options and hoped for a coordinated response. Certainly all three stakeholders shared a common interest in preserving Lesotho's preferential trade status, if at all possible. But short of that best-case scenario—an outcome not to be taken for granted—the options available to them varied considerably, and the consistency of their respective interests was far from clear.

The Government

A more challenging policy environment was difficult to imagine. The government in Lesotho was obliged by the crisis to reconsider its approach to the exchange rate, foreign investment promotion, and engagement with the norms and rules of world markets.

Some exporters, who bore the brunt of the currency appreciation, urged the government to reconsider linking its currency to the strengthening rand. Government officials were reluctant even to consider undoing the peg.[80] "Lesotho is a small country with a limited capacity to fight with international markets over the value of the currency," argued Thahane.[81] Another possibility was to move in the opposite direction by tightening the bond. If Lesotho moved to a full currency union with South Africa, perhaps by unilaterally adopting the rand as its currency, the government might thereby eliminate the interest rate differential between the two economies.

As the margins of manufacturers were squeezed further, the LNDC responded with more tax breaks, lower rents, and coordinated wage bargaining. Local manufacturers appreciated the efforts of the government to insulate their operations from the downturn. The government also re-introduced the Duty Credit Certification Scheme (DCCS), a complicated system within the SACU that provided incentives for exporters in the form of duty credit. Apparel firms in Lesotho thereby received DCCS certificates, the value of which could be applied to any duties that applied to imports. For Lesotho's firms, which already enjoyed a variety of incentives regarding duties in imported inputs provided by the government in Maseru, the DCCS proved a welcome windfall. Firms typically sold their DCCS certificates to a South African clothing importing firm for 15% to 20% of their value, and no extra effort was required of them.[82]

The finance ministry also considered offering a wage subsidy for exporters: the government would value a company's current wage bill at a base exchange rate (7.5 maloti per U.S. dollar had been suggested) and grant a subsidy whenever the loti fell below the base exchange rate.[83] Then, in February 2006, Thahane proposed the most impressive incentive to date—a zero percent corporate tax on income generated from exporting manufactured goods outside of the customs union.[84]

Tallying all of the subsidies and incentives, compared to the prospect of essentially no corporate tax revenues from the apparel manufacturers, some observers wondered why Lesotho's government seemed so intent on paying the firms to remain. The government saw things very differently, however. In the words of the finance minister, "for the government the only alternative to paying for incentives for foreign investors is to pay for unemployment benefits. The return from the employment foreign investors create is potentially much larger. With what should I compare the taxes foregone? The wages of 50,000 workers."[85] Articulating a strategy for the inevitable endgame, Thahane reflected that "the important thing is not to have the textile and apparel industry forever. That is not realistic. We are facing stiff competition from China, Bangladesh, and India. We must milk this industry while we diversify."[86] The alternatives being discussed in 2006 included horticulture, sandstone, and tourism.

One other solution the government considered was the possibility of encouraging investors from China to build a cotton knit fabric mill. "Our relationship with China and Chinese investors is critical," observed Thahane, "and we also feel that Chinese-funded and managed textile production in Lesotho will be strategically useful for them."[87] The advantages of such a mill for Lesotho would be twofold. First, it would make Lesotho's duty-free access to the U.S. market independent of AGOA's rules of origin, since most cloth would be sourced in-country. Second, it would reduce the cost of production by freeing Lesotho factories from the need to import cloth from East Asia at relatively high cost. Fabric costs represented approximately 40%–60% of total costs for the typical garment factory, versus 30% for wages. The Taiwanese and Chinese-owned companies supported the idea of a fabric mill to reduce costs.[88] One of the labor unions was similarly supportive.[89] The idea appeared to be economically feasible—an LNDC/ComMark study estimated that the country consumes a minimum of 22,000 tons of cotton cloth every year, mostly fabric-dyed, and that such volume appeared to be sufficient to support a cotton fabric mill.[90] By early 2006, no commitment from China had been made. Hopes were raised, however, by the continuing engagement of African states by both China and Taiwan—and indeed their rivalry on the continent.[91] (See **Exhibits 14** and **15**.)

The Manufacturers

Chen argued that marketing and the diversification of buyers were important challenges for the Taiwanese and Chinese producers represented by the LTEA. Chen indicated that Asian manufacturers in Lesotho relied excessively on contacts in Taiwan, Hong Kong, and Singapore: "The marketing is still handled in Asia. We've subcontracted the manufacturing to Africa." She emphasized that "marketing is our weak point. We generally produce on a CMT basis. I have a partner in Hong Kong, who handles marketing and finance."[92]

Beginning in 2005, some firms based in Lesotho dealt with these various pressures by negotiating with their parent companies to become "Free on Board" (FOB), rather than CMT, producers. Rather than merely receiving fabric for existing orders and then literally cutting, making, and trimming the garments, FOB firms had the increased flexibility to source their own fabric and (hopefully) to negotiate lower prices. CMT firms essentially were subcontractors, whereas FOB firms were wholly-owned subsidiaries. Additionally, whereas CMT firms experienced only the downside of currency appreciation (squeezed sales abroad), FOB firms benefited from the upside as well (cheaper imported inputs). With these new decision rights, FOB firms in Lesotho achieved greater flexibility, but also bore new risks—the effects of exchange-rate swings on input prices and the possible inconsistency of orders from buyers.[93] (For a comparison of the two cost structures, see **Exhibit 16**.)

Chen also worried about the cost differences between their manufacturing plants and those based in mainland China. Specifically, she believed that high wages in Lesotho put them at a disadvantage. While Lesotho's employers paid on average $98 per month, her partners in mainland China paid "between $60–$80 a month." In Vietnam a worker got about "$40 a month."[94] Chinese labor compensation in textiles in 2002 averaged $73 a month (with regional labor costs varying between $60 and $80), while the average monthly wage in Lesotho, in contrast, was $98.[95]

The Unions and the Workers

For the unions and workers, the constant comparisons with Chinese wage rates grated. According to the General Secretary of LECAWU, "I understand that it's basically slavery there. We can't compete with that."[96] Because the exchange-rate appreciation had increased so dramatically the dollar value of their Maloti wages, union leaders felt that continuing to squeeze the workers would not significantly improve the competitiveness of the industry.

Although cross-country productivity data were elusive, most observers were certain that productivity might be significantly improved. The government considered expanding training schemes for textile workers. "The best way to reduce poverty in Lesotho is to rely on that asset which labor owns in abundance—muscle. But that asset is not there until you invest in it—skills and technology transform muscle into something useable and valuable."[97] The lack of training opportunities within the industry, however, was a complaint of both major trade unions. As the textile industry declined, officials discussed ways to help the displaced workers.

Maraisane worried that the government had made a terrible, and indelible, error in promoting the industry beyond a sustainable growth trajectory. By 2004 AGOA had helped to create a textile export powerhouse in Lesotho, which sent $467 million worth of clothing to the United States. But the AGOA textile provisions would soon expire. "In the next few years, the industry will shrink back to 20,000 workers, from 57,000 at its height," predicted Maraisane. "What will these people do? We would have been better off sticking with the firms that have been here all along. The government has put all of its eggs in one basket."[98]

Finally, the decisions of the U.S. government and the big buyers would affect the future of the industry and the economy of the mountain kingdom. In 2006 the U.S. Congress was considering extending the Special Rule for a few more years. The buyers would decide whether to continue to buy Lesotho even when their prices were higher because Lesotho had been essentially branded as labor-friendly. With enough coordination among the government, the manufacturers, and the unions, both of those outcomes could be influenced. The U.S. Congress could be lobbied again. The European market could be reconsidered. The Lesotho brand could be enhanced and marketed. Did the policy makers, managers, and union leaders know what they wanted? And would they cooperate to get it? Should preservation of Lesotho's preferential trade status prove unattainable, would a coordinated response by these stakeholders even remain possible?

Exhibit 1   Lesotho's National Income Accounts

	1995	1996	1997	1998	1999	2000	2001	2002	2003	2004	2005
GDP (% real change pa^a)	4.4	10.0	8.1	-4.6	0.2	1.3	3.2	3.8	3.3	3.0	0.8
Nominal GDP (US$ billions at PPP)	2.7	3.2	3.5	3.5	3.6	3.8	4.1	4.3	4.6	4.9	5.0
Structure of GDP											
Private consumption (% of GDP)	120	119	114	113	103	102	102	120	119	101	93
Government consumption (% of GDP)	18	16	17	21	20	18	18	18	18	13	14
Gross fixed investment (% of GDP)	61	58	55	49	48	43	43	42	38	32	30
Stockbuilding (% of GDP)	-1	0	-1	-2	-1	-3	-3	-2	0	-1	-1
Exports of G&S (% of GDP)	21	24	27	27	24	28	42	51	49	42	42
Imports of G&S (% of GDP)	120	118	112	107	95	88	100	103	96	88	79
GDP per head											
GDP per head (US $)	552	551	589	506	515	502	418	410	633	958	1,050
GDP per head ($ at PPP)	1,586	1,842	2,028	2,000	2,044	2,114	2,270	2,411	2,551	2,700	2,760
Real GDP growth per head (% pa)	3.2	8.7	6.3	-5.7	-0.3	0.2	2.6	3.8	3.3	3.0	-0.2
National savings											
Gross national savings rate (%)	25.9	26.3	27.7	15.6	22.4	22.9	28.1	22.9	26.3	27.1	24.4
Structure of the Economy											
Agriculture/GDP	18	19	16	18	17	19	18	17	17	16	16
Industry/GDP	39	40	42	39	41	41	42	43	44	44	44
Services/GDP	43	42	41	43	41	40	40	40	40	40	39
Government budget											
Budget balance (% of GDP)	3.2	3.4	1.9	-3.8	-5.2	-3.3	-0.7	-4.4	-2.9	6.2	0.6
Inflation											
Consumer prices (% change pa; av^b)	9.2	9.3	5.0	9.6	7.5	6.2	-9.7	33.9	6.7	5.1	4.7

Source: Adapted from Economist Intelligence Unit (EIU).

Note: Some data for 2004 and 2005 was estimated by the EIU.

^a per annum

^b average

Exhibit 2   Lesotho's Balance of Payments (in millions of US dollars)

	1995	1996	1997	1998	1999	2000	2001	2002	2003	2004	2005
Current account	-323	-303	-269	-280	-221	-151	-95	-127	-135	-76	-93
Trade balance	-825	-812	-828	-673	-607	-517	-400	-406	-519	-595	-610
Goods: exports fob	*160*	*187*	*196*	*193*	*173*	*211*	*279*	*357*	*475*	*707*	*749*
Goods: imports fob	*-985*	*-999*	*-1,024*	*-866*	*-779*	*-728*	*-679*	*-763*	*-994*	*-1,302*	*-1,358*
Services: balance	-22	-13	19	1	-6	0	-9	-21	-35	-32	-39
Income: balance	314	334	337	234	244	226	179	178	250	303	284
Current transfers: balance	210	189	202	157	148	139	135	122	170	248	272
FDI											
Inward direct investment	275	288	268	265	163	118	117	84	116	124	na
International Reserves											
International reserves	457	461	572	575	500	418	387	406	460	503	573
Memorandum Items											
Workers' remittances	411	388	379	295	276	252	209	184	184	na	na

Source: Adapted from Economist Intelligence Unit (EIU) data.

Note: Some data for 2004 and 2005 were estimated by the EIU.

Exhibit 3 Lesotho: Direction of Trade, 1999–2003 (in millions of maloti)

	1999 Imports	1999 Exports	2000 Imports	2000 Exports	2001 Imports	2001 Exports	2002 Imports	2002 Exports	2003 Imports	2003 Exports
World	5,288.8	1,054.1	5,611.2	1,468.3	6,399.8	2,426.0	8,517.5	3,739.9	8,411.6	3,557.3
Africa	4,737.7	555.0	4,876.9	607.5	5,306.0	899.1	6,270.3	856.4	7,242.7	695.6
Common customs area	4,736.4	554.5	4,309.3	606.9	5,296.6	897.0	6,261.7	856.0	7,234.1	689.7
Other Africa	1.3	1.6	6.9	0.7	3.0	2.1	1.6	0.2	8.6	5.9
Europe	97.8	2.1	45.8	1.8	46.5	3.5	93.2	8.1	12.1	3.7
European Union	83.7	1.9	42.7	1.8	44.5	3.5	82.5	7.8	8.9	3.7
Belgium	4.1	0.2	1.4	0.2	0.4	0.1	3.9	0.0	0.0	0.0
Denmark	1.5	0.4	0.8	0.0	1.7	0.0	9.2	0.0	1.3	0.0
France	4.3	0.0	0.4	0.0	2.9	0.1	4.6	0.0	0.1	0.0
Germany	23.7	1.2	6.4	0.7	20.9	0.0	9.4	2.2	0.1	0.6
Greece	--	--	--	--	--	--	4.7	0.0	3.2	0.0
Italy	17.5	0.0	5.5	0.0	5.0	0.0	16.0	0.0	0.1	0.0
Spain	3.3	0.0	6.7	0.0	11.9	0.0	11.3	0.9	0.2	0.0
Netherlands	1.7	0.0	3.1	0.0	0.0	0.0	0.0	0.0	2.7	2.0
United Kingdom	27.6	0.1	14.1	0.9	0.6	0.0	24.9	0.0	1.4	1.2
Portugal	0.0	0.0	4.3	0.0	0.0	3.2	0.0	4.6	0.0	0.0
Turkey	--	--	--	--	--	--	2.2	--	1.4	--
Other Europe	14.1	0.2	3.1	0.0	2.0	0.0	3.8	0.3	1.8	0.0
North America	50.0	494.9	104.8	858.3	41.7	1,522.5	53.4	2,874.6	15.1	2,849.1
Canada	41.9	5.7	97.2	22.5	34.5	35.0	12.1	15.9	0.6	19.7
United States	8.1	489.2	7.6	835.8	7.2	1,487.5	41.3	2,858.7	14.5	2,829.4
Asia	372.4	0.2	526.0	0.6	953.3	0.9	2,021.6	0.8	1,141.7	8.9
Japan	23.3	0.0	34.6	0.0	11.6	0.4	33.2	0.0	11.3	1.2
Hong Kong SAR	31.0	0.1	70.3	0.0	224.3	0.0	483.8	0.0	401.3	0.9
China	0.2	0.1	0.0	0.0	74.2	0.0	355.7	0.0	241.8	0.2
Taiwan	192.2	0.0	294.6	0.6	527.1	0.0	913.2	0.8	367.6	0.7
Other	125.7	0.0	126.5	0.0	109.8	0.5	192.5	0.0	119.7	5.8
Oceania	30.9	0.9	57.7	0.1	52.2	0.0	79.0	0.0	32.0	0.0

Source: Central Bank of Lesotho.

Exhibit 4   Basotho Employment in South Africa

	Basotho Mine Workers in South Africa	All Basotho Laborers in South Africa	Total Lesotho Labor Force
1920	10,439		
1930	22,306		
1940	52,044		
1950	34,467		
1960	48,842		
1970	63,988		
1980	96,308		
1989	100,529	126,264	673,284
1990	99,707	127,386	690,789
1991	93,897	122,188	708,750
1992	93,519	119,596	727,177
1993	89,940	116,129	746,084
1994	89,237	101,032	765,482
1995	87,935		
1996	81,357		
1997	76,361		
1998	60,450		
1999	52,188		
2000	58,224		
2001	60,175		
2002	62,125		
2003	59,241		
2004	56,357		
2005	54,171		

Source: Adapted from Godfrey Kanyenze, "African Migrant Labour Situation in Southern Africa," presented at the ICTU-AFRO Conference on Migrant Labor, Nairobi, March 2004; LECAWU, "Current Labor Market Conditions in Lesotho," mimeo, 2004, p. 4; and Ntsau Lekhetho, "Lesotho migrant workers lose 2000 jobs as low gold price knocks SA producers," *Business Report*, June 30, 2005. (2001 and 2003 figures are interpolated.)

Exhibit 5   Lesotho Highlands Water Project

	Royalty Receipts for Water Exports (million rand)	Electricity Production, GW-Hours	Value of Electricity Production (million rand)	Exports as % of Electricity Production
1999–2000	146.93	386.44	41.68	16.8%
2000–2001	158.05	371.57	44.13	3.4%
2001–2002	182.95	372.95	44.76	5.6%
2002–2003	205.91	377.93	43.25	9.4%

Source: Adapted from Lesotho Highlands Development Authority, *Annual Report, 2002-2003* (Maseru: Lesotho Highlands Development Authority, 2004), Tables 2 and 3.

Exhibit 6 Lesotho's Exports to the United States (in thousands of current dollars)

	Total Exports	Textile Exports	AGOA- Eligible Exports
1989	18,924	16,338	na
1990	24,860	24,516	na
1991	27,185	27,014	na
1992	52,388	50,752	na
1993	55,721	55,088	na
1994	62,737	62,407	na
1995	61,909	61,705	na
1996	74,257	71,169	na
1997	86,605	80,633	na
1998	100,244	82,376	na
1999	110,814	87,851	na
2000	140,150	114,925	na
2001	217,165	163,502	128,769
2002	321,475	271,431	313,043
2003	393,056	324,970	366,726
2004	467,047	387,153	446,535

Source: Data from U.S. International Trade Commission. (1996 data are interpolated.)

Exhibit 7 Share of AGOA Apparel Exports to the United States in 2003, by country

Countries	m² Equivalent	% Share of AGOA Exports
Lesotho	32,483,869	35.9%
Madagascar	17,273,746	19.1%
Swaziland	16,760,712	18.5%
Kenya	15,220,512	16.8%
Namibia	3,992,015	4.4%
Malawi	2,490,863	2.8%
Botswana	1,039,037	1.1%
Ethiopia	544,653	0.6%
Cape Verde	309,521	0.3%
Uganda	305,952	0.3%
Mozambique	86,714	0.1%
Ghana	68,539	0.1%
TOTAL	90,576,133	100.0%

Source: Adapted from Global Development Solutions, "Value Chain Analysis of Selected Strategic Sectors in Lesotho," mimeo, June 7, 2004, Table 3.

Exhibit 8   Apparel Employment in Lesotho

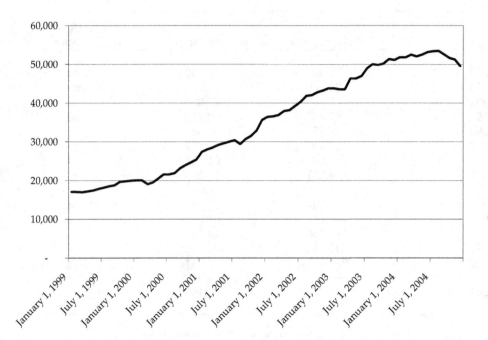

Source: Data provided by the Lesotho National Development Corporation to the authors.

Exhibit 9   Lesotho Wage Rates, 2004–2005, in Maloti (roughly 6.6 per US dollar as of August 2005)

Sector	Monthly Wage (Maloti)	Weekly Wage (Maloti)	Daily Wage (Maloti)
Manufacturing			
Trainee	621.00	155.00	34.00
Trained	650.00	163.00	36.00
Construction			
Construction worker	722.00	180.00	38.00
Construction machine operator	1,257.00	301.00	69.00
Wholesale Retail			
Wholesaler, bakery, supermarket, furniture shop	642.00	186.00	39.00
Retailers			
Mini-supermarket, café, food caterer	722.00	181.00	38.00
Hotels			
Motel, Lodge	742.00	186.00	39.00
Restaurants	722.00	181.00	38.00
Service Sector			
Security	911.00	228.00	47.00
Funeral parlour	742.00	186.00	39.00
Small Business	444.00	110.00	23.00
Domestic Worker	221.00	56.00	12.00
General Minimum Wage	650.00	163.00	36.00

Source: Labour Code Wages (Amendment) Order 2004, Legal Notice No. 177; *Government Gazette*, Vol. XLIX, September 28, 2004.

Exhibit 10   South African Rand per Dollar, January End-of-Month Quotation

	Rand per Dollar
1998	4.93
1999	6.06
2000	6.33
2001	7.78
2002	11.44
2003	8.65
2004	6.85
2005	5.93

Source: 1998–2001 data from http://www.economist.com/ markets/currency/md_conv.cfm. 2002–05 data from Statement to Parliament by the Honourable Mpho Malie, Minister of Trade and Industry, Co-operative and Marketing, on Lesotho's Export Textiles and Garment Industry, February 2005.

Exhibit 11   Comparative Labor Compensation, China and Lesotho (in US dollars)

	People's Republic of China			Kingdom of Lesotho	
	All Urban Manufacturing	Private Urban Manufacturing	CAGR, Private	Private Urban Manufacturing	CAGR
1990	$0.31	$0.42			
1991	$0.34	$0.50	19%		
1992	$0.37	$0.54	8%		
1993	$0.43	$0.56	4%		
1994	$0.44	$0.58	4%		
1995	$0.47	$0.61	5%		
1996	$0.49	$0.63	3%		
1997	$0.51	$0.66	5%	$0.37	-6%
1998	$0.54	$0.65	-2%	$0.35	-4%
1999	$0.62	$0.74	14%	$0.33	1%
2000	$0.71	$0.83	12%	$0.34	-11%
2001	$0.82	$0.92	11%	$0.30	-19%
2002	$0.94	$1.03	11%	$0.24	37%
2003				$0.33	37%
2004				$0.46	39%
2005				$0.49	7%

Source: Chinese data calculated from data in Judith Banister, "Manufacturing Earnings and Compensation in China," *Monthly Labor Review*, August 2005, p. 28 and p. 35. Lesotho data adapted from Christopher Maloney, *All Dressed Up With No Place to Go?: Lesotho's Rollercoaster Experience with Apparel*, MPA/ID SYPA, Kennedy School of Government, Harvard University, spring 2006. The Lesotho data for 2004 and 2005 include an estimated 4.5% (or 2¢ per hour) for worker training expenses under the DCCS scheme.

Exhibit 12   Average Labor Compensation in Manufacturing, Various Countries, Mid-2005

	U.S. Dollars per hour
Lesotho	$ 0.49
Nicaragua	$ 0.67
Vietnam (2001)	$ 0.69
China (2002)[a]	$ 0.94
Honduras	$ 1.08
Guatemala	$ 1.32
El Salvador	$ 1.35
Costa Rica	$ 2.25
Chile	$ 2.50
Mexico[b]	$ 2.60
Taiwan (2001)	$ 5.18
Korea (201)	$ 5.69
Singapore (2001)	$ 6.72
European Union (2001)	$14.13
United States	$16.50

Source: Data for Costa Rica, El Salvador, Guatemala, Honduras, and Nicaragua are from Nicaragua International Investment Promotion Agency. Data for Chile, Mexico, and the United States are from INEGI. Data for China are from Judith Banister, "Manufacturing Earnings and Compensation in China," *Monthly Labor Review* (August 2005), pp. 22-40, Table 10, and are for 2002 and exclude TVEs. Data for Vietnam are from U.S. International Trade Commission and are for 2001. Data for the European Union, Korea, Singapore and Taiwan are from "China: Awakening Giant," *Southwest Economy*, Issue 5 (September/October 2003), Federal Reserve Bank of Dallas, and are for 2001.

[a]Average wages in the privately-owned Chinese textile industry were $0.63 per hour in 2002. Average wages in the Township and Village Enterprises (TVE) sector were $0.41 per hour.

[b]Average wages in the Mexican textile industry were $1.90 per hour in mid-2005.

Exhibit 13   U.S. Trade with Sub-Saharan Africa (in $ millions)

	2001	2002	2003	2004
U.S. Exports	6,941.8	6,026.1	6,870.9	8,565.7
U.S. Imports	21,286.8	17,891.4	25,633.3	35,874.9

Source: Compiled from official statistics of the U.S. Department of Commerce.

Exhibit 14   China's Trade with Africa, 2001–2005 (in billions of dollars)

	Exports to Africa	% Change	Imports from Africa	% Change
2000	5.1		5.5	
2001	6.0	19%	4.7	-14%
2002	7.0	16%	5.3	13%
2003	10.2	46%	8.4	57%
2004	13.9	36%	15.6	87%
2005	18.7	35%	21.1	35%

Source: Adapted from "Friend or Forager?" *The Financial Times*, February 23, 2006.

Exhibit 15   Chinese Trade with Africa in 2005, by Country

Exports to Africa		Imports from Africa	
South Africa	20%	Angola	31%
Nigeria	12%	South Africa	16%
Egypt	10%	Sudan	12%
Algeria	7%	Congo	11%
Sudan	7%	Equatorial Guinea	7%
Others	43%	Others	23%

Source: Adapted from "Friend or Forager?" *The Financial Times*, February 23, 2006.

Exhibit 16   Estimates of Cost Structure for Lesotho Apparel Firms, 2005 (in US dollars)

	Traditional CMT Manufacturers	Integrated FOB Firm	
	Cost Structure	Cost Structure	Value per Fleece Sweatshirt
Profit	4%	4%	$0.10
Labor compensation	50%	20%	$0.50
Packaging	20%	8%	$0.20
Fabric	na	50%	$1.25
Transport costs	9%	6%	$0.15
Utilities + Rent + Other overhead	16%	12%	$0.30
	100%	100%	$2.50

Source: Adapted from Christopher Maloney, *All Dressed Up With No Place to Go?: Lesotho's Experience with Apparel FDI*, MPA/ID SYPA, Kennedy School of Government, Harvard University, Spring 2006.

Note: Value per fleece sweatshirt is approximated. The costs are calculated with the exchange rate in 2005.

Endnotes

[1] The best and most comprehensive recent overview is Christopher Maloney, *All Dressed Up With No Place to Go?: Lesotho's Rollercoaster Experience with Apparel*, MPA/ID SYPA, Kennedy School of Government, Harvard University, spring 2006. Additionally, the authors are grateful for Christopher's sharing his data, findings, and considerable expertise as we were writing.

[2] J. M. Mohapeloa, *Tentative British Imperialism in Lesotho* (Maseru, Lesotho: Morija Museum and Archives, 2002), p. 16.

[3] Ibid., p. 339.

[4] Ibid., pp. 146, 356.

[5] Francis Makoa, "Political Instability in Post-Military Lesotho: The Crisis of the Basotho Nation-state?" *African Security Review* 5, no. 3 (1996).

[6] John Spence, *Lesotho: The Politics of Dependence* (London: Oxford, 1963), pp. 55-56.

[7] Mohapeloa, p. 359.

[8] Lesotho Chamber of Commerce and Industry, Association of Lesotho Employers, and Sechaba Consultants, *Lesotho 1998: Assessment of Damages to Business and Loss of Employment*, November 1998.

[9] South Africa's mining labor force totaled 673,000 in 1987. Jim Cobbe, "Lesotho: Will the Enclave Empty?" Migration Policy Institute Working Paper, 2004.

[10] See ibid.; Department for International Development, "Lesotho Garment Industry Subsector Study," *Government of Lesotho*, January 2002, p. 12.

[11] See Lesotho Highlands Water Project (LHWP), "Frequently Asked Questions," LHWP Web site, http://www.lhwp.org.ls/faqs/default.htm, accessed March 7, 2006; Theo Sparreboom and Pete Sparreboom-Burger, "Migrant worker remittances in Lesotho," International Labor Organization Working Paper No. 16, 1997, p. 6.

[12] Department of Water Affairs and Forestry (DWAF)—South Africa, "Overview of the Lesotho Highlands Water Project," DWAF Web site, http://www.dwaf.gov.za/orange/Up_Orange/lhwpover.htm, accessed March 7, 2006.

[13] Ryan Hoover, "Pipe Dreams: The World Bank's Failed Efforts to Restore Lives and Livelihoods of Dam-Affected People in Lesotho," *International Rivers Network*, 2001, p. 2.

[14] Ibid., p. 12.

[15] Ibid., p. 41; LHWP, "Frequently Asked Questions."

[16] "Small place, big wave," *The Economist*, September 19, 2002; Lesotho Highlands Water Project (LHWP), "Overview of the Lesotho Highlands Water Project (LHWP)," LHWP Web site, http://www.lhwp.org.ls/overview/default.htm, accessed March 7, 2006.

[17] Agata Pawlowska, "Formulating a PSD Strategy for Lesotho," mimeo, June 10, 2004, p. 9.

[18] Frank Baffoe, "Work For Developing Industrialisation Master Plan For Lesotho," *Ministry of Trade and Industry, Co-Operatives, and Marketing*, Maseru, Lesotho, September 2004, p. 3.

[19] Department for International Development, p. 14.

[20] Ibid., pp. 14–15.

[21] UNCTAD, "Investment Policy Review—Lesotho," *United Nations*, 2003, p. 14.

[22] Maloney, p. 4.

[23] See Regina Abrami, "Worker Rights and Global Trade: The U.S.-Cambodia Bilateral Textile Trade Agreement," HBS Case No. 703-034 (Boston: Harvard Business School Publishing, 2003).

[24] Ibid., p. 5.

[25] Department for International Development, p. 15.

[26] "Summary of AGOA I," African Growth and Opportunity Act (AGOA) Web site, http://www.agoa.gov/agoa_legislation/agoa_legislation.html, accessed March 7, 2006.

[27] Daniel Maraisane, General Secretary, Lesotho Clothing & Allied Workers Union (LECAWU), interview by authors, Maseru, Lesotho, July 28, 2005.

[28] An extraordinarily clear description of this complicated mix of policies is in Maloney, p. 5. Also see "Summary of AGOA I"; Alex Fryer, "GOP Legislators, McDermott Join Forces on Africa-trade Bill; Unusual Alliance Aided by Rocker Bono in Bid to Renew Law Set to Expire," *Seattle Times*, May 19, 2004.

[29] Authors' interview with Maraisane.

[30] Department for International Development, p. 19.

[31] Authors' interview with Maraisane.

[32] Department for International Development, p. 17.

[33] John Gay and David Hall, *Poverty and Livelihoods in Lesotho, 2000*, Sechaba Consultants, Maseru, Lesotho, June 2000, p. 78.

[34] Statement to Parliament by the Honourable Mpho Malie, Minister of Trade and Industry, Co-operative and Marketing, on Lesotho's Export Textiles and Garment Industry, February 2005.

[35] Lesotho National Development Corporation (LNDC), "Investors Guide," LNDC Web site, http://www.lndc.org.ls/IG.htm, accessed March 7, 2006.

[36] Statement to Parliament by the Honourable Mpho Malie.

[37] Maloney, pp. 31-32.

[38] Department for International Development, p. 25.

[39] Ibid., p. 21.

[40] *Labour Code (Amendment) Act 2000*, Authority of His Majesty the King, Kingdom of Lesotho.

[41] Jennifer Chen, Managing Director, Shining Century Limited, interview by authors, Maseru, Lesotho, July 28, 2005.

[42] Authors' interview with Maraisane.

[43] Report of the Inter-Ministerial Task Team on Maintaining Foreign Direct Investment in Lesotho's Textiles and Apparel Industry, Government working document C3(2004/6) 188, September 21, 2004, p. 10.

[44] Abrami, p. 6.

[45] US-China Business Council (USCBC), "China WTO/PNTR: Raising Wages, Improving Chinese Labor Standards and Safeguarding U.S. Workers," USCBC Web site, March 9, 2000, http://www.uschina.org/public/wto/b4ct/raising.html, accessed March 7, 2006.

[46] "China's people problem," *The Economist*, April 14, 2005.

[47] David Barboza and Keith Bradsher, "China Braces for Speculation in the Yuan," *The New York Times*, July 23, 2005.

[48] Authors' interview with Chen. An analysis of the new wage rate, as of January 2006, can be found in Vietnamnet Bridge, "Government sets new minimum wage for foreign firms," Vietnamnet Bridge Web site, January 7, 2006, http://english.vietnamnet.vn/social/2006/01/530227, accessed March 7, 2006 (source: VNA).

[49] ProNicaragua, "Investment Opportunities: Textiles and Apparels," ProNicaragua Web site, http://www.pronicaragua.org/index.php?option=com_content&task=view&id=14&Itemid=28, accessed March 7, 2006.

[50] "3rd Country Fabrics: Options for Lesotho's Textiles and Garment Industries," LNDC/ComMark discussion paper, July 14, 2005, p. 5.

[51] Department for International Development, p. 39.

[52] Ibid.

[53] John Haycock, Report on the Productivity Audit and Training Needs Analysis for the Garment Industry in Lesotho, ComMark Trust, November 2003, p. 5. See also Maloney, p. 20.

[54] Amanda Hilligas, "The Elimination of Quotas Under the World Trade Organization Agreement on Textiles and Clothing: The Impact on Lesotho," USAID, mimeo, February 23, 2005, p. 13.

[55] *Transit Transport Issues in Landlocked and Transit Developing Countries*, Landlocked Developing Countries Series, No. 1, Economic and Social Commission for Asia and the Pacific, United Nations, 2003, p. 59.

[56] Ibid., p. 74.

[57] Authors' interview with Chen.

[58] Haycock, pp. 2, 6.

[59] Ibid., pp. 7–8.

[60] Ibid., p. 9.

[61] Ibid., p. 8.

[62] HIV/AIDS Behavioral Surveillance Survey: Lesotho 2002, USAID 2002, p. 16.

[63] Ibid.

[64] Ibid., pp. 1-2.

[65] Central Intelligence Agency (CIA), "The World Fact Book: Lesotho," CIA Web site, http://www.cia.gov/cia/publications/factbook/geos/lt.html, accessed March 7, 2006.

[66] Timothy T. Thahane, Minister of Finance and Development Planning, Kingdom of Lesotho, interview by authors, Maseru, Lesotho, July 28, 2005.

[67] Michael Wines, "Women in Lesotho Become Easy Prey for HIV," *The New York Times*, July 20, 2004.

[68] Authors' interview with Chen.

[69] Maloney, p. 35.

[70] In 2004, UNITE joined with the Hotel Employees and Restaurant Employees (HERE) International Union, forming UNITE HERE.

[71] BBC News, "Gap hit by 'sweatshop' protests," BBC News Web site, November 21, 2002, http://news.bbc.co.uk/1/hi/business/2497957.stm, accessed March 7, 2006.

[72] Sean Ansett, Director, Global Partnerships, the Gap Inc., interview by authors, August 22, 2005. In September 2005, Sean Ansett left the Gap Inc.

[73] Ibid.

[74] Authors' interview with Maraisane.

[75] Authors' interview with Ansett.

[76] UNCTAD, "Investment Policy Review: Lesotho," 2003, p. 56.

[77] AGOA.info, "Lesotho Weaves Its Way From Rags to Riches," AGOA.info Web site, August 1, 2003, http://agoa.info/?view=.&story=news&subtext=124, accessed March 7, 2006 (source: Business Day).

[78] UNCTAD, p. 56.

[79] Authors' interview with Maraisane.

[80] For a discussion, see Maloney, pp. 39-40.

[81] Authors' interview with Thahane.

[82] Maloney, pp. 49-50.

[83] Report of the Inter-Ministerial Task Team on Maintaining Foreign Direct Investment in Lesotho's Textiles and Apparel Industry, p. 19.

[84] *Results Do Matter*, Budget speech to Parliament for the 2006/2007 Fiscal Year by the Honorable Timothy T. Thahane, Minister of Finance and Development Planning, February 8, 2006, p. 9.

[85] Authors' interview with Thahane.

[86] Ibid.

[87] Ibid.

[88] Authors' interview with Chen.

[89] Macaefa Billy, General Secretary of the Factory Workers Union (Fawu) and MP for the Worker's Party, Kingdom of Lesotho, interview by authors, Maseru, Lesotho, July 27, 2005.

[90] Paul Theron, RPA Consulting, "Determining Lesotho's Knitted Fabric Requirements," *LNDC-ComMark Lesotho Apparel Project*, December 2004, p. 11.

[91] See, for example, "Friend or Forager? How China is Winning the Resources and Loyalties of Africa," *The Financial Times*, February 23, 2006.

[92] Authors' interview with Chen.

[93] See especially Maloney, pp. 29-31.

[94] Authors' interview with Chen.

[95] Basic Chinese wage rates in textiles are from Judith Banister, "Manufacturing Employment and Compensation in China," *Bureau of Labor Statistics*, Table 6. Regional variations are from the authors' interview with Chen.

[96] Authors' interview with Maraisane.

[97] Authors' interview with Thahane.

[98] Authors' interview with Maraisane.

DEBORA SPAR

NICHOLAS BARTLETT

Life, Death, and Property Rights:
The Pharmaceutical Industry Faces AIDS in Africa

At the start of the twenty-first century, AIDS (Acquired Immune Deficiency Syndrome) was poised to become the most deadly disease known to humanity. In the 20 years since its first documented outbreaks, 24.4 million people had died from AIDS, while over 40 million were living with the disease.[1] Rapidly spreading around the world, AIDS had proliferated in countries where basic factors including education and safer sex practices were at a minimum, with 95% of infections occurring in the developing world.[2] In certain countries in sub-Saharan Africa as many as one in three adults tested positive for HIV (Human Immunodeficiency Virus), the virus that eventually causes AIDS. In South Africa alone, in the year 2000, there were an estimated 4,700,000 people infected with HIV/AIDS.[3] Terrifyingly, many experts believed that worse was yet to come. With infection rates continuing to increase in many areas and treatment woefully inadequate for the vast majority of those infected, AIDS threatened the developing world with an epidemic of unprecedented magnitude.

There were, to be sure, treatments for AIDS. While a cure remained frustratingly elusive decades after the disease first emerged, scientists and pharmaceutical firms had managed to concoct a series of increasingly effective drugs that enhanced the quality of life for many AIDS victims and transmuted what had once been a certain sentence of death. The drugs were complicated to administer, however, and extremely expensive—roughly $10,000 to $15,000 per person, per year. In Africa, where average annual per capita incomes ranged from $450 to $8,900, they were essentially unaffordable.

Not surprisingly, then, the death toll in Africa had begun by the 1990s to plague the world's pharmaceutical firms as well. Across Africa and into the developed nations, doctors and AIDS activists clamored for an industrywide response to the AIDS epidemic. Pharmaceutical companies, they argued, needed to lower the prices they charged for AIDS drugs in Africa. They needed to make their drugs more accessible and to ensure that even the poorest victims could benefit from cutting-edge research. Where the companies were unwilling or unable to comply with these demands, the activists argued, local pharmaceutical firms should be able to step into the gap, selling generic versions of the sought-after drugs.

Such "solutions" were anathema to the established Western pharmaceutical industry. These were firms, after all, that spent millions of dollars on research and development; firms that often spent years, or decades, perfecting the treatments they discovered. In their home markets, these firms were

---

Professor Debora Spar and Research Associate Nicholas Bartlett prepared this case. This case was developed from published sources. HBS cases are developed solely as the basis for class discussion. Cases are not intended to serve as endorsements, sources of primary data, or illustrations of effective or ineffective management.

protected by patent systems that enabled them to recover the development costs of their drugs. They were not simply going to turn around and distribute their product for free. Moreover, the patents that protected the Western pharmaceutical firms were part of a broader system of intellectual property rights—a system based on the sanctity of privately owned information and enshrined in the newly created rules of the World Trade Organization. If the pharmaceutical companies relented in the face of Africa's epidemic, they risked denting the entire global structure of intellectual property rights. For if drugs were free—or cheap, or copied—in Africa, why not books or music or software? Indeed, why stop in Africa? There were poor people everywhere, and millions who were dying from AIDS.

The stakes of AIDS in Africa, therefore, were immense. If the pharmaceutical companies did nothing, they risked the lives of millions and a massive blow to their global standing and reputation. But if they lowered prices in Africa or weakened their patent rights, they risked destroying the system that sustained them; the system that, arguably, enabled them to save the very people who were now organizing against them.

Prelude to Catastrophe: The Emergence of AIDS in the United States

The first wave of the AIDS epidemic was concentrated in the United States, and particularly in the cities of New York and San Francisco, where a group of otherwise healthy gay men began in the early 1980s to develop a rare form of cancer. Suspecting that an unknown virus might be to blame, scientists began to look for the culprit and transmission mechanism. Quickly, they realized this strange new disease traveled through direct physical contact: blood transfusions, sharing needles, perinatility (from mother to child during childbirth), and sexual contact, both homosexual and heterosexual. Nevertheless, because AIDS was first discovered in the gay community and remained concentrated there for some time, it swiftly became known as the "gay disease" and was associated, almost entirely at first, with homosexual activity.

In the 1980s, the disease spread through the United States at an alarming rate: 100,000 people tested positive for AIDS in the first eight years of testing, with an additional 100,000 cases identified just two years later.[4] Because scientists were unable to define an effective medical treatment for this mysterious virus, death rates were extremely high and patients rarely survived for more than 10 years.

This initial phase of infection was characterized by a general lack of information, widespread fear, and an inability or unwillingness to deal with the extent of the problem in the United States. In a sign of the times, Ryan White, a 13-year-old hemophiliac with AIDS, had to attend middle school classes by phone after being barred from his Indiana school in 1985. The superintendent justified his decision by explaining, "With all the things we do and don't know about AIDS, I just decided not to do it. There are a lot of unknowns and uncertainties, and then you have the inherent fear that would generate among classmates."[5] The U.S. government, meanwhile, did little to stem public fears. President Reagan waited six years after the initial outbreak of AIDS to address the topic publicly and the United States was among the last of the major Western industrialized nations to launch a coordinated education campaign.

Soon, however, it became clear that AIDS was not an isolated problem of the United States. In 1983, 33 countries reported AIDS infection and by 1987 that number had increased to 127. In 1984 the Ugandan Minister of Health asked the World Health Organization for assistance in battling AIDS, and the United Kingdom formed a special cabinet committee to investigate the disease. That same year, the Zambian Ministry of Health launched a national AIDS education campaign. It would do little to stop the spread of the virus, though, which swiftly claimed the life of the president's son.

As the effects of AIDS swept across the world, activists in the United States finally propelled the disease into the public spotlight. In 1987, a group of mostly gay protestors created ACT UP (AIDS Coalition to Unleash Power), a "diverse, non-partisan group of individuals united in anger and committed to direct action to end the AIDS crisis."[6] In "zap" demonstrations designed to attract media attention and raise public awareness, ACT UP members staged "die-ins," harassed politicians, and picketed corporate buildings. Seven demonstrators broke into the New York Stock Exchange in 1989, where they chained themselves to railings to protest the high prices of AIDS treatment. In a less confrontational but equally influential campaign, Elizabeth Glaser, wife of TV's "Starsky and Hutch" star Paul Glaser, took the cause to Washington during her well-publicized battle with the disease in the late 1980s. Infected by a blood transfusion during childbirth before transmitting the disease to her two children, Glaser became a marquee celebrity spokesperson for the disease, lobbying to raise money and challenging the public's conception of AIDS as a "gay" or "drug-user" disease.

Before long, increased awareness and scientific breakthrough began to make some headway against the disease. Through a combination of preventive campaigns and improved treatment, health care officials greatly reduced the rate of transmission while boosting the quality of care provided to those with AIDS. By the mid-1990s, the rate of infection in the U.S. appeared to have peaked, dropping from nearly 80,000 new cases diagnosed in 1993 to just 21,700 in 2000.[7] While more people in the United States were living with HIV and AIDS than ever before, doctors had found a menu of ways to check the spread of the disease in the body and thus to slow the inevitable pace of death.

Some of this improvement, to be sure, was due to preventive measures that the activists had helped bring to light: blood screening, needle exchange programs, and promotion of condom use. But much was the result of a slow but steady onslaught against the virus itself. In the 20 years that followed the discovery of AIDS, scientists had still not succeeded in curing the disease or formulating an effective vaccine against it. But they had made great strides in understanding and treating both AIDS and HIV. Essentially, HIV spreads in a patient's body by targeting cells that normally clear foreign pathogens. As these cells replicate, the HIV virus eventually—often rapidly—devastates the immune system of its victim. HIV develops into full-blown AIDS when the virus has spread to such a degree that it disrupts the basic function of the immune system. Patients die from diseases that their immune systems can no longer prevent, rather than from AIDS itself.

Initially, scientists struggling with the HIV/AIDS virus were forced to treat only the disease's symptoms, focusing for instance on the pneumonia that felled so many patients in the latter stages of AIDS. In 1986, however, the U.S. Food and Drug Administration (FDA) approved the first AIDS-specific drug, an antiviral medication known as zidovudine or AZT, which worked by inhibiting one of the enzymes involved with replication. Several years later, scientists developed a new class of drugs, called protease inhibitors, that attempted to stop already infected cells from further spreading the HIV virus. Both AZT and the protease inhibitors represented a quantum leap in treatment quality, and it was their usage that began, by the early 1990s, to reduce the toll of AIDS. However, as the drugs were increasingly prescribed, the virus itself began to mutate, morphing into new and more drug-resistant strains. In response, doctors backed away from the once-promising "monotherapies" and began to attack AIDS with what became known as HAART (Highly Active Antiviral Therapy), a combination of drugs designed to combat the virus at various levels.

By the late 1990s, the HAART approach seemed to be working. AIDS infection rates had plummeted in the United States and infected patients were living longer, healthier lives. While a diagnosis of AIDS was still devastating to the victim, it was no longer the death sentence it had been a decade ago. Infected patients such as basketball great Magic Johnson or *New Republic* editor Andrew Sullivan were living normal and productive lives, and had reclaimed their position in society. HAART, however, was far from perfect. It was, in its early days, extremely complicated, demanding that patients take over 20 pills a day in accordance with a rigid schedule. Second, the cost of these pills was exorbitant, reaching $10,000–$15,000 a year for patients in the United States. And finally, all this medicine still did not get at the root cause of the disease: HAART treated AIDS, but it didn't cure it.

The Second Wave: AIDS and the Developing World

Just as the United States was beginning to stem the HIV/AIDS crisis within its own borders, infection rates in much of the rest of the world began spinning out of control. By the year 2000, 25.3 million people with HIV/AIDS lived in Africa, while South and Southeast Asia and Latin America hosted 6.1 million and 1.4 million, respectively.[8] In many of these regions, heterosexual contact was the primary method of transmission; indeed, 55% of sub-Saharan Africans infected were women.[9] In the year 2001 alone, the virus infected 3.4 million new victims in Africa, raising the sub-continent's percentage of total adults infected to 8.4%.[10] In Zimbabwe, where over 30% of the adult population tested positive for HIV, the demographic toll of the disease had already been felt, pushing the country's once-robust rate of population growth down to zero. Starting in 2003, the populations of Zimbabwe, Botswana, and South Africa were actually predicted to decline by .1%–.3% a year.[11] Similar declines were likely to sweep across the continent, as other countries watched their HIV cases develop into full-blown AIDS.

In South Africa, home to the largest HIV-positive population in the world, the prognosis was particularly grim. Already staggering under the burdens of poverty and a grossly unequal distribution of wealth, South Africa had seen AIDS ravage its population in the late 1990s: 20% of the adult population was infected with HIV in the year 2000, with 500,000 new cases reported in that year alone. A total of 4.7 million suffered from the disease, which had also become the leading cause of death.[12] Predictions for the future were terrifying. Fueled by a lack of information about the disease and continued high-risk behavior (a 1998 survey found that only 16% of women used a condom in the last encounter with their nonspouse sexual partner), health care officials predicted that HIV infection rates could hit 7.5 million by 2010, with 635,000 people dying that year from the disease.[13] The vast majority of those affected would be between 15 and 29 years old, with half infected before they turned 25, and half dead before 35.[14]

Beyond this unspeakable death toll, experts also feared broader setbacks to South Africa, including a reduction in life expectancy, a decrease in educational opportunities for its citizens, and growing socioeconomic disparities. Various reports noted that the economic, political, and social fallout of the epidemic could be enormous, ranging from a decimated workforce (including a 40% to 50% loss of employees in certain sectors) to declining growth and an impending crisis for a healthcare system unequipped to deal with millions of sick and dying.[15] Most disturbing, perhaps, was the disease's expected toll on the next generation of South Africans. Because of the nature of its transmission, AIDS tended to infect both parents of a family, and thus to leave a staggering number of orphans in its wake. By 2010 experts predicted that there could be nearly 2 million AIDS orphans in South Africa. How would the country, already pushed to its fiscal limits, provide either physical or emotional care to these swelling ranks of children? "Everybody is scared," wrote the author of one USAID report. "We're moving into uncharted territory."[16]

Sadly, the countries hit hardest by the HIV/AIDS epidemic were also those least able to provide their citizens with adequate treatment. In most of the developing world, HIV-positive populations did not have access to the most rudimentary health care or doctors, let alone the ultra-expensive antiviral drugs regularly prescribed in the United States. Indeed, conditions in these countries often precluded all but the most basic care. Doctors were scarce across the developing world, storage and distribution systems rare, and education about the disease often sorely limited. Under these conditions, even the limited funding that did flow to HIV/AIDS treatment was often wasted, with the World Bank estimating that for every $100 that African governments spent on drugs, only $12 worth of medicine reached the patient.[17] In many countries, moreover, the social stigma that surrounded AIDS kept infected people from seeking assistance and allowed their governments to turn a blind eye to the disease. The most notorious example of this behavior occurred in South Africa, the heart of the epidemic, where President Thabo Mbeki stubbornly refused to increase his country's spending on medical treatment, arguing that poverty, poor diet, and other social ills were to blame.[18]

Others, however, were not so complacent, nor were they prepared to blame Africa's ills solely on the African context. Instead, raging rates of death and infection on the continent were linked, not illogically, to the things Africa lacked: drugs, in particular, and the means to afford them. And from this vantage point, the weight of blame fell heavily on the pharmaceutical industry.

The Pharmaceutical Industry and Intellectual Property Rights

Over the course of the twentieth century, Western pharmaceutical companies had transformed themselves from anonymous, low-profit chemical suppliers into high profile, top-performing firms. They earned billions of dollars, employed thousands of the world's leading scientists, and made the drugs that saved lives. Many factors had contributed to the pharmaceutical industry's success— medical advances, government support, and a capital market eager to oblige. At the center of the industry, though, and close to the heart of all industry executives sat the patent system, a legal bulwark protecting—some might even say permitting—the development of drugs.

First devised in fifteenth-century Venice, patents were intended to repay their holders for the effort and expenses incurred during a product's development: if a glassblower pioneered a new method for shaping glass, for example, or a craftsman built a better compass, the republic wanted to ensure that they could reap the commercial benefits of their work. So Venice granted its patent holders a window of market exclusivity for their product, a kind of government-sanctioned temporary monopoly. Over subsequent centuries, justification for patents varied from recognizing the "natural right" of an inventor's ownership of ideas to providing a practical way for governments to promote and reward innovation. Such motives figured prominently in the early history of the United States. Story has it that the Constitutional Convention adjourned one afternoon to watch John Frich's steamboat undergo tests on the Delaware River. Hoping to safeguard the freedom of individuals and the enterprises they were creating, many of the founding fathers of the United States saw the implementation of a federal patent system as a sensible way of defending emerging American industry. And thus, to "encourage the progress of science and the useful arts,"[19] America's legislators enshrined a system of patents in the U.S. constitution.[20]

Not all Americans, however, favored laws that restricted the dissemination of ideas. Indeed, many argued that patents were an invidious form of regulation, one that favored commerce over the greater development of humankind. As Thomas Jefferson, an early proponent of freely flowing ideas, famously reasoned:

> He who receives an idea from me, receives instruction himself without lessening mine; as he who lights his taper at mine, receives light without darkening me. That ideas should freely spread from one to another over the globe, for the moral and mutual instruction of man, and improvement of his condition, seems to have been peculiarly and benevolently designed by nature. . . . Inventions then cannot, in nature, be a subject of property.[21]

Such poetic objection, though, remained rare. Several decades after Jefferson's argument, President Lincoln appeared to speak for the nation when he noted that "the Patent System added the fuel of interest to the fire of genius."[22] Patents enjoyed permanent inclusion in the laws of the United States.

For the pharmaceutical industry, however, this system of protection was initially irrelevant. For patents were designed to protect research—innovation—and the pharmaceutical trade in the early United States had little to do with discovery. Instead, the drug industry was largely composed of small, low-profile firms that supplied pharmacists with the bulk chemicals they used to produce formulaic mixtures. Indeed, until the turn of the twentieth century, "patented drugs" were simply those marketed under a trademarked name—often the most dubious drugs or "elixirs" available.

Events in the 1930s and 1940s, however, brought drastic change to the pharmaceutical industry. In 1932, a German pharmacologist discovered Prontosil, a sulfanilamide drug with significant antibacterial properties. Suddenly, it appeared that scientific research could lead to direct cures; that chemistry and discovery could pave the path to drugs. Accordingly, the U.S. government poured $3 million into a massive research and production effort during World War II, involving more than 20 companies and several universities in a coordinated research effort.[23] These initial funds flowed primarily to war-specific concerns and led, over time, to the development of yellow fever and typhus vaccines and the discovery of oral saline therapies to help exhausted soldiers on the battlefields. After the war, research efforts widened, leading to a widely heralded stream of pharmaceutical breakthroughs: antibiotics in the 1940s, steroids in the 1950s, and birth control pills in the 1960s. Far more efficacious than the elixirs of earlier years, these new drugs flooded the U.S. market, bringing massive improvements in medicine and (with birth control pills especially) significant social change.[24] They also brought a correspondingly large improvement in the fortunes of pharmaceutical companies and a newfound interest in patents.

By the 1970s, the U.S. pharmaceutical industry was completely transformed. Companies such as Merck and Pfizer, once humble chemical suppliers, had become corporate giants, with armies of in-house scientists and a major commitment to research and development. (See **Exhibit 4a** for the growth of research and development expenses.) They had arsenals of proprietary drugs (such as Merck's Pepcid and Abbott Labs' erythromycin) that were distributed through complex networks and supported by sophisticated promotion campaigns. And they had a patent system, enshrined since the eighteenth century, which gave each company 20 years of exclusive control over the drugs that it developed.[25] As of 1980, U.S. pharmaceutical companies were spending just under $2 billion annually for research and development.[26] By 2001, the $170 billion U.S. pharmaceutical market was easily the largest in the world, a combination of high demand (Americans consumed relatively large amounts of drugs), high quality, and prices that remained stubbornly aloof from government regulation. U.S. pharmaceutical firms, together with European players such as Novartis and Bayer, were among the largest corporations in the world and easily among the most profitable: between 1994 and 1998, after-tax profits in the drug industry averaged 17% of sales, or three times higher than industrywide averages.[27]

Not surprisingly, representatives of the industry explained these profit levels as evidence of their products' power: pharmaceutical companies made money because they made products that worked; products that customers wanted to buy at almost any cost. Moreover, the industry argued, drug prices were high because they had to be. Each drug, after all, was the product of an increasingly expensive research process, one that was inherently fraught with uncertainty. For each drug that Pfizer, say, developed, there were roughly 5,000 compounds that Pfizer researchers had tested and abandoned in the laboratory.[28] And even those compounds that did prove promising were subjected to a long and tedious process of testing and regulation. Under guidelines established by the U.S. Food and Drug Administration (FDA), no drug could be sold in the U.S. market until it underwent three stages of successful clinical testing and survived a rigorous approval procedure. Only one in 20 trial-phase drugs was eventually approved for public use, and even successful candidates often took 10 years and 50,000 pages of documentation to win FDA approval.[29] The total cost of this process was reported to be between $500 million and $880 million.[30] No wonder, industry representatives argued, that drug prices were high. No wonder drugs demanded years of patent protection to recoup their research costs. Or as one industry expert explained, "You have to relativize this. A company can support some research without being paid off, but not much. Especially with the pressure on shareholder value."[31]

To be sure, not all observers shared the pharmaceutical industry's analysis of its own economics. Indeed, criticism of the industry was rife in the 1980s and 1990s, and eventually assumed a fairly predictable course. Periodically, critics (such as the early AIDS activists) would decry the industry's high profits and the prices it charged for life-saving drugs. During the Clinton administration, there was a burst of concern about the trend of drug prices and an intense, if ill-fated, attempt to increase regulation of the industry.[32] In other instances, critics complained that drug companies spent more on advertising than on research, and that Americans, stimulated perhaps by this marketing blitz, were taking drugs unnecessarily.[33] One study, for example, revealed that two-thirds of the people taking allergy-fighting Claritin did not in fact have allergies.[34] Moreover, the critics also claimed that pharmaceutical firms vastly overstated their drug development costs: according to Ralph Nader's consumer advocacy organization, R&D costs for an average drug totaled only between $57 million and $71 million throughout the 1990s.[35]

In general, however, the structure of the U.S. pharmaceutical industry did not cause Americans undue concern. Although drug prices in the United States were substantially higher than they were elsewhere—nearly triple average drug prices in Spain and Greece, for example—Americans (and their insurers) seemed willing to pay, or at least unwilling to fight.[36] Or as one industry expert noted, "In reality, if a drug is going to save a life, we will find a way to afford it."[37] Moreover, the skeleton that supported the U.S. drug industry—the U.S. patent system—was itself almost entirely immune from dissent. Even if Americans resisted high drug prices, it appeared, and even if they resented the companies that charged these prices, they weren't willing to topple the underlying system. For most Americans believed, like Lincoln, in the inviolability of intellectual property rights and in the advantages of combining "interest" with "genius."

Going Global: The International Battlefield for Intellectual Property Rights

Elsewhere in the world, attitudes toward intellectual property rights were quite different. Some countries had strong patent laws for pharmaceuticals, but mixed them with a regulatory structure that kept drug prices low. Others had licensing requirements or weaker laws that led to lower prices and, often, the development of a generic pharmaceutical industry. And some had no patent laws, no domestic drug industry, and relied entirely on foreign imports.

For countries that lacked a domestic pharmaceutical industry, looser patent laws made sense. In these countries, there was often a sense that the nation simply could not afford either to develop new medications on its own or to pay the high prices that patented drugs commanded elsewhere. Instead, it was economically more efficient simply to allow local firms to copy high-priced imports, reproducing their chemical composition without having to bear the costs of research and development. Such strategies also paid significant social dividends, since they led almost inevitably to cheaper and more accessible drugs. After India loosened its patent laws, for example, drug prices in that country were often more than 90% lower than those in the OECD states.[38] Similarly, after local drug companies began producing a generic version of Pfizer's antifungal Fluconazole, prices dropped within months from $7.00 per dose to just 60 cents.[39]

Occasionally, weaker property rights actually led over time to the creation of a substantial generic industry, as occurred in India, Turkey, and Argentina. India's growth was particularly notable, since it took place only after 1970, when the country scaled down its patent laws in order to reduce drug prices. Elsewhere, countries that otherwise adhered to strict protection of intellectual property made a specific exception in the pharmaceutical sector, arguing that health concerns trumped property rights in this industry. Such was the case, for example, in Canada throughout the 1980s, where the government historically offered compulsory licenses for any drug imported into the country. After paying a government-determined royalty payment (generally 4%) to the patent holder, local Canadian firms were free to produce their own version of the drug, even if it was still on patent in its home market. Brazil had a similar system, requiring foreign patent holders to produce their drugs locally and charge locally mandated prices.

In the initial phase of post-war pharmaceutical growth, this diffusion of national systems functioned relatively well. Nations fashioned their laws to suit their own needs, and pharmaceutical firms adapted to their local circumstances: where property rights were strong and markets large (as in the United States and Great Britain), well-funded drug companies made both substantial profits and significant breakthroughs. Where rights were weak and patients poor, pharmaceutical firms were either generic (as in India or Brazil) or nonexistent.

As the major Western drug manufacturers began to go global, however, they also began a decades-long campaign to bring Western-style property rights to the developing world. Led by Pfizer and its politically active chairman, Edmund T. Pratt, Jr., the companies negotiated for these rights with individual governments, lobbied to have them embedded under the auspices of WIPO— the World Intellectual Property Organization—and formed international alliances with other knowledge-based industries, such as software and publishing.[40] They ran advertising campaigns and held extensive meetings, striving to convince foreign officials of the urgency of their plight.

And in the end, the pharmaceutical companies essentially returned to Washington. In 1988, the U.S. Congress amended the Trade and Tariff Act of 1984, authorizing the U.S Trade Representative (USTR) to take retaliatory action against any country believed to be guilty of failing to protect U.S. companies' intellectual property rights through a provision known as "Special 301." Justifying the policy by arguing that "we don't work for" consumers in patent-violating countries such as Argentina and South Korea, the USTR compiled annual lists of suspected violators and threatened unilateral sanctions unless these countries conformed with the dictates of U.S. law. In response, countries—including Argentina, Thailand, Brazil, Italy, and Korea—swiftly tightened their patent and copyright laws. At an ideological level, several of these states continued to assert the superiority of their former systems. But pressure from the United States was sufficient to compel a regulatory change of heart.

In the meantime, the pharmaceutical lobby also labored to include intellectual rights on the World Trade Organization's agenda. Allying with other developed nations during the Uruguay Round of GATT (General Agreement on Tariffs and Trade) negotiations, U.S. officials successfully added intellectual property rights to the slate of new requirements. Under a provision known as TRIPS (for trade-related intellectual property rights), all countries that wanted to join the newly created World Trade Organization (WTO) would henceforth be required to grant a minimum of 20-year patent protection in most fields of medicine. Despite loopholes allowing for the compulsory licensing of drugs in some cases and the concession of a 10-year implementation period for the least-developed countries, TRIPS marked a landmark achievement in the pharmaceutical industry's quest for global patent protection. "TRIPS," claimed one industry specialist, "is the most important international agreement on intellectual property this century."[41]

Debate, however, continued to rage. In many parts of the world, both government officials and public opinion maintained that U.S.-style patent rights were ill-suited to their countries' circumstances—that they were unfair, unrealistic, and ultimately damaging to public health. Indeed, despite their formal adherence to TRIPS, many countries still argued that health had to take precedence over profits, and that all countries (including the United States) should be able to license patented drugs in case of medical emergency. Healthcare experts also stressed that generic production posed far less of a threat than industry representatives suggested. Indeed, in most parts of the world, people simply could not afford patented drugs and would not purchase them under any circumstances. In areas such as sub-Saharan Africa, for example, where per capita expenditure on drugs rarely topped $100 a year, activists stressed that "the purchasing power of 1.2 billion people living on US$1 a day simply does not constitute a commercial incentive to research and development."[42]

Yet the pharmaceutical companies remained firm. Snug behind the protection of both U.S. law and TRIPS, they maintained the intellectual purity of their position. Without patent protection, no company could afford to take the financial risks that drug development demanded. And without drugs and drug research, millions of people would suffer.

Back to Africa

At the turn of the century, the AIDS situation in Africa remained grim. Even as AIDS-related deaths in the developed world were plummeting at last; and even though nonprofit groups such as Doctors Without Borders were trying to distribute drugs to small clusters of Africans, the vast majority of Africa's AIDS patients remained without treatment. In 2001, 25 million Africans were HIV-positive, roughly half of whom were medically eligible for combination treatments such as HAART.[43] Only 25,000 of these patients had received antiretroviral drugs, however—a tiny portion when compared to Western standards.[44] In Uganda, for example, only about 1,000 patients, or 0.1% of the infected population, had received the prescribed triple therapy; in Malawi, the number was only 30.[45] Without drugs, these patients were also essentially without hope. And thus the AIDS epidemic continued to ravage Africa and to wreak an escalating havoc on a continent already beset with troubles.

It wasn't long, therefore, before Africa spawned AIDS activists of its own—patients or their supporters who struggled to find some way of attacking, or at least forestalling, the disease's deadly hold. Like their Western predecessors, the activists spread a wide net at first, cajoling governments and the media to take notice of their plight. But eventually they focused on the easiest and most obvious target: the pharmaceutical companies whose drugs held the prospect of survival.

Although these groups were split to some extent by their negotiating tactics, they shared a common underlying complaint—the same complaint that had initially motivated ACT UP a decade earlier in the United States. Simply put, the activists charged that the AIDS plague in Africa was due, at least in part, to the actions of Western drug firms. It was the drug companies, they claimed, that consciously held prices beyond the grasp of most Africans; the drug companies that refused to allow lower-priced versions of their product. It was the drug companies that hid behind the veneer of Western patent laws and used international pressure to preserve their own profits. And while the companies reaped profits from high-priced AIDS drugs, millions of Africans were dying.

Central to the activists' complaint was the problem of prices. In the developed world, the typical price of HAART treatment in 1999 remained at the staggering level of $10,000–$15,000. Much of this cost, however, was assumed either by government insurance plans (in Canada and Europe) or by private insurance (in the United States). In Africa, where both public and private insurance schemes were scarce, pricing drugs at Western levels essentially meant pricing them far beyond the reach of nearly all potential patients: at $10,000, virtually no one in Africa, or indeed anywhere in the developing world, could afford HAART-style treatment. Accordingly, AIDS activists and patients in Africa accused the Western drug companies of using their pricing policies to "wage an undeclared drugs war" against the developing world.[46] By refusing to lower their prices, the activists charged, pharmaceutical firms were directly responsible for millions of unnecessary deaths and for allowing AIDS to spread unchecked across the continent. "There are drugs," argued one prominent AIDS consultant, "there is unimaginable wealth in this world, and the people who have the money are refusing to help."[47] Echoed another: "The poor have no consumer power, so the market has failed them. I'm tired of the logic that says, 'He who can't pay, dies.'"[48]

What particularly infuriated many Africa-based activists was the pharmaceutical companies' reluctance to endorse generic substitutes for their product. Typically, branded drugs from the developing world were sold in Africa and elsewhere as lower-priced copies—there were generic antibiotics, for example, and ulcer-fighting medicines rather than the branded products that prevailed in the West. Sometimes these drugs were produced by Western firms, and sometimes by generic producers based in India, Argentina, or Brazil. Nearly always, though, the generic drugs were legally generic (even by U.S. standards) since the original patents had already expired. AIDS drugs, however, were different: they were new, they were often experimental, and nearly all of them remained protected by Western patents in their home markets. In the case of these drugs, therefore, Western companies were reluctant to permit generic production—even if generic firms could arguably produce the same drug at a substantially reduced price. For the companies, this was simply accepted practice. But for the activists, it was greed that led to murder. Industry experts estimated that generic competition in the AIDS drug market could lead to an immediate 50%–90% reduction in drug prices.[49]

Already, a handful of countries had formally embraced generic solutions. In India, for example, local firms were legally permitted to produce patented medicines as long as they could develop a new means of producing them, and in Thailand, the government actively encouraged the production of generic AIDS drugs.[50] The most dramatic policy, though, came from Brazil, where a controversial "Free Drugs for All" program provided a compelling example of low-priced, large-scale antiretroviral treatment. Launched in 1997, this government-sponsored initiative offered a variety of HAART therapies, for free, to all AIDS patients. Using generic drugs produced by its own local industry, the government spent only $4,716 per patient per year—compared with $12,000 for similar therapy in the United States. By the turn of the century, over 90,000 patients had received treatment and infection rates were plummeting in Brazil.[51] AIDS-related deaths had fallen by half since 1996 and the government actually appeared to be saving money: according to official estimates, treatment under the Free Drugs program had kept 146,000 people out of the hospital and saved the country $422 million in averted hospital charges.[52] Overjoyed with their success, health officials argued that Brazil demonstrated both the efficacy of generic solutions and the economic feasibility of treating even very poor patients. "The simplistic argument that treating AIDS is expensive is no longer convincing," asserted one well-placed observer, "In Brazil, the cost of the investment is economically positive."[53] Even more impressive, perhaps, was that Brazil had not completely abandoned the recognition of international patents. Indeed, under pressure from the United States, Brazil only permitted the generic production of antiretroviral drugs commercialized before 1997. Half of its per-patient cost came from the importation of more recently patented treatments.

As word of Brazil's success spread, health workers in Africa urged a similar response. They argued that drugs had to be made available on the continent in large quantities and at reduced prices, meaning that the pharmaceutical companies would have to either cut their prices or agree to generic production of still-patented treatments. In South Africa, seeds of a future battle were sown on December 12, 1997, when President Nelson Mandela signed a series of key amendments to the South African Medicines Act. Initiated by the controversial South African Health Minister, Nkosazana Zuma, the amendments gave the health minister authority to break international patents and import or manufacture generic drugs.[54] As part of a larger plan to improve the sorry state of healthcare in a country that paid some of the highest drug prices in the world, Zuma pledged, "I will not sacrifice the public's right to health on the altar of vested interests."[55]

In May of 1999, the World Health Assembly (the policymaking body of the World Health Organization) passed a resolution that declared public health concerns "paramount" in intellectual property issues related to pharmaceuticals. When U.S. Vice President Gore visited Africa in the summer of 1999, AIDS was a constant refrain; in South Africa, the vice president was actually booed in public for his pro-patent stance. Under attack from mounting public criticism, U.S. President Clinton announced in late 1999 that the United States would no longer impose sanctions on developing countries seeking cheaper AIDS treatment. But U.S. pharmaceutical companies, which obviously bore the brunt of any policy relaxation, were far from being convinced. On the contrary, they continued to stress that the problem of AIDS in Africa had little to do with either the cost or availability of cutting-edge treatments. Africans were dying, they insisted, because of Africa's own problems.

View from the Pharmaceuticals

It was not easy, of course, for the pharmaceutical industry to respond dispassionately to the criticism that erupted in the late 1990s. People in the industry genuinely believed that they were saving lives, not harming them, and they felt that the criticism was seriously misplaced. So they tried to build a careful and compelling case, one that shifted the spotlight away from their own activities.

According to the major pharmaceutical producers, the slow spread of AIDS treatment in Africa had little to do with either the price or availability of AIDS drugs. Instead, it was due simply to endemic features of the African landscape: to the lack of clean water in many areas, to poor medical infrastructure and limited information, and to stubborn political and social issues that local authorities either could not, or would not, address. Industry executives claimed, for example, that government officials in Africa were far less committed to the AIDS struggle than their public pronouncements might suggest and that corruption remained a corroding influence across the African continent. To support this contention, industry advocates pointed to the World Bank study that found that, for every $100 that certain African governments spent on drugs, only $12 worth of medicine actually reached the patient.[56] Under such conditions, the industry argued, making drugs more widely available would not necessarily make Africans healthier; instead, drugs might simply be stolen and resold elsewhere in the world. As Dr. Josef Decosas, director of the Southern Africa AIDS Training Program, put it: "Virtually all African countries have centralized drug import and distribution centers, and most of them are broken or corrupted. Even if you make these drugs available for free, the systems to deliver them are not there."[57] In early 2001, an estimated 50% of drug stocks were reported stolen from South African public hospitals and clinics.[58]

Pharmaceutical companies also emphasized the sheer difficulty of distributing AIDS drugs across the African continent. Transportation links in the region were relatively scarce, as were basic elements of a medical infrastructure. Without clinics to support the treatments, they argued, and health-care workers to administer them, regimes like HAART simply wouldn't work. Indeed, to be successful, HAART-style therapies demanded support programs, palliative care, and preventive treatments—none of which could be easily established in most parts of Africa. Moreover, because AIDS preyed on the immune system, patients on HAART treatment were prone to opportunistic infections and needed to depend on a regime of regular tests and monitoring—a regime which, again, would be difficult to implement in the African context. Burroughs Wellcome, for example, which manufactured the AIDS-fighting compound AZT, had concluded in the late 1990s that Africa lacked the laboratory support necessary to administer its own drug safely.[59] Similarly, Britain's GlaxoSmithKline had funded a study demonstrating the difficulties of adhering to an AIDS treatment regime, with the number of pills, side effects, and food restrictions all cited as problems.[60] Although the study was not specific to Africa, other industry representatives used it and similar data to imply that poorer patients from other cultures might not be able to adhere to the demands of an AIDS regime. Even USAID director Andrew Natsios articulated this controversial sentiment when he justified his organization's decision not to fund antiretroviral treatment by observing that African AIDS patients "don't know what Western time is" and thus would be unable to take treatments effectively.[61]

Pharmaceutical executives also pointed to the difficulty of maintaining effective treatment in poverty. Taking care of AIDS, they noted, entailed more than just taking drugs. Patients also had to take care of their general health, getting proper nutrition and exercise and avoiding other diseases. Where people lived in poverty, all of these environmental conditions became considerably more difficult to sustain—to a point where even the most powerful drugs might be rendered useless. Indeed, failed treatment, as one health worker noted, "can become a vicious circle—no food, no money—so they can't take their medicine properly, so they get opportunistic diseases, so they can't work, they get depressed and that leads them further away from treatment."[62] Under these conditions, scientists feared that resistant strains of the HIV virus could easily evolve, thwarting efforts at long-term control.[63] Moreover, while AIDS under any circumstance was a treacherous, deadly disease, Africa was still plagued by other ills—river blindness, tuberculosis, measles, typhoid, malaria—that were relatively easy to treat. "In view of the competing demands of other health problems," therefore, many industry observers concluded that wide-scale HAART treatment in Africa was both unwise and possibly dangerous.[64]

Finally, although pharmaceutical companies were reluctant to engage in detailed price discussions, they were generally willing to defend their position on both patents and pricing. Essentially, the industry argued that high prices and long-term patents were a critical element of their business, regardless of where this business occurred. If they lowered prices for AIDS drugs, decreased revenues in this area would drive innovation to other, more lucrative diseases. Pharmaceutical companies would stop investing in AIDS research, and AIDS patients, over the long run, would suffer. Moreover, once the sanctity of patents was undermined in Africa or for AIDS, what would stop this loosening trend from continuing elsewhere, in European markets, for example, or for equally potent (and profitable) cancer-fighting drugs? The Western patent system, industry representatives urged, had facilitated the emergence of research-driven companies and life-saving scientific breakthroughs. If patents were undermined in Africa, then they would swiftly be undermined elsewhere in the global economy. And without patents, research across the global economy would suffer.

Ultimately, the problem of AIDS in Africa, argued the pharmaceutical industry, was a problem for governments and society. Tackling AIDS meant tackling education. It meant talking about subjects (sexual behavior, gender norms) that were still taboo in many places. And it meant spending money—public money—in places where funds were scarce. None of these tasks were the responsibility of the world's pharmaceutical firms. Instead, as a senior drug lobbyist had reasoned earlier in the decade:

> The predominant contribution that the research-based pharmaceutical industry could reasonably be expected to make is in their predominant area of competence—research and development. The broader responsibility for ensuring that such products are delivered to those they could benefit should be born by society, particularly government.[65]

Africa's AIDS activists, however, were not content to leave their burden with either government or society. Instead, pointing to success stories such as Brazil and Thailand, they insisted that large-scale drug treatment was imminently feasible in Africa. "The limiting factor for us," stated the nonprofit Doctors Without Borders, "is price."[66] Similarly, leaders from various health NGOs argued that while conditions in poor countries precluded treatment for some, most major cities in the developing world would be fully equipped to handle AIDS patients if they had access to affordable tests and drugs.[67]

In late 2000, Joep Lange, a negotiator at nonprofit International Antiviral Therapy Evaluation, articulated his frustration at industry representatives' reaction to plans that would have expanded treatment by extending business discounts for drugs distributed to employees:

> They laughed at us. The [pharmaceutical] companies are not interested. They don't want to treat a million people tomorrow. They say, "We want to do it responsibly," but there's a lot of window dressing there. They don't know what could be the repercussions: Their whole price structure could collapse. They are scared to death.[68]

Exhibit 1   International Rates of HIV / AIDS among Adults, 2000

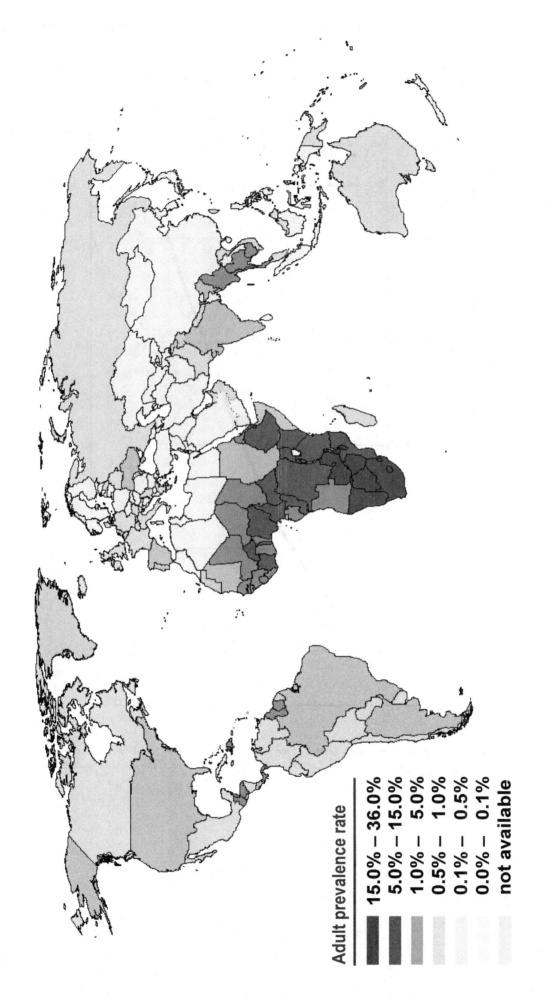

Adult prevalence rate

15.0% — 36.0%
5.0% — 15.0%
1.0% — 5.0%
0.5% — 1.0%
0.1% — 0.5%
0.0% — 0.1%
not available

Source: Adapted from UNAIDS, Report on the Global 2000 Epidemic, June 2000, p. 14.

Exhibit 2   Comparison of Annual AIDS-Related Deaths, 1982–2000

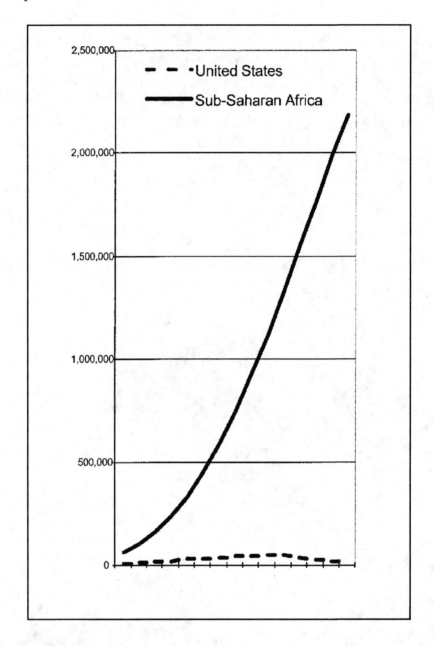

Source: "Consensus Statement on Antiretroviral Treatment for AIDS in Poor Countries," Individual Members of the Faculty at Harvard University, March 2001, p. 27, Center for International Development website, www.cid.harvard.edu, accessed October 27, 2005.

Exhibit 3   Changes in Life Expectancy in Selected African Countries, 1950–2005

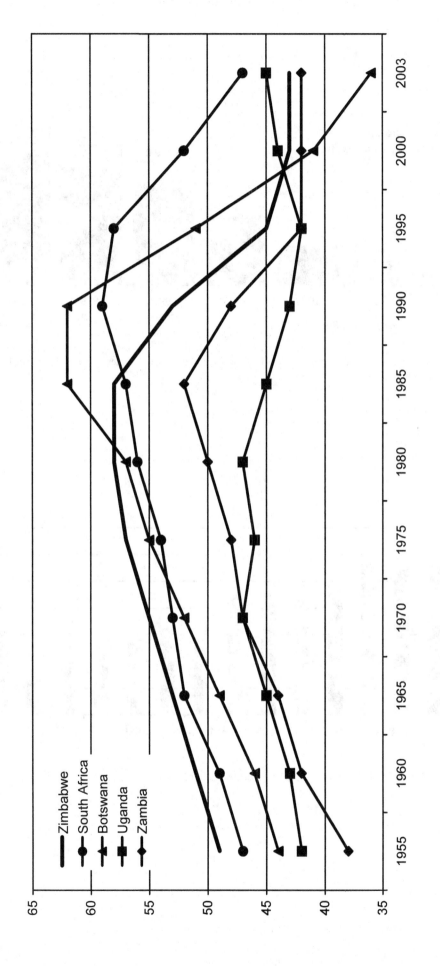

Source: Adapted from UNAIDS and WHO, *AIDS Epidemic*, December 2001, p. 9.

Exhibit 4a   R&D Expenditures for U.S. Research-Based Pharmaceutical Companies, 1980–2000[a]

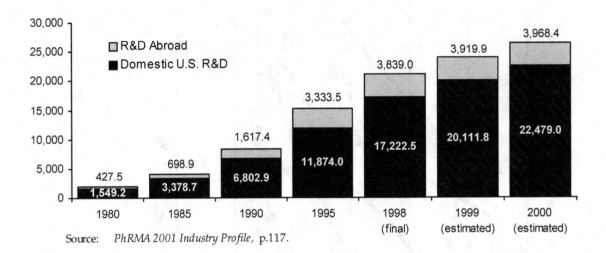

Source: *PhRMA 2001 Industry Profile*, p.117.

[a]Domestic R&D includes U.S. and foreign pharmaceutical spending in the United States.   R&D abroad includes U.S. companies' foreign expenditures.

Exhibit 4b   FDA New Drug Approval Times, 1986–2000

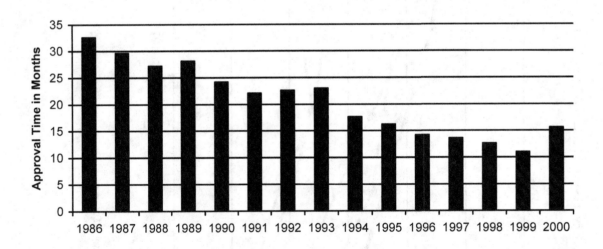

Source: Adapted from PhRMA, *2001 Industry Profile*, p. 25. (Data provided by the FDA.)

Exhibit 5 Profitability of Fortune 500 Drug Industry Compared with Fortune 500 Average, 1970–2000

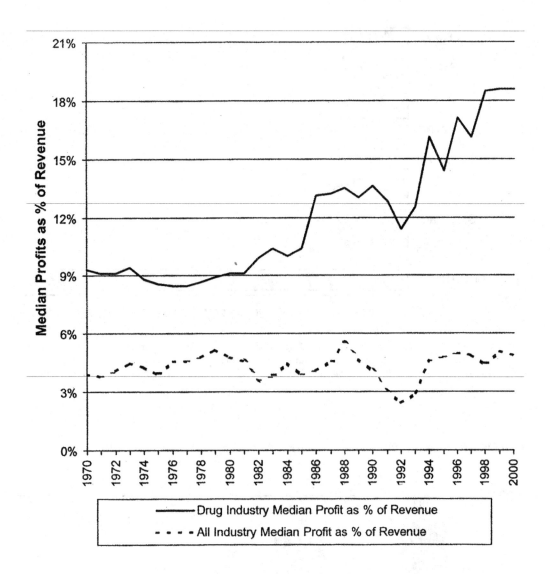

Source: "Rx R&D Myths: The Case Against the Drug Industry's R&D 'Score Card,'" Public Citizen Congress Watch, July 2001, p. 12.

Exhibit 6a   Development of 152 Global Drugs by Country of Origin, 1975–1994

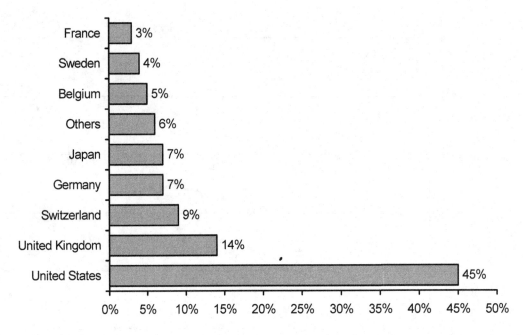

Source: Adapted from "Why Do Prescription Drugs Cost So Much…and Other Questions About Your Medicines," Pharmaceutical Research and Manufacturers of America, p. 16.   Original source: P.E. Barral, *20 Years of Pharmaceutical Research Results Throughout The World: 1975–94* (Paris: Rhone-Poulenc Rorer Foundation, 1996).

Exhibit 6b   New Drugs Placed on the Market According to Nationality of the Company, 1975-1999

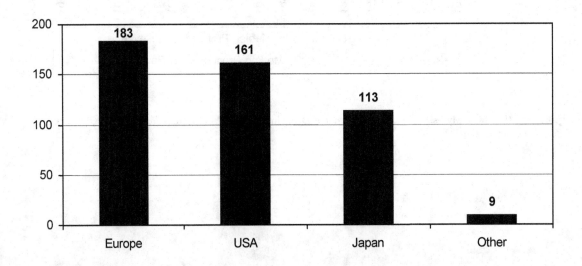

Source: Adapted from European Federation of Pharmaceutical Industries and Associations, *The Pharmaceutical Industry in Figures 2000*, p. 22.

Exhibit 7   Drug Price Comparisons

A. Prices for Selected Drugs and Their Generic Equivalents in Pakistan and India, 1997[a]

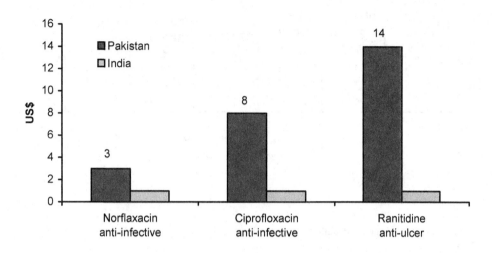

B. Prices for Selected Drugs and their Generic Equivalents in South Africa and Brazil, 2000[b]

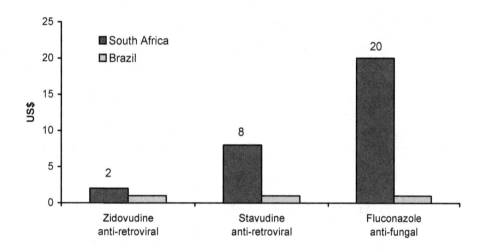

Source: Adapted from "Patent Injustice: How World Trade Rules Threaten the Health of Poor People," Oxfam Briefing Paper, 2001, pp. 26–27.

[a]Prices for patented drugs in Pakistan as a multiple of India's generic equivalents.

[b]Prices for patented drugs in South Africa as a multiple of Brazil's generic equivalents.

Exhibit 8   Drug Price Ratios between Selected Countries, 2000

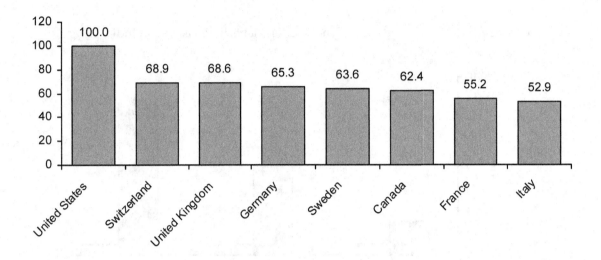

Source: Adapted from Canada's Patented Medicine Prices Review Board Annual Report 2000, p. 21.

Endnotes

[1] UNAIDS and WHO, "AIDS Epidemic Update," December 2001, p. 3.

[2] Karen Stanecki, "The AIDS Pandemic in the Twenty-First Century: The Demographic Impact in Developing Countries." Paper presented at the XIIIth International AIDS Conference, Durban, South Africa, July 9–14, 2000, p. 1.

[3] See Rachel L. Swarns, "Newest Statistics Show AIDS Still Spreading in South Africa," *The New York Times*, March 21, 2001, p. A8.

[4] United States Department of Health and Human Services Press Release, "AIDS Education," March 26, 1992.

[5] "School Bars 13-year-old Victim of AIDS," *Houston Chronicle*, August 1, 1985, p.9.

[6] From their website: http://www.actupny.org. Their slogan: "We advise and inform. We demonstrate. We are not silent."

[7] Center for Disease Control, "HIV AIDS Surveillance Report," Year-end Edition, vol. 12, no. 2, p. 9.

[8] UNAIDS and WHO, "AIDS Epidemic Update," p. 3.

[9] Stanecki, "The AIDS Pandemic in the Twenty-First Century," p. 2.

[10] UNAIDS and WHO, "AIDS Epidemic Update," p. 3.

[11] Stanecki, p.3.

[12] Ravi Nessman, "Yet Another AIDS Death as Government Argues over Statistics," Associated Press Newswire, November 9, 2001.

[13] ABT Associates, The Impending Catastrophe: A Research Book on the Emerging HIV/AIDS Epidemic in South Africa (Lovelife, 2000), pp. 7–9, 20.

[14] Ibid., p. 8.

[15] Ibid., p. 4.

[16] Steve Sternberg, "Number of AIDS Orphans to Reach 29 Million in 10 Years," *USA Today*, July 14, 2000, p. 8A. *Children on the Brink*, a report from the U.S. Agency for International Development, predicts that 29 million children 14 or younger will have lost at least one parent by 2010.

[17] From http://world.phrma.org. accessed November 15, 2001.

[18] "Deadly Meddling," *The Economist*, November 3, 2001.

[19] U.S. Constitution, Art. I, §8.

[20] These constitutional provisions were subsequently included in the Patent Act of 1790.

[21] Cited in Lawrence Lessig, *Code and Other Laws of Cyberspace* (New York: Basic Books, 1999), p. 132.

[22] *The Collected Works of Abraham Lincoln*, edited by Ray P. Basler (New Brunswick, Rutgers University Press, 1953), p. 363.

[23] This wartime funding marked the start of a continued government commitment to medical research. Between 1945 and 1965, appropriations for the NIH, measured in constant 1988 dollars, rose from $26 million to $4 billion. In 2002 dollars, this was about $14 billion. "Industry Sponsored Research at Duke," INSIDE, Duke University Medical Center, August 31, 1998 volume 7, no. 17.

[24] See Lynn S. Baker, *The Fertility Fallacy: Sexuality in the Post-Pill Age* (Philadelphia: Saunders Press, 1981).

[25] Originally spanning only 14 years from the date of issue, patent length was extended to 17 years in 1861 and then to 20 in 1994.

[26] PhRMA Annual Report, 2001–2002, p. 13.

[27] Standard and Poor's Industry Survey, "Healthcare: Pharmaceuticals," December 16, 1999, p. 26.

[28] See Robert Hunter, "Crack the Code and Profit from Genomics: Research Promises Great Medical Advances but Outlook for Stocks is Hazy," *The Wall Street Journal Europe*, January 19, 2001, p. 26.

[29] See Standard and Poor's Industry Survey, "Healthcare: Pharmaceuticals," 2001, pp. 20, 22.

[30] See John Carey and Amy Barrett, "Drug Prices: What's Fair," *BusinessWeek*, December 10, 2001, p. 64; and "Tufts Center for the Study of Drug Development Pegs Cost of New Prescription Medicine at $802 Million," Press Release, Tufts Center for the Study of Drug Development, November 30, 2001.

[31] Quoted in Donald McNeil, "Drug Companies and the Third World: Study in Neglect," *The New York Times*, May 21, 2000, p. 6.

[32] See, for example, Dana Priest, "Health Care Price Caps Considered; In Separate Move, White House Prepares New Medicare Limits," *The Washington Post*, February 14, 1993, p. A1.

[33] Between 1997 and 2001, for example, U.S. direct-to-consumer drug advertising rose from $859 million to $2.49 billion. See Thomas M. Burton, "Backlash Is Brewing among Companies Who Believe Flashy Ads Drive up Costs," *The Wall Street Journal*, March 13, 2002, p. B1. Likewise, Pfizer's marketing and administrative expenses accounted for 39% of expenses in 2000, while R&D accounted for just 17%. See Gardiner Harris, "Drug Firms, Stymied in the Lab, Become Marketing Machines," *The Wall Street Journal*, July 6, 2000, p. 1.

[34] Carey and Barrett, p. 63.

[35] See "Rx R&D Myths: The Case Against the Drug Industry's Scare Card," Public Citizen Congress Watch, July 2001.

[36] For more on price differentials, see Willis Emmons, "Note on the Pharmaceutical Industry," HBS No. 729-002 (Boston: Harvard Business School Publishing, 1998).

[37] Quoted in Carey and Barrett, p. 66.

[38] See "Fatal Side Effects: Medicine Patents Under the Microscope," Oxfam, 2000, p. 18.

[39] Reported in Carmen Perez-Casas, "HIV/AIDS Medicines Pricing Report. Setting Objectives: Is There a Political Will?" *Médecines Sans Frontiéres*, July 6, 2000, p. 10.

[40] See Lynn Sharp Paine, "Pfizer: Protecting Intellectual Property in a Global Marketplace," HBS No. 392-073.

[41] Quoted in Frances Williams, "The GATT Deal: Developing Nations Give Way on Patents—Intellectual Property," *The Financial Times*, December 16, 1993, p. 4.

[42] "Fatal Side Effects: Medicine Patents Under the Microscope," Oxfam, February 2001, p. 5.

[43] Bristol-Myers Squibb Announces Accelerated Program to Fight HIV/AIDS in Africa (company press release), March 14, 2001, p.1.

[44] Howard Hiatt, "Learn From Haiti," *The New York Times*, December 6, 2001.

[45] Markus Haacker, *Providing Health Care to HIV Patients in Southern Africa*, IMF Policy Discussion Paper, March, 2001, p. 12.

[46] See Donald G. McNeil, "Oxfam Joins Campaign to Cut Drug Prices for Poor Nations," *The New York Times*, February 13, 2001, p. A5.

[47] Siddarth Dube, quoted in Michael Spector, "India's Plague: Cheaper Drugs May Help Millions Who Have AIDS, but How Many Will They Hurt?" *The New Yorker*, December 17, 2001, p. 83.

[48] Dr. James Orbinski, International President, Doctors Without Borders, quoted in Donald G. McNeil, "Drug Makers and 3rd World: Study in Neglect," *The New York Times*, May 21, 2000, p. 6.

[49] See Merrill Goozner, "Third World Battles for AIDS Drugs: U.S. Firms Oppose Generic Licensing," *Chicago Tribune*, April 28, 1999, p. 12.

[50] On India, see Kevin Watkins, "Patent the Poor Will Lose," *The Guardian*, October 13, 2000. For Thailand, see Marwaan Macan-Markar, "Health: Thailand has Capacity to Test WTO Deal on Generic Drugs," *Inter Press Service*, November 15, 2001.

[51] There were only 540,000 total infections in 2000, half as many as the World Health Organization had predicted only six years earlier. See Tina Rosenberg, "Look at Brazil," *The New York Times Magazine*, January 28, 2001.

[52] "Drug Companies versus Brazil: The Threat to Public Health," Oxfam Great Britain, London, May 2001, p. 5.

[53] Pedro Chequer of UNAIDS, quoted in Andrew Downie, "AIDS Drugs Offered Free in Brazil," *Christian Science Monitor*, December 6, 2000, p.6.

[54] See Donald G. McNeil, "South Africa's Bitter Pill for World's Drug Makers," *The New York Times*, March 29, 1998, p. C1.

[55] Quoted in Lynn Duke, "Activist Health Minister Draws Foes in South Africa," *The Washington Post*, December 11, 1998, p. A41.

[56] Cited at http://world.phrma.org/challenges.health.infra.html, accessed March 2002.

[57] Quoted in Thomas Friedman, "It Takes a Village," *The New York Times*, April 27, 2001, p. 25.

[58] "A War over Drugs and Patents," *The Economist*, March 10, 2001, p. 44.

[59] See Barton Gellman, "An Unequal Calculus of Life and Death," *The Washington Post*, December 27, 2000.

[60] In that study, 62% of 292 questioned patients reported having "problems keeping up with their treatment." AIDS Drug Regime Considered Too Hard to Follow, *Agence France Presse*, March 15, 2001.

[61] Amir Attaran, Kenneth Freedberg and Martin Hirsch, "Dead Wrong on AIDS," *The Washington Post*, June 15, 2001.

[62] Tina Rosenberg, "Look at Brazil."

[63] See Spector, "India's Plague," p. 82.

[64] See for example, industry comments quoted in Gellman, "An Unequal Calculus of Life and Death, p. A1.

[65] Quoted in Gellman, "An Unequal Calculus of Life and Death," p. A18.

[66] Quoted in McNeil, "Drug Makers and 3rd World," *The New York Times*, May 21, 2000, p. 6. This comment referred more generally to the situation facing all drugs in Africa.

[67] Merrill Goozner, "Third World Battles for AIDS Drugs: U.S. Firms Oppose Generic Licensing," *Chicago Tribune*, April 28, 1999, p. 16.

[68] Quoted in Barton Gellman, "A Turning Point That Left Millions Behind," *The Washington Post*, December 28, 2000, p. A18.

Competition Policy in the European Union and the Power of Microsoft

In early 2001, Mario Monti had to decide what to do about Microsoft. Monti had started his professional career as a professor of monetary economics at Bocconi University in Milan. While there, he had been a columnist for the newspaper *Corriere della Sera* and had joined the Board of Directors of several leading Italian firms including Fiat. Then, as Commissioner for the Single market, Monti had become famous for rescinding the tax-free status of duty-free shops at airports and harbors despite furious protests and even street demonstrations by workers in the affected industries. He had argued that these duty-free shops merely allowed affluent travelers to avoid sales taxes and that the resulting losses in tax revenues for the member states were substantial.[1] Finally, in September 1999, nine years after helping to draft Italy's first Competition law, Monti became the European Competition Commissioner at age 56. He was now arguably "the most powerful man in Europe," or at least that was how he had described his predecessor, Karel van Miert.[2]

Monti had several options concerning Microsoft. He could seek to fine Microsoft for violations of the European Union's competition law, or to force the company to alter the way it carried out its business. If he sought fines, he could set them as high as ten percent of Microsoft's worldwide annual sales of $23 billion. Some observers saw this case as too ambitious. On the other hand, large fines and severe restrictions on this company would certainly send the message to other companies that the EU was serious about competition. Maybe it would be wiser to let the United States take the lead, to wait for a final resolution of the related suit that the US government had brought against Microsoft. Or maybe the best choice would be to work out some sort of compromise with the firm, an agreement to stop the investigation if Microsoft agreed to share certain information with its competitors.

Competition Law or Antitrust

Laws seeking to prevent competitive abuses were born in North America during the deflation of the late 19th century when associations between competitors became more common. Some of these associations were informal and involved no explicit contract, while others were effectively mergers under the legal form of "trusts." Perhaps because the documents creating these mergers were not public, all these associations were called trusts and attacked together. Some trusts were accused of raising prices while others were accused of lowering prices so much that firms had to choose between closing down and becoming trust members. Many commentators alleged that trusts whose prices

---

Research Associate Michelle Kalka prepared this case from published sources under the supervision of Professor Julio J. Rotemberg as the basis for class discussion rather than to illustrate either effective or ineffective handling of an administrative situation.

---

were low intended to raise their prices later. Other commentators fumed at the lobbying efforts carried out by large trusts to avoid being regulated.[3] In the US presidential election of 1888, both parties had platforms against trusts, and in 1890, despite the opposition of economists who tended to see big business as efficient, the Sherman Act became law. Both the government and private parties filed suits under this Act, which remained the foundation of US antitrust law, and the resulting judgments by the Supreme Court clarified the implications of the Act's fairly broad sentences (**see exhibit 1**.) Still, even in 2001, it was often difficult to predict the outcome of antitrust suits in the US.

In justifying their decisions, Supreme Court justices attributed a variety of goals to the Sherman Act. These included the protection of consumers, the prevention of excessive political influence by large firms, and the economic survival of "small dealers and worthy men whose lives had been spent in [business]."[4] While some antitrust authorities argued that antitrust laws ought to aim only at increasing consumer welfare and economic efficiency, many past Court decisions were difficult to explain in this light. It proved particularly hard, for instance, to use economic reasoning to justify the court-mandated prohibition of all agreements between producers and retailers (or wholesalers) about the price at which retailers could resell goods that they purchased from producers.[5] [6]

Mergers

Mergers were circumscribed after the passage of the Sherman Act, an unsurprising development given the Act's prohibition of "combinations." By 2001, the Department of Justice and the Federal Trade Commission were determining which of these two agencies would review any particular merger. Both agencies used the same blueprint, or "guidelines," to determine whether mergers were acceptable. The reasoning underlying these guidelines was to forbid mergers that gave too much market power to individual firms within a "relevant market."

Whether a firm was judged to have market power depended, in part, on its market share in the relevant market. A firm's market share, however, tended to fall as one expanded the range of products included in its market. For example, Sun Microsystems' 1998 market share in high-end servers, its specialty, was larger than its share in the overall market for servers. The US merger guidelines sought to address this issue by including in the relevant market all close substitutes in either consumption or production. They determined that a set of products constituted a relevant market if a "hypothetical monopolist" who sold all these products could profitably raise its prices by 5-10% over prices prevailing under more competitive conditions. Because this method was based on studying counterfactual outcomes, it often involved the statistical analysis of market and survey data.

Other Contracts or Informal Arrangements among Competitors

The Sherman Act reflected the suspicion that informal agreements among firms led to similar outcomes as those caused by mergers. Thus, shortly after the passage of this law, the Supreme Court declared that Section 1 rendered automatically illegal any agreement among competing firms to fix prices or to share the market. This stood in marked contrast with past European practice. Explicit cartel contracts stipulating the behavior of competitors were enforced by the German courts before World War II, for example. The Netherlands was long known as a "cartel paradise," because, until a 1997 EU Directive, all Dutch cartels were assumed legal unless expressly forbidden.[7] One justification given for these agreements was that they prevented bankruptcies in recessions and preserved small and medium sized businesses. In principle, British competition law was more similar to its American counterpart, but enforcement was lax. Italy simply had no law concerning competition until 1990.

In the period from the end of World War II to about 1990, European cartels were most stringently limited in Germany. Under allied occupation, Germany passed a decartelization law in 1947 and then replaced it with a competition law in 1958. [8] This law outlawed many conceivable agreements among firms, though it gave legal protection to certain types of cartels if they received explicit clearance by the Federal Cartel Office (FCO.) These laws were vigorously enforced. For example, in 1991 the FCO uncovered an illegal price-fixing cartel among 12 leading German wholesalers of pharmaceutical products and fined them a total of $23.7 million.

Nevertheless, many Germans in 2001 still looked to cartels to protect mainstays of German culture from the feared blandness thought to accompany the unregulated market. In 1999, for instance, Germany's powerful alliance of 5000 booksellers mobilized to fight the end of a 100-year tradition of price-fixing agreements between publishers and booksellers. Politicians in Bavaria united across party lines in the battle against Brussels' effort to break the price-fixing cartel, warning that it would lead to the end of Germany's thriving small independent book stores. "It's unacceptable for books to be treated the same as soap," insisted Friederike Harmgarth, head of public relations and cultural affairs for the German publisher, Bertelsmann. [9]

Other proscribed business practices in the United States

Even though it is true that two of the three largest US companies at the beginning of the 20th century were broken up by government regulators, a large market share was not in and of itself illegal. Section 2 of the Sherman Act condemned "monopolization," not monopoly itself. Monopolies were tolerated both when protected by patents and when, in Judge Learned Hand's words, they resulted from "superior skill, foresight, and industry."[10] What the courts found unacceptable were business practices that they were unable to explain as rational except insofar as they weakened competitors.

The courts often proscribed arrangements where firms "tied" sales by requiring purchasers of one product to purchase a second as well. The US case law on tying evolved over time. In its early decisions on tying, the Supreme Court treated all tying contracts as illegal, irrespective of market power. In 1947, it denied a firm called *International Salt* the right to require that its purchasers of industrial salt dispensers also buy its salt. The Court expressed no interest in the market power of this company in either the salt market or the market for salt dispensing equipment, even though the company faced considerable competition in both. In 1958, Justice Black reaffirmed this presumption against tying by reasserting that "tying agreements serve hardly any purpose beyond the suppression of competition."[11] More recently, US courts have outlawed tying only when presented with evidence that it was used to extend monopoly power from the tying product to another product. Firms have thus been exonerated unless it was proved that they had monopoly power in the tying product.

Other business practices associated with the acquisition of market power could also be illegal in the United States. One such practice consisted of charging different prices to different customers if these customers were themselves businesses. This practice was allowed, however, when the price differences could be ascribed to either cost differences or to "competitive conditions."

Competition Policy in the European Union

The first Europe-wide rules governing competition were those incorporated in the 1951 Treaty of Paris, among Belgium, France, Germany, Italy, the Netherlands, and Luxembourg, which created the European Coal and Steel Community (ECSC). Article 65 of this treaty prohibited agreements between firms that distorted "normal competition" in these two critical industries, while Article 66 controlled mergers and outlawed the abuse of economic power. These provisions appeared to have had little practical impact, however. In particular, the governing body of the ECSC rarely considered competitive conditions in these industries to be "normal," so it frequently interfered by setting minimum and maximum prices and assigning output quotas to individual firms.[12]

A much more significant step towards economic integration among these states took place when the Treaty of Rome went into effect on January 1, 1958. This treaty created the European Commission and significantly reduced trade barriers among the member states. Articles 85 and 86 of this new treaty dealt with competition and resembled somewhat Articles 65 and 66 of the 1951 treaty. As a result of later EU policy, individual European states later passed competition laws that, while not wholly identical to Articles 85 and 86, were similar in spirit.[13]

Article 86 constrained the actions of firms with a "dominant" position while Section 1 of Article 85 limited the legality of cartels (**see exhibit 2.**) At the same time, Section 3 of Article 85 contained a broadly worded exception for inter-firm agreements that increased economic efficiency. Firms that wished to take advantage of this provision had to obtain permission to do so from the European Commission. The Commission also had to approve mergers of firms that engaged in trade among member states. Mergers which "create or strengthen a dominant position as a result of which effective competition would be significantly impeded" could be blocked by the Commission. The national European authorities only dealt with mergers that involved firms whose geographic scope was relatively narrow.

These Articles were often rationalized on the grounds that they were necessary for achieving European integration. As the Commission put it, "Competition is an important tool for achieving the goal of, and maintaining, an internal market, in particular via the enforcement of rules ensuring that the regulatory barriers to trade that have been removed are not replaced by private ... restrictions having the same effect." More recently, the Commission also emphasized that competition was desirable because it "enhances consumer welfare and creates an efficient allocation of resources."[14]

Procedure

After the ratification of the Treaty of Rome, the European Commission became responsible both for proposing new legislation and for enforcing European law. By 2001, there were 20 Commissioners appointed by member governments at the top of this Commission. The Commission also included administrative bodies called Directorate Generals, which were presided over by individual Commissioners. The Commissioner for Competition was effectively the head of Directorate General Competition (DG COMP), which dealt with mergers and violations of Articles 85 and 86. DG COMP was also charged with ensuring that "state aid," a name given to subsidies and tax breaks provided by national governments, did not distort competition excessively.

DG COMP could begin investigating violations of Articles 85 and 86 either as a result of its own exploration of industry conduct, or in response to complaints made by consumers or competitors. In either case, DG COMP had broad powers of investigation. It could request information from any firm concerning all aspects of the market and its conduct and activities. There were penalties for false, delayed, or incomplete returns. If DG COMP became concerned that information would be hidden or destroyed, the Competition Commissioner could authorize a surprise raid, which would be carried out with the help of the local police.[15]

The formal phase of the proceedings against a company started when DG COMP issued a Statement of Objections. The firm was then asked to submit a written response. An oral hearing could also be scheduled if the firm desired it, though statements at these hearings were not made under oath. In 1982, to counter criticism against the Commission for unfairness and lack of due process, a Hearing Officer was appointed to supervise these hearings.[16] After the firm's reply was examined, DG COMP could reach an informal settlement with the firm. Alternatively, if the DG wrote a draft decision, it presented the draft to the Advisory Committee on Restrictive Practices and Monopolies. This Committee was composed of expert representatives from each Member State. It gave advice but its decisions were not binding on DG COMP or the Commission. After further consultations, the Commission could issue formal decisions, which had to be approved by a majority of the 20 Commissioners. Such decisions included the reasoning of the Commission as well as its proposed remedy. Formal decisions could be appealed first to the Court of First Instance and then to the European Court of Justice.[17] In practice, these Courts seldom questioned the Commission's economic analysis, including its definition of the relevant market.

Unlike American trustbusters, the European Commission could not bring criminal charges and threaten offenders with jail, but it could forbid individual practices and could fine companies up to 10% of their yearly worldwide sales. Although actual antitrust fines have all been smaller than this legal maximum, they have been substantial. In 1998, then-Competition Commissioner Van Miert imposed a new record of fines totaling $480 million on companies involved in five cartel cases (Alloy Surcharge, Pre-Insulated Pipes, British Sugar, Greek Ferries, and Taca.) In September 1999, Monti fined a group of shipping companies controlling freight across the Atlantic $314 million. The Commission was also pursuing fines on Roche and other companies for raising vitamin prices in a worldwide conspiracy first uncovered in the United States.

The Commissioner

Immediately upon taking office, Mario Monti began seeking to reform DG COMP. He declared, "We have to rethink and modernize the architecture of our competition weaponry."[18] He vowed to pursue cartels more aggressively and asserted, "Cartels are cancers on the open market economy, which forms the very basis of our community... In the words of Adam Smith, there is a tendency for competitors to conspire. I am determined to strengthen our fight against cartels."[19] Monti intended to increase his staff of about 500 and strengthen the Commission's powers of investigation so that it would be allowed to search private homes. He also sought to increase the fines against companies that were slow to respond to requests for information.[20]

Monti wished to strengthen the principle of subsidiarity – which required that decisions be taken at the lowest practical level - by having national courts and national competition authorities enforce Articles 85 and 86 even for firms that traded among Member States. DG COMP and the national competition authorities would cooperate in determining which agency ought to clear a particular merger or pursue a particular violation. DG COMP would play a leading role, however, and would take over precedent-setting cases or cases where it disagreed with the national authorities. This reform could increase the penalties for violators because the formation of cartels was a criminal violation subject to jail sentences in several countries. By letting national authorities approve practices under Section 3 of Article 85, these reforms could also reduce the Commission's backlog, which involved 1,200 unprocessed cases as of January 2000. Many worried, though, that this shift of power would lead to inconsistent decisions. A member of the European Parliament agonized that the "Commission [would] be flying blind by giving [policy] back to the national authorities."[21]

DG COMP's merger directorate became more active under Monti. While its official guidelines continued to forbid mergers that created or strengthened dominant positions, its investigations rose from 12 in 1990 and 110 in 1995, to 292 in 1999. In 2000, it had already scrutinized 231 deals by the end of August. By early 2001, only 13 deals had been blocked since 1990, but three of those had been under Super Mario, as he was referred to in the press (**see exhibit 3**.) One well-publicized deal he squashed, together with the US Department of Justice, was WorlCom's bid for Sprint.[22]

Many members of the business and investment community were openly critical of Monti's reign. One advisor to a deal that did not survive DG COMP scrutiny said, "The European Commission is acting like a blunderbuss in forcing through legislation without any apparent regard to the commercial basis of the businesses they are examining."[23] Some managers questioned the accountability of the European system, its transparency and its consistency from one commissioner to the next, and the increasing uncertainty big regulators brought to commercial decisions. A senior partner at a London anti-trust firm said, "Basically Brussels has got you... When you are trying to get a deal through you can try and push them, you can try and call their bluff, but there is no bluff. They hold all the cards. They will hold your feet to the fire in getting what they want... The point is there is no effective form of appeal in Europe once a deal is blocked. You can go to the European Court of Justice but that will take you three years, it's very expensive and it seems the judges won't overturn a Commission decision."[24] Moreover, according to managers, it was rare for the EU to provide informal guidance before a deal was announced. There was also some criticism from within the Commission. In September 2000, the head of the Competition directorate, John Temple Lang, resigned on the grounds that Monti was unwilling to give firms targeted for anti-trust violations a stronger voice during investigations.[25]

Monti recognized the political character of his post. According to Van Miert, "In the Commission, you need a good assessment of the facts and the legal situation behind your decision—that's 90 per cent of the work, but you also have to take account of politics too."[26] An aide to Monti said, "Competition gives you big power, but he is still convinced he has to explain it in a proper way. He would hate to be accused of not being even-handed."[27] With regard to public opinion, Monti believed that consumers did not give the European Union enough credit for making their lives easier, and sought to help them make this connection. "Even the things they do see, like dramatic decreases in prices for telecoms and air fares, they hardly relate to EU-generated liberalization."[28]

Microsoft

Microsoft was a US-based producer of operating systems and applications software, mainly for Intel-compatible personal computers and Intel-based servers. Operating systems were designed to issue commands to a computer's hardware, while applications generally affected the hardware only by first issuing instructions to the operating system. A key element of an operating system's design was thus the set of instructions, often known as "applications program interfaces" (APIs), that allowed applications to communicate with the operating system. Some applications also contained APIs, and these allowed other applications to communicate with them.

In fiscal 2000, Microsoft's revenue totaled $22.9 billion, its net income was $9.4 billion, and its R&D budget equaled $3.8 billion. Desktop applications were responsible for 40% of company revenue, or $9.3 billion.[29] Microsoft Office, which combined a number of programs including Word, Excel and PowerPoint, accounted for 83% of desktop applications revenue in calendar 2000. New users were responsible for 37% of this figure, while upgrades bought by existing users accounted for 63%. Second to applications, desktop operating systems were responsible for 31% of Microsoft revenue, or $7.0 billion, about 80% of which came from sales to PC Original Equipment Manufacturers (OEMs.)[30] Since 1990, Microsoft had a greater than 90% worldwide market share in the market for operating systems designed for Intel-compatible PCs.

While critics complained that Microsoft developed few truly original technologies itself, there was no doubt that it continually sought to add new features to its products. Microsoft regularly introduced new versions of its existing programs and heavily advertised their new features. Microsoft's applications and operating systems were developed, and succeeded, in tandem. Thus, Microsoft's word processing program, Word, was unable to compete successfully against the market leaders WordStar and WordPerfect until Microsoft succeeded in getting users to adopt the Windows user interface for its operating system. When Windows finally succeeded, with version 3.0 released in 1990, Word for Windows rapidly eclipsed the popular program WordPerfect, which took much longer to develop a version that took advantage of the Windows user interface.[31] By the year 2001, WordPerfect was so weakened that Microsoft acquired 24.6% of the stock of its parent company for $135 million. The development of Word for Windows may have been facilitated by the collaboration between Microsoft's operating systems and applications groups. In March 1995, Microsoft CEO Bill Gates declared that "there is no Chinese wall" separating them, and continued, "We don't block input going in either direction."[32]

Because Microsoft knew that selling operating systems with new features required that developers incorporate these features into applications, Microsoft spent considerable resources educating outside developers about Microsoft APIs. Nonetheless, some outside developers felt that they were at a disadvantage relative to developers that worked for Microsoft. They claimed that Microsoft developers had access to "undocumented calls," that is, to methods for accessing operating system functions that were not revealed to outsiders.[33] In addition, some non-Microsoft software developers complained that when Microsoft introduced upgrades, it made a considerably larger effort to create and maintain interoperability with its own applications than it did to maintain interoperability with the software of others. Avie Tevanian of Apple, in particular, complained that Microsoft provided poor support for Apple's QuickTime after Microsoft embedded DirectX, its competing set of routines for handling multimedia files, into Internet Explorer 4.0. Microsoft, on the other hand, responded that it tried to help Apple and that QuickTime's difficulties when running with Internet Explorer 4.0 stemmed from Apple's unwillingness to follow Microsoft's advice.[34] [35]

Microsoft started selling operating systems for servers in 1993, when it introduced Windows NT. Servers played two roles that distinguished them from desktop personal computers. First, many organizations connected the desktop computers of their employees in networks run by servers because such an arrangement gave the organization's members access to additional resources. These resources could include remote computing, storage of shared or individual files, email, and printing facilities. Second, servers were also used to deliver information over either the Internet or organizational Intranets. Because traffic at certain Internet sites was extremely heavy, many web sites used several servers that were themselves linked to one another.

Microsoft's operating systems for servers incorporated a number of features that had previously only been available on separate products. For example, the Windows 2000 Server included a "Web Server" whose functions were similar to those of the popular open-source Apache program that many enterprises used to host web pages. Windows 2000 also included an evolving set of features called "Active Directory." These features facilitated the control of networks by allowing system managers to see all the resources in a network and easily modify their properties, including the access that different individuals had to these resources. At the same time, desktops running Windows could use their own version of Active Directory to locate the resources to which they had access.

The European Objections against Microsoft

The EU's Statement of Objections delivered to Microsoft on August 3, 2000 focused on the server market. Its accompanying press release read

> Microsoft has a market share of about 95% in the market for personal computer (PC) operating systems (OS) and thus enjoys practically undisputed market dominance. Most

PCs today are embedded into networks, which are controlled by servers. Interoperability, i.e. the ability of the PC to talk to the server, is the basis for network computing. Interoperability can only function if the operating systems running on the PC and on the server can talk to each other through links or so-called interfaces. To enable competitors of Microsoft to develop server operating systems which can talk to the dominant Windows software for PCs, interface information—technical information and even limited parts of the software source code of the Windows PC OS—must be known. Without interoperating software and as a result of the overwhelming Microsoft dominance in the computer software market, computers running on Windows operating systems would be *de facto* obliged to use Windows server software if they wanted to achieve full interoperability...

Sun Microsystems alleged, in a complaint in December 1998 and in subsequent submissions, that the near monopolistic position of Microsoft in the PC operating system market creates an obligation on Microsoft to disclose its interfaces to enable interoperability with non-Microsoft server software. This obligation would cover the OSs distributed by Microsoft at the time when Sun's request for disclosure of interface information was refused in October 1998, i.e. Windows 95, 98, NT4.0 and all subsequent updates. Sun alleges that the launch of Windows 2000 on 17 February 2000, was a final step in Microsoft's strategy to strengthen the effects of its refusal to supply interface information with the intention of driving all serious competitors out of the server software market. Sun claims that Microsoft has applied a policy of discriminatory licensing by distinguishing between its competitors according to a so-called "friend-enemy" scheme...

The Commission was given evidence that Microsoft did not carry out its obligation to disclose sufficient interface information about its PC operating system. The Commission believes that Microsoft gave information only on a partial and discriminatory basis to some of its competitors. It refused to supply interface information to competitors like Sun Microsystems.[36]

Microsoft executives agreed that several features of the Windows 2000 desktop operating system would only work when this desktop (or client) was connected to a Windows 2000 server. In November 1999, PC Week interviewed Microsoft President Steve Ballmer about Windows 2000 and asked, "But most of the value added you'll get from the client is tied to the features in the server, like Active Directory or Intellimirror[1], isn't it?" He responded, "I'd say 60 percent [of enhancements] you'd probably get without the server -- [features like] reliability and infrared..."[37]

The disclosures of information by Microsoft that led to this complaint were confidential at the beginning of 2001. However, Cisco Systems had a widely publicized partnership with Microsoft to extend the use of Active Directory. Separately, Sun's director of enterprise architecture Dave Douglas claimed in a 1999 interview that Cisco had access to the Windows 2000 source code.[38]

For Microsoft to be found guilty of violating Article 86, the Commission would have to find that it was a dominant firm. While firms were often found to be dominant when their market share in the relevant market was in the 40-50% range, the Commission was actually interested in evidence of market power.[39] Microsoft might thus have used the argument it employed in the related but different US antitrust case to deny that it had monopoly power. During that case, the Dean of the

---

[1] Intellimirror updates the files residing in clients and servers whenever they reconnect with one another.

Sloan School of Management, Richard Schmalensee, who was employed by Microsoft as an expert witness, affirmed under oath: "Microsoft does not have monopoly power in the PC operating system market alleged by Plaintiffs--or in any relevant antitrust market in which Windows is licensed."[40] His logic was that Microsoft needed to worry constantly about the possibility that other firms would introduce innovative substitutes and thereby drastically reduce the demand for the products sold by Microsoft. By contrast, expert witnesses employed by the US Department of Justice argued that Microsoft's market power in PC operating systems was substantial and that, in particular, the firm would not lose appreciable revenues if it raised the price of these operating systems by 5%.

By February 2001, Microsoft had responded to the Commission's complaint. A hearing would probably follow and Mario Monti would have to make a decision. A decision in favor of Sun might be similar to the 1984 settlement with International Business Machines (IBM.) In that settlement, IBM ended a four-year legal dispute with the Commission by agreeing to license compatibility information regarding its mainframe computers to all who requested it, for a flat and modest fee (see below for additional details.)

Jean-Philippe Courtois, president of Microsoft Europe in Paris, maintained that "this proceeding has nothing to do with the consumer, but with a complaint from a competitor".[41] Microsoft lawyer John Frank stated, "Sun's complaint is based on their desire to gain access to our technical trade secrets. We don't believe that the law requires Microsoft, or any other company, to share its secrets with direct competitors. Every company should be able to choose the partners with which it collaborates."[42] Microsoft attorney Brad Smith added that forced licensing "would dramatically reduce the incentive to innovate and [would] reduce competition over the medium to long term." [43] Microsoft further maintained that software and hardware developers already had access to all the information they needed to build compatible products. It claimed that companies that found the APIs published by Microsoft insufficient could manipulate Microsoft programs to extract further information using the procedure sanctioned by the 1991 European Software Directive (see below.) Many observers, however, doubted that this procedure would provide good and timely information about the roughly 30 million lines of source code in Windows 2000.

At stake in this investigation was one of the most robust growth markets for computer technology. IT sector analyst International Data Corporation estimated that worldwide sales of server software approached $6 billion in 2000, and were set to grow by up to 15 percent a year over the next five years. In 2000, sales of Microsoft's Windows NT equaled 38 percent of that total. Variants of Unix, a 31-year old multi-user operating system offered by many manufacturers including Sun, had sales which accounted, in total, for 53 percent of total revenue.[44] Sun also championed Java, a programming language it developed which allowed programs to be downloaded from servers and run on a wide variety of hardware/operating system combinations. Sun had been eager to obtain the Windows 2000 source code to update Java.

Emphasizing the importance of this case, Monti commented, "The Commission welcomes all genuine innovation and advances in computer technology, wherever they come from, as highly positive developments for consumers and industry alike. Effective protection of copyrights and patents is most important for technological progress. However, we will not tolerate the extension of existing dominance into adjacent markets through the leveraging of market power by anti-competitive means and under the pretext of copyright protection. All companies that want to do business in the European Union must play by its antitrust rules and I'm determined to act for their rigorous enforcement."[45]

Information Sharing and Standards in Europe

The 1984 IBM Precedent on Information Sharing

In the mid-1970s, IBM's competitors in Europe complained that the company was inhibiting their operation by refusing to provide early information about how to link non-IBM equipment to IBM's System 370, its most popular computer model. IBM made this information public only when its products were shipped, even though the products started to be sold much earlier. Competitors complained that they had to wait until IBM products actually reached Europe to reverse-engineer them for the purpose of building printers, disk drives, and other computers that would be compatible with IBM designs.[46]

These competitors sought to tame IBM by using two approaches. The first was an ultimately unsuccessful attempt at securing an international agreement on common technical standards governing interfaces between electronic information systems. The second, and more successful tactic, was to complain to the Commission. In 1973, prompted by these complaints and by the antitrust action launched by the US Justice Department five years earlier, the Commission began an investigation. In 1980, it filed suit against IBM for abusing its dominant position.

The Carter Administration (1977-81) had encouraged the Commission to pursue the case. However, when the Reagan Administration dropped the US case in January 1982, it urged the Commission to follow suit. Nonetheless, in an April 1982 news conference, Competition Commissioner Frans Andriessen reacted by proclaiming that the Commission was "proceeding as dynamically as before."[47] He disclosed that he had discussed the case in October in Washington with William Baxter, the Assistant Attorney General in charge of the Justice Department's antitrust division, and that, subsequent to that discussion, the European Community had received a "diplomatic note" from the Commerce Department outlining the Reagan Administration's view that a decision against IBM might hamper the operations of American computer companies in Europe.[48] Douglas E. Rosenthal, a partner at the Washington law firm of Sutherland, Asbill & Brennan, said, "I think this is as important an antitrust investigation as the Common Market has had in its history. The Community for years has been critical of US antitrust enforcement, which they saw as highly political. This is the first case that raises the same concerns in reverse."[49]

IBM poured tremendous resources into this European case, matched only by its efforts in fighting the antitrust suit in the US.[50] It lobbied intensively in European capitals to get the case dropped. IBM's central objection was that the Commission was seeking to force it to give proprietary design information to its competitors, enabling its rivals to copy its products as soon as they were announced. IBM claimed that this mandatory disclosure constituted unwarranted interference in its commercial freedom and would deprive the company of its just commercial rewards from its investment in research and development.[51] With the Reagan Administration as a vocal ally, IBM asserted that such a disclosure policy would enable Japanese manufacturers such as Fujitsu and Hitachi to obtain technical information in Europe and use it against IBM all over the world.[52]

Neither the Commission nor IBM wanted the situation to end in a formal decision by the Commission. For IBM's part, aside from the inevitable large fine the company would face, a Commission decision would have marked the first time an independent administrative body had ever found the company guilty of a breach of antitrust law. IBM also knew that a court case would damage its efforts to present itself as a "European" company. If classified as European, it would be eligible to join Esprit, the $1.5 billion EEC-backed research and development program intended to help Europe's electronics industry compete with the US and Japan. As part of Esprit, IBM would receive a share of government orders and research aid.[53] A Commission decision against IBM could also open the way to private legal actions and damages claims by its competitors.[54]

On the other side, the Commission worried that IBM would appeal its judgement to the European Court of Justice (ECJ) and that the Court was likely to take several years to decide. During this waiting period, the Court would almost certainly suspend any constraints the Commission had imposed on the company. Moreover, the Commission was not confident it would prevail in the ECJ. Stated one independent Brussels lawyer, "It has gone far beyond being a normal anti-trust proceeding—it has become a political battle. The debate is no longer over legal rights or wrongs, but over whether the Commission has the stomach for a major confrontation with IBM or will simply put its tail between its legs and retreat."[55] While the Commission was composing a judgement, it was simultaneously continuing to pursue negotiations with IBM.

In early August 1984, with both sides eager to bring this matter to a close, Competition Commissioner Andriessen and IBM's senior vice president and general counsel Nicholas Katzenbach negotiated a settlement. The agreement applied only to IBM's 370 model range, its peripherals and the models that were set to replace the 370 when it was discontinued. The Commission believed that sales of these products accounted for some 80% of IBM's revenues in the EC.[56]

The agreement required that, within four months of announcing a new product in Europe, IBM disclose technical interface information so that rival companies could have adequate time to produce hardware and software products compatible with IBM machines. IBM was also required to provide competitors with "adequate and timely" technical information on IBM's Systems Network Architecture, a set of rules and procedures that IBM computers used to communicate, making it easier for disparate computer systems to "talk" with IBM machines. Rival manufacturers would be charged a "reasonable" sum for all this information. IBM maintained the right to conceal any information about the basic workings of its computers that could be valuable to rival manufacturers of mainframe computers.

Industry and legal experts contended that it was far from clear that IBM lost this battle. For one, IBM never admitted to violating Community law. In addition, IBM had already accelerated the process of giving out technical information on how its computers communicated and on its interfaces to select groups. Some experts even asserted that the concessions were in IBM's interest, and would bring the giant company's products into even more widespread use. David Moschella, an industry analyst at the International Data Corporation, said that the agreement would "help promote IBM as an industry standard."[57]

The 1991 Decompilation Directive

The debate surrounding interfaces and standards erupted again around 1989, this time in the context of software. This new debate concerned the degree to which it was permissible to analyze a program to create a new program that was interoperable with the first. Opponents of such analyses, including IBM, Apple and the Digital Equipment Corporation, argued that software interfaces were protected by copyright. Moreover, they claimed that the actual analysis that was needed to obtain these interfaces constituted an additional infringement.

On the other side of the debate was the European Committee for Interoperable Systems (Ecis), which was backed by companies such as Bull, Olivetti, and a European subsidiary of Fujitsu. It argued that an interface was an *idea*, and copyright protection for such ideas would reduce competition. In copyright law, only *expressions of ideas* receive protection. The usual justification for not protecting ideas was that such protection would slow progress too much. Probably for the same reason, the expression of an idea was not protected if it was so inescapably linked to an idea that the idea could not be expressed in any other way. [58]

Ecis supported decompilation as a legitimate way of understanding interfaces. Decompilation involved copying a program's code, translating it by computer into human-readable assembly code, and analyzing it to build a picture of the program's source code. According to Ecis, unless companies were allowed to perform this type of reverse engineering, the company that built the interface would have too much control.

IBM argued instead that once someone began decompiling, there was nothing to prevent the decompiler from unscrambling the entire program. Code in hand, the decompiler could easily claim to have found a "bug which needs repairing," make a few changes, and sell the amended program as a new product. While similar practices were already widespread, IBM did not want decompiling to have the extra sanction of Community law.[59]

In its 1991 Directive, the Commission crafted a compromise. Computer programs were classified as literary works, and were granted copyright protection provided they passed a test of originality, that is, provided they were not copied. The copyright holder was given a series of exclusive rights, the most important of which was the right to reproduce, adapt, and distribute to the public the work which the program constituted.[60] Under Community Law, then, the piracy of computer programs was equated with the illicit copying of books, sheet music, or films. On the other hand, there were two narrow exceptions permitting some reverse engineering. The first allowed anyone to observe, study, and test a program, but only where this occurred in the normal course of running it. This provided only a very limited understanding of how a program worked. The second exception allowed decompilation, but only for the purpose of writing an interoperable program. The understanding of programs through decompilation could only be used to build an interface to that program, but for no other purpose.[61]

In the US, there were a handful of court decisions regarding decompilation before 2001. While these decisions were somewhat inconsistent, they did tend to allow decompilation for the purpose of obtaining interface information. In two notable cases, *Sega Enterprises, Ltd. v. Accolade, Inc.* and *Atari Games Corp. v. Nintendo of America, Inc.*, the courts essentially ruled that decompilation was permissible when it was a necessary step in the development of a compatible computer program.[62]

European Standards in Mobile Telephones

While European firms were pushing the Commission to force IBM to release interface information, they also were hoping that the Commission would spearhead a drive to secure common technical standards for electronic information systems. This hope was fueled in part by Europe's telecommunications monopolies, which had long acted as powerful enforcers of national standards.

In the late 1980s, the European Community recognized that a new common digital cellular telephone network could improve on the incompatible national analog cellular networks. Thus, Tjakko Schuringa, director of communications at the high-technology division of the European Commission, set up an ad hoc working group which would include European manufacturers and representatives from the PTT (Postal, Telephone, and Telegraph) agencies.[63] This independent organization was named the Groupe Speciale pour les Services Mobiles, or GSM. The state-owned PTTs of 16 European countries—Norway, Sweden, Finland, Denmark, Ireland, Belgium, the Netherlands, West Germany,

France, Switzerland, Austria, Portugal, Spain, Italy, Greece, and Turkey— as well as the two private PTT's from the UK, collaborated in the GSM.

On September 7, 1987, 13 of the 18 carriers signed a Memorandum of Understanding and announced plans to implement a pre-operational digital cellular network, while the remaining five were "active observers." The object of the 13 carriers was to select, in cooperation with equipment vendors, the technologies necessary for supporting the future pan-European digital cellular radio network. On February 29, 1988, the GSM sent out about 3,000 pages of common technical specifications to a total of 92 equipment suppliers. These suppliers were compiled from a list of vendors chosen by each carrier. Soon afterward, each of the 13 carriers sent out requests to their preferred suppliers for quotes on pre-operational networks to fit these specifications. The first order for the fully operational digital mobile telephone infrastructure was made on July 5, 1988.[64]

The US experience was quite different. In late 1987, the FCC charged the Cellular Telecommunications Industry Association (CTIA), a Washington, DC based organization representing 93% of the American cellular industry, with the task of evaluating the trials of the new digital technology. The trials were to be conducted by AT&T, Ericsson, International Mobile Machines, Motorola, and Northern Telecom. The CTIA would report its findings to the Telecommunications Industry Association (TIA), which would choose the new digital standard.[65]

The CTIA essentially had to chose between two technologies, TDMA and CDMA. CDMA was a newer and potentially better technology, but was not yet ready for commercial deployment. Before CDMA began attracting industry attention, the CTIA endorsed TDMA in late 1990 and received accolades from the FCC for developing a self-imposed standard, rather than relying on outside forces. However, delays in getting TDMA phones to market gave companies such as Qualcomm the time to refine CDMA technology and in the summer of 1993, the TIA published an interim standard for CDMA. Thus, the industry ended up with two standards.

TDMA and CDMA were incompatible. However, as "dual-mode" standards, both could access analog cellular when digital service was unavailable. Therefore, industry observers worried that the schism over standards could force carriers to continue to provide inferior analog service simply for interoperability reasons. Jim Mullins, director of networking for cellular products at Hughes Network Systems, said of the US, "We who have half the world's cellular users look like we don't know what we're doing." Ashok Trivedi, however, director of cellular planning business development at Northern Telecom, Inc., remarked, "With digital, North America has said, 'Let the best technology win,' rather than be bound by the first."[66]

Different companies offering cellular service to customers adopted different standards. PacTel Cellular, Bell Atlantic, and US West committed themselves to CDMA, while Cellular One adopted TDMA. Ameritech declared TDMA to be inferior to analog and announced its intention to delay indefinitely its transition to digital cellular until it could test CDMA. Sometime later, VoiceStream Wireless offered GSM service in the US and proclaimed that its phones could be used worldwide. At the beginning of 2001, several firms were migrating from TDMA to GSM, both because they hoped this migration would ease the transition towards more advanced offerings and because GSM handset prices were lower.

Differences and Similarities between Europe and the United States

The Browser Case against Microsoft in the US

Rather than focusing on servers as in the EU, the related US antitrust case against Microsoft focused on browsers for personal computers. One similarity between the cases, however, was that they both involved the accusation that Microsoft had extended its monopoly in PC operating systems into new products. In addition, as in Europe, several of Microsoft's competitors urged the US government to pursue the case[2]. In particular, Sun Microsystems spent $3 million to fund "Project Sherman," a biweekly gathering of paid antitrust experts that met for three months to help craft the legal argument that would convince the government to sue Microsoft.[67]

In 1998, the US Department of Justice and 20 states filed their antitrust suit. Microsoft was accused of pressuring Netscape to split the browser market in a cartel-like arrangement. When Netscape refused, Microsoft responded by giving away its browser while also bribing and threatening customers to favor its browser over Netscape's. The government claimed that these actions were predatory and constituted an illegal monopolization because they were not rationally profit maximizing except insofar as they removed the threat that Netscape's browser posed for Microsoft. Microsoft was also charged with illegal tying for incorporating a browser into Windows 98. According to the government, Microsoft treated Netscape's browser as a threat because it feared that applications developers would use Netscape's API's instead of Microsoft's, thus undermining Microsoft's monopoly in operating systems.

After months of testimony, US District Court Judge Thomas Penfield Jackson essentially agreed with these charges. In interviews with journalists, Judge Jackson said he found Apple and Netscape's executives believable when they complained about Microsoft's threats, while he found many of Microsoft's witnesses less credible.[68] He thus dismissed most of Microsoft's arguments including its assertion that the browser and the operating system constituted an integrated product (like the left and the right shoe in a pair of shoes) which worked better when installed together. Jackson also disagreed with Microsoft's claim that its copyright entitled it to impose restrictions on OEMs, and stated that "a copyright holder is not by reason thereof entitled to employ the perquisites in ways that directly threaten competition."[69]

Microsoft was not accused of violating the law by either charging different prices for the same product or by withholding information. However, in his "Findings of Fact," Jackson noted that Microsoft used both these tactics to pressure IBM to reduce its support for software products that competed with Microsoft's own offerings.[70] When IBM did not comply with Microsoft's wishes, Microsoft withheld a license for Windows 95, delayed the release of the "golden master" code IBM needed for its product planning and development, and charged IBM significantly more for Windows than other major OEMs, including Compaq, Dell, and Hewlett-Packard.

Jackson also found that Microsoft withheld technical information from Netscape to punish it for its refusal to split the browser market with Microsoft. Even though Netscape requested certain Windows 95 APIs as early as June 1995, Microsoft did not release this crucial technical information to Netscape

---

[2] Ironically, an academic study claimed that the stock prices of Microsoft's competitors fell together with Microsoft's around those days where newspapers carried stories that suggested Microsoft would be hurt by this case (See George Bittlingmayer and Thomas Hazlett "DOS Kapital", Journal of Financial Economics, 2000).

until late October, months after Windows 95's August debut. As a result of this delay, Netscape missed most of the holiday selling season.[71]

As part of his proposed remedy, Jackson ordered Microsoft to sever its operating systems business from its applications business, which would also sell browsers. The two new businesses created from the split would be prohibited from giving each other any technical information that was not simultaneously made available to competitors. In addition, the company selling operating systems would have to disclose to its competitors in a "timely manner" all APIs and technical information which the company used internally to create products that interoperated with its operating systems.

Some analysts wondered whether Judge Jackson applied the US antitrust laws in a way that was appropriate for markets with such strong "network effects" as operating systems and browsers. In these markets, users may benefit so much from adopting a popular product that only one supplier can survive. Firms may then only have a choice between stopping production of a particular product line, and doing what is necessary to become a monopoly supplier. The question that arises, then, is whether it is preferable to have separate monopolies or to let a firm like Microsoft gain a monopoly in several products. Many economists reasoned that when consumers all wish to buy a bundle of several products at once, the bundle is cheaper when it is provided by a single monopolist than when each product in the bundle is provided by a separate monopolist. Their argument was that, in the latter case, each monopolist had a larger incentive to raise prices because it could ignore the negative effect of his own price increase on the sales of the others.

US-Europe Convergence?

In the years just preceding 2001, EU and US antitrust officials sought to increase their collaboration when evaluating proposed mergers and acquisitions. Regulators from the two antitrust regimes signed an agreement in 1998 to promote more extensive information sharing. In assessing the recent WorlCom/Sprint merger, the two staffs kept in close contact and met the companies jointly several times in Washington and in Brussels.

International collaboration in mergers may have become necessary for merging firms. In a proposed merger in 2000, Montreal-based Alcan Aluminium complained that it had to make 16 separate filings in eight languages and pay $100,000 in filing fees to satisfy the various nations that might be affected by the deal with France's Pechiney and Switzerland's Alusuisse Lonza Group. In a lawyers' conference in Italy, Monti stated that "competition policy, and specifically international cooperation in competition policy, have an important role to play if we are to avoid resentment against globalization and a protectionist backlash." [72]

In September 2000, in one of his last speeches as head of the Antitrust Division for the US Department of Justice, Joel Klein expressed optimism for increased future US/EU antitrust collaboration: "The confidence that we're acting based on a common approach toward a common objective is what makes our bilateral approach work."[73] Patrick Lynch, an antitrust expert who represented IBM and Microsoft in European antitrust disputes dating to the 1970s, believed that the gap between American and European antitrust policies shrunk considerably in recent years, partly because of greater collaboration between US and EU authorities: "What I see [in Europe] is a growing acceptance of the economic theories that have been the driving force in US antitrust laws for the past 30 years."[74]

Other antitrust experts were not as optimistic. Tom Rosch, former chairman of the American Bar Association's antitrust section, contended that Americans and Europeans had fundamentally different views about antitrust: "The US, whose laws reflect a free-market-inspired skepticism about government regulation, tends to concentrate on price-fixing and other forms of anti-competitive behaviors that lead to higher prices. In Europe, on the other hand, there is a much more entrenched tradition of government-regulation, and officials have focused on preserving competition in the marketplace, sometimes regardless of its effect on prices." Some analysts also argued that Europeans were more likely to use antitrust laws as a "pretense" to protect jobs.[75]

The EU proposed adding two "core principles" of antitrust policy to the WTO agreement. The first of these required transparency in the antitrust enforcement process while the second required non-discrimination among firms of different national origin. Monti also wanted the WTO to host meetings where antitrust authorities would engage in "voluntary peer reviews" of each other's policies. He thought this would strengthen the national competition authorities and "contribute to ... the spread of a competition culture."[76] Joel Klein, by contrast, thought that the differences among countries would make it hard to agree on "sound" competition rules for the WTO. As he put it "Because it would be so hard to achieve meaningful consensus, the lowest common denominator would prevail. Any WTO standard would probably end up legitimizing weak and ineffective competition laws."[77] He thus preferred to focus on bilateral cooperation. In any event, as Mario Monti considered his response to Microsoft, he needed to take into account how this response would affect one of the relationships he wanted to strengthen, namely that between EU and US competition authorities.

Exhibit 1: The Sherman Act of 1890 (selections)

1. Every contract, combination in the form of trust or otherwise, or conspiracy, in restraint of trade or commerce among the several States, or with foreign nations, is declared to be illegal. Every person who shall make any such contract or engage in any such combination or conspiracy shall be deemed guilty of a misdemeanor, and, on conviction thereof, shall be punished by fine not exceeding five thousand dollars, or by imprisonment not exceeding one year, or by both said punishments, in the discretion of the court.

2. Every person who shall monopolize, or attempt to monopolize, or combine or conspire with any other person or persons, to monopolize any part of the trade or commerce among the several States, or with foreign nations, shall be deemed guilty of a misdemeanor, and, on conviction thereof, shall be punished by fine not exceeding five thousand dollars, or by imprisonment not exceeding one year, or by both said punishments, in the discretion of the court.

4. The several circuit courts of the United States are hereby invested with jurisdiction to prevent and restrain violations of this Act; and it shall be the duty of the several district attorneys of the United States, in their respective districts, under the discretion of the Attorney General, to institute proceedings in equity to prevent and restrain such violations. Such proceedings may be by way of petition setting forth the case and praying that such violation shall be enjoined or otherwise prohibited. When the parties complained of shall have been duly notified of such petition the court shall proceed, as soon as may be, to the hearing and determination of the case; and pending such petition and before final decree, the court may at any time make such temporary restraining order or prohibition as shall be deemed just in the premises.

6. Any property owned under any contract or by any combination, or pursuant to any conspiracy (and being the subject thereof) mentioned in section one of this Act, and being in the course of transportation from one State to another, or to a foreign country, shall be forfeited to the United States, and may be seized and condemned by like proceedings as those provided by law for the forfeiture, seizure, and condemnation of property imported into the United States contrary to law.

7. Any person who shall be injured in his business or property by any other person or corporation, by reason of anything forbidden or declared to be unlawful by this Act, may sue therefor in any circuit court of the United States in the district in which the defendant resides or is found, without respect to the amount in controversy, **and shall recover threefold the damages by him sustained,** and the costs of suit, including a reasonable attorney's fee. (emphasis added)

Exhibit 2: Articles 85 and 86 of the Treaty of Rome

Article 85

1. The following shall be prohibited as incompatible with the common market: all agreements between undertakings[3], decisions by associations of undertakings and concerted practices which may affect trade between member states and which have as their object or effect the prevention, restriction, or distortion of competition within the common market, and in particular those which:

    a. directly or indirectly fix purchase or selling prices or any other trading conditions;
    b. limit or control production, markets, technical development, or investment;
    c. share markets or sources of supply;
    d. apply dissimilar conditions to equivalent transactions with other trading parties, thereby placing them at a competitive disadvantage;
    e. make the conclusion of contracts subject to acceptance by the other parties of supplementary obligations which, by their nature or according to commercial usage, have no connection with the subject of such contracts.

2. Any agreements or decisions prohibited pursuant to this article shall be automatically void.

3. The provisions of paragraph 1 may, however, be declared inapplicable in the case of:

    ■ any agreement or category of agreements between undertakings;
    ■ any decision or category of decisions by associations of undertakings;
    ■ any concerted practice or category of concerted practices;

    which contributes to the production or distribution of goods or to promoting technical or economic progress, while allowing consumers a fair share of the resulting benefit, and which does not:

    a. impose on the undertakings concerned restrictions which are not indispensable to the attainment of these objectives;
    b. afford such undertakings the possibility of eliminating competition in respect of a substantial part of the products in question.

Article 86

Any abuse by one or more undertakings of a dominant position within the common market or in a substantial part of it shall be prohibited as incompatible with the common market in so far as it may affect trade between Member States. Such abuse may, in particular, consist in:

    a. directly or indirectly imposing unfair purchase or selling prices or other unfair trading conditions;
    b. limiting production, markets or technical development to the prejudice of consumers;
    c. applying dissimilar conditions to equivalent transactions with other trading parties, thereby placing them at a competitive disadvantage;
    d. making the conclusion of contracts subject to acceptance by other parties of supplementary obligations which, by nature or according to commercial usage, have no connection with the subject of such contracts.

---

[3] Undertaking means firm or concern.

Exhibit 3: Mergers in the EU, 1990-2000

	1990	1991	1992	1993	1994	1995	1996	1997	1998	1999	2000
Approved	7	53	53	54	85	101	116	123	215	236	297
Approved with Changes	0	6	7	2	4	6	3	9	17	27	40
Sent to Member States	0	0	1	1	1	0	3	7	4	5	6
Denied	0	1	0	0	1	2	3	1	2	1	2
TOTAL	7	60	61	57	91	109	125	140	238	270	345

Source: European Merger Control, Council Regulation 4064/89, Statistics
http://europa.eu.int/comm/competition/mergers/cases/stats.html

Exhibit 4: Shipments, Server Operating Environments

	Europe 1997		Europe 1998		Worldwide 1997		Worldwide 1998		Worldwide 1999		Worldwide 2000	
	Shipments	Share (%)	Shipments	Share (%)	Shipments	Share (%)	Shipments	Share (%)	Shipments	Share (%)	Shipments	Share (%)
Unix, Multiuser												
Compaq/Digital-UX[a]	11,955	1.0	9,500	0.7	33,000	0.9	25,000	0.6	31,000	0.6	34,000	0.6
HP HP-UX	28,752	2.3	36,659	2.6	76,000	2.2	94,000	2.2	105,000	1.9	126,000	2.1
IBM AIX & IBM AIX SP	32,975	2.6	59,308	4.1	97,000	2.8	113,000	2.5	113,000	2.1	125,000	2.0
SCO OpenServer[a]	102,329	8.2	88,794	6.2	232,000	6.7	215,000	4.9	194,000	3.6	124,000	2.0
SCO UnixWare[a]	18,317	1.5	37,917	2.6	65,000	1.9	114,000	2.6	119,000	2.2	93,000	1.5
Siemens Reliant	10,022	0.8	9,074	0.6	13,000	0.4	11,000	0.2	n.a.	n.a.	n.a.	n.a.
Sun Solaris SPARC	36,174	2.9	59,281	4.1	105,000	3.0	156,000	3.5	186,000	3.4	262,000	4.3
Sun Solaris (x86)[a]	18,965	1.5	11,001	0.8	25,000	0.7	28,000	0.6	n.a.	n.a.	n.a.	n.a.
Other	31,711	2.5	23,158	1.6	82,000	2.3	67,000	1.7	78,000	1.4	62,000	1.0
Total Unix	**291,200**	**23.3**	**334,620**	**23.3**	**728,000**	**20.9**	**828,000**	**18.8**	**826,000**	**15.2**	**826,000**	**13.5**
Microsoft Windows NT Server[a]	380,400	30.5	506,100	35.2	1,226,000	35.3	1,687,000	38.3	2,086,000	38.4	2,508,000	40.9
Novell NetWare[a]	315,180	25.2	311,263	21.7	927,000	26.7	1,004,000	22.8	1,064,000	19.6	1,030,000	16.8
Linux, Multiuser[a,b]	96,000	7.7	181,218	12.6	240,000	6.9	697,000	15.8	1,322,000	24.3	1,645,000	26.9
IBM OS/2 Server[a]	145,200	11.6	85,674	6.0	220,000	6.3	131,000	3.0	n.a.	n.a.	n.a.	n.a.
Other NOS	20,588	1.6	17,502	1.2	135,000	3.9	57,000	1.3	140,000	2.6	116,000	1.9
TOTAL	**1,248,568**	**100.0%**	**1,436,377**	**100.0%**	**3,476,000**	**100.0%**	**4,404,000**	**100.0%**	**5,437,000**	**100.0%**	**6,125,000**	**100.0%**

a: Used, at least partially, with Intel-based servers. b: Includes only paid shipments.

Source: International Data Corporation

Exhibit 5: Shipments, Server Operating Systems, by Country, 1998

	Total Unix	IBM OS/2	Linux, Multiuser[a]	Microsoft Windows NT Server	Novell Netware	Other NOS	TOTAL
Germany	81,340	23,855	61,615	99,612	91,915	2,222	360,559
United Kingdom	73,991	13,318	40,681	104,584	77,816	3,978	314,368
France	58,259	10,830	19,028	73,908	36,229	4,143	202,397
Italy	41,190	8,781	10,873	52,325	16,030	989	130,188
Netherlands	11,696	3,805	9,967	24,996	26,845	1,530	78,839
Belgium	8,086	2,342	1,812	15,188	10,076	490	37,994
Sweden	11,480	1,756	3,624	25,378	7,570	935	50,743
Denmark	5,861	1,610	1,906	17,537	4,097	613	31,624
Norway	4,174	878	1,812	12,322	4,258	589	24,033
Finland	5,771	732	3,624	9,885	4,731	467	25,210
Switzerland	10,870	4,098	4,624	17,110	9,683	468	46,853
Austria	4,640	2,049	906	10,597	5,894	182	24,268
Spain	9,993	9,366	13,498	24,943	10,618	653	69,071
Portugal	2,114	1,464	1,812	6,826	2,706	104	15,026
Greece	1,909	351	1,812	3,847	1,206	52	9,177
Ireland	3,246	439	3,624	7,042	1,589	87	16,027
TOTAL	334,620	85,674	181,218	506,100	311,263	17,502	1,436,377

a: Includes only paid shipments.

Source: International Data Corporation

Exhibit 6: Revenue, Server Operating Environments, 1997 & 1998

	Europe				Worldwide			
	1997		1998		1997		1998	
	Revenue ($m)	Share (%)	Revenue ($m)	Share (%)	Revenue ($m)	Share (%)	Revenue ($m)	Share (%)
Unix, Multiuser	1,019.2	50.8	1,132.4	49.3	2,548.0	58.0	2,831.0	56.6
Microsoft Windows NT Server	570.6	28.4	721.0	31.4	1,100.0	25.0	1,390.0	27.8
Novell Netware	358.3	17.8	397.0	17.3	621.0	14.1	688.0	13.7
IBM OS/2 Server	38.7	1.9	27.7	1.2	58.7	1.3	35.0	0.7
Linux, Multiuser	3.9	0.2	9.3	0.4	54.0	1.2	29.0	0.6
Other NOS	16.7	0.8	9.0	0.4	13.0	0.3	31.0	0.6
TOTAL	2,007.4	100.0%	2,296.4	100.0%	4,394.7	100.0%	5,004.0	100.0%

Source: International Data Corporation

[1] Alistair Osborne, "Last Orders for Booze Cruisers," *Daily Telegraph*, Feb. 20, 1999, p. 31.

[2] Andrew Osborn, "Mild Mannered Monti Seeks Superpowers: Competition Chief Flexes Muscles to Take on the Mega-Corporations," *Guardian*, Sept. 19, 2000, p. 25.

[3] New York Times, February 1888, various issues.

[4] United States v. Trans-Missouri Freight Association, 166 U.S. 290, 323 (1897).

[5] Robert H. Bork, *The Antitrust Paradox: A Policy at War with Itself* (New York and Toronto: The Free Press, A Division of Macmillan, 1993), 91.

[6] Louis Kaplow, *Antitrust, Law and Economics, and the Courts, in* The Political Economy of the Sherman Act: The First One Hundred Years 238 (E. Thomas Sullivan ed., 1991).

[7] Jeremy Gray, "The Youngest Watchdog Shows Its Teeth," *Financial Times*, Nov. 5, 1998, Section Finance p. 3.

[8] David J. Gerber, *Law and Competition in Twentieth Century Europe: Protecting Prometheus* (Oxford: Clarendon Press, 1998), 269.

[9] Carol J. Williams, "EU Push to End Price-Fixing Puts Germany's Booksellers in a Bind," *Los Angeles Times*, Apr. 10, 1999, p. A5.

[10] Aluminum Co. of America v. United States, 148 F.2d 416, 430 (2nd Circuit 1945).

[11] Northern Pacific Railway v. United States, 356 U.S. 1, 6 (1958) (quoting Standard Oil Co. v. United States, 337 U.S. 293, 305-6 (1911)).

[12] F.M. Scherer, *Industrial Market Structure and Economic Performance*, (Chicago: Rand McNally College Publishing Company, 2nd ed. 1980), 508.

[13] The 1999 Treaty of Amsterdam gave these Articles numbers 81 and 82, respectively.

[14] European Commission, "XXV Report on Competition Policy", 1995 and "Guidelines on Vertical Restraints," in *Official Journal of the European Communities* Oct. 13, 2000.

[15] Tim Frazer, *Monopoly, Competition and the Law: The Regulation of Business Activity in Britain, Europe and America*, (Hertfordshire: Harvester Wheatsheaf, 2nd ed. 1992), 44.

[16] Michelle Cini and Lee McGowan, *Competition Policy in the European Union*, (London: Macmillan Press Ltd, 1998), 107.

[17] Frazer, p. 45.

[18] Deborah Hargreaves, "Monti Sets Out to Modernise the Weapons in EU's Fight to Promote Competition," *Financial Times*, Oct. 26, 1999, p. 12.

[19] Osborn, *Guardian*, Sept. 19, 2000, p.25.

[20] Ibid.

[21] "Competition Policy: Parliament Votes for Commission Reforms," *European Report*, Jan. 19, 2000.

[22] Damian Reece, "The Blocker of Brussels EMI and Time Warner Abandoned their Merger Plans before the EU Intervened, Under Mario Monti Europe's Competition Policy Is Becoming Ever More Hard Line, " *Sunday Telegraph*, Oct. 8, 2000, p. 6.

[23] Ibid.

[24] Ibid.

[25] James Gwynn, "Good News for Microsoft," *Scotsman*, Sept. 5, 2000, Section Business p. 3.

[26] Deborah Hargreaves, "Monti Shows His Tough Streak," *Financial Times*, Mar. 6, 2000, p. 23.

[27] Ibid.

[28] Hargreaves, *Financial Times*, Oct. 26, 1999, p. 12.

[29] Henry Blodget and Justin Baldauf, "Microsoft: Wherefore Are Thou, Long-Term Growth?," *Merrill Lynch & Co.*, Feb. 8, 2001, p. 6.

[30] Ibid., p. 11.

[31] Daniel Ichbiah and Susan L. Knepper, *The Making of Microsoft: How Bill Gates and His Team Created the World's Most Successful Software Company* (Rocklin, California: Prima Publishing, 1991), 133.

[32] Don Clark, "Microsoft Will Keep Making Products for Apple's Macintosh," *Wall Street Journal*, Mar. 22, 1995, p. B6.

[33] Michael A. Cusumano and Richard Selby, *Microsoft Secrets: How the World's Most Powerful Software Company Creates Technology, Shapes Markets, and Manages People* (New York: The Free Press, A Division of Simon & Schuster, 1995), 169.

[34] Direct Testimony of Avadis Tevanian Jr., U.S. v. Microsoft, at 98-102.

[35] Direct Testimony of Eric Engstrom, U.S. v. Microsoft, at 113-120.

[36] Press Release, European Commission, "Commission Opens Proceedings Against Microsoft's Discriminatory Licensing and Refusal to Supply Software Information," Aug. 3, 2000.

[37] See http://www.zdnet.com/eweek/stories/general/0,11011,1018247,00.html.

[38] See http://www.microsoft.com/NTServer/nts/news/msnw/cisco.asp and "Sun Produces a Cascade for Win NT Services" Inter@ctive Week, January 18, 1999.

[39] Cini and McGowan, p. 87.

[40] Direct Testimony of Richard L. Schmalensee, U.S. v. Microsoft, at Section III.

[41] "Microsoft Under Attack from Europe," *Irish Times*, Aug. 7, 2000.

[42] http://www.microsoft.com/freedomtoinnovate/newsletter/finnews_082200.htm

[43] Brandon Mitchener and Kevin J. Delaney, "Microsoft Submits Defense in Europe Antitrust Case—Firm Claims Existing Laws Already Guarantee Rivals Sufficient Information," *Wall Street Journal*, Nov. 20, 2000, p. A21.

[44] Gwynn, *Scotsman*, Sept. 5, 2000, Section Business, p. 3.

[45] Press Release, European Commission, Aug. 3, 2000.

[46] David E. Sanger, "Europeans Aim Action at IBM," *New York Times*, Apr. 26, 1984, p. D1.

[47] John Tagliabue, "Common Market Says It Will Push IBM Suit," *New York Times*, Apr. 3, 1982, Section 2, p. 31.

[48] Ibid.

[49] Sanger, *New York Times*, Apr. 26, 1984, p. D1.

[50] Ibid.

[51] Guy de Jonquieres, "Waiting for the Other Side to Blink First; Europe's Largest Anti-trust Case," *Financial Times*, June 29, 1984, Section 1, p. 22.

[52] Sanger, *New York Times*, Apr. 26, 1984, p. D1.

[53] De Jonquieres, *Financial Times*, June, 29, 1984, Section 1, p. 22.

[54] Paul Cheeseright and Guy de Jonquieres, "IBM Faces EEC Fines for Guarding Product Secrecy," *Financial Times*, Apr. 26, 1984, Section 1, p. 1.

[55] De Jonquieres, *Financial Times*, June 29, 1984, Section 1, p. 22.

[56] Paul Lewis, "IBM to Give Data to Rivals, Settling European Trust Case," *New York Times*, Aug. 3, 1984, p. A1.

[57] Eric N. Berg, "Accord Called a Compromise," *New York Times*, Aug. 3, 1984, p. D14.

[58] Honorable Jon O. Newman, *New Lyrics for an Old Melody: The Idea/ Expression Dichotomy in the Computer Age*, 17 Cardozo Arts & Ent. L.J. 691 (Fall 1999).

[59] Ibid.

[60] Brian Napier, "Light at the End of Europe's Software Tunnel," *Financial Times*, Apr. 18, 1991, p. 10.

[61] Andrew Christie, "It May Be Compatible, but Is It Legal?," *The Independent*, June 24, 1991, p. 20.

[62] Lawrence D. Graham, *Legal Battles that Shaped the Computer Industry* (Connecticut and London: Quorum Books, 1999), 117.

63 Sabine Krueger and Peter Heywood, "Newsfront: International Ad Hoc Standards Group Seeks Common Ground for Private ISDNs," *Data Communications*, Dec. 1, 1987.

64 Raymond Boult, "Europeans Unite to Build Digital Cellular Network," *Network World*, Jan. 23, 1989, p. 1.

65 Jack Shandle, "Sizzling Markets Speed Vendors in Drive to Digital Cellular," *Electronics*, Feb. 1, 1989.

66 "Debate Rages over Cellular Technologies," *Network World*, Aug. 2, 1993, p. 23.

67 Ken Auletta, *World War 3.0: Microsoft and Its Enemies* (Toronto and New York: Random House, 2001), 8.

68 John R. Wilke, "For Antitrust Judge, Trust, or Lack of It, Really Was the Issue," *Wall Street Journal*, June 8, 2000, p. A1.

69 U.S. Judge Thomas Penfield Jackson, *"Conclusions of Law,"* U.S. v. Microsoft; Apr. 3, 2000, Federal District Court for the District of Columbia, 8.

70 U.S. Judge Thomas Penfield Jackson, *"Findings of Fact,"* U.S. v. Microsoft; Nov. 5, 1999, Federal District Court for the District of Columbia, at 132.

71 Ibid., at 91.

72 Evelyn Iritani, "Global Mergers Pushing the Boundaries of Antitrust Law Regulation," *Los Angeles Times*, Nov. 5, 2000, p. C1.

73 Joel I. Klein, "Time for a Global Competition Initiative?," Address at the EC Merger Control 10th Anniversary Conference (Sept. 14, 2000).

74 Iritani, *Los Angeles Times*, Nov. 5, 2000, at C1.

75 Ibid.

76 Communication from the European Community and its Member States to the Working Group on the Interaction between Trade and Competition Policy, World Trade Organization, July 12, 1999.

77 "No Monopoly on Antitrust," *Financial Times*, Feb. 13, 1998, p. 20.